Juan Aparicio • C. A. Knox Lovell • Jesus T. Pastor • Joe Zhu
Editors

Advances in Efficiency and Productivity II

Springer

Editors
Juan Aparicio
Center of Operations Research
Miguel Hernandez University
Elche, Alicante, Spain

C. A. Knox Lovell
School of Economics
University of Queensland
Brisbane, QLD, Australia

Jesus T. Pastor
Center of Operations Research
Miguel Hernandez University
Elche, Alicante, Spain

Joe Zhu
Foisie Business School
Worcester Polytechnic Institute
Worcester, MA, USA

ISSN 0884-8289 ISSN 2214-7934 (electronic)
International Series in Operations Research & Management Science
ISBN 978-3-030-41617-1 ISBN 978-3-030-41618-8 (eBook)
https://doi.org/10.1007/978-3-030-41618-8

This Springer imprint is published by the registered company Springer Nature Switzerland AG
The registered company address is: Gewerbestrasse 11, 6330 Cham, Switzerland

Contents

Part I
Background

Introduction

Juan Aparicio, C. A. Knox Lovell, Jesus T. Pastor, and Joe Zhu

Abstract We begin by providing contextual background of this book, the second in a series. We continue by proclaiming the importance of efficiency and productivity, for businesses, industries, and nations. We then summarize the chapters in the book, which consist of an equal number of advances in the analytical foundations of efficiency and productivity measurement and advances in empirical applications that illustrate the significance of efficiency and productivity.

Keywords Efficiency · Productivity · Analytical advances · Empirical applications

1 Background

The Santander Chair of Efficiency and Productivity was created at the Miguel Hernandez University (UMH) of Elche, Spain, at the end of year 2014. Its aim was, and continues to be, the promotion of specific research activities among the international academic community. This Research Chair was assigned to the UMH Institute CIO (Center of Operations Research). The funding of the Chair by *Santander Universidades* constitutes one more example of the generosity and the vision of this organization, which supports a network of over 1407 Ibero-American universities and over 19.9 million students and academicians. Professor Knox Lovell, Honorary Professor of Economics at the University of Queensland, Australia, was appointed Director of the Chair. The Advisory Board of the Chair consists of four members, two of them on behalf of *Santander Universidades*, Mr. José María García de los Ríos and Mr. Joaquín Manuel Molina, and the other two on behalf of the UMH, Ph.D. Juan Aparicio, appointed as Co-Director, and Ph.D. Lidia Ortiz, the Secretary of the Chair.

During 2015 and 2016, the Chair organized eight Efficiency/Productivity Seminars for starting new programs with researchers interested in a variety of topics such as education, municipalities, financial risks, regional cohesion, meta-heuristics, renewable energy production, food industry, and endogeneity. During 2015, an International Workshop on Efficiency and Productivity was organized. The Workshop contributions of 15 relevant researchers and research groups made it possible to conceive the first book in this series, *Advances in Efficiency and Productivity*, with the inestimable support of Professor Joe Zhu, the Associate Series Editor for the Springer International Series in Operations Research and Management Sciences.

During 2017–2019, the Chair organized ten seminars on topics such as financial efficiency, conditional efficiency applied to municipalities, analysis of the change in productivity through dynamic approaches, measures of teacher performance in education, meta-heuristic approaches, centralized reallocation of human resources, evaluation of the impact of public policies, and comparative evaluation of the performance of the innovation in the European Union. Additionally, in June 2018, a second International Workshop on Efficiency and Productivity was organized in the city of Alicante, and the contributions of the participants are collected in this volume, naturally entitled *Advances in Efficiency and Productivity II*. Professor Joe Zhu has graciously agreed to join the editors of this volume.

J. Aparicio (✉) · J. T. Pastor
Center of Operations Research (CIO), University Miguel Hernández of Elche, Elche, Alicante, Spain
e-mail: j.aparicio@umh.es

C. A. K. Lovell
Centre for Efficiency and Productivity Analysis, University of Queensland, Brisbane, Australia

J. Zhu
School of Business, Worcester Polytechnic Institute, Worcester, MA, USA

J. Aparicio et al. (eds.), *Advances in Efficiency and Productivity II*, International Series in Operations Research & Management Science 287, https://doi.org/10.1007/978-3-030-41618-8_1

2 Advances in Efficiency and Productivity

The title of this book, like the title of the first book, is generic, but the two substantive components, efficiency and productivity, are of great concern to every business and economy, and to most regulators as well. The first word in the title is the theme of the book and of the 2018 International Workshop on Efficiency and Productivity that spawned it. The presentations at the workshop, and the chapters in this book, truly do advance our understanding of efficiency and productivity.

The theoretical definition of *efficiency* involves a comparison of observed inputs (or resources) and outputs (or products) with what is optimal. Thus, technical efficiency is the ratio of observed to minimum input use, given the level of outputs produced, or as the ratio of observed to maximum output production, given the level of input use, or any of several combinations of the two, with or without additional constraints. Each type of technical efficiency is conditional on the technology in place, and each is independent of prices. In contrast, economic efficiency is price-dependent and typically is defined as the ratio of observed to minimum cost, given outputs produced and input prices paid, or as the ratio of observed to maximum revenue, given inputs used and output prices received. There are variants of these definitions based on different measures of value, such as the ratio of observed to maximum profit, but all take the form of a comparison of observed values with optimal values, conditional on the technology in place. It is also possible, and useful for conveying financial information to managements, to convert all ratios above, technical and economic, to differences expressed in units of the relevant currency. Indeed many important recent analytical advances, including some in this book, measure economic performance in terms of differences rather than ratios.

The principal challenge in efficiency measurement is the definition of minimum, maximum, or optimum, each of which is a representation of the unobserved production technology, which therefore must be estimated. The analytical techniques developed in this book provide alternative ways of defining optimum, typically as a (technical) production frontier or as an (economic) cost, revenue, or profit frontier, and alternative ways of measuring efficiency relative to an appropriate frontier. The concept of frontiers, and deficits or gaps or inefficiencies relative to them, plays a prominent role in the global warming and climate change literature, reflecting the fact that some nations are more at risk than others.

The theoretical definition of *productivity* coincides with the common sense notion of the ratio of observed output to observed input. This definition is straightforward on the rare occasion in which a producer uses a single input to produce a single output. The definition is more complicated otherwise, when multiple outputs in the numerator must be aggregated using weights that reflect their relative importance, and multiple inputs in the denominator must be aggregated in a similar fashion, so that productivity is again the ratio of two scalars, aggregate output and aggregate input. The time path of aggregate output is an output quantity index, and the time path of aggregate input is an input quantity index. Productivity growth is then defined as the rate of growth of the ratio of an output quantity index to an input quantity index or, equivalently, as the rate of growth of an output quantity index less the rate of growth of an input quantity index. Market prices are natural choices for weights in the two indexes, provided they exist and they are not distorted by market power, regulatory or other phenomena. As with efficiency measurement, productivity measurement can be expressed in terms of differences rather than ratios, in which case productivity indexes become productivity indicators. Also as with efficiency measurement, many important recent analytical advances, including some in this book, measure productivity performance with difference-based indicators rather than with ratio-based indexes.

Two challenges must be overcome, or at least addressed, in productivity measurement. The first involves the mathematical structure of the aggregator functions employed to convert individual outputs and inputs to output indexes or indicators and input indexes or indicators. This challenge is mentioned frequently in this book. The second is an extension of the first and occurs when prices do not exist or are unreliable indicators of the relative importance of corresponding quantities. In this case, productivity and its rate of growth must be estimated, rather than calculated from observed quantities and prices. The analytical techniques developed in this book provide alternative methods for estimating productivity and productivity change through time or productivity variation across producers.

The concepts of efficiency and productivity are significant beyond academe and characterize two important dimensions of the performance of businesses and economies, as evidenced by the following examples:

- The financial performance of businesses depends on the efficiency with which they conduct their operations. Statista, a financial statistics provider, has ranked the banking systems in selected European countries by their cost-income ratio, the ratio of the cost of running operations to operating income, a traditional measure of operating efficiency in banking. In 2018 it found Belgian banks to be the most cost-efficient, with a cost-income ratio of 38.1%, and German banks to be the least cost-efficient, with a cost-income ratio of 81.8%. The five most efficient national banking systems had an average cost-income ratio of 44.3%, while the five least efficient national banking systems had an average ratio of 69.4%. It seems worthwhile to search for an explanation for the variation in national operating efficiency, if only in an effort to shore up the financial performance of the laggard banking systems, some of which are very large.

- The relative prosperity of economies depends in large part on their productivity growth. According to the OECD, labor productivity (real GDP per hour worked) has grown faster in Germany than Italy since the turn of the century. Not coincidentally, according to the World Bank, GDP per capita also has grown faster in Germany than in Italy during the same time period. Many of the sources of the productivity gaps are well known, but a decade of experience suggests that they are difficult to rectify. As an aside to ponder, Italy lags Germany by far less on the 2019 World Happiness Index than it does by GDP per capita.

To be useful, efficiency and productivity must be not just well defined and satisfy a reasonable set of axioms, but they must be capable of measurement using quantitative techniques. Many popular concepts, such as cost-income ratios, labor productivity, and GDP per capita, can be calculated directly from company reports and country national accounts. When the data constraint prohibits direct calculation, empirical efficiency and/or productivity analysis is required. Such analyses typically are based on either a mathematical programming technique known as data envelopment analysis (DEA) or an econometric technique known as stochastic frontier analysis (SFA). Both types of estimation construct best practice frontiers, technical or economic, that bound the data from above or below, more or less tightly, and these frontiers provide empirical approximations to the theoretical optima referred to above. Both types of estimation, but especially DEA, are analyzed and employed throughout this book.

3 The Contents of the Book

Fortuitously the contributions divide themselves evenly between theoretical advances in the analysis of efficiency and productivity and empirical applications of efficiency and productivity analysis. The theoretical advances appearing in Sect. 1.3.1 address a wide range of modeling issues, and the empirical applications appearing in Sect. 1.3.2 address a similarly wide range of policy-relevant topics.

3.1 Analytical Advances

The analytical advances in the study of efficiency and productivity considered in the studies contained in this section are wide-ranging and explore a variety of model specification issues with important empirical ramifications. The three studies in Sect. 1.3.1.1 refer to production activities in general, whether modeled parametrically or nonparametrically. The four studies in Sect. 1.3.1.2 characterize production activities modeled nonparametrically, with DEA and its numerous extensions.

3.1.1 Modeling Advances

The concept of cross-efficiency uses the mean of the optimal weights of all DMUs in a sample, rather than those of a target DMU, to evaluate the efficiency of a target DMU in a DEA exercise. Originally introduced to estimate technical cross-efficiency, the concept recently has been extended to the estimation of economic, cost and profit, cross-efficiency, both of which decompose into technical and allocative cross-efficiencies. In chapter "New Definitions of Economic Cross-Efficiency" Aparicio and Zofio exploit duality theory to provide further economic extensions of the cross-efficiency concept to revenue, profit, and profitability to reflect alternative managerial objectives. They then place economic cross-efficiency in a panel data context, which leads naturally to extensions of a cost Malmquist productivity index and a profit Luenberger productivity indicator, which provide alternative frameworks for the evaluation of economic cross-efficiency change and its decomposition into technical and economic sources. The authors provide an empirical application to a sample of Iranian branch banks.

Theoretical and empirical production analysis incorporating the generation of undesirable outputs within a nonparametric framework has traditionally treated undesirable outputs as being weakly disposable. However recent research has discredited this influential approach, since it is incompatible with the materials balance principle. Alternative nonparametric approaches have been developed that do incorporate the materials balance principle, and in chapter "Modelling Pollution-Generating Technologies: A Numerical Comparison of Non-parametric Approaches" Dakpo, Jeanneaux and Latruffe consider the properties of four approaches to production analysis incorporating undesirable outputs, the family of weak disposability models, the family of eco-efficiency models, and a pair of models that incorporate the materials balance principle. Their theoretical and numerical analyses lead to a preference for a category of multi-equation models in which the global production technology is contained in the intersection of an intended outputs sub-technology and an undesirable outputs sub-technology. Further analysis is required to distinguish among models within this category.

Conventional wisdom asserts that most index numbers do not satisfy the desirable circularity, or transitivity, property. In chapter "Local Circularity of Six Classic Price Indexes" Pastor and Lovell challenge conventional wisdom, by considering six popular index numbers commonly used to measure price change. They acknowledge the validity of conventional wisdom, provided the property must be satisfied *globally*, over all possible nonnegative prices, not just the prices in a data set, and through all time periods included in a data set. However they also show that, although each of these index numbers fails to satisfy circularity globally, each can satisfy circularity *locally*, on a restricted data domain involving both the observed price mix and three consecutive time periods. Although the conditions for local circularity are demanding, the probability that a data set satisfies local circularity is not zero. They also distinguish necessary and sufficient conditions for local circularity, satisfied by Laspeyres and Paasche indexes, and sufficient conditions, satisfied by the geometric Laspeyres and geometric Paasche indexes and the Fisher and Törnqvist indexes.

3.1.2 Extensions of DEA

DEA was developed to analyze the relative performance of a comparable group of DMUs. Comparability requires DMUs to use similar inputs to produce similar outputs in similar operating environments, a stringent requirement that is rarely satisfied. If heterogeneity is ignored, some DMUs are unfairly disadvantaged in the exercise. Alternative adjustments to the DEA methodology have been proposed to account for heterogeneity, particularly in the operating environment. In chapter "Evaluating Efficiency in Non-homogeneous Environments" Avilés-Sacoto, Cook, Güemes-Castorena and Zhu develop and empirically test an adjusted DEA model designed to provide a fair evaluation of DMUs operating in different environments or belonging to different groups. The adjustment compensates disadvantaged DMUs for their excessive use of inputs by assuming that a proportion of their inputs is used to cope with a difficult environment or group rather than to produce intended outputs. The trick is to estimate this proportion, which the authors do with their adjusted DEA model, which provides estimates of both production efficiency and compensation efficiency. A sample of Mexican economic activities is used to illustrate the workings of the model.

Endogeneity occurs when an explanatory variable is correlated with the error term. This is a common problem in stochastic frontier analysis (SFA), in which endogeneity involves correlation between input use and the inefficiency error component, which causes biased and inconsistent parameter estimates. Endogeneity has suffered from relative neglect in DEA, but it exists and has similar dire consequences, particularly when endogeneity involves strong positive correlation. In chapter "Testing Positive Endogeneity in Inputs in Data Envelopment Analysis" Aparicio, Ortiz, Santin and Sicilia provide a new robust statistical test of the presence of endogeneity resulting from either positive or negative correlation between each input and the efficiency level *prior to conducting an output-oriented DEA analysis*. A Monte Carlo analysis shows their test successfully detects endogenous inputs, the inclusion of which would otherwise adversely affect the performance of output-oriented DEA. An empirical application to a sample of Uruguayan public schools illustrates the ability of the model to detect positive endogeneity linked to students' socioeconomic status.

A sample may not be representative of the population from which it is drawn. This makes the use of sample weights important when using sample information to conduct inference about the population, and although the use of sample weights is common in econometrics, it is less so in nonparametric frontier analysis. This is particularly unfortunate if, for example, the sample is not representative of the population due to the exclusion of best performers from the sample. In chapter "On the Estimation of Educational Technical Efficiency from Sample Designs: A New Methodology Using Robust Nonparametric Models" Aparicio, González, Santin and Sicilia propose a methodological strategy for incorporating sample weight information when using robust nonparametric order-α methods to improve the estimation of nonparametric production frontiers. The authors conduct a Monte Carlo analysis to explore the consequences for inference about the population frontier and the population average efficiency of not incorporating sample weight information.

The selection of variables to be included in a relative performance evaluation is an old and important one in empirical research. The problem has attracted considerable attention in DEA, particularly when the Delphi method exploiting expert opinion is not available. Two recommended strategies involve assignment of unconditional probabilities of inclusion in a DEA model or assuming the Principle of Maximum Entropy as a measure of uncertainty. In chapter "Robust DEA Efficiency Scores: A Heuristic for the Combinatorial/Probabilistic Approach" Aparicio and Monge adopt a probabilistic approach to variable selection, by calculating robust efficiency scores based on these two recommended strategies. Using data from the OECD PISA international educational achievement database, the authors calculate computational times and distances among radial scores, cross-efficiency scores, unconditional scores, and entropy scores.

3.2 Empirical Applications

The empirical applications of efficiency and productivity analysis appearing in this section examine a number of industries, sectors, and countries, illustrating the widespread empirical relevance of the analytical techniques appearing in Sect. 1.3.1. The three studies in Sect. 1.3.2.1 explore three very different economic issues using three disparate collections of individual production units from the USA, Spain, and the EU. The four studies in Sect. 1.3.2.2 explore a similarly wide range of economic issues using aggregate data from Peru, Spain, the EU and 39 countries.

3.2.1 Individual Production Units

Corporate social responsibility (CSR) has attracted intense interest in academe, particularly as it relates to corporate financial performance. A Google search on the linkage between the two returned about 160,000 results. In chapter "Corporate Social Responsibility and Firms' Dynamic Productivity Change" Kapelko changes the orientation from financial to economic by examining the impact of CSR on corporate dynamic productivity change. CSR data are obtained from a popular database and contain the usual environmental, social, and governance (ESG) components. Productivity change is estimated from a novel specification of a dynamic Luenberger productivity indicator that incorporates costly partial adjustment of quasi-fixed inputs. A bootstrap regression model is used to relate dynamic productivity change to CSR and its components. Using a large unbalanced panel of US firms during 2004–2015, Kapelko finds a modest positive impact of CSR and two of its components, S and G, and a modest negative impact of E, on dynamic productivity change, after controlling for a number of firm and other effects.

An important research topic concerns how markets value the ability of firms to increase intangible assets that create a gap between their market value and their book value and enhance the information value of the former. Intangible assets may include a risk indicator, as an outcome of a firm's business model, and a bank economic performance indicator, as an outcome of a firm's production plan. In chapter "Probability of Default and Banking Efficiency: How Does the Market Respond?" Curi and Lozano-Vivas examine a large sample of European banks before and after the financial crisis. They measure market value with Tobin's Q (the ratio of the sum of the market value of equity and book value of liabilities to the asset replacement cost), they specify a business model of minimizing probability of default, and they specify a production plan of maximizing cost-efficiency. Probability of default is obtained from a popular database, and cost-efficiency is estimated using DEA. Empirical findings are based on a regression of Tobin's Q on probability of default and cost-efficiency. Controlling for bank and other effects, they find bank valuation to be significantly influenced by both probability of default and cost-efficiency, with probability of default becoming more important and cost-efficiency less important, after the crisis.

Land consolidation (LC) involves land reallocation to reduce fragmentation, and rural planning to enhance infrastructure provision, and has been proposed as a way of adding new farmland, improving land productivity and agricultural competitiveness, and promoting sustainable land use. In chapter "The Impact of Land Consolidation on Livestock Production in Asturias' Parishes: A Spatial Production Analysis" Álvarez, Orea and Pérez-Méndez study the impact of LC processes on milk and beef production, and the number of farms, in a detailed geospatial sample of Asturian parishes since 2000. They model production technology with a set of translog distance functions, which they estimate using spatial panel data econometric techniques with controls for three LC indicators. They find a positive impact of LC processes on production, due to both direct effects (within parish) and indirect (spatial effects generated in neighboring parishes) spillover effects.

3.2.2 Aggregates of Production Units

Gross domestic product (GDP) is a narrow measure of economic well-being, and GDP growth is an equally narrow measure of social economic progress. The relative merits of the two measures have been debated for nearly a century. One popular measure of social economic progress is the social progress index (SPI), defined as the arithmetic mean of three noneconomic component factors of human needs, well-being, and opportunity. Each factor has four sub-factors, each having multiple indicators. The SPI typically is used to compare the performance of nations. However in chapter "A Novel Approach to

Computing a Regional Social Progress Index" Charles, Gherman and Tsolas apply it to 26 regions in Peru in 2015. They develop a novel two-phase method for computing a regional SPI. The first phase aggregates indicators into sub-factors and sub-factors into three factors for each region, using a two-stage objective general index. In the second phase, radial and non-radial DEA programs are used to construct regional SPIs. The two rankings are significantly positively correlated, especially at the upper (coastal regions) and lower (jungle regions) tails of the two distributions.

Estimating the impact of public infrastructure on private productivity has been a popular research topic for decades. Infrastructure can influence productivity directly, as an input at least partly under the control of individual producers, and indirectly by promoting resource reallocation among producers, preferably from less productive to more productive producers. In chapter "A Two-Level Top-Down Decomposition of Aggregate Productivity Growth: The Role of Infrastructure" Orea, Álvarez-Ayuso and Servén decompose aggregate labor productivity growth into direct and indirect effects. They then apply production and duality theory to a stochastic translog production frontier to implement the decomposition of labor productivity growth. They decompose labor productivity growth into size and substitution effects, a technical change effect, and direct and indirect infrastructure effects, the latter captured by the effect of infrastructure on the production efficiency of individual producers. They use a balanced panel of 5 industries in 39 countries over 15 years to estimate the effects of within-industry variables (size, substitution, and technical change) and 4 reallocation variables associated with infrastructure provision. Among their many findings is that telecommunications networks facilitate both within-industry productivity and resource reallocation among industries.

The Kyoto Protocol requires nations to establish binding targets for greenhouse gas emissions, in an effort to keep global warming within 2 °C of preindustrial levels. The EU has adopted such a target, which requires its reliance on fossil fuels to generate electricity and derived heat. In chapter "European Energy Efficiency Evaluation Based on the Use of Superefficiency Under Undesirable Outputs in SBM Models" R. Gómez-Calvet, Conesa, A. R. Gómez-Calvet and Tortosa-Ausina study the productivity performance of the electricity and derived heat sector in 28 EU nations during 2008–2012. Unlike many productivity studies, they include both desirable output, electricity and derived heat obtained from nonrenewable sources, and undesirable output, CO_2-equivalent greenhouse gas emissions, together with three inputs, primary energy consumed, installed capacity, and the number of employees. Analytically the authors follow Tone by specifying production technology with a superefficiency variant of a slacks-based DEA model. They then specify a Malmquist productivity index derived from the efficiencies obtained from the DEA model, which they decompose into efficiency change and technical change. They find wide variation in estimated productivity change, and its components, across countries.

The efficiency with which municipalities deliver public goods is an important research topic. Two requirements for credible inference are a representative and comprehensive set of performance indicators and a reliable estimation strategy. In chapter "Measuring Global Municipal Performance in Heterogeneous Contexts: A Semi-nonparametric Frontier Approach" Cordero, Diaz-Caro and Polo study the service delivery performance of a sample of medium-size Catalonian municipalities during 2005–2012 containing the financial crisis. Their data set contains five services (and a composite indicator of all five), three inputs, and four contextual variables (including the size of municipal debt) that may influence service delivery efficiency. Their estimation technique is the increasingly popular StoNED, which combines some virtues of DEA and SFA, as modified to incorporate contextual variables. Among their empirical findings are (i) efficiency varies directly with municipality size, (ii) efficiency has declined through time for all municipality sizes, and (iii) coastal municipalities are significantly more efficient than other municipalities.

Acknowledgments We gratefully acknowledge the support of *Banco Santander* (*Santander Universidades*) for the organization of the 2018 Workshop on Efficiency and Productivity in Alicante, as well as the assistance of the members of the Advisory Board of the Chair who were engaged in its design and development. We would also like to express our gratitude to Springer Nature and to Lidia Ortiz for the help provided during the editing of the book. Finally, we thank our authors for their participation at the Workshop and their contributions to this book.

Part II
Methodological Advances

New Definitions of Economic Cross-efficiency

Juan Aparicio and José L. Zofío

Abstract Overall efficiency measures were introduced in the literature for evaluating the economic performance of firms when reference prices are available. These references are usually observed market prices. Recently, Aparicio and Zofío (*Economic cross-efficiency: Theory and DEA methods*. ERIM Report Series Research in Management, No. ERS-2019-001-LIS. Erasmus Research Institute of Management (ERIM). Erasmus University Rotterdam, The Netherlands. http://hdl.handle.net/1765/115479, 2019) have shown that the result of applying cross-efficiency methods (Sexton, T. R., Silkman, R. H., & Hogan, A. J. (1986). Data envelopment analysis: Critique and extensions. In R. H. Silkman (Ed.), *Measuring efficiency: An assessment of data envelopment analysis, new directions for program evaluation* (Vol. 32, pp. 73–105). San Francisco/London: Jossey-Bass), yielding an aggregate multilateral index that compares the technical performance of firms using the shadow prices of competitors, can be precisely reinterpreted as a measure of economic efficiency. They termed the new approach "economic cross-efficiency." However, these authors restrict their analysis to the basic definitions corresponding to the Farrell (*Journal of the Royal Statistical Society, Series A, General 120*, 253–281, 1957) and Nerlove (*Estimation and identification of Cobb-Douglas production functions*. Chicago: Rand McNally, 1965) approaches, i.e., based on the duality between the cost function and the input distance function and between the profit function and the directional distance function, respectively. Here we complete their proposal by introducing new economic cross-efficiency measures related to other popular approaches for measuring economic performance, specifically those based on the duality between the profitability (maximum revenue to cost) and the generalized (hyperbolic) distance function and between the profit function and either the weighted additive or the Hölder distance function. Additionally, we introduce panel data extensions related to the so-called cost-Malmquist index and the profit-Luenberger indicator. Finally, we illustrate the models resorting to data envelopment analysis techniques—from which shadow prices are obtained and considering a banking industry dataset previously used in the cross-efficiency literature.

Keywords Data envelopment analysis · Overall efficiency · Cross-efficiency

1 Introduction

In a recent contribution, Aparicio and Zofío (2019) link the notions of overall economic efficiency and cross-efficiency by introducing the concept of economic cross-efficiency. Overall economic efficiency compares optimal and actual economic performance. From a cost perspective and following Farrell (1957), cost-efficiency is the ratio of minimum to actual (observed) cost, conditional on a certain quantity of output and input prices. From a profit perspective, Chambers et al. (1998) define the so-called Nerlovian inefficiency as the normalized difference between maximum profit and actual (observed) profit, conditional on both output and input prices.

Cost and profit efficiencies can in turn be decomposed into technical and allocative efficiencies by resorting to duality theory. In the former case, it can be shown that Shephard input distance function is dual to the cost function and, for *any*

J. Aparicio (✉)
Center of Operations Research (CIO), Universidad Miguel Hernandez de Elche, Elche, Alicante, Spain
e-mail: j.aparicio@umh.es

J. L. Zofío
Department of Economics, Universidad Autónoma de Madrid, Madrid, Spain

Erasmus Research Institute of Management, Erasmus University, Rotterdam, The Netherlands

J. Aparicio et al. (eds.), *Advances in Efficiency and Productivity II*, International Series in Operations Research & Management Science 287, https://doi.org/10.1007/978-3-030-41618-8_2

reference prices, cost-efficiency is always smaller or equal to the value of the input distance function (Färe and Primont 1995). Consequently, as the distance function can be regarded as a measure of technical efficiency, whatever (residual) difference may exist between the two can be attributed to allocative efficiency. Likewise, in the case of profit inefficiency, Chambers et al. (1998) show that the directional distance function introduced by Luenberger (1992) is dual to the profit function and, for *any* reference prices, (normalized) maximum profit minus observed profit is always greater than or equal to the directional distance function. Again, since the directional distance function can be regarded as a measure of technical inefficiency, any difference corresponds to allocative inefficiency.

In this evaluation framework of economic performance, the reference output and input prices play a key role. In applied studies, the use of market prices allows studying the economic performance of firms empirically. However, in the duality approach just summarized above, reference prices correspond to those shadow prices that equate the supporting economic functions (cost and profit functions) to their duals (input or directional distance functions). Yet there are many other alternative reference prices, such as those that are assigned to each particular observation when calculating the input and directional distance functions in empirical studies. An example are the optimal weights that are obtained when solving the "multiplier" formulations of data envelopment analysis (DEA) programs that, approximating the production technology, yield the values of the technical efficiencies.

This set of weights can be used to cross-evaluate the technical performance of a particular observation with respect to its counterparts. That is, rather than using its own weights, the technical efficiency of an observation can be reevaluated using the weights corresponding to other units.[1] This constitutes the basis of the cross-efficiency methods initiated by Sexton et al. (1986). Taking the mean of all bilateral cross-evaluations using the vector of all (individual) optimal weights results in the cross-efficiency measure. Aparicio and Zofío (2019) realized that if these weights were brought into the duality analysis underlying economic efficiency, by considering them as specific shadow prices, the cross-efficiency measure can be consistently reinterpreted as a measure of economic efficiency and, consequently, could be further decomposed into technical and allocative efficiencies.

In particular, and under the customary assumption of input homotheticity (see Aparicio and Zofío 2019), cross-efficiency analysis based on the shadow prices obtained when calculating the input distance function results in the definition of the Farrell cost cross-efficiency. Likewise, it is possible to define the Nerlovian profit cross-inefficiency considering the vector of optimal shadow prices obtained when calculating the directional distance function. One fundamental advantage of the new approach based on shadow prices is that these measures are well-defined under the assumption of variable returns to scale; i.e., they always range between zero and one, in contrast to conventional cross-efficiency methods that may result in negative values. This drawback of the cross-efficiency methodology is addressed by Lim and Zhu (2015), who devise an ad hoc method to solve it, based on the translation of the data. The proposal by Aparicio and Zofío (2019) also takes care of the anomaly effortlessly while opening a new research path that connects the economic efficiency and cross-efficiency literatures.

This chapter follows up this new avenue of research by extending the economic cross-efficiency model to a number of multiplicative and additive definitions of economic behavior and their associated technological duals. From an economic perspective, this is quite relevant since rather than minimizing cost or maximizing profit, and due to market, managerial, or technological constraints, firms may be interested, for example, in maximizing revenue or maximizing profitability. As the economic goal is different, the underlying duality that allows a consistent measurement of economic cross-efficiency is different. For example, for the revenue function, the dual representation of the technology is the output distance function (Shephard 1953), while for the profitability function it is the generalized distance function (Zofío and Prieto 2006). Moreover, since the generalized distance function nests the input and output distance functions as particular cases (as well as the hyperbolic distance function), we can relate the cost, revenue, and profitability cross-efficiency models. Also, since a duality relationship may exist between a given supporting economic function and several distance functions, alternative economic cross-efficiency models may coexist. We explore this situation for the profit function. Besides the already mentioned model for profit efficiency measurement and its decomposition based on the directional distance function, an alternative evaluation can be performance relying on the weighted additive distance function (Cooper et al. 2011) or the Hölder distance function (Briec and Lesourd 1999). We present these last two models and compare them to the one based on the directional distance function. We remark the results of these models differ because of the alternative normalizing constraints that the duality relationship imposes. Hence researchers and practitioners need to decide first on the economic approach that is relevant for their study—cost, revenue, profit, and profitability—and then, among the set of suitable distance functions complying with the required duality conditions, choose the one that better characterizes the production process. Related to the DEA

[1] This cross-efficiency evaluation with respect to alternative peers results in smaller technical efficiency scores, because DEA searches for the most favorable weights when performing own evaluations.

methods that we consider in this chapter to implement the economic cross-efficiency models, it is well-known that the use of radial (multiplicative) distance functions projects observations to subsets of the production possibility set that are not Pareto-efficient because nonradial input reductions and output increases may be feasible (i.e., slacks). As for additive distance functions, the use of the weighted additive distance function in a DEA context ensures that efficiency is measured against the strongly efficient subset of the production possibility set, while its directional and Hölder counterparts do not. Thus, the choice of distance function is also critical when interpreting results. For example, in the event that slacks are prevalent, this source of technical inefficiency will be confounded with allocative inefficiency when decomposing profit inefficiency. Of course, other alternative models of economic cross-efficiency could be developed in terms of alternative distance functions. And some of them could even generalize the proposals presented here, such as the profit model based on the loss distance function introduced by Aparicio et al. (2016), which nests all the above additive functions.

Finally, in this chapter we also extend the economic cross-efficiency model to a panel data setting where firms are observed over time. For this we rely on existing models that decompose cost or profit change into productivity indices or indicators based on quantities, i.e., the Malmquist productivity index or Luenberger productivity indicator, and their counterpart price formulations. As the Malmquist index or Luenberger indicator can be further decomposed into efficiency change and technological change components, we can further learn about the sources of cost or profit change. As for the price indices and indicators, they can also be decomposed so as to learn about the role played by allocative efficiency. We relate this panel data framework to the cross-efficiency model and, by doing so, introduce the concept of economic cross-efficiency change. In this model, the cost-Malmquist and profit-Luenberger definitions proposed by Maniadakis and Thanassoulis (2004) and Juo et al. (2015), using market prices to determine cost change and profit change, are modified following the economic cross-efficiency rationale that replaces the former by the set of shadow prices corresponding to all observations, which results in a complete evaluation of the economic performance observations over time—to the extent that a complete set of alternative prices is considered.

This chapter is structured as follows. In the next section, we introduce the notation and recall the economic cross-efficiency model proposed by Aparicio and Zofío (2019). In the third section, we present the duality results that allow us to extend the analytical framework to the notion of profitability cross-efficiency based on the generalized distance function and how it relates to the partially oriented Farrell cost and revenue cross-efficiencies. We also introduce two alternative models of profit cross-efficiency based on the weighted additive and Hölder distance functions. A first proposal of economic cross-inefficiency for panel data models based on the cost-Malmquist index and profit-Luenberger indicator is proposed in Sect. 4. In Sect. 5, we illustrate the empirical implementation of the existing and new definitions of economic cross-efficiency through data envelopment analysis and using a dataset of bank branches previously used in the literature. Finally, relevant conclusions are drawn in Sect. 6, along with future venues of research in this field.

2 Background

In this section, we briefly introduce the notion of (standard) cross-efficiency in data envelopment analysis and review the concept of economic cross-efficiency. Let us consider a set of n observations (e.g., firms or decision-making units, DMUs) that use m inputs, whose (nonnegative) quantities are represented by the vector $X \equiv (x_1, \ldots, x_m)$, to produce s outputs, whose (nonnegative) quantities are represented by the vector $Y \equiv (y_1, \ldots, y_s)$. The set of data is denoted as $\{(X_j, Y_j), j = 1, \ldots, n\}$. The technology or production possibility set is defined, in general, as $T = \left\{(X, Y) \in R_+^{m+s} : X \text{ can produce Y}\right\}$.

Relaying on data envelopment analysis (DEA) techniques, T is approximated as $T_c = \left\{(X, Y) \in R_+^{m+s} : \sum_{j=1}^{n} \lambda_j x_{ij} \le x_i, \forall i, \sum_{j=1}^{n} \lambda_j y_{rj} \ge y_r, \forall r, \lambda_j \ge 0, \forall j\right\}$. This corresponds to a production possibility set characterized by constant returns to scale (CRS). Allowing for variable returns to scale (VRS) results in the following definition: $T_v = \left\{(X, Y) \in R_+^{m+s} : \sum_{j=1}^{n} \lambda_j x_{ij} \le x_i, \forall i, \sum_{j=1}^{n} \lambda_j y_{rj} \ge y_r, \forall r, \sum_{j=1}^{n} \lambda_j = 1, \lambda_j \ge 0, \forall j\right\}$—see Banker et al. (1984).[2]

Let us now introduce the notion of Farrell cross-efficiency.

[2]Based on these technological characterizations, in what follows we define several measures that allow the decomposition of economic cross-efficiency into technical and allocative components. As it is now well-established in the literature, we rely on the following terminology: We refer to the different *factors* in which economic cross-efficiency can be decomposed *multiplicatively* as efficiency measures (e.g., Farrell cost-efficiency). Numerically, the greater their value, the more efficient observations are. For these measures, one is the upper bound signaling an efficient behavior. Alternatively, we refer to the different *terms* in which economic cross-*in*efficiency can be decomposed *additively* as *in*efficiency measures (e.g.,

2.1 Farrell (Cost) Cross-efficiency

In DEA, for firm k, the radial input technical efficiency assuming CRS is calculated through the following program:

$$
\begin{aligned}
ITE_c(X_k, Y_k) = \max_{U,V} & \frac{\sum_{r=1}^{s} u_r y_{rk}}{\sum_{i=1}^{m} v_i x_{ik}} \\
s.t. & \\
& \frac{\sum_{r=1}^{s} u_r y_{rj}}{\sum_{i=1}^{m} v_i x_{ij}} \leq 1, \; j = 1, \ldots, n, \; (1.1) \\
& u_r \geq 0, \quad r = 1, \ldots, s, \; (1.2) \\
& v_i \geq 0, \quad i = 1, \ldots, m. \; (1.3)
\end{aligned}
\tag{1}
$$

Although (1) is a fractional problem, it can be linearized as shown by Charnes et al. (1978). $ITE_c(X_k, Y_k)$ ranges between zero and one. Hereinafter, we denote the optimal solution obtained when solving (1) as $\left(V_k^*, U_k^*\right)$.

Model (1) allows firms to choose their own weights on inputs and outputs in order to maximize the ratio of a weighted (virtual) sum of outputs to a weighted (virtual) sum of inputs. In this manner, the assessed observation is evaluated in the most favorable way, and DEA provides a self-evaluation of the observation by using input and output weights that are unit-specific. Unfortunately, this fact hinders obtaining a suitable ranking of firms based on their efficiency score, particularly for efficient observations whose $ITE_c(X_k, Y_k)$. In contrast to standard DEA, a cross-evaluation strategy is suggested in the literature (Sexton et al. 1986, and Doyle and Green 1994). In particular, the (bilateral) cross input technical efficiency of unit l with respect to unit k is defined by:

$$
CITE_c(X_l, Y_l | k) = \frac{U_k^* \cdot Y_l}{V_k^* \cdot X_l} = \frac{\sum_{r=1}^{s} u_{rk}^* y_{rl}}{\sum_{i=1}^{m} v_{ik}^* x_{il}}. \tag{2}
$$

$CITE_c(X_l, Y_l|k)$ also takes values between zero and one and satisfies $CITE_c(X_l, Y_l|l) = ITE_c(X_l, Y_l)$.[3]

Given the observed n units in the data sample, the traditional literature on cross-efficiency postulates the aggregation of the bilateral cross input technical efficiencies of unit l with respect to all units k, $k = 1, \ldots, n$, through the arithmetic mean. This results in the definition of the multilateral notion of cross input technical efficiency of unit l:

$$
CITE_c(X_l, Y_l) = \frac{1}{n}\sum_{k=1}^{n} CITE_c(X_l, Y_l | k) = \frac{1}{n}\sum_{k=1}^{n} \frac{U_k^* \cdot Y_l}{V_k^* \cdot X_l} = \frac{1}{n}\sum_{k=1}^{n} \frac{\sum_{r=1}^{s} u_{rk}^* y_{rl}}{\sum_{i=1}^{m} v_{ik}^* x_{il}}. \tag{3}
$$

Before presenting the notion of economic cross-efficiency, we need to briefly recall the main concepts related to the measurement of economic efficiency through frontier analysis, both in multiplicative form (Farrell 1957) and in additive manner (Chambers et al. 1998). We start considering the Farrell radial paradigm for measuring and decomposing cost-efficiency. For the sake of brevity, we state our discussion in the input space, defining the input requirement set $L(Y)$ as the set of nonnegative inputs $X \in R_+^m$ that can produce nonnegative output $Y \in R_+^s$, formally $L(Y) = \left\{X \in R_+^m : (X, Y) \in T\right\}$, and the isoquant of $L(Y) : IsoqL(Y) = \{X \in L(Y) : \varepsilon < 1 \Rightarrow \varepsilon x \notin L(Y)\}$. Let us also denote by $C_L(Y, W)$ the minimum cost of producing the output level Y given the input market price vector $W \in R_{++}^m : C_L(Y, W) = \min\left\{\sum_{i=1}^{m} w_i x_i : X \in L(Y)\right\}$.

Nerlovian profit inefficiency). Now the greater their numerical value, the greater the *in*efficiency, with zero being the lower bound associated to an efficient behavior.

[3] For a list of relevant properties, see Aparicio and Zoffo (2019).

The standard (multiplicative) Farrell approach views cost-efficiency as originating from technical efficiency and allocative efficiency. Specifically, we have:

$$\underbrace{\frac{C_L(Y,W)}{\sum_{i=1}^{m} w_i x_i}}_{\text{Cost Efficiency}} = \underbrace{\frac{1}{D_L^I(X,Y)}}_{\text{Technical Efficiency}} \cdot \underbrace{AE_L^F(X,Y;W)}_{\text{Allocative Efficiency}}, \tag{4}$$

where $D_L^I(X,Y) = \sup\{\theta > 0 : X/\theta \in L(Y)\}$ is the Shephard input distance function (Shephard 1953) and allocative efficiency is defined residually. We use the subscript L to denote that we do not assume a specific type of returns to scale. Nevertheless, we will refer to $C_c(Y,W)$ and $D_c^I(X,Y)$ for CRS and $C_v(Y,W)$ and $D_v^I(X,Y)$ for variable returns to scale (VRS) when needed. Additionally, it is well-known in DEA that the inverse of $D_L^I(X,Y)$ coincides with $ITE_L(X_k,Y_k)$. For the particular case of CRS program (1), $ITE_c(X_k,Y_k) = D_c^I(X,Y)^{-1}$.

Considering actual common market prices for all firms within an industry, then the natural way of comparing the performance of each one would be using the left-hand side in (4). We then could assess the obtained values for each firm since we were using the same reference weights (prices) for all the observations, creating a market-based ranking. This idea inspired Aparicio and Zofío (2019), who suggest that cross-efficiency in DEA could be also defined based on the notion of Farrell's cost-efficiency. In particular, for a given set of *any* reference prices (e.g., shadow prices, market prices, or other imputed prices), they define the Farrell (cost) cross-efficiency of unit l with respect to unit k as:

$$FCE_L(X_l, Y_l | k) = \frac{C_L(Y_l, V_k^*)}{\sum_{i=1}^{m} v_{ik}^* x_{il}}, \tag{5}$$

where $L \in \{c,v\}$ denotes either constant or variable returns to scale.

As in (4), $FCE_L(X_l,Y_l|k) = \frac{1}{D_L(X_l,Y_l)} \cdot AE_L^F(X_l,Y_l;V_k^*)$. Therefore, Farrell cross-efficiency of unit l with respect to unit k corrects the usual technical efficiency, the inverse of the Shephard distance function, through a term with meaning of (shadow) allocative efficiency.

Given the observed n units, the traditional literature on cross-efficiency suggests to aggregate bilateral cross-efficiencies through the arithmetic mean to obtain the multilateral notion of cross-efficiency. In the case of the Farrell cross-efficiency, this yields:

$$FCE_L(X_l,Y_l) = \frac{1}{n}\sum_{k=1}^{n} FCE_L(X_l,Y_l|k) = \frac{1}{n}\sum_{k=1}^{n} \frac{C_L(Y_l,V_k^*)}{\sum_{i=1}^{m} v_{ik}^* x_{il}}. \tag{6}$$

Additionally, $FCE_L(X_l, Y_l)$ can be always decomposed (under any returns to scale) into (radial) technical efficiency and a correction factor defined as the arithmetic mean of n shadow allocative efficiency terms. That is,

$$FCE_L(X_l,Y_l) = \frac{1}{n}\sum_{k=1}^{n} FCE_L(X_l,Y_l|k) = \frac{1}{n}\sum_{k=1}^{n} \frac{C_L(Y_l,V_k^*)}{\sum_{i=1}^{m} v_{ik}^* x_{il}} = ITE_L(X_l,Y_l)\cdot\frac{1}{n}\sum_{k=1}^{n} AE_L^F(X_l,Y_l;V_k^*), \tag{7}$$

with $ITE_L(X_l, Y_l)$ and $AE_L^F(X_l,Y_l;V_k^*)$, $L \in \{c,v\}$, denoting constant and variable returns to scale technical and (shadow) allocative efficiencies, respectively.

We note that $FCE_L(X_l, Y_l)$ satisfies two very interesting properties:

First, assuming the existence of perfectly competitive input markets resulting in a single equilibrium price for each input (i.e., firms are price takers), if we substitute (shadow) prices by these market prices in (7), then $FCE_L(X_l, Y_l)$ precisely coincides with $C_L(Y_l,W) / \sum_{i=1}^{m} w_i x_{il}$, which is Farrell's measure of cost inefficiency (4). Hence, economic cross-efficiency offers a "natural" counterpart to consistently rank units when reference prices are unique for all units. This property is not satisfied in general by the standard measure of cross-efficiency, if both input and output market prices are used as weights;

i.e., $CITE_c(X_l, Y_l) = \frac{\sum_{r=1}^{s} p_r y_{rl}}{\sum_{i=1}^{m} w_i x_{il}} \neq \frac{C_c(Y_l, W)}{\sum_{i=1}^{m} w_i x_{il}}$. Indeed Aparicio and Zofío (2019) show that besides market prices, input homotheticity is required for the equality to hold; otherwise $CITE_c(X_l, Y_l) \geq FCE_c(X_l, Y_l)$. Nevertheless, we also remark that the concept of economic cross-efficiency can accommodate firm-specific market prices if some degree of market power exists and firms are price makers in the inputs markets. In that case, individual firms' shadow prices would be substituted by their market counterparts in (7). This connects our proposal to the extensive theoretical and empirical economic efficiency literature considering individual market prices, e.g., Ali and Seiford (1993).

Second, as previously remarked, $FCE_L(X_l, Y_l)$ is well-defined, ranging between zero and one, even under variable returns to scale. This property is not verified in general by the standard cross-efficiency measures (see Wu et al. 2009; Lim and Zhu 2015). This is quite relevant because traditional measures may yield negative values under variable returns to scale, which is inconsistent and hinders the extension of cross-efficiency methods to technologies characterized by VRS.

An interesting by-product of the economic cross-efficiency approach is that by incorporating the economic behavior of firms in the formulations (e.g., cost minimizers in $FCE_v(X_l, Y_l)$), the set of weights represented by the shadow prices are reinterpreted as market prices, rather than their usual reading in terms of the alternative supporting technological hyperplanes that they define and against which technical inefficiency is measured. This solves some recent criticism raised against the cross-efficiency methods, since shadow prices could be then considered as specific realizations of market prices, e.g., see Førsund (2018a, b) and Olesen (2018).

Next, we briefly introduce the Nerlovian cross-inefficiency.

2.2 Nerlovian (Profit) Cross-inefficiency

Now, we recall the concepts of profit inefficiency and its dual graph measure corresponding to the directional distance function (Chambers et al. 1998).

Given the vector of input and output market prices $(W, P) \in R_+^{m+s}$, and the production possibility set T, the profit function is defined as: $\Pi_T(W, P) = \max_{X,Y} \left\{ \sum_{r=1}^{s} p_r y_r - \sum_{i=1}^{m} w_i x_i : (X, Y) \in T \right\}$. In what follows, let $\Pi_c(W, P)$ and $\Pi_v(W, P)$ be the maximum profit given the CRS technology T_c and the VRS technology T_v, respectively.

Profit inefficiency *à la Nerlove* for firm k is defined as maximum profit (i.e., the value of the profit function given market prices) minus observed profit, normalized by the value of a prefixed reference vector $(G^x, G^y) \in R_+^{m+s}$. By duality, the following inequality is obtained (Chambers et al. 1998):

$$\frac{\Pi_T(W, P) - \left(\sum_{r=1}^{s} p_r y_{rk} - \sum_{i=1}^{m} w_i x_{ik} \right)}{\sum_{r=1}^{s} p_r g_r^y + \sum_{i=1}^{m} w_i g_i^x} \geq \vec{D}_T \left(X_k, Y_k; G^x, G^y \right). \tag{8}$$

where $\vec{D}_T(X_k, Y_k; G^x, G^y) = \max_{\beta} \{\beta : (X_k - \beta G^x, Y_k + \beta G^y) \in T\}$ is the directional distance function. As for the Farrell approach, profit inefficiency can be also decomposed into technical inefficiency and allocative inefficiency, where the former corresponds to the directional distance function:

$$\frac{\Pi_T(W, P) - \left(\sum_{r=1}^{s} p_r y_{rk} - \sum_{i=1}^{m} w_i x_{ik} \right)}{\sum_{r=1}^{s} p_r g_r^y + \sum_{i=1}^{m} w_i g_i^x} = \vec{D}_T \left(X_k, Y_k; G^x, G^y \right) + AI_T^N \left(X_k, Y_k; W, P; G^x, G^y \right). \tag{9}$$

The subscript T in $\Pi_T(W, P)$, $\vec{D}_T(X_k, Y_k; G^x, G^y)$ and $AI_T^N(X_k, Y_k; W, P; G^x, G^y)$ implies that we do not assume a specific type of returns to scale. Nevertheless, as before we will use $\vec{D}_c(X_k, Y_k; G^x, G^y)$ and $AI_c^N(X_k, Y_k; W, P; G^x, G^y)$ for CRS and $\vec{D}_v(X_k, Y_k; G^x, G^y)$ and $AI_v^N(X_k, Y_k; W, P; G^x, G^y)$ for VRS.

In the case of DEA, when VRS is assumed, the directional distance function is determined through (10):

$$\begin{aligned} \vec{D}_v(X_k, Y_k; G^x, G^y) = \max_{\beta,\lambda} \ & \beta \\ s.t \ & \sum_{j=1}^{n} \lambda_j x_{ij} \leq x_{ik} - \beta g_i^x, \quad i = 1, \ldots, m \\ & \sum_{j=1}^{n} \lambda_j y_{rj} \geq y_{rk} + \beta g_r^y, \quad r = 1, \ldots, s, \\ & \sum_{j=1}^{n} \lambda_j = 1, \\ & \lambda_j \geq 0, \quad j = 1, \ldots, n. \end{aligned} \tag{10}$$

whose dual is:

$$\begin{aligned} \min_{U,V,\alpha} \ & -\sum_{r=1}^{s} u_r y_{rk} + \sum_{i=1}^{m} v_i x_{ik} + \alpha \\ s.t. \ & \sum_{r=1}^{s} u_r y_{rj} - \sum_{i=1}^{m} v_i x_{ij} - \alpha \leq 0, \ j = 1, \ldots, n, \\ & \sum_{r=1}^{s} u_r g_r^y + \sum_{i=1}^{m} v_i g_i^x = 1, \\ & U \geq 0_s, V \geq 0_m. \end{aligned} \tag{11}$$

Let us also denote the optimal solutions of problem (11) as $\left(\vec{V}_k^*, \vec{U}_k^*, \vec{\alpha}_k^*\right)$.

Aparicio and Zofío (2019) defined the Nerlovian cross-inefficiency of unit l with respect to unit k as:

$$NCI_v\left(X_l, Y_l; G^x, G^y \,|k\right) = \frac{\Pi\left(\vec{V}_k^*, \vec{U}_k^*\right) - \left(\sum_{r=1}^{s} \vec{u}_{rk}^* y_{rl} - \sum_{i=1}^{m} \vec{v}_{ik}^* x_{il}\right)}{\sum_{r=1}^{s} \vec{u}_{rk}^* g_r^y + \sum_{i=1}^{m} \vec{v}_{ik}^* g_i^x} = \frac{\vec{\alpha}_k^* - \left(\sum_{r=1}^{s} \vec{u}_{rk}^* y_{rl} - \sum_{i=1}^{m} \vec{v}_{ik}^* x_{il}\right)}{\sum_{r=1}^{s} \vec{u}_{rk}^* g_r^y + \sum_{i=1}^{m} \vec{v}_{ik}^* g_i^x}. \tag{12}$$

As usual, the arithmetic mean of (12) for all observed units yields the final Nerlovian cross-inefficiency of unit l:

$$NCI_v\left(X_l, Y_l; G^x, G^y\right) = \frac{1}{n} \sum_{k=1}^{n} NCI_v\left(X_l, Y_l; G^x, G^y \,|k\right). \tag{13}$$

Invoking (9), we observed once again that the Nerlovian cross-inefficiency of firm l is a "correction" of the original directional distance function value for the unit under evaluation, where the modifying factor can be interpreted as (shadow) allocative inefficiency:

$$\begin{aligned} NCI_v\left(X_l, Y_l; G^x, G^y\right) = \ & \vec{D}_v\left(X_0, Y_0; G^x, G^y\right) \\ & + \frac{1}{n} \sum_{k=1}^{n} AI_v^N\left(X_l, Y_l; \vec{V}_k^*, \vec{U}_k^*; G^x, G^y\right). \end{aligned} \tag{14}$$

Finally, these authors showed that the approach by Ruiz (2013), based on the directional distance function under CRS, is a particular case of (14).

3 New Economic Cross-(in)efficiency Measures

3.1 Profitability Cross-efficiency

We now extend the previous framework of economic cross-(in)efficiency to a set of new measures which can be decomposed either multiplicatively or additively. We start with the notion of profitability—corresponding to Georgescu-Roegen's (1951) "return to the dollar," defined as the ratio of observed revenue to observed cost. We then show that it can be decomposed into a measure of economic efficiency represented by the generalized distance function introduced by Chavas and Cox (1999) and a factor defined as the geometric mean of the allocative efficiencies corresponding to the n shadow prices. Let us define maximum profitability as $\mathrm{P}_T(W,P) = \max\limits_{X,Y}\left\{\sum\limits_{r=1}^{s} p_r y_r / \sum\limits_{i=1}^{m} w_i x_i : (X,Y) \in T\right\}$. Zofío and Prieto (2006) proved that:

$$\frac{P \cdot Y_k / W \cdot X_k}{\mathrm{P}_T(W,P)} \leq D_c^G(X_k, Y_k; \gamma), \tag{15}$$

where $D_c^G(X_k, Y_k; \gamma) = \inf\left\{\delta : \left(\delta^{\gamma} X_k, Y_k/\delta^{1-\gamma}\right) \in T\right\}$, $0 \leq \gamma \leq 1$, is the generalized distance function and $P \cdot Y_k = \sum\limits_{r=1}^{s} p_r y_{rk}$ and $W \cdot X_k = \sum\limits_{i=1}^{m} w_i x_{ik}$.

We remark that the generalized distance function in expression (15), rather than being defined to allow for either constant or variable returns to scale as in the previous models, is characterized by the former. The reason is that the production technology exhibits local constant returns to scale at the optimum; hence maximum profitability is achieved at loci representing most productive scale sizes in Banker et al. (1984) terminology. This provides the rationale to develop the duality underlying expression (15) departing from such technological specification. We further justify this choice in what follows when recalling the variable returns to scale technology so as to account for scale efficiency.

The generalized distance function $D_c^G(X_k, X_k; \ \gamma)$ can be calculated relying on DEA by solving the following nonlinear problem:

$$\begin{aligned} D_c^G(X_k, Y_k; \gamma) = \min_{\delta,\lambda} \ & \delta \\ \text{s.t.} \ & \\ & \sum_{j=1}^{n} \lambda_j x_{ij} \leq \delta^{1-\gamma} x_{ik}, \qquad i = 1, \ldots, m, \\ & \sum_{j=1}^{n} \lambda_j y_{rj} \geq \tfrac{y_{rk}}{\delta^{\gamma}}, \qquad r = 1, \ldots, s, \\ & \lambda_j \geq 0, \qquad j = 1, \ldots, n, \end{aligned} \tag{16}$$

Following the Farrell and Nerlovian decompositions (7) and (14), it is possible to define allocative efficiency as a residual from expression (15):

$$\frac{P \cdot Y_k / W \cdot X_k}{\mathrm{P}_T(W,P)} = D_c^G(X_k, Y_k; \ \gamma) \cdot AE_c^G(X_k, Y_k; W, P; \gamma), \tag{17}$$

where $AE_c^G(X_K, Y_K; W, P; \gamma) = \frac{P \cdot \hat{Y}_k / W \cdot \hat{X}_k}{\mathrm{P}_T(W,P)}$ with $\hat{X}_k = D_c^G(X_k, Y_k; \ \gamma) X_k$ and $\hat{Y}_k = Y_k / D_c^G(X_k, Y_k; \ \gamma)$.[4] So, allocative efficiency, which is a measure that in the Farrell approach essentially captures the comparison of the rate of substitution between production inputs with the ratio of market prices at the production isoquant given the output level Y_k, is, in this case, the profitability calculated at the (efficient) projection linked to the generalized model.

As previously mentioned, since the technology may be characterized by variable returns to scale, it is possible to bring its associated directional distance function $D_v^G(X_k, X_k; \ \gamma)$ into (17)—calculated as in (16) but adding the VRS constraint $\sum_{j=1}^{n} \lambda_j = 1$. This allows decomposing productive efficiency into two factors, one representing "pure" VRS technical

[4] Färe et al. (2002) defined this relationship in terms of the hyperbolic distance function; i.e., $D_c^H(X_k, Y_k) = \min\limits_{\delta,z}\left\{\delta : \sum\limits_{j=1}^{n} \lambda_j X_j \leq \delta X_k, \frac{Y_k}{\delta} \leq \sum\limits_{j=1}^{n} \lambda_j Y_j, \lambda_j \geq 0, j = 1, \ldots, n\right\}$.

efficiency and a second one capturing scale efficiency: i.e., $D_c^G(X_k, X_k; \gamma) = D_v^G(X_k, X_k\ \gamma) \cdot SE^G(X_k, X_k; \gamma)$, where $SE^G(X_k, X_k; \gamma) = D_c^G(X_k, X_k; \gamma) / D_v^G(X_k, X_k; \gamma)$. Defining expression (15) under constant returns to scale enables us to individualize the contribution that scale efficiency makes to profitability efficiency. Otherwise, had we directly relied on the directional distance function defined under variable returns to scale in (15), scale inefficiency would had been confounded with allocative efficiency in (17).

Reinterpreting the left-hand side of (15) in the framework of cross-efficiency, we next define a new economic cross-efficiency approach that allows us to compare the (bilateral) performance of firms l with respect to firm k using the notion of profitability:

$$PCE_c(X_l, Y_l;\ \gamma\,|k) = \frac{U_k^* \cdot Y_l / V_k^* \cdot X_l}{\mathrm{P}_T\left(V_k^*, U_k^*\right)}, \tag{18}$$

where, once again, $\left(V_k^*, U_k^*\right)$ are the shadow prices associated with the frontier projections generated by $D_c^G(X_k, X_k;\ \gamma)$.

To aggregate all cross-efficiencies in a multiplicative framework, we depart on this occasion from standard practice and use the geometric mean, whose properties make the aggregation meaningful when consistent (transitive) bilateral comparisons of performance in terms of productivity are pursued; see Aczél and Roberts (1989) and Balk et al. (2017). Hence:

$$PCE_c(X_l, Y_l;\ \gamma) = \left(\prod_{k=1}^{n} \frac{U_k^* \cdot Y_l / V_k^* \cdot X_l}{\mathrm{P}_T\left(V_k^*, U_k^*\right)}\right)^{1/n}, \tag{19}$$

As in the Farrell and Nerlovian models (7) and (14), we can decompose $PCE_c(X_l, Y_l;\ \gamma)$ according to technical and allocative criteria, thereby obtaining:

$$PCE_c(X_l, Y_l;\ \gamma) = D_c^G(X_k, Y_k;\ \gamma) \cdot \left(\prod_{k=1}^{n} AE_c^G\left(X_k, Y_k; V_k^*, U_k^*; \gamma\right)\right)^{1/n} \tag{20}$$

Based on this decomposition, the role played by VRS technical efficiency and scale efficiency can be further individualized since $D_C^G(X_k, X_k; \gamma) = D_v^G(X_k, X_k; \gamma) \cdot SE^G(X_k, X_k; \gamma)$.

We now obtain some relevant relationships between the profit and profitability cross-(in)efficiencies. Relaying on Färe et al. (2002) and Zofío and Prieto (2006), it is possible to show that under constant returns to scale, maximum feasible profit is zero, $\Pi_c(W, P) = 0$ (if $\Pi_c(W, P) < +\infty$), and, therefore, maximum profitability is one, $\mathrm{P}_c(W, P) = 1$.[5] Also, it is a well-known result that, under CRS, $ITE_c(X_k, Y_k) = D_c^G(X_k, Y_k;\ 0)$.[6] Combining both conditions, it is possible to express (17) as follows:

$$\frac{P \cdot Y_k}{W \cdot X_k} = ITE_c(X_k, Y_k) \cdot AE_c^G(X_k, Y_k; W, P;\ 0). \tag{21}$$

Now, in the usual cross-efficiency context considering k's shadow prices $\left(V_k^*, U_k^*\right)$when evaluating the performance of firm l, we first have that the standard input-oriented bilateral cross-efficiency can be interpreted as a profitability measure: $CITE_c(X_l, Y_l\,|k) = \frac{U_k^* \cdot Y_l}{V_k^* \cdot Y_l}$. Second, $CITE_c(X_l, Y_l) = \frac{1}{n}\sum_{k=1}^{n} \frac{U_k^* \cdot Y_l}{V_k^* \cdot X_l}$ is the arithmetic mean of the n individual profitabilities [see (3)]. Additionally, by (21), we obtain the following decomposition of $CITE_c(X_l, Y_l)$:

$$CITE_c(X_l, Y_l) = \frac{1}{n}\sum_{k=1}^{n} \frac{U_k^* \cdot Y_l}{V_k^* \cdot X_l} = ITE_c(X_l, Y_l) \cdot \left[\frac{1}{n}\sum_{k=1}^{n} AE_c^G\left(X_l, Y_l; V_k^*, U_k^*:\ \gamma = 0\right)\right]. \tag{22}$$

Hence, under the assumption of CRS, $CITE_c(X_l, Y_l)$ can be decomposed as $FCE_L(X_l, Y_l)$ into two technical and allocative factors, expression (7). Indeed, CRS implies that the production technology is input homothetic, and Aparicio and Zofío (2019) show in their Theorem 1 that in this (less restrictive) case, $CITE_c(X_l, Y_l) = FCE_c(X_l, Y_l)$, and therefore (22) coincides

[5] Aparicio and Zofío (2019) show in their Lemma 2 that given an optimal solution to problem (1), $\left(V_k^*, U_k^*\right)$, then $\Pi_c\left(V_k^*, U_k^*\right) = 0$, i.e., maximum profit equal to infinitum can be discarded.

[6] In terms of the hyperbolic distance function, $ITE_c(X_k, Y_k) = D_c^H(X_k, Y_k)^2$.

with (7). Consequently, as in the latter expression, the classical input cross-inefficiency measure is equal to the self-appraisal score of firm l, $ITE_c(X_l, Y_l)$, modified by the mean of its (shadow) generalized allocative efficiencies. Note also that, as per (20), technical efficiency can be decomposed into VRS and scale efficiencies: $ITE_c(X_l, Y_l) = ITE_v(X_l, Y_l) \cdot SE^F(X_l, Y_l)$.

Finally, it is also worth mentioning that the profit and profitability dualities and their associated economic cross-inefficiencies, including their decompositions, can be directly related in the case of CRS. Following Färe et al. (2002, 673), the precursor of expression (15) in terms of the profit function is:

$$\Pi_T(W, P) \geq \frac{P \cdot Y_l}{D_c^G(X_l, Y_l;\ \gamma)^{\gamma}} - D_c^G(X_l, Y_l;\ \gamma)^{1-\gamma} W \cdot X_l. \tag{23}$$

Since $\Pi_T(W, P) = 0$ in the case of CRS, expression (15) is easily derived from (23) and vice versa. However, under VRS, $\Pi_T(W, P)$ is not nil and we cannot obtain the duality-based inequality (15), with the left-hand side not depending on any efficiency measure (distance function) and the right-hand side not depending on prices. This shows, once again, the importance of defining multiplicative economic cross-efficiency measures under the assumption of VRS.

3.2 Farrell (Revenue) Cross-efficiency

Following the same procedure set out to define the Farrell (cost) cross-efficiency, $FCE_L(X_l, Y_l)$in (6), we can develop an output-oriented approach in terms of the radial output technical efficiency, $OTE_c(X_k, Y_k)$under CRS calculated through a DEA program corresponding to the inverse of (1)—see Ali and Seiford (1993)—and the revenue function. As usual, $OTE_v(X_k, Y_k)$ may be computed under VRS adding the constraint $\sum_{j=1}^{n} \lambda_j = 1$.

The standard output technical cross-efficiency of l based on the optimal weights—shadow prices—of k, $\left(V_k^*, U_k^*\right)$, defines as:

$$COTE_c(X_l, Y_l \,|k) = \frac{V_k^* \cdot X_l}{U_k^* \cdot Y_l} = \frac{\sum_{i=1}^{m} v_{ik}^* x_{il}}{\sum_{r=1}^{s} u_{rk}^* y_{rl}}, \tag{24}$$

The introduction of the Farrell (revenue) cross-efficiency requires defining the output requirement set $P(X)$ as the set of nonnegative outputs $Y \in R_+^s$ that can be produced with nonnegative inputs $X \in R_+^m$, formally $P(X) = \left\{Y \in R_+^s : (X, Y) \in T\right\}$, and the isoquant of $P(X) : Isoq\ P(X) : = \{Y \in P(X) : \varepsilon > 1 \Rightarrow \varepsilon Y \notin P(X)\}$. Let us also denote by $R_L(X, P)$ the maximum revenue obtained from using input level X given the output market price vector $P \in R_{++}^s$: $R_L(X, P) = \max_Y \left\{\sum_{i=1}^{s} p_s y_s : Y \in P(X)\right\}$. The standard revenue definition and decomposition is given by:

$$\underbrace{\frac{R_L(X, P)}{\sum_{i=1}^{s} p_s y_s}}_{\text{Revenue Efficiency}} = \underbrace{\frac{1}{D_L^O(X, Y)}}_{\text{Technical Efficiency}} \cdot \underbrace{AE_L^F(X, Y; P)}_{\text{Allocative Efficiency}}, \tag{25}$$

where $D_L^O(X, Y) = \inf\{\phi > 0 : Y/\phi \in P(X)\}$ is the Shephard output distance function (Shephard 1953) and allocative efficiency is defined residually. Again, we use the subscript L to stress that revenue efficiency can be defined with respect to different returns to scale.

Consequently, considering shadow prices, the Farrell (revenue) cross-efficiency of firm l with respect to firm k is:

$$FRE_L(X_l, Y_l \,|k) = \frac{R_L\left(X_l, U_k^*\right)}{U_k^* \cdot Y_l} = \frac{R_L\left(X_l, U_k^*\right)}{\sum_{r=1}^{s} u_{rk}^* y_{rl}}, \tag{26}$$

with $L \in \{c, v\}$ denoting constant and variable returns to scale, respectively.

As in (25), $FRE_L(X_l, Y_l|k) = \frac{1}{D_L^O(X_l,Y_l)} \cdot AE_L^F(X_l, Y_l; U_k^*)$. Therefore, Farrell revenue cross-efficiency corrects the usual technical efficiency, the inverse of Shephard output distance function, through a term capturing (shadow) allocative efficiency.

As in the case of the Farrell cost cross-efficiency (6), we could aggregate all individual revenue cross-efficiencies following the standard approach that relies on the arithmetic mean. However, in the current multiplicative framework, we rely on our preferred choice for the geometric mean, already used in the profitability approach. This yields:

$$FRE_L(X_l, Y_l) = \left(\prod_{k=1}^{n} FRE_L(X_l, Y_l|k)\right)^{1/n} = \left(\prod_{k=1}^{n} \frac{R_L(X_l, U_k^*)}{U_k^* \cdot Y_l}\right)^{1/n}, \tag{27}$$

which can be further decomposed into technical and allocative components:

$$FRE_L(X_l, Y_l) = \left(\prod_{k=1}^{n} \frac{R_L(X_l, U_k^*)}{U_k^* \cdot Y_l}\right)^{1/n} = OTE_L(X_l, Y_l) \cdot \left(\prod_{k=1}^{n} AE_L^F(X_l, Y_l; U_k^*)\right)^{1/n}. \tag{28}$$

We now combine the cost and revenue approaches of economic cross-efficiency and relate it to the profitability cross-efficiency definition. Assume first that the $FCE_L(X_l, Y_l)$ in (6) is defined using the geometric mean as aggregator—so it is consistent with $FRE_L(X_l, Y_l)$ in (27). Then, given that $FCE_L(X_l, Y_l)$ depends on (shadow) input prices but not on (shadow) output prices and vice versa for $FRE_L(X_l, Y_l)$, we suggest to mix both approaches to introduce yet another new cross-efficiency measure under the Farrell paradigm.

$$FE_L(X_l, Y_l) = \frac{FCE_L(X_l, Y_l)}{FRE_L(X_l, Y_l)} = \frac{\left(\prod_{k=1}^{n} \frac{C_L(Y_l, V_k^*)}{V_k^* \cdot X_l}\right)^{1/n}}{\left(\prod_{k=1}^{n} \frac{R_L(X_l, U_k^*)}{U_k^* \cdot Y_l}\right)^{1/n}} = \frac{ITE_L(X_l, Y_l) \cdot \left(\prod_{k=1}^{n} AE_L^F(X_l, Y_l; V_k^*)\right)^{1/n}}{OTE_L(X_l, Y_l) \cdot \left(\prod_{k=1}^{n} AE_L^F(X_l, Y_l; U_k^*)\right)^{1/n}}. \tag{29}$$

$FE_L(X_l, Y_l)$ is related to $CITE_c(X_l, Y_l|k)$ under CRS:

$$FE_c(X_l, Y_l) = \frac{\left(\prod_{k=1}^{n} \frac{U_k^* \cdot Y_l}{V_k^* \cdot X_l}\right)^{1/n}}{\left(\prod_{k=1}^{n} \frac{R_c(X_l, U_k^*)}{C_c(Y_l, V_k^*)}\right)^{1/n}} = \frac{\left(\prod_{k=1}^{n} CITE_c(X_l, Y|k)\right)^{1/n}}{\left(\prod_{k=1}^{n} \frac{R_c(X_l, U_k^*)}{C_c(Y_l, V_k^*)}\right)^{1/n}}. \tag{30}$$

The value of (30) must be closed to:

$$\left(\prod_{k=1}^{n} CITE_c(X_l, Y|k)\right)^{1/n} / \left(\prod_{k=1}^{n} \mathrm{P}_T(V_k^*, U_k^*)\right)^{1/n}. \tag{31}$$

Additionally, $FE_L(X_l, Y_l)$ always takes values between zero and one, while $FE_L(X_l, Y_l) \leq \frac{ITE_L(X_l, Y_l)}{OTE_L(X_l, Y_l)}$, under any returns to scale assumed.

At this point, it is worth mentioning that analogous results to the Farrell cost cross-efficiency can be derived for the cross output technical efficiency and revenue efficiency when output homotheticity is assumed; i.e., $COTE_c(X_l, Y_l|k) = FRE_c(X_l, Y_l|k)$. However, $COTE_c(X_l, Y_l) \neq FRE_c(X_l, Y_l)$ in general if $COTE_c(X_l, Y_l)$ is defined as usual by additive aggregation, and $FRE_c(X_l, Y_l)$ is defined through multiplicative aggregation.

3.3 *Profit Cross-inefficiency Based on the (Weighted) Additive Distance Function*

This section introduces a measure of economic cross-efficiency based on the weighted additive distance function, which constitutes an alternative to the Nerlovian definition based on the directional distance function.

Cooper et al. (2011) proved that:

$$\frac{\Pi_T(W,P)-\left(\sum_{r=1}^{s}p_r y_{rk}-\sum_{i=1}^{m}w_i x_{ik}\right)}{\min\left\{\frac{w_1}{a_{1k}},\ldots,\frac{w_m}{a_{mk}},\frac{p_1}{b_{1k}},\ldots,\frac{p_s}{b_{sk}}\right\}}\geq WA_T(X_k,Y_k;A_k,B_k), \tag{32}$$

where:

$$WA_v(X_k,Y_k;A_k,B_k)=\max_{S,H,\lambda_j}\left\{A_k\cdot S+B_k\cdot H:\sum_{j=1}^{n}\lambda_j x_{ij}\leq x_{ik}-s_i,\forall i,\ y_{rk}+h_r\leq\sum_{j=1}^{n}\lambda_j y_{rj},\right.$$
$$\left.\sum_{j=1}^{n}\lambda_j=1,\lambda_j\geq 0,\ j=1,\ldots,n,\ \ S\geq 0_m, H\geq 0_s\right\} \tag{33}$$

is the weighted additive model in DEA. In particular, A_k and B_k are prefixed input and output weights, respectively. As in the Nerlovian approach (8), the left-hand side of (32) measures profit inefficiency, defined as maximum profit (i.e., the value of the profit function at the market prices) minus observed profit, normalized by the minimum of the ratios of market prices to their corresponding prefixed weights. Based on (32), and assuming variable returns to scale, profit inefficiency for firm k can be decomposed as follows:

$$\frac{\Pi_V(W,P)-\left(\sum_{r=1}^{s}p_r y_{rk}-\sum_{i=1}^{m}w_i x_{ik}\right)}{\min\left\{\frac{w_1}{a_{1k}},\ldots,\frac{w_m}{a_{mk}},\frac{p_1}{b_{1k}},\ldots,\frac{p_s}{b_{sk}}\right\}}=WA_v(X_k,Y_k;A_k,B_k)+AI_V^W(X_k,Y_k;W,P;A_k,B_k). \tag{34}$$

Substituting market prices by shadow prices[7] in evaluating firm l with respect to firm k, we obtain:

$$WACI_V(X_l,Y_l;A_l,B_l\,|k)=\frac{\Pi_v\left(V_k^*,U_k^*\right)-\left(\sum_{r=1}^{s}u_{rk}^* y_{rl}-\sum_{i=1}^{m}v_{ik}^* x_{il}\right)}{\min\left\{\frac{v_{1k}^*}{a_{1l}},\ldots,\frac{v_{mk}^*}{a_{ml}},\frac{u_{1k}^*}{b_{1l}},\ldots,\frac{u_{sk}^*}{b_{sl}}\right\}}. \tag{35}$$

Aggregating all profit cross-inefficiencies through the arithmetic mean, given the additive framework, allows us to define the new profit cross-inefficiency measure based on the weighted additive approach:

$$WACI_v(X_l,Y_l;A_l,B_l)=\frac{1}{n}\sum_{k=1}^{n}\frac{\Pi_v\left(V_k^*,U_k^*\right)-\left(\sum_{r=1}^{s}u_{rk}^* y_{rl}-\sum_{i=1}^{m}v_{ik}^* x_{il}\right)}{\min\left\{\frac{v_{1k}^*}{a_{1l}},\ldots,\frac{v_{mk}^*}{a_{ml}},\frac{u_{1k}^*}{b_{1l}},\ldots,\frac{u_{sk}^*}{b_{sl}}\right\}} \tag{36}$$

which can be decomposed as (34), yielding:

$$WACI_v(X_l,Y_l;A_l,B_l)=WA_v(X_l,Y_l;A_l,B_l)+\frac{1}{n}\sum_{k=1}^{n}AI_V^W\left(X_l,Y_l;V_k^*,U_k^*;A_l,B_l\right) \tag{37}$$

Therefore $WACI_T(X_l,Y_l;A_l,B_l)$ coincides with the sum of the original technical inefficiency measure of firm l, determined by the weighted additive model, and a correction factor capturing (shadow) allocative inefficiencies.

It is worth mentioning that, among all the approaches mentioned in this chapter, the weighted additive model is unique such that it measures technical efficiency with respect to the strongly efficient frontier, resorting to the notion of Pareto-Koopmans efficiency.

[7]Shadow prices are obtained for DMU_k through the linear dual of program (33).

3.4 *Profit Cross-inefficiency Measure Based on the Hölder Distance Function*

In this section, we introduce a profit cross-inefficiency measure based on the Hölder distance function, thereby relating two streams of the literature: cross-efficiency and least distance. Hölder distance functions were firstly introduced with the aim of relating the concepts of technical efficiency and metric distances (Briec 1998).

The Hölder norms ℓ_q ($q \in [1, \infty]$) are defined over a g-dimensional real normed space as follows:

$$\| \|_q : Z \to \|Z\|_q = \begin{cases} \left(\sum_{j=1}^{g} |z_j|^q \right)^{1/q} & \text{if q} \in [1, \infty[\\ \max_{j=1,\dots,g} \{|z_j|\} & \text{if q} = \infty \end{cases}, \tag{38}$$

where $Z = (z_1, \dots, z_g) \in R^g$. From (38), Briec (1998) defines the Hölder distance function for firm k with vector of inputs and outputs (X_k, Y_k) as follows:

$$D_{\| \|_q}(X_k, Y_k) = \inf_{X,Y} \left\{ \|((X_k, Y_k)) - (X, Y)\|_q : (X, Y) \in \partial(T) \right\}. \tag{39}$$

Model (39) minimizes the distance from (X_k, Y_k) to the weakly efficient frontier of the technology, denoted as $\partial(T)$, and is interpreted as a measure of technical inefficiency. Other related paper where Hölder distance functions have also been used linked to the weakly efficient frontier is Briec and Lesourd (1999).

After introducing some notation and definitions, we are ready to show that we can derive a difference-form measure of profit inefficiency from a duality result proven in Briec and Lesourd (1999).

Proposition 1 Let (X_k, Y_k) an input-output vector in T. Let ℓ_t be the dual space of ℓ_q with $1/q + 1/t = 1$. Then:

$$D_{\| \|_q}(X_k, Y_k) = \inf_{D,H} \left\{ \Pi_T(D, H) - \left(\sum_{r=1}^{s} h_r y_{rk} - \sum_{i=1}^{m} d_i x_{ik} \right) : \|(D, H)\|_t \geq 1, D \geq 0_m, H \geq 0_s \right\}.$$

Proof See Proposition 3.2 in Briec and Lesourd (1999). ■

By Proposition 1, it is obvious that if the input-output market prices (W, P) are such that $\|(W, P)\|_t \geq 1$, then $\Pi_T(W, P) - \left(\sum_{r=1}^{s} p_r y_{rk} - \sum_{i=1}^{m} w_i x_{ik} \right) \geq D_{\| \|_q}(X_k, Y_k)$. We are then capable of obtaining the usual difference-form measure of profit inefficiency in the left-hand side of the inequality and the Hölder distance function in the right-hand side, showing that it is possible to decompose overall inefficiency through $D_{\| \|_q}(X_k, Y_k)$. However, as with the previous proposals (8) and (32), profit inefficiency must be normalized (deflated) in order to obtain an appropriate measure—see Aparicio et al. (2016). Accordingly, we propose the following solution, which was proven in Aparicio et al. (2017a)

Proposition 2 Let (X_k, Y_k) an input-output vector in T. Let ℓ_t be the dual space of ℓ_q with $1/q + 1/t = 1$. Let $(W, P) \in R^{m+s}_{++}$. Then:

$$\frac{\Pi_T(W, P) - \left(\sum_{r=1}^{s} w_r y_{rk} - \sum_{i=1}^{m} p_i x_{ik} \right)}{\|(W, P)\|_t} \geq D_{\| \|_q}(X_k, Y_k). \tag{40}$$

As before, departing from (40), and assuming variable returns to scale, profit inefficiency for firm k can be decomposed as follows:

$$\frac{\Pi_T(W, P) - \left(\sum_{r=1}^{s} p_r y_{rk} - \sum_{i=1}^{m} w_i x_{ik} \right)}{\|(W, P)\|_t} = D_{\| \|_q}(X_k, Y_k) + AI_V^{\| \|_q}(X_k, Y_k; W, P). \tag{41}$$

Considering shadow prices[8] rather than market prices when evaluating firm l with respect to firm k, we obtain:

$$HCI_V\left(X_l, Y_l\,|k\right) = \frac{\Pi_v\left(V_k^*, U_k^*\right) - \left(\sum_{r=1}^{s} u_{rk}^* y_{rl} - \sum_{i=1}^{m} v_{ik}^* x_{il}\right)}{\left\|\left(V_k^*, U_k^*\right)\right\|_t} \tag{42}$$

Then, aggregating all profit cross-inefficiencies through the arithmetic mean yields the new profit cross-efficiency measured based on the Hölder distance function:

$$HCI_v\left(X_l, Y_l\right) = \frac{1}{n}\sum_{k=1}^{n} \frac{\Pi_v\left(V_k^*, U_k^*\right) - \left(\sum_{r=1}^{s} u_{rk}^* y_{rl} - \sum_{i=1}^{m} v_{ik}^* x_{il}\right)}{\left\|\left(V_k^*, U_k^*\right)\right\|_t} \tag{43}$$

which, once again, can be decomposed as (41), thereby obtaining:

$$HCI_v\left(X_l, Y_l\right) = D_{\|\|_q}\left(X_k, Y_k\right) + \frac{1}{n}\sum_{k=1}^{n} AI_V^{\|\|_q}\left(X_l, Y_l; V_k^*, U_k^*\right) \tag{44}$$

4 Extensions of Economic Cross-(in)efficiency to Panel Data

We now briefly introduce extensions of the economic cross-efficiency models related to panel data with the aim of comparing the evolution of firms' performance over time. To this end, we rely on two proposals related to the Farrell (cost) and Nerlovian (profit) approaches. For the former, Maniadakis and Thanassoulis (2004) introduce the so-called cost-Malmquist index:

$$CM\left(X_l^t, Y_l^t; X_l^{t+1}, Y_l^{t+1}\right) = \left[\left(\frac{W^t \cdot X^{t+1}/C_c^t\left(Y^{t+1}, W^t\right)}{W^t \cdot X^t/C_c^t\left(Y^t, W^t\right)}\right) \cdot \left(\frac{W^{t+1} \cdot X^{t+1}/C_c^{t+1}\left(Y^{t+1}, W^{t+1}\right)}{W^{t+1} \cdot X^t/C_c^{t+1}\left(Y^t, W^{t+1}\right)}\right)\right]^{1/2}, \tag{45}$$

where the superscripts t and t + 1 denote two different periods of time.

If we translate (45) to the cross-efficiency context considering shadow prices (those associated with the radial model in DEA), we get the following:

$$CM_c\left(X_l^t, Y_l^t; X_l^{t+1}, Y_l^{t+1}\,|k\right) = \left[\left(\frac{V_k^{*t} \cdot X_l^{t+1}/C_c^t\left(Y_l^{t+1}, V_k^{*t}\right)}{V_k^{*t} \cdot X_l^t/C_c^t\left(Y_l^t, V_k^{*t}\right)}\right) \cdot \left(\frac{V_k^{*t+1} \cdot X_l^{t+1}/C_c^{t+1}\left(Y_l^{t+1}, V_k^{*t+1}\right)}{V_k^{*t+1} \cdot x^{lt}/C_c^{t+1}\left(Y_l^t, V_k^{*t+1}\right)}\right)\right]^{1/2}. \tag{46}$$

In this way, we can introduce and decompose the cost-Malmquist cross-efficiency index for firm l as the geometric mean of $CM_c\left(X_l^t, Y_l^t; X_l^{t+1}, Y_l^{t+1}\,|k\right)$ for all k:

$$CM_c\left(X_l^t, Y_l^t; X_l^{t+1}, Y_l^{t+1}\right) = \left(\prod_{k=1}^{n} CM_c\left(X_l^t, Y_l^t; X_l^{t+1}, Y_l^{t+1}\,|k\right)\right)^{1/n} = \frac{ITE_c^t\left(X_l^t, Y_l^t\right)}{ITE_c^{t+1}\left(X_l^{t+1}, Y_l^{t+1}\right)} \cdot \Delta_l^F, \tag{47}$$

where Δ_l^F is a mix of technological, allocative efficiency and price changes over time.

For the Nerlovian cross-efficiency approach, Juo et al. (2015) define the change of normalized profit inefficiency from period t to period $t+1$ and propose its decomposition into different sources. In particular, these authors introduce a profit-Luenberger indicator:

[8] These shadow prices come from the optimization model that appears in Proposition 1.

$$\Pi L_T\left(X_l^t, Y_l^t; X_l^{t+1}, Y_l^{t+1}; G_l^x, G_l^y\right) = \frac{1}{2}\left\{\left[\frac{\Pi_T^t(W^t,P^t)-(P^t\cdot Y^t-W^t\cdot X^t)}{W^t\cdot G^x+P^t\cdot G^y} - \frac{\Pi_T^t(W^t,P^t)-(P^t\cdot Y^{t+1}-W^t\cdot X^{t+1})}{W^t\cdot G^x+P^t\cdot G^y}\right] + \left[\frac{\Pi_T^{t+1}(W^{t+1},P^{t+1})-(P^{t+1}\cdot Y^t-W^{t+1}\cdot X^t)}{W^{t+1}\cdot G^x+P^{t+1}\cdot G^y} - \frac{\Pi_T^{t+1}(W^{t+1},P^{t+1})-(P^{t+1}\cdot Y^{t+1}-W^{t+1}\cdot X^{t+1})}{W^{t+1}\cdot G^x+P^{t+1}\cdot G^y}\right]\right\}. \tag{48}$$

Accordingly, this definition can be reformulated for firm l in terms of the shadow prices of firm k (those related to the directional distance function), thereby obtaining:

$$\Pi L_T\left(X_l^t, Y_l^t; X_l^{t+1}, Y_l^{t+1}; G_l^x, G_l^y\,|k\right) = \frac{1}{2}\left\{\left[\frac{\Pi_T^t(V_k^{*t},U_k^{*t})-(U_k^{*t}\cdot Y_l^t-V_k^{*t}\cdot X_l^t)}{V_k^{*t}\cdot G_l^x+U_k^{*t}\cdot G_l^y} - \frac{\Pi_T^t(V_k^{*t},U_k^{*t})-\left(U_k^{*t}\cdot Y_l^{t+1}-V_k^{*t}\cdot X_l^{t+1}\right)}{V_k^{*t}\cdot G_l^x+U_k^{*t}\cdot G_l^y}\right] + \left[\frac{\Pi_T^{t+1}\left(V_k^{*t+1},U_k^{*t+1}\right)-\left(U_k^{*t+1}\cdot Y_l^t-V_k^{*t+1}\cdot X_l^t\right)}{V_k^{*t+1}\cdot G_l^x+U_k^{*t+1}\cdot G_l^y} - \frac{\Pi_T^{t+1}\left(V_k^{*t+1},U_k^{*t+1}\right)-\left(U_k^{*t+1}\cdot Y_l^{t+1}-V_k^{*t+1}\cdot X_l^{t+1}\right)}{V_k^{*t+1}\cdot G_l^x+U_k^{*t+1}\cdot G_l^y}\right]\right\}, \tag{49}$$

and the final profit-Luenberger cross-inefficiency indicator for firm l is defined as:

$$\Pi L_T\left(X_l^t, Y_l^t; X_l^{t+1}, Y_l^{t+1}; G_l^x, G_l^y\right) = \frac{1}{n}\sum_{k=1}^{n} \Pi L_T\left(X_l^t, Y_l^t; X_l^{t+1}, Y_l^{t+1}; G_l^x, G_l^y\,|k\right). \tag{50}$$

Following Juo et al. (2015), ΠL_T can be decomposed into several components, mainly a Luenberger productivity indicator, which ultimately corresponds to a profit-based Bennet quantity indicator, and a price change term incorporating allocative inefficiency (see Balk 2018). Likewise, the Luenberger productivity indicator may be decomposed into efficiency change and technical change. In particular, efficiency change coincides with the difference $DDF_T^t\left(X_l^t, Y_l^t; G_l^x, G_l^y\right) - DDF_T^{t+1}\left(X_l^{t+1}, Y_l^{t+1}; G_l^x, G_l^y\right)$. In this way, the profit-Luenberger cross-inefficiency for firm l would be decomposed into the change experienced by the DEA self-appraisal scores, the directional distance function value for firm l in times t and t + 1, and a (shadow) correction factor Δ_l^N:

$$\Pi L_T\left(X_l^t, Y_l^t; X_l^{t+1}, Y_l^{t+1}; G_l^x, G_l^y\right) = \left[DDF_T^t\left(X_l^t, Y_l^t; G_l^x, G_l^y\right) - DDF_T^{t+1}\left(X_l^{t+1}, Y_l^{t+1}; G_l^x, G_l^y\right)\right] + \Delta_l^N. \tag{51}$$

As for other panel data economic cross-(in)efficiency models that can be related to existing literature, we note that a profitability efficiency change measure based on shadow prices, i.e., $PCE_c(X_l, Y_l;\ \gamma)$, can be defined in terms of the Fisher index following Zofío and Prieto (2006). Also, following Aparicio et al. (2017b), it is possible to define a profit efficiency change measure using the economic cross-inefficiency model based on the weighted additive distance function $WACI_v(X_l, Y_l; A_l, B_l)$—alternative to the profit-Luenberger indicator in (49).

5 Numerical Examples: An Application to Banking Data

To illustrate the new cross-(in)efficiency measures and their empirical implementation, we rely on a database on 20 Iranian branch banks observed in 2001, previously used by Akbarian (2015) to present a novel model that ranks observations combining cross-efficiency and analytic hierarchy process (AHP) methods. The database was compiled originally by Amirteimoori and Kordrostami (2005), who discuss the statistical sources and selected variables. Following these authors, the production process is characterized by three inputs and three outputs. Inputs are I.1) number of staff (personnel), I.2) number of computer terminals, and I.3) branch size (square meters of premises). On the output side, the following variables are considered: O.1) deposits, O.2) amount of loans, and O.3) amount of charge. All output variables are stated in ten million of current Iranian rials. The complete (normalized) dataset can be found in Amirteimoori and Kordrostami (2005:689), while Table 1 shows the descriptive statistics for all these variables.

Table 1 Descriptive statistics for inputs and outputs, 2001

	Inputs			Outputs		
	Staff (#)	Computer terminals (#)	Space (m^2)	Deposits	Loans	Charge
Average	0.738	0.713	0.368	0.191	0.549	0.367
Median	0.752	0.675	0.323	0.160	0.562	0.277
Minimum	0.372	0.550	0.120	0.039	0.184	0.049
Maximum	1.000	1.000	1.000	1.000	1.000	1.000
Stand. dev.	0.160	0.138	0.207	0.200	0.261	0.257

Source: Amirteimoori and Kordrostami (2005)

In the empirical application, we illustrate the most representative multiplicative and additive models of economic cross-efficiency. In particular the Farrell cost model is based on the inverse of the input distance function, the profit approach based on the directional distance function (Nerlove), the weighted additive distance function, and the Hölder distance function, as well as the profitability definition based on the generalized distance function. We leave the Farrell revenue model and panel data implementations of the cost-Malmquist index and profit-Luenberger indicator as exercises to the interested readers.

5.1 *Farrell (Cost) and Nerlovian (Profit) Economic Cross-efficiency*

For comparison purposes, we calculate the economic cross-efficiency scores corresponding to the Farrell (cost) and the Nerlovian (profit) economic definitions introduced by Aparicio and Zofío (2019). In the first set of columns of Table 2, under the "Technical (in)efficiency – Distance functions" heading, we report the results for the original Farrell input-oriented model that radially measures technical efficiency for bank k as in (1) but allowing for variable returns to scale (VRS), i.e., $ITE_v(X_l, Y_l)$—see Ali and Seiford (1993) for the multiplier formulation of the program. The ranking of banks in the left column is precisely based on these values, which serves us as benchmark. As many as 12 banks (60% of the observations) are technically efficient, exemplifying the poor discriminatory power of conventional DEA models in small samples and the need for cross-efficiency methods.[9] The duality between the cost function and the inverse of the input distance function allows to introduce the bilateral cost cross-efficiency of firm l using the shadow prices of firm k, expression (5). Taking the arithmetic mean of all bilateral cross-inefficiencies yields the Farrell cross-efficiency measure (6), $FCE_v(X_l, Y_l)$, which is reported in the first (leftmost) column of the second group of results under the heading "Economic cross (in)-efficiencies." Here, it is interesting to remark that despite the use of cross-efficiency methods, several banks are still tied in the first place with a cost cross-efficiency score of one. Finally, the difference between the cost-based economic cross-efficiency measure and the input technical efficiency corresponds to the average of the allocative inefficiencies obtained for the n shadow prices: $\frac{1}{n}\sum_{k=1}^{n} AE_v^F\left(X_l, Y_l; V_k^*\right)$, (7). The values are reported once again in the first (left) column of the third group of results under the heading "Allocative (in)efficiency." Comparing technical and allocative efficiencies, we observe that the second component is a comparatively larger source of inefficiency.

The second set of results reported in Table 2 corresponds to the Nerlovian (profit) cross-efficiency. The values of the directional distance function under variable returns to scale, $\overrightarrow{D}_v\left(X_k, Y_k; G^x, G^y\right)$, are calculated with the customary choice of directional vector corresponding to the observed input and output quantities, $(G^x, G^y) = (X_l, Y_l)$. We see that the same 12 banks are efficient and that the ranking for the inefficient observations is almost the same, except for banks #18 and #6, whose position is reversed. On this occasion, based on the duality between the profit function and the directional distance function, we can define the bilateral cross-inefficiency measure (12), and aggregating all bilateral cross-inefficiencies through the arithmetic mean yields the Nerlovian profit cross-inefficiency, $NCI_v(X_l, Y_l; G^x, G^y)$ in (13), which is reported in the second column of the second group of results. Contrary to the Farrell cost cross-efficiency, none of the banks are Nerlovian cross-efficient. As before, the difference between profit cross-inefficiency and the technical efficiency score of the bank under evaluation (represented by the directional distance function) yields the average of allocative inefficiencies,

[9]The number of technically efficient banks reduces to seven under constant returns to scale, the standard assumption in the cross-efficiency literature.

Table 2 Economic cross-efficiency decompositions

		Technical (in)efficiency—distance functions						Economic cross-(in)efficiency					Allocative (in)efficiency				
Ranking	Bank	ITE_v	$\vec{D}^F_v$	D^G_c	D^G_v	WA_v	$D_{\|\|\|_q}$	FCE_v	NCI_v	PCE_c	$WADD_v$	HCI_v	AE^F_v	AI^N_v	AE^G_v	AI^W_v	$AI^{\|\|\|_q}_v$
		(1)	(10)	(16)	(16)+VRS	(33)	(39)	(6)	(13)	(19)	(35)	(43)	(7)	(14)	(20)	(37)	(44)
1	1	1.000	0.000	1.000	1.000	0.000	0.000	0.749	0.659	0.526	13.700	0.196	0.749	0.659	0.526	13.700	0.196
2	3	1.000	0.000	0.991	1.000	0.000	0.000	1.000	0.522	0.670	8.998	0.160	1.000	0.522	0.676	8.998	0.160
3	4	1.000	0.000	1.000	1.000	0.000	0.000	1.000	0.333	0.772	2.000	0.097	1.000	0.333	0.772	2.000	0.097
4	7	1.000	0.000	1.000	1.000	0.000	0.000	1.000	0.330	0.864	2.943	0.091	1.000	0.330	0.864	2.943	0.091
5	8	1.000	0.000	0.798	1.000	0.000	0.000	0.736	1.119	0.345	18.180	0.230	0.736	1.119	0.432	18.180	0.230
6	9	1.000	0.000	0.789	1.000	0.000	0.000	0.979	1.071	0.529	9.153	0.155	0.979	1.071	0.670	9.153	0.155
7	10	1.000	0.000	0.289	1.000	19.648	0.000	0.694	2.498	0.176	62.712	0.262	0.694	2.498	0.608	43.064	0.262
8	12	1.000	0.000	1.000	1.000	0.000	0.000	1.000	0.502	0.791	4.024	0.125	1.000	0.502	0.791	4.024	0.125
9	15	1.000	0.000	1.000	1.000	0.000	0.000	1.000	1.115	0.656	4.734	0.020	1.000	1.115	0.656	4.734	0.020
10	17	1.000	0.000	1.000	1.000	0.000	0.000	1.000	0.932	0.625	12.500	0.173	1.000	0.932	0.625	12.500	0.173
11	19	1.000	0.000	0.408	1.000	0.000	0.000	0.896	2.500	0.257	17.575	0.214	0.896	2.500	0.628	17.575	0.214
12	20	1.000	0.000	1.000	1.000	0.000	0.000	0.916	0.582	0.649	8.040	0.134	0.916	0.582	0.649	8.040	0.134
13	2	0.969	0.024	0.833	0.952	1.732	0.012	0.711	0.521	0.490	19.946	0.224	0.733	0.497	0.588	18.214	0.212
14	5	0.927	0.043	0.899	0.918	2.556	0.018	0.796	0.596	0.617	8.016	0.181	0.859	0.553	0.686	5.460	0.163
15	13	0.923	0.052	0.817	0.901	2.036	0.028	0.788	0.681	0.574	8.280	0.191	0.853	0.629	0.703	6.244	0.163
16	18	0.896	0.104	0.473	0.802	9.951	0.060	0.767	2.026	0.303	25.732	0.224	0.856	1.922	0.639	15.781	0.164
17	6	0.882	0.096	0.748	0.820	1.572	0.052	0.739	0.506	0.556	9.528	0.179	0.838	0.410	0.744	7.956	0.127
18	16	0.813	0.146	0.639	0.738	3.459	0.071	0.665	0.914	0.392	12.140	0.253	0.818	0.768	0.613	8.681	0.182
19	11	0.796	0.151	0.604	0.731	2.446	0.072	0.678	0.826	0.414	9.414	0.243	0.852	0.675	0.685	6.968	0.171
20	14	0.695	0.281	0.470	0.535	4.843	0.168	0.576	0.914	0.350	16.157	0.288	0.829	0.633	0.746	11.314	0.120
	Average	0.945	0.045	0.788	0.920	2.412	0.024	0.835	0.957	0.528	13.689	0.182	0.880	0.912	0.665	11.276	0.158
	Median	1.000	0.000	0.825	1.000	0.000	0.000	0.792	0.754	0.543	9.471	0.186	0.858	0.646	0.663	8.840	0.163
	Minimum	0.695	0.000	0.289	0.535	0.000	0.000	0.576	0.330	0.176	2.000	0.020	0.694	0.330	0.432	2.000	0.020
	Maximum	1.000	0.281	1.000	1.000	19.648	0.168	1.000	2.500	0.864	62.712	0.288	1.000	2.500	0.864	43.064	0.262
	Stand. dev.	0.088	0.075	0.232	0.130	4.736	0.043	0.142	0.649	0.186	13.038	0.066	0.103	0.654	0.095	9.003	0.054

Source: Own elaboration

Table 3 Rank correlations of cross-(in)efficiencies

	FCE_v (6)	NCI_v (13)	PCE_c (19)	$WADD_v$ (35)	HCI_v (43)
FCE_v	1.0000				
NCI_v	0.3133	1.0000			
PCE_c	0.7909*	0.7499*	1.0000		
$WADD_v$	0.6713*	0.6431*	0.8932*	1.0000	
HCI_v	0.9170*	0.5004*	0.8853*	0.8101*	1.0000

Spearman coefficients
Notes: Correlations are calculated once the (additive) economic cross-inefficiency scores are multiplied by -1, so the rankings are based on the same numerical interpretation, i.e., the greater the value, the higher the position in the ranking
Source: Own elaboration
*p-$value < 0.01$

$\frac{1}{n}\sum_{k=1}^{n} AI_v^N\left(X_l, Y_l; \overrightarrow{V}_k^*, \overrightarrow{U}_k^*; G^x, G^y\right)$ in (14). In this model, allocative inefficiency is almost the sole responsible of overall economic cross-inefficiency on average.

One wonders if the previously observed similarity in the technical efficiency rankings based on the input and directional distance functions extends to their respective economic cross-(in)efficiencies. As shown in Table 3, the Spearman rank correlation between these results turns out to be rather low: $\rho(FCE_v(X_l, Y_l), NCI_v(X_l, Y_l; G^x, G^y)) = 0.3131$, not being statistically significant at the usual levels of confidence. The low correlation would be expected, as this simply shows how different rankings can be depending on the cross-(in)efficiency models that are compared, in particular whether (i) they correspond to a multiplicative or additive definition of economic efficiency and whether (ii) they are based on a partial dimension of the production process and corresponding economic objective (e.g., input orientation and cost minimization) versus a complete characterization that takes into account both inputs and outputs and a maximizing profit behavior. In this case, the Farrell and Nerlovian economic cross-efficiency models differ in both aspects, and therefore a weak correlation could be anticipated.

5.2 New Measures of Economic Cross-(in)efficiency

Subsequently, in the third column of the first group of results in Table 2, we find the generalized distance function, $D_c^G(X_k, Y_k; \gamma)$ in (16), representing the technical part of the profitability cross-efficiency model, $PCE_c(X_l, Y_l; \gamma)$ in (19). To obtain these results, we have chosen $\gamma = 0.5$, a value that weights equally inputs and outputs when projecting the banks to the production frontier and therefore is neutral. Both the technical and economic cross-efficiency scores corresponding to this multiplicative approach are significantly lower than those reported for the Farrell cost cross-efficiency model. The reason is that profitability cross-efficiency is measured under the constant returns to scale (CRS) characterization of the production technology, while the rest of cross-efficiencies allow for VRS. Thus, the efficiency scores are smaller in the profitability model. This difference can be attributed to scale inefficiencies. For this reason, we present in the fourth column the directional distance function under variables returns to scale, $D_v^G(X_k, Y_k; \gamma)$. This allows calculation of the magnitude of the scale efficiency as $SE^G(X_k, X_k; \gamma) = D_c^G(X_k, X_k; \gamma)/D_v^G(X_k, X_k; \gamma)$. On average, scale inefficiency is 0.8565, which means that if banks were to produce at one of the most productive scale sizes (Banker et al. 1984), they could yield about 15% more quantity of outputs with a similar reduction in the quantity of inputs employed. Also, looking at the subset of 12 banks that are efficient under VRS, as many as 5 are scale inefficient (#3, #8, #9, #10, and #19). Moving on to profitability cross-efficiency, $PCE_c(X_l, Y_l; \gamma)$ is reported in the third column of the second group of results. Despite the fact that the profit cross-efficiency takes into account both the input and output dimensions of the production process, its ranking of banks correlates positively with that corresponding to the Farrell cost definition, showing the compatibility of these two multiplicative measures in the current application: $\rho(FCE_v(X_l, Y_l), PCE_c(X_l, Y_l; \gamma)) = 0.7909$—statistically significant at the 1% level. Completing the results for this measure, the ratio of the profitability cross-efficiency measure to the generalized distance function corresponds to the allocative efficiency factor, $\left(\prod_{j=1}^{n} AE_c^G(X_k, Y_k; V_k^*, U_k^*; \gamma)\right)^{1/n}$ in (20), presented in the third column of the third group of results. Looking at the average of the technical and allocative components, the weight of the latter term is relatively larger than the former (as in the multiplicative Farrell cost model).

We now focus on the last two alternative definitions of profit cross-inefficiency based on the duality between the profit function and either the weighted additive distance function or the Hölder distance functions, respectively. The results corresponding to the former, $WA_v(X_k, Y_k; A_k, B_k)$ in (33), are shown in the fifth column of the first group of results. Because of its different normalization constraint, its values are significantly larger than those observed for the—also additive—directional distance function $\overrightarrow{D}_v(X_k, Y_k; G^x, G^y)$, with bank #10 performing rather poorly. The values of the profit cross-inefficiency corresponding to this model, $WACI_v(X_l, Y_l; A_l, B_l)$ in (35), can be found in the fourth column of the second group of results, while its associated allocative inefficiency in the same column of the third group of results, i.e., $\frac{1}{n}\sum_{k=1}^{n} AI_V^W\left(X_l, Y_l; V_k^*, U_k^*; A_l, B_l\right)$, in (37).

As for the Hölder distance function, $D_{\|\|_q}(X_k, Y_k)$ in (39), underlying the last definition of profit cross-inefficiency, we choose as reference the infinitum norm, ℓ_∞—see Aparicio et al. (2016). This makes this function equal to the directional distance function when the directional vector is unit-valued, i.e., $(G^x, G^y) = (1, \ 1)$. For that reason, the results can be readily compared to those previously reported for the directional distance function: $\overrightarrow{D}_v(X_k, Y_k; G^x, G^y)$ with $(G^x, G^y) = (X_l, Y_l)$. This also extends to the comparison between the Hölder and Nerlovian profit cross-inefficiencies. The results for the Hölder distance function are reported in the last (rightmost) column of the first group of results, with the 12 technically efficient banks exhibiting, once again, zero-valued scores. Finally, the Hölder cross-inefficiency scores, $HCI_v(X_l, Y_l)$ in (43), and its corresponding allocative inefficiencies, $\frac{1}{n}\sum_{k=1}^{n} AI_V^{\|\|_q}\left(X_l, Y_l; V_k^*, U_k^*\right)$ in (44), are shown in the last (rightmost) columns of the second and third group of results, respectively. As in the Nerlovian profit model, the allocative component is the main source of inefficiency.

The compatibility between rankings resulting from the same economic efficiency definition (i.e., profit) is rather high, with the Spearman correlations in the range set by $\rho(NCI_v(X_l, Y_l; G^x, G^y), HCI_v(X_l, Y_l)) = 0.5004$ and $\rho(WA_v(X, Y; A, B), HCI_v(X_l, Y_l)) = 0.8101$—both statistically significant as identified in Table 3. Scanning through all coefficients, it is the ranking based on the profitability cross-inefficiency the one with the higher correlations with either its multiplicative or additive alternatives. This is a relevant result since the profitability ranking is based on constant returns to scale while its alternatives are created under the assumption of variable returns. This suggests that the rankings are not significantly affected by the existence of scale inefficiencies. On the other side, it seems that it is the ranking based on the Nerlovian profit cross-inefficiency the one that correlates less with any of its alternatives. Also, and rather surprisingly, the rankings from the multiplicative, partially oriented, Farrell (cost) cross-efficiency and the additive Hölder (profit) cross-inefficiency are those presenting the highest (and significant) correlation: $\rho(FCE_v(X_l, Y_l)\ HCI_v(X_l, Y_l)) = 0.9170$. The relative values for the technical and allocative inefficiencies follow the exact same pattern in the previous Nerlovian and weighted additive models.

6 Summary and Conclusion

This study extends the existing definitions of economic cross-(in)efficiency proposed by Aparicio and Zofío (2019) by introducing a new set of multiplicative and additive measures that can be obtained from the duality relationship between alternative representations of economic behavior and their distance function technological counterparts. Economic cross-(in)efficiency measures the performance of firms in terms of a set of reference prices that could correspond to either market prices, shadow prices, or any other imputed prices. When market prices are available, it can be shown that for homothetic technologies, the process of benchmarking corresponds to the usual economic efficiency definitions, e.g., *à la* Farrell regarding cost-efficiency or *à la* Nerlove in the case of profit inefficiency. However, mirroring cross-inefficiency methods, it is possible to adapt this framework by considering the complete set of shadow prices that are obtained when evaluating the technical efficiency of all firms within the sample. This overall economic measure can be interpreted as the capability of firms to behave optimally by reaching minimum cost or maximum profit for a wide range of prices. The new methodology is particularly relevant in studies where market prices are not readily available because of the institutional framework (e.g., public services such as education, health, safety, etc.), but yet a robust ranking of observations based on their performance is demanded by decision-makers and stakeholders.

The combination of the economic and cross-efficiency literatures solves some of the weaknesses of the standard approaches based on DEA for ranking observations, as when there is a large set of them that are technically efficient, resulting in ties for the first place. Cross-efficiency methods were introduced in part to solve that drawback, yet they have been only applied under the assumption of constant returns to scale because of the negative scores that may be obtained when the technology is characterized by variable returns to scale. The economic cross-(in)efficiency methodology solves this problem in a natural way, without proposing ad hoc methods such as those based on data translations (Lim and Zhu 2015). Also, recent critics which raised against cross-efficiency methods regarding the (unrealistic) interpretation of the DEA multipliers as sensible shadow prices (Førsund 2018a, 2018b) can now be addressed under the new paradigm, since they can be understood as actual realizations of possible market prices.

To be consistent in the definition of economic cross-(in)efficiency, a duality relationship between a supporting economic function and its corresponding distance function is required. This allows the decomposition in a subsequent stage of economic cross-efficiencies into technical efficiency (the actual value of the distance function) and a residual defined as either the arithmetic or geometric mean of the allocative (in)efficiency residuals. Following this scheme, we introduce two new multiplicative definitions of economic cross-efficiency. The first one relates the profitability function, defined as the ratio of revenue to costs (Georgescu-Roegen 1951), and the generalized distance function (Chavas and Cox 1999). The second one can be seen as a particular case of the former that relates the revenue function and the output distance function (Shephard 1953)—just as the Farrell cost cross-efficiency approach. We also present two alternative additive definitions of economic cross-inefficiencies based in the duality between the profit function and either the weighted additive distance function (Cooper et al. 2011) or the Hölder distance function (Briec and Lesourd 1999). In passing we note that these two distance functions are particular cases of the loss function introduced by Aparicio et al. (2016), which could be eventually used to develop the most general model of economic cross-inefficiency. All these and previous models of economic cross-efficiency correspond to a cross-sectional evaluation of performance, but they can be extended to panel data. In this case the change on cost-efficiency over time can be combined with our proposed reinterpretation of cross-efficiency methods to yield, thereby obtaining the counterpart to the so-called cost-Malmquist (Maniadakis and Thanassoulis 2004) and profit-Luenberger indicators (Juo et al. 2015). Following the same procedure, these variations can be decomposed into quantity productivity indices or indicators and a residual capturing the role played by changes in prices (i.e., allocative efficiency change) and technological change.

We show also that the new models can be implemented empirically using DEA techniques. For this, we rely on a database of financial institutions previously used in the cross-efficiency literature. The results show the suitability of adopting the economic cross-(in)efficiency approach to rank observations according to their productive performance and its decomposition into its technical and allocative sources. For this particular application, we find that results are in general compatible across models (particularly for the relative weight of technical and allocative (in)efficiencies), resulting in rather high Spearman correlations. This result is also observed for models that are quite dissimilar in principle, i.e., those based on a partial orientation such as the Farrell cost cross-efficiency and the input distance function and a complete characterization of the production process based on the profit function and the Hölder distance function. Nevertheless, the correlation between the former and the Nerlovian economic cross-efficiency is in turn the lowest across all models. This shows that, as with any efficiency and productivity study, the choice of the appropriate reference model is critical when assessing performance.

We conclude suggesting some paths for further research related to both the economic efficiency and the cross-efficiency literature that could be brought to the new models of economic cross-efficiency. Regarding the former, it is well-known that if technologies are non-homothetic, the standard decompositions of economic efficiency fail to correctly characterize technical and allocative inefficiency. Within the non-DEA approach, Aparicio et al. (2015) show that, for non-homothetic technologies, the radial contractions (expansions) of the input (output) vectors resulting in efficiency gains do not maintain allocative (in)efficiency constant along the firm's projection to the production frontier (isoquants). This implies that they cannot be solely interpreted as technical efficiency reductions. From the perspective of, for example, the Farrell cost-efficiency decomposition in this study, this result invalidates the residual nature of allocative efficiency and justifies the use of flexible distance functions (i.e., directional, weighted additive, Hölder, etc.) with a choice of directional vector capable of keeping allocative efficiency constant along the projections. As for cross-efficiency, it is well-known that there exist alternative optima for the DEA models, which may result in different cross-efficiency scores. To overcome this situation, weights restrictions could be employed as suggested by Ramón et al. (2010). Yet another possibility is the adoption of secondary goals such as the so-called benevolent and aggressive approaches proposed by Sexton et al. (1986) and Doyle and Green (1994). See also Liang et al. (2008a) and Lim (2012) for further refinements. It is also possible to adopt a game cross-efficiency approach as in Liang et al. (2008b). All these are relevant qualifications and natural extensions that would result in the consolidation and improvement of cross-efficiency methods, making their diffusion to wider audiences more likely.

Acknowledgments J. Aparicio and J. L. Zofío thank the financial support from the Spanish Ministry of Economy and Competitiveness (Ministerio de Economía, Industria y Competitividad), the State Research Agency (Agencia Estatal de Investigación), and the European Regional Development Fund (Fondo Europeo de Desarrollo Regional) under grant no. MTM2016-79765-P (AEI/FEDER, UE).

References

Aczél, J., & Roberts, F. S. (1989). On the possible merging functions. *Mathematical Social Sciences, 17*, 205–243.

Akbarian, D. (2015). Ranking all DEA-efficient DMUs based on cross efficiency and analytic hierarchy process methods. *Journal of Optimization, 2015*, 594727, 10 pages.

Ali, A. I., & Seiford, L. M. (1993). The mathematical programming approach to efficiency analysis. In H. O. Fried, C. A. K. Lovell, & S. S. Schmidt (Eds.), *The measurement of productive efficiency: Techniques and applications* (pp. 120–159). New York, Oxford: Oxford University Press.

Amirteimoori, A., & Kordrostami, S. (2005). Efficient surfaces and an efficiency index in DEA: A constant returns to scale. *Applied Mathematics and Computation, 163*(2), 683–691.

Aparicio, J., & Zoffo, J. L. (2019). *Economic cross-efficiency: Theory and DEA methods*. ERIM Report Series Research in Management, No. ERS-2019-001-LIS. Erasmus Research Institute of Management (ERIM). Erasmus University Rotterdam, The Netherlands. http://hdl.handle.net/1765/115479

Aparicio, J., Pastor, J. T., & Zofio, J. L. (2015). How to properly decompose economic efficiency using technical and allocative criteria with non-homothetic DEA technologies. *European Journal of Operational Research, 240*(3), 882–891.

Aparicio, J., Borras, J., Pastor, J. T., & Zoffo, J. L. (2016). Loss distance functions and profit function: General duality results. In J. Aparicio, C. A. Knox Lovell, & J. T. Pastor (Eds.), *Advances in efficiency and productivity* (pp. 76–91). New York: Springer.

Aparicio, J., Pastor, J. T., Sainz-Pardo, J. L., & Vidal, F. (2017a). Estimating and decomposing overall inefficiency by determining the least distance to the strongly efficient frontier in data envelopment analysis. *Operational Research*, 1–24. https://doi.org/10.1007/s12351-017-0339-0.

Aparicio, J., Borras, F., Ortiz, L., Pastor, J.T., & Vidal, F. (2017b). Luenberger-type indicators based on the weighted additive distance function. *Annals of Operations Research*, 1–19. https://doi.org/10.1007/s10479-017-2620-2.

Balk, B. M. (2018). Profit-oriented productivity change: A comment. *Omega, 78*, 176–178.

Balk, B. M., de Koster, M. B. M., Kaps, C., & Zoffo, J. L. (2017). *An evaluation of cross-efficiency methods, applied to measuring warehouse performance*. ERIM Report Series Research in Management No. ERS-2017-015-LIS, Erasmus Research Institute of Management (ERIM), Erasmus University Rotterdam, The Netherlands. http://hdl.handle.net/1765/103185

Banker, R. D., Charnes, A., & Cooper, W. W. (1984). Some models for estimating technical and scale inefficiencies in data envelopment analysis. *Management Science, 30*(9), 1078–1092.

Briec, W. (1998). Hölder distance function and measurement of technical efficiency. *Journal of Productivity Analysis, 11*(2), 111–131.

Briec, W., & Lesourd, J. B. (1999). Metric distance function and profit: Some duality results. *Journal of Optimization Theory and Applications, 101*(1), 15–33.

Chambers, R. G., Chung, Y., & Färe, R. (1998). Profit, directional distance functions and Nerlovian efficiency. *Journal of Optimization Theory and Applications, 98*(2), 351–364.

Charnes, A., Cooper, W. W., & Rhodes, E. (1978). Measuring the efficiency of decision making units. *European Journal of Operational Research, 2*(6), 429–444.

Chavas, J.-P., & Cox, T. M. (1999). A generalized distance function and the analysis of production efficiency. *Southern Economic Journal, 66*(2), 295–318.

Cooper, W. W., Pastor, J. T., Aparicio, J., & Borras, F. (2011). Decomposing profit inefficiency in DEA through the weighted additive model. *European Journal of Operational Research, 212*(2), 411–416.

Doyle, J. R., & Green, R. H. (1994). Efficiency and cross-efficiency in DEA: Derivations, meanings, and uses. *Journal of the Operational Research Society, 45*, 567–578.

Färe, R., & Primont, D. (1995). *Multi-output production and duality: Theory and applications*. Boston: Kluwer Academic.

Färe, R., Grosskopf, S., & Zaim, O. (2002). Hyperbolic efficiency and return to the dollar. *European Journal of Operational Research, 136*(3), 671–679.

Farrell, M. J. (1957). The measurement of productive efficiency. *Journal of the Royal Statistical Society, Series A, General, 120*, 253–281.

Førsund, F. R. (2018a). Economic interpretations of DEA. *Socio-Economic Planning Sciences, 61*, 9–15.

Førsund, F. R. (2018b). Cross-efficiency: A critique. *Data Envelopment Analysis Journal, 4*, 1–25.

Georgescu-Roegen, N. (1951). The aggregate linear production function and its application to von Newman's economic model. In T. Koopmans (Ed.), *Activity analysis of production and allocation* (pp. 98–115). New York: Wiley.

Juo, J. C., Fu, T. T., Yu, M. M., & Lin, Y. H. (2015). Profit-oriented productivity change. *Omega, 57*, 176–187.

Liang, L., Wu, J., Cook, W. D., & Zhu, J. (2008a). Alternative secondary goals in DEA cross-efficiency evaluation. *International Journal of Production Economics, 113*(2), 1025–1030.

Liang, L., Wu, J., Cook, W. D., & Zhu, J. (2008b). The DEA game cross-efficiency model and its Nash equilibrium. *Operations Research, 56*(5), 1278–1288.

Lim, S. (2012). Minimax and maximin formulations of cross-efficiency in DEA. *Computers and Industrial Engineering, 62*(3), 726–731.

Lim, S., & Zhu, J. (2015). DEA cross-efficiency evaluation under variable returns to scale. *Journal of the Operational Research Society, 66*(3), 476–487.

Luenberger, D. G. (1992). New optimality principles for economic efficiency and equilibrium. *Journal of Optimization Theory and Applications, 75*(2), 221–264.

Maniadakis, N., & Thanassoulis, E. (2004). A cost Malmquist productivity index. *European Journal of Operational Research, 154*(2), 396–409.

Nerlove, M. (1965). *Estimation and identification of Cobb-Douglas production functions*. Chicago: Rand McNally.

Olesen, O. B. (2018). Cross efficiency analysis and extended facets. *Data Envelopment Analysis Journal, 4*, 27–64.

Ramón, N., Ruiz, J. L., & Sirvent, I. (2010). On the choice of weights profiles in cross-efficiency evaluations. *European Journal of Operations Research, 207*, 1564–1572.

Ruiz, J. L. (2013). Cross-efficiency evaluation with directional distance functions. *European Journal of Operational Research, 228*(1), 181–189.

Sexton, T. R., Silkman, R. H., & Hogan, A. J. (1986). Data envelopment analysis: Critique and extensions. In R. H. Silkman (Ed.), *Measuring efficiency: An assessment of data envelopment analysis, new directions for program evaluation* (Vol. 32, pp. 73–105). San Francisco/London: Jossey-Bass.

Shephard, R. W. (1953). *Cost and production functions*. Princeton: Princeton University Press.

Wu, J., Liang, L., & Chen, Y. (2009). DEA game cross-efficiency approach to Olympic rankings. *Omega, 37*(4), 909–918.

Zofío, J. L., & Prieto, A. M. (2006). Return to dollar, generalized distance function and the Fisher productivity index. *Spanish Economic Review, 8*(2), 113–138.

Evaluating Efficiency in Nonhomogeneous Environments

Sonia Valeria Avilés-Sacoto, Wade D. Cook, David Güemes-Castorena, and Joe Zhu

Abstract The conventional DEA methodology is generally designed to evaluate the relative efficiencies of a set of *comparable* decision-making units (DMUs). An appropriate setting is one where all DMUs use the same inputs, produce the same outputs, experience the same operating conditions, and generally operate in similar environments. In many applications, however, it can occur that the DMUs fall into different groups or categories, where the efficiency scores for any given group may be significantly different from those of another group. Examples include sets of hospitals with different patient mixes, groups of bank branches with differing customer demographics, manufacturing plants where some have been upgraded or modernized and others not, and so on. In such settings, if one wishes to evaluate an entire set of DMUs as a single group, this necessitates modifying the DEA structure such as to make allowance for what one might deem different environmental conditions or simply inherent inequities. Such a modification is presented herein and is illustrated using a particular example involving business activities in Mexico. While we do carry out a detailed analysis of these businesses, it is important to emphasize that this paper's principal contribution is the methodology, not the particular application to which the methodology is applied.

Keywords DEA · Nonhomogeneous DMUs · Compensation · Disadvantaged DMUs

1 Introduction

Data envelopment analysis (DEA), developed by Charnes et al. (1978), is a tool for evaluating the relative efficiencies of a set of decision-making units (DMUs), in the presence of multiple inputs and multiple outputs. Over the 35+ years since that seminal work appeared, there has been an enormous growth in research in this area. A number of surveys on this subject have appeared in recent years, including Liu et al. (2016), Cook and Seiford (2009), Cook et al. (2010), Paradi and Zhu (2013), and others.

Generally, DEA is applied to DMUs operating in the same environment, meaning that they constitute a homogeneous set. In such a situation, efficiency scores and accompanying projections to the best practice frontier should be a realistic portrayal of the technical efficiency standing of each DMU; this should mean that targets or projections are relatively achievable.

S. V. Avilés-Sacoto (✉)
Industrial Engineering Department, Institute of Innovation in Logistics, SCM—CATENA, Universidad San Francisco de Quito (USFQ). Diego de Robles entre Francisco de Orellana y Pampite, Quito, Ecuador

Instituto Tecnológico y de Estudios Superiores de Monterrey I.T.E.S.M., Monterrey, Nuevo León, Mexico

Schulich School of Business, York University, Toronto, ON, Canada
e-mail: svaviless@usfq.edu.ec

W. D. Cook
Schulich School of Business, York University, Toronto, ON, Canada
e-mail: wcook@schulich.yorku.ca

D. Güemes-Castorena
InstitutoTecnológico y de Estudios Superiores de Monterrey I.T.E.S.M., Monterrey, Nuevo León, Mexico
e-mail: guemes@itesm.mx

J. Zhu
School of Business, Worcester Polytechnic Institute, Worcester, MA, USA
e-mail: jzhu@WPI.EDU

J. Aparicio et al. (eds.), *Advances in Efficiency and Productivity II*, International Series in Operations Research & Management Science 287, https://doi.org/10.1007/978-3-030-41618-8_3

Many applications of DEA, however, involve situations where the DMUs fall into what might be seen as different groups: bank branches in different geographical areas, large branches versus small branches, hospitals that cater to different age groups, manufacturing plants falling into different technology upgrades, etc. In such settings, one group of DMUs can have an *advantage* over those DMUs in another group. Consider, for example, the case of bank branches falling into two groups, namely, those with a wealthy customer base (the rich branches) with significant investments in mutual funds, mortgages, etc. and the remaining branches that cater to poorer customers who purchase few financial services products. In such a setting, if investments constitute one of the outputs of the branches, then one might expect that the majority of efficient DMUs will come from the group of rich branches, while most poor branches will be declared as inefficient, possibly *very* inefficient. The recommended projections for poor branches may, in all likelihood, be unattainable, in that they can only reach the frontier by becoming rich branches.

In the current paper, we consider the situation where DMUs are a set of economic activities in Mexico. Example activities are shrimp fishing; silver mining; tanning and finishing leather; wholesale trade of red meat; generation, transmission, and distribution of electricity; and others. These economic activities fall into a number of distinct groups according to their three-digit SIC codes. For purposes of our analysis, we have chosen to view the DMUs as falling into three groups. Unlike the case where DMUs constitute a rather homogeneous set (hospitals in similar settings, bank branches in a given area with similar environmental circumstances in terms of customer mix, etc.), it happens that when one performs a conventional DEA analysis on the entire set of activities, the average DEA scores for the three groups are substantially different from one another. As a result, one might argue that those DMUs in the best performing group are in a more favorable position to achieve "efficient" status than is true of the DMUs in the other groups. This situation points to the need to adjust the DEA methodology to provide for a more fair setting in terms of efficiency evaluation.

Section 2 develops a modified version of the radial projection DEA model aimed at providing a fairer evaluation for "disadvantaged" DMUs. As an illustration, Sect. 3 describes the data set for the 800+ economic activities in Mexico which we wish to evaluate from an efficiency standpoint. While we provide some summary results for the entire set of 800+ business activities, we focus initially on a small subset of 42 of these, aimed at bringing clarity in explaining our methodology. More to the point, it is, for example, useful to observe both the conventional efficiency scores and the adjusted scores; the smaller sample of DMUs permits this, while for the full set of DMUs, such detail is more cumbersome to display. Conclusion and recommendations follow in Sect. 4.

2 A Model for Fair Evaluation of DMUs in Different Environments or Groups

The conventional input-oriented methodology of Charnes et al. (1978) provides an efficiency score for each of a set of similar decision-making units. Efficiency evaluation therein is based upon a set of inputs $\{x_{ij}\}_{i=1}^{I}$ and outputs $\{y_{rj}\}_{r=1}^{R}$, and the resulting efficiency score is given by the proportional reduction θ in each of the inputs (the input-oriented model) needed in order for the DMU in question to reach the efficient frontier. This idea can, as well, be applied in an output-oriented setting which provides for a proportional expansion in outputs rather than a reduction in inputs. In our problem setting involving economic activities, output expansion rather than input reduction is more appropriate.

The original work of Charnes et al. (1978) is based on a constant returns to scale (CRS) technology wherein for any DMU j is in the production possibility set, any new DMU created by proportionally scaling both the inputs and outputs of j will also be in the production possibility set. The CRS model is generally appropriate in settings where DMUs do not appear in a wide range of "sizes." An important extension of the CRS model is the variable returns to scale (VRS) model of Banker et al. (1984). In situations such as the one discussed in this paper, size of DMU is an inherent feature, and as a result we employ the VRS technology.

The output-oriented VRS (multiplier) model takes the following form:

$$
\begin{aligned}
&\text{Min } \left(\sum_i v_i x_{ij_0} + v_o\right) / \sum_r u_r y_{rj_0} \\
&\textit{Subject to} \\
&\left(\sum_i v_i x_{ij} + v_o\right) / \sum_r u_r y_{rj} \geq 1 \\
&u_r, v_i \geq \varepsilon, \quad v_o \textit{ unrestricted in } \text{sign}
\end{aligned}
\tag{1}
$$

Applying the usual Charnes and Cooper (1962) transformation, this nonlinear fractional programming problem can be converted to linear format as per (2):

$$\begin{aligned}
&\text{Min } \sum_i \upsilon_i x_{ij_0} + \upsilon_o \\
&Subject\ to \\
&\sum_r \mu_r y_{rj_0} = 1 \\
&\left(\sum_i \upsilon_i x_{ij} + \upsilon_o\right) - \sum_r \mu_r y_{rj} \geq 0, \ \forall j \\
&\mu_r, \upsilon_i \geq \varepsilon, \quad \upsilon_o \ unrestricted\ in\ \text{sign}
\end{aligned} \tag{2}$$

As discussed above, the intended settings to which such a model is to be applied are normally those where differences in DEA scores are purely a reflection of differences in technical efficiency and where each inefficient DMU can have a reasonable expectation of achieving full or nearly full efficiency status. In a case such as the bank branch setting discussed above, however, something in addition to technical efficiency and/or managerial capability may account for some of the observed differences in performance between the two groups of DMUs.

For notational purposes, let $N1$ and $N2$ denote the proposed or observed advantaged and disadvantaged groups, respectively; in our hypothetical bank branch setting, N1 would represent the rich branches and $N2$ the poor branches. In this setting, it can be claimed (possibly by branch management) that the poorer branches are being unfairly treated in having to be compared to their rich counterparts, and generally such a dichotomy would reveal itself by way of the efficiency scores arising from a DEA model such as (2). More to the point, the claim of a set of DMUs being disadvantaged would normally arise from an observation that the efficiency scores for that (disadvantaged) group appear to be substantially worse than those for the advantaged group.

2.1 Some Relevant Literature

It must be noted here that the concept of DMUs falling into different groups is not entirely un-researched. There is a substantial literature, for example, on the use of meta-frontier production functions in situations where firms are operating under different technologies. See, for example, Battase et al. (2004). That approach is one where each subset of DMUs (e.g., N1 and N2) is subjected to its own separate DEA analysis. A consequence of performing separate analyses on two or more groups results, of course, in the generation of as many frontiers. This does not, however, by itself, help to obtain a measure of the extent to which one group is disadvantaged relative to another group. In our case, however, we choose to evaluate the entire set (N1 and N2 combined), thereby allowing for the development of an actual measure of the *extent* to which N2 is disadvantaged.

Along somewhat the same line, the work of Banker and Morey (1986) on categorical variables views the problem of DMUs as falling into "nested" groups. To demonstrate, and using our terminology herein, suppose we have groups N1, N2, N3, for example, where N3 is the most disadvantaged, N2 the second most disadvantaged, and N1 the most advantaged. The categorical variable approach would see N3 DMUs evaluated only against other N3 DMUs, N2 DMUs against all units in N2 and N3, and finally N1 DMUs evaluated against DMUs in all three sets. In our current setting, however, we wish to create an environment, as described above, wherein all DMUs are evaluated against one another as a single group.

Another somewhat related line of literature is that due to Seiford and Zhu (2003) on context-dependent DEA. There, it is demonstrated that one can obtain multiple frontiers against which to evaluate DMUs. Specifically, one first applies the DEA model and obtains a frontier. The efficient units derived are then removed from the set of DMUs, and the model is applied again with the reduced set, leading to a second-level frontier, which is again removed from the set, and so on. The process terminates when no DMUs are left to be evaluated. The purpose of having the multiple frontiers is to be able to compare any given DMU against multiple peers leading to measures of attractiveness and progress for that DMU. In our setting, however, our purpose is to obtain an objective measure of the extent to which one subset of DMUs is advantaged or disadvantaged as compared to another subset, and then use that measure to adjust the disadvantaged set such as to create a fairer context within which to measure technical efficiency.

One area of DEA research of interest herein, and relating to the idea of a level playing field, is that where a three-stage approach is implemented. Specifically, the first stage involves a standard DEA analysis being carried out on a set of DMUs, followed by a second stage where the obtained DEA scores are regressed against a set of environmental variables with the intention of *explaining* differences in the first stage scores. In stage 3, the DEA scores are adjusted using the stage 2 results. As an example of this procedure, see Fried et al. (2002).

In another direction, Apriciao and Santin (2018) develop a Malmquist-type index for measuring group performance over time. In addition, the reader is referred to a number of important surveys of research in DEA including Emrouznejad, Parker, and Tavares (2008), Cook and Seiford (2009), and Liu et al. (2013).

In the examples described above such as those involving bank branches in different locations or branches serving different demographics, and where there is a believed advantage/disadvantage in one category versus another, the definition of the groupings N1, N2, etc. becomes relatively obvious. Specifically, one groups the entities (DMUs) according to the feature (e.g., location) that is believed to be creating the claimed inequity (disadvantage/advantage). In many situations, however, the question as to an appropriate set of groups is not so clear, as is the case regarding the performance of the various business activities discussed in the section to follow. In such a setting, one would need to rely on expertise in the appropriate government agencies such as the Department of Industry, Trade, and Commerce. As a starting point, a decision would normally be made as to the makeup of the most advantaged group N1. This decision would identify (1) which three-digit groups are closest to the frontier in terms of the average scores in those groupings and (2) which groups have historically been the best performers. It is, of course, recognized that certain members of particular advantaged three-digit groups may be poor performers, regardless of their "advantaged status."

Having decided on the DMU-membership of N1, a decision would next be made as to the makeup of N2 and so on. Support for a claimed advantage/disadvantage for DMUs in one group versus another might reasonably be based on the average efficiencies $\overline{e}_{N1}$ and $\overline{e}_{N2}$ for those two groups. Viewed from a purely statistical standpoint, one might offer the hypothesis that the two groups of DMUs are not drawn from the same population, which can be a signal that the conventional DEA model may fail to provide a proper framework within which to measure technical efficiency. The question then arises as to what "adjustments" should be implemented such as to give a fair chance to both (all) groups of DMUs in the sense that the adjusted average scores for the groups will display a greater degree of similarity to one another, hence be seen as leading to a *level playing field* for all DMUs. As well, it would be hoped that some efficient units will come from each of the groups, and for inefficient branches, frontier projections will be reasonably achievable.

One way of making for a more level playing field is to argue that the advantaged DMUs (say bank branches) have more of an additional input, such as "wealth of customers," and, therefore, this added advantage should be recognized. Alternatively, one can propose that to facilitate an evaluation that is "fair," there is a need to "compensate" disadvantaged DMUs. For example, staff in poor branches may devote as much time to marketing mutual funds as is the case in rich branches, but the outcome for poor branches is less profitable. In this case, an allowance that recognizes resources expended on unrewarded ventures (customers who are approached, but do not purchase) might be appropriate.

To formalize the compensation concept, let us assume, as discussed above, that the DMUs can be divided into two identifiable groups, namely, an advantaged group N1 and a disadvantaged group N2. We discuss the multigroup scenario later. For a disadvantaged DMU j_o, we argue that only a fraction α_{ij_o} of that DMU's input x_{ij_o} should be needed to generate its outputs, if it did *not* find itself in a disadvantageous situation. In other words, we might claim that a portion 1-α_{ij_o} of x_{ij_o} is dedicated to *coping with* an unaccommodating $\alpha_{ij_o}\alpha_{ij_o}$ environment; in the bank branch setting, 1-α_{ij_o} might reasonably represent the portion of resource x_{ij_o} expended on customers, but with no positive payoff.

Revisiting (2) above, we might consider a reformulation of that model as per (3). Here, α_{ij_o} is treated as a decision variable lying in a prescribed range [*a*, 1]; we assume of course that $0 \leq a \leq 1$. Let us refer to *a* as the *reduction parameter*. This problem would then be solved for each DMU $j_o \in N2$:

$$
\begin{aligned}
&\text{Min } \sum_i \upsilon_i \alpha_{ij_o} x_{ij0} + \upsilon_o \\
&Subject\ to \\
&\sum_r \mu_r y_{rj0} = 1 \\
&\left(\sum_i \upsilon_i x_{ij} + \upsilon_o\right) - \sum_r \mu_r y_{rj} \geq 0, \quad j \in N_1 \\
&\left(\sum_i \upsilon_i \alpha_{ij_o} x_{ij} + \upsilon_o\right) - \sum_r \mu_r y_{rj} \geq 0, \quad j \in N_2 \\
&a \leq \alpha_i \leq 1 \\
&\mu_r, \upsilon_i \geq \varepsilon, \quad \upsilon_o\ unrestricted\ in\ \text{sign}
\end{aligned}
\tag{3}
$$

We note that adjustments in inputs by way of α_{ij_o} apply only to the disadvantaged DMUs in N2.

The idea here is to adjust (reduce) inputs of DMUs in N2 so as to push those DMUs closer to the frontier and in the process hopefully bring the average efficiency score for N2 closer to that of N1. A problem with this model is that once an adjusted DMU hits the frontier, further adjustment then pushes the frontier "up," meaning that DMUs in N1 can become less efficient. At the same time, efficiency improvement for inefficient DMUs in N2 may not materialize even with input reduction, as such reduction is happening to peer DMUs at the same rates, especially those that have already reached the frontier and are moving that frontier up. As a result, model (3) is unlikely to bring about the desired fair and level playing field.

One way of moving the average efficiency of DMUs in N2 closer to that of N1 is to *fix* the frontier generated by the solution of (2). In other words, undertake the adjustment to DMUs while requiring that those adjusted units remain within the production possibility set (PPS) generated by (2). In that regard, let J denote the set of efficient DMUs generated by (2). We point out that some members of both N1 and N2 may appear in J. Now, for each inefficient DMU $j_o \in N_2$, consider problem (4):

$$\text{Min} \sum_i \upsilon_i \alpha_{ij_o} x_{ij_0} + \upsilon_o \tag{4a}$$

$$\textit{Subject to} \quad \sum_r \mu_r y_{rj_0} = 1 \tag{4b}$$

$$\sum_i \upsilon_i \alpha_{ij_o} x_{ij_0} + \upsilon_o - \sum_r \mu_r y_{rj_0} \geq 0 \tag{4c}$$

$$\left(\sum_i \upsilon_i x_{ij} + \upsilon_o\right) - \sum_r \mu_r y_{rj} \geq 0, \quad j \in J \tag{4d}$$

$$a \leq \alpha_{ij_o} \leq 1, \quad \forall i \tag{4e}$$

$$\mu_r, \upsilon_i \geq \varepsilon, \ \forall r, i, \quad \upsilon_o \ \textit{unrestricted in} \text{ sign} \tag{4f}$$

Here constraints (4d) define the PPS for the overall DEA model given by (2). At the same time, whatever reduction in inputs occurs, the resulting *adjusted* DMU j_o should lie within that PPS, as expressed by (4c).

Clearly model (4) is nonlinear by virtue of the fact that α_i is a decision variable. To linearize this problem, define a change of variables $\gamma_{ij_o} = \upsilon_i \alpha_{ij_o}$. Further, notice that $a \leq \alpha_{ij_o} \leq 1$ implies that $\upsilon_i a \leq \upsilon_i \alpha_{ij_o} \leq \upsilon_i$, hence, $\upsilon_i a \leq \gamma_{ij_o} \leq \upsilon_i$.

Thus, (4) can be written in linear format as:

$$\text{Min} \sum_i \gamma_{ij_o} x_{ij_0} + \upsilon_o \tag{5a}$$

$$\textit{Subject to} \quad \sum_r \mu_r y_{rj_0} = 1 \tag{5b}$$

$$\sum_i \gamma_{ij_o} x_{ij_0} + \upsilon_o - \sum_r \mu_r y_{rj_0} \geq 0 \tag{5c}$$

$$\left(\sum_i \upsilon_i x_{ij} + \upsilon_o\right) - \sum_r \mu_r y_{rj} \geq 0, \quad j \in J \tag{5d}$$

$$\upsilon_i a \leq \gamma_{ij_o} \leq \upsilon_i, \quad \forall i \tag{5e}$$

$$\mu_r, \upsilon_i, \gamma_{ij_o} \geq \varepsilon, \ \forall r, i, \quad \upsilon_o \ \textit{unrestricted in} \text{ sign} \tag{5f}$$

We point out that the optimal values for $\hat{\alpha}_{ij_o}$ are derived from $\hat{\alpha}_{ij_o} = \hat{\gamma}_{ij_o}/\hat{\upsilon}_i$.

Arguably, there is still a potential problem with model (5) in two respects:

First, in the current form of (5c), it is possible that for the chosen value of the parameter a, DMU j_o may not only project onto the frontier but also may push the frontier *up*, as was true of model (3). To address this, we suggest replacing constraint (5c) by:

$$\sum_i \gamma_{ij_o} x_{ij_0} + \upsilon_o - \sum_r \mu_r y_{rj_0} \geq \varepsilon \tag{5c'}$$

Here, ε is a small positive number that permits j_o to be adjusted arbitrarily close to the frontier without touching it, hence without distorting it.

Second, for the chosen parameter a, one or more of the adjusted components of x_i, namely $\alpha_i x_i$, may hit the frontier or bump against the ε in (5a) before (5e) becomes binding. In other words, there may be alternate optima for (5). To insure that the largest value of $\hat{\alpha}_{\hat{i}}$ results from the projection (hence, the least adjustment in the inputs occurs), we suggest that the objective function (5a) be modified to Min $\sum_i \gamma_{ij_o} x_{ij_0} + \upsilon_o - \varepsilon \sum_i (\gamma_{ij_o} - a\upsilon_i)$. Thus, we suggest the following modified version of (5):

$$\text{Min} \sum_i \gamma_{ij_o} x_{ij_0} + \upsilon_o - \varepsilon \sum_i (\gamma_{ij_o} - a\upsilon_i) \tag{6a}$$

$$\textit{Subject to} \quad \sum_r \mu_r y_{rj_0} = 1 \tag{6b}$$

$$\sum_i \gamma_{ij_o} x_{ij_0} + \upsilon_o - \sum_r \mu_r y_{rj_0} \geq \varepsilon \tag{6c}$$

$$\left(\sum_i \upsilon_i x_{ij} + \upsilon_o\right) - \sum_r \mu_r y_{rj} \geq 0, \quad j \in J \tag{6d}$$

$$\upsilon_i a \leq \gamma_{ij_o} \leq \upsilon_i b, \quad \forall i \tag{6e}$$

$$\mu_r, \upsilon_i, \gamma_{ij_o} \geq \varepsilon, \quad \forall r, i, \quad \upsilon_o \textit{ unrestricted in } \text{sign} \tag{6f}$$

Model (6) will adjust only DMUs in N2, unlike model (3), meaning that the scores for members of N1 arising from (2) are the final scores for that group.

It must be noted that the reduction parameter a is treated here as a parameter. So, the objective is to choose a value for a such that the resulting average $\overline{e}_{N2}$ of the efficiency scores for members of N2 is *close* to the average score $\overline{e}_{N1}$ for N1. It is suggested that the simple *half interval* method can be used here to find an appropriate value a. Specifically, we apply the following algorithm:

Algorithm:

Step 1: Choose as a starting value for a, the midpoint 0.5 of the [0, 1] interval, solve (6) for each member of N2, and compute the average score $\overline{e}_{N2}$. If $\overline{e}_{N2}$ is above $\overline{e}_{N1}$ and not yet close enough to $\overline{e}_{N1}$, then go to Step2. If $\overline{e}_{N2}$ is below $\overline{e}_{N1}$ and deemed not yet close enough to $\overline{e}_{N1}$, go to Step 3. Otherwise go to Step 4.

Step 2: At iteration k, set a_k equal to the midpoint of the unfathomed lower interval [0, a_{k-i}] and repeat the process described in Step 1.

Step 3: At iteration k, set a_k equal to the midpoint of the unfathomed upper interval [a_{k-i}, 1] and repeat the process described in Step 1.

Step 4: The appropriate parameter a has been determined.

The authors recognize that there is no definitive measure of the degree to which the two averages would be deemed to be "close", any more than what an appropriate value of ε in constraint (6f) should be. For empirical purposes, we have chosen as our "closeness parameter" a value of 0.005.

2.2 The Case of Multiple Levels of Disadvantaged DMUs

In many situations, the DMUs may appear in multiple groups at different levels in a disadvantaged sense. The application to be discussed in Sect. 3 presents one such situation. In that case, we examine the economic activities as lying in three groups which we designate as N1, N2, and N3. There, N2 is seen as being disadvantaged relative to N1, while N3 is presented as being disadvantaged relative to both N1 and N2. The approach described above for the case of two groups of DMUs N1 and N2 can be immediately extended to the case of more than two groups since we base the compensation idea on average efficiency scores. Specifically, we derive a different reduction parameter a, for each of the disadvantaged groups. More is discussed on this in Sect. 3.

2.3 Compensation Efficiency

The purpose of solving model (6) is to generate a set of adjusted efficiency scores for disadvantaged DMUs (those in N2) such that those adjusted scores have an average that is at or near the average of the scores of the members of the advantaged group. In the process of generating these adjusted scores, a set of proportions α_{ij_o} corresponding to the inputs x_{ij_o} is created. These proportions reflect the needed reductions in these inputs. The reduction parameter a for an inefficient DMU j_o in a disadvantaged group provides a rough measure of the combined effect of these input reductions which we shall call the *level of compensation* afforded that DMU. It generally coincides with the α_{ij_o} being allocated to the primary task of the DMU, namely, the production of the outputs. The remaining $1-\alpha_{ij_o}$ is directed to the secondary task of "coping with the unfavorable environment" in which the DMU finds itself. One might postulate, as well, that a reasonable measure of compensation is simply the difference between the efficiency scores arising from models (2) and (6). However, these scores may not be directly comparable given that they arise from different projections. That being said, it is therefore pertinent to develop a more formal measure of compensation in the form of an efficiency score. In other words, we wish to evaluate the relative *degree* of compensation not only in terms of the reduction parameter a but also in terms of the quantities of aggregate inputs diverted away from the production of that DMU's outputs. To formalize this idea, we again emphasize that the disadvantaged DMU j_o is in two lines of "business": a primary business of generating outputs $\left\{y_{rj_o}\right\}_{r=1}^{R}$ and a secondary business of coping with an unaccommodating environment. To express this requirement in quantitative terms, we create an additional output or compensation variable, which we designate as a unit indicator (variable) $y_{R+1j_o}=1$. This concept is somewhat similar to adding a dummy variable to a regression model to capture environmental, categorical, or demographic factors such as discussed in Fried et al. (2002). The value of resources transferred to that compensation variable is then given by $\sum_i v_i\left(1-\alpha_{ij_o}\right)x_{ij_o}$.

We, therefore, propose the following model as a mechanism for evaluating the efficiency of the compensation accorded DMU j_o relative to its peers:

$$
\begin{aligned}
&e_{comp} = \text{ Min } \left[\sum_i v_i\left(1-\alpha_{ij_o}\right)x_{ij_o}+v_o\right]/u_r y_{R+1j_o}\\
&Subject\ to\\
&\sum_i v_i\left(1-\alpha_{ij}\right)x_{ij}+v_o\Big]/u_r y_{R+1j}\geq 1,\quad \forall j\in N2\\
&v_{i,}\ ,u_{R+1}\geq 0,\ \ v_o\ unrestricted
\end{aligned}
\tag{7}
$$

We note that the parameters α_{ij} are those arising from model (6) and the relationship $\hat{\alpha}_{ij_o}=\hat{\gamma}_{ij_o}/\hat{v}_i$

In a VRS sense, our efficiency score from (7), for the compensation line of business, is the ratio of inputs consumed here to the value of the output generated.

Since there is a single output variable y_{rj_o} equal to unity for each DMU in N2, we may view (7) in the simpler linear format:

$$\begin{aligned} e_{comp} = \ & \text{Min} \left[\sum_i v_i \left(1 - \alpha_{ij_o}\right) x_{ij_o} + v_o \right] \\ & Subject\ to \\ & \sum_i v_i \left(1 - \alpha_{ij}\right) x_{ij} + v_o \Big] \geq 1, \quad \forall j \in N2 \\ & v_{i,} \ \geq 0, \ \ v_o \ unrestricted \end{aligned} \tag{8}$$

The scores arising from this output-oriented model provide an aggregate measure of the compensation accorded the DMU in question.

In the following section, we discuss the application of these models to a set of economic activities.

3 Application

The above methodology is illustrated using a data set relating to the full set of business activities in Mexico. These activities cover the spectrum of primary, secondary, and tertiary activities. Before proceeding, we point out again that data envelopment analysis (DEA), as proposed by Charnes et al. (1978), involves the derivation of efficiency scores of a set of *comparable* decision-making units relative to one another. “The units under study are understood to be similar in that they are undertaking similar activities and producing comparable products or services, so that a common set of outputs can be defined” (Dyson et al. 2001).

Normally, the efficiency measurement exercise is conducted using sets of supplied inputs and outputs for the DMUs in question. However, for this particular analysis, the set of DMUs might be seen as being nonhomogeneous, especially because they do “different” things. Some produce primary products, while others provide welfare services for the inhabitants of the country. Some economic activities hold a significant advantage in relation to others, because they can produce more due to the technology or to advanced and specialized processes. Thus, it will be necessary to adapt the conventional DEA methodology so that dissimilar DMUs can be compared on an equal footing. The INEGI —from the Spanish Instituto Nacional de Estadistica y Geografia—is an autonomous agency of the Mexican government, dedicated to the maintenance and coordination of the National Statistical Information System and Geographic from that country. This institution is responsible for conducting the economic census every 5 years.

For this study, inputs and outputs should reflect objectively the real situation involving the economy of the country, thus providing for meaningful efficiency scores. We have used several variables that are quantifiable and comparable and hence should have logical cause-effect relationships (Tong and Liping 2009).

There are approximately 800+ economic activities in Mexico, to be considered as the DMUs for this analysis. The numbers of DMUs vary and generally increase over time, due mainly to improvements in technology and to the development of some processes that in the past were not available. Previous econometric studies done in Mexico show that a way to classify the economic activities is by three main sectors, namely, primary, secondary, and tertiary. These are defined as (see Parra Leyva 2000):

Primary sector: agriculture, farming, timber, fishing, and hunting
Secondary sector: manufacturing, construction, mining, electricity, and oil
Tertiary sector: commerce, services, and transport

For purposes of this study, and due to the lack of information for the primary sector, we include only fishing from that sector.

Currently, economic activities are denoted by a code which comes from North American Industry Classification System (NAICS). The objective of NAICS (SCIAN from the Spanish “Sistema de Clasificaci6n Industrial de America del Norte”—Mexico) is to provide a unique, consistent, and updated system for the collection, analysis, and presentation of statistics on economic activities, reflecting the structure and framework of the Mexican economy. The starting point for our analysis is the selection of appropriate variables considered as inputs and outputs and forming the basis for measuring the performance of each economic activity in the country. Examples of this are those used by Byrnesa and Storbeck (2000) who used macroeconomic data on outputs (domestic product measures) and inputs (labor and investment or capital); they employed traditional DEA models to compare the economic performance of major cities in China.

Although research in these areas is broad, there is rather wide agreement among many authors that the most important variables to be considered are:

Inputs: labor, capital, salaries, fixed assets
Outputs: production and the net added value

We use these in the study herein.

We approach the analysis in two parts. Part 1 examines in detail a sample of 41 of these activities, while Part 2 goes on to evaluate the full population from which the sample was drawn. We approach the problem in this manner to provide greater transparency as to how the methodology works. More to the point, we want to show in detail the performance scores of DMUs before and after the level playing fields are created and as well display the reduction parameters involved. At the same time, it is useful to present the compensation efficiency for disadvantaged DMUs. The sample set of DMUs provides a clear picture that cannot be easily displayed for the entire 800+ set.

3.1 Part 1: Measuring Efficiency for a Sample of DMUs

Table 1 displays the data on 41 business activities. Here, the units of measurement for these variables are in thousands of Mexican pesos, except for labor which is expressed as the numbers of persons employed.

Table 2 presents various analysis results. Shown in column 4 are the VRS output efficiencies for the set of activities (DMUs) arising from model (2); these have been grouped according to their three-digit SIC codes. For each three-digit subgroup, the average score has been computed and appears in column 5.

Application of the methodology described in the previous section requires deciding on what will constitute the groupings of DMUs N1, N2, N3, etc. In some settings, as explained earlier, the groups will have been predetermined such as would be the case of a comparison of bank branches in one jurisdiction versus another. While in the current situation one might consider applying the methodology to one sector of the economy relative to other sectors, we have chosen to take a different course of action. Our objective is to provide for what we deem a level playing field for all DMUs; hence, the choice of groups is based on three-digit code average efficiencies. This being the case, there is no particular objective definition of what the cutoff score should be to distinguish which DMUs to include in each of the groups N1, N2, N3, etc. For purposes of the analysis carried out, we used the ranges $1 \leq \overline{e}_{N1} \leq 1.5$, $1.5 < \overline{e}_{N2} \leq 2.5$, and $2.5 < \overline{e}_{N3}$, in selecting three-digit industries from the full set of evaluated DMUs.

Using these three ranges for the average efficiency scores, the first column of Table 2 indicates in which of the three sets each average belongs. For example, N1 contains industry code 238, N2 contains industry code 326, and N3 contains industry code 485. The VRS model (2) was applied to the set of 41 DMUs, and the resulting scores appear in column 4.

We point out that the efficiency score for any member of the 41 DMUs within the full set of 800+ peer DMUs *differs* from the score that DMU receives against its 40 peers; hence, the average scores reported in Table 2 differ from the averages when the above referenced ranges $1 \leq \overline{e}_{N1} \leq 1.5$, $1.5 < \overline{e}_{N2} \leq 2.5$, and $2.5 < \overline{e}_{N3}$ were being applied.

Using the efficient DMUs appearing in column 4, and for a chosen value of the reduction parameter a, model (6) is solved for each inefficient DMU in N2. Using the resultant scores arising from (6), their average is computed, and the size of this average is compared to that of the DMUs in N1. Following the algorithm presented in the previous section and solving (6) for the selected values of the reduction parameter, the process terminates when the averages for N1 and N2 are deemed to be sufficiently close. For demonstration, we have defined "close" to mean within a difference of at most 0.005. Table 3 displays the average efficiency scores for selected values of the reduction parameter. At a value of $a = 95$, the average N2 score is at 1.0113, which we have taken to be sufficiently close to the N1 average score of 1.0139.

This process is now repeated for N3 versus N1, and the results are shown in Table 3.

Table 4 shows the final efficiency scores for the full set of 41 DMUs arising from (6).

We note that the solutions to (6) yield the α_{ij_o}, hence the percentages $1 - \alpha_{ij_o}$, for all i and j. The latter are used to compute the portions of inputs diverted to the compensation efficiency model (8); efficiency scores arising from (8) are given in Table 5.

Table 1 Input and output data for a sample of 41 economic activities in Mexico

DMU	Code	Economic activity	Total employed persons	Total earnings[a]	Gross fixed capital formation[a]	Total fixed assets[a]	Gross total produc-tion[a]	Gross value added census[a]
1	238110	Work foundation	5204	193685.8618	3495208.679	461841.6403	1168758.765	10379372.23
2	238120/238121/ 238122 (2003 y 2008)	Installation of structures and foundations (concrete and steel)	7001	282333.1121	3492852.59	320230.0118	1926586.436	10535483.1
3	238130	Masonry work	1143	60889.53942	3479299.416	63785.15514	375239.1542	10119170.33
4	238190	Other outside building works	571	26672.6106	3473335.899	36923.63433	168790.5185	10045942.69
5	238210	Electrical systems in buildings	8596	634365.0246	3519561.472	625517.9816	3536663.636	11495598.84
6	238221/238140 (1998)	Plumbing and gas facilities	3211	167096.3717	3494542.203	195633.9039	993775.0143	10364350.09
7	238222	Facilities of central air-conditioning systems and heating	4606	291843.6078	3491968.491	358849.3042	1798414.636	10684629.98
8	238290	Other facilities and equipment in buildings	1025	63322.70295	3475927.747	667735.6357	3830509.693	11268834.05
9	238311	False wall installation and isolation	1500	90738.86414	3475917.168	86126.43242	681675.698	10215949.79
10	238312	Plastering work	408	17189.31798	3472228.129	17765.1163	108263.6867	10009797.36
11	238320	Paint work and other wall coverings	1096	67776.4501	3476015.401	74738.92486	333322.2451	10112850.15
12	238330	Flexible placement and wood floors	256	8966.434286	3471999.926	25498.34473	82973.8988	9991932.5
13	238340	Placement of ceramic and tile floors	236	10560.83647	3474986.218	21213.86113	53097.37101	9989367.855
14	238350	Making carpentry work place construction	314	7703.00279	3472844.732	18735.35915	53928.57594	9990335.075

15	238390	Other finishing works in buildings	2262	126325.0142	3484082.623	154197.5824	734520.685	10275689.24
16	238910	Preparation of land for construction	4304	174268.9146	3553412.67	828832.219	1580507.462	10554795.77
17	238990	Other specialized works for construction	3721	140095.813	3540603.047	354274.6545	1065081.818	10375856.99
18	326110	Manufacture of plastic bags and flexible films without support	31796	3417287.496	4332083.939	13319484.74	28139991.08	18012062.64
19	326120	Making pipes and fittings rigid plastic without support	7814	927663.9966	3661845.621	3125102.338	7549637.924	12371244.53
20	326130	Making rigid plastic laminate unsupported	4602	501207.5059	3542422.63	1161664.809	4108644.464	11572648.52
21	326140	Manufacturing of foam and polystyrene products	10787	735469.7699	3681652.478	3404205.841	7523863.015	12598618.37
22	326150	Manufacturing of foam and urethane products	4771	345885.5299	3530550.001	1664658.65	5490985.115	12816196.08
23	326160	Manufacture of plastic bottles	16614	1267362.339	5324420.213	9126447.28	19022569.17	15861037.27
24	326191	Manufacture of plastic goods for home	19464	1608392.121	3883715.375	4896369.821	10716008.83	13915464.6
25	326192	Manufacturing of plastic auto parts	21367	3384873.526	4569598.481	9783014.544	26225704.96	22384622.23
26	326193	Manufacture of plastic containers and boxes with and without support	12168	1232294.559	3820132.731	3702721.758	7496954.644	12762807.03
27	326194	Making other items plastic industrial goods use without reinforcement	24013	2317228.574	3790297.008	4381442.9	9759822.415	14074679.64
28	326195/326198 (2008)	Making other articles of reinforced plastic	4997	356889.1719	3576707.566	901712.2674	3129509.236	10930897.86

(continued)

Table 1 (continued)

DMU	Code	Economic activity	Total employed persons	Total earnings[a]	Gross fixed capital formation[a]	Total fixed assets[a]	Gross total produc-tion[a]	Gross value added census[a]
29	326199	Manufacture of other plastic products	17312	1319852.175	3434127.206	1908390.605	5371132.92	12562272.04
30	326211	Tire manufacturing and cameras	4637	1098092.744	3786614.015	4170078.065	6434481.298	11507974.73
31	326212	Revival of wheels	2306	174306.6967	3471162.676	376525.2549	1150760.911	10304946.14
32	326220	Manufacture of rubber bands and rubber and plastic hoses	7040	697993.0064	3566523.039	1118650.709	3406611.802	11269489.95
33	326290	Other rubber product manufacturing	22235	2163939.271	3732942.357	4054984.896	11573499.49	14458031.36
34	485111	Bus transportation of urban and suburban passenger	109596	7368208.557	4529272.951	25730601.52	32069781.4	26083966.27
35	485113	Urban transport and suburban passenger in trolleybuses and trains	3628	819622.4684	3534557.92	6930329.799	495860.5912	10100707
36	485114	Transport of urban and suburban passenger in metro	15131	4538312.428	5343749.506	36436437.92	4803182.681	11791386.9
37	485210	Long-distance and rural transport of passengers	63949	8177079.767	5334766.447	20814795.11	38464612.71	27050240.49
38	485320	Car rental with driver	318	31433.14794	3474498.074	155368.8258	188283.0298	10078875.02
39	485410	School and personal transportation	12076	767808.1755	3774428.55	2924774.393	3487001.409	11623339.93
40	485510	Bus rental with driver	675	43177.31798	3474034.111	190976.1337	187757.1037	10055497.01
41	485990	Another land transport of passengers	6419	131723.3124	3499343.545	688613.9922	1131053.798	10397882.41

[a]Thousands of Mexican pesos

Table 2 VRS efficiency scores in three groups within a sample of 41 industries

Group	DMU	SCIAN code	Efficiency score	Average score from efficiency score
N1	1	238110	1.0565	1.0139
N1	2	238120/238121/238122 (2003 y 2008)	1.0114	
N1	3	238130	1.0023	
N1	4	238190	1.0098	
N1	5	238210	0.9999	
N1	6	238221/238140 (1998)	1.0091	
N1	7	238222	1.0129	
N1	8	238290	1.0000	
N1	9	238311	0.9999	
N1	10	238312	0.9999	
N1	11	238320	1.0052	
N1	12	238330	1.0000	
N1	13	238340	0.9999	
N1	14	238350	0.9999	
N1	15	238390	1.0083	
N1	16	238910	1.0953	
N1	17	238990	1.0350	
N2	18	326110	1.0000	1.0678
N2	19	326120	1.1250	
N2	20	326130	1.0459	
N2	21	326140	1.1056	
N2	22	326150	1.0000	
N2	23	326160	1.0000	
N2	24	326191	1.1668	
N2	25	326192	0.9990	
N2	26	326193	1.1933	
N2	27	326194	1.1127	
N2	28	326195/326198 (2008)	1.0749	
N2	29	326199	0.9999	
N2	30	326211	1.1521	
N2	31	326212	1.0322	
N2	32	326220	1.0762	
N2	33	326290	1.0000	
N3	34	485111	1.0000	1.1501
N3	35	485113	1.2324	
N3	36	485114	1.6252	
N3	37	485210	0.9999	
N3	38	485320	1.0038	
N3	39	485410	1.2189	
N3	40	485510	1.0298	
N3	41	485990	1.0910	

3.2 *Part: 2 Efficiency Results for Full Set of DMUs*

The methodology was applied to the set of 800+ business activities, and the three-digit code average VRS efficiency scores (from the running of model (2)) appear in Table 6. Note that the average scores have been arranged in increasing order. The three ranges used here to identify $N1$, $N2$, and $N3$ are $1 \leq \overline{e}_{N1} \leq 2.5$, $2.5 < \overline{e}_{N2} \leq 3.5$, and $3.5 < \overline{e}_{N3}$, respectively. Those industry groupings falling into the sets N1, N2, and N3 are displayed in the table as well. Again, model (6) was applied for various values of the reduction parameter, and average scores were computed as shown in Table 7. The final values of the reduction parameter a selected are highlighted. The $1 - \alpha_{ij_o}$parameters were then used in the running of model (8).

Table 3 Average efficiency scores for various input reduction parameters

N1	A(N2)	N2	A(N3)	N3
1.0139	Original	1.0678	Original	1.1501
	0.8	1.0000	0.95	1.1075
	0.9	1.0000	0.94	1.1027
	0.94	1.0031	0.90	1.0790
	0.95	1.0113	0.80	1.0686
	0.96	1.0191	0.70	1.0338
			0.65	1.0071
			0.66	1.0142

At a value of $a = .95$, the average N2 score is at 1.0113, which we have taken to be sufficiently close to the N1 average score of 1.0104

Table 4 Efficiency scores for the disadvantaged groups following input reduction

Group	DMU	Code	Efficiency score
N2	18	326110	1.000000011
N2	19	326120	1.000000026
N2	20	326130	1.000000004
N2	21	326140	1.000000116
N2	22	326150	1.000000006
N2	23	326160	1.000000000
N2	24	326191	1.017491566
N2	25	326192	1.000000004
N2	26	326193	1.098622836
N2	27	326194	1.000000026
N2	28	326195/326198 (2008)	1.000000069
N2	29	326199	1.000000000
N2	30	326211	1.086800853
N2	31	326212	1.000000000
N2	32	326220	1.000000029
N2	33	326290	1.000000000
N3	34	485111	1.000000000
N3	35	485113	1.000000000
N3	36	485114	1.291912758
N3	37	485210	1.000000007
N3	38	485320	1.000000001
N3	39	485410	1.000000031
N3	40	485510	1.000000000
N3	41	485990	1.000000000

4 Conclusion

This paper examines the problem of applying data envelopment analysis in what can be deemed nonhomogeneous environments. The setting for this is often one where the decision-making units fall into distinct groups, wherein the average performance of one group is significantly different from that of another group. In some circumstances, groupings may be well defined by size, technology type, demographics, and so on, while in others there may be no obvious explanation for observed differences in performance. Here, we look specifically at a set of economic activities in Mexico and make the observation that when activities are grouped into three-digit industry codes, vastly different average efficiency scores arise.

Table 5 Compensation efficiency from model (3.8)

Group	DMU	Code	Economic activity	Efficiency	Average
N2	18	326110	Manufacture of plastic bags and flexible films without support	1.059100121	1.020028439
N2	19	326120	Making profiles, pipes, and fittings rigid plastic without support	1.012675308	
N2	20	326130	Making rigid plastic laminate unsupported	1.004790572	
N2	21	326140	Manufacturing of foam and polystyrene products	1.013424768	
N2	22	326150	Manufacturing of foam and urethane products	1.004497053	
N2	23	326160	Manufacture of plastic bottles	1.042558801	
N2	24	326191	Manufacture of plastic goods for home	1.026659292	
N2	25	326192	Plastic auto parts manufacturing	1.051513373	
N2	26	326193	Manufacture of plastic containers and boxes	1.018798091	
N2	27	326194	Making other items plastic industrial goods use without reinforcement	1.031488224	
N2	28	326195	Making other articles of reinforced plastic	1.004052366	
N2	29	326199	Manufacture of other plastic products	1.000000000	
N2	30	326211	Tire manufacturing and cameras	1.014869396	
N2	31	326212	Revival of wheels	1.000000004	
N2	32	326220	Manufacture of rubber bands and rubber and plastic hoses	1.007272564	
N2	33	326290	Other rubber products manufacturing	1.028755105	
N3	34	485111	Bus transportation of urban and suburban passenger	2.139532908	1.508680111
N3	35	485113	Urban transport and suburban passenger in trolleybuses and trains	1.299779455	
N3	36	485114	Transport of urban and suburban passenger in metro	1.880529053	
N3	37	485210	Long distance and rural transport of passengers	2.036933826	
N3	38	485320	Car rental with driver	1.000000000	
N3	39	485410	School and personal transportation	1.301718121	
N3	40	485510	Bus rental with driver	1.19159612	
N3	41	485990	Another land transport of passengers	1.219351422	

While there is no convenient one-dimensional explanation for such large discrepancies, it is clear that the usual homogeneity that characterizes most DEA applications is not present in this very heterogeneous environment. The new DEA methodology developed herein is designed to compensate disadvantaged groups of DMUs relative to a base "advantaged" group.

The developed model can be regarded as a mechanism for separating a DMU's pure technical inefficiency from a score that is partially explainable by environmental inequities or imbalances. The methodology constructs, for each member of a disadvantaged group, two measures. The first of the measures, via model (6), is intended to capture a "fair" evaluation of that DMU's technical efficiency; it accomplishes this by undertaking a reduction of that unit's inputs, with the purpose being to bring it to a point where it can be fairly compared to other "advantaged" DMUs. The second measure, arising from model (8), provides a compensation score that describes the extent to which the DMU has been disadvantaged.

The ideas presented here can potentially lend important insights into the performance of business activities over time. One of the models used to look at time series data is that based on the Malmquist index. Using the compensation methodology, together with Malmquist indexes, a more realistic portrayal of concepts like frontier shifts may be captured. This is the subject of future research.

Table 6 Average efficiency scores across all economic activities

DMU group	Three-digit code	Average score	Economic activity	Group	DMU group	Three-digit code	Average score	Economic activity	Group
1	211	1.00000000	Oil and gas extraction	N1	42	435	3.618050378	Wholesale of machinery, furniture, and equipment for agricultural, industrial, and service activities	N3
2	521	1.000000059	Central banking	N1	43	621	3.615879289	Outpatient medical services and related services	N3
3	551	1.226451352	Corporate and business management	N1	44	237	3.654372794	Construction of civil engineering works or heavy work	N3
4	236	1.241549125	Construction	N1	45	436	3.803739191	Wholesale truck	N3
5	533	1.358059559	Rental service trademarks, patents, and franchises	N1	46	461	3.802959968	Retail sale of food, beverages, and snuff	N3
6	221	1.532982457	Generation, transmission, and supply of electricity	N1	47	464	3.890381245	Retail trade of articles for health care	N3
7	481	1.708797053	Air transportation	N1	48	326	3.834826196	Manufacture of plastic and rubber	N3
8	523	1.842863739	Exchange activities and finance investment	N1	49	213	3.935310209	Services incidental to mining	N3
9	512	1.908699863	Film and video industry and sound industry	N1	50	332	3.959782371	Manufacture of metal products	N3
10	524	1.927474983	Company finance, insurance, and pensions	N1	51	562	3.971825394	Waste management and remediation services	N3
11	522	2.154905431	Credit institutions and financial intermediation no stock market	N1	52	541	3.582181194	Professional, scientific, and technical services	N3

12	511	2.381718504	Edition of publications and software, except through the Internet	N1	53	238	4.105575213	Expert work for construction	N3
13	325	2.458426044	Chemical industry	N1	54	327	4.138044452	Manufacture of products based on nonmetallic minerals	N3
14	483	2.552941514	Water transportation	N2	55	482	4.196683388	Rail transportation	N3
15	334	2.605664296	Manufacture of computer equipment, communication, measurement, and other equipment, electronic components, and accessories	N2	56	531	3.820320861	Real estate services	N3
16	711	2.675850952	Artistic services and sporting and other related services	N2	57	212	4.266795816	Mining of metal ores and nonmetallic except oil and gas	N3
17	431	2.728408807	Wholesale of food, beverages, and snuff	N2	58	622	4.27367441	Hospitals	N3
18	311	2.647936968	Food industry	N2	59	315	4.284128538	Manufacture of clothing	N3
19	433	2.807266288	Wholesale of pharmaceutical products, perfume, clothing accessories, items for recreation, and appliances	N2	60	515	4.292904108	Radio and television, except through the Internet	N3
20	519	2.818924659	Other information services	N2	61	321	4.310692201	Timber industry	N3

(continued)

Table 6 (continued)

DMU group	Three-digit code	Average score	Economic activity	Group	DMU group	Three-digit code	Average score	Economic activity	Group
21	337	2.83035335	Manufacture of furniture and related products	N2	62	484	4.333120595	Trucking	N3
22	336	2.851138763	Manufacture of transport equipment	N2	63	467	4.362168386	Retail of hardware, hardware store, and glasses	N3
23	432	2.96595929	Wholesale of textiles and footwear	N2	64	465	4.383251261	Retail of stationery, for recreation and other articles of personal use	N3
24	462	2.976344567	Retail in supermarkets and department	N2	65	222	4.434820957	Water and gas supply pipeline to the final consumer	N3
25	331	3.094199504	Basic metal industries	N2	66	339	4.472652488	Other manufacturing	N3
26	324	3.095799577	Manufacture of products of petroleum and coal	N2	67	112	4.54241835	Livestock (animal aquaculture)	N3
27	312	2.743283737	Beverage industry and snuff	N2	68	114	4.670060676	Fishing, hunting, and trapping (fishing only)	N3
28	517	2.748209733	Other telecommunications	N2	69	811	4.513613742	Repair and maintenance services	N3
29	722	3.172100621	Services in preparation of food and drink	N2	70	323	3.517204196	Printing and allied industries	N3
30	335	3.197533944	Manufacture of electric generation equipment and electrical appliances and accessories	N2	71	316	4.761988905	Manufacture of leather products, leather and substitutes materials, except apparel	N3
31	624	3.284392263	Other social services	N2	72	493	4.82894125	Store service	N3
32	485	3.318420556	Land passenger transportation, except by rail	N2	73	488	3.95784415	Services related to transport	N3

33	434	3.386932184	Wholesale of agricultural raw materials for industry and waste materials	N2	74	611	4.575328735	Educational services	N3
34	333	3.457962467	Manufacture of machinery and equipment	N2	75	313	5.433178388	Manufacture of textile inputs	N3
35	463	3.548634015	Retail sale of textiles, clothing accessories, and footwear	N3	76	623	3.914760922	Residences of social assistance and health care	N3
36	466	3.555210405	Retail sale of household appliances, computers, and articles for interior decoration	N3	77	812	5.657601189	Personal services	N3
37	492	3.566666911	Courier and mail services	N3	78	314	5.267111796	Manufacture of textiles, except apparel	N3
38	561	3.564382459	Support services for businesses	N3	79	713	4.571843383	Entertainment services in recreational facilities and other recreational services	N3
39	532	3.5797794	Rental services of movable property	N3	80	518	6.283449196	Access providers' Internet search services on the network and information processing services	N3
40	468	3.579047763	Retail trade of motor vehicles, parts, fuel, and lubricants	N3	81	487	6.631283051	Tourist transportation	N3
41	322	3.582494499	Paper industry	N3	82	721	4.636817045	Temporary accommodation services	N3

Table 7 Average efficiency scores for various input reduction parameters

N1	A(N2)	N2	A(N3)	N3
2.0914	Original	2.9717	Original	4.1101
	0.8	1.0001	0.8	1.1767
	0.9	1.4467	0.9	1.5963
	0.92	1.8014	0.92	1.7600
	0.95	1.6303	0.95	2.1457
	0.97	2.0543	0.97	2.5842

References

Aparicio, J., & Santin, D. (2018). A note on measuring group performance over time with pseudo-panels. *European Journal of Operational Research, 267*(1), 227–235.

Banker, R., Charnes, A., & Cooper, W. W. (1984). Some models for estimating technical and scale efficiencies in data envelopment analysis. *Management Science, 30*, 1078–1092.

Banker, R. D., & Morey, R. (1986). The use of categorical variables in data envelopment analysis. *Management Science, 32*(12), 1613–1627.

Battase, G., Rao, D., & O'Donnell, C. (2004). A metafrontier production function for estimation of technical efficiencies and technology gaps for firms operating under different technologies. *Journal of Productivity Analysis, 21*(1), 91–103.

Byrnesa, P. E., & Storbeck, J. E. (2000). Efficiency gains from regionalization: Economic development in China revisited. *Socio-Economic Planning Sciences, 34*, 141–154.

Charnes, A., & Cooper, W. W. (1962). Programming with linear fractional functionals. *Naval Research Logistics Quarterly, 9*, 67–88.

Charnes, A., Cooper, W. W., & Rhodes, E. (1978). Measuring the efficiency of decision making units. *European Journal of Operational Research, 2*, 429–444.

Cook, W. D., Liang, L., & Zhu, J. (2010). Measuring performance of two-stage network structures by DEA: A review and future perspective. *Omega, 38*, 423–430.

Cook, W. D., & Seiford, L. M. (2009). Data envelopment analysis (DEA)-thirty years on. *European Journal of Operational Research, 192*(1), 1–17.

Dyson, R. G., Allen, R., Camanho, A. S., Podinovski, V. V., Sarrico, C. S., & Shale, E. A. (2001). Pitfalls and protocols in DEA. *European Journal of Operational Research, 132*, 245–259.

Emrouznejad, A., Parker, B. R., & Tavares, G. (2008). Evaluation of research in efficiency and productivity: A survey and analysis of the first 30 years of scholarly literature in DEA. *Socio-Economic Planning Sciences, 42*(3), 151–157.

Fried, H. O., Lovell, C. A. K., Schmidt, S. S., & Yaisawarng, S. (2002). Accounting for environmental effects and statistical noise in data envelopment analysis. *Journal of Productivity Analysis, 17*(1–2), 157–174.

Instituto Nacional de Estadistica y Geografáa - INEGI. (2009). *Glosario de Censos Económicos*. Aguascalientes, Mexico. Retrieved from: https://www.inegi.org.mx/app/glosario/default.html?p=ce09

Liu, J. S., Lu, L. Y. Y., & Lu, W. M. (2016). Research fronts in data envelopment analysis. *Omega, 58*, 33–45.

Liu, J. S., Lu, L. Y. Y., Lu, W. M., & Lin, B. J. Y. (2013). Data envelopment analysis 1978–2010: A citation-based literature survey. *Omega, 41*(1), 3–15.

Paradi, J., & Zhu, H. (2013). A survey on bank branch efficiency and performance research with data envelopment analysis. *Omega-International Journal of Management Science, 41*, 61–79.

Parra Leyva, G. (2000). *Economic growth in Mexico: A regional approach.* (PhD.), Cornell University United States.

Seiford, L., & Zhu, J. (2003). Context-dependent data envelopment analysis-measuring attractiveness and progress. *Omega, 31*(5), 397–408.

Tong, L., & Liping, C. (2009). *Research on the Evaluation of Innovation Efficiency for China's Regional Innovation System by Utilizing DEA.* Paper presented at the 2009 International Conference on Information Management, Innovation Management and Industrial Engineering. http://0ieeexplore.ieee.org.millenium.itesm.mx/stamp/stamp.jsp?tp=&arnumber=5369923

Testing Positive Endogeneity in Inputs in Data Envelopment Analysis

Juan Aparicio, Lidia Ortiz, Daniel Santin, and Gabriela Sicilia

Abstract Data envelopment analysis (DEA) has been widely applied to empirically measure the technical efficiency of a set of schools for benchmarking their performance. However, the endogeneity issue in the production of education, which plays a central role in education economics, has received minor attention in the DEA literature. Under a DEA framework, endogeneity arises when at least one input is correlated with the efficiency term. Cordero et al. (*European Journal of Operational Research* 244:511–518, 2015) highlighted that DEA performs well under negative and moderate positive endogeneity. However, when an input is highly and positively correlated with the efficiency term, DEA estimates are misleading. The aim of this work is to propose a new test, based on defining a grid of input flexible transformations, for detecting the presence of positive endogeneity in inputs. To show the potential ability of this test, we run a Monte Carlo analysis evaluating the performance of the new approach in finite samples. The results show that this test outperforms alternative statistical procedures for detecting positive high correlations between inputs and the efficiency term. Finally, to illustrate our theoretical findings, we perform an empirical application on the education sector.

Keywords Data envelopment analysis · Endogeneity · Education

1 Introduction

Data envelopment analysis (DEA) is a nonparametric methodology for estimating technical efficiency of a set of decision-making units (DMUs) from a dataset of inputs and outputs. This methodology is fundamentally based on linear mathematical programming and allows a piece-wise linear production frontier enveloping the input-output observations to be determined. DEA is a widespread technique in many different fields for determining efficiency, from banking to education sectors.[1] The main reason for its extensive use is its flexibility. DEA estimates the production frontier based only on few axiomatic assumptions (i.e., monotonicity and concavity) but without assuming a priori a particular functional form for the underlying production technology or about the inefficiency distribution. That is, the "best-practice frontier" is drawn from the observed data resulting from an underlying and unknown data generating process (DGP). Thus, the estimated technical efficiency score for each observed DMU in the sample is a relative measure computed by it distance to the frontier.

DEA was introduced by Charnes et al. (1978) and Banker et al. (1984), and since its appearance, numerous research contributions have dealt with different relevant issues for studying its behavior under different synthetic scenarios. For example, Pedraja-Chaparro et al. (1997) study the effects of introducing weight restrictions in DEA estimations, Zhang

[1]For a review of the DEA impact in theoretical and empirical applications, see, for example, Emrouznejad and Yang (2018). It is worth noting that the fifth application field of DEA in 2015 and 2016 was "public policies" where endogeneity issues tend to appear.

J. Aparicio (✉) · L. Ortiz
Center of Operations Research (CIO). Miguel Hernandez University of Elche (UMH), Elche, Alicante, Spain
e-mail: j.aparicio@umh.es

D. Santin
Department of Applied Economics, Public Economics and Political Economy, Complutense University of Madrid, Complutense Institute of Economic Analysis, Madrid, Spain

G. Sicilia
Department of Economics and Public Finance, Autonomous University of Madrid, Madrid, Spain

J. Aparicio et al. (eds.), *Advances in Efficiency and Productivity II*, International Series in Operations Research & Management Science 287, https://doi.org/10.1007/978-3-030-41618-8_4

and Bartels (1998) investigate the effect of sample size on mean technical efficiency scores, Holland and Lee (2002) measure the influence of random noise on efficiency estimation, Muñiz et al. (2006) analyze different alternatives to introduce non-discretionary inputs, or Banker and Chang (2006) evaluate how to identify and delete outliers in efficiency estimations. All this research has the common target of evaluating DEA performance for improving its robustness in empirical applications (Cook and Seiford 2009; Liu et al. 2013).

However, there is an issue that has been relatively overlooked in the DEA literature: the role of endogeneity in production processes. DEA is frequently used for benchmarking DMUs in order to detect best and worst performers for learning good managerial practices, reallocating resources based on performance, and introducing rankings to boost performance. However, on certain occasions some inputs for explaining outputs, such as motivation or the quality of some inputs, might be unobserved. When some observed input is correlated with the unobserved factor, the endogeneity problem arises causing biased estimations. Intuitively this means, for example, that more observed input produces a higher technical efficiency because the hidden unobserved input is also raising output levels that the researcher perceives as more efficiency. When using nonparametric techniques for measuring technical efficiency, Peyrache and Coelli (2009) [PC2009] formalize this example arguing that the presence of endogeneity within a production process is relevant when the efficiency term is not exogenously distributed with respect to some of the inputs or, in other words, when there is a correlation between the input and the efficiency term (Bifulco and Bretschneider 2001; PC2009).

The potential distortions that the presence of endogeneity might cause on the estimation of technical efficiency using DEA have been barely studied[2] (Gong and Sickles 1992; Orme and Smith 1996; Bifulco and Bretschneider 2001, 2003; Ruggiero 2003, 2004; Cordero et al. 2015; Cazals et al. 2016; Simar et al. 2016; Santin and Sicilia 2017; Mastromarco and Simar 2018). Running a Monte Carlo experiment, Cordero et al. (2015) evaluated DEA performance simulating the correlation between the inputs and the efficiency term under different directions and intensities. The authors concluded that DEA performs well under negative and low positive endogeneity. However, when an input is highly and positively correlated with the efficiency term, DEA estimates become misleading. This decline in DEA performance is driven by the misidentification of the most inefficient units with a low endogenous input level.

These findings take on greater significance, because this kind of positive correlation is likely to be found in several production processes where DEA is applied to empirically evaluate the performance of DMUs, for instance, in the education sector (De Witte and Lopez-Torres 2017) or in the provision of public services (Mayston 2016). Therefore, overlooking this problem could lead to misleading efficiency estimates and, thus, to inappropriate performance-based recommendations.

Drawing on this evidence, the first question that arises is how to detect this problem when we suspect the presence of endogeneity in a particular empirical setting. Although in the econometric literature this has been widely studied, there are only a handful of previous works that have addressed this issue in the nonparametric frontier analysis field. Wilson (2003) briefly surveys simple nonparametric tests of independence that can be used in the context of efficiency estimation and provides some empirical examples to illustrate their use. His Monte Carlo results show that these tests have poor size and low power properties in moderate sample sizes. Based on Wilson's work, PC2009 propose a semi-parametric Hausman-type asymptotic test for linear independence (uncorrelation) of all inputs and outputs included in the DEA model. Using a Monte Carlo experiment, they show that this test for uncorrelation has superior size and power properties in finite samples, relative to the independence tests discussed in Wilson (2003).

However, all these tests have two important drawbacks that makes them useless for the purpose of detecting the presence of endogenous inputs with a positive correlation with the efficiency term. Firstly, the null hypothesis of these tests includes all the inputs and outputs contained in the DEA model. Thus, we cannot identify which specific inputs (or outputs) are endogenous or exogenous in the production process in order to deal only with the endogenous ones. Secondly, these tests are two-sided tests. Consequently, it is not feasible for disentangling if inputs are positively or negatively correlated with efficiency. This is particularly difficult to be corrected in the PC2009 approach because they resort to a quadratic form, a Wald statistic, for their test of linear independence, which does not allow the sign of the underlying correlation to be dealt with.

Finally, Santín and Sicilia (2017) provide a simple statistical heuristic procedure to classify each input type included in the DEA model, based on comparing the expected correlation coefficients between the efficiency term and each input under the assumption that a setting is exogenous or endogenous. The authors define different cutoff points from their Monte

[2]Endogeneity is receiving a growing interest in the parametric world of production frontiers as well. See, for example, Solis et al. (2007), Kumbhakar et al. (2009), Greene (2010), Mayen et al. (2010), Perelman and Santin (2011), Bravo-Ureta et al. (2012), and Crespo-Cebada et al. (2014) for studying different solutions for dealing with endogeneity when comparing different groups of DMUs in applications related with agriculture, health, or education. Different directions for researching about the endogeneity issues on parametric and nonparametric production frontiers estimations can be found in the *Journal of Econometrics* (2016) volume 190, where issue 2 is fully devoted to discussing and analyzing problems related with endogeneity.

Carlo experiment using the quartiles criterion to label the degree of endogeneity in empirical data. This proposed detection procedure is significantly less robust than a statistical test, because, as in every heuristic, there is no theoretical or statistical basis for defining the cutoff points that characterize the type of inputs.

The aim of this paper is to provide a new robust statistical test to identify the presence of positive endogenous inputs before running the DEA analysis. This test is rooted in the semi-parametric Hausman-type asymptotic test for linear independence (uncorrelation) proposed by PC2009. In particular, our approach will invoke and exploit some results proved by PC2009. In order to empirically evaluate its performance in finite samples, we run a Monte Carlo experiment following the experimental design used in Cordero et al. (2015). To illustrate the application of the test and its empirical implications, we apply it to the database used in Santín and Sicilia (2017).

The chapter is organized as follows: Sect. 2 briefly revises the literature on detection of endogeneity in inputs in DEA, paying special attention to the PC2009 test, on which our approach is mainly based. Section 3 introduces the new test for dealing with positive endogeneity. Section 4 describes the results of a Monte Carlo experiment to test its performance in finite samples. Section 5 describes the empirical application of this test (practitioners). Section 6 provides conclusions and directions for future research.

2 Notation and Background

In this section, we define the production technology, show how it can be estimated through nonparametric techniques, introduce a formal definition of uncorrelation, and briefly review some results from PC2009, which is the main precursor of the methodology that we propose in this chapter.

The usual starting point of the modern theory of production is the production technology, also called production possibility set, i.e., all production plans available for the producer. Given a set of postulates about the features of the production technology, several functions of great interest from an economic perspective can be derived and characterized (the production function, the cost function, etc.).

Formally, let $\boldsymbol{x} \in R_+^m$ denote a vector of inputs and $\boldsymbol{y} \in R_+^s$ a vector of outputs; the production possibility set T is given by

$$T = \left\{(\boldsymbol{x}, \boldsymbol{y}) \in R_+^{m+s} : \boldsymbol{x} \text{ can produce } \boldsymbol{y}\right\}. \tag{1}$$

In this paper, we assume that T is a subset of R_+^{m+s} that satisfies the following axioms (see Färe et al. 1985):

(A1) No free lunch: if $\boldsymbol{x} = \boldsymbol{0}_m$ then $\boldsymbol{y} = \boldsymbol{0}_s$;
(A2) $T(\boldsymbol{x}) : \{(\boldsymbol{u},\boldsymbol{y}) \in T : \boldsymbol{u} \leq \boldsymbol{x}\}$ is bounded $\forall \boldsymbol{x} \in R_+^m$;
(A3) $(\boldsymbol{x},\boldsymbol{y}) \in T$, $(\boldsymbol{x}, -\boldsymbol{y}) \leq (\boldsymbol{x}', -\boldsymbol{y}') \Rightarrow (\boldsymbol{x}',\boldsymbol{y}') \in T$, i.e., inputs and outputs are freely disposable;
(A4) T is a closed set;
(A5) T is a convex set.

Efficiency evaluation in production has been a relevant topic for managers and policy makers. The objective of such assessment is to analyze the efficiency of a set of observations, called DMUs (decision-making units), in recognition of their autonomy in setting their input and output levels, by comparing their performance with respect to the boundary of a production possibility set and using to that end a sample of other observations operating in a similar technological environment. The standard methods to measure technical efficiency of production need to explicitly or implicitly determine the boundary of the underlying technology, which constitutes the reference benchmark. Its estimation allows the corresponding technical inefficiency value for each DMU to be calculated as the deviation of each production plan to the frontier of the production possibility set.

Regarding the determination of the technology in practice, Farrell (1957) was the first in showing, for a single output and multiple inputs, how to estimate an isoquant enveloping all the observations. This line of research, initiated by Farrell, was later taken up by Charnes et al. (1978) and Banker et al. (1984), resulting in the development of the data envelopment analysis (DEA) approach, in which the determination of the frontier is only restricted via its axiomatic foundation, mainly convexity and minimal extrapolation.

Data envelopment analysis (DEA) is a mathematical programming, nonparametric technique commonly used to measure the relative performance of a set of DMUs. Additionally, DEA does not need to suppose a particular functional form for the production function. Technical efficiency may be easily evaluated with multiple inputs and outputs and it also produces relevant benchmarking information from a managerial point of view.

Let us assume that we have observed a sample of n units: $\{(\boldsymbol{x}_k, \boldsymbol{y}_k)\}_{k=1}^{n}$. The i-th input, $i = 1, \ldots, m$, of observation $(\boldsymbol{x}_k, \boldsymbol{y}_k)$ will be denoted as x_{ki}, while the r-th output, $r = 1, \ldots, s$, of observation $(\boldsymbol{x}_k, \boldsymbol{y}_k)$ will be denoted as y_{kr}. Using data envelopment analysis, T is estimated as

$$T_c = \left\{(\boldsymbol{x}, \boldsymbol{y}) \in R_+^{m+s} : \sum_{h=1}^{n} \lambda_h x_{hi} \leq x_i, \forall i, \sum_{h=1}^{n} \lambda_h y_{hr} \leq y_r, \forall r, \lambda_h \geq 0, \forall h\right\} \tag{2}$$

under constant returns to scale (CRS) and as

$$T_v = \left\{(\boldsymbol{x}, \boldsymbol{y}) \in R_+^{m+s} : \sum_{h=1}^{n} \lambda_h x_{hi} \leq x_i, \forall i, \sum_{h=1}^{n} \lambda_h y_{hr} \leq y_r, \forall r, \sum_{h=1}^{n} \lambda_h = 1, \lambda_h \geq 0, \forall j\right\} \tag{3}$$

under variable returns to scale (VRS) (Banker et al. 1984).

Since its introduction, DEA has witnessed the definition of many different technical efficiency measures: radial (equiproportional) and non-radial, oriented and non-oriented, and so on. Perhaps, the most famous is the radial measure (see Charnes et al. 1978; Banker et al. 1984). In particular, its output-oriented version for a DMU$_0$ under VRS can be computed through the following linear programming model:

$$\begin{aligned} &\text{Max } \varphi_0 \\ &s.t. \\ &\sum_{h=1}^{n} \lambda_h x_{hi} \leq x_{ki}, \quad i = 1, \ldots, m \\ &\sum_{h=1}^{n} \lambda_h y_{hr} \geq \varphi_0 y_{0r}, \; r = 1, \ldots, s \\ &\sum_{h=1}^{n} \lambda_h = 1, \\ &\lambda_h \geq 0, \quad h = 1, \ldots, n \end{aligned} . \tag{4}$$

In this paper, with the aim of introducing a stochastic representation of the production possibility set, let us consider the density function $f(\boldsymbol{x},\boldsymbol{y}) \geq 0$, where $\boldsymbol{x} \in R_+^m$ represents the input vector and $\boldsymbol{y} \in R_+^s$ denotes the output vector, such that $\int_{R_+^{m+s}} f(\boldsymbol{x}, \boldsymbol{y})\, d\boldsymbol{x} d\boldsymbol{y} = 1$. We define the support associated with the above density function as follows, which may be interpreted as the technology or the production possibility set related to some industry in production economics:

$$T = \left\{(\boldsymbol{x}, \boldsymbol{y}) \in R_+^{m+s} : f(\boldsymbol{x}, \boldsymbol{y}) > 0\right\}. \tag{5}$$

As we mentioned, technical efficiency is a notion related to the "distance" from an input-output vector $(\boldsymbol{x},\boldsymbol{y}) \in T$ to some specific part of the boundary of the set T. A way of defining this specific subset is resorting to the compliment of T, denoted as $\overline{T}$, and the closure of both T and $\overline{T}$:

$$\partial T = \left\{\left[T \cap cl\left(\overline{T}\right)\right] \cup \left[cl(T) \cap \overline{T}\right]\right\}. \tag{6}$$

The most usual axioms assumed on the production possibility set, shown before, are now translated to the stochastic world as follows (see, e.g., Kumbhakar and Lovell 2000): (A1) no free lunch, if $f(\boldsymbol{x}, \boldsymbol{0}_s) > 0$ and $f(\boldsymbol{0}_m, \boldsymbol{y}) > 0$ then $\boldsymbol{y} = \boldsymbol{0}_s$; (A2) T is bounded, for each $\boldsymbol{x} \in R_+^m$ exist $\boldsymbol{y} \in R_+^s$ such that $f(\boldsymbol{x},\boldsymbol{y}) = 0$; (A3) free disposability, if $f(\boldsymbol{x},\boldsymbol{y}) > 0$ then $f(\boldsymbol{u},\boldsymbol{v}) > 0$ for each $(-\boldsymbol{u},\boldsymbol{v}) \leq (-\boldsymbol{x},\boldsymbol{y})$; (A4) T is closed, for a succession of points $(\boldsymbol{x}_t,\boldsymbol{y}_t) \to (\boldsymbol{x},\boldsymbol{y})$, if $f(\boldsymbol{x}_t,\boldsymbol{y}_t) > 0 \; \forall t$ then $f(\boldsymbol{x},\boldsymbol{y}) > 0$; (A5) convexity, if $f(\boldsymbol{x},\boldsymbol{y}) > 0$ and $f(\boldsymbol{u},\boldsymbol{v}) > 0$, then $f(\alpha \boldsymbol{x} + (1-\alpha)\boldsymbol{u}, \alpha \boldsymbol{y} + (1-\alpha)\boldsymbol{v}) > 0 \; \forall \alpha \in [0, 1]$.

The above axioms represent the usual statistical restrictions on a stochastic data generating process (DGP). Additionally, we assume that the sample observations $(\boldsymbol{x}_k,\boldsymbol{y}_k)$, $k = 1, \ldots, n$, are realizations of identically and independently distributed random variables $(\boldsymbol{X}, \boldsymbol{Y})$ with density function $f(\boldsymbol{X}, \boldsymbol{Y})$.

A well-known measure of technical efficiency is the Shephard distance function (Shephard 1953). In general, the Shephard output distance function is defined as $\theta = \inf\{\delta : (\boldsymbol{x},\boldsymbol{y}/\delta) \in T\}$, which is translated to our stochastic context as $\theta = \inf\{\delta : f(\boldsymbol{x},\boldsymbol{y}/\delta) > 0\}$.

Now, we turn to the problem of endogeneity in the estimation of technical efficiency. In the statistical context, endogeneity arises when the assumption that all inputs are uncorrelated with the error term does not hold (see, e.g., Greene 2003). In the context of the measurement of technical efficiency using nonparametric techniques, this concept implies a correlation between an input and the efficiency term (Bifulco and Bretschneider 2001; Orme and Smith 1996; PC2009).

At this point, we introduce the notion of uncorrelation or linear independence between the efficiency score and inputs and outputs.

Definition 1 The efficiency score θ is uncorrelated if and only if $E[\theta|\boldsymbol{x},\boldsymbol{y}] = E[\theta]$.

In the above definition, $E[.]$ denotes the expected value of a random variable while $E[.|.]$ denotes the conditional expected value.

Next, we restrict the above definition for introducing uncorrelation with respect to a specific input i, $i = 1, \ldots, m$, which will be key throughout the text.

Definition 2 [Input-specific uncorrelation] The efficiency score θ is uncorrelated with respect to input i, $i = 1, \ldots, m$, if and only if $E[\theta|x_i] = E[\theta]$.

In an output-oriented framework, the most usual techniques for measuring efficiency make the implicit assumption that the degree of technical inefficiency of a DMU is independent of the inputs of the unit. For example, in stochastic frontier analysis (SFA), the property of consistency of the estimators of the slope parameters determined by the corrected ordinary least squares (COLS) can be affected if there is a correlation between the efficiency term and the regressors. In the case of DEA, the efficiency scores may be severely impaired if the efficiency term is highly and positively correlated with one of the inputs. Such positive correlation is frequently observed in production processes where DEA is in widespread use. For example, the education sector is a good example where positive endogeneity very frequently arises due to the school self-selection problem (see De Witte and Lopez-Torres 2017; Schlotter et al. 2011; Webbink 2005). In all these contexts, the empirical estimation of technical efficiency using DEA models could lead to misleading efficiency estimates and thus to inappropriate performance-based recommendations for policy makers.

Before showing the methodology proposed by PC2009, which is the main precursor of this chapter, it will be useful to discuss some properties of weighted average estimators of average technical efficiency. Let us consider the following statistic ϕ:

$$\phi = \sum_{k=1}^{n} w_k \theta_k, \quad \sum_{k=1}^{n} w_k = 1, \tag{7}$$

where θ_k, $k = 1, \ldots, n$, is the efficiency of observation k and w_k, $k = 1, \ldots, n$, are random weights defined as function of the sample observations $(\boldsymbol{x}_k, \boldsymbol{y}_k)$, $k = 1, \ldots, n$. In particular, we assume that $w_k(\boldsymbol{x}_k, \boldsymbol{y}_k) = \frac{g(\boldsymbol{x}_k, \boldsymbol{y}_k)}{\sum_{k=1}^{n} g(\boldsymbol{x}_k\ \boldsymbol{y}_k)}$, where $g : R^{m+s} \to R$ is a generic function. In this way, (7) can be rewritten as

$$\phi = \sum_{k=1}^{n} \left(\frac{g(\boldsymbol{x}_k, \boldsymbol{y}_k)}{\sum_{k=1}^{n} g(\boldsymbol{x}_k, \boldsymbol{y}_k)} \right) \theta_k. \tag{8}$$

Next, we show that ϕ, which is a linear aggregator function of the efficiency scores with weights that sum up to one, is a consistent estimator of the average efficiency only if uncorrelation holds.

Proposition 1 [PC2009] If the efficiency score is statistically uncorrelated from the arguments of the function $g(\boldsymbol{x},\boldsymbol{y})$, then the statistic (8) satisfies the consistency property $\phi \xrightarrow{P} E[\theta]$.

Obviously, Proposition 1 can be extended to the case of input-specific uncorrelation. Let us consider the input i', $i' = 1, \ldots, m$. Then, we can define, as in (8), a statistic dependent of a function of the values observed for the input i' and the efficiency scores associated with the sample observations:

$$\phi_{i'} = \sum_{k=1}^{n} \left(\frac{g(x_{ki'})}{\sum_{k=1}^{n} g(x_{ki'})} \right) \theta_k. \tag{9}$$

So, in the same line with the PC2009 proposition, it is possible to prove the following lemma:

Lemma 1 If the efficiency score is statistically input-specific uncorrelated with respect to input i, then the statistic (9) satisfies the consistency property $\phi_i \xrightarrow{P} E[\theta]$.

Proof $\phi_i = \sum_{k=1}^{n}\left(\frac{g(x_{ki})}{\sum_{k=1}^{n} g(x_{ki})}\right)\theta_k = \frac{\sum_{k=1}^{n}\theta_k g(x_{ki})}{\sum_{k=1}^{n} g(x_{ki})} = \frac{\sum_{k=1}^{n}\theta_k g(x_{ki})/n}{\sum_{k=1}^{n} g(x_{ki})/n} \xrightarrow{P} \frac{E[\theta g]}{E[g]}$, where the limit is a consequence of the consistency of the sample mean and Slutsky's theorem (see Greene 1997). Finally, by hypothesis, the efficiency score is statistically input-specific uncorrelated with respect to input i, which implies that $E[\theta g] = E[\theta]E[g]$. Therefore, $\phi_i \xrightarrow{P} E[\theta]$.

The proof of the consistency of ϕ in Proposition 1 allowed PC2009 to construct a test for "full" uncorrelation based on the Wald statistic, full in the sense of being uncorrelated regarding inputs and outputs. We next show this particular test.

Although the function $g(\boldsymbol{x},\boldsymbol{y})$ is general enough to encompass an infinity of possibilities, PC2009 (PC) simplify it considering that $g(\boldsymbol{x},\boldsymbol{y})$ is directly equal to one of the inputs or one of the outputs. In this way, they define $m + s$ different statistics as

$$\phi_i^{In-PC} = \frac{\sum_{k=1}^{n} x_{ki}\theta_k}{\sum_{k=1}^{n} x_{ki}}, i = 1, \ldots, m \tag{10}$$

and

$$\phi_r^{Out-PC} = \frac{\sum_{k=1}^{n} y_{kr}\theta_k}{\sum_{k=1}^{n} y_{kr}}, r = 1, \ldots, s. \tag{11}$$

From the central limit theorem, the sample mean of the efficiencies $\overline{\theta} = \frac{\sum_{k=1}^{n}\theta_k}{n}$ is a consistent estimator of $E[\theta]$, and from Proposition 1, (10) and (11) are also consistent estimators of the same parameter under the hypothesis of uncorrelation. Consequently, the differences $\phi_i^{In-PC} - \overline{\theta}, i = 1, \ldots, m$, and $\phi_r^{Out-PC} - \overline{\theta}, r = 1, \ldots, s$, converge in probability to zero if uncorrelation holds. Finally, by defining $\boldsymbol{d} = \left[\left(\phi_1^{In-PC} - \overline{\theta}\right), \ldots, \left(\phi_m^{In-PC} - \overline{\theta}\right), \left(\phi_1^{Out-PC} - \overline{\theta}\right), \ldots, \left(\phi_s^{Out-PC} - \overline{\theta}\right)\right]$, it is possible to check uncorrelation by means of the following test:

$$\begin{cases} H_0 : E[\boldsymbol{d}] = \boldsymbol{0}_{m+s} \\ H_1 : E[\boldsymbol{d}] \neq \boldsymbol{0}_{m+s} \end{cases}. \tag{12}$$

(12) can be solved through the Wald statistic $W = \boldsymbol{d}'\left[\widehat{Var(\boldsymbol{d})}\right]^{-1}\boldsymbol{d}$, which is asymptotically distributed as a chi-square with $m + s$ degrees of freedom.

Finally, the PC2009 procedure is executed in three steps for the semi-parametric setting. First, we must estimate individual efficiencies θ_k by applying nonparametric DEA techniques (the well-known output-oriented radial model). Although we do not have the true efficiencies, the DEA estimator, for the radial (Shephard) approach, is consistent, and, therefore, it can be considered suitable for dealing with these situations (Simar and Wilson 2000). Second, the covariance matrix $Var(\boldsymbol{d})$ must be estimated using bootstrap (Efron and Tibshirani 1993). In the final third step, the Wald statistic must be computed and compared with the corresponding chi-square.

3 A New Methodology for Testing Input-Specific Uncorrelation in DEA

As was mentioned in the introduction, Wilson (2003) explored a number of relatively simple independence tests that can be used in the context of efficiency estimation and provides some empirical examples to illustrate their use. However, his

Monte Carlo results show that these tests have poor size and low power properties in moderate sample sizes. Based on this work, PC2009 proposed a semi-parametric Hausman-type asymptotic test for linear independence of all inputs and outputs included in the DEA model. Using a Monte Carlo experiment, they showed that this test has good size and power properties in finite samples.

However, since the null hypothesis of these proposed tests include all the inputs and outputs at the same time, we cannot directly identify which inputs are endogenous or exogenous in the production process. Moreover, we cannot discern if inputs are positively or negatively correlated with efficiency using the PC2009 approach since they resorted to a quadratic form statistic, a Wald test, which does not allow the sign of the correlations to be dealt with. Note that, as Cordero et al. (2015) showed, it is only the presence of medium or high "positive" correlation that damages DEA performance. So, it is key in the analysis to identify this kind of correlation between inputs and the true efficiency before trying to correct DEA estimates.

This section aims to contribute to this literature by proposing a statistical procedure to identify the presence of positive endogenous inputs in empirical production problems based on the previous results and work by PC2009.

A little exploited point of the results by PC2009, mainly the expression of their statistic (8) and Proposition 1, is that the function g is very flexible. In fact, both Proposition 1 and Lemma 1 hold for any function g under the hypothesis of uncorrelation. One can imagine that, even in the case of dealing with an actual positively correlated input, there will be certain functions g that will benefit the detection of the problem (positive endogeneity) and others that do not. Note that, in the description of their procedure, PC2009 selected a particular and simple function g (see the expressions of statistics (10) and (11)). However, in this paper, we suggest exploiting this flexibility, checking the hypothesis of input-specific uncorrelation through a set of transformations (i.e., specifying different functions g) of the input to be evaluated.

In order to materialize this idea, we focus our attention on a flexible specification of g. In particular, although there are other possibilities,[3] we resort to the expression of a translog function with a single argument. In this way, we consider

$$g\left(x_{ki'}\right) = \alpha_0 x_{ki'}^{\alpha_1} x_{ki'}^{\frac{1}{2}\alpha_2 \ln(x_{ki'})} = \alpha_0 x_{ki'}^{\alpha_1 + \frac{1}{2}\alpha_2 \ln(x_{ki'})}. \tag{13}$$

Given that we cannot computationally check uncorrelation through Lemma 1 for all $g\left(x_{ki'}\right)$ generated from all possible combinations $(\alpha_0, \alpha_1, \alpha_2)$, we suggest to consider a finite grid of points for $(\alpha_0, \alpha_1, \alpha_2)$. After that, for each particular combination $\left(\alpha_0', \alpha_1', \alpha_2'\right)$, we can compute the mean of the efficiencies and the statistic $\phi_{i'}$ in (9) . However, we only have two sample values to be used for testing input-specific uncorrelation (one value for $\phi_{i'}$ and another one for $\overline{\theta}$), which is clearly insufficient. Consequently, we recommend applying the bootstrap procedure on the data sample to generate a vector of values for $\phi_{i'}$ and a vector of values of mean efficiencies with a size sufficiently large.

As in other situations where the results are subject to the sample size, the bootstrap (Efron 1979) provides a smart alternative for making statistical inferences. Simar and Wilson (1998) introduce an algorithm to implement the bootstrap in the framework of data envelopment analysis. The algorithm offers an approximation of the sampling distribution of the difference between the DEA estimator and the parameter (the true efficiency score when a radial measure is utilized) in a multi-output multi-input context. Once these approximations are determined, confidence intervals and testing procedures may be implemented.

After applying the bootstrap technique, it is possible to compare the values of both vectors (a vector of values for $\phi_{i'}$ and a vector of values of mean efficiencies) in a statistical way for each particular combination $\left(\alpha_0', \alpha_1', \alpha_2'\right)$. For example, it could be used a paired-samples T-test. Note that the test must be one-sided in order to identify the sign of the specific correlation, if it is presented in the data.

According to this procedure, we obtain a p-value for each combination $\left(\alpha_0', \alpha_1', \alpha_2'\right)$ of the grid, denoted as $p\left(\alpha_0', \alpha_1', \alpha_2'\right)$. Finally, we suggest taking the mean of all the p-values as an approximation of the final p-value for the test of endogeneity that we present in this paper.

The test problem that we want to solve for input $i, i = 1, \ldots, m$, is as follows:

$$\begin{cases} H_0 : E\left[\phi_{i'} - \overline{\theta}\right] \leq 0 \\ H_1 : E\left[\phi_{i'} - \overline{\theta}\right] > 0 \end{cases}. \tag{14}$$

In practice, with empirical data, we proceed in several steps as follows:

1. Randomly generate a grid of combinations $\left(\alpha_0^q, \alpha_1^q, \alpha_2^q\right)$, $q = 1, \ldots, Q$.

[3]Other possibilities of flexible functions to be used in order to represent $g\left(x_{ki'}\right)$ could be the Taylor polynomials or trigonometric functions based on sine and cosine. Nevertheless, checking these other alternatives falls outside the scope of this paper.

2. Randomly draw a bootstrap sample with replacement $\left(\boldsymbol{x}_k^b, \boldsymbol{y}_k^b\right)$, $k = 1, \ldots, n$, from the empirical dataset $(\boldsymbol{x}_k, \boldsymbol{y}_k)$, $k = 1, \ldots, n$.[4]
3. Compute the efficiency scores using DEA. In particular, it is necessary to solve n LP models as (15) in the case of assuming variable returns to scale (Banker et al. 1984):

$$\begin{aligned}\frac{1}{\hat{\theta}_k^b} = \text{Max}\ & \varphi_k^b \\ s.t.\ & \\ & \sum_{h=1}^{n} \lambda_h^b x_{hi}^b \le x_{ki}^b, \quad i = 1, \ldots, m \\ & \sum_{h=1}^{n} \lambda_h^b y_{hr}^b \ge \varphi_k^b y_{kr}^b, \ r = 1, \ldots, s \\ & \sum_{h=1}^{n} \lambda_h^b = 1, \\ & \lambda_h^b \ge 0, \qquad h = 1, \ldots, n\end{aligned} \quad (15)$$

In the case of assuming constant returns to scale (Charnes et al. 1978), the model to be solved would be (16):

$$\begin{aligned}\frac{1}{\hat{\theta}_k^b} = \text{Max}\ & \varphi_k^b \\ s.t.\ & \\ & \sum_{h=1}^{n} \lambda_h^b x_{hi}^b \le x_{ki}^b, \quad i = 1, \ldots, m \\ & \sum_{h=1}^{n} \lambda_h^b y_{hr}^b \ge \varphi_k^b y_{kr}^b, \ r = 1, \ldots, s \\ & \lambda_h^b \ge 0, \qquad h = 1, \ldots, n\end{aligned} \quad (16)$$

4. Determine the mean of the efficiency scores: $\overline{\theta}^b = \frac{\sum_{k=1}^{n} \hat{\theta}_k^b}{n}$.
5. Compute $\phi_{i'}^b\left(\alpha_0^q, \alpha_1^q, \alpha_2^q\right) = \sum_{k=1}^{n} \left(\frac{g\left(x_{ki'}^b\right)}{\sum_{k=1}^{n} g\left(x_{ki'}^b\right)} \right) \hat{\theta}_k^b$, where $g\left(x_{ki'}\right) = \alpha_0^q x_{ki'}^{\alpha_1^q + \frac{1}{2}\alpha_2^q \ln(x_{ki'})}$.
6. Repeat steps 2 to 5 B times in order to obtain two bootstrap sets: $\left\{\phi_{i'}^1\left(\alpha_0^q, \alpha_1^q, \alpha_2^q\right), \ldots, \phi_{i'}^B\left(\alpha_0^q, \alpha_1^q, \alpha_2^q\right)\right\}$ and $\left\{\overline{\theta}^1, \ldots, \overline{\theta}^B\right\}$.
7. Determine $p\left(\alpha_0^q, \alpha_1^q, \alpha_2^q\right) = P\left(\frac{\overline{d}}{s_d/\sqrt{B}} > t_{B-1}\right)$, where $\overline{d}$ is the arithmetic mean of $d_b = \phi_{i'}^b\left(\alpha_0^q, \alpha_1^q, \alpha_2^q\right) - \overline{\theta}^b$, $b = 1, \ldots, B$, s_d is its sample standard deviation, and t_{B-1} denotes T-student random variable with $B - 1$ degrees of freedom.
8. Calculate the final p-value of the test as $\frac{1}{Q} \sum_{q=1}^{Q} p\left(\alpha_0^q, \alpha_1^q, \alpha_2^q\right)$.

Next, in Fig. 1, we illustrate the different steps that have to be carried out in order to determine the final p-value for the new test of positive endogeneity in data envelopment analysis.

Finally, it is worth mentioning that our approach could be extended to non-radial measures in the context of data envelopment analysis. In contrast to the parametric world, where the measurement of technical efficiency is based upon a few measures, essentially the Shephard distance functions and the directional distance functions, DEA researchers have introduced many different technical efficiency measures such as the Russell input and output measures of technical efficiency and their graph extension (Färe et al. 1985), the additive model (Charnes et al. 1985), the range-adjusted measure (Cooper et al. 1999) and the enhanced Russell graph (Pastor et al. 1999), or, more recently, the bounded adjusted measure (Cooper et al. 2011). Nevertheless, this extension needs a further development that is beyond the scope of this paper.

[4] Bootstrapping is a kind of resampling where big numbers of samples of the same size as the original one are repeatedly drawn, "with replacement," from the observed sample (see, e.g., Simar and Wilson 1998).

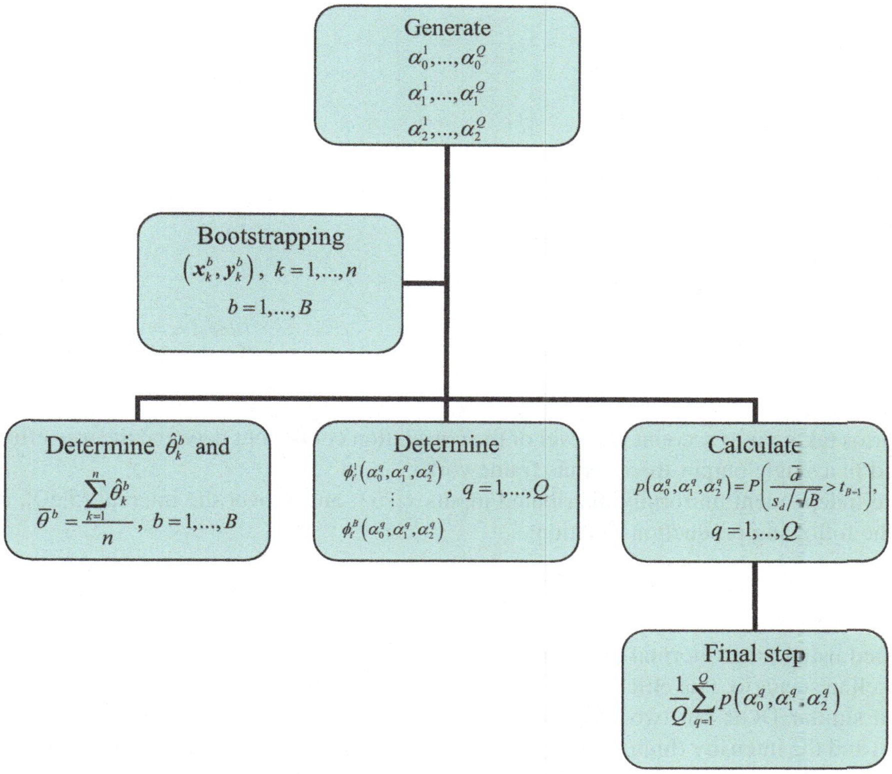

Fig. 1 Scheme of the steps of the algorithm to determine the p-value of the test

Table 1 Rejection rates for the uncorrelation test in PC2009

		Size of test		
Rejection rate		0.10	0.05	0.01
Correlation (ρ)	**0.0**	0.111 (0.058)	0.047 (0.029)	0.010 (0.004)
	0.1	0.432 (0.186)	0.320 (0.112)	0.152 (0.029)
	0.2	0.901 (0.431)	0.856 (0.301)	0.730 (0.102)
	0.3	0.990 (0.739)	0.988 (0.584)	0.970 (0.301)
	0.4	1.000 (0.930)	1.000 (0.856)	1.000 (0.594)
	0.5	1.000 (0.991)	1.000 (0.969)	1.000 (0.871)

Source: PC2009
Notes: $n = 70$. Seven variables. One thousand replications. In brackets are the results obtained in Wilson (2003)

4 Monte Carlo Experiment

In this section, we test the performance of the statistical procedure proposed in this work in finite samples through some Monte Carlo simulations. Particularly, it is interesting, from a methodological point of view, to compare how the new procedure works in comparison with other similar approaches proposed in the literature. To do that, we measure the accuracy of the proposed test by comparing its rejection rates under different assumptions regarding the level of correlation between inputs and the efficiency. Bearing in mind the results of the test proposed by PC2009 and Wilson (2003), we summarize the main results of their experiments in Table 1. The values in brackets are the results obtained by Wilson (2003) for testing independence and not just uncorrelation. Under the null hypothesis, the Wilson test has an acceptance rate that is too high (thus, indicating incorrect size) and increases quite slowly for larger values of the correlation coefficient (poor power). On the contrary, the power of the test proposed by PC2009 increases sharply with the value of the correlation coefficient, as one would wish.

As we have discussed above, we have proposed the statistical procedure in this work for testing for both positive and negative correlation between each input and the efficiency level. To evaluate the performance of this method, we generate

Table 2 Rejection rates for the uncorrelation test

		Size of test		
Rejection rate		0.10	0.05	0.01
Correlation (ρ)	**−0.8**	0.000	0.000	0.000
	−0.4	0.000	0.000	0.000
	−0.2	0.010	0.000	0.000
	0.0	0.245	0.200	0.115
	0.2	0.755	0.695	0.625
	0.4	0.985	0.975	0.965
	0.6	1.000	1.000	1.000
	0.8	1.000	1.000	1.000

Notes: $n = 100$. Output-oriented model. $B = 100$. Two hundred replications. Grid = 400 combinations

eight different scenarios taking into account the level of the correlation coefficient between the true efficiency and inputs. All datasets were defined in a single output-three inputs framework.

We consider three independent uniformly distributed inputs x_1, x_2, and $x_3$over the interval [5,50], and then we generate the output through the following production function:

$$y = x_1^{0.3} x_2^{0.35} x_3^{0.35} \exp(-u) \tag{17}$$

where u was generated using a half-normal distribution $u \approx |N(0; 0.30)|$ and $0 < \exp(-u) < 1$ is the vector of technical efficiency. In the baseline scenario, this efficiency is generated independently from all inputs. The remaining scenarios were developed through a similar DGP, but two factors were allowed to vary in order to generate different settings: the sign (negative or positive) and the intensity (high, medium, or weak) of the ρ Pearson's correlation coefficient between u and x_3.[5] Particularly, we use the following eight correlation coefficients: $\rho = (-0.8, -0.4, -0.2, 0.0, 0.2, 0.4, 0.6, 0.8)$. All scenarios were replicated for a sample size of 100 DMUs. Finally, for each scenario, we run the test we proposed in this work using $B = 100$, and taking into account the obtained p-value, we decide whether or not to reject the null hypothesis. We undertake a Monte Carlo experiment with 200 replicates; consequently, all rejection rates are computed in each replication and finally averaged to obtain the results presented in Table 2.

From Table 2, we find extremely low rejection rates when the correlation coefficient is negative, which implies that the test does not properly reject the null hypothesis under the presence of negative correlation which in fact does not represent a problem in the context of DEA (see Cordero et al. 2015). On the contrary, as we expected, the test correctly detects the positive sign of the correlation, rejecting correlations greater or equal to zero at a substantial rate. Moreover, similar to PC2009, the power of the test increases speedily with the value of the correlation coefficient, as desired (Fig. 2). Particularly, under the assumption of a moderate positive correlation between the true efficiency and one input ($\rho = 0.4$), the proposed statistical procedure shows rejection rates equal or greater than 0.965 for all sizes of the test, which implies that it is powerful enough to detect this scenario. This is a significant desirable result since only the presence of moderate positive correlation impairs the performance of DEA.

5 An Empirical Application

In this section, we illustrate how the new methodology works through an empirical example. The aim is to check the goodness of the new approach comparing its results with respect to those obtained by applying the heuristic proposed by Santin and Sicilia (2017). To do that, we use the same real dataset utilized in that paper, which is focused on the education sector, where the endogeneity problem is frequently observed due to school self-selection (see, e.g., Webbink 2005 or Cordero et al. 2018).

Regarding the data, we analyze 71 Uruguayan public schools included in the Programme for International Student Assessment (PISA) 2012 database (OECD 2013). The PISA target population is composed of students who are aged between 15 and 16 years old at the time of the assessment, all of whom were born in the same year. PISA measures their performance in mathematics, reading, and science. Given that home and socioeconomic context and school factors have influence on

[5]See Cordero et al. (2015) for the detailed procedure to generate the specific correlation coefficient between u and x_3.

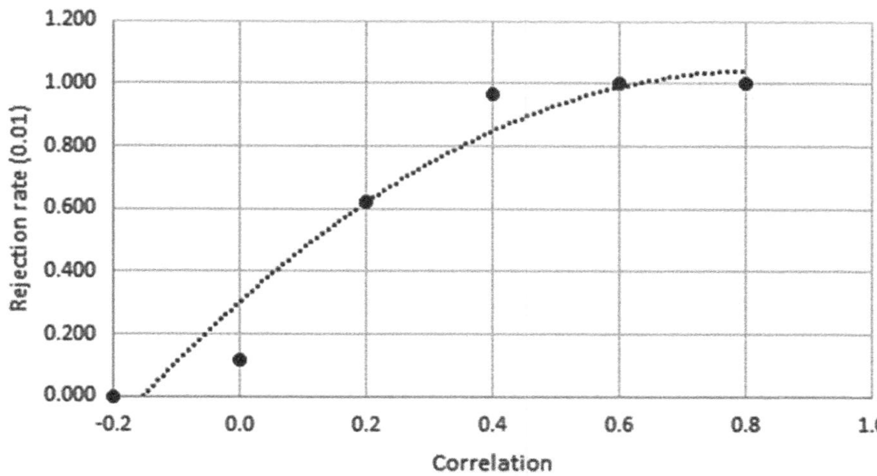

Fig. 2 Rejection rates, different from zero, for the uncorrelation test introduced in this paper (0.01). $n = 100$. Grid = 400 combinations

Table 3 Descriptive statistics of output and input variables of Uruguayan schools in PISA 2012

Variable	Mean	Std. dev.	Min.	Max.
Output				
Maths	382.7	44.2	270.9	466.5
Inputs				
ESCS	2.20	0.42	1.35	3.29
SCMATEDU	4.50	1.11	2.30	6.57
PROPCERT	0.52	0.20	0.15	0.94

Source: Santin and Sicilia (2017)

students' performance, PISA also collects information about students' personal background and schools' environment, for which purpose two questionnaires are administered, one addressed to school principals and another to students. These surveys have taken place every 3 years since the year 2000 focusing on one of the above three areas each time.

The Uruguayan case is interesting because it has historically held a leading position in Latin America in terms of educational achievement. However, the major budgetary effort in education made by the government at the beginning of the twenty-first century has not been accompanied by effective reforms and policies to improve educational outcomes. The result is that in PISA 2012, Uruguay was placed in third position among Latin American countries in the three areas assessed behind Mexico and Chile. Additionally, the variance of test scores among students attending Uruguayan public schools is higher than in other countries, which emphasizes the high social segmentation of the education system. Families from high socioeconomic status self-select in the best public schools with a higher resource level as the perceived quality of teaching and the availability of resources. This fact opens the door for a potential endogeneity problem when analyzing the efficiency of schools.[6]

As PISA 2012 focused on mathematics, we select the schools' average result in mathematics (*Maths*) as the output of the educational process. Regarding educational inputs, we select three variables to represent the classical inputs in education economics required to carry out the learning process: students' quality (raw material), teachers (human capital), and infrastructure (physical capital). Firstly, we use the quality of material educational resources at the school (SCMATEDU), an index built from the school principal's responses to seven questions related to the scarcity or lack of laboratory equipment, institutional materials, computers, the Internet, educational software, library materials, and, finally, audiovisual resources, in order to record the school's physical capital. The higher the index, the better the quality of the school's material. Secondly, we include the proportion of fully certified teachers (PROPCERT). This reflects the quality of teachers and therefore the school's human capital. The index is constructed as the ratio of the total number of certified teachers (with a teaching degree) to the total number of teachers in the school. Finally, we include the school's socioeconomic context, computed as the average students' index of economic, social, and cultural status (ESCS) developed by PISA analysts to indicate students' socioeconomic status. In Table 3, we report the descriptive statistics for all the selected variables mentioned above.

[6]For an extensive discussion about the challenges and problem that Uruguay faces regarding its education system, see Santín and Sicilia (2015).

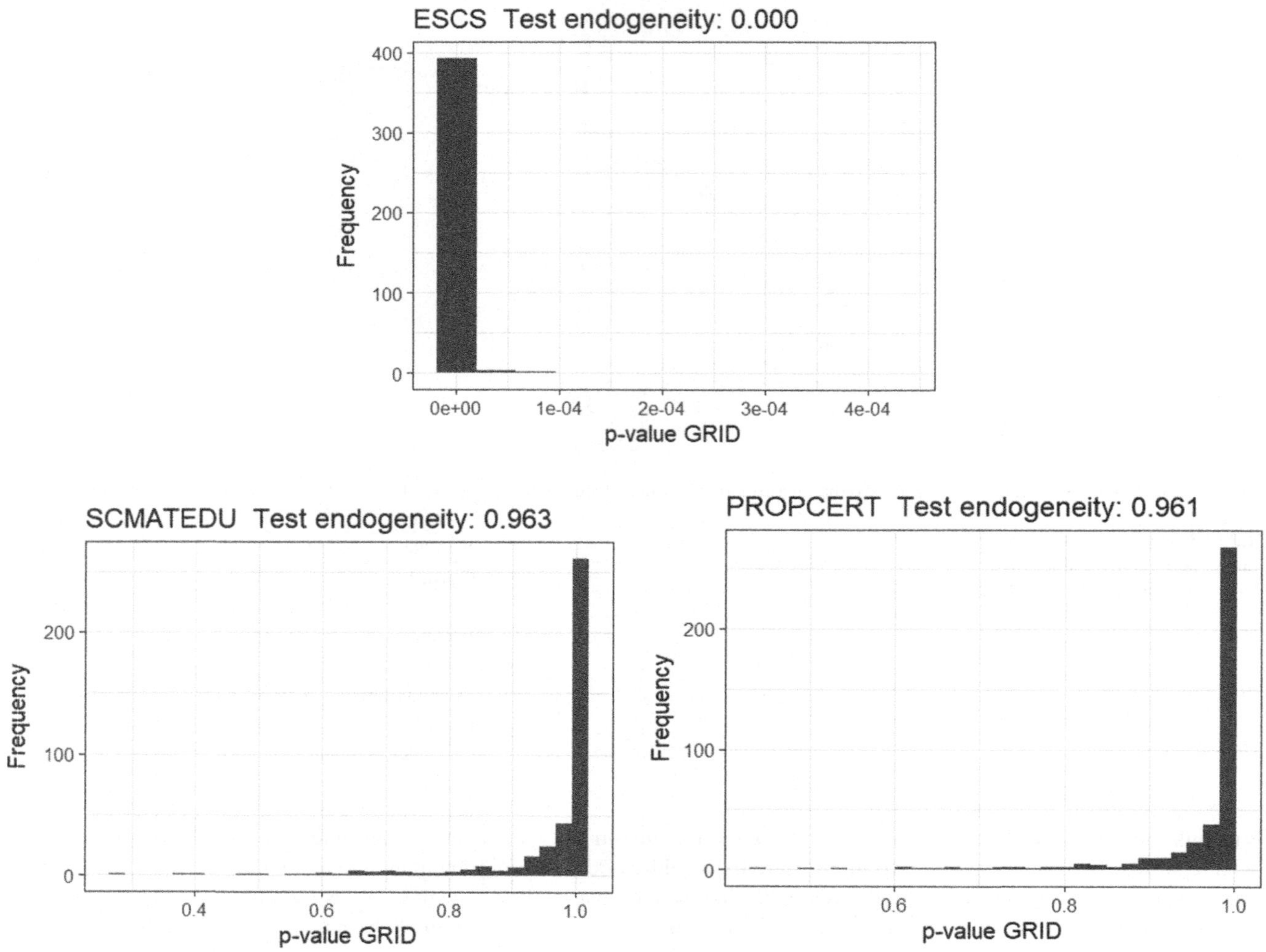

Fig. 3 p-values GRID. Input classification using the test proposed to identify endogenous inputs using conventional DEA. Sample size $n = 71$. The BCC-DEA was estimated following and output orientation. Bootstrap replicates $B = 100$. Grid = 400 combinations

Table 4 Input classification using the test proposed to identify endogenous inputs

Variable	p-value	Classification
ESCS	0.000	We detect positive endogeneity
SCMATEDU	0.963	We do not detect positive endogeneity
PROPCERT	0.961	We do not detect positive endogeneity

Note: Sample size $n = 71$. The BCC-DEA was estimated following and output orientation. Bootstrap replicates $B = 100$. Grid = 400 combinations

We use the procedure explained in Sect. 3 to detect the presence of positive correlation associated with each of the three inputs. In Fig. 3 and Table 4, we report the results we have obtained. Following these findings, the school socioeconomic level (ESCS) appears to be a positive endogenous input, since we reject the null hypothesis. However, in the case of SCMATEDU and PROPCERT, we do not detect problems of positive endogeneity. These results coincide with those obtained by the heuristic method proposed by Santin and Sicilia (2017) applied to the same dataset (Table 5). It is important to note the complementarity between our statistical procedure and this heuristic, since while the first one follows the traditional logic of Hausman (1978) for testing for uncorrelation, the second one allows the intensity of the correlation between the input and the efficiency score to be determined. For example, in the case of ESCS input in the empirical application, we detect the presence of positive correlation using our test, but we cannot distinguish if it is low, moderate, or high which is crucial for practitioners to decide whether or not it is necessary to correct the DEA efficiency estimates for endogeneity.

Table 5 Input classification using the heuristic by Santin and Sicilia (2017)

Variable	γ	Classification
ESCS	0.803	Highly positive correlation
SCMATEDU	0.119	Exogenous or negatively correlated
PROPCERT	0.285	Low positive correlation

Notes: Conventional DEA. Sample size $n = 71$. The BCC-DEA was estimated following and output orientation. Bootstrap replicates $B = 2000$

6 Conclusion

Although endogeneity is currently one of the biggest concerns in microeconomics, so far it has not received much attention in the DEA literature. Recently, Cordero et al. (2015) was the bearer of good and bad news for DEA practitioners: the technique appears to be robust in the presence of negative and slightly positive endogeneity, but a significant positive correlation between one input and the true efficiency level severely biases DEA performance. Unfortunately, as such a positive correlation is frequently observed in different production contexts, the key issue is to deal with this problem in empirical applications. In this paper, we propose a statistical procedure that will allow practitioners to identify potential endogenous inputs when they suspect that there might be some significant positive endogeneity in their setting. The new approach is based on previous results of PC2009.

Our Monte Carlo simulations show that the new procedure correctly detects the sign of the correlation. Additionally, the power of the test increases speedily with the value of the correlation coefficient, as desired. Moreover, through an empirical application on Uruguayan public schools, we showed that our approach produces results that are consistent with respect to the result obtained in Santin and Sicilia (2017) by means of the application of a heuristic.

Finally, this paper should be construed as an initial step to encourage academics and practitioners to continue contributing to this line of research, since more research is still needed in different directions not only to detect the presence of this problem in empirical applications but also to deal with it to improve DEA performance.

Acknowledgments J. Aparicio and L. Ortiz thank the financial support from the Spanish Ministry of Economy and Competitiveness (Ministerio de Economía, Industria y Competitividad), the State Research Agency (Agencia Estatal de Investigacion), and the European Regional Development Fund (Fondo Europeo de DEsarrollo Regional) under grant MTM2016-79765-P (AEI/FEDER, UE). D. Santín and G. Sicilia acknowledge the funding received from the Spanish Ministry of Economy and Competitiveness (Ministerio de Economía, Industria y Competitividad) project referenced ECO2017-83759-P.

References

Banker, R. D., & Chang, H. (2006). The super-efficiency procedure for outlier identification, not for ranking efficient units. *European Journal of Operational Research, 175*(2), 1311–1320.

Banker, R. D., Charnes, A., & Cooper, W. W. (1984). Some models for estimating technical and scale inefficiencies in data envelopment analysis. *Management Science, 30*(9), 1078–1092.

Bifulco, R., & Bretschneider, S. (2001). Estimating school efficiency: A comparison of methods using simulated data. *Economics of Education Review, 20*(5), 417–429.

Bifulco, R., & Bretschneider, S. (2003). Response to comment on estimating school efficiency. *Economics of Education Review, 22*(6), 635–638.

Bravo-Ureta, B. E., Greene, W., & Solís, D. (2012). Technical efficiency analysis correcting for biases from observed and unobserved variables: an application to a natural resource management project. *Empirical Economics, 43*(1), 55–72.

Cazals, C., Fève, F., Florens, J. P., & Simar, L. (2016). Nonparametric instrumental variables estimation for efficiency frontier. *Journal of Econometrics, 190*(2), 349–359.

Charnes, A., Cooper, W. W., & Rhodes, E. (1978). Measuring the efficiency of decision making units. *European Journal of Operational Research, 2*(6), 429–444.

Charnes, A., Cooper, W. W., Golany, B., Seiford, L., & Stutz, J. (1985). Foundations of data envelopment analysis for Pareto-Koopmans efficient empirical production functions. *Journal of Econometrics, 30*(1–2), 91–107.

Cook, W. D., & Seiford, L. M. (2009). Data envelopment analysis (DEA)–Thirty years on. *European Journal of Operational Research, 192*(1), 1–17.

Cooper, W. W., Park, K. S., & Pastor, J. T. (1999). RAM: A range adjusted measure of inefficiency for use with additive models, and relations to other models and measures in DEA. *Journal of Productivity Analysis, 11*(1), 5–42.

Cooper, W. W., Pastor, J. T., Borras, F., Aparicio, J., & Pastor, D. (2011). BAM: A bounded adjusted measure of efficiency for use with bounded additive models. *Journal of Productivity Analysis, 35*(2), 85–94.

Cordero, J. M., Santín, D., & Sicilia, G. (2015). Testing the accuracy of DEA estimates under endogeneity through a Monte Carlo simulation. *European Journal of Operational Research, 244*(2), 511–518.

Cordero, J. M., Cristobal, V., & Santín, D. (2018). Causal inference on education policies: A survey of empirical studies using PISA, TIMSS and PIRLS. *Journal of Economic Surveys, 32*(3), 878–915.

Crespo-Cebada, E., Pedraja-Chaparro, F., & Santín, D. (2014). Does school ownership matter? An unbiased efficiency comparison for regions of Spain. *Journal of Productivity Analysis, 41*(1), 153–172.

De Witte, K., & Lopez-Torres, L. (2017). Efficiency in education: A review of literature and a way forward. *Journal of the Operational Research Society, 68*(4), 339–363.

Efron, B. (1979). Bootstrap methods: Another look at the jackknife. *Annals of Statistics, 7*(1), 16.

Efron, B., & Tibshirani, R. J. (1993). *An introduction to the bootstrap*. New York: Chapman & Hall.

Emrouznejad, A., & Yang, G. L. (2018). A survey and analysis of the first 40 years of scholarly literature in DEA: 1978–2016. *Socio-Economic Planning Sciences, 61*, 4–8.

Färe, R., Grosskopf, S., & Lovell, C. A. K. (1985). *The measurement of efficiency of production*. Boston: Kluwer Nijhof Publishing.

Farrell, M. J. (1957). The measurement of productive efficiency. *Journal of the Royal Statistical Society: Series A (General), 120*(3), 253–281.

Gong, B.-H., & Sickles, R. C. (1992). Finite sample evidence on the performance of stochastic frontiers and data envelopment analysis using panel data. *Journal of Econometrics, 51*(1), 259–284.

Greene, W. H. (1997). *Econometric analysis*. Upper Saddle River: Prentice Hall.

Greene, W. H. (2003). *Econometric analysis* (Fifth ed.). New Jersey: Pearson Education.

Greene, W. H. (2010). A stochastic frontier model with correction for sample selection. *Journal of Productivity Analysis, 34*(1), 15–24.

Hausman, J. A. (1978). Specification tests in econometrics. *Econometrica, 46*(6), 1251–1271.

Holland, D. S., & Lee, S. T. (2002). Impacts of random noise and specification on estimates of capacity derived from data envelopment analysis. *European Journal of Operational Research, 137*, 10–21.

Kumbhakar, S. C., & Lovell, C. A. K. (2000). *Stochastic frontier analysis*. Cambridge: Cambridge University Press.

Kumbhakar, S. C., Tsionas, M., & Sipilainen, T. (2009). Joint estimation of technology choice and technical efficiency: An application to organic and conventional dairy farming. *Journal of Productivity Analysis, 31*(3), 151–162.

Liu, J. S., Lu, L. Y., Lu, W.-M., & Lin, B. J. (2013). Data envelopment analysis 1978–2010: A citation-based literature survey. *Omega, 41*(1), 3–15.

Mastromarco, C., & Simar, L. (2018). Globalization and productivity: A robust nonparametric world frontier analysis. *Economic Modelling, 69*, 134–149.

Mayen, C. D., Balagtas, J. V., & Alexander, C. E. (2010). Technology adoption and technical efficiency: Organic and conventional dairy farms in the United States. *American Journal of Agricultural Economics, 92*(1), 181–195.

Mayston, D. J. (2016). Data envelopment analysis, endogeneity and the quality frontier for public services. *Annals of Operations Research, 250*, 185–203.

Muñiz, M., Paradi, J., Ruggiero, J., & Yang, Z. (2006). Evaluating alternative DEA models used to control for non-discretionary inputs. *Computers and Operations Research, 33*, 1173–1183.

OECD. (2013). *PISA 2012 assessment and analytical framework: Mathematics, reading, science, problem solving and financial literacy*. Paris: OECD Publishing

Orme, C., & Smith, P. (1996). The potential for endogeneity bias in data envelopment analysis. *Journal of the Operational Research Society, 47*(1), 73–83.

Pastor, J. T., Ruiz, J. L., & Sirvent, I. (1999). An enhanced DEA Russell graph efficiency measure. *European Journal of Operational Research, 115*(3), 596–607.

Pedraja-Chaparro, F., Salinas-Jimenez, J., & Smith, P. (1997). On the role of weight restrictions in data envelopment analysis. *Journal of Productivity Analysis, 8*, 215–230.

Perelman, S., & Santin, D. (2011). Measuring educational efficiency at student level with parametric stochastic distance functions: An application to Spanish PISA results. *Education Economics, 19*(1), 29–49.

Peyrache, A., & Coelli, T. (2009). Testing procedures for detection of linear dependencies in efficiency models. *European Journal of Operational Research, 198*(2), 647–654.

Ruggiero, J. (2003). Comment on estimating school efficiency. *Economics of Education Review, 22*(6), 631–634.

Ruggiero, J. (2004). Performance evaluation when non-discretionary factors correlate with technical efficiency. *European Journal of Operational Research, 159*(1), 250–257.

Santín, D., & Sicilia, G. (2015). Measuring the efficiency of public schools in Uruguay: Main drivers and policy implications. *Latin American Economic Review, 24*(1), 5.

Santin, D., & Sicilia, G. (2017). Dealing with endogeneity in data envelopment analysis applications. *Expert Systems with Applications, 68*, 173–184.

Schlotter, M., Schwerdt, G., & Woessmann, L. (2011). Econometric methods for causal evaluation of education policies and practices: A non-technical guide. *Education Economics, 19*(2), 109–137.

Shephard, R. W. (1953). *Cost and production functions*. Princeton: Princeton University Press.

Simar, L., & Wilson, P. W. (1998). Sensitivity analysis of efficiency scores: How to bootstrap in nonparametric frontier models. *Management Science, 44*(1), 49–61.

Simar, L., & Wilson, P. W. (2000). Statistical inference in nonparametric frontier models: The state of the art. *Journal of Productivity Analysis, 13*, 49–78.

Simar, L., Vanhems, A., & Van Keilegom, I. (2016). Unobserved heterogeneity and endogeneity in nonparametric frontier estimation. *Journal of Econometrics, 190*(2), 360–373.

Solis, D., Bravo-Ureta, B. E., & Quiroga, R. E. (2007). Soil conservation and technical efficiency among hillside farmers in Central America: A switching regression model$_*$. *Australian Journal of Agricultural and Resource Economics, 51*(4), 491–510.

Webbink, D. (2005). Causal effects in education. *Journal of Economic Surveys, 19*(4), 535–560.

Wilson, P. W. (2003). Testing independence in models of productive efficiency. *Journal of Productivity Analysis, 20*(3), 361–390.

Zhang, Y., & Bartels, R. (1998). The effect of sample size on the mean efficiency in DEA with an application to electricity distribution in Australia, Sweden and New Zealand. *Journal of Productivity Analysis, 9*, 187–204.

Modelling Pollution-Generating Technologies: A Numerical Comparison of Non-parametric Approaches

K Hervé Dakpo, Philippe Jeanneaux, and Laure Latruffe

Abstract In this chapter, we compare the existing non-parametric approaches that account for undesirable outputs in technology modelling. The approaches are grouped based on Lauwers' (Ecological Economics 68:1605–1614, 2009) seminal three-group classification and extended to a fourth group of recent models grounded on the estimation of several sub-technologies depending on the type of the outputs. With this fourth group of models, we provide a new complete picture of pollution-technologies modelling in the non-parametric framework of data envelopment analysis (DEA). We undertake a numerical comparison of the most recent models – the approach based on materials balance principle and weak G-disposability and the multiple equation technologies, namely, the by-production model and its various extensions, as well as the unified framework of natural and managerial disposability. The results reveal that the weak G-disposability and the unified natural and managerial disposability perform poorly compared to the multiple equation models. In addition, simulation fails to explicitly discriminate between the various multiple equation models.

Keywords Eco-efficiency · Undesirable outputs · Materials balance principle · By-production · Non-parametric technology modelling

1 Introduction

Firms' production process inevitably results in residual outputs and, therefore, often implies the deterioration of environmental quality. Over the years it has become important to measure firms' environmental performance. It can help policy-makers design the most effective policy schemes (subsidies, taxes, permits, etc.) to encourage firms to internalise pollution in their decision-making. It can also provide new opportunities for firms which engage in the adoption of environmentally friendly behaviour by boosting their brand image (Tyteca 1997). A number of environmental performance indicators exist, such as indicators provided by Life Cycle Assessment (LCA), business-specific measures, environmental accounting measures or indicators based on the theory of productive efficiency (see the review by Tyteca (1996)). We focus here on the latter approach based on the estimation of production frontier (see Shephard (1970), Färe (1988) or Coelli et al. (2005)). Contrary to many indicators which provide partial measures of the performance (e.g. greenhouse gas emissions per euro, non-renewable energy consumption per ton of product, etc.), the frontier-based measures give a global performance ratio which accounts for all inputs and outputs of production processes. Based on the neoclassical production function theory and especially on activity analysis (also referred to as non-parametric data envelopment analysis (DEA) (Charnes et al 1978)), productive efficiency measures offer several advantages, such as consistent standardisation allowing the comparison of several decision-making units (DMU) using scores comprised between zero and one and important flexibility (Färe et al. 1996; Tyteca 1996).

The introduction of undesirable outputs (e.g. pollution) in a production technology has grown in importance at the beginning of the 1980s with Pittman's (1983) work. His approach was based on index numbers theory (Caves et al. 1982) which requires price information for undesirable outputs. In Pittman's (1983) work, these prices were based on observed

K. H. Dakpo (✉)
Economie Publique, INRA, AgroParisTech, Université Paris-Saclay, Grignon, France
e-mail: k-herve.dakpo@inra.fr

P. Jeanneaux
VetAgro Sup, UMR Territoires, Lempdes, France

L. Latruffe
INRA, UMR GREThA, Université de Bordeaux, Pessac, France

J. Aparicio et al. (eds.), *Advances in Efficiency and Productivity II*, International Series in Operations Research & Management Science 287, https://doi.org/10.1007/978-3-030-41618-8_5

values of marketable permits, on taxes and on shadow prices estimated in previous studies. In general, however, prices of undesirable goods are unavailable. For example, pollution is a non-marketed good for which it is challenging to compute all abatement costs. In cases where price information about undesirable outputs is available, it is imprecise and unreliable since many abatement costs are not accounted for, such as efforts required to change the production process or '... time spent by managers dealing with environmental regulators and regulations ...' (Berman and Bui 2001, p 498).

In this context, the advantage of activity analysis models, and the flow of formulations and extensions that have been proposed, lies in their quantity-based information only. The difference between the different methodological developments of activity models relates to the disposability assumptions associated with undesirable outputs (free or weak disposability, weak G-disposability, natural and managerial disposability, conditional free and costly disposability)[1] or to the physical properties that must hold in the production technology (law of matter/energy conservation). In other words, the divergence among results obtained from the various non-parametric models is certainly due to the way undesirable outputs are incorporated or to the paradigms embedded in the technology.

In this regard, a seminal paper is the one by Lauwers (2009), who proposes a classification of the non-parametric methodologies on frontier modelling with the inclusion of undesirable outputs, into three different groups. A first group includes environmentally adjusted production efficiency (EAPE) models, namely, models that consider pollution as output under the weak disposability assumption (Fare et al. 1986, 1989) or where pollution is treated as a free disposable input (Hailu and Veeman 2001; Haynes et al. 1993). The second group includes frontier eco-efficiency (FEE) models. These models relate to the normalised undesirable output approach discussed by Tyteca (1996, p 295) 'in which the desirable outputs and the inputs are no longer considered explicitly, but are rather implicitly accounted for', and link economic outcomes to environmental damages. The third group proposed in Lauwers (2009) includes models incorporating material balance principle (MBP) in environmental performance assessment, namely, MBP-adjusted efficiency (MBP-AE) models. As argued by Lauwers (2009), MBP reconciles the production technology with the physical laws of mass conservation. More recently, Dakpo et al. (2016) provided an extensive up-to-date critical review of major methodologies developed within the non-parametric framework of DEA to account for undesirable outputs. The authors included in their review the recent models that rely on the estimation of separate sub-technologies, one for the good outputs and another for the undesirable outputs, which we coin multiple equation environmentally adjusted efficiency (M3E) models (Førsund 2017; Murty et al. 2012; Dakpo 2015).

The aim of this chapter is to contribute to the literature that compares the existing non-parametric approaches accounting for bad output in technology modelling. More specifically, our contribution is to provide an up-to-date numerical comparison of the models and to conclude on their respective benefits or shortcomings. While the existing literature has focused on comparing the approaches from a theoretical point of view, or on applying a single approach to data, here we apply several approaches to the same data.[2]

For this, we firstly clarify the concept of eco-efficiency. In the literature on environmental performance, many concepts (environmental intensity or productivity, eco-efficiency, ecological efficiency, environmental efficiency) are interchangeably used to represent the same notion even though there are scientific differences between them. This is, for instance, the case of the eco-efficiency concept which has been associated by Chen and Delmas (2012) and Chen (2013) to EAPE models though the concept is more related to FEE models, while in Dyckhoff and Allen (2001), ecological efficiency, environmental efficiency and eco-efficiency have been used to capture the same notions. After our terminology clarification, we secondly provide a numerical comparison of approaches based on the intuitive classification of models made by Lauwers (2009), which we extend to a fourth group of models relying on separate sub-technologies. We believe this extension to a fourth group of models will enlighten the philosophy behind the modelling of pollution-generating technologies and also explain the choices of models for our numerical comparison. Besides, this group taxonomy can allow almost exhaustively classify existing models in non-parametric productive efficiency assessment.

This chapter is organised as follows. We provide in Sect. 2 some background and clarification of terminology. In Sect. 3 we explain the various models, based on the above-mentioned classification. In Sect. 4 we present and discuss the numerical results of several simulations, and in Sect. 5 we provide some concluding remarks.

[1]The free or strong disposability simply relates the classical monotonicity condition. About the other disposability assumptions, they will be explained in the next sections.

[2]It is worth mentioning that a first attempt in this framework of comparing several polluting technologies modelling can be found in Dakpo et al. (2014) where the authors have considered greenhouse gas emissions in livestock farming.

2 A Glance at Eco-efficiency Definition

In performance benchmarking the concept of eco-efficiency emerged in the beginning of the 1990s (Schaltegger and Sturm 1990; Schmidheiny 1992), as a suitable tool for linking economic value to environmental impact in a sustainability framework (Mickwitz et al. 2006). The notion of eco-efficiency is defined by the World Business Council for Sustainable Development (WBCSD) as '... the delivery of competitively priced goods and services that satisfy human needs and bring quality of life, while progressively reducing ecological impacts and resource intensity throughout the life-cycle to a level at least in line with the Earth's estimated carrying capacity'. In the same line, other definitions of eco-efficiency have been proposed in the literature. For instance, according to Schaltegger and Burritt (2000, pp 22, 24), 'eco-efficiency ensures that ecological and economic matters are integrated in the environmental accounting framework'. This implies that eco-efficiency is reached in a system where ecological resources are used as inputs to meet economic goals (outputs). Thus, eco-efficiency in a normative sense represents a situation where a decision-making unit (DMU) produces more value with fewer environmental impacts (Huppes and Ishikawa 2005a). For Schaltegger and Burritt (2000), eco-efficiency is the cross efficiency between economic and ecological dimensions, and it is also referred to as economic-ecological efficiency or E^2 efficiency. In relation to sustainable development, this concept is the ratio between economic performance and environmental performance. In light of this definition, various pollution intensity ratios have been used, such as pollution per unit of value added, and some of them being grounded on LCA.[3] Hence, environmental performance is not eco-efficiency per se, but is a component of eco-efficiency. Table 1 summarises the construction of eco-efficiency. Each component of eco-efficiency is a value (in the case of economic efficiency) or an impact (in the case of environmental efficiency) related to a functional unit which is a reference to which both value and impact are related.

As underlined by Kuosmanen (2005, p 15), many variations of the eco-efficiency concept defined as 'the ratio of economic value added to the environmental damage index' have been proposed. Huppes and Ishikawa (2005a) discussed four types of eco-efficiency-related concepts (environmental productivity, environmental intensity, environmental improvement cost and environmental cost-effectiveness), depending on whether the focus is on economic value or on environmental impact. The major challenge with eco-efficiency is the aggregation of environmental impacts. Huppes and Ishikawa (2005b) explained how individual or collective preferences (revealed or stated) can be used for such aggregation. Based on the literature on productive efficiency, Kuosmanen and Kortelainen (2005) used DEA to find data-driven weights for the aggregation of environmental pressures for the eco-efficiency concept in the same way as Huppes and Ishikawa (2005b). However, the measures provided in Kuosmanen and Kortelainen (2005) are relative measures similar to the scores obtained in productive efficiency analysis and thus are different from the traditional eco-efficiency ratios.

Clearly, the concept of eco-efficiency has become very popular despite its ambiguous definition: it has been used to 'refer to a target, it can refer to an indicator, or it can refer to a tool. Quantitative indicators of eco-efficiency can differ in terms of meaning and/or units', as underlined by Heijungs (2007, p 80). Schaltegger and Burritt (2000, p 49) also noticed that 'in practice, the term has been given different meanings and, as a result, has little precision'. Heijungs (2007, p 87) suggested that 'the noun efficiency refers to the degree of optimality of a system. It can be a quantitative indicator, in which case it

Table 1 Eco-efficiency construction path

Economic dimension	Ecological dimension
Economic efficiency ↓ Net present value (NPV) per functional unit	Ecological (or environmental) efficiency ↓ Environmental impact added (EIA) per functional unit
Economic-ecological efficiency or eco-efficiency ↓	
EIA per NPV	

Source: Adapted from Schaltegger and Burritt (2000, p 359)

[3] LCA is a method that allows quantifying and identifying sources of environmental impacts of a product or a system from 'cradle to grave' (Ekvall et al. 2007). It means that these impacts are evaluated from the extraction of the natural resources till their elimination or disposal as waste.

is a dimensionless pure number, measured on a ratio scale, bounded between 0 and 1, and with higher values signifying a higher degree of optimality. Alternatively, it can be a qualitative relative indicator, measured on an ordinal scale, and again with higher values signifying a higher degree of optimality'. Based on this, our understanding is that the eco-efficiency measure of Kuosmanen and Kortelainen (2005) is close to the scientific definition of an efficiency measure (that is to say, a dimensionless measure), while the other measures are rather eco-productivity measures.

3 Classification of the Existing Methodologies

As explained above, Lauwers (2009) classified into three groups the different non-parametric approaches incorporating pollution in production technologies that existed at the time of his review. This classification is sensible and intuitive, and therefore we follow it here.

3.1 Environmentally Adjusted Production Efficiency (EAPE) Models

In this classification, the first group, called by the author 'environmentally adjusted production efficiency' (EAPE), refers to approaches that treat pollution as input or as output under the weak disposability assumption (WDA). Considering that pollution generates social costs, some authors recommend introducing bad outputs as extra inputs and assume their free disposability, since this accounts for the consumption of natural resources that is necessary for their disposal (e.g. Dyckhoff and Allen 2001; Prior 2006).[4] However, the WDA implies that reducing bad outputs is not without cost; good outputs also need to be reduced for a given level of inputs since resources must be diverted to abatement activities in order to mitigate the pollution level (Chung et al. 1997; Fare et al. 2007; Kuosmanen and Podinovski 2009). Lauwers (2009, p 1608) showed the limits of these models and argued, for the example of non-point source nitrogen pollution in agriculture, that this pollution is 'calculated from conventional inputs and outputs using a nutrient balance equation'. Considering pollution as input or output is likely to raise some problems such as mathematical infeasibility, as shown by Coelli et al. (2007). The physical laws and the mass conservation equation imply that the levels of bad outputs can be assessed using some technical coefficients that convert inputs, good outputs and bad outputs into a common mass. Even if we can make these models compatible with the mass conservation law, their fundamental drawback lies in the inappropriate trade-offs present in the productive technology (see Dakpo et al. (2016) for more details). Many types of approaches can also be classified in this category like non-radial directional distance function (Zhou et al. 2012), additive efficiency index (Chen and Delmas 2012), range-adjusted measure (Sueyoshi and Goto 2011) and other slacks-based measures (Lozano and Gutierrez 2011; Tone 2004). All these models also suffer from the same limits aforementioned in this category, and more importantly they can be viewed as a generalisation of the model that treats pollution as an input.

3.2 Frontier Eco-efficiency (FEE) Models

The second group of models defined by Lauwers (2009) includes 'frontier eco-efficiency' (FEE) models, discussed in Kortelainen and Kuosmanen (2004), where environmental pressures are used as inputs to explain production value-added. This approach is very similar to the ecological efficiency model presented in Korhonen and Luptacik (2004). However, as stressed by Dakpo et al. (2016), the FEE models are based on an incomplete representation of the production technology. Tyteca (1997, p 188) argued that 'the absence of "true" inputs [...] can be criticized since firms that produce identical levels of outputs and discharge identical levels of pollutants, while using different levels of inputs, will be considered equally efficient'. Another weakness of the FFE models arises in the case where value-added is used as the economic outcome. Since value-added is production value minus intermediate consumption ($VA = p'y - w'x$), inputs are implicitly introduced in the technology.[5] Since environmental impacts are treated as inputs, the production technology properties would thus allow meaningless substitutions between inputs. It seems that FEE models may be useful in the case of data limitation which is actually a salient issue in this framework of modelling polluting technologies.

[4]In the same vein, Reinhard et al. (1999) discussed an early way of treating undesirable outputs by using proxies, namely, environmentally detrimental inputs that generate pollution and need to be reduced (such as nitrogen excess). Scheel (2001) introduced 'nonseparating efficiency measures' where bad outputs and good outputs are considered simultaneously and bad outputs are introduced as negative outputs.

[5]The production technology can be described as $T = \{(VA, b) | \, b \text{ can produce } VA\}$: alternatively b can produce $p'y - w'x$. Hence inputs are implicitly considered.

3.3 MBP-Adjusted Efficiency (MBP-AE) Models

The third group proposed by Lauwers (2009) is made up of the materials balance-based models, in which both economic and environmental outcomes are seen as outputs of the same production set (Coelli et al. 2007). These models are related to the first two laws of thermodynamics.[6] In this category, we find the first model originally proposed by Lauwers et al. (1999) and further improved in Coelli et al. (2007). The model minimises the levels of bad outputs, and the problem is solved analogously to a cost minimisation program using the mass balance equation. The boundary of the objective function is equivalent to what the authors called an 'iso-environmental cost line' (in allusion to the commonly known iso-cost line). Hampf and Rødseth (2015) recently introduced the weak G-disposability model which is also based on the MBP, but from a different perspective. This new approach is a classic production technology augmented with bad outputs as well as a constraint that ensures mass conservation. This constraint relates inputs' excesses and good outputs' shortfalls to undesirable outputs' excesses using the conservation law. Models in this third group improve to some extent the EAPE models (first group),[7] but nevertheless have important shortcomings. Hampf and Rødseth (2015) demonstrated that, under some assumptions, the weak G-disposability approach is equivalent to the WDA, an approach which is in itself questionable as explained above. Furthermore, Dakpo et al. (2016) argued that the weak G-disposability approach might generate unusual trade-offs between inputs and outputs. Førsund (2009) also underlined that the mass conservation equation does not explicitly show how residuals are generated. This does not preclude that MBP are not inherent in most production processes, but it implies that meaningful economic properties cannot be derived by resorting to the physical identity of mass conservation.

3.4 Multiple Equation Environmentally Adjusted Efficiency (M3E) Models

In addition to the three groups of approaches suggested by Lauwers (2009), we add here a fourth group of more recent models, namely, models grounded on the multiple equation production concept originally discussed in Frisch (1965) (multiple equation environmentally adjusted efficiency (M3E)). As put forward by Førsund (2009), a production process generating undesirable outputs is complex and is actually made of several sub-processes. In this category of models, Murty et al. (2012) proposed the by-production approach where the global technology lies at the intersection of an intended outputs' sub-technology and an unintended (i.e. undesirable) outputs' sub-technology. The rationale of this by-production approach lies in the separation of the inputs into two groups: the non-polluting inputs (also called non-materials inputs) and the polluting inputs that is to say inputs that generate pollution (also called materials inputs). Murty et al. (2012) posited costly disposability for undesirable outputs, which implies that for a given level of polluting input, it is possible to generate a minimum level of pollution; however, the presence of inefficiencies can lead to the generation of more than this minimum level. In this modelling framework, free disposability is maintained for good outputs and non-polluting inputs. Free disposability of good outputs implies that it is possible to produce lower levels of these outputs with the same amount of inputs. Free disposability of non-polluting inputs means that it is possible to produce the same amount of outputs using higher levels of these inputs. As for polluting inputs, they globally violate the free disposability assumption since larger amounts of these inputs imply that more pollution is generated. Murty (2015) recently discussed the conditional free and costly disposability assumptions referring to these inputs. The conditional free disposability captures changes in the minimum amount of pollution that can be generated given that higher levels of materials inputs are possible due to their free disposability under the intended outputs' sub-technology. The conditional costly disposability implies that lower levels of materials inputs attainable under the unintended outputs' sub-technology inevitably affect the maximum amount of good outputs that is produced under the intended outputs' sub-technology. In the case of two-technology system, graphically on Fig. 1, the frontier of the good outputs is the upper curve, while the lower curve shows the frontier for bad outputs' generation. Inputs are denoted $x \in \mathbb{R}_+^K$, good outputs $y \in \mathbb{R}_+^Q$, and bad outputs $b \in \mathbb{R}_+^R$. DMU_o lies in the inner regions of both sub-technologies. To be operationally (or economically) efficient, this DMU needs to be projected on the north-west side of the intended outputs' sub-technology. On the other hand, the DMU needs to be projected on the south-east side of the frontier of unintended outputs' sub-technology to become environmentally efficient.

[6]The first law of thermodynamics gives the principle of mass/energy conservation, that is to say 'what goes in, comes out'. The second law, also known as the law of entropy, states that using polluting inputs will inevitably result in pollution generation.

[7]For the FEE models, Lauwers (2009) argued that introducing the materials balance is less problematic.

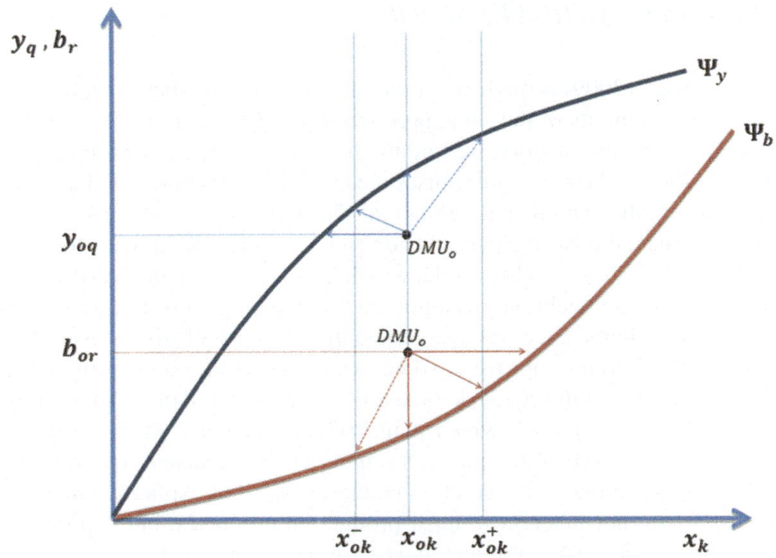

Fig. 1 By-production representation with one polluting input x_k, one good output y_q, one bad output b_r and two sub-technologies, one for the good output (Ψ_y) and one for the bad output (Ψ_b)

One limitation of the by-production approach is that independence between benchmarks of the two sub-technologies is maintained by Murty et al. (2012) in their operationalisation of the approach with the non-parametric methodology (DEA). This independence weakens Murty et al.'s (2012) approach and may provide inconsistent results. To circumvent this shortcoming, Dakpo (2015) developed an extension by introducing an interconnectedness relation (which he called 'dependence constraints') relative to the pollution-generating inputs between the two sub-technologies involved in the by-production approach. Recently, Førsund (2017) has re-discussed the multiple equation framework where non-materials inputs (service inputs) play an important role in the unintended outputs' sub-technology's dematerialisation. In other words, they are useful to mitigate unintended outputs. In addition to the by-production approaches, we also include in this fourth group of models the one proposed in Sueyoshi et al. (2010) and Sueyoshi and Goto (2010), reflecting two different adaptation strategies that can be followed by the DMU's manager: natural disposability, where the manager chooses to reduce the consumption of inputs as the strategy for decreasing pollution, and managerial disposability, where managerial efforts (such as implementing cleaner technologies or substituting clean inputs for polluting ones) result in an increase in the consumption of inputs but simultaneously in a reduction in the pollution generated. In the case of the latter disposability assumptions, the authors also considered two independent sub-technologies. Moreover, they considered a unified framework, which was criticised in Dakpo et al. (2016) arguing that it may create situations where bad outputs are treated as inputs or where all inputs are considered as good outputs that need to be increased.

4 Numerical Comparison of the Approaches

For the numerical comparison, we apply here Monte Carlo (MC) simulations which are well-known tools largely used in the literature of performance benchmarking to assess the quality of a modelling (see, e.g. Andor and Hesse (2013); Badunenko and Mozharovskyi (2019); Kuosmanen and Johnson (2010); Nieswand and Seifert (2018)). In the case of this chapter, we provide a follow-up of the work done by Hampf (2018) who considered MC simulations to compare several pollution-adjusted technologies, namely, inverse and translation of bad outputs technologies, bad output modelled as input or WDA and weak G-disposability technologies. The conclusion of Hampf (2018) is that in most scenarios the weak G-disposability model provides more accurate results. We thereby provide numerical illustrations for two groups of models: the materials balance principle-based weak G-disposability model[8] and the by-production model along the lines of Murty et al. (2012), Dakpo (2015) and Førsund (2017). For a more complete picture, we also consider the unified framework of natural and managerial disposability as formulated in Sueyoshi and Goto (2010). We do not consider EAPE models like the ones relying on WDA or the ones treating pollution as inputs because of the theoretical and practical limits associated with these models and also considering the results discussed in Hampf (2018). We then go further than the latter article, by accounting for additional relevant and recent models. Finally, we ignore here the FEE model since the objective of this model cannot compare directly with all the other models retained for our analysis. As previously explained, FEE models rely on value added as the good output and pollution as the bad output. Yet all the models compared here do not require the value added. Therefore, to have the same ground for comparison, the FEE models have been omitted.

4.1 Simulation Framework

Let us recall that $x \in \mathbb{R}_{+}^{K}$, $y \in \mathbb{R}_{+}^{Q}$, and $b \in \mathbb{R}_{+}^{R}$ are the vectors of inputs, good outputs and bad outputs, respectively. For simplicity, in our numerical application, we use $K = 2$ where x_1 is the materials input and x_2 the service input, $Q = 1$ and $R = 2$. The number of DMUs is set to $(i = 1, \ldots, N)$. Adapting the Hampf (2018) MC approach, the following production functions are considered:

$$y_i = x_{1i}^{\alpha_1} (z_i x_{2i})^{\alpha_2} \exp\left(-u_{yi} + v_{yi}\right) \tag{1}$$

and

$$b_{ji} = x_{1i}^{\gamma}((1 - z_i) x_{2i} + 1)^{-1} \exp\left(u_{bji} + v_{bji}\right) \qquad j = 1, 2 \tag{2}$$

where u_{yi} and v_{bji} are, respectively, the inefficiency of the good output and of both undesirable outputs and the MC simulations are drawn from a multivariate half-normal distribution $|\mathcal{N}(0, \mathbf{\Sigma}_1)|$where

$$\mathbf{\Sigma}_1 = \begin{bmatrix} \sigma_{uy}^2 & \sigma_{uyb_1} & \sigma_{uyb_2} \\ \sigma_{uyb_1} & \sigma_{ub_1}^2 & \sigma_{ub_1b_2} \\ \sigma_{uyb_2} & \sigma_{ub_1b_2} & \sigma_{ub_2}^2 \end{bmatrix} \tag{3}$$

where σ_{uy}^2 and σ_{ubj}^2 are chosen in advance and the covariance is computed such that

$$\sigma_{uyb_1} = \sigma_{uyb_2} = \sigma_{ub_1b_2} = \rho_1 \tag{4}$$

The noise variables v_{yi} and v_{bji} are also drawn from a multivariate normal distribution $\mathcal{N}(0, \mathbf{\Sigma}_2)$ with a variance-covariance matrix as

$$\mathbf{\Sigma}_1 = \sigma_v^2 \begin{bmatrix} 1 & \rho_2 & \rho_2 \\ \rho_2 & 1 & \rho_2 \\ \rho_2 & \rho_2 & 1 \end{bmatrix} \tag{5}$$

Following Badunenko and Mozharovskyi (2019), x_1 and x_2 are drawn from a doubly truncated normal distribution such that

$$\begin{bmatrix} x_1 \\ x_2 \end{bmatrix} \sim \mathcal{N}_{((0,0)',(10,5)')} \left(\begin{bmatrix} 2 \\ 1.5 \end{bmatrix}, \begin{bmatrix} \sigma_{x_1}^2 & 0.5\sqrt{\sigma_{x_1}^2 \sigma_{x_1}^2/3} \\ 0.5\sqrt{\sigma_{x_1}^2 \sigma_{x_1}^2/3} & \sigma_{x_1}^2/3 \end{bmatrix} \right) \tag{6}$$

[8]We do not consider the environmental efficiency measured by Coelli et al. (2007) using the materials balance since the estimation of the iso-environmental lines can work with only one bad output. In the case of several pollutants, it would require aggregation weights, which, as pointed out in Hoang and Rao (2010), may not meet universal acceptance.

Table 2 MC simulations parameters

Parameters	Values
(α_1, α_2)	$\{(0.45, 0.35), (0.5, 0.5)\}$
$\left(\sigma_{uy}^2, \sigma_{ub1}^2, \sigma_{ub2}^2, \sigma_v^2, \sigma_{x1}^2\right)$	$(0.49, 0.16, 0.1, 0.02, 25)$
$\rho_1 = \rho_2$	0.5
z_i	$z_i \in \{1, Uniform(0, 1)\}$
γ	$\{1, 2\}$
N	$\{50, 100, 200, 500\}$
$L =$ # of replications	500

In Eqs. (1) and (2), $1 - z_i$ indicates the share of the service input that is shifted from the production of the good output to the mitigation of undesirable outputs (Hampf 2018). As such $z_i \in [0, 1]$ and when $z_i = 1$ no abatement takes place. The parameter γ in Eq. (2) is used here for modelling either a linear ($\gamma = 1$) or a non-linear ($\gamma = 2$) emission-generating process. Table 2 displays the values chosen for the various parameters that will be used in the numerical simulations.

Given the values of $\alpha_1$and α_2 in Table 2, the production function of the good output is a Cobb-Douglas function with constant returns to scale (CRS) when $(\alpha_1, \alpha_2) = (0.5, 0.5)$ and decreasing returns to scale (DRS) when $(\alpha_1, \alpha_2) = (0.45, 0.35)$. Since we use here activity analysis for the efficiency computation, we also consider a scenario where the noise variable v is not included in Eqs. (1) and (2). To compare the performance of different estimators, we use the following measures:

- Mean absolute deviation (MAD)

$$MAD = \frac{1}{nL} \sum_{l=1}^{L} \sum_{i=1}^{N} \left| \hat{E}_{il} - E_{il} \right| \tag{7}$$

where $\hat{E}$ is the estimated efficiency score and E the true efficiency score. For this measure, the lower the better.

- Mean deviation (MD) or bias

$$MD = \frac{1}{nL} \sum_{l=1}^{L} \sum_{i=1}^{N} \left(\hat{E}_{il} - E_{il} \right) \tag{8}$$

About the *MD* the closer to zero the better.

- Mean squared error (MSE)

$$MSE = \frac{1}{nL} \sum_{l=1}^{L} \sum_{i=1}^{N} \left(\hat{E}_{il} - E_{il} \right)^2 \tag{9}$$

For a well-performing model, *MSE* is lower as possible.

- Upward bias (UB)

$$UB = \frac{1}{nL} \sum_{l=1}^{L} \sum_{i=1}^{N} \mathbb{1} \left(\hat{E}_{il} \geq E_{il} \right) \tag{10}$$

The expected value for this statistic is 0.5 and a value less or greater will indicate underestimation or overestimation, respectively, of efficiencies.

- Mean Spearman rank correlation (MRC)

$$MRC = \frac{1}{L}\sum_{l=1}^{L} \frac{\sum_{i=1}^{N}\left(\hat{e}_{il} - \overline{\hat{e}}_{il}\right)\left(e_{il} - \overline{\hat{e}}_{il}\right)}{\sqrt{\sum_{i=1}^{N}\left(\hat{e}_{il} - \overline{\hat{e}}_{il}\right)^2 \sum_{i=1}^{N}\left(e_{il} - \overline{\hat{e}}_{il}\right)^2}} \tag{11}$$

where the efficiencies E are converted into rank efficiencies e. We expect a higher correlation for a model that is performing closer to the original simulation.

4.2 Estimation of Pollution-Generating Technologies Using Activity Analysis

As previously mentioned, several models have been retained for this comparison regarding the new classification of pollution-generating technologies modelling.

(i) Materials balance principle and the weak G-disposability (Weak G)

This model has been formulated and used in Hampf and Rødseth (2015) and Rødseth (2015). It is grounded on the materials balance principle which is accounted for through a summing up condition. The proposed model writes as follows:

$$\begin{aligned}
HR_0 = \max_{s_y, s_{b_j}, \lambda} & \; s_y + \sum_{j=1}^{R} s_{b_j} \\
s.t. \; x_{1o} - s_{x_1} &= \sum_{i=1}^{N} \lambda_i x_{1i} \\
x_{2o} &\geq \sum_{i=1}^{N} \lambda_i x_{2i} \\
y_o + s_y &= \sum_{i=1}^{N} \lambda_i y_i \\
b_{jo} - s_{b_j} &= \sum_{i=1}^{N} \lambda_i b_{ij} \\
a_j s_{x_1} &= s_{b_j} \\
\sum_{i=1}^{N} \lambda_i &= 1 \\
\lambda &\geq 0
\end{aligned} \tag{12}$$

where a_j is the material content coefficient associated with the materials input. To obtain the value of a_j, we simply divide the amount of pollutant b_j by the amount of the materials input x_1. In this case, the material content varies with the different observations. The efficiency scores can be retrieved by calculating $\left(b_{jo} - s_{b_j}\right)/b_{jo}$ for the bad output and $y_o/(y_o + s_y)$ for the good output.

(ii) Multiple equation technology

In this framework, several models have been discussed in the literature. Murty et al. (2012) proposed the by-production approach which basically splits the global technology into two sub-technologies: one corresponding to the good output and the second to the undesirable output. In terms of activity analysis, this model writes as

$$
\begin{aligned}
MRL1_0 = & \max_{s_y, s_{b_j}, \lambda, \mu} s_y + \sum_{j=1}^{R} s_{b_j} \\
s.t.\ & x_{1o} \geq \sum_{i=1}^{N} \lambda_i x_{1i} \\
& x_{2o} \geq \sum_{i=1}^{N} \lambda_i x_{2i} \\
& y_o + s_y = \sum_{i=1}^{N} \lambda_i y_i \\
& x_{1o} \leq \sum_{i=1}^{N} \mu_i x_{1i} \\
& b_{jo} - s_{b_j} = \sum_{i=1}^{N} \mu_i b_{ij} \\
& \sum_{i=1}^{N} \lambda_i = 1 \\
& \sum_{i=1}^{N} \mu_i = 1 \\
& \lambda, \mu \geq 0
\end{aligned}
\tag{13}
$$

In (13) each sub-technology is associated with an intensity variable λ or μ. Dakpo (2015) argued that model (13) assumes some independence between the two sub-technologies involved and suggested to add some constraints that equalise the benchmarks of the materials input. The proposed model is

$$
\begin{aligned}
DA1_0 = & \max_{s_y, s_{b_j}, \lambda, \mu} s_y + \sum_{j=1}^{R} s_{b_j} \\
s.t.\ & same\ constraints\ as\ in\ (13) \\
& \sum_{i=1}^{N} \lambda_i x_{1i} = \sum_{i=1}^{N} \mu_i x_{1i} \\
& \lambda, \mu \geq 0
\end{aligned}
\tag{14}
$$

In a recent article, Førsund (2017) insisted on the role of service inputs (non-materials inputs) in the bad output sub-technology as dematerialisation. We account for this argument and propose a modification of the previous models:

$$
\begin{aligned}
FOR\ 1_0 = & \max_{s_y, s_{b_j}, \lambda, \mu} s_y + \sum_{j=1}^{R} s_{b_j} \\
s.t.\ & x_{1o} \geq \sum_{i=1}^{N} \lambda_i x_{1i} \\
& x_{2o} \geq \sum_{i=1}^{N} \lambda_i x_{2i} \\
& y_o + s_y = \sum_{i=1}^{N} \lambda_i y_i \\
& x_{1o} \leq \sum_{i=1}^{N} \mu_i x_{1i} \\
& x_{2o} \geq \sum_{i=1}^{N} \mu_i x_{2i} \\
& b_{jo} - s_{b_j} = \sum_{i=1}^{N} \mu_i b_{ij} \\
& \sum_{i=1}^{N} \lambda_i = 1 \\
& \sum_{i=1}^{N} \mu_i = 1 \\
& \lambda, \mu \geq 0
\end{aligned}
\tag{15}
$$

With regard to the role of service input and the discussion in Dakpo and Lansink (2019), the following model is also considered here:

$$
\begin{aligned}
DA2_0 = & \max_{s_y, s_{b_j}, \lambda, \mu} s_y + \sum_{j=1}^{R} s_{b_j} \\
s.t.\ & \text{same constraints as in (15)} \\
& \sum_{i=1}^{N} \lambda_i x_{1i} = \sum_{i=1}^{N} \mu_i x_{1i} \\
& \sum_{i=1}^{N} \lambda_i x_{2i} = \sum_{i=1}^{N} \mu_i x_{2i} \\
& \lambda, \mu \geq 0
\end{aligned}
\tag{16}
$$

One concept that has been discussed in Frisch (1965) is the factorially determined production technology where the degree of assortment (number of outputs minus number of independent equations) equals zero. To account for this concept, we consider here the following models:

$$
\begin{aligned}
MRL2_0 = & \max_{s_y, s_{b_j}, \lambda, \mu_j} s_y + \sum_{j=1}^{R} s_{b_j} \\
s.t.\ & x_{1o} \geq \sum_{i=1}^{N} \lambda_i x_{1i} \\
& x_{2o} \geq \sum_{i=1}^{N} \lambda_i x_{2i} \\
& y_o + s_y = \sum_{i=1}^{N} \lambda_i y_i \\
& x_{1o} \leq \sum_{i=1}^{N} \mu_{ji} x_{1i} \\
& b_{jo} - s_{b_{j1}} = \sum_{i=1}^{N} \mu_{ji} b_{i1} \\
& \sum_{i=1}^{N} \lambda_i = 1 \\
& \sum_{i=1}^{N} \mu_{ji} = 1 \\
& \lambda, \mu_j \geq 0
\end{aligned}
\tag{17}
$$

and

$$
\begin{aligned}
FOR2_0 = & \max_{s_y, s_{b_j}, \lambda, \mu} s_y + \sum_{j=1}^{R} s_{b_j} \\
s.t.\ & x_{1o} \geq \sum_{i=1}^{N} \lambda_i x_{1i} \\
& x_{2o} \geq \sum_{i=1}^{N} \lambda_i x_{2i} \\
& y_o + s_y = \sum_{i=1}^{N} \lambda_i y_i \\
& x_{1o} \leq \sum_{i=1}^{N} \mu_{ji} x_{1i} \\
& x_{2o} \geq \sum_{i=1}^{N} \mu_{ji} x_{2i} \\
& b_{jo} - s_{b_j} = \sum_{i=1}^{N} \mu_{ji} b_{ij} \\
& \sum_{i=1}^{N} \lambda_i = 1 \\
& \sum_{i=1}^{N} \mu_{ji} = 1 \\
& \lambda, \mu_j \geq 0
\end{aligned}
\tag{18}
$$

And considering the aforementioned dependence constraints, we also have

$$\begin{aligned} DA3_0 = & \max_{s_y, s_{b_j}, \lambda, \mu} s_y + \sum_{j=1}^{R} s_{b_j} \\ s.t.\ & \text{same constraints as in (18)} \\ & \sum_{i=1}^{N} \lambda_i x_{1i} = \sum_{i=1}^{N} \mu_{ji} x_{1i} \\ & \sum_{i=1}^{N} \lambda_i x_{2i} = \sum_{i=1}^{N} \mu_{ji} x_{2i} \\ & \lambda, \mu_j \geq 0 \end{aligned} \tag{19}$$

Finally, in this category of multiple equation production technology, we also examine the unified framework of natural and managerial disposability discussed in Sueyoshi and Goto (2010) which summarises as

$$\begin{aligned} SUE_0 = & \max_{s_y, s_{b_j}, \lambda} s_y + \sum_{j=1}^{R} s_{b_j} \\ s.t.\ & x_{ko} - s_{x_k}^{-} + s_{x_k}^{+} = \sum_{i=1}^{N} \lambda_i x_{ki} \\ & y_o + s_y = \sum_{i=1}^{N} \lambda_i y_i \\ & b_{jo} - s_{b_j} = \sum_{i=1}^{N} \lambda_i b_{ij} \\ & \sum_{i=1}^{N} \lambda_i = 1 \\ & s_{x_k}^{-} \leq M z_k^{-} \\ & s_{x_k}^{+} \leq M z_k^{+} \\ & z_k^{+} + z_k^{-} \leq 1 \\ & \left(z_k^{+}, z_k^{-}\right) \in \{0, 1\} \\ & \lambda \geq 0 \end{aligned} \tag{20}$$

where M is a sufficiently large number that need to be chosen.

4.3 Results of Monte Carlo Simulations

First we present the global results which consider all the 64 scenarios considered. Three efficiency scores are calculated: one for the good output and two for the bad outputs. The global results for each of the efficiency scores are presented in Tables 3, 4, and 5.

Overall, the multiple equation technologies, namely, the by-production approach and its diverse extensions, perform better than the model assuming weak G-disposability and also than the model combining natural and managerial disposability. For

Table 3 Finite sample performance of the estimates of the efficiency of $\boldsymbol{y}$ (good output) for the different models

Models	*MAD*	*MD*	*MSE*	*UB*	*MRC*
HR	0.425	0.422	0.228	0.992	0.166
*MRL*1	0.128	0.016	0.035	0.614	0.631
*DA*1	0.138	0.03	0.041	0.63	0.594
*FOR*1	0.128	0.016	0.035	0.615	0.631
*DA*2	0.147	0.045	0.046	0.649	0.573
*MRL*2	0.128	0.016	0.035	0.615	0.631
*FOR*2	0.127	0.016	0.035	0.615	0.631
*DA*3	0.145	0.043	0.045	0.648	0.577
SUE	0.353	0.308	0.17	0.892	0.296

Table 4 Finite sample performance of the estimates of the efficiency of $\boldsymbol{b}_1$ (first bad output) for the different models

Models	*MAD*	*MD*	*MSE*	*UB*	*MRC*
HR	0.332	−0.11	0.152	0.43	0.087
*MRL*1	0.207	−0.108	0.075	0.449	0.472
*DA*1	0.207	−0.108	0.076	0.45	0.468
*FOR*1	0.168	0	0.05	0.588	0.432
*DA*2	0.17	0.007	0.051	0.599	0.418
*MRL*2	0.2	−0.141	0.075	0.399	0.513
*FOR*2	0.154	−0.038	0.045	0.53	0.486
*DA*3	0.157	−0.028	0.046	0.545	0.468
SUE	0.482	−0.438	0.283	0.111	0.207

Table 5 Finite sample performance of the estimates of the efficiency of $\boldsymbol{b}_2$ (second bad output) for the different models

Models	*MAD*	*MD*	*MSE*	*UB*	*MRC*
HR	0.341	−0.16	0.161	0.408	0.079
*MRL*1	0.217	−0.13	0.083	0.44	0.433
*DA*1	0.217	−0.129	0.083	0.44	0.429
*FOR*1	0.166	−0.021	0.049	0.576	0.399
*DA*2	0.167	−0.015	0.049	0.585	0.386
*MRL*2	0.215	−0.166	0.086	0.383	0.471
*FOR*2	0.159	−0.061	0.047	0.507	0.444
*DA*3	0.16	−0.052	0.048	0.522	0.429
SUE	0.519	−0.482	0.323	0.106	0.182

Table 6 Finite sample performance of the estimates of the efficiency of $\boldsymbol{y}$ (good output) for the different models when $z_i = 1$

Models	*MAD*	*MD*	*MSE*	*UB*	*MRC*
HR	0.434	0.433	0.235	1	0.154
*MRL*1	0.096	0.063	0.021	0.782	0.756
*DA*1	0.107	0.076	0.028	0.791	0.712
*FOR*1	0.096	0.063	0.021	0.782	0.757
*DA*2	0.12	0.093	0.034	0.814	0.682
*MRL*2	0.096	0.063	0.021	0.782	0.756
*FOR*2	0.096	0.063	0.021	0.782	0.757
*DA*3	0.117	0.089	0.033	0.811	0.69
SUE	0.385	0.371	0.194	0.958	0.276

Table 7 Finite sample performance of the estimates of the efficiency of $\boldsymbol{b}_1$ (first bad output) for the different models when $z_i = 1$

Models	*MAD*	*MD*	*MSE*	*UB*	*MRC*
HR	0.315	−0.084	0.138	0.449	0.082
*MRL*1	0.097	0.04	0.019	0.733	0.665
*DA*1	0.097	0.04	0.019	0.733	0.658
*FOR*1	0.116	0.069	0.027	0.774	0.58
*DA*2	0.12	0.077	0.028	0.786	0.559
*MRL*2	0.078	−0.007	0.013	0.654	0.74
*FOR*2	0.093	0.023	0.019	0.702	0.656
*DA*3	0.098	0.035	0.021	0.72	0.63
SUE	0.477	−0.435	0.276	0.105	0.226

instance, for these latter models, the *MAD*, *MD* and *MSE* statistics are the highest in absolute value, while *UB* is the furthest to 0.5, and finally the Spearman correlation coefficients are the lowest. Moreover, though it is not easy to discriminate between the different multiple equation models that better perform, the case of the factorially determined technology, in light of what has been proposed by Førsund (2017), seems to be more robust. The model with dependence constraints provides intermediate results. Results considering the case with no abatement possibilities ($z_i = 1$) are presented in Tables 6, 7, and 8. The results are pretty similar to the global results except for the *MRL*2 model which seems to perform better given the different performance ratios. When abatement is explicitly included in the simulation ($z_i = Uniform(0, 1)$), the results, shown in Tables 9, 10, and 11, are still pretty similar except that models with dependence constraints seem to be the ones with the

Table 8 Finite sample performance of the estimates of the efficiency of $\boldsymbol{b_2}$ (second bad output) for the different models when $z_i = \mathbf{1}$

Models	*MAD*	*MD*	*MSE*	*UB*	*MRC*
HR	0.322	−0.134	0.145	0.424	0.074
*MRL*1	0.094	0.03	0.017	0.725	0.636
*DA*1	0.094	0.03	0.017	0.724	0.63
*FOR*1	0.108	0.056	0.022	0.765	0.557
*DA*2	0.111	0.062	0.023	0.775	0.537
*MRL*2	0.08	−0.019	0.014	0.636	0.707
*FOR*2	0.09	0.008	0.017	0.683	0.625
*DA*3	0.094	0.019	0.018	0.7	0.601
SUE	0.514	−0.479	0.316	0.099	0.201

Table 9 Finite sample performance of the estimates of the efficiency of $\boldsymbol{y}$ (good output) for the different models when $z_i = \boldsymbol{Uniform}(\mathbf{0}, \mathbf{1})$

Models	*MAD*	*MD*	*MSE*	*UB*	*MRC*
HR	0.416	0.411	0.221	0.985	0.179
*MRL*1	0.16	−0.032	0.048	0.447	0.505
*DA*1	0.169	−0.015	0.054	0.469	0.476
*FOR*1	0.159	−0.031	0.048	0.447	0.505
*DA*2	0.174	−0.004	0.057	0.484	0.464
*MRL*2	0.159	−0.032	0.048	0.447	0.506
*FOR*2	0.159	−0.031	0.048	0.447	0.506
*DA*3	0.173	−0.004	0.057	0.485	0.465
SUE	0.32	0.245	0.145	0.825	0.316

Table 10 Finite sample performance of the estimates of the efficiency of $\boldsymbol{b_1}$ (first bad output) for the different models when $z_i = \boldsymbol{Uniform}(\mathbf{0}, \mathbf{1})$

Models	*MAD*	*MD*	*MSE*	*UB*	*MRC*
HR	0.349	−0.136	0.166	0.411	0.091
*MRL*1	0.316	−0.255	0.131	0.166	0.28
*DA*1	0.317	−0.256	0.132	0.166	0.278
*FOR*1	0.22	−0.069	0.073	0.403	0.283
*DA*2	0.22	−0.063	0.073	0.413	0.277
*MRL*2	0.322	−0.276	0.136	0.145	0.287
*FOR*2	0.215	−0.1	0.071	0.358	0.316
*DA*3	0.216	−0.092	0.071	0.37	0.306
SUE	0.488	−0.44	0.29	0.118	0.188

Table 11 Finite sample performance of the estimates of the efficiency of $\boldsymbol{b_2}$ (second bad output) for the different models when $z_i = \boldsymbol{Uniform}(\mathbf{0}, \mathbf{1})$

Models	*MAD*	*MD*	*MSE*	*UB*	*MRC*
HR	0.36	−0.186	0.177	0.392	0.085
*MRL*1	0.34	−0.289	0.149	0.155	0.229
*DA*1	0.34	−0.289	0.149	0.156	0.228
*FOR*1	0.224	−0.097	0.075	0.386	0.24
*DA*2	0.224	−0.092	0.075	0.395	0.234
*MRL*2	0.35	−0.312	0.157	0.13	0.235
*FOR*2	0.227	−0.13	0.078	0.331	0.263
*DA*3	0.226	−0.123	0.077	0.343	0.256
SUE	0.525	−0.484	0.331	0.113	0.163

lower mean deviation (bias). We then do the same exercise to see whether the linearity in polluting technology matters ($\gamma \in \{1, 2\}$). Results, shown in Tables 12, 13, 14, 15, 16, and 17, are still similar to the global ones. Finally, whether noise is included or not in the model, results, shown in Tables 18, 19, 20, 21, 22, and 23, also exhibit almost similar patterns than in the global results.

Table 12 Finite sample performance of the estimates of the efficiency of $\boldsymbol{y}$ (good output) for the different models when $\gamma = 1$

Models	*MAD*	*MD*	*MSE*	*UB*	*MRC*
HR	0.425	0.423	0.228	0.993	0.176
*MRL*1	0.128	0.016	0.035	0.614	0.631
*DA*1	0.138	0.031	0.041	0.63	0.594
*FOR*1	0.127	0.016	0.035	0.614	0.632
*DA*2	0.142	0.038	0.043	0.64	0.584
*MRL*2	0.128	0.016	0.035	0.614	0.631
*FOR*2	0.128	0.016	0.035	0.614	0.631
*DA*3	0.142	0.038	0.043	0.64	0.585
SUE	0.357	0.307	0.174	0.883	0.281

Table 13 Finite sample performance of the estimates of the efficiency of $\boldsymbol{b}_1$ (first bad output) for the different models when $\gamma = 1$

Models	*MAD*	*MD*	*MSE*	*UB*	*MRC*
HR	0.316	−0.079	0.139	0.463	0.108
*MRL*1	0.209	−0.143	0.08	0.401	0.503
*DA*1	0.21	−0.142	0.081	0.403	0.501
*FOR*1	0.168	−0.046	0.052	0.512	0.459
*DA*2	0.17	−0.038	0.053	0.525	0.446
*MRL*2	0.21	−0.173	0.083	0.354	0.528
*FOR*2	0.163	−0.079	0.051	0.456	0.493
*DA*3	0.165	−0.069	0.052	0.471	0.476
SUE	0.429	−0.385	0.228	0.116	0.242

Table 14 Finite sample performance of the estimates of the efficiency of $\boldsymbol{b}_2$ (second bad output) for the different models when $\gamma = 1$

Models	*MAD*	*MD*	*MSE*	*UB*	*MRC*
HR	0.322	−0.129	0.145	0.439	0.104
*MRL*1	0.223	−0.163	0.09	0.394	0.462
*DA*1	0.223	−0.163	0.09	0.394	0.46
*FOR*1	0.172	−0.066	0.054	0.5	0.42
*DA*2	0.173	−0.059	0.054	0.511	0.41
*MRL*2	0.227	−0.197	0.095	0.341	0.486
*FOR*2	0.172	−0.103	0.056	0.435	0.452
*DA*3	0.172	−0.094	0.056	0.45	0.439
SUE	0.463	−0.426	0.261	0.11	0.21

Table 15 Finite sample performance of the estimates of the efficiency of $\boldsymbol{y}$ (good output) for the different models when $\gamma = 2$

Models	*MAD*	*MD*	*MSE*	*UB*	*MRC*
HR	0.424	0.422	0.228	0.992	0.156
*MRL*1	0.128	0.016	0.035	0.614	0.631
*DA*1	0.138	0.03	0.041	0.63	0.594
*FOR*1	0.128	0.016	0.035	0.615	0.631
*DA*2	0.152	0.051	0.048	0.658	0.562
*MRL*2	0.128	0.016	0.035	0.615	0.631
*FOR*2	0.127	0.016	0.034	0.615	0.632
*DA*3	0.149	0.048	0.046	0.656	0.57
SUE	0.349	0.31	0.166	0.901	0.311

5 Conclusion

In this chapter, we compared the non-parametric approaches available to account for undesirable outputs in technology modelling. The approaches were grouped based on Lauwers' (2009) seminal three-group classification, to which we added a fourth group of recent models grounded on the estimation of several sub-technologies depending on the type of outputs (good or bad). We undertook a numerical comparison of the most recent models – the approach based on materials balance

Table 16 Finite sample performance of the estimates of the efficiency of b_1 (first bad output) for the different models when $\gamma = 2$

Models	*MAD*	*MD*	*MSE*	*UB*	*MRC*
HR	0.348	−0.141	0.164	0.397	0.065
*MRL*1	0.204	−0.073	0.07	0.498	0.442
*DA*1	0.204	−0.074	0.07	0.497	0.436
*FOR*1	0.167	0.046	0.048	0.665	0.405
*DA*2	0.169	0.051	0.049	0.673	0.39
*MRL*2	0.19	−0.11	0.066	0.445	0.499
*FOR*2	0.145	0.003	0.039	0.605	0.479
*DA*3	0.149	0.012	0.04	0.619	0.46
SUE	0.536	−0.49	0.339	0.107	0.172

Table 17 Finite sample performance of the estimates of the efficiency of b_2 (second output) for the different models when $\gamma = 2$

Models	*MAD*	*MD*	*MSE*	*UB*	*MRC*
HR	0.361	−0.191	0.177	0.376	0.054
*MRL*1	0.211	−0.096	0.076	0.486	0.404
*DA*1	0.211	−0.096	0.076	0.487	0.399
*FOR*1	0.16	0.024	0.043	0.652	0.377
*DA*2	0.162	0.029	0.044	0.66	0.361
*MRL*2	0.202	−0.134	0.076	0.425	0.456
*FOR*2	0.145	−0.019	0.039	0.579	0.437
*DA*3	0.148	−0.01	0.039	0.593	0.419
SUE	0.576	−0.537	0.385	0.102	0.154

Table 18 Finite sample performance of the estimates of the efficiency of y (good output) for the different models in the absence of noise

Models	*MAD*	*MD*	*MSE*	*UB*	*MRC*
HR	0.426	0.424	0.229	0.993	0.164
*MRL*1	0.12	0.036	0.032	0.747	0.671
*DA*1	0.13	0.049	0.039	0.756	0.633
*FOR*1	0.12	0.036	0.032	0.748	0.672
*DA*2	0.141	0.062	0.043	0.764	0.609
*MRL*2	0.12	0.036	0.032	0.748	0.672
*FOR*2	0.12	0.036	0.032	0.748	0.671
*DA*3	0.139	0.061	0.042	0.765	0.613
SUE	0.356	0.316	0.172	0.901	0.294

Table 19 Finite sample performance of the estimates of the efficiency of b_1 (first bad output) for the different models in the absence of noise

Models	*MAD*	*MD*	*MSE*	*UB*	*MRC*
HR	0.325	−0.095	0.147	0.447	0.088
*MRL*1	0.194	−0.086	0.071	0.584	0.531
*DA*1	0.194	−0.086	0.071	0.584	0.524
*FOR*1	0.157	0.022	0.047	0.71	0.481
*DA*2	0.16	0.028	0.047	0.715	0.464
*MRL*2	0.177	−0.114	0.068	0.575	0.584
*FOR*2	0.134	−0.011	0.039	0.691	0.551
*DA*3	0.139	−0.003	0.041	0.696	0.528
SUE	0.479	−0.435	0.28	0.112	0.208

principle and the weak G-disposability and the by-production model along with its extensions (dependence constraints and service inputs), as well as the unified framework of natural and managerial disposability.

The results revealed that the model under the weak G-disposability assumption and the one that unifies natural and managerial disposability performed poorly compared to the multiple equation models. However, the simulation results provided here failed to discriminate between those different models, since depending on the statistics and the parameters, each one of the M3E models performs better. This suggests that further assumptions or possibly further theoretical and methodological discussion are necessary to discriminate between the well-performing models. Finally, it is worth mentioning

Table 20 Finite sample performance of the estimates of the efficiency of b_2 (second bad output) for the different models in the absence of noise

Models	*MAD*	*MD*	*MSE*	*UB*	*MRC*
HR	0.333	−0.145	0.155	0.423	0.078
*MRL*1	0.202	−0.105	0.078	0.578	0.503
*DA*1	0.202	−0.105	0.078	0.579	0.499
*FOR*1	0.154	0.003	0.044	0.701	0.459
*DA*2	0.156	0.009	0.045	0.706	0.441
*MRL*2	0.188	−0.134	0.077	0.567	0.557
*FOR*2	0.135	−0.03	0.04	0.678	0.521
*DA*3	0.139	−0.023	0.041	0.683	0.5
SUE	0.516	−0.478	0.32	0.107	0.184

Table 21 Finite sample performance of the estimates of the efficiency of y (good output) for the different models in the presence of noise

Models	*MAD*	*MD*	*MSE*	*UB*	*MRC*
HR	0.423	0.42	0.227	0.991	0.168
*MRL*1	0.135	−0.004	0.037	0.481	0.59
*DA*1	0.145	0.012	0.044	0.503	0.556
*FOR*1	0.135	−0.004	0.037	0.481	0.59
*DA*2	0.153	0.027	0.048	0.534	0.537
*MRL*2	0.135	−0.004	0.037	0.481	0.591
*FOR*2	0.135	−0.004	0.037	0.481	0.591
*DA*3	0.152	0.025	0.047	0.531	0.541
SUE	0.35	0.301	0.167	0.883	0.298

Table 22 Finite sample performance of the estimates of the efficiency of b_1 (first bad output) for the different models in the presence of noise

Models	*MAD*	*MD*	*MSE*	*UB*	*MRC*
HR	0.339	−0.125	0.157	0.413	0.086
*MRL*1	0.219	−0.13	0.08	0.315	0.414
*DA*1	0.22	−0.13	0.08	0.316	0.412
*FOR*1	0.178	−0.022	0.053	0.467	0.382
*DA*2	0.179	−0.014	0.054	0.484	0.372
*MRL*2	0.222	−0.169	0.081	0.224	0.442
*FOR*2	0.173	−0.065	0.05	0.37	0.422
*DA*3	0.174	−0.054	0.051	0.394	0.408
SUE	0.486	−0.441	0.286	0.11	0.206

Table 23 Finite sample performance of the estimates of the efficiency of b_2 (second bad output) for the different models in the presence of noise

Models	*MAD*	*MD*	*MSE*	*UB*	*MRC*
HR	0.349	−0.175	0.167	0.392	0.081
*MRL*1	0.232	−0.154	0.088	0.302	0.363
*DA*1	0.232	−0.154	0.088	0.302	0.36
*FOR*1	0.179	−0.044	0.053	0.45	0.338
*DA*2	0.178	−0.038	0.053	0.464	0.33
*MRL*2	0.242	−0.197	0.094	0.199	0.385
*FOR*2	0.182	−0.092	0.054	0.337	0.368
*DA*3	0.181	−0.081	0.054	0.36	0.357
SUE	0.523	−0.485	0.327	0.105	0.18

that the simulations conducted here are related to non-parametric models and cannot be used in the case of parametric models. However, the theoretical discussion about each model is still valid whatever the estimation method is.

Acknowledgements The authors are grateful to the European FP7 project FLINT and to the European research collaboration TRUSTEE for funding this research.

References

Andor, M., & Hesse, F. (2013). The StoNED age: The departure into a new era of efficiency analysis? A monte carlo comparison of StoNED and the "oldies" (SFA and DEA). *Journal of Productivity Analysis, 41*, 85–109.

Badunenko, O., & Mozharovskyi, P. (2019). Statistical inference for the Russell measure of technical efficiency. *Journal of the Operational Research Society, 71*(**3**), 517–527.

Berman, E., & Bui, L. T. M. (2001). Environmental regulation and productivity: Evidence from oil refineries. *Review of Economics and Statistics, 83*, 498–510.

Caves, D. W., Christensen, L. R., & Diewert, W. E. (1982). The economic-theory of index numbers and the measurement of input, output, and productivity. *Econometrica, 50*, 1393–1414.

Charnes, A., Cooper, W. W., & Rhodes, E. (1978). Measuring the efficiency of decision making units. *European Journal of Operational Research, 2*, 429–444.

Chen, C.-M. (2013). Evaluating eco-efficiency with data envelopment analysis: An analytical reexamination. *Annals of Operations Research, 214*, 49–71.

Chen, C. M., & Delmas, M. A. (2012). Measuring eco-inefficiency: A new frontier approach. *Operations Research, 60*, 1064–1079.

Chung, Y. H., Fare, R., & Grosskopf, S. (1997). Productivity and undesirable outputs: A directional distance function approach. *Journal of Environmental Management, 51*, 229–240.

Coelli, T. J., Rao, D. S. P., O'Donnell, C. J., & Battese, G. E. (2005). *An introduction to efficiency and productivity analysis*. New York: Springer.

Coelli, T., Lauwers, L., & Van Huylenbroeck, G. (2007). Environmental efficiency measurement and the materials balance condition. *Journal of Productivity Analysis, 28*, 3–12.

Dakpo, K. H. (2015). On modeling pollution-generating technologies: A new formulation of the by-production approach. In *EAAE PhD workshop*. Rome, Italy.

Dakpo, K. H., & Lansink, A. O. (2019). Dynamic pollution-adjusted inefficiency under the by-production of bad outputs. *European Journal of Operational Research, 276*, 202–211.

Dakpo, H. K., Jeanneaux, P., & Latruffe, L. (2014). Inclusion of undesirable outputs in production technology modeling: The case of greenhouse gas emissions in French meat sheep farming. In S. LERECO (Ed.), *Working Paper* (Vol. 14-08): INRA – Agro Campus Ouest.

Dakpo, K. H., Jeanneaux, P., & Latruffe, L. (2016). Modelling pollution-generating technologies in performance benchmarking: Recent developments, limits and future prospects in the nonparametric framework. *European Journal of Operational Research, 250*, 347–359.

Dyckhoff, H., & Allen, K. (2001). Measuring ecological efficiency with data envelopment analysis (DEA). *European Journal of Operational Research, 132*, 312–325.

Ekvall, T., Assefa, G., Björklund, A., Eriksson, O., & Finnveden, G. (2007). What life-cycle assessment does and does not do in assessments of waste management. *Waste Management, 27*, 989–996.

Färe, R. (1988). *Fundamentals of production theory*. New York: Springer-Verlag Berlin.

Fare, R., Grosskopf, S., & Pasurka, C. (1986). Effects on relative efficiency in electric-power generation due to environmental controls. *Resources and Energy, 8*, 167–184.

Fare, R., Grosskopf, S., Lovell, C. A. K., & Pasurka, C. (1989). Multilateral productivity comparisons when some outputs are undesirable – a nonparametric approach. *Review of Economics and Statistics, 71*, 90–98.

Färe, R., Grosskopf, S., & Tyteca, D. (1996). An activity analysis model of the environmental performance of firms—application to fossil-fuel-fired electric utilities. *Ecological Economics, 18*, 161–175.

Fare, R., Grosskopf, S., & Pasurka, C. A. (2007). Environmental production functions and environmental directional distance functions. *Energy, 32*, 1055–1066.

Førsund, F. R. (2009). Good modelling of bad outputs: Pollution and multiple-output production. *International Review of Environmental and Resource Economics, 3*, 1–38.

Førsund, F. R. (2017). Multi-equation modelling of desirable and undesirable outputs satisfying the materials balance. *Empirical Economics, 54*, 67–99.

Frisch, R. (1965). *Theory of production*. Dordrecht: Reidel Publishing Company.

Hailu, A., & Veeman, T. S. (2001). Non-parametric productivity analysis with undesirable outputs: An application to the Canadian pulp and paper industry. *American Journal of Agricultural Economics, 83*, 605–616.

Hampf, B. (2018). Measuring inefficiency in the presence of bad outputs: Does the disposability assumption matter? *Empirical Economics, 54*, 101–127.

Hampf, B., & Rødseth, K. L. (2015). Carbon dioxide emission standards for U.S. power plants: An efficiency analysis perspective. *Energy Economics, 50*, 140–153.

Haynes, K. E., Ratick, S., Bowen, W. M., & Cummings-Saxton, J. (1993). Environmental decision models: US experience and a new approach to pollution management. *Environment International, 19*, 261–275.

Heijungs, R. (2007). From thermodynamic efficiency to eco-efficiency. In G. Huppes & M. Ishikawa (Eds.), *Quantified eco-efficiency* (Vol. 22, pp. 79–103). Dordrecht: Springer Netherlands.

Hoang, V. N., & Rao, D. S. P. (2010). Measuring and decomposing sustainable efficiency in agricultural production: A cumulative exergy balance approach. *Ecological Economics, 69*, 1765–1776.

Huppes, G., & Ishikawa, M. (2005a). Eco-efficiency and its terminology. *Journal of Industrial Ecology, 9*, 43–46.

Huppes, G., & Ishikawa, M. (2005b). A framework for quantified eco-efficiency analysis. *Journal of Industrial Ecology, 9*, 25–41.

Korhonen, P. J., & Luptacik, M. (2004). Eco-efficiency analysis of power plants: An extension of data envelopment analysis. *European Journal of Operational Research, 154*, 437–446.

Kortelainen, M., & Kuosmanen, T. (2004). Measuring eco-efficiency of production: A frontier approach. In Department of Economics, Washington University St. Louis, MO, EconWPA working paper no. 0411004.

Kuosmanen, T. (2005). Measurement and analysis of eco-efficiency – an economist's perspective. *Journal of Industrial Ecology, 9*, 15–18.

Kuosmanen, T., & Johnson, A. L. (2010). Data envelopment analysis as nonparametric least-squares regression. *Operations Research, 58*, 149–160.
Kuosmanen, T., & Kortelainen, M. (2005). Measuring eco-efficiency of production with data envelopment analysis. *Journal of Industrial Ecology, 9*, 59–72.
Kuosmanen, T., & Podinovski, V. (2009). Weak disposability in nonparametric production analysis: Reply to Färe and Grosskopf. *American Journal of Agricultural Economics, 91*, 539–545.
Lauwers, L. (2009). Justifying the incorporation of the materials balance principle into frontier-based eco-efficiency models. *Ecological Economics, 68*, 1605–1614.
Lauwers, L., Van Huylenbroeck, G., & Rogiers, G. (1999). Technical, economic and environmental efficiency analysis of pig fattening farms. In *9th European congress of agricultural economists*. Warsaw, Poland.
Lozano, S., & Gutierrez, E. (2011). Slacks-based measure of efficiency of airports with airplanes delays as undesirable outputs. *Computers & Operations Research, 38*, 131–139.
Mickwitz, P., Melanen, M., Rosenström, U., & Seppälä, J. (2006). Regional eco-efficiency indicators–a participatory approach. *Journal of Cleaner Production, 14*, 1603–1611.
Murty, S. (2015). On the properties of an emission-generating technology and its parametric representation. *Economic Theory, 60*, 243–282.
Murty, S., Russell, R. R., & Levkoff, S. B. (2012). On modeling pollution-generating technologies. *Journal of Environmental Economics and Management, 64*, 117–135.
Nieswand, M., & Seifert, S. (2018). Environmental factors in frontier estimation – a Monte Carlo analysis. *European Journal of Operational Research, 265*, 133–148.
Pittman, R. W. (1983). Multilateral productivity comparisons with undesirable outputs. *Economic Journal, 93*, 883–891.
Prior, D. (2006). Efficiency and total quality management in health care organizations: A dynamic frontier approach. *Annals of Operations Research, 145*, 281–299.
Reinhard, S., Lovell, C. A. K., & Thijssen, G. (1999). Econometric estimation of technical and environmental efficiency: An application to Dutch dairy farms. *American Journal of Agricultural Economics, 81*, 44–60.
Rødseth, K. L. (2015). Axioms of a polluting technology: A materials balance approach. *Environmental and Resource Economics, 67*, 1–22.
Schaltegger, S., & Burritt, R. (2000). *Contemporary environmental accounting: Issues, concepts and practice*. Sheffield: Greenleaf.
Schaltegger, S., & Sturm, A. (1990). Ökologische rationalität: Ansatzpunkte zur ausgestaltung von ökologieorientierten managementinstrumenten. *Die Unternehmung, 44*, 273–290.
Scheel, H. (2001). Undesirable outputs in efficiency valuations. *European Journal of Operational Research, 132*, 400–410.
Schmidheiny, S. (1992). *Changing course: A global business perspective on development and the environment* (Vol. 2). Cambridge, MA: MIT press.
Shephard, R. W. (1970). *Theory of cost and production functions*. Princeton: Princeton University Press.
Sueyoshi, T., & Goto, M. (2010). Should the US clean air act include CO2 emission control?: Examination by data envelopment analysis. *Energy Policy, 38*, 5902–5911.
Sueyoshi, T., & Goto, M. (2011). Measurement of returns to scale and damages to scale for DEA-based operational and environmental assessment: How to manage desirable (good) and undesirable (bad) outputs? *European Journal of Operational Research, 211*, 76–89.
Sueyoshi, T., Goto, M., & Ueno, T. (2010). Performance analysis of US coal-fired power plants by measuring three DEA efficiencies. *Energy Policy, 38*, 1675–1688.
Tone, K. (2004). Dealing with undesirable outputs in DEA: A slacks-based measure (SBM) approach. *Nippon Opereshonzu, Risachi Gakkai Shunki Kenkyu Happyokai Abusutorakutoshu, 2004*, 44–45.
Tyteca, D. (1996). On the measurement of the environmental performance of firms— a literature review and a productive efficiency perspective. *Journal of Environmental Management, 46*, 281–308.
Tyteca, D. (1997). Linear programming models for the measurement of environmental performance of firms—concepts and empirical results. *Journal of Productivity Analysis, 8*, 183–197.
Zhou, P., Ang, B. W., & Wang, H. (2012). Energy and CO2 emission performance in electricity generation: A non-radial directional distance function approach. *European Journal of Operational Research, 221*, 625–635.

On the Estimation of Educational Technical Efficiency from Sample Designs: A New Methodology Using Robust Nonparametric Models

Juan Aparicio, Martín González, Daniel Santín, and Gabriela Sicilia

Abstract Average efficiency is popular in the empirical education literature for comparing the aggregate performance of regions or countries using the efficiency results of their disaggregated decision-making units (DMUs) microdata. The most common approach for calculating average efficiency is to use a set of inputs and outputs from a representative sample of DMUs, typically schools or high schools, in order to characterize the performance of the population in the analyzed education system. Regardless of the sampling method, the use of sample weights is standard in statistics and econometrics for approximating population parameters. However, weight information has been disregarded in the literature on production frontier estimation using nonparametric methodologies in education. The aim of this chapter is to propose a preliminary methodological strategy to incorporate sample weight information into the estimation of production frontiers using robust nonparametric models. Our Monte Carlo results suggest that current sample designs are not intended for estimating either population production frontiers or average technical efficiency. Consequently, the use of sample weights does not significantly improve the efficiency estimation of a population with respect to an unweighted sample. In order to enhance future efficiency and productivity estimations of a population using samples, we should define an independent sampling design procedure for the set of DMUs based on the population's production frontier.

Keywords Technical efficiency · Sample designs · Education sector · Non-parametric partial frontiers

1 Introduction

Large-scale assessment surveys have played a growing role in educational research over the last three decades. Broadly defined, large-scale assessments are standardized surveys of cognitive skills in different subjects that provide comparable data about many different students, schools, and, in short, education systems in one region, country, or even several countries around the world. Because both home and school play an important role in how students learn, large-scale surveys also collect extensive information about such background factors at individual, teacher, and school level. Some of the best-known international databases worldwide are the Programme for International Student Assessment (PISA), the Trends in International Mathematics and Science Study (TIMSS), or the Progress in International Reading Literacy Study (PIRLS). Additionally, in many developed countries, ministries of education gather similar data for analyzing their educational systems.

Researchers can use this information for three important purposes. First, educational databases are useful for making cross-country comparisons of the achievements of different education systems, as well as for introducing the quality of human capital in economic growth regressions (Hanushek and Kimko 2000; De La Fuente 2011; Hanushek and Woessmann 2012). Second, these databases are analyzed for disentangling the causal effects of educational policies, law changes, and different social factors on educational outcomes through the use of counterfactuals (Strietholt et al. 2014; Cordero et al.

J. Aparicio (✉) · M. González
Center of Operations Research (CIO). Miguel Hernandez University of Elche (UMH), Elche (Alicante), Spain
e-mail: j.aparicio@umh.es

D. Santín
Department of Applied Economics, Public Economics and Political Economy, Complutense University of Madrid, Complutense Institute of Economic Analysis, Madrid, Spain

G. Sicilia
Department of Economics and Public Finance, Autonomous University of Madrid, Madrid, Spain

J. Aparicio et al. (eds.), *Advances in Efficiency and Productivity II*, International Series in Operations Research & Management Science 287, https://doi.org/10.1007/978-3-030-41618-8_6

2018). Finally, large-scale assessment surveys are used for measuring technical efficiency through production frontiers in order to benchmark the most successful educational policies (Afonso and Aubyn 2005, 2006; De Jorge and Santín 2010; Agasisti and Zoido 2018). This latter research line is the focus of this chapter, also addressed in recent related publications by Aparicio et al. (2017a, b), Aparicio et al. (2018), and Aparicio and Santín (2018).

Furthermore, the use of representative samples of a population is an extremely widespread practice in statistics. Multiple methods have been developed for characterizing a population through a sample (see Hedayat and Sinha 1991; Särndal et al. 1992). There are some reasons for introducing weight designs in educational databases. First, sampling could oversample or undersample some major school types within the population. For example, the sample could include schools from major, albeit small, territories or regions, which, depending on the sampling method applied, could be either not well represented or overly significant when results are averaged to draw conclusions about the population. Second, school sizes vary across the school population. Therefore, average results at school level hide the fact that the analysis covers all students at some schools and just a group of students at others. Finally, weighting is used to address non-response issues from some schools.

However, the sample weights that appear in many educational databases have been repeatedly ignored in econometrics. Recently, Lavy (2015) investigated whether instruction time has a positive impact on academic performance across countries using unweighted PISA 2006 data pooled at student level. Jerrim et al. (2017, p. 54) reanalyzed Lavy's data, running the same regression analysis with the PISA final weights to capture the population size of each country. Their results show that the effect of an additional hour of instruction is almost 50% greater in developed countries and 40% smaller in Eastern European countries than Lavy's estimations. As a result, the parameters estimated from a sample might not be representing the population under study.

The same problem could affect production frontiers applied to educational databases when researchers assume that the average efficiency results for an unweighted sample can be straightforwardly identified as a good estimation for the population. So far, extensions have not been developed to incorporate the sample weights when estimating the production frontier and the efficiency scores for comparing the performance of different sets of schools.

Under the production frontier framework, there are basically two potential concerns affecting the estimation of technical efficiency. First, there is a representativeness problem, since only the weighted sample is representative of the population. Thus, sample weights are necessary to make valid estimates and inferences about any population parameter from the sample. Therefore, a straightforward adjustment could be to expand the sample to the population using the sample weights. Basically, this means including these weights to compute the aggregate (average) efficiency of the sector (region, country, etc.) and ensure that the entire population is represented. Second, the DMUs included in the analysis are only one of many possible sampling realizations of the population. Because not all DMUs have the same probability of inclusion in the sample, the omission of best-performers information might affect the shape of the estimated true production frontier. The potential misidentification of the true frontier also impairs the estimation of individual efficiency scores, since they are computed as the relative distance to the estimated frontier.

PISA, TIMSS, and PIRLS are based on multistage probability proportional to size (PPS) sampling schemes. Basically, the sampling design is composed of two stages. First, schools are randomly selected from different strata taking into account the size of the schools. Second, students are randomly selected within each sampled school. As a result, each school and each student have different probabilities of being included in the sample, i.e., different sample weights.[1] This makes weighting information crucial for getting unbiased estimates of population characteristics. As stated in the PISA 2015 Technical Report (OECD 2017, p. 116): "Survey weights are required to analyse PISA data, to calculate appropriate estimates of sampling error and to make valid estimates and inferences of the population"... "While the students included in the final PISA sample for a given country were chosen randomly, the selection probabilities of the students vary. Survey weights must be incorporated into the analysis to ensure that each sampled student appropriately represents the correct number of students in the full PISA population." For this reason, it could be misleading to extrapolate results from sample to population regardless of weighting. This problem can also arise in other sectors, like health, banking, agriculture, etc., where the use of samples is commonplace too.

How can we deal with weights in production frontiers? Nonparametric methods, and especially data envelopment analysis, have been applied for measuring efficiency much more often than parametric methods in the education literature. Their extensive application is a consequence of their flexibility, as there is no theoretical education production function (Levin 1974) and few assumptions are needed to envelop the best performers. Nonparametric methods do not explicitly estimate the parameters of a production technology. Instead, they determine an efficiency index reflecting how much use each unit makes of its available resources based on a mathematical model implicitly describing the estimated technology.

[1] For a detailed explanation of this sampling design, see chapter "Testing Positive Endogeneity in Inputs in Data Envelopment Analysis" of the PISA 2015 Technical Report.

Taking insights from the conditional quantile-based approach proposed by Aragon et al. (2005), this paper provides a preliminary methodological strategy to incorporate the information of sample weights into the estimation of the production frontier using robust nonparametric models. The final aim is to enhance the estimation of the technical efficiency of a population of DMUs using a representative sample and its weights as is common practice in education. The reason why we select Aragon et al. (2005), among other possibilities, is that it allows extending the standard frontier analysis to contexts with sample weights[2] in a simple way.

The remainder of the paper is organized as follows: In Sect. 2, we discuss the main methodological issues related to the estimation of nonparametric production from sample designs. In Sect. 3 we propose a method to add the sample weights to the estimation of robust nonparametric frontier models. Section 4 is devoted to check the performance of this method through a Monte Carlo experiment. Finally, Sect. 5 outlines the main conclusions.

2 Methodological Issues

In this section, we briefly review the main nonparametric frontier estimators, their robust estimation through partial frontiers, and some key notions about finite population sampling in statistics before extending Aragon et al.'s approach (2005) to the context where information on the sampling design is available. See also Daouia and Simar (2007) and Daraio and Simar (2007).

2.1 Nonparametric Frontier Models

In frontier analysis, most of the nonparametric approaches—free disposal hull (FDH) and data envelopment analysis (DEA)— are based upon enveloping the set of observations from above to let the data speak for themselves, as well as requiring certain properties (like monotonicity). According to economic theory (Koopmans 1951; Debreu 1951; Shephard 1953), the production set, where the activity is described by a set of m inputs $x \in R_+^m$ used to produce a set of p outputs $y \in R_+^p$, is defined as the set of all physically producible activities given a certain knowledge $(x, y)\, \Psi = \left\{(x, y) \in R_+^{m+p} : x \text{ can produce } y\right\}$ (see also Pastor et al. 2012).

In this paper, we assume that Ψ is a subset of R_+^{m+p} that satisfies the following postulates (see Färe et al. 1985):

(P1) $\Psi \neq \varnothing$;
(P2) $\Psi(x) : \{(u, y) \in \Psi : u \leq x\}$ is bounded $\forall x \in R_+^m$;
(P3) $(x, y) \in \Psi$, $(x, -y) \leq (x', -y') \Rightarrow (x', y') \in \Psi$, i.e., inputs and outputs are freely disposable;
(P4) is a closed set;
(P5) is a convex set.

A certain activity (observation) is considered to be technically inefficient if it is possible to either expand its output bundle y without requiring any increase in its inputs x or contract its input bundle without requiring a reduction in its outputs. The capacity for expanding the output bundle reflects output-oriented inefficiency. Likewise, potential input savings indicate input-oriented inefficiency. Exactly which of these two orientations is selected depends on the analyzed empirical framework. On the one hand, it is assumed, in the case of input-oriented contexts, that the output bundle (like the number of patients to be treated at a hospital) is fixed or given by the demand side. Hence, it is reasonable to save on the use of inputs to contain costs. In this case, determining input-oriented technical efficiency measurements by scaling down x (the frontier of Ψ) as far as possible is the most rational first step. On the other hand, when the input bundle is predetermined (like land at a farm), output-oriented technical efficiency measurements would appear to be a better option.

For simplicity's sake, we assume in this paper that firms, schools if we refer to the education sector, cannot change their inputs in the short run or that they are given. Consequently, output orientation is the best choice, and we will evaluate their performance based on the assessment of the production of outputs from a certain level of inputs. In this context, it is common

[2] In the DEA literature, we can find some references that include weights like, for example, Allen et al. (1997) and Färe and Zelenyuk (2003). However, they do not consider sample weights from sample designs.

practice to work with the notion of requirement set. The requirement set, denoted as $Y(x)$, is the set of all outputs that a firm can produce using $x \in R_+^m$ as inputs. Mathematically speaking, $Y(x) = \{y \in R_+^p : (x, y) \in \Psi\}$.

Assumptions on the data generating process (DGP) encompass the statistical model, which defines how the observations in Ψ are generated. There are many alternatives. However, since nonparametric methods for estimating frontiers have no need of parametric assumptions about the DGP, we will simply assume that the production process, which generates the set of observations $\Theta_n = \{(x_i, y_i) : i = 1, \ldots, n\}$, is defined by the joint distribution of the random vector $(X, Y) \in R_+^m \times R_+^p$, where X represents the random inputs and Y represents the random outputs. Where Ψ is equal to the support of the distribution of (X, Y) and $p = 1$, another way to define the production frontier is through the notion of production function. The production function, denoted as φ, is characterized for a given level of inputs $x \in R_+^m$ by the upper boundary of the support of the conditional distribution of the univariate Y given $X \leq x$, i.e., $\varphi(x) = \sup \{y \in R_+ : F(y|x) < 1\}$, where $F(y|x)$ is the conditional distribution function of Y given $X \leq x$. The inequality $X \leq x$ should be interpreted componentwise. We owe this formulation of the production function to Cazals et al. (2002), and it is useful for expressing the customary notion of production function by distribution functions.

Regarding the practical determination of the technology from a data sample, economists before Farrell (1957) used to parametrically specify the corresponding production functions (e.g., a Cobb-Douglas function) and apply ordinary least squares (OLS) regression analysis to estimate an "average" production function, assuming that disturbance terms had zero mean. However, the notion of production function moves away from the concept of average. In this respect, Farrell (1957) was the first author to show how to estimate an isoquant enveloping all the observations and, therefore, was the first to econometrically implement the idea of production frontier.

The line of research initiated by Farrell in 1957 was later taken up by Charnes et al. (1978) and Banker et al. (1984), resulting in the development of the data envelopment analysis (DEA) approach, where the determination of the frontier is only constrained by its axiomatic foundation and the property of convexity plays a major role. Additionally, Deprins et al. (1984) introduced a more general version of the DEA estimator, depending exclusively upon the free disposability assumption of inputs and outputs and neglecting convexity. Indeed, the two main nonparametric frontier techniques in the literature nowadays are DEA and FDH. In the case of DEA, the frontier estimator is, as already mentioned, constructed as the smallest polyhedral set that contains the observations and satisfies free disposability, whereas FDH makes fewer assumptions than DEA. Graphically, the convex hull of the FDH estimate is the same as the DEA estimate of the production technology.

Aigner and Chu (1968) reported a more natural follow-on from previous research by econometricians than DEA and FDH. They showed how to apply a technique based on mathematical programming to yield an envelope "parametric" Cobb-Douglas production function by controlling the sign of the disturbance terms and, consequently, following the standard definition of production function. A more general parametric approach is the stochastic frontier analysis (SFA) by Aigner et al. (1977) and Meeusen and Van den Broeck (1977).

Generally speaking, two different approaches have been introduced in the literature: deterministic frontier models, like DEA and FDH, which assume with probability one that all the observations in Θ_n belong to Ψ, and stochastic frontier models, like SFA, where, due to random noise, some observations may be outside of Ψ.

2.2 Nonparametric Robust Estimators: Partial Frontiers

Nonparametric deterministic frontier models, like DEA and FDH, are very attractive because they depend on very few assump*tions. However, by definition, they are very sensitive to extreme values. To solve this problem, Cazals et al. (2002) and Aragon et al. (2005) proposed robust nonparametric frontier techniques. In this section, we briefly review the main features of these two approaches.

Cazals et al. (2002) introduced the notion of expected maximal output frontier of order $m \in \mathrm{N}^*$, where N^* denotes the set of all integers $m \geq 1$. It is defined as the expected maximum achievable level of output across m units drawn from the population using less than a given level of inputs. Formally, for a fixed integer $m \in \mathrm{N}^*$ and a given level of inputs $x \in R_+^m$, the order-m frontier is defined as

$$\varphi_m(x) = E\left[\max\left(Y^1, \ldots, Y^m\right)\right] = \int_0^\infty \left(1 - [F(y|x)]^m\right) dy, \tag{1}$$

where $(Y^1, \ldots, Y^m)$ are m independent identically distributed random variables generated by the distribution of Y, given $X \leq x$. Its nonparametric estimator is defined by $\hat{\varphi}_m(x) = \int_0^\infty \left(1 - \left[\hat{F}(y|x)\right]^m\right) dy$, which is based upon the estimation of the distribution function. In particular, $\hat{F}(y|x) = \hat{F}(x, y)/\hat{F}(x)$ is the empirical version of the conditional distribution function of Y given $X \leq x$, with $\hat{F}(x, y) = \frac{1}{n}\sum_{i=1}^{n} 1(X_i \leq x, Y_i \leq y)$ and $\hat{F}(x) = \frac{1}{n}\sum_{i=1}^{n} 1(X_i \leq x)$. Cazals et al. (2002) were also able to rewrite the FDH estimator of the production function in terms of the conditional distribution function as $\hat{\varphi}_{FDH}(x) = \sup\left\{y \in R_+ : \hat{F}(y|x) < 1\right\} = \max_{i:X_i \leq x}\{Y_i\}$.

By definition, the order-m frontier does not envelop all the observations in the sample. Consequently, it is more robust to extreme values and outliers than the standard FDH estimator. Additionally, using an appropriate selection of m as a function of the sample size, $\hat{\varphi}_m(x)$ estimates the production function $\varphi(x)$ while, at the same time, retaining the asymptotic properties of the FDH estimator.

Later, Aragon et al. (2005) proposed a nonparametric estimator of the production function that is, as they demonstrated, more robust to extreme values than the standard DEA and FDH estimators and the nonparametric order-m frontier by Cazals et al. (2002). This model is based upon quantiles of the conditional distribution of Y given $X \leq x$. These conditional quantiles define a natural notion of a partial production frontier in place of the order-m frontier. Moreover, Aragon et al. (2005) proved that their estimators satisfy most of the good properties of the order-m estimator.

In particular, the quantile production function of order α, $\alpha \in [0, 1]$, given a certain level of inputs $x \in R_+^m$, can be defined as

$$q_\alpha(x) = F^{-1}(\alpha|x) = \inf\{y \in R_+ : F(y|x) \geq \alpha\}. \tag{2}$$

This conditional quantile is the production threshold exceeded by $100(1-\alpha)\%$ of units that use less than the level x of inputs. Notice that, by the traditional production function definition, $\varphi(x)$ coincides with the order-one quantile production function, i.e., $\varphi(x) = q_1(x)$.

The natural way of estimating $q_\alpha(x)$ is to substitute the conditional distribution function by its empirical estimation $\hat{F}(\cdot|x)$:

$$\hat{q}_\alpha(x) = \hat{F}^{-1}(\alpha|x) = \inf\left\{y \in R_+ : \hat{F}(y|x) \geq \alpha\right\}. \tag{3}$$

This estimator may be computed explicitly as follows (see Aragon et al. 2005): Let $s_x = \left\{i_1, \ldots, i_{n_x}\right\}$ be the subset of observations in the data sample such that $X_i \leq x$, where $n_x = \sum_{i=1}^{n} 1(X_i \leq x)$, i.e., the number of elements in s_x. Hence, $Y_{i_1}, \ldots, Y_{i_{n_x}}$ corresponds to the outputs observed in s_x, while $Y_{(i_1)}, \ldots, Y_{(i_{n_x})}$ are their ordered values. Additionally, it is assumed that the labels $i_1, \ldots, i_{n_x}$ contain no information as to the ordering of the values of $Y_{i_1}, \ldots, Y_{i_{n_x}}$. For example, it is not necessarily true that $Y_{i_j} < Y_{i_k}$ for $j < k$. However, $Y_{(i_j)} \leq Y_{(i_k)}$ for all $j \leq k$. We also assume that $n_x \neq 0$.

The estimation of the conditional distribution function is

$$\hat{F}(y|x) = \frac{\sum_{i:X_i \leq x} 1(Y_i \leq y)}{n_x} = \frac{\sum_{j=1}^{n_x} 1\left(Y_{(i_j)} \leq y\right)}{n_x}. \tag{4}$$

Hence,

$$\hat{F}(y|x) = \begin{cases} 0, & \text{if } y < Y_{(i_1)} \\ k/n_x, & \text{if } Y_{(i_k)} \leq y < Y_{(i_{k+1})},\ 1 \leq k \leq n_x - 1 \\ 1, & \text{if } y \geq Y_{(i_{n_x})} \end{cases} \tag{5}$$

Consequently, for any $\alpha > 0$, we have that

$$\hat{q}_\alpha(x) = \begin{cases} Y_{(i_{\alpha n_x})}, & \text{if } \alpha n_x \in \mathrm{N}^* \\ Y_{([\alpha n_x]+1)}, & \text{otherwise} \end{cases}, \tag{6}$$

where $[\alpha n_x]$ is the largest integer less than or equal to αn_x. Consequently, the conditional empirical quantile $\hat{q}_\alpha(x)$ is computed as the simple empirical quantile of $Y_{i_1}, \ldots, Y_{i_{n_x}}$. Additionally, note that $\varphi(x) = q_1(x) = Y_{(i_{n_x})} = \max_{i:X_i \leq x}\{Y_i\}$, i.e., it is equal to the FDH estimation.

In this research, we extend Aragon et al.'s notion of α-quantile production function (Aragon et al. 2005) in order to deal with situations where the data sample is the result of applying a particular sampling design on a finite population.

2.3 Sampling Designs on a Finite Population

Let us now assume that the first stage of the production process generates a finite population of production units $\Theta_N = \{(X_i, Y_i) : i = 1, \ldots, N\}$. For simplicity's sake, let the i-th element be represented by its label i. Thus, we denote the finite population as $U = \{1, \ldots, N\}$. Additionally, we assume that we are an observer outside the production process. Hence, the values X_i and Y_i, $i = 1, \ldots, N$, are unknown to us. Let us also suppose that, in a second stage, we select a subset of the population, called a sample and denoted as $s \subseteq U$, with the aim of estimating some parameters associated with the population. Specifically, we are able to observe and collect the values of X_i and Y_i for all $i \in s$. In particular, as is very common in social science, we consider samples that are realized by a probabilistic (randomized) selection scheme.

Given a sample selection scheme, it is possible, although not always simple, to establish the probability of selecting a specified sample s. We shall use the notation $p(s)$ for this probability. In this way, we assume that there is a function $p(\cdot)$ such that $p(s)$ gives the probability of selecting s under the scheme in use. The function $p(\cdot)$ is usually called the sampling design in finite population sampling theory. This notion plays a central role because it determines the essential statistical properties (sampling distribution, expected value, and variance) of random quantities calculated from the data sample (estimators) in order to estimate certain population parameters or functions of parameters.

For a given sampling design $p(\cdot)$, we can regard any sample s as the outcome of a set-valued random variable S, whose probability distribution is specified by the function $p(\cdot)$. Let Γ be the set of all samples. Thus the cardinal of Γ is 2^N if we consider the empty set as well as U itself. Then we have that $\Pr(S = s) = p(s)$ for any $s \in S$. Because $p(\cdot)$ is a probability distribution on the set Γ, we have (i) $p(s) \geq 0$, $s \in S$, and (ii) $\sum_{s \in \Gamma} p(s) = 1$. Note that the probability of some (usually many) of the 2^N samples contained in Γ is equal to zero. The subset of Γ composed of any samples for which $p(s)$ is strictly positive constitutes the set of possible samples. They are the only ones that can be drawn given the specified design.

The sample size, denoted as n_s, is the number of elements in s. Note that n_s depends on the sample and is not, therefore, necessarily the same for all possible samples. If, in fact, all possible samples have the same size, then the sample size is denoted, as usual, as n. For example, Bernoulli sampling can generate different sample sizes, while simple random sampling without replacement always yields the same sample size (Särndal et al. 1992). For simplicity's sake, we will assume hereafter that all possible samples have the same size n.

An interesting feature of a finite population of N units is that each unit can be given different probabilities of inclusion in the sample. The sampling statistician often takes advantage of the identifiability of the population unit by deliberately attaching different inclusion probabilities to the various elements. This is one way to get more accurate estimates, for example, by using strata, clusters, or some known auxiliary variable related to the size of the population units.

Given a sampling design $p(\cdot)$, the probability that unit k was included in a sample, denoted π_k, is obtained from the given design $p(\cdot)$ as $\pi_k = \Pr(k \in S) = \sum_{s:k \in s} p(s)$.

One very usual parameter to be estimated in these contexts is the total of a population, defined for a response variable Z as $t_z = \sum_{i \in U} Z_i$. An unbiased estimator of t_z, under any sampling design, is the so-called π estimator, which resorts to the use of the inclusion probabilities of the units belonging to the data sample. In particular, it is expressed as follows:

$$\hat{t}_{\pi z} = \sum_{i \in s} \frac{Z_i}{\pi_i}. \tag{7}$$

The π estimator expands the values collected in the sample by increasing the importance of the observed population units. Because the sample contains fewer elements than the original population, an expansion is required to reach the level for the total population. The i-th unit, when present in the sample, will represent $1/\pi_i$ population units. As it is unbiased, the π estimator is the cornerstone of the main estimators in finite population sampling theory. Formulations of the variance and estimations of the variance of the π estimator can be found in many textbooks (see, e.g., Särndal et al. 1992 and Hedayat and Sinha 1991). Horvitz and Thompson (1952) were the first authors to use this expansion principle to estimate the total of a population, on which ground the π estimator is also called the Horvitz-Thompson (HT) estimator in the literature.

3 An Adaptation of the Order-α Quantile-Type Frontier for Dealing with Sampling Designs

In this framework, we adapt the estimation of the order-α quantile production function, $\alpha \in [0, 1]$, to work with a data sample derived from a sampling design $p(\cdot)$. The results reported in this section are completely new.

The conditional distribution function of the survey variable Y given $X \leq x$ in a finite population of size N is defined as follows:

$$F_U(y|x) = \frac{\sum_{i=1}^{N} 1(X_i \leq x, Y_i \leq y)}{N_x}, \tag{8}$$

where $N_x = \sum_{i=1}^{N} 1(X_i \leq x)$ represents the number of units in the population such that $X \leq x$.

Notice that, from the point of view of finite population sampling, $F_U(y|x)$ is a population parameter since it is defined through the unknown values of survey variables X and Y for all the population units U. At the same time, $F_U(y|x)$ could be considered the empirical estimation of $F(y|x)$ (see Sect. 2) for the original production process from the N generated observations, which are, as already pointed out, unknown to us.

Note also that the estimation process linked to the quantile production function described above could be applied to U instead of the observed s in order to determine an estimation for $q_\alpha(x)$. In this case, $\hat{F}(y|x)$ should be substituted by $F_U(y|x)$.

In our framework, however, we are an observer outside the production process. Consequently, the values X_i and Y_i, $i = 1, \ldots, N$, are unknown to us. It implies that we cannot apply the estimation process by Aragon et al. (2005) for the quantile production function directly on U. Instead, we select a subset of the population $s \subseteq U$ and try to accurately estimate some population parameters of interest, like $F_U(y|x)$.

To do this, note first that $t_{I(x,y)} = \sum_{i=1}^{N} 1(X_i \leq x, Y_i \leq y)$ is really the total of the population for the binary membership indicator variable $I(x, y)$ defined as

$$I_i(x, y) = \begin{cases} 1, & \text{if } X_i \leq x \text{ and } Y_i \leq y \\ 0, & \text{otherwise} \end{cases}. \tag{9}$$

Additionally, $N_x = \sum_{i=1}^{N} 1(X_i \leq x)$ is the total of the population for the binary membership indicator variable $I(x)$ defined as

$$I_i(x) = \begin{cases} 1, & \text{if } X_i \leq x \\ 0, & \text{otherwise} \end{cases}. \tag{10}$$

Then, $F_U(y|x) = t_{I(x,y)}/N_x$ is the ratio of two population totals. The HT estimator can estimate each total without bias. Hence, we propose the following estimator for $F_U(y|x)$:

$$\hat{F}_U(y|x) = \frac{\sum_{i \in s} 1(X_i \leq x, Y_i \leq y)/\pi_i}{\sum_{i \in s} 1(X_i \leq x)/\pi_i} = \frac{\sum_{j=1}^{n_x} 1\left(Y_{(i_j)} \leq y\right)/\pi_{(i_j)}}{\sum_{j=1}^{n_x} 1/\pi_{i_j}}. \tag{11}$$

Using (first-order) Taylor linearization of the ratio $\hat{F}_U(y|x)$, we get

$$\hat{F}_U(y|x) \approx F_U(y|x) + \frac{1}{N_x} \sum_{i \in s} \frac{I_i(x, y) - F_U(y|x) I_i(x)}{\pi_i}. \tag{12}$$

This implies that $E\left[\hat{F}_U(y|x)\right] \approx E\left[F_U(y|x)+\frac{1}{N_x}\sum_{i\in s}\frac{I_i(x,y)-F_U(y|x)I_i(x)}{\pi_i}\right] = F_U(y|x)+\frac{1}{N_x}E\left[\sum_{i\in s}\frac{I_i(x,y)-F_U(y|x)I_i(x)}{\pi_i}\right]$.

And $E\left[\sum_{i\in s}\frac{I_i(x,y)-F_U(y|x)I_i(x)}{\pi_i}\right] = E\left[\sum_{i\in s}\frac{I_i(x,y)}{\pi_i} - F_U(y|x)\sum_{i\in s}\frac{I_i(x)}{\pi_i}\right] = E\left[\sum_{i\in s}\frac{I_i(x,y)}{\pi_i}\right] - F_U(y|x)\,E\left[\sum_{i\in s}\frac{I_i(x)}{\pi_i}\right] =$ $t_{I(x,y)} - F_U(y|x)\,N_x = t_{I(x,y)} - \frac{t_{I(x,y)}}{N_x}N_x = 0$, which means that $E\left[\hat{F}_U(y|x)\right] \approx F_U(y|x)$.

In other words, the estimator $\hat{F}_U(y|x)$ is approximately unbiased for $F_U(y|x)$, which is, at the same time, the estimator that Aragon et al. (2005) would use for approximating $F(y|x)$.

Moreover, $\hat{F}_U(y|x)$ may be expressed as

$$\hat{F}_U(y|x) = \begin{cases} 0, & \text{if } y < Y_{(i_1)} \\ \dfrac{\sum_{j=1}^{k} 1/\pi_{(i_j)}}{\sum_{j=1}^{n_x} 1/\pi_{i_j}}, & \text{if } Y_{(i_k)} \le y < Y_{(i_{k+1})},\ 1 \le k \le n_x - 1 \\ 1, & \text{if } y \ge Y_{(i_{n_x})} \end{cases}. \tag{13}$$

Let us now introduce some new notation. Let $W_k = \sum_{j=1}^{k} 1/\pi_{(i_j)}$. Additionally, let $q_{\alpha,U}(x)$ be the empirical quantile of Y calculated from Y_i, $i \in U$ such that $X_i \le x$.

Then, following Aragon et al.'s (2005) approach, an estimator of $q_{\alpha,U}(x)$ would be $\hat{q}_{\alpha,U}(x) = Y_{(i_k)}$, where k, $1 \le k \le n_x$, is the smallest index such that $W_k \ge \alpha W_{n_x}$, for $\alpha > 0$.

In the extreme case of $\alpha = 1$, i.e., when the quantile to be estimated is equal to the maximum, note that $\hat{q}_{1,U}(x) = Y_{(i_{n_x})} = \max_{i:X_i \le x}\{Y_i\}$. This means that the estimation of the traditional production function constructed from the N population units is equal to the standard FDH estimation calculated from n observations, regardless of the sampling design.

The following proposition establishes that any sampling design that generates identical inclusion probabilities for all the elements of the population produces the same quantile production function estimator as Aragon et al.'s (2005) approach applied directly to the n observations, i.e., without using the information contained in π_i, $i \in U$.

Proposition 1 Let $p(\cdot)$ such that $\pi_i = \pi\ \forall i \in U$, then $\hat{q}_{\alpha,U}(x) = \hat{q}_\alpha(x)$ for any $\alpha > 0$.

Proof From (11), $\hat{F}_U(y|x) = \frac{\sum_{i\in s} 1(X_i\le x, Y_i\le y)/\pi_i}{\sum_{i\in s} 1(X_i\le x)/\pi_i} \underbrace{=}_{\text{by hypothesis}} \frac{\sum_{i\in s} 1(X_i\le x, Y_i\le y)/\pi}{\sum_{i\in s} 1(X_i\le x)/\pi} = \frac{\sum_{i\in s} 1(X_i\le x, Y_i\le y)}{\sum_{i\in s} 1(X_i\le x)} = \frac{\sum_{i:X_i\le x} 1(Y_i\le y)}{n_x}$, since $n_x = \sum_{i=1}^{n} 1(X_i \le x)$. By expression (4), we have that $\hat{F}_U(y|x)$ is equal to $\hat{F}(y|x)$ in Aragon et al. (2005). Consequently, $\hat{q}_{\alpha,U}(x) = \hat{q}_\alpha(x)$ for any $\alpha > 0$.

Several well-known sampling designs satisfy the hypothesis in Proposition 1, including Bernoulli sampling, simple random sampling without replacement, and systematic sampling. The following result establishes that, under these designs, our approach generates the same estimations as the approach by Aragon et al. (2005).

Corollary 1 Applying Bernoulli sampling (BE), simple random sampling without replacement (SRS), and systematic sampling (SS), $\hat{q}_{\alpha,U}(x) = \hat{q}_\alpha(x)$ for any $\alpha > 0$.

As a consequence of Corollary 1, BE, SRS, and SS generate the same estimation for the quantile production function of order $\alpha > 0$ as by directly applying Aragon et al.'s approach (Aragon et al. 2005) without taking into account that the sample has been drawn from a finite population U. Hence, if a researcher's database is built from the above sampling design types, then it suffices, as suggested by Aragon et al. (2005), to determine the empirical quantile of observations in the sample such that $X \le x$. The problem arises when the data used in the empirical study come from a sampling design with non-equal inclusion probabilities. For example, the sampling statisticians in the famous PISA report resort to random schemes based on inclusion probabilities proportional to a positive and known auxiliary variable, such as the number of students in each school. This means that the inclusion probabilities vary across the population units and, therefore, the hypothesis stated in Proposition 1 does not hold. The effect of this deviation on the estimation of the quantiles is something that warrants detailed investigation due to the importance of reports like PISA. Indeed, the PISA technical report states that "While the students included in the final PISA sample for a given country were chosen randomly, the selection probabilities of the students vary. Survey weights must therefore be incorporated into the analysis to ensure that each sampled student represents the appropriate number of students in the full PISA population" (OECD 2017).

The above process of estimation is able to generate a point estimation for the population quantile $q_{\alpha,U}(x)$. However, a confidence interval of this parameter sometimes has to be used to make other inference types. Next, we propose an approximate confidence interval for the population quantile $q_{\alpha,U}(x)$.

Our approach is inspired by Woodruff (1952). This method was used by Woodruff (1952) for confidence intervals of medians, although it can be generalized to other quantiles. In our context, the approach requires computing a confidence interval for $F_U(y|x)$. Assuming that these values are F_l and F_u, the confidence interval for $q_{\alpha,U}(x)$, namely, (q_l, q_u), is implicitly defined by the equations $\hat{F}_U(q_l|x) = F_l$ and $\hat{F}_U(q_u|x) = F_u$.

In order to determine a confidence interval for the population parameter $F_U(y|x)$, we first need to propose an estimation of the variance of the estimator $\hat{F}_U(y|x)$. Following Särndal et al. (1992), an approximate variance of the π estimator of the ratio of two totals is

$$V\left(\hat{F}_U(y|x)\right) \approx \frac{1}{N_x^2}\sum_{i\in U}\sum_{j\in U}\Delta_{ij}\frac{I_i(x,y)-F_U(y|x)I_i(x)}{\pi_i}\frac{I_j(x,y)-F_U(y|x)I_j(x)}{\pi_j}, \tag{14}$$

which can be estimated through

$$\hat{V}\left(\hat{F}_U(y|x)\right) \approx \frac{1}{\left(\sum_{j=1}^{n_x}1/\pi_{i_j}\right)^2}\sum_{i\in s}\sum_{j\in s}\tilde{\Delta}_{ij}\frac{I_i(x,y)-\hat{F}_U(y|x)I_i(x)}{\pi_i}\frac{I_j(x,y)-\hat{F}_U(y|x)I_j(x)}{\pi_j}, \tag{15}$$

where $\Delta_{ij} = \pi_{ij} - \pi_i\pi_j$, $\tilde{\Delta}_{ij} = \Delta_{ij}/\pi_{ij}$ and $\pi_{ij} = \Pr(i \in S, j \in S)$.

Then, a confidence interval for $F_U(y|x)$ at the approximate level $1 - \beta$ can be computed as

$$\hat{F}_U(y|x) \pm z_{1-\beta/2}\left[\hat{V}\left(\hat{F}_U(y|x)\right)\right]^{1/2}, \tag{16}$$

where $z_{1-\beta/2}$ is the constant exceeded with probability $\beta/2$ by the $N(0, 1)$ random variable.

Let us define the following two elements, which we will use to define the confidence interval:

$$F_l = \hat{F}_U(y|x) - z_{1-\beta/2}\left[\hat{V}\left(\hat{F}_U(y|x)\right)\right]^{1/2} \tag{17}$$

and

$$F_u = \hat{F}_U(y|x) + z_{1-\beta/2}\left[\hat{V}\left(\hat{F}_U(y|x)\right)\right]^{1/2}. \tag{18}$$

Then, a confidence interval for $q_{\alpha,U}(x)$ at the approximate level $1 - \beta$ is (q_l, q_u) with $q_l = Y_{(i_l)}$, where l, $1 \le l \le n_x$, is the largest index such that $W_l \le F_l W_{n_x}$, and $q_u = Y_{(i_u)}$, where u, $1 \le u \le n_x$, is the largest index such that $W_u \le F_u W_{n_x}$. The problem in this case is that we need to know not only π_i but also π_{ij} to determine the approximate confidence interval. Unfortunately, the database owner (e.g., the OECD for PISA) does not always provide this information.

4 Monte Carlo Experiment

In order to test the performance of the proposed method, we perform a Monte Carlo experiment applied to three different scenarios assuming different sample designs. As discussed in Sect. 3, it is common in the educational context to observe complex sample designs where the probabilities of inclusion in the sample are not equal across the population units. Particularly, most large-scale international educational assessments (e.g., PISA, TIMSS, PIRLS, etc.) are based on a probability proportional to size (PPS) design, where the inclusion probabilities are proportional to a positive and known auxiliary variable (e.g., the number of students in each school).

4.1 Experimental Design

To carry out the experiment, we replicate Aragon et al.'s Example 1 (2005). Thus, the data generation process is rooted in a Cobb-Douglas log-linear single-input single-output model given by $Y = X^{0.5}\exp^{-U}$, where the input X is uniformly distributed between (0,1) and the efficiency component U is exponentially distributed with mean $\left(\frac{1}{3}\right)$. Finally, the true frontier is defined by $\varphi(x) = x^{0.5}$.

All scenarios in this Monte Carlo experiment are based on a PPS design with a population size (N) equal to 1000. First, we compute a scenario assuming that the sample is drawn using a PPS design and the auxiliary variable T_j is not correlated with the efficiency level (referred to hereinafter as the *non-informative design* scenario). The second scenario is generated drawing the sample from a PPS design and assuming that the auxiliary variable T_j is highly correlated with the level of efficiency by $T_j = (\exp^{-U})^4$ (referred to hereinafter as the *informative design* scenario). Finally, the third scenario is simulated using a two-stage sampling design. In this scenario, half of the sample is drawn using an *informative design*, and the second half of the sample is drawn using a simple random sample (SRS) design (referred to hereinafter as the *two-stage design* scenario). In this scenario, we use the first half of the sample only to estimate the frontier and the second half of the sample only to estimate the average efficiency.

We replicate each scenario for different sample sizes (50, 100, 300, and 500), i.e., we simulate four different sampling fractions $f = \frac{n}{N}$. In large-scale international assessment, we usually observe sample sizes of around 50 schools. This is usually no more than 10% of the population at country level. However, there are some exceptions where f can be very large (even equal to 1), for example, when some countries expand the sample at regional level. In this vein, we aim to simulate different sample sizes to dimension the problem according to the sampling fraction.

For each dataset, we estimate the population quantile frontier $\hat{q}_{\alpha,U}(x)$ and the individual efficiency score $\hat{\theta}_j$ for each observation included in the sample $j = 1, 2, \ldots, n$ by running the order-α quantile-type frontier model proposed by Aragon et al. (2005) (referred to hereinafter as the order-α model) and our proposed adaptation of this model to include the sample weights (referred to hereinafter as the AGSS model) for $\alpha = 0.8$, $\alpha = 0.9$, and $\alpha = 1$. Finally, for each dataset, we estimate the average population efficiency μ from the sample, both omitting (which is the standard practice) and accounting for inclusion probabilities. Thus, we define the following estimators:

$$\hat{\mu}^{order-\alpha} = \frac{1}{n}\sum_{j=1}^{n}\hat{\theta}_j^{order-\alpha} \tag{19}$$

$$\hat{\mu}^{order-\alpha,\pi} = \frac{1}{n}\sum_{j=1}^{n}\frac{1}{\pi_j}\hat{\theta}_j^{order-\alpha} \tag{20}$$

$$\hat{\mu}^{AGSS} = \frac{1}{n}\sum_{j=1}^{n}\hat{\theta}_j^{AGSS} \tag{21}$$

$$\hat{\mu}^{AGSS,\pi} = \frac{1}{n}\sum_{j=1}^{n}\frac{1}{\pi_j}\hat{\theta}_j^{AGSS} \tag{22}$$

Note that we use only the half of the sample drawn from a SRS design to estimate the population average efficiency in the *two-stage* sampling design. This means that the probabilities of inclusion are identical for all observations, and, consequently, it is not necessary to take this information into account. Thus, for this sampling design, we only provide the estimators $\hat{\mu}^{order-\alpha}$ and $\hat{\mu}^{AGSS}$.

In summary, we simulate 36 scenarios (three sample designs, four sampling fractions, and three levels of α). In order to make the results more reliable, we undertook a Monte Carlo experiment, where B, the number of replicates, is 100. Therefore, all measures were computed in each replication and then averaged to get the results reported in the next section.

4.2 Results

4.2.1 Results on the Population Quantile-Type Frontier Estimation

In order to dimension the effect of taking into account the sample weights to estimate the order-α quantile-type frontier in finite population samples, we compare the results from both the *order-α* and *AGSS* models. To do this, we compute the mean square error (MSE) for each model:

$$MSE = \frac{1}{n}\sum_{j=1}^{n}\left(\hat{q}_{\alpha,U}(x)_j - q_{\alpha,U}(x)_j\right)^2, \tag{23}$$

where $q_{\alpha,\,U}(x)_j$ is the population quantile-type frontier of order α evaluated at unit j and $\hat{q}_{\alpha,U}(x)_j$ is the estimation of this order-αfrontier at the same point. Note that, for $\alpha = 1$, the quantile production $q_1(x)$coincides with the production function $\varphi(x)$. Results from this analysis are shown in Table 1. To illustrate the above ideas, we report the results for the population production frontier estimation from one particular simulation. Figures 1, 2, and 3 show these results for the *non-informative* design, *informative* design, and *two-stage* design ($\alpha = 0.9$ and $n = 50$, $n = 300$, respectively). Note that these results are plotted merely for illustrative purposes, since they represent only one simulation. To properly compare model performance, we also compare the MSE of the Monte Carlo simulation.

The first remarkable result from the Monte Carlo experiment is that, in the extreme case of $\alpha = 1$, i.e., when the quantile to be estimated is equal to the maximum (last two columns of Table 1), we obtain the same estimation of the population production function with both models, regardless of the sample design. Consequently, from now on, we will focus on the results for $\alpha < 1$.

In the *non-informative* scenario, the results demonstrate that the order-αmodel proposed by Aragon et al. (2005) performs reasonably well. In other words, the omission of different probabilities of inclusion does not, in this case, pose a problem in terms of population frontier identification provided that they are independent of the efficiency. Moreover, the inclusion of the sample weights through the adaptation of the order-αmodel leads to larger MSE values.

Conversely, when the auxiliary variable in the PPS design is informative, i.e., it is correlated with the efficiency of the units in the population (e.g., larger schools are more efficient than smaller ones), failure to include the probability of inclusion information in the model significantly impairs the estimation of the population frontier for all levels of α and sample sizes. Figures 2 and 3 illustrate this result. Note that if we compare both PPS informative designs, the most pronounced improvements of considering the sample weights are observed in the *informative* scenario, because all the units included in the sample are used to estimate the frontier in this case. However, only half of the sample is used to identify the population frontier in the *two-stage* dataset.

Table 1 Mean square error for the estimation of the population frontier from PPS sample designs

	$\alpha = 0.8$		$\alpha = 0.9$		$\alpha = 1$	
	Order-α	AGSS	Order-α	AGSS	Order-α	AGSS
Non-informative						
$n = 50$	0.095	0.103	0.089	0.095	0.168	0.168
$n = 100$	0.093	0.102	0.088	0.096	0.152	0.152
$n = 300$	0.079	0.087	0.074	0.082	0.102	0.102
$n = 500$	0.060	0.070	0.055	0.063	0.063	0.063
Informative						
$n = 50$	0.250	0.144	0.156	0.102	0.052	0.052
$n = 100$	0.400	0.159	0.241	0.099	0.044	0.044
$n = 300$	1.028	0.200	0.579	0.104	0.015	0.015
$n = 500$	1.626	0.226	0.910	0.093	0.000	0.000
Two-stage						
$n = 50$	0.161	0.133	0.104	0.083	0.054	0.054
$n = 100$	0.245	0.151	0.151	0.090	0.053	0.053
$n = 300$	0.549	0.192	0.322	0.094	0.035	0.035
$n = 500$	0.838	0.169	0.481	0.089	0.022	0.022

Note: Mean values after 100 replications

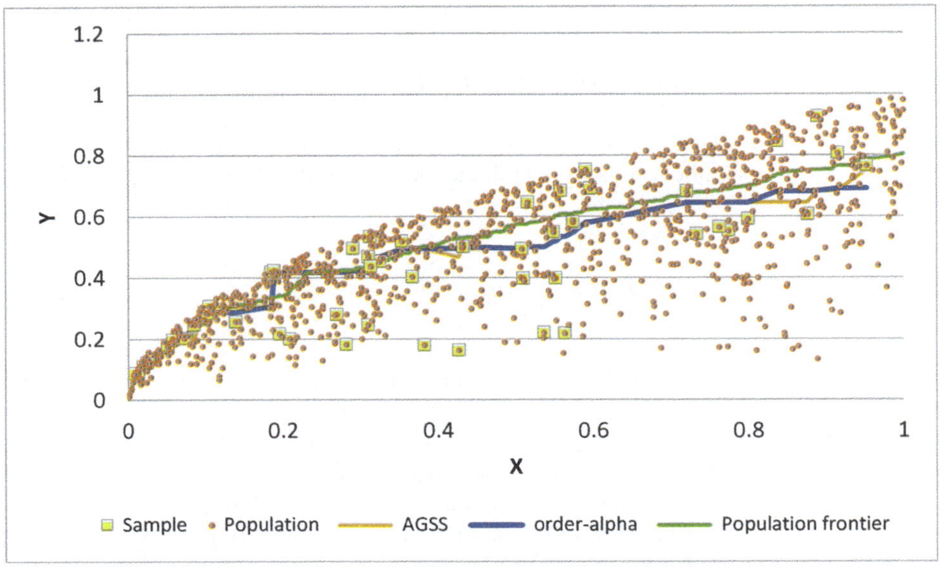

Panel (a) Non-informative design n=50 *and* $\alpha = 0.9$

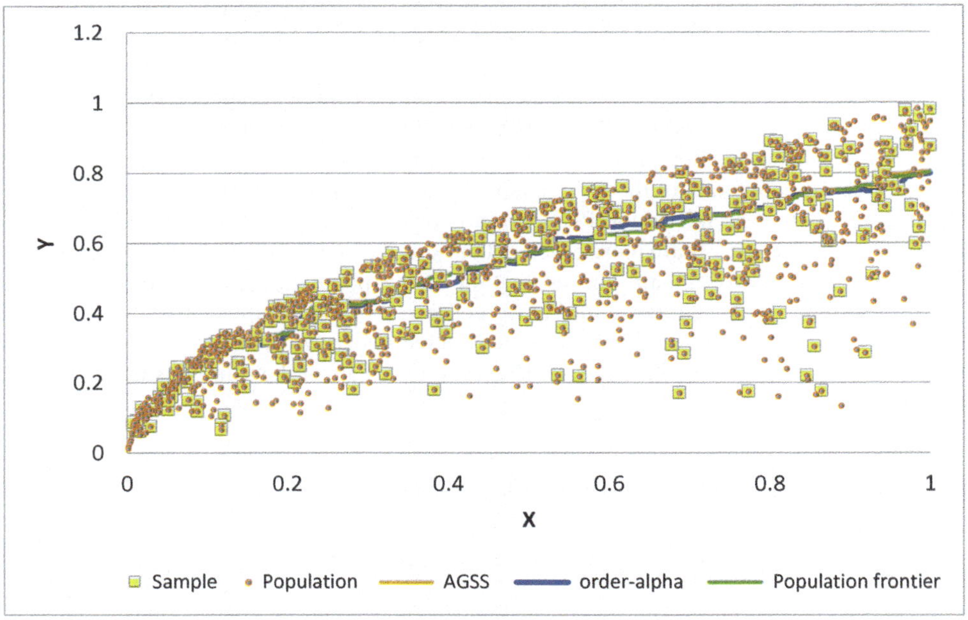

Panel (b) Non-informative design n=300 *and* $\alpha = 0.9$

Fig. 1 Estimation of the population production frontier using the order-α and AGSS models, non-informative design. Panel (**a**) Non-informative design $n = 50$ and $\alpha = 0.9$. Panel (**b**) Non-informative design $n = 300$ and $\alpha = 0.9$

Finally, an interesting finding in both *informative* designs for $\alpha < 1$ is that the MSE also increases as the sample size increases. This means that the negative effect of omitting information about different sample weights across the sample intensifies in these contexts as the sample size increases. The accurate estimation of the population production frontier is extremely important when we set out to measure technological change over time or compare the performance between different sectors or groups of units. In these contexts, if there is any previous evidence about the potential correlation between the auxiliary variable and population efficiency, it would be recommendable to use the AGSS model instead of overlooking the probabilities of inclusion. In fact, since there is not a substantial difference in the MSE between both models in the *non-informative* scenario, it might be preferable, if there is any inkling, even if there is no robust evidence, of such a correlation, to include, rather than omit, the sample weights.

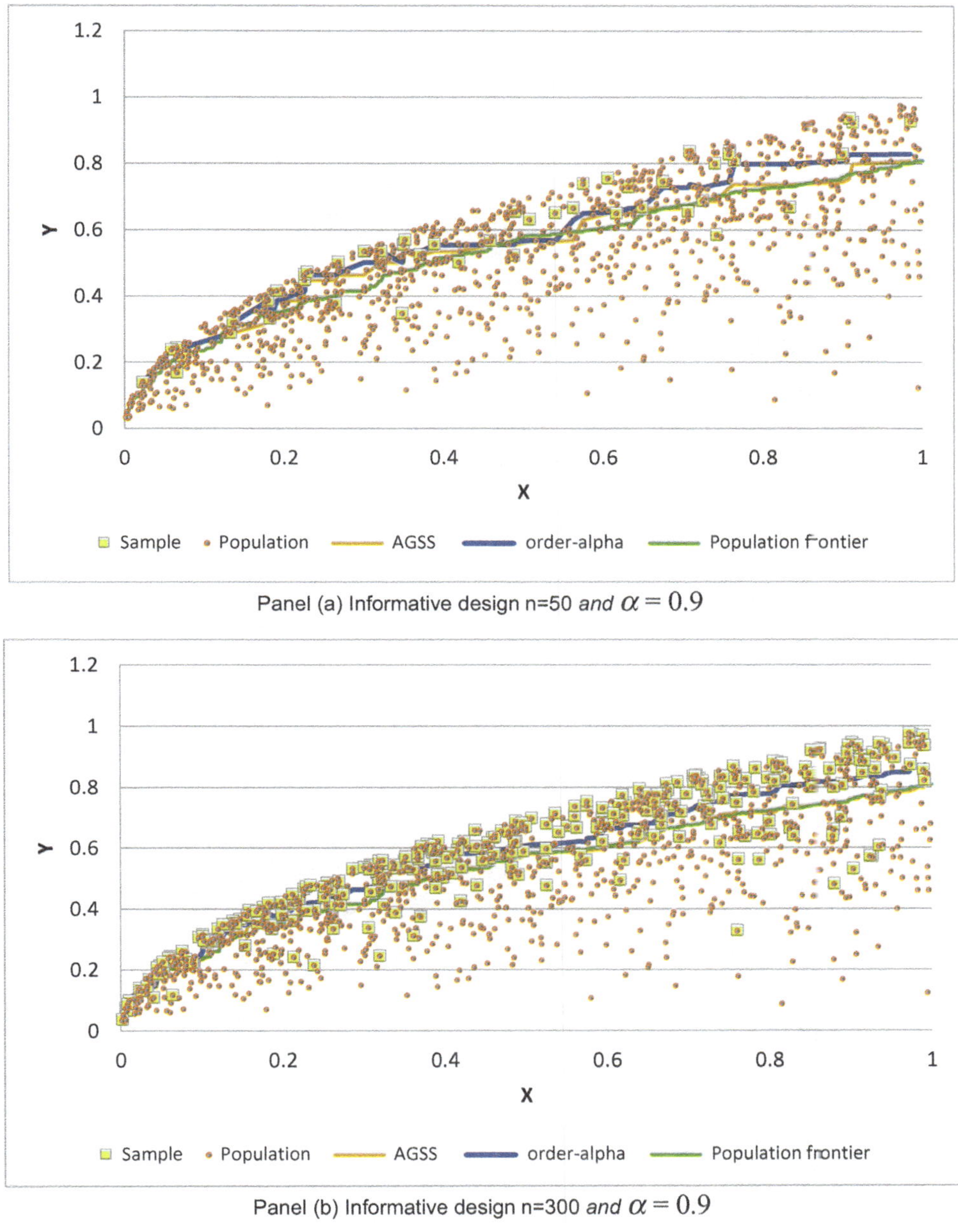

Fig. 2 Estimation of the population production frontier using the order-α and AGSS models, *informative* design. Panel (**a**) Informative design $n = 50$ and $\alpha = 0.9$. Panel (**b**) Informative design $n = 300$ and $\alpha = 0.9$

4.2.2 Results on the Population Average Efficiency

We are also interested in exploring the effect of taking into account the existence of different probabilities of inclusion π_j when we aggregate the individual efficiencies to estimate the population average efficiency μ. To do this, we compute, after the 100 replications, the mean bias relative to the true population average efficiency μ for each estimator $\hat{\mu}$ (Eqs. 19, 20, 21, and 22):

$$Bias = \frac{\sum_{b=1}^{100} \hat{\mu}_b - \mu_b}{100}$$

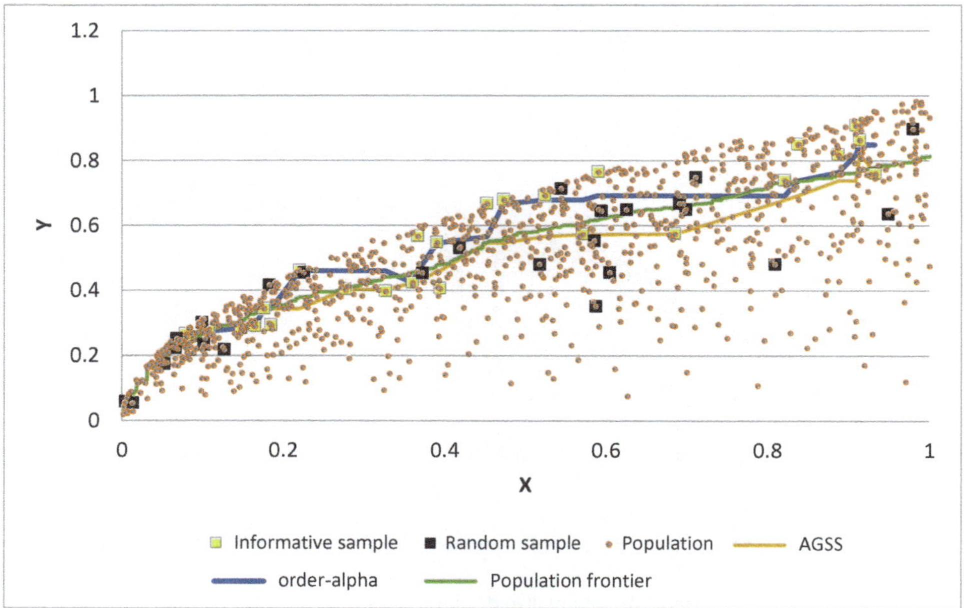

Panel (a) Two-stage design n=50 *and* $\alpha = 0.9$

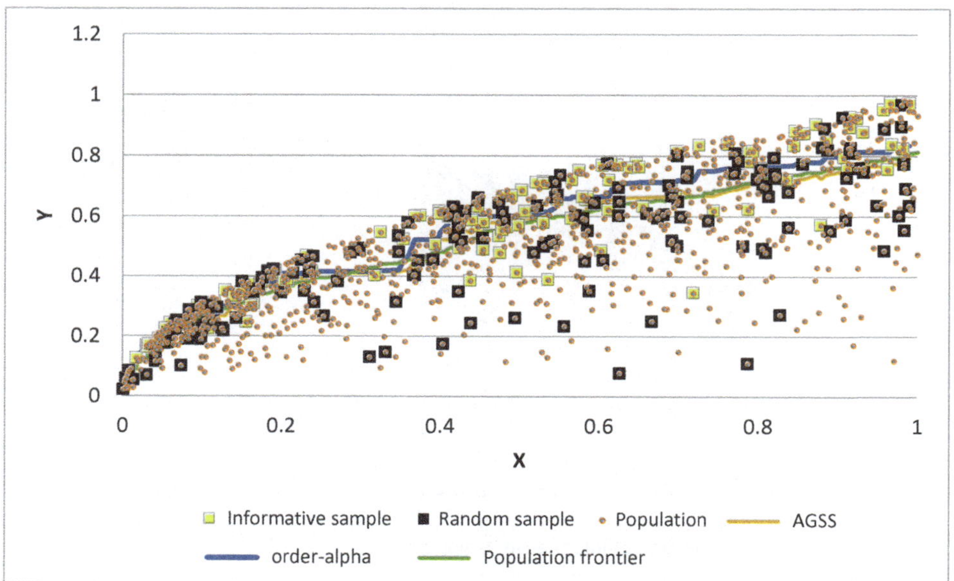

Panel (b) Two-stage design n=300 *and* $\alpha = 0.9$

Fig. 3 Estimation of the population production frontier using the order-α and AGSS models, two-stage design. Panel (**a**) Two-stage design $n = 50$ and $\alpha = 0.9$. Panel (**b**) Two-stage design $n = 300$ and $\alpha = 0.9$

and the MSE relative to the true population efficiency μ:

$$MSE = \frac{\sum_{b=1}^{100} \left(\hat{\mu}_b - \mu_b\right)^2}{100}. \tag{24}$$

Note that, for $\alpha < 1$, some observations will be located above the quantile frontier $q_\alpha(x)$, i.e., the efficiency level of these units will be lower than 1. Then, the parameterμ and the estimators $\hat{\mu}$ could also take values smaller than 1, leading to a positive or a negative bias. Results for the bias and the MSE are shown in Tables 2 and 3, respectively.

Table 2 Bias for the estimation of the population average efficiency

	Non-informative				*Informative*				*Two-stage*			
	Order-α	Order-α (π)	AGSS	AGSS(π)	Order-α	Order-α (π)	AGSS	AGSS(π)	Order-α	Order-α (π)	AGSS	AGSS(π)
$\alpha = \mathbf{0.8}$												
$n = 50$	−0.002	−0.008	0.006	0.002	−0.107	0.135	−0.194	−0.028	0.054	–	−0.032	–
$n = 100$	−0.017	−0.012	−0.015	−0.009	−0.115	0.084	−0.208	−0.003	0.087	–	0.005	–
$n = 300$	−0.011	−0.009	−0.012	−0.010	−0.120	0.086	−0.208	−0.041	0.101	–	−0.008	–
$n = 500$	−0.010	−0.009	−0.012	−0.010	−0.121	0.068	−0.211	−0.054	0.108	–	0.001	–
$\alpha = \mathbf{0.9}$												
$n = 50$	−0.020	−0.026	−0.017	−0.021	−0.151	0.108	−0.215	−0.017	0.004	–	−0.054	–
$n = 100$	−0.032	−0.026	−0.029	−0.023	−0.158	0.054	−0.226	0.017	0.045	–	−0.017	–
$n = 300$	−0.022	−0.020	−0.022	−0.020	−0.163	0.062	−0.227	−0.031	0.065	–	−0.014	–
$n = 500$	−0.017	−0.016	−0.022	−0.020	−0.163	0.041	−0.229	−0.048	0.078	–	−0.004	–
$\alpha = \mathbf{1}$												
$n = 50$	−0.151	−0.157	−0.151	−0.157	−0.313	−0.036	−0.313	−0.036	−0.189	–	−0.189	–
$n = 100$	−0.122	−0.115	−0.122	−0.115	−0.299	−0.067	−0.299	−0.067	−0.114	–	−0.114	–
$n = 300$	−0.069	−0.067	−0.069	−0.067	−0.280	−0.028	−0.280	−0.028	−0.053	–	−0.053	–
$n = 500$	−0.046	−0.045	−0.046	−0.045	−0.274	−0.044	−0.274	−0.044	−0.024	–	−0.024	–

Note: Mean values after 100 replications

Table 3 Mean square error for the estimation of the population average efficiency

	Non-informative				*Informative*				*Two-stage*			
	Order-α	Order-α (π)	AGSS	AGSS(π)	Order-α	Order-α (π)	AGSS	AGSS(π)	Order-α	Order-α (π)	AGSS	AGSS(π)
$\boldsymbol{\alpha = 0.8}$												
$n = 50$	0.005	0.007	0.006	0.008	0.000	0.274	0.047	0.087	0.030	–	0.027	–
$n = 100$	0.003	0.004	0.003	0.004	0.018	0.155	0.053	0.437	0.017	–	0.011	–
$n = 300$	0.001	0.001	0.001	0.001	0.019	0.090	0.051	0.049	0.013	–	0.004	–
$n = 500$	0.000	0.000	0.001	0.001	0.019	0.040	0.052	0.022	0.013	–	0.003	–
$\boldsymbol{\alpha = 0.9}$												
$n = 50$	0.006	0.009	0.006	0.010	0.032	0.313	0.061	0.145	0.028	–	0.030	–
$n = 100$	0.003	0.004	0.003	0.004	0.035	0.173	0.066	0.490	0.012	–	0.011	–
$n = 300$	0.001	0.001	0.001	0.001	0.036	0.105	0.065	0.074	0.007	–	0.003	–
$n = 500$	0.000	0.001	0.001	0.001	0.036	0.044	0.066	0.032	0.007	–	0.002	–
$\boldsymbol{\alpha = 1}$												
$n = 50$	0.022	0.027	0.022	0.027	0.123	0.342	0.123	0.342	0.065	–	0.065	–
$n = 100$	0.012	0.012	0.012	0.012	0.113	0.220	0.113	0.220	0.024	–	0.024	–
$n = 300$	0.003	0.003	0.003	0.003	0.101	0.137	0.101	0.137	0.006	–	0.006	–
$n = 500$	0.001	0.001	0.001	0.001	0.097	0.061	0.097	0.061	0.002	–	0.002	–

Note: Mean values after 100 replications

As in the previous case, for $\alpha = 1$, the results from both models are equal. Thus, we will focus on $\alpha < 1$. In the first scenario, the *non-informative* design, both the bias and the MSE results show that omission of the sample weights is, in this case, the best strategy for estimating the population average efficiency for all sample sizes and levels of α.

In the *informative* design, the bias and MSE lead to different conclusions. In terms of bias, it appears to be better to take into account the information on the probabilities of inclusion to estimate the population frontier and then aggregate the individual efficiencies to estimate the population average efficiency. This result holds for all sample sizes and both levels of $\alpha = 0.8$ and $\alpha = 0.9$. However, if we focus on the MSE, the conclusion is the exact opposite. In this case, the estimator $\hat{\mu}^{order-\alpha}$performs best for all sample sizes and levels of α, which means that it is more accurate to ignore this information. Note that, in this scenario, there is a trade-off between population frontier estimation accuracy and population average efficiency. With a view to population frontier estimation accuracy, it would be necessary to include the sample weights (i.e., using the AGSS model). However, this implies a considerable deterioration in terms of the MSE in the estimation of the population average efficiency.

Finally, the *two-stage* design addresses this trade-off. In this context, it is also more accurate to include the probabilities of inclusion in the model for estimating the population average efficiency for all sample sizes and levels of α, and there are no contradictory results between bias and MSE. Moreover, the estimation of the population average efficiency μ from this sampling design is much more accurate than the *informative* design, regardless of the estimator that we use. This finding is notable in terms of public policy design, since large-scale assessment surveys are usually used to measure technical efficiency through production frontiers. However, current sample designs (PPS) are not designed for estimating either population production frontiers or average technical efficiency. If there is any previous evidence (e.g., earlier studies) indicating that there is any correlation between the auxiliary variable (e.g., school size) and the efficiency of the schools in the population, it would be advisable to define a *two-stage* sampling design instead of a standard PPS to enhance future population efficiency and productivity estimations using samples. This issue is even more important when the aim of the analysis is to compare school performance over time (i.e., technological change) or different educational sectors (e.g., public and private schools).

5 Concluding Remarks

Nowadays, it is quite common to find educational databases based on complex sampling designs used to minimize survey costs and improve the precision of the estimates of some parameters of interest for the population. However, the use of the information provided by sample weights has been repeatedly overlooked in the literature on production frontier estimation, leading to estimations (from sample data) that are not representative of the population under study. In this research, we develop an extension of robust nonparametric order-α frontier methods to incorporate sample weight information into the estimation of the population production frontier. Monte Carlo results show that when the auxiliary variable in the PPS sample design contains information about the level of efficiency in the population, the estimation of the population frontier can be improved if the nonparametric model accounts for information on sample weights. In this context, however, the PPS sample design should be transformed into a *two-stage* sampling design in order to properly estimate the average educational efficiency for the target population.

This research should be regarded as a foundation stone for addressing the issue of incorporating sample weight information into the estimation of technical efficiency. More research is needed in several directions to explore other potential solutions for improving the accuracy of nonparametric estimations. Probably, the most straightforward and intuitive alternative is to explore the potential of incorporating sample weight information into the conventional bootstrap methodology (Simar and Wilson 1998). In particular, it is important to test its validity and performance, since the basic assumption of this method (i.e., observed data in the sample come from independent and identically distributed random variables) does not hold in the case of complex sampling designs in finite populations. Another fruitful line of research would be to address this issue in the parametric framework, for example, by incorporating sample weights into the corrected ordinary least square (COLS) model.

Acknowledgments The authors are greatly indebted to Fundación Ramon Areces for supporting and encouraging mutual collaboration on productivity analysis in education as part of projects *La medición de la eficiencia de la educacion primaria y de sus determinantes en España y en la Union Europea: un análisis con TIMSS-PIRLS 2011* (D. Santín) and *Evaluación de la eficiencia en la producción educativa a partir de diseños muestrales* (J. Aparicio, M. González and G. Sicilia).

References

Afonso, A., & Aubyn, M. S. (2005). Non-parametric approaches to education and health efficiency in OECD countries. *Journal of Applied Economics, 8*(2), 227–246.

Afonso, A., & Aubyn, M. S. (2006). Cross-country efficiency of secondary education provision: A semi-parametric analysis with non-discretionary inputs. *Economic Modelling, 23*(3), 476–491.

Agasisti, T., & Zoido, P. (2018). Comparing the efficiency of schools through international benchmarking: Results from an empirical analysis of OECD PISA 2012 data. *Educational Researcher, 47*(6), 352–362.

Aigner, D. J., & Chu, S. F. (1968). On estimating the industry production function. *American Economic Review, 58*, 826–839.

Aigner, D. J., Lovell, C. A. K., & Schmidt, P. (1977). Formulation and estimation of stochastic frontier production functions. *Journal of Econometrics, 6*, 21–37.

Allen, R., Athanassopoulos, A., Dyson, R. G., & Thanassoulis, E. (1997). Weights restrictions and value judgements in Data Envelopment Analysis: Evolution, development and future directions. *Annals of Operations Research, 73*, 13–34.

Aparicio, J., & Santin, D. (2018). A note on measuring group performance over time with pseudo-panels. *European Journal of Operational Research, 267*(1), 227–235.

Aparicio, J., Cordero, J. M., & Pastor, J. T. (2017a). The determination of the least distance to the strongly efficient frontier in data envelopment analysis oriented models: Modelling and computational aspects. *Omega, 71*, 1–10.

Aparicio, J., Crespo-Cebada, E., Pedraja-Chaparro, F., & Santín, D. (2017b). Comparing school ownership performance using a pseudo-panel database: A Malmquist-type index approach. *European Journal of Operational Research, 256*(2), 533–542.

Aparicio, J., Cordero, J. M., Gonzalez, M., & Lopez-Espin, J. J. (2018). Using non-radial DEA to assess school efficiency in a cross-country perspective: An empirical analysis of OECD countries. *Omega, 79*, 9–20.

Aragon, Y., Daouia, A., & Thomas-Agnan, C. (2005). Nonparametric frontier estimation: A conditional quantile-based approach. *Econometric Theory, 21*(2), 358–389.

Banker, R. D., Charnes, A., & Cooper, W. W. (1984). Some models for estimating technical and scale inefficiencies in data envelopment analysis. *Management Science, 30*(9), 1078–1092.

Cazals, C., Florens, J. P., & Simar, L. (2002). Nonparametric frontier estimation: A robust approach. *Journal of Econometrics, 106*(1), 1–25.

Charnes, A., Cooper, W. W., & Rhodes, E. (1978). Measuring the efficiency of decision making units. *European Journal of Operational Research, 2*(6), 429–444.

Cordero, J. M., Cristobal, V., & Santín, D. (2018). Causal inference on education policies: A survey of empirical studies using PISA, TIMSS and PIRLS. *Journal of Economic Surveys, 32*(3), 878–915.

Daouia, A., & Simar, L. (2007). Nonparametric efficiency analysis: A multivariate conditional quantile. *Journal of Econometrics, 140*, 375–400.

Daraio, C., & Simar, L. (2007). Conditional nonparametric frontier models for convex and nonconvex technologies: A unifying approach. *Journal of Productivity Analysis, 28*, 13–32.

De Jorge, J., & Santín. (2010). Determinantes de la eficiencia educativa en la Unión Europea. *Hacienda Pública Española, 193*, 131–155.

De La Fuente, A. (2011). Human capital and productivity. *Nordic Economic Policy Review, 2*(2), 103–132.

Debreu, G. (1951). The coefficient of resource utilization. *Econometrica, 19*(3), 273–292.

Deprins, D., Simar, L., & Tulkens, H. (1984). Measuring labor inefficiency in post offices. In M. Marchand, P. Pestieau, & H. Tulkens (Eds.), *The performance of public enterprises: Concepts and measurements* (pp. 243–267). Amsterdam: North-Holland.

Färe, R., & Zelenyuk, V. (2003). On aggregate Farrell efficiencies. *European Journal of Operational Research, 146*, 615–620.

Färe, R., Grosskopf, S., & Lovell, C. A. K. (1985). *The measurement of efficiency of production*. Boston: Kluwer Nijhof Publishers.

Farrell, M. J. (1957). The measurement of productive efficiency. *Journal of the Royal Statistical Society Series A (General), 120*(3), 253–290.

Hanushek, E. A., & Kimko, D. D. (2000). Schooling, labor-force quality, and the growth of nations. *American Economic Review, 90*(5), 1184–1208.

Hanushek, E. A., & Woessmann, L. (2012). Do better schools lead to more growth? Cognitive skills, economic outcomes, and causation. *Journal of Economic Growth, 17*(4), 267–321.

Hedayat, A. S., & Sinha, B. K. (1991). *Design and inference in finite population sampling*. New York: Wiley.

Horvitz, D. G., & Thompson, D. J. (1952). A generalization of sampling without replacement from a finite universe. *J. Amer. Statist. Assoc. 47*(**260**), 663–685.

Jerrim, J., Lopez-Agudo, L. A., Marcenaro-Gutierrez, O. D., & Shure, N. (2017). What happens when econometrics and psychometrics collide? An example using the PISA data. *Economics of Education Review, 61*, 51–58.

Koopmans, T. C. (1951). Analysis of production as an efficient combination of activities. In T. C. Koopmans (Ed.), *Activity analysis of production and allocation* (pp. 33–97). New York: Wiley.

Lavy, V. (2015). Do differences in schools' instruction time explain international achievement gaps? Evidence from developed and developing countries. *The Economic Journal, 125*, 397–424.

Levin, H. M. (1974). Measuring efficiency in educational production. *Public Finance Quarterly, 2*(1), 3–24.

Meeusen, W., & van den Broeck, J. (1977). Efficiency estimation from Cobb-Douglas production functions with composed error. *International Economic Review, 18*, 435–444.

OECD. (2017). *PISA 2015 technical report*, OECD, Paris.

Pastor, J. T., Lovell, C. K., & Aparicio, J. (2012). Families of linear efficiency programs based on Debreu's loss function. *Journal of Productivity Analysis, 38*(2), 109–120.

Särndal, C. E., Swensson, B., & Wretman, J. (1992). *Model assisted survey sampling*. Springer Science and Business Media, New York.

Shephard, R. W. (1953). *Cost and production functions*. Princeton University Press, Princeton.

Simar, L., & Wilson, P. W. (1998). Sensitivity analysis of efficiency scores: How to bootstrap in nonparametric frontier models. *Management Science, 44*(1), 49–61.

Strietholt, R., Gustafsson, J. E., Rosen, M., & Bos, W. (2014). Outcomes and causal inference in international comparative assessments. In R. Stietholt, W. Bos, J. E. Gustafsson, & M. Rosen (Eds.), *Educational policy evaluation through international comparative assessments*. New York: Waxman, Münster.

Woodruff, R. S. (1952). Condence intervals for medians and other position measures. *J. Amer. Statist. Assoc. 47*, 635–646.

Local Circularity of Six Classic Price Indexes

Jesús T. Pastor and C. A. Knox Lovell

Abstract In this paper, we characterize local circularity for the Laspeyres, Paasche, and Fisher price indexes. In the first two cases, we begin by deriving a sufficient condition for achieving circularity that establishes that at least one of two proposed equalities must hold. We end up showing that the sufficient condition is also necessary. We continue with the Fisher price index that is the geometric mean of the two, and we find a sufficient circularity condition that is a direct consequence of the corresponding sufficient conditions for its two component indexes. However, we also show that, unlike its Laspeyres and Paasche components, this sufficient circularity condition for the Fisher price index is not necessary. We reach different conclusions when we extend our investigation to the circularity properties of the geometric Laspeyres, geometric Paasche, and Törnqvist price indexes, for which none of the proposed sufficient conditions is necessary. Throughout, we distinguish local circularity, which all six price indexes satisfy, from global circularity, which none of the price indexes satisfies.

Keywords Price index · Local circularity

JEL Classification C43

1 Introduction

Price indexes are used to estimate the general price level of an economy, and its rate of change is used to estimate the rate of inflation. An early price index was proposed by German economist Etienne Laspeyres (1871). Shortly thereafter, German statistician Hermann Paasche (1874) proposed an alternative price index.

If the question to answer is how much an n-items basket purchased in the base period would cost in the comparison period, the answer requires data on the quantities purchased and their prices in the base period and their prices in the comparison period. This information generates the Laspeyres price index, defined as

$$L(0,t) = \frac{\sum_{i=1}^{n} p_{it} q_{i0}}{\sum_{i=1}^{n} p_{i0} q_{i0}}, \tag{1}$$

in which the base period is identified with the subindex 0 and the comparison period is identified as t, where t can take any integer value between 1 and T.

If, instead, we consider the n-items basket purchased in the comparison period and want to compare its actual cost with what it would have cost in the base period, we require data on the quantities purchased and their prices in the comparison period and their prices in the base period. This information generates the Paasche price index, defined as

J. T. Pastor
Centro de Investigación Operativa, Universidad Miguel Hernández, Alicante, Spain
e-mail: jtpastor@umh.es

C. A. K. Lovell (✉)
Centre for Efficiency and Productivity Analysis, School of Economics, University of Queensland, St Lucia, QLD, Australia
e-mail: k.lovell@uq.edu.au

J. Aparicio et al. (eds.), *Advances in Efficiency and Productivity II*, International Series in Operations Research & Management Science 287, https://doi.org/10.1007/978-3-030-41618-8_7

$$P(0,t) = \frac{\sum_{i=1}^{n} p_{it} q_{it}}{\sum_{i=1}^{n} p_{i0} q_{it}}. \tag{2}$$

Since $L(0,t)$ usually overestimates the rate of price change due to substitution bias, and, for the same reason, $P(0,t)$ usually underestimates it, the American economist Irving Fisher (1922) proposed to use the geometric mean of the two as a more accurate price index. Fisher's "ideal" price index is defined as[1]

$$F(0,t) = \sqrt{L(0,t) \cdot P(0,t)}. \tag{3}$$

The only disadvantage of the Fisher price index relative to its two components is that it requires data on quantities, as well as prices, from both periods.

With more than two time periods, circularity becomes a desirable property of an index number. It is also a demanding property, requiring the product of the index value in situation *b* relative to situation *a* and the index value in situation *c* relative to situation *b* to equal the index value in situation *c* relative to situation *a*, without going through the intermediate situation *b*. We interpret this property as being a *global* requirement, and we consider situations to be time periods, so that an index number I satisfies the circularity property if, and only if, $\mathrm{I}(0,t)\cdots\mathrm{I}(t,t+1) = \mathrm{I}(0,t+1)\ \forall\, p \in R^n_{++},\ q \in R^n_{++}$.[2] None of the price indexes we consider satisfies the circularity property globally.[3] Indeed, Funke et al. (1979) have shown that a price index satisfies monotonicity and homogeneity of degree zero in prices, linear homogeneity in comparison period prices, the identity property, and commensurability, which all of our price indexes satisfy, and the circular test, which none of our price indexes satisfies, if and only if it has the restrictive Cobb-Douglas form.

However, empirical time series price and quantity data do not typically span R^n_{++}, which prompts a search for a *local* circularity property for each of the price indexes. In subsequent sections, we demonstrate that each of the price indexes does satisfy a local circularity property, although these local circularity properties are demanding.

In this paper, we investigate the ability of the three price indexes introduced above to satisfy the circularity property locally, over a restricted price and quantity domain. The paper is organized as follows. In Sect. 2 we derive a sufficient condition for the Laspeyres price index to satisfy circularity. We then show that this sufficient condition is also necessary and that it exhausts the set of necessary and sufficient conditions. In Sect. 3 we conduct the same analysis for the Paasche price index, and we obtain an economically similar and exhaustive, necessary, and sufficient condition for the Paasche price index to satisfy circularity. In Sect. 4 we merge the previous two analyses to provide a complete and exhaustive sufficient condition for the Fisher price index to satisfy circularity, and we show by way of a numerical example that, unlike its Laspeyres and Paasche components, this sufficient condition is not necessary. In Sect. 5 we briefly discuss three additional price indexes, the Törnqvist price index and its geometric Laspeyres and geometric Paasche components.[4] None of these indexes satisfies the circularity property globally, and we develop sufficient conditions for each of them to satisfy circularity, although none of the sufficient conditions is necessary. A motivation for considering these three price indexes is that the US Bureau of Labor Statistics has replaced the Laspeyres formula with a geometric Laspeyres formula in an effort to reduce substitution bias in the calculation of some lower-level indexes and a Törnqvist formula to calculate upper-level indexes, in the US consumer price index (CPI). Section 6 contains a summary of our findings and some suggestions for future research.

[1]Fisher (1922; 241) has an interesting history of the use of the qualifier "ideal" to describe his index.

[2]A reviewer has pointed out, correctly, that this is a definition of transitivity, not circularity. However, if a transitive index number satisfies the identity test, then transitivity and circularity are identical properties. Since all six of our classic price indexes satisfy the identity test, we follow Balk and Althin (1996) by referring to the more popular circularity property.

[3]Fisher, whose "ideal" index satisfies a large number of desirable properties but fails the circularity property, claimed that the property "... is theoretically a mistaken one ... and ... a *perfect* fulfillment of this so-called circular test should really be taken as proof that the formula that fulfils it is erroneous" (1922; 271, emphasis in the original).

[4]Eichhorn and Voeller (1976; 8), Diewert (2004; 308), and Balk (2008; Sect. 3.3.3) all present the geometric Laspeyres and geometric Paasche indexes without attributing their discovery to any author(s).

2 Local Circularity of the Laspeyres Price Index

We begin by providing a characterization of the circularity property for the Laspeyres price index in Definition 1, and we continue by using this characterization to establish a sufficient condition for circularity to hold in Proposition 1. We then prove in Propositions 2 and 3 that this sufficient condition is also necessary.

Considering base period 0 and any subsequent periods t and $t+1$, the Laspeyres price index satisfies the circularity property if $L(0,t) \cdot L(t,t+1) = L(0,t+1)$. Using (1), the circularity property can be expressed as

$$\frac{\sum_{i=1}^{n} p_{it}q_{i0}}{\sum_{i=1}^{n} p_{i0}q_{i0}} \cdot \frac{\sum_{i=1}^{n} p_{i(t+1)}q_{it}}{\sum_{i=1}^{n} p_{it}q_{it}} = \frac{\sum_{i=1}^{n} p_{i(t+1)}q_{i0}}{\sum_{i=1}^{n} p_{i0}q_{i0}}. \tag{4}$$

Eliminating the term $\sum_{i=1}^{n} p_{i0}q_{i0}$ that appears in the denominator of both sides and moving the term $\sum_{i=1}^{n} p_{it}q_{i0}$ to the right side of the equality, we obtain an alternative circularity characterization.

Definition 1 Circularity property for the Laspeyres price index:

$$\frac{\sum_{i=1}^{n} p_{i(t+1)}q_{it}}{\sum_{i=1}^{n} p_{it}q_{it}} = \frac{\sum_{i=1}^{n} p_{i(t+1)}q_{i0}}{\sum_{i=1}^{n} p_{it}q_{i0}}. \tag{5}$$

The only difference between the ratios on the two sides of (5) is the quantities; on the left side period t quantities weight price changes, while on the right side period 0 quantities weight price changes. Let us observe that expression (5) requires information on prices of periods t and $t+1$ and quantities of periods 0 and t. Because the Laspeyres price index does not satisfy this property globally, in Sect. 2.1 we develop a sufficient condition for local circularity.

2.1 *A Sufficient Local Circularity Condition for the Laspeyres Price Index*

Proposition 1 establishes a sufficient condition for the Laspeyres price index to satisfy circularity.

Proposition 1 The Laspeyres price index is circular if at least one of the following pairs of equalities holds:

(L1) $q_{it} = \gamma_{t0} \cdot q_{i0}$, $i = 1, \ldots, n$, $\gamma_{t0} > 0$, or
(L2) $p_{i(t+1)} = \mu_{(t+1)t} \cdot p_{it}$, $i = 1, \ldots, n$, $\mu_{(t+1)t} > 0$,

in which γ_{t0} and $\mu_{(t+1)t}$ are independent of i.

Proof If equality (L1) holds, the left side of (5) can be written as

$$\frac{\sum_{i=1}^{n} p_{i(t+1)}q_{it}}{\sum_{i=1}^{n} p_{it}q_{it}} = \frac{\sum_{i=1}^{n} p_{i(t+1)}(\gamma_{t0} \cdot q_{i0})}{\sum_{i=1}^{n} p_{it}(\gamma_{t0} \cdot q_{i0})} = \frac{\gamma_{t0} \cdot \left(\sum_{i=1}^{n} p_{i(t+1)}q_{i0}\right)}{\gamma_{t0} \cdot \left(\sum_{i=1}^{n} p_{it}q_{i0}\right)},$$

and after cancelling $\gamma_{t0} > 0$ in the numerator and denominator of the right side, we obtain exactly the right side of (5), and so circularity holds.

If, alternatively, equality (L2) holds, the left side of (5) becomes

$$\frac{\sum_{i=1}^{n} p_{i(t+1)}q_{it}}{\sum_{i=1}^{n} p_{it}q_{it}} = \frac{\sum_{i=1}^{n} \mu_{(t+1)t} \cdot p_{it}q_{it}}{\sum_{i=1}^{n} p_{it}q_{it}} = \frac{\mu_{(t+1)t} \cdot \sum_{i=1}^{n} p_{it}q_{it}}{\sum_{i=1}^{n} p_{it}q_{it}} = \mu_{(t+1)t},$$

and applying the same transformations to the right side of (5), we obtain the same result and, as a consequence, both sides of (5) are equal to $\mu_{(t+1)t}$ and circularity holds.

Comments

1. The two equalities of Proposition 1 are similar. (L1) states that all quantities in period t must be in the same proportion as their period 0 values, i.e., $\frac{q_{it}}{q_{i0}} = \gamma_{t0}, i = 1, \ldots, n$. (L2) states that all prices in period $t + 1$ must be in the same proportion as their period t values, i.e., $\frac{p_{it+1}}{p_{it}} = \mu_{(t+1)t}, i = 1, \ldots, n$. Moreover, the proportionality factor, $\mu_{(t+1)t} = \frac{p_{it+1}}{p_{it}}, i = 1, \ldots, n$, satisfies $\mu_{(t+1)t} = L(t, t + 1)$, as the proof of (L2) shows.
2. The sufficient condition is demanding, requiring either equal quantity mixes in periods 0 and t or equal price mixes in periods t and $t + 1$. Thus, the probability that a data set comprising three consecutive time periods satisfies circularity is low but cannot be discarded.
3. If preferences or technology is of Leontief form and if agents are price-taking cost minimizers, then (L1) is satisfied and a Laspeyres price index is circular and is a Konüs (1924) "true" cost-of-living index with no substitution bias.[5]

2.2 The Sufficient Condition Is Also Necessary

We begin by reviewing the $n = 2$ case. Since it is unrealistic, we continue by reviewing the $n \geq 2$ case. Our aim is to prove that the sufficient condition is also necessary. Moreover, we will also establish that (L1) and (L2) are exhaustive, in the sense that there is no possibility of finding any other condition that is necessary for achieving circularity.

Proposition 2 Let us assume that the Laspeyres price index for $n = 2$ is circular. Then at least one of the two equations in the sufficient condition in Proposition 1 is necessary.

Comment In other words, for $n = 2$, the Laspeyres price index is circular if, and only if, condition (L1) holds or, alternatively, condition (L2) holds. There is no other necessary and sufficient condition that guarantees circularity, with the only exception being the juxtaposition of both conditions (L1) and (L2).

Proof According to (5), Laspeyres circularity is achieved if

$$\frac{\sum_{i=1}^{2} p_{i(t+1)}q_{it}}{\sum_{i=1}^{2} p_{it}q_{it}} = \frac{\sum_{i=1}^{2} p_{i(t+1)}q_{i0}}{\sum_{i=1}^{2} p_{it}q_{i0}},$$

or, equivalently, if

$$\left(\sum_{i=1}^{2} p_{i(t+1)}q_{it}\right) \cdot \left(\sum_{i=1}^{2} p_{it}q_{i0}\right) = \left(\sum_{i=1}^{2} p_{i(t+1)}q_{i0}\right) \cdot \left(\sum_{i=1}^{2} p_{it}q_{it}\right).$$

The left side equals $(p_{1(t+1)}q_{1t} + p_{2(t+1)}q_{2t}) \cdot (p_{1t}q_{10} + p_{2t}q_{20})$, and the right side equals $(p_{1(t+1)}q_{10} + p_{2(t+1)}q_{20}) \cdot (p_{1t}q_{1t} + p_{2t}q_{2t})$. Each of the two products gives rise to four summands. The first one on each side and the last one on each side are equal and can be cancelled. As a consequence, the second equality can be reduced to $(p_{1(t+1)}q_{1t}p_{2t}q_{20} + p_{2(t+1)}q_{2t}p_{1t}q_{10}) = (p_{1(t+1)}q_{10}p_{2t}q_{2t} + p_{2(t+1)}q_{20}p_{1t}q_{1t})$. Grouping on the left side the first two

[5] In the index number literature, this result linking a price index with an aggregator function states that a Laspeyres price index is "exact" for a Leontief aggregator function. As Diewert (1981; 182) notes, this relationship has been known for a very long time, although it has not previously been associated with satisfaction of local circularity.

terms of both sides and on the right side the remaining second terms, we get

$$\left(p_{1(t+1)}q_{1t}p_{2t}q_{20} - p_{1(t+1)}q_{10}p_{2t}q_{2t}\right) = \left(p_{2(t+1)}q_{20}p_{1t}q_{1t} - p_{2(t+1)}q_{2t}p_{1t}q_{10}\right),$$

or, equivalently,

$$p_{1(t+1)}p_{2t}\left(q_{1t}q_{20} - q_{10}q_{2t}\right) = p_{2(t+1)}p_{1t}\left(q_{1t}q_{20} - q_{10}q_{2t}\right). \tag{6}$$

This equality holds if $(q_{1t}q_{20} - q_{10}q_{2t}) = 0$ or, equivalently, if $\frac{q_{1t}}{q_{10}} = \frac{q_{2t}}{q_{20}}$, which is exactly equality (L1) of Proposition 1. In this case, (L1) is necessary. Alternatively, if (L1) is not necessary, which means that $(q_{1t}q_{20} - q_{10}q_{2t}) \neq 0$, we can cancel this term in (6) to obtain the equality $p_{1(t+1)}p_{2t} = p_{2(t+1)}p_{1t}$ or, equivalently, $\frac{p_{1(t+1)}}{p_{1t}} = \frac{p_{2(t+1)}}{p_{2t}}$, which is exactly equality (L2) of Proposition 1. In this case, (L2) is necessary. ■.

Comment As a summary, (L1) is necessary or, if it is not, (L2) is necessary. Since there is no other possibility, the condition is not only necessary and sufficient but also exhaustive. We reiterate that this conclusion does not exclude the possibility that both equalities (L1) and (L2) hold.

Proposition 3 extends Proposition 2 to the general $n \geq 2$ case.

Proposition 3 Let us assume that for $n \geq 2$, the corresponding Laspeyres price index is circular. Then the sufficient condition in Proposition 1 is also necessary.

Proof The proof is by induction over the number of goods. The proof for $n = 2$ appears in Proposition 2. Let us assume that Proposition 3 is true for $(n - 1)$, and let us prove that it also holds for n, which completes the proof. According to (5), let us assume that the corresponding Laspeyres price index is circular, i.e.,

$$\frac{\sum_{i=1}^{n} p_{i(t+1)}q_{it}}{\sum_{i=1}^{n} p_{it}q_{it}} = \frac{\sum_{i=1}^{n} p_{i(t+1)}q_{i0}}{\sum_{i=1}^{n} p_{it}q_{i0}}.$$

We need to prove that at least one of the equalities in Proposition 1, (L1) or (L2), holds. Since we are assuming that the Laspeyres price index for $(n - 1)$ is circular, the following equality holds:

$$\frac{\sum_{i=1}^{n-1} p_{i(t+1)}q_{it}}{\sum_{i=1}^{n-1} p_{it}q_{it}} = \frac{\sum_{i=1}^{n-1} p_{i(t+1)}q_{i0}}{\sum_{i=1}^{n-1} p_{it}q_{i0}}. \tag{7}$$

Additionally, we know that, for $(n - 1)$, at least one of the two equalities is necessary, that is, either

$$q_{it} = \gamma_{t0} \cdot q_{i0},\ i = 1, \ldots, n-1,\ \gamma_{t0} > 0,$$

or

$$p_{i(t+1)} = \mu_{(t+1)t} \cdot p_{it},\ i = 1, \ldots, n-1,\ \mu_{(t+1)t} > 0.$$

What we need to prove is that, assuming that the Laspeyres price index is circular for n-items, at least one of the two equalities in Proposition 1 holds.

More precisely, assuming that (5) holds, which expresses that circularity holds for n-items, let us prove that exactly the same condition, either (L1) or (L2), which we assume is necessary for $(n - 1)$, is also necessary for n. The equality

$$\frac{\sum_{i=1}^{n} p_{i(t+1)}q_{it}}{\sum_{i=1}^{n} p_{it}q_{it}} = \frac{\sum_{i=1}^{n} p_{i(t+1)}q_{i0}}{\sum_{i=1}^{n} p_{it}q_{i0}},$$

can be rewritten by transposing the two denominators and grouping terms to obtain

$$\left(\sum_{i=1}^{n-1} p_{i(t+1)}q_{it} + p_{n(t+1)}q_{nt}\right)\left(\sum_{i=1}^{n-1} p_{it}q_{i0} + p_{nt}q_{n0}\right)$$
$$= \left(\sum_{i=1}^{n-1} p_{it}q_{it} + p_{nt}q_{nt}\right)\left(\sum_{i=1}^{n-1} p_{i(t+1)}q_{i0} + p_{n(t+1)}q_{n0}\right).$$

Eliminating the parentheses yields

$$\left(\sum_{i=1}^{n-1} p_{i(t+1)}q_{it}\sum_{i=1}^{n-1} p_{it}q_{i0} + p_{n(t+1)}q_{nt}\sum_{i=1}^{n-1} p_{it}q_{i0} + p_{nt}q_{n0}\right.$$
$$\left.\sum_{i=1}^{n-1} p_{i(t+1)}q_{it} + p_{nt}q_{n0}p_{n(t+1)}q_{nt}\right)$$
$$= \left(\sum_{i=1}^{n-1} p_{i(t+1)}q_{i0}\sum_{i=1}^{n-1} p_{it}q_{it} + p_{n(t+1)}q_{n0}\sum_{i=1}^{n-1} p_{it}q_{it} + p_{nt}q_{nt}\right.$$
$$\left.\sum_{i=1}^{n-1} p_{i(t+1)}q_{i0} + p_{nt}q_{nt}p_{n(t+1)}q_{n0}\right).$$

Since the first terms of each side are equal and the last terms of each side are also equal, we can eliminate them. Transposing the original second term of the right side to the left side and the original third term of the left side to the right side yields

$$p_{n(t+1)}q_{nt}\sum_{i=1}^{n-1} p_{it}q_{i0} - p_{n(t+1)}q_{n0}\sum_{i=1}^{n-1} p_{it}q_{it} = p_{nt}q_{nt}$$
$$\sum_{i=1}^{n-1} p_{i(t+1)}q_{i0} - p_{nt}q_{n0}\sum_{i=1}^{n-1} p_{i(t+1)}q_{it}.$$

Grouping and reordering the two sides yields

$$p_{n(t+1)}\left(\sum_{i=1}^{n-1} p_{it}\left[q_{i0}q_{nt} - q_{n0}q_{it}\right]\right) = p_{nt}\left(\sum_{i=1}^{n-} p_{i(t+1)}\left[q_{i0}q_{nt} - q_{n0}q_{it}\right]\right).$$

Moving the right side term to the left, we get finally

$$\sum_{i=1}^{n-1}\left(\left[p_{n(t+1)}p_{it} - p_{nt}p_{i(t+1)}\right]\cdot\left[q_{i0}q_{nt} - q_{n0}q_{it}\right]\right) = 0. \tag{8}$$

Expression (8) holds for the Laspeyres price index for n goods, assuming it is circular, whatever the value of the prices and quantities in each period are. This means that, initially, we can imagine situations in which some of the summands are positive and the rest negative or zero and that we have to discard the possibility that part of the summands are all positive – or all negative – and the rest zero. Let us recall that we are seeking a necessary condition that works for any kind of summand.

Let us start by assuming that equality (L1) holds for $(n-1)$ goods, and let us prove that if circularity holds for $(n-1)$ goods, as given in (7), then necessarily (L1) holds for n goods. Since our proof is by induction, we know in advance that $\frac{q_{it}}{q_{i0}} = \gamma_{t0}, i = 1, \ldots, n-1$, and, consequently, the $(n-1)$ expressions $[q_{i0}q_{nt} - q_{n0}q_{it}]$ of equality (8) can be rewritten as $q_{i0}[q_{nt} - \gamma_{t0}q_{n0}] \geq 0, i = 1, \ldots, n-1$. Hence, since $[p_{n(t+1)}p_{it} - p_{nt}p_{i(t+1)}], i = 1, \ldots, n-1$, can take any positive, negative, or zero value, the only way to guarantee that, under any circumstances, (8) holds is that $[q_{nt} - \gamma_{t0}q_{n0}] = 0$ or, equivalently, that equality (L1) holds for the entire basket of n goods.

Alternatively, let us assume that equality (L2) holds for $(n - 1)$ items, i.e., $p_{i(t+1)} = \mu_{(t+1)t} \cdot p_{it}$, $i = 1, \ldots, n - 1$, $\mu_{(t+1)t} > 0$. In this case, the $(n - 1)$ bracketed terms in (8) dealing with prices can be rewritten as $[p_{n(t+1)}p_{it} - p_{nt}p_{i(t+1)}] = = [p_{n(t+1)}p_{it} - p_{nt}\mu_{(t+1)t}p_{it}] = p_{it}[p_{n(t+1)} - \mu_{(t+1)t}p_{nt}]$, $i = 1, \ldots, n - 1$. Applying the same reasoning developed above for the quantities, the only way to guarantee that (8) holds for any set of prices is that $[p_{n(t+1)} - \mu_{(t+1)t}p_{nt}] = 0$ or, equivalently, that equality (L2) holds for n-items. Proposition 3 is proved.■

In this section, we have developed a necessary and sufficient condition, given in Proposition 1, for the Laspeyres price index to satisfy the circularity property. This condition requires either prices to vary proportionately in periods t and $t + 1$ or quantities to vary proportionately in periods 0 and t. In Sect. 3 we turn to the Paasche price index.

3 Local Circularity of the Paasche Price Index

Following exactly the same steps as in Sect. 2, we provide a characterization of the circularity property for the Paasche price index in Definition 2, and we continue by using this characterization to establish a sufficient condition for circularity to hold in Proposition 4. We then prove in Propositions 5 and 6 that this sufficient condition is also necessary.

Considering base period 0 and any subsequent periods t and $t + 1$, the Paasche price index satisfies the circularity property if $P(0, t) \cdot P(t, t + 1) = P(0, t + 1)$. Using (2), the circularity property can be expressed as

$$\frac{\sum_{i=1}^{n} p_{it}q_{it}}{\sum_{i=1}^{n} p_{i0}q_{it}} \cdot \frac{\sum_{i=1}^{n} p_{i(t+1)}q_{i(t+1)}}{\sum_{i=1}^{n} p_{it}q_{i(t+1)}} = \frac{\sum_{i=1}^{n} p_{i(t+1)}q_{i(t+1)}}{\sum_{i=1}^{n} p_{i0}q_{i(t+1)}}. \tag{9}$$

Eliminating the expression $\sum_{i=1}^{n} p_{i(t+1)}q_{i(t+1)}$ that appears in the numerator of both sides of (9) and moving the expression $\sum_{i=1}^{n} p_{it}q_{i(t+1)}$ to the right side of the equality, we obtain an alternative circularity characterization.

Definition 2 Circularity property for the Paasche price index:

$$\frac{\sum_{i=1}^{n} p_{it}q_{it}}{\sum_{i=1}^{n} p_{i0}q_{it}} = \frac{\sum_{i=1}^{n} p_{it}q_{i(t+1)}}{\sum_{i=1}^{n} p_{i0}q_{i(t+1)}}. \tag{10}$$

The only difference between the ratios on the two sides of (10) is the quantities: on the left side period t quantities weight price changes, while on the right side period $t + 1$ quantities weight price changes. Moreover, the prices involved correspond to periods 0 and t. If we compare the Paasche circularity property in (10) with the Laspeyres circularity property in (5), it is clear that, although they have a similar structure, the subindexes involved appear interchanged between prices and quantities. The Paasche price index does not satisfy this circularity property globally, but it does satisfy the circularity condition locally, as we show in Sect. 3.1.

3.1 A Sufficient Circularity Condition for the Paasche Price Index

Proposition 4 establishes a sufficient condition for the Paasche price index to satisfy circularity.

Proposition 4 The Paasche price index is circular if at least one of the following pairs of equalities holds:

(P1) $q_{i(t+1)} = \gamma_{(t+1)t} \cdot q_{it}$, $i = 1, \ldots, n$, $\gamma_{(t+1)t} > 0$, or
(P2) $p_{it} = \mu_{t0} \cdot p_{i0}$, $i = 1, \ldots, n$, $\mu_{t0} > 0$,

where $\gamma_{(t+1)t}$ and μ_{t0} are independent of i.

Proof The proof follows exactly the same steps as developed in the proof of Proposition 1 for the Laspeyres price index and is left to the reader.

Comments

1. Proposition 4 states through equality (P1) that if the quantity mixes in periods t and $t+1$ are equal or, alternatively through equality (P2), if the price mixes in periods 0 and t are equal, then the Paasche price index satisfies circularity. Let us observe that the circularity condition for Laspeyres price index introduced in Proposition 1 is similar to the circularity condition for the Paasche price index in Proposition 4, with two notable differences: the two periods – 0 and t – in which the quantity mixes must be equal for Laspeyres circularity (see (L1)) are exactly the two periods in which the price mixes must be equal for Paasche circularity (see (P2)), and the two periods – t and $t+1$ – in which the price mixes must be equal for Laspeyres circularity (see (L2)) are exactly the two periods in which the quantity mixes must be equal for Paasche circularity (see (P1)).
2. As we noted above for the Laspeyres price index, the sufficient condition for circularity of the Paasche price index is also demanding, and the probability of it being satisfied is low but positive.
3. If preferences or technology is of Leontief form and if agents are price-taking cost minimizers, then (P1) is satisfied and a Paasche price index is circular and joins the Laspeyres price index as a Konüs (1924) "true" cost-of-living index with no substitution bias.

3.2 The Sufficient Condition Is Also Necessary

Following the same strategy as above, we begin by assuming $n = 2$ and continue by assuming $n \geq 2$, with a goal of proving that the sufficient condition is also necessary. We will also establish that (P1) and (P2) are exhaustive, in the sense that it is not possible to find any other equality that is necessary for achieving circularity of the Paasche price index.

Proposition 5 Let us assume that the Paasche price index for $n = 2$ is circular. Then at least one of the two equalities in Proposition 4 is necessary.

Proof According to (10), Paasche circularity is achieved if

$$\frac{\sum_{i=1}^{n} p_{it}q_{it}}{\sum_{i=1}^{n} p_{i0}q_{it}} = \frac{\sum_{i=1}^{n} p_{it}q_{i(t+1)}}{\sum_{i=1}^{n} p_{i0}q_{i(t+1)}}.$$

Following the same steps as in Proposition 2, we end up with the following equality, which is equivalent to (10):

$$p_{10}p_{2t}\left(q_{1(t+1)}q_{2t} - q_{1t}q_{2(t+1)}\right) = p_{20}p_{1t}\left(q_{1(t+1)}q_{2t} - q_{1t}q_{2(t+1)}\right). \tag{11}$$

This equality holds trivially if $(q_{1(t+1)}q_{2t} - q_{1t}q_{2(t+1)}) = 0$ or, equivalently, if $\frac{q_{1(t+1)}}{q_{1t}} = \frac{q_{2(t+1)}}{q_{2t}}$, which is exactly equality (P1) of Proposition 4. In this case, (P1) is necessary. Otherwise, we can cancel the parenthetical expression in (11) and obtain the equality $p_{10}p_{2t} = p_{20}p_{1t}$, which can be expressed exactly as equality (P2). This proves necessity of (P2) in case (P1) does not hold. ■

Comment Summarizing, (P1) is necessary or, if it is not, (P2) is necessary. Since there is no other possibility, the condition is not only necessary and sufficient but also exhaustive. As in the Laspeyres case, this conclusion does not exclude the possibility that both equalities (P1) and (P2) hold.

Proposition 6 extends Proposition 5 to the general $n > 2$ case.

Proposition 6 Let us assume that for $n \geq 2$, the Paasche price index is circular. Then the sufficient condition in Proposition 4 is also necessary.

Proof The proof follows exactly the same steps as the proof of Proposition 3, considering the subindexes associated with the Paasche price index instead of the subindexes associated with the Laspeyres price index, and is left to the reader.

In this section, we have developed a necessary and sufficient condition for the Paasche price index to satisfy circularity. This condition is essentially the same as that for the Laspeyres price index to satisfy circularity, with time periods interchanged between prices and quantities. In Sect. 4 we will combine this condition with the analogous condition for the Laspeyres price index to satisfy circularity to develop a circularity condition for their geometric mean, the Fisher price index. However, we also show that this combined circularity condition, while sufficient, is not necessary.

4 Local Circularity of the Fisher Price Index

Let us introduce the circularity property for the Fisher price index. Considering base period 0 and any subsequent pair of periods t and $t+1$, the Fisher price index satisfies circularity if $F(0,t)\cdot F(t,t+1)=F(0,t+1)$, which, using (3), we reformulate as

$$\sqrt{L(0,t)\cdot P(0,t)}\cdot\sqrt{L(t,t+1)\cdot P(t,t+1)}=\sqrt{L(0,t+1)\cdot P(0,t+1)}.$$

Since the square root is a strictly increasing function, this equality can be reformulated and reordered as

$$[L(0,t)\cdot L(t,t+1)]\cdot[P(0,t)\cdot P(t,t+1)]=L(0,t+1)\cdot P(0,t+1)\,. \tag{12}$$

This equality can be expressed in terms of prices and quantities, by multiplying on the left side the two left side fractions of (4) with the two left side fractions of (9) and on the right side the fractions of the right sides of (4) and (9). Moreover, since (4) and (9) have been simplified in (5) and (10), we can multiply the last two equalities in an orderly fashion and get the following circularity characterization.

Definition 3 Circularity property for the Fisher price index:

$$\frac{\sum_{i=1}^{n} p_{i(t+1)}q_{it}}{\sum_{i=1}^{n} p_{it}q_{it}}\cdot\frac{\sum_{i=1}^{n} p_{it}q_{it}}{\sum_{i=1}^{n} p_{i0}q_{it}}=\frac{\sum_{i=1}^{n} p_{i(t+1)}q_{i0}}{\sum_{i=1}^{n} p_{it}q_{i0}}\cdot\frac{\sum_{i=1}^{n} p_{it}q_{i(t+1)}}{\sum_{i=1}^{n} p_{i0}q_{i(t+1)}}. \tag{13}$$

The Fisher price index does not satisfy this property globally, but as a direct consequence of (13), (5), and (10), we can enunciate the next proposition, which establishes a local circularity condition.

Proposition 7 A sufficient circularity condition for the Fisher price index:

If both the Laspeyres and the Paasche price indexes are circular, then the Fisher price index is also circular.

Proof Obvious. ∎

Comments

1. According to the circularity characterizations derived for the Laspeyres and Paasche price indexes (5) and (10), Proposition 7 can also be expressed as follows:

   "If $\frac{\sum_{i=1}^{n} p_{i(t+1)}q_{it}}{\sum_{i=1}^{n} p_{it}q_{it}}=\frac{\sum_{i=1}^{n} p_{i(t+1)}q_{i0}}{\sum_{i=1}^{n} p_{it}q_{i0}}$ and $\frac{\sum_{i=1}^{n} p_{it}q_{it}}{\sum_{i=1}^{n} p_{i0}q_{it}}=\frac{\sum_{i=1}^{n} p_{it}q_{i(t+1)}}{\sum_{i=1}^{n} p_{i0}q_{i(t+1)}}$ hold, then the Fisher price index is circular."

2. Thus, the juxtaposition of sufficient conditions associated with the Laspeyres and Paasche price indexes constitutes a sufficient condition for circularity of the Fisher price index. Since we have introduced two equalities in Proposition 1, each of which is sufficient for circularity of the Laspeyres price index, and, similarly, two equalities in Proposition 4, each of which is sufficient for circularity of the Paasche price index, we are able to combine them to obtain four pairs of equalities, each of which guarantees circularity of the Fisher price index, as the next proposition shows.
3. The Fisher price index satisfies circularity and is a Konüs "true" cost-of-living index with no substitution bias if preferences or technology is of Leontief form and agents are price-taking cost minimizers. The Fisher price index is a Konüs "true" cost-of-living index with no substitution bias under more general conditions, if preferences or technology

is homothetic quadratic, but we are unable to prove circularity in this more general setting. Note that the quadratic specfication generalizes the Leontief specification.[6]

Proposition 8 The Fisher price index is circular if any of the four pairs of circularity conditions holds:

(F1) Conditions (L1) and (P1);
(F2) Conditions (L1) and (P2);
(F3) Conditions (L2) and (P1), or
(F4) Conditions (L2) and (P2).

Comments

1. (F1) is a pair of conditions involving only quantities. (L1) states that $q_{it} = \gamma_{t0} \cdot q_{i0}, i = 1, \ldots, n, \gamma_{t0} > 0$, and (P1) states that $q_{i(t+1)} = \gamma_{(t+1)t} \cdot q_{it}, i = 1, \ldots, n, \gamma_{(t+1)t} > 0$. Therefore, (F1) can be reformulated as:
   (F1) $q_{i(t+1)} = \gamma_{(t+1)t} \cdot q_{it} = \gamma_{(t+1)t} \cdot \gamma_{t0} \cdot q_{i0}, i = 1, \ldots, n, \gamma_{t0} > 0, \gamma_{(t+1)t} > 0$, or, in words, the three quantity mixes of periods 0, *t*, and $t + 1$ must be the same. Let us observe that, in this case, $q_{i(t+1)}$ is directly related to q_{i0}. If we define a new positive constant $\gamma_{(t+1)0}$ as $\gamma_{(t+1)0} : \gamma_{(t+1)t} \cdot \gamma_{t0}$, so $\gamma_{(t+1)0}$ is precisely the proportionality factor that relates $q_{i(t+1)}$ with q_{i0}.
2. A similar situation arises with (F4), but now the pair of conditions involves only prices. Therefore, (F4) can be reformulated as follows:
   (F4) $p_{i(t+1)} = \mu_{(t+1)t} \cdot p_{it} = \mu_{(t+1)t} \cdot \mu_{t0} \cdot p_{i0}, i = 1, \ldots, n, \mu_{(t+1)t} > 0, \mu_{t0} > 0$, or, in words, the three price mixes of periods 0, *t*, and $t + 1$ must be the same. Again, the direct relationship between $p_{i(t+1)}$ and p_{i0} is given through the new proportionality factor $\mu_{(t+1)0} : \mu_{(t+1)t} \cdot \mu_{t0}$.
3. Conditions (F1) ($q_{i(t+1)} = \gamma_{(t+1)0} \cdot q_{i0}$) and (F4) ($p_{i(t+1)} = \mu_{(t+1)0} \cdot p_{i0}$) illustrate the informal definition of circularity in Sect. 1, by providing scenarios in which the rate of quantity change or the rate of price change between situations 0 and $t + 1$ can be calculated directly "... without going through the intermediate situation ..." *t*.
4. Each of the two remaining sufficient conditions for guaranteeing circularity, (F2) and (F3), requires the same quantity mix and the same price mix in the same pair of subsequent periods, either 0 and *t* or *t* and $t + 1$, respectively. More explicitly,

   (F2) requires (L1) $q_{it} = \gamma_{t0} \cdot q_{i0}, i = 1, \ldots, n, \gamma_{t0} > 0$, and
   (P2) $p_{it} = \mu_{t0} \cdot p_{i0}, i = 1, \ldots, n, \mu_{t0} > 0$, while
   (F3) requires (L2) $p_{i(t+1)} = \mu_{(t+1)t} \cdot p_{it}, i = 1, \ldots, n, \mu_{(t+1)t} > 0$, and
   (P1) $q_{i(t+1)} = \gamma_{(t+1)t} \cdot q_{it}, i = 1, \ldots, n, \gamma_{(t+1)t} > 0$.

5. Circularity condition (F2) implies constancy of expenditure shares $S_i = p_i \cdot q_i / \sum_{i=1}^{n} p_i \cdot q_i$ in periods *t* and 0, while condition (F3) implies constancy of expenditure shares in periods $t + 1$ and *t*. Constancy of expenditure shares is rationalized by Cobb-Douglas preferences or technology.
6. If preferences or technology is homothetic and if agents are price-taking cost minimizers, then (P2) drives (L1) and (F2) is satisfied, and (L2) drives (P1) and (F3) is satisfied, and in both cases the Fisher price index is circular.

The Sufficient Circularity Condition Is Not Necessary
The sufficient condition of Proposition 8 is not necessary, since it may happen that the Fisher price index is circular but neither of its Laspeyres and Paasche components is circular, as the following counterexample shows.

A Numerical Counterexample
To simplify things, we will assume $n = 2$, since if the sufficient condition for circularity is not necessary for $n = 2$, it is not necessary for $n \geq 2$. We are going to assign numerical values to prices and quantities in periods 0, *t*, and $t + 1$ as follows:

$$p_{10} = 90, p_{20} = 109; p_{1t} = 100, p_{2t} = 100; p_{1(t+1)} = 200, p_{2(t+1)} = 120.$$

$$q_{10} = 40, q_{20} = 100; q_{1t} = 100, q_{2t} = 200; q_{1(t+1)} = 180, q_{2(t+1)} = 200.$$

Since the three price vectors are not proportional and the three quantity vectors are not proportional, the necessary conditions for the Laspeyres and Paasche price indexes are not satisfied, which means, according to Propositions 3 and 6, that neither price index is circular. However, we are going to show that the circularity property for the Fisher price index (13) does hold.

[6]Diewert (1981; 184) notes that this result, apart from circularity, is also very old.

The value of the left side of (13) is

$$\frac{\sum_{i=1}^{2} p_{i(t+1)}q_{it}}{\sum_{i=1}^{2} p_{it}q_{it}} \cdot \frac{\sum_{i=1}^{2} p_{it}q_{it}}{\sum_{i=1}^{2} p_{i0}q_{it}} = \frac{(200 \cdot 100 + 120 \cdot 200)}{(100 \cdot 100 + 100 \cdot 200)} \cdot \frac{(100 \cdot 100 + 100 \cdot 200)}{(90 \cdot 100 + 109 \cdot 200)}$$

$$= \frac{44 \cdot 300}{30 \cdot 308} = \frac{10}{7},$$

and the value of the right side of (13) is

$$\frac{\sum_{i=1}^{n} p_{i(t+1)}q_{i0}}{\sum_{i=1}^{n} p_{it}q_{i0}} \cdot \frac{\sum_{i=1}^{n} p_{it}q_{i(t+1)}}{\sum_{i=1}^{n} p_{i0}q_{i(t+1)}} = \frac{(200 \cdot 40 + 120 \cdot 100)}{(100 \cdot 40 + 100 \cdot 100)} \cdot \frac{(100 \cdot 180 + 100 \cdot 200)}{(90 \cdot 180 + 109 \cdot 200)}$$

$$= \frac{20 \cdot 380}{14 \cdot 380} = \frac{10}{7}.$$

Since the two fractions are equal, the Fisher price index is circular, even though neither Laspeyres nor Paasche component is circular, as claimed.

Comment As a consequence of the above counterexample, the juxtaposition of any pair of necessary conditions for circularity of the Laspeyres and Paasche price indexes does not constitute a necessary condition for circularity of the Fisher price index.

5 Local Circularity of the Geometric Laspeyres, Geometric Paasche, and Törnqvist Price Indexes

We noted in the introduction that the US Bureau of Labor Statistics (BLS) has modified its consumer price indexes (CPIs) by introducing a geometric version of the Laspeyres formula to calculate lower-level price indexes accounting for approximately 61% of consumer spending. The objective has been to incorporate consumer substitution among commodities within categories, thereby reducing the upward bias of the Laspeyres formula, which assumes no substitution. BLS calculates that this change has reduced annual increases in its CPIs by between 0.2% and 0.3% points. The BLS has also introduced a Törnqvist formula to calculate upper-level price indexes that allow for even more flexible substitution possibilities among categories. This provides ample motivation for examining the circularity properties of the Törnqvist price index and its two components, the geometric Laspeyres and the geometric Paasche.[7]

We now introduce three additional price indexes, the geometric Laspeyres price index

$$\mathrm{GL}\,(0,t) = \prod\nolimits_{i=1}^{n} \left(\frac{p_{it}}{p_{i0}}\right)^{S_{i0}}, \tag{14}$$

the geometric Paasche price index

$$\mathrm{GP}\,(0,t) = \prod\nolimits_{i=1}^{n} \left(\frac{p_{it}}{p_{i0}}\right)^{S_{it}}, \tag{15}$$

and the geometric mean of the two, the price index introduced by Finnish statistician Leo Törnqvist (1936)[8]

[7]Greenlees (2006) and Rippy (2014) provide historical, institutional, and theoretical background. Johnson et al. (2006) provide empirical evidence on the reduction in the substitution bias.

[8]As a reviewer has reminded us, Balk (2008; 26) notes that the Törnqvist index was introduced not by Törnqvist (1936) but by Törnqvist and Törnqvist (1937).

$$T(0,t) = \sqrt{GL(0,t) \cdot GP(0,t)} = \prod_{i=1}^{n} \left(\frac{p_{it}}{p_{i0}}\right)^{1/2(S_{i0}+S_{it})}, \tag{16}$$

in which expenditure shares $S_{ir} = p_{ir} \cdot q_{ir} / \sum_{i=1}^{n} p_{ir} \bullet q_{ir}$, $r = 0, t$. The only disadvantage of the Törnqvist price index over its two component price indexes is that it requires knowledge of quantity data as well as price data from both periods. The introduction of expenditure shares adds a new dimension to the analysis of circularity.

For the geometric Laspeyres price index in (14), circularity is achieved when the following equality holds: $\prod_{i=1}^{n} \left(\frac{p_{it}}{p_{i0}}\right)^{S_{i0}} \cdot \prod_{i=1}^{n} \left(\frac{p_{i(t+1)}}{p_{it}}\right)^{S_{it}} = \prod_{i=1}^{n} \left(\frac{p_{i(t+1)}}{p_{i0}}\right)^{S_{i0}}$. Eliminating the denominators of the first and the last products and transposing the numerator of the first product, we obtain the following circularity characterization.

Definition 4 Circularity property for the geometric Laspeyres price index:

$$\prod_{i=1}^{n} \left(\frac{p_{i(t+1)}}{p_{it}}\right)^{S_{it}} = \prod_{i=1}^{n} \left(\frac{p_{i(t+1)}}{p_{it}}\right)^{S_{i0}}, \tag{17}$$

which should be compared with (5), the circularity property for the Laspeyres price index, which involves prices from the same periods t and $t+1$, but quantities rather than expenditure shares from periods 0 and t.

The only difference between the left and right sides involves expenditure shares, which leads to

Proposition 9 The geometric Laspeyres price index is circular if at least one of the following equalities holds:

(GL1) $S_{it} = \alpha_{t0} \cdot S_{i0}$, $i = 1, \ldots, n, > 0$, or
(GL2) $p_{i(t+1)} = \mu_{(t+1)t} \cdot p_{it}$, $i = 1, \ldots, n$, $\mu_{(t+1)t} > 0$,

in which α_{t0} and $\mu_{(t+1)t}$ are independent of i.

Proof

If (GL1) holds, and since $\sum S_{i0} = \sum S_{it} = 1$, the only admissible value for α_{t0} is $\alpha_{t0} = 1$, and so $S_{it} = S_{i0}$, $i = 1, \ldots, n$, and the equality holds.
If (GL2) holds, the circularity property becomes $\mu_{(t+1)t}{}^{\sum S_{it}} = \mu_{(t+1)t}{}^{\sum S_{i0}}$, and since $\sum S_{i0} = \sum S_{it} = 1$, the equality holds.

Comments

1. In contrast to (L1), which holds quantity ratios fixed and allows no substitution when price ratios change, (GL1) holds expenditure shares fixed and allows equi-proportionate substitution when price ratios change.
2. If preferences or technology has Cobb-Douglas structure and if agents are price-taking cost minimizers, (GL1) holds and the geometric Laspeyres price index is circular and is a Konüs "true" cost-of-living index with no substitution bias.
3. (GL2) is equivalent to (L2).

Curiously enough, the condition required in (L1), relating quantities from periods 0 and t, and a new condition, relating prices from the same two periods 0 and t, considered together also constitute a sufficient condition for the circularity of the geometric Laspeyres price index, as the next proposition shows.

Proposition 10 The geometric Laspeyres price index is circular if the next two equalities hold:

(GL3) $q_{it} = \gamma_{t0} \cdot q_{i0}$, $i = 1, \ldots, n$, $\gamma_{t0} > 0$, and
$p_{it} = \mu_{t0} \cdot p_{i0}$, $i = 1, \ldots, n$, $\mu_{t0} > 0$.

Proof Since $S_{it} = \frac{p_{it}q_{it}}{\sum_{i=1}^{n} p_{it}q_{it}}$, $i = 1, \ldots, n$, resorting to the first equality of (GL3), we get $S_{it} = \frac{p_{it}(\gamma_{t0} \cdot q_{i0})}{\sum_{i=1}^{n} p_{it}(\gamma_{t0} \cdot q_{i0})} = \frac{p_{it}q_{i0}}{\sum_{i=1}^{n} p_{it}q_{i0}}$, $i = 1, \ldots, n$. Introducing the second equality of (GL3) in the last fraction, we obtain $S_{it} = \frac{p_{it}q_{i0}}{\sum_{i=1}^{n} p_{it}q_{i0}} = \frac{(\mu_{t0} \cdot p_{i0})q_{i0}}{\sum_{i=1}^{n} (\mu_{t0} \cdot p_{i0})q_{i0}} = \frac{p_{i0}q_{i0}}{\sum_{i=1}^{n} p_{i0}q_{i0}} = S_{i0}$, $i = 1, \ldots, n$, which means that (GL1) is satisfied and, consequently, thanks to Proposition 9, circularity holds. ■

Comment (GL3) is more demanding than (GL1).

Unfortunately, none of the three considered conditions is necessary, as shown by means of the next

Counterexample 1 The easiest counterexample that can be built corresponds to $n = 2$, recalling that if sufficiency is not necessary for $n = 2$, it is not necessary for $n \geq 2$. Since the geometric Laspeyres price index is circular, it satisfies equality (17). In this particular case, we need to know the values of $p_{1(t+1)}$, $p_{2(t+1)}$; p_{1t}, p_{2t}, for checking (GL2), as well as the values of S_{1t}, S_{2t}, and S_{10}, S_{20}, for checking (GL1). Let us start with (GL1). Since $S_{it} = \frac{p_{it}q_{it}}{\sum_{i=1}^{2} p_{it}q_{it}}$, $i = 1, 2$, we consider the next values: $p_{1t} = 20$, $q_{1t} = 200$; $p_{2t} = 20$, $q_{2t} = 300$. Consequently, we get $S_{1t} = \frac{4000}{10000} = \frac{2}{5}$, which means that $S_{2t} = 1 - S_{1t} = \frac{3}{5}$. Similarly, since $S_{i0} = \frac{p_{i0}q_{i0}}{\sum_{i=1}^{n} p_{i0}q_{i0}}$, $i = 1, 2$, we define $p_{10} = 10$, $q_{10} = 150$; $p_{20} = 12$, $q_{20} = 250$, getting $S_{10} = \frac{1500}{4500} = \frac{1}{3}$, and $S_{20} = 1 - S_{10} = \frac{2}{3}$. Since there is no proportionality between the vectors $(S_{10}, S_{20}) = \left(\frac{1}{3}, \frac{2}{3}\right)$ and $(S_{1t}, S_{2t}) = \left(\frac{2}{5}, \frac{3}{5}\right)$, (GL1) fails. Moreover, introducing the values $p_{1(t+1)} = 30$, $p_{2(t+1)} = 12$, we find also that the price vectors $(p_{1t}, p_{2t}) = (20, 20)$ and $(30, 12)$ are not proportional, which means that (GL2) fails. Finally, (GL3) fails also because it implies (GL1).

For the geometric Paasche price index in (15), circularity is achieved if the following equality holds: $\prod_{i=1}^{n}\left(\frac{p_{it}}{p_{i0}}\right)^{S_{it}} \cdot \prod_{i=1}^{n}\left(\frac{p_{i(t+1)}}{p_{it}}\right)^{S_{i(t+1)}} = \prod_{i=1}^{n}\left(\frac{p_{i(t+1)}}{p_{i0}}\right)^{S_{it}}$. Eliminating the denominators of the first and the last products and transposing the numerator of the first product, we obtain the following circularity characterization.

Definition 5 Circularity property for the geometric Paasche price index:

$$\prod_{i=1}^{n}\left(\frac{p_{i(t+1)}}{p_{it}}\right)^{S_{i(t+1)}} = \prod_{i=1}^{n}\left(\frac{p_{i(t+1)}}{p_{it}}\right)^{S_{it}}, \tag{18}$$

which should be compared with (10), the circularity property for the Paasche price index, which involves prices from the same periods 0 and t, but quantities rather than expenditure shares from periods t and $t + 1$.

The only difference between the left and right sides of (18) involves expenditure shares, which leads to

Proposition 11 The geometric Paasche price index is circular if at least one of the following conditions holds:

(GP1) $S_{i(t+1)} = \alpha_{(t+1)t} \cdot S_{it}$, $i = 1, \ldots, n, > 0$, or
(GP2) $p_{it} = \mu_{t0} \cdot p_{i0}$, $i = 1, \ldots, n, > 0$,

in which $\alpha_{(t+1)t}$ and μ_{t0} are independent of i.

Proof If condition (GP1) holds, and since $\sum S_{i(t+1)} = \sum S_{it} = 1$, the only admissible value for $\alpha_{(t+1)t}$ is $\alpha_{(t+1)t} = 1$, and so $S_{i(t+1)} = S_{it}$, i = 1, …, n, and the circularity property holds.

If condition (GP2) holds, the circularity property becomes $\mu_{t0}{}^{\sum S_{i(t+1)}} = \mu_{t0}{}^{\sum S_{it}}$, and since $\sum S_{i(t+1)} = \sum S_{it} = 1$, the circularity property holds. ■

Comments

4. If preferences or technology has Cobb-Douglas structure and if agents are price-taking cost minimizers, (GP1) holds and the geometric Paasche price index is circular and is a Konüs "true" cost-of-living index with no substitution bias.
1. (GP2) is equivalent to (P2).

Curiously enough, the condition required in (P1), relating quantities from periods t and $t + 1$, and a new condition, relating prices from the same two periods $t + 1$ and t, when considered together also constitute a sufficient condition for the circularity of the geometric Paasche index, as the next proposition shows.

Proposition 12 The geometric Paasche price index is circular if the next two equalities hold:

(GP3) $q_{i(t+1)} = \gamma_{(t+1)t} \cdot q_{it}$, $i = 1, \ldots, n$, $\gamma_{(t+1)t} > 0$, and
$p_{i(t+1)} = \mu_{(t+1)t} \cdot p_{it}$, $i = 1, \ldots, n$, $\mu_{(t+1)t} > 0$.

Proof Since $S_{i(t+1)} = \frac{p_{i(t+1)}q_{i(t+1)}}{\sum_{i=1}^{n} p_{i(t+1)}q_{i(t+1)}}$, $i = 1, \ldots, n$, resorting to the first equality of (GP3), we get $S_{it} = \frac{p_{i(t+1)}(\gamma_{(t+1)t} \cdot q_{it})}{\sum_{i=1}^{n} p_{i(t+1)}(\gamma_{(t+1)t} \cdot q_{it})} = \frac{p_{i(t+1)}q_{it}}{\sum_{i=1}^{n} p_{i(t+1)}q_{it}}$, $i = 1, \ldots, n$. Introducing the second equality of (GP3) in the last fraction, we obtain

$S_{it} = \frac{p_{i(t+1)}q_{it}}{\sum_{i=1}^{n} p_{i(t+1)}q_{it}} = \frac{\mu_{(t+1)t}\cdot p_{it}q_{it}}{\sum_{i=1}^{n} \mu_{(t+1)t}\cdot p_{it}q_{it}} = \frac{p_{it}q_{it}}{\sum_{i=1}^{n} p_{it}q_{it}} = S_{it}, i = 1, \ldots, n$, which means that (GP1) is satisfied and, consequently, thanks to Proposition 11, circularity holds. ■

Comment (GP3) is more demanding than (GP1).

Unfortunately, none of the three considered sufficient conditions is necessary, as shown by means of the next counterexample. As explained for the geometric Laspeyres price index, we only need to consider (GP1) and (GP2).

Counterexample 2 The easiest counterexample that can be built corresponds to $n = 2$. Let us consider values for prices and quantities that guarantee local circularity of the GP index, i.e., GP satisfies equality (18). In this particular case, we need to know the values of $p_{1t}, p_{2t}, p_{10}, p_{20}$ for checking (GP2), as well as the values of $S_{1(t+1)}, S_{2(t+1)}$, and S_{1t}, S_{2t}, for checking (GP1). Let us start with (GP1). Since $S_{i(t+1)} = \frac{p_{i(t+1)}q_{i(t+1)}}{\sum_{i=1}^{n} p_{i(t+1)}q_{i(t+1)}}, i = 1, 2$, we consider the next values: $p_{1(t+1)} = 30$, $q_{1(t+1)} = 300$; $p_{2(t+1)} = 20$, $q_{2(t+1)} = 600$. Consequently, $S_{1(t+1)} = \frac{9000}{21000} = \frac{3}{7}$, which means that $S_{2(t+1)} = 1 - S_{1(t+1)} = \frac{4}{7}$. Similarly, since $S_{it} = \frac{p_{it}q_{it}}{\sum_{i=1}^{2} p_{it}q_{it}}, i = 1, 2$, we define $p_{1t} = 20, q_{1t} = 200; p_{2t} = 20, q_{2t} = 300$, yielding $S_{1t} = \frac{4000}{10000} = \frac{2}{5}$, and $S_{2t} = 1 - S_{1t} = \frac{3}{5}$. Since there is no proportionality between the vectors $(S_{1t}, S_{2t}) = \left(\frac{2}{5}, \frac{3}{5}\right)$ and $\left(S_{1(t+1)}, S_{2(t+1)}\right) = \left(\frac{3}{7}, \frac{4}{7}\right)$, (GL1) fails. Moreover, introducing the values $p_{10} = 10, p_{20} = 12$ we find also that the vectors $(p_{1t}, p_{2t}) = (20, 20)$ and $(10, 12)$ are not proportional, which means that (GP2) fails.

Definition 6 Circularity property for the Törnqvist price index:

$$\prod\left(\frac{p_{i(t+1)}}{p_{it}}\right)^{S_{it}} \cdots \prod\left(\frac{p_{it}}{p_{i0}}\right)^{S_{it}} = \prod\left(\frac{p_{i(t+1)}}{p_{it}}\right)^{S_{i0}} \cdots \prod\left(\frac{p_{it}}{p_{io}}\right)^{S_{i(t+1)}}. \tag{19}$$

Proposition 13 If both the geometric Laspeyres and the geometric Paasche price indexes are circular, then the Törnqvist price index is also circular.

Proof Obvious. ■

Next, because GL has three circularity conditions, and GP has three circularity conditions, it follows that Törnqvist has nine circularity conditions.

Proposition 14 The Törnqvist price index is circular if any of the nine pairs of circularity conditions hold:

(T1) Conditions (GL1) and (GP1)
(T2) Conditions (GL1) and (GP2)
(T3) Conditions (GL1) and (GP3)
(T4) Conditions (GL2) and (GP1)
(T5) Conditions (GL2) and (GP2)
(T6) Conditions (GL2) and (GP3)
(T7) Conditions (GL3) and (GP1)
(T8) Conditions (GL3) and (GP2)
(T9) Conditions (GL3) and (GP3)

Comments

1. (T1) and (T5) illustrate the informal definition of circularity in Sect. 1.
2. (T1) involves expenditure shares of periods 0, t, and $t + 1$. $[S_{it} = \alpha_{t0} \cdot S_{i0}, i = 1, \ldots, n, \alpha_{t0} > 0] \wedge [S_{i(t+1)} = \alpha_{(t+1)t} \cdot S_{it}, i = 1, \ldots, n, \alpha_{(t+1)t} > 0] \Rightarrow [S_{i(t+1)} = \alpha_{(t+1)0} \cdot S_{i0}]$. Since the only admissible values for α_{t0} and $\alpha_{(t+1)t}$ are $\alpha_{t0} = \alpha_{(t+1)t} = 1$, (T1) implies constant expenditure shares on $[0, t + 1]$.
3. (T2) involves expenditure shares and prices of periods 0 and t: $[S_{it} = \alpha_{t0} \cdot S_{i0}, i = 1, \ldots, n, \alpha_{t0} > 0] \wedge [\alpha_{t0} = 1] \wedge [p_{it} = \mu_{t0} \cdot p_{i0}, i = 1, \ldots, n, \mu_{t0} > 0] \Rightarrow [q_{it} = \gamma_{t0} \cdot q_{i0}, i = 1, \ldots, n, \gamma_{t0} > 0]$. Consequently, $\gamma_{t0} = \frac{\sum_{i=1}^{n} p_{it}q_{it}}{\sum_{i=1}^{n} p_{i0}q_{i0}}$.
4. (T3) involves expenditure shares of periods 0 and t and quantities of periods t and $t + 1$: $S_{it} = \alpha_{t0} \cdot S_{i0}, i = 1, \ldots, n, \alpha_{t0} > 0$, and $q_{i(t+1)} = \gamma_{t(t+1)} \cdot q_{it}, i = 1, \ldots, n, \gamma_{t(t+1)} > 0$. No further relationship can be established.

5. (T4) involves prices and expenditure shares from periods t and $t + 1$. Similar to (T2), $[p_{i(t+1)} = \mu_{(t+1)t} \cdot p_{it}, i = 1, \ldots, n, \mu_{(t+1)t} > 0] \wedge [S_{i(t+1)} = \alpha_{(t+1)t} \cdot S_{it}, i = 1, \ldots, n, \alpha_{(t+1)t} > 0] \wedge [\alpha_{(t+1)t} = 1] \Rightarrow [q_{i(t+1)} = \gamma_{t(t+1)} \cdot q_{it}, i = 1, \ldots, n, \gamma_{t(t+1)} > 0]$. Consequently, $\gamma_{t(t+1)} = \frac{\sum_{i=1}^{n} p_{i(t+1)} q_{i(t+1)}}{\sum_{i=1}^{n} p_{it} q_{it}}$.
6. (T5) involves prices of periods 0, t, and $t + 1$. $[p_{i(t+1)} = \mu_{(t+1)t} \cdot p_{it}, i = 1, \ldots, n, \mu_{(t+1)t} > 0] \wedge [p_{it} = \mu_{t0} \cdot p_{i0}, i = 1, \ldots, n, \mu_{t0} > 0] \Rightarrow p_{i(t+1)} = \mu_{(t+1)0} \cdot p_{i0}$, where $\mu_{(t+1)0} = \mu_{(t+1)t} \cdot \mu_{t0} > 0$. Hence, (T5) implies constant price mixes on $[0, t + 1]$.
7. (T6) involves prices of periods t and $t + 1$ as well as quantities of the same two periods. No further relationship can be established.
8. (T7) involves quantities and prices of periods 0 and t as well as expenditure shares of periods t and $t + 1$: $q_{it} = \gamma_{t0} \cdot q_{i0}, i = 1, \ldots, n, \gamma_{t0} > 0, p_{it} = \mu_{t0} \cdot p_{i0}, i = 1, \ldots, n, \mu_{t0} > 0$ and $S_{i(t+1)} = \alpha_{(t+1)t} \cdot S_{it}, i = 1, \ldots, n, \alpha_{(t+1)t} > 0$. As a consequence, $S_{it} = \frac{p_{it} q_{it}}{\sum_{i=1}^{2} p_{it} q_{it}} = \frac{p_{it} \mu_{t0} q_{i0}}{\sum_{i=1}^{2} p_{it} \mu_{t0} q_{i0}} = \frac{\gamma_{t0} p_{i0} q_{i0}}{\sum_{i=1}^{2} \gamma_{t0} p_{i0} q_{i0}} = S_{i0}, \forall i$, which means that the expenditure shares must be constant on $[0, t + 1]$.
9. (T8) involves quantities and prices of periods t and $t + 1$, establishing constant quantity and price mixes for them.
10. (T9) involves quantities and prices from periods 0, t, and $t + 1$, establishing constant quantity and price mixes for them.
11. The comment that follows Proposition 9 together with the comment that follows Proposition 11 shows that (T5) of Proposition 14 is coincident with (F4) of Proposition 8, which gives rise to the next joint sufficient condition.

Proposition 15 The conditions (L2) and (P2) are sufficient for guaranteeing the circularity of both the Fisher and the Törnqvist price indexes.

The Sufficient Condition Is Not Necessary
The sufficient condition in Proposition 14 is not necessary, as the following numerical counterexample shows.

Counterexample 3 Based on Counterexamples 1 and 2, it is easy to derive a new one just by gathering all the values for prices and quantities considered there. Just as a reminder, we provide here again the proposed data for a basket of just two items:

$p_{10} = 10, q_{10} = 150; p_{20} = 12, q_{20} = 250, p_{1t} = 20, q_{1t} = 200; p_{2t} = 20, q_{2t} = 300$, and $p_{1(t+1)} = 30, q_{1(t+1)} = 300; p_{2(t+1)} = 20, q_{2(t+1)} = 600$. These data, as shown in the two mentioned counterexamples, guarantee that any of the sufficient expressions for the geometric Laspeyres and the geometric Paasche do not hold. Hence, any juxtaposition of them will not hold either. Therefore, Proposition 14 establishes nine different sufficient conditions that guarantee that the Törnqvist index satisfies circularity that, unfortunately, are not necessary.

6 Conclusions

In Sect. 2 we have developed a sufficient circularity condition for the Laspeyres price index that requires either the same quantity mix in periods 0 and t or, alternatively, the same price mix in periods t and $t + 1$. We further have proved necessity as well as exhaustiveness of this condition: the only possible necessary and sufficient condition for achieving circularity of the Laspeyres price index is the one we have developed. Unsurprisingly, in Sect. 3 we have also been able to discover an economically similar necessary and sufficient condition that guarantees circularity of the Paasche price index. This condition requires either the same quantity mix in periods t and $t + 1$ or, alternatively, the same price mix in periods 0 and t.

In Sect. 4 we have analyzed circularity of the Fisher price index. We have been able to develop only a sufficient condition, in Proposition 7, that is based directly on the definition of the Fisher price index as the square root of the product of Laspeyres and Paasche price indexes. However, this sufficient condition is not necessary, as we have shown through a numerical counterexample in which the Fisher price index is circular, but neither of its components is circular. In Proposition 8, we have expressed the sufficient condition as a set of four pairs of equalities obtained from the sufficient conditions for its Laspeyres and Paasche components. Since none of these pairs of equalities is necessary, as shown in the same counterexample, there is room for extending this research trying to find a necessary and sufficient condition for circularity of the Fisher price index.

In Sect. 5 we have briefly analyzed circularity of the Törnqvist price index and its geometric Laspeyres and geometric Paasche components. Our findings differ only in details from our findings in Sects. 2, 3, and 4, involving either prices and expenditure shares or quantities and expenditure shares. In a departure from the Laspeyres and Paasche price indexes in Sects. 2 and 3, sufficient conditions for circularity are not necessary for the geometric Laspeyres and geometric Paasche price indexes. Consistent with the Fisher price index in Sect. 4, sufficient conditions for circularity are not necessary for the Törnqvist price index. Additionally, our final proposition identifies a joint sufficient condition that guarantees circularity of both the Fisher price index and the Törnqvist price index. As with the Fisher price index, our inability to prove necessity of any set of sufficient conditions opens up the possibility of extending this research by seeking necessary and sufficient conditions for circularity of the Törnqvist price index and its two component indexes.

We conclude on an empirical note. As we have observed, the circularity conditions for any of the six price indexes we have considered are demanding and are unlikely to be satisfied over extended time periods. To paraphrase Fisher, this prompts an investigation into an *imperfect* satisfaction of circularity. Many writers, most notably Balk (1998), have identified conditions under which empirical index numbers provide "reasonable approximations" to their theoretical counterparts. Brea et al. (2011) have considered a variation on this theme by testing empirically the ability of an empirical Fisher price index and a theoretical Malmquist quantity index to provide a reasonable approximation to satisfaction of the product test. Using US agricultural data, they found the approximation to be quite reasonable; they were unable to reject the hypothesis that the product test is satisfied for revenue change or for cost change, but they were (barely) able to reject the hypothesis that the product test is satisfied for profitability change. Subsequently, Grifell-Tatjé and Lovell (2016) analyzed the ability of theoretical Malmquist quantity indexes and empirical Fisher price indexes and also of empirical Fisher quantity indexes and theoretical Konüs price indexes, to satisfy the product test with revenue change, cost change, and profitability change. They found the product test gaps to depend on the magnitudes of the relevant allocative inefficiencies. We believe a worthwhile extension of our current research would be to test empirically some of our propositions, Propositions 8 and 14 in particular. Proposition 8 (F1) and Proposition 14 (T1) state sufficient conditions for Fisher and Törnqvist price indexes to satisfy circularity. These conditions are demanding, as we have noted, requiring constant quantity mixes or constant expenditure shares on $[0, t + 1]$, respectively. However, we believe it is worth investigating whether approximate satisfaction of these conditions would generate approximate circularity, and reduced chain drift, of the respective price indexes. This would be particularly informative in interspatial comparisons.

Acknowledgment The authors are grateful to an extremely perceptive reviewer, whose comments on our original submission contributed to substantial improvements in the revision.

The authors are also grateful to the financial support from the Spanish Ministry for Economy and Competitiveness (*Ministerio de Economía, Industria y Competitividad*), the State Research Agency (*Agencia Estatal de Investigacion*), and the European Regional Development Fund (*Fondo Europeo de Desarrollo Regional*) under grant MTM2016-79765-P (AEI/FEDER, UE).

References

Balk, B. (1998). *Industrial price, quantity and productivity indices*. Dordrecht: Kluwer Academic Publishers.

Balk, B. (2008). *Price and quantity index numbers*. Cambridge: Cambridge University Press.

Balk, B., & Althin, R. (1996). A new, transitive productivity index. *Journal of Productivity Analysis, 7*, 19–27.

Brea, H., Grifell-Tatjé, E., & Lovell, C. A. K. (2011). Testing the product test. *Economics Letters, 113*, 157–159.

Diewert, W. E. (1981). Chapter 7: The economic theory of index numbers: A survey. In A. Deaton (Ed.), *Essays in the theory and measurement of consumer behaviour in honour of Sir Richard Stone*. Cambridge: Cambridge University Press.

Diewert, W. E. (2004). Chapter 16: The axiomatic and stochastic approaches to index number theory. In *Consumer price index manual: Theory and practice*. Geneva: International Labour Office.

Eichhorn, W., & Voeller, J. (1976). *Theory of the price index*. Heidelberg: Springer.

Fisher, I. (1922). *The making of index numbers: A study of their varieties, tests, and reliability*. Boston: Houghton Mifflin.

Funke, H. G., Hacker, G., & Voeller, J. (1979). Fisher's circular test reconsidered. *Schweizerische Zeitschrift für Volkswirtschaft und Statistik, 115*, 677–687.

Greenlees, J. S. (2006). The BLS response to the Boskin Commission Report. *International Productivity Monitor, 12*, 23–41.

Grifell-Tatjé, E., & Lovell, C. A. K. (2016). Chapter 5: Exact relationships between fisher indexes and theoretical indexes. In J. Aparicio, C. A. K. Lovell, & J. T. Pastor (Eds.), *Advances in efficiency and productivity* (Springer International Series in Operations Research & Management Science) (Vol. 249). Cham, Switzerland: Springer Nature.

Johnson, D. S., Reed, S. B., & Stewart, K. J. (2006, May 10). Price measurement in the United States: a decade after the Boskin report. *Monthly Labor Review*.

Konüs, A. A. (1924). The problem of the true index of the cost of living. *Econometrica, 7*, 10–29. (1939 translation).

Laspeyres, E. (1871). Die Berechnung einer Mittleren Waarenpreissteigerung. *Jahrbücher für Nationalökonomie und Statistik, 16*, 296–314.

Paasche, H. (1874). Ueber die Preisentwicklung der Letzten Jahre nach den Hamburger Börsennotierungen. *Jahrbücher für Nationalökonomie und Statistik, 23*, 168–178.
Rippy, D. (2014, April). The first hundred years of the consumer price index: a methodological and political history. *Monthly Labor Review*, pp. 1–45. https://doi.org/10.21916/mlr.2014.13.
Törnqvist, L. (1936). The Bank of Finland's consumption price index. *Bank of Finland Monthly Bulletin, 16* 27–34.
Törnqvist, L., & Törnqvist, E. (1937). Vilket är Förhållandet Mellan Finska Markens och Svenska Kronans Köpkraft? *Ekonomiska Samfudets Tidskrift, 39*, 1–39.

Robust DEA Efficiency Scores: A Heuristic for the Combinatorial/Probabilistic Approach

Juan Aparicio and Juan F. Monge

Abstract In this paper, we present a comparison of robust efficiency scores for the scenario in which the specification of the inputs/outputs to be included in the data envelopment analysis (DEA) model is modeled with a probability distribution, through the traditional cross-efficiency evaluation procedure. We evaluate the ranking obtained from these scores and analyze the robustness of these rankings, in such a way that any changes respect the set of units selected for the analysis. The probabilistic approach allows us to obtain two different robust efficiency scores: the unconditional expected score and the expected score under the assumption of maximum entropy principle. The calculation of these efficiency scores involves the resolution of an exponential number of linear problems. We also present an algorithm to estimate the robust scores in an affordable computational time.

Keywords Data envelopment analysis · Model specification · Efficiency measurement · Robustness

1 Introduction

Data envelopment analysis (DEA) was introduced by Charnes et al. (1978) as a methodology for measuring the efficiency of productive units. DEA provides an efficiency score for each unit under evaluation; this is done by a weighted sum of the inputs and outputs involved in the production process. The selection of the inputs and outputs to be included in the DEA model will determine the technological frontier of the units to be compared, which shows the great importance that the selection of inputs and outputs has in the DEA models.

In many cases, the experience provided by experts is the only tool available for the correct selection of inputs/outputs in a DEA model. However, very often, there are variables for which the expert does not have a firm criterion of inclusion or exclusion in the DEA model; see Pastor et al. (2002). The situation in which the variables that should be included in the DEA model and that would determine the technological frontier are not available in a reliable way is a very relevant research field in DEA. Some works have been carried out with the objective of analyzing and discussing which variables are the most appropriate to consider for inclusion in the DEA model and therefore used for the comparison of the productive units; see, for example, Banker (1993, 1996), Sirvent et al. (2005), Edirisinghe and Zhang (2010), Natajara and Johnson (2011), Wagner and Shimshak (2007), Jenkins and Anderson (2003), Eskelinen (2017), and Luo et al. (2012).

A different methodology to those presented in the works mentioned above is presented in the work (Landete et al. 2017). In this work, the authors define robust scores in the sense that not all variables have the same importance or probability of selection. The importance of a variable (input/output) is determined by the weight (probability of inclusion in the DEA model) provided by a panel of experts. The natural extension that the authors (Landete et al. 2017) propose to the case in which the preferences of the experts are not known is the calculation of the scores assuming some distribution on the

The authors thank the financial support from the Spanish Ministry for Economy and Competitiveness (Ministerio de Economía, Industria y Competitividad), the State Research Agency (Agencia Estatal de Investigación), and the European Regional Development Fund (Fondo Europeo de Desarrollo Regional) under grant MTM2016-79765-P (AEI/FEDER, UE).

J. Aparicio (✉) · J. F. Monge
Center of Operations Research, Miguel Hernández University, Elche (Alicante), Spain
e-mail: j.aparicio@umh.es; monge@umh.es

J. Aparicio et al. (eds.), *Advances in Efficiency and Productivity II*, International Series in Operations Research & Management Science 287, https://doi.org/10.1007/978-3-030-41618-8_8

probabilities of inclusion in the DEA model or assuming the principle of maximum entropy as a measure of uncertainty. The following sections will address in detail what these so-called robust scores consist of.

Although DEA provides a classification of the productive units according to their efficiency score, the selection of the optimal weights for each unit so that its score is as beneficial as possible means that the comparison between units cannot be carried out according to just the score obtained through DEA. With the aim of comparing the productive units and their subsequent ranking, in the seminal work (Sexton et al. 1986) and later (Doyle and Green 1994), the term cross-efficiency is introduced. Cross-efficiency is a pairwise comparison, in which each productive unit is evaluated not only with the weights that are favorable in the DEA model but with the weights of the other units. To calculate a unit score, the weights of all the units are used, which allows a comparison of the units, since all of them end up being evaluated with the same weights.

The methodology proposes the average of the scores obtained when evaluated with the weights of all units as an efficiency score for a unit. The importance of the cross-efficiency score lies in the obtention of homogeneous scores, all units evaluated with the same weights, which allows the comparison of the units and the determination of an efficiency ranking between the units.

In the following sections, the main concepts in data envelopment analysis, the cross-efficiency of units and robust scores, will be presented, proposing the use of the latter as a measure of comparison between units in cases in which cross-efficiency is not considered as a valid methodology.

Finally, a process for estimating robust scores is presented for the case in which these scores cannot be solved computationally.

2 DEA and Cross-Efficiency Evaluation

Cross-efficiency has been widely developed for the Charnes, Cooper, and Rhodes model (CCR) (Charnes et al. 1978) in its two variants, input orientation and output orientation. Consider that you want to evaluate a set of n DMUs that use a set of m inputs in their production processes to produce s outputs. The set of inputs and outputs can be represented by vectors (X_j, Y_j), $j = 1, \cdots, n$ where X is the matrix $m \times n$ of inputs and Y the matrix $s \times n$ of outputs. If we consider the output orientation in the DEA CCR model, the efficiency of a DMU_0 is the optimal value of the following problem:

$$\begin{aligned} \min \quad & \phi_0 = \frac{v'X_0}{u'Y_0} \\ \text{s.t.} \quad & \frac{v'X_j}{u'Y_j} \geq 1 \qquad j = 1, \dots, n \\ & v \geq 0_m, u \geq 0_s \end{aligned} \tag{1}$$

Problem (1) is the CCR model in its fractional version, a problem that can be solved by optimizing the following linear problem:

$$\begin{aligned} \min \quad & v'X_0 \\ \text{s.t.} \quad & u'Y_0 = 1 \\ & -v'X_j + u'Y_j \leq 0 \qquad j = 1, \dots, n \\ & v \geq 0_m, u \geq 0_s \end{aligned} \tag{2}$$

The solutions obtained by solving the problem (2) are used in the cross- evaluation of the DMU units. Formally, if $(v_1^k, v_2^k, \cdots, v_m^k, u_1^k, u_2^k, \cdots, v_s^k)$ is the optimal solution of the problem (2) for the unit k, DMU_k, the efficiency of the unit j, DMU_j, with the weights of unit k is:

$$E_{kj} = \frac{v^k Y_j}{u^k X_j}$$

In this way, the cross efficiency of the DMU_j is defined as the average of the efficiencies obtained using the weights of the other units, i.e.,

$$\overline{E}_j = \frac{1}{n}\sum_{k=1}^{n} E_{kj}, \qquad \forall j = 1, \cdots, n.$$

The cross-efficiency score provides a peer evaluation of each DMU_j, and these values are commonly used to establish a ranking among the units evaluated. The theoretical framework in the cross-evaluation of units in DEA has been restricted to DEA models with constant returns to scale (CRS). The use of the cross-efficiency methodology in the evaluation of units under variable returns to scale (VRS) presents several drawbacks, for example, the possible occurrence of negative scores for some units.

Lim and Zhu (2015) present a methodology for estimating cross-efficiency scores in VRS models. By translating the variables of the model and changing the origin of coordinates, they achieve cross-evaluation of the units in variable returns to scale models.

Model (2) under variable returns to scale is:

$$\begin{aligned} \min \quad & v'X_0 + \psi \\ \text{s.t.} \quad & u'Y_j = 1 \\ & -v'X_j + u'Y_j - \psi \geq 0 \qquad j = 1, \ldots, n \\ & v \geq 0_m, u \geq 0_s \\ & \psi \text{ free in sign} \end{aligned} \tag{3}$$

The authors (Lim and Zhu 2015) propose the evaluation of unit j with the weights of unit k for the calculation of cross-efficiency through the expression:

$$E_{kj} = \frac{v^k Y_j}{u^k X_j + \psi}.$$

A problem that is widely treated in cross-evaluation is the existence of optimal alternatives (weights) in models (2) and (3). The presence of alternatives implies that the evaluation of a unit j with the weights of unit k will depend to a large extent on the optimal solution selected for unit k, among the possible alternatives.

There is a multitude of procedures in the literature for the selection of weights among the different optimal alternatives. Practically all ways for selecting the weights to be used in the cross-evaluation can be classified into two approaches, the benevolent approach (selection of the most favorable weights for the unit evaluated) and the aggressive approach (selection of the most unfavorable weights for the unit evaluated). Some references in cross-evaluation are Ruiz (2013), Lim and Zhu (2015), Ramon et al. (2010, 2011), and Ruiz and Sirvent (2012).

In Ruiz (2013), the author proposes a model for the determination of the most favorable weights (benevolent case) among the alternative weights of unit k. The adaptation of the model for the case of variable returns to scale is as follows:

$$\begin{aligned} \min \quad & \sum_{j=1}^{n} \alpha_j^k \\ \text{s.t.} \quad & u^{k'} Y_k = 1 \\ \text{s.t.} \quad & v^{k'} X_k + \psi = \phi_k \\ & -v^{k'} X_j + \phi_j u^{k'} Y_j - \psi + \alpha_j^k = 0 \qquad j = 1, \ldots, n \\ & v^k \geq 0_m, u^k \geq 0_s \\ & \alpha_j^k \geq 0, \forall j \\ & \epsilon \text{ free in sign} \end{aligned} \tag{4}$$

Model (4) considers all the optimal solutions of model (3) for unit k. The decision variables α_j^k represent the cross-efficiency deviations E_{kj} with respect to the efficiency score ϕ_j.

The model presented in Ruiz (2013), and the extension (4) presented here in the case of variable returns to scale, allows the determination of the most favorable weights for each unit among the optimal alternatives that may exist.

The determination of unique weights under an aggressive approach would require maximization in the objective function of the problem (4), but unfortunately, this change results in cases in which cross-efficiency is not bounded, that is, the problem (max (4)) may have no optimal solution.

3 Robust *Scores*

Robust scores were introduced in Landete et al. (2017) as an efficiency measure that allows each variable to be associated with a certain selection probability in the DEA model. The methodology assumes that each variable (input/output) has an associated inclusion probability in the DEA model; if we denote the set of variables considered by $\mathcal{C} = \{z_1, z_2, \cdots, z_q\}$, and assume that the probability that the variable z_c selected in the DEA model is p_c, then the expected efficiency score is defined as:

$$E_p(\Phi) = \sum_{b \in \{0,1\}^q} \left(\prod_{c=1}^{q} p_c^{b_c} (1 - p_c)^{(1-b_c)} \right) \phi_o^b,$$

where $b = (b_1, \cdots, b_q)$ represents the vector of Bernoulli random variables, where each b_c variable takes the value 1 if the variable z_c is selected in the DEA model, and ϕ_o^b the DEA efficiency score with the specified variables by the realization of vector b.

In order to obtain the robust efficiency score $E_p(\Phi)$, it is necessary to have the probability vector p_c, a vector that in our opinion ought to be provided by a panel of experts, who will indicate which variables are suitable for inclusion in the DEA model and the probability or weight of those variables. If information on the selection probabilities of the variables in the DEA model is not available, we can assume some probability distribution associated with those probabilities. In this context, the authors in Landete et al. (2017) presented two robust scores: the maximum entropy score and the unconditional score.

3.1 *The Maximum Entropy Score*

The entropy score follows the principle of maximum entropy enunciated by Shannon (1948). In the context of the calculation of probabilities, entropy is the measure of information provided by p, where high entropy values correspond to greater uncertainty or less information, i.e., the principle of maximum entropy is used in statistics to obtain the values of the uncertain parameters that less information presuppose on the parameters. In this context, if we do not have information from a panel of experts on the inclusion probabilities of each variable in the DEA model, and following the statistical principle of maximum entropy, the score that that makes less assumptions about these probabilities is that which is obtained considering that the selection probabilities of the variables are all equal and equal to 1/2. In this case, the maximum entropy score is given by the expression:

$$E^e(\Phi) = \frac{1}{2^q} \sum_{b \in \{0,1\}^q} \phi_o^b. \tag{5}$$

The maximum entropy score is the result of calculating the average of all scores obtained using the DEA model for all possible specifications given the set of variables $\mathcal{C}$. Note that the number of possible specifications is an exponential number, exactly 2^q, where q is the cardinality of set $\mathcal{C}$.

3.2 *The Unconditional* Score

A different approach to the principle of maximum entropy is that the uncertain parameter assumes a known probability distribution, in our case the selection probability of each variable. Under the assumption that the selection probabilities are unknown, we can obtain the unconditional score assuming the uniform distribution in the interval (0,1) for the probabilities p_c. In this case, the efficiency score coincides with the maximum entropy score.

A similar approach is to assume that the selection probabilities for each of the variables are equal, although unknown. In this context of equality in the selection probability of the variables and assuming a uniform distribution in the interval (0, 1), the unconditional score would be given by the expression:

$$E_{\overline{u}}(\Phi) = \frac{1}{q+1} \sum_{b \in \{0,1\}^q} \frac{1}{\binom{q}{\sum_c b_c}} \phi_o^b, \tag{6}$$

or alternatively by

$$E_{\overline{u}}(\Phi) = \frac{1}{q+1} \sum_{i=0}^{q} \left(\sum_{b \in \{0,1\}^q : \sum_c b_c = i} \frac{1}{\binom{q}{i}} \phi_o^b \right). \tag{7}$$

The unconditional score $E_{\overline{u}}(\Phi)$ can be seen as weighted average of the efficiency scores for all possible specifications. See in the article by Landete et al. (2017) the definition of robust scores, as well as an example of application and the interpretation of each of them in the DEA context.

4 Estimation of Robust Scores

In this section, a method of estimating robust scores is proposed. Given the large number of problems that must be solved for calculating robust, entropy, and unconditional scores, there needs to be some sort of methodology to facilitate their calculation.

The calculation of robust scores implies the resolution of the DEA model for each unit under evaluation and for each configuration/selection of variables (inputs/outputs). In total, the number of problems to be solved is of the order $n \cdot 2^q$.

The proposal made in this work is the resolution for each unit of a subset of the 2^q possible configurations of variables (inputs and outputs). It is proposed not to solve a DEA model for each possible configuration but for a representative sample of the possibility set. A priori, the most appropriate seems to consider a simple random sampling without replacement in the set of possible configurations $\{0, 1\}^q$, although we will see later that stratified sampling provides better results when the aim is to estimate the unconditional score.

4.1 *Simple Random Sampling (SRS)*

Simple random sampling (SRS) is the easiest random sampling and the one that serves as a reference for the rest of statistical sampling. SRS consists of enumerating the units of the population and randomly selecting a subset of these units.

For the estimation of the entropy score and the unconditional score, the study population consists of all the possible specifications of the DEA model, i.e., all possible configurations (inputs/outputs) given the set of variables $\mathcal{C} = \{z_1, z_2, \cdots, z_q\}$. The total number of configurations is 2^q, which corresponds to the number of subsets that can be extracted from set $\mathcal{C}$.

Once the sample size m has been determined, and the m configurations randomly selected from the total configurations, the entropy score estimator (5) will be given by means of the sample average of the scores obtained for each subset of inputs/outputs, that is:

$$\hat{E}^e(\Phi) = \frac{1}{m}\sum_{l=1}^{m}\phi_0^{b^l}, \tag{8}$$

where b^l represents the subset of inputs/outputs considered in the $l-th$ sample extraction of the power set of $\mathcal{C}$, $\mathcal{P}(\mathcal{C})$, and $\phi_o^{b^l}$ the efficiency score obtained through the DEA model with the variables defined by the configuration given by b^l.

For the estimation of the unconditional score after performing a simple random sampling, the estimator would be the weighted sample mean of the scores obtained for each subset of inputs/outputs, that is:

$$\hat{E}_{\overline{u}}(\Phi) = \frac{1}{q+1}\sum_{l=1}^{m}\frac{1}{\binom{q}{\sum_c b_c^l}}\phi_o^{b^l}. \tag{9}$$

4.2 *Stratified Sampling (SS)*

In stratified sampling, a population is first divided into subpopulations called strata, and within each stratum, an independent sampling is performed. If we observe the expression (7) of the unconditional score calculation, we can see that the unconditional score is the arithmetic mean of the scores obtained for the configurations (inputs/outputs) of equal cardinality, i.e., we can consider all the configurations of variables with the same number of variables as a stratum, take a sample from said stratum, and then calculate the unconditional score estimator as the average of the estimated scores in each of the strata.

The unconditional score estimator will be given by the expression:

$$\hat{E}_{\overline{u}}(\Phi) = \frac{1}{q+1}\sum_{l=0}^{q}\left(\sum_{l=1}^{m_q}\frac{1}{m_q}\phi_o^{b^l}\right), \tag{10}$$

where m_q is the sample size in each stratum.

5 Comparison of Rankings: Kendall tau Distance

The ordering of elements is a problem that has been present in many fields of science for centuries, for example, in economics, it is sought to order consumer preferences, in computer science, it is sought to order the tasks to be executed on a computer, or, much more recently, web search engines sort the results of a search based on certain user preferences and companies that offer their services. Although the fields of application of linear ordering are very wide, they all must have a distance function that allows us to measure, for example, how close two orderings or rankings of elements are. Among the different distance measurements that can be considered, the Kendall tau distance is commonly used for comparing rankings.

Given two permutations, orderings or rankings, π_1 and π_2 of n elements, the Kendall tau distance between these permutations is defined as the number of pairwise disagreements between both permutations. The following definition formally presents the Kendall tau distance.

Definition 1 The Kendall tau distance between two permutations π_1 and π_2 is given by:

$$d(\pi_1, \pi_2) = |\{(i,j) : i < j, ((\pi_1(i) < \pi_1(j) \wedge \pi_2(i) > \pi_2(j)) \\ \vee ((\pi_1(i) > \pi_1(j) \wedge \pi_2(i) < \pi_2(j))))\}|$$

where, $\pi_1(i)$ and $\pi_2(i)$ are the positions of element i in π_1 and π_2 respectively.

The Kendall tau distance is a metric in the set of permutations of n elements. The greater the Kendall tau distance between two permutations, the more different they are. For example, in the ordering of three elements, the distance from permutation 123 to permutations 132, 231, and 321 is 1, 2, and 3, respectively. The greatest distance between two permutations of n elements is $n(n-1)/2$ and corresponds to the distance between a permutation and the same in reverse order. This upper bound in distance between the permutations allows to normalize the Kendall tau distance as the number of disagreements between the two permutations with respect to the maximum possible number, i.e.,

$$\frac{d(\pi_1, \pi_2)}{n(n-1)/2}.$$

6 PISA: Case of Application

The Organization for Economic Cooperation and Development (OECD) is a common forum in which member countries work together sharing experiences and seeking solutions to common problems. Within the multitude of activities developed by the (OECD), the *Programme for International Student Assessment* (PISA) is a triennial report whose objective is to evaluate the education systems of OECD member countries.

The report is prepared by measuring the attitudes and knowledge of 15-year-old students. To make the report (PISA), a sample of schools in each country is selected, and within each selected school, a sample of students is chosen. The report measures the abilities of students in reading, mathematics, and science and also collects different types of indicators, about the school as well as the students themselves.

For the evaluation of the techniques proposed in the previous sections and in order to compare the different scores presented in this work, the data from the PISA report for the year 2012 have been selected. The variables considered for the DEA analysis are as follows:

Outputs

PVMATH: average score of the students of each school in mathematics skills.
PVREAD: average score of the students of each school in reading skills.
PVSCIE: average score of the students of each school in science skills.

Inputs

SCMATEDU: index of quality of schools, educational resources.
ESCS: average socioeconomic status by school.
PRFAL100: number of teachers per 100 pupils.
SCHAUTON: index of school autonomy, ongoing variable provided by PISA 2012 at a school level.
RESPRES2: continuous index. Measures the degree of responsibility in hiring teachers, setting salaries, formulating school budgets, etc.
RATCOMP: index measuring the availability of computers.
DISCLIMA: index that measures the student's work environment, high values indicate a better disciplinary climate.
STUDCLIM: index related to the student, high values indicate a positive behavior of the student.
TEACCLIM: index related to the teacher, high values indicate positive teacher behavior.
SCMATBUI2: index of the quality of the schools, physical infrastructure, high values indicate a better quality infrastructure.

6.1 Robust Scores vs Cross-Efficiency

This section aims to analyze and compare robust scores (entropy and unconditional) against cross-efficiency. In order to make the comparison, the sample of 13,494 schools of the PISA report for the year 2012 was taken, considering as variables those presented in the previous section.

Table 1 shows the number of problems and the time required to obtain each of the different calculated scores, radial score, entropy score, unconditional score, and cross-efficiency. We can observe that obtaining entropy scores and unconditional scores requires a very high computational time, 64 h, given the large number of problems that must be solved. In this application, for each of the 13,494 units evaluated (schools), $2^{13} = 8192$, different problems must be resolved, one for each possible subset of variables, resulting in a total of more than 110 million problems.

Table 1 Total computational time and number of problems to solve, for each approach

	Time	N_{prob}
Φ^R : Radial scores	2 min 3 s	13,494
$\overline{E}$: Cross-efficiency scores	2 h 32 min 42 s	26,988
$E^e(\Phi)$: Entropy scores	64 h 19 min 28 s	110,542,848
$E_{\overline{u}}(\Phi)$: Unconditional scores	64 h 19 min 28 s	110,542,848

Table 2 Linear correlation between different scores

	ϕ^R	$\overline{E}$	$E^e(\Phi)$	$E_{\overline{u}}(\Phi)$
ϕ^R: Radial scores	1	0.439	0.872	0.903
$\overline{E}$: Cross-efficiency scores	0.439	1	0.390	0.397
$E^e(\Phi)$: Entropy scores	0.872	0.390	1	0.997
$E_{\overline{u}}(\Phi)$: Unconditional scores	0.903	0.397	0.997	1

Table 3 Kendall-tau distance between different rankings

	ϕ^R	$\overline{E}$	$E^e(\Phi)$	$E_{\overline{u}}(\Phi)$
ϕ^R: Radial scores	0	28.88%	16.04%	13.85%
$\overline{E}$: Cross-efficiency scores	28.88%	0	32.57%	31.98%
$E^e(\Phi)$: Entropy scores	16.04%	32.57%	0	2.29%
$E_{\overline{u}}(\Phi)$: Unconditional scores	13.85%	31.98%	2.29%	0

Note also that although the number of problems to be solved for the calculation of cross- efficiency, 26,988 problems in total, half of them for the calculation of the radial efficiency score and the other half for the weights to be used in the calculation of cross-efficiency, the computational time is very high. This is because the problems to be solved for the calculation of the weights, using the benevolent model (4), are not as straightforward as the radial efficiency problems, using the VRS model (3).

Once the scores are obtained, we can measure the relationship between them. Table 2 shows the linear correlation between the different scores for the 13,494 units evaluated. We can observe that the correlation between the cross-efficiency of the units evaluated and their radial efficiency is low, 0.439, while there is a much greater relationship between radial efficiency and the robust scores 0.872 and 0.903.

The first result that we can obtain is that robust scores provide efficiency measures with a high relation to radial efficiency for each DMU. Using these robust scores to make a ranking of the units evaluated would allow us to obtain a ranking of units with a high correlation with the original radial efficiencies of each unit. Also, noteworthy is the high degree of linear correlation between the entropy score and the unconditional score, presenting a close correlation 1, exactly 0.997. Next we will see that both scores provide rankings of very close units.

In addition to comparing efficiency scores, it is interesting to compare the rankings that these scores provide. Table 3 shows the Kendall tau normalized distances $(d(\pi_1, \pi_2)/n(n-1)/2)\%$ between the rankings resulting from ordering the units by means of their scores.

The first result that we can highlight is that the distance between the ranking created from the radial scores and the cross-efficiency is 28.88%, which indicates that the ranking provided by the cross-efficiency has a dissimilarity close to 29% with respect to the ordering of the units through their radial efficiency score. The entropy and unconditional scores provide rankings closer to the ordering of the units through their radial efficiency, with normalized distances of 16.04% and 13.85%, respectively.

The other relevant conclusion is that the rankings provided by cross-efficiency and robust scores differ by approximately 32%, the latter being very close to each other, only differing by 2.29%.

Figure 1 shows the distribution of radial, entropy, and unconditional scores for the units evaluated. The representation of cross-efficiencies appears in Fig. 2; since the scores are significantly higher, the representation has been carried out separately.

Figures 3 and 4 show the box diagrams for the different scores. We can see how cross-efficiency provides efficiency values far higher than the rest of the scores. A graph similar to the box diagrams are Figs. 5 and 6, where the densities associated with each of the box diagrams are observed.

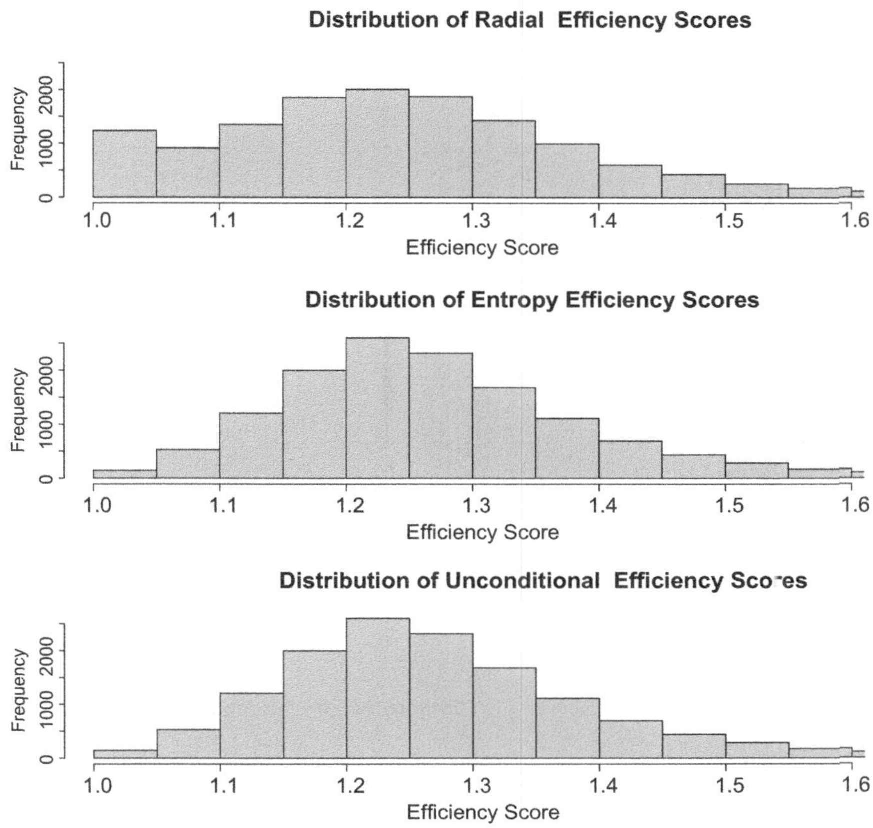

Fig. 1 Distribution of efficiency scores: radial, entropy, and unconditional scores

Fig. 2 Distribution of the cross-efficiency scores

6.2 Robustness Analysis

This section presents an analysis on the robustness of the scores obtained in the previous section. Basically, the robust scores provide an efficiency score that takes into account all the subsets of possible variables in the DEA model, meaning that each unit is evaluated with all variables, not just with the more favorable variables (inputs/outputs). In this sense, the score

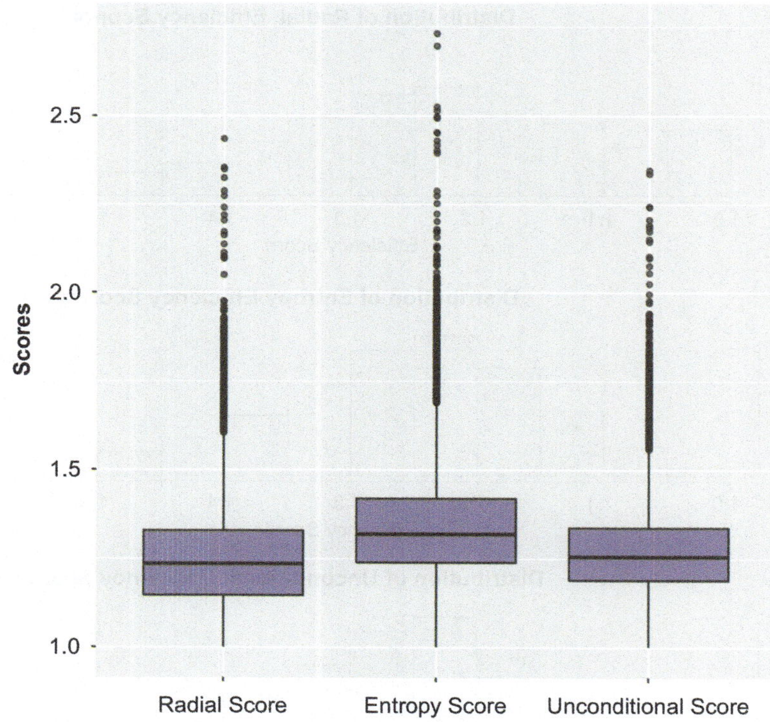

Fig. 3 Distribution of efficiency scores: radial, entropy, and unconditional scores

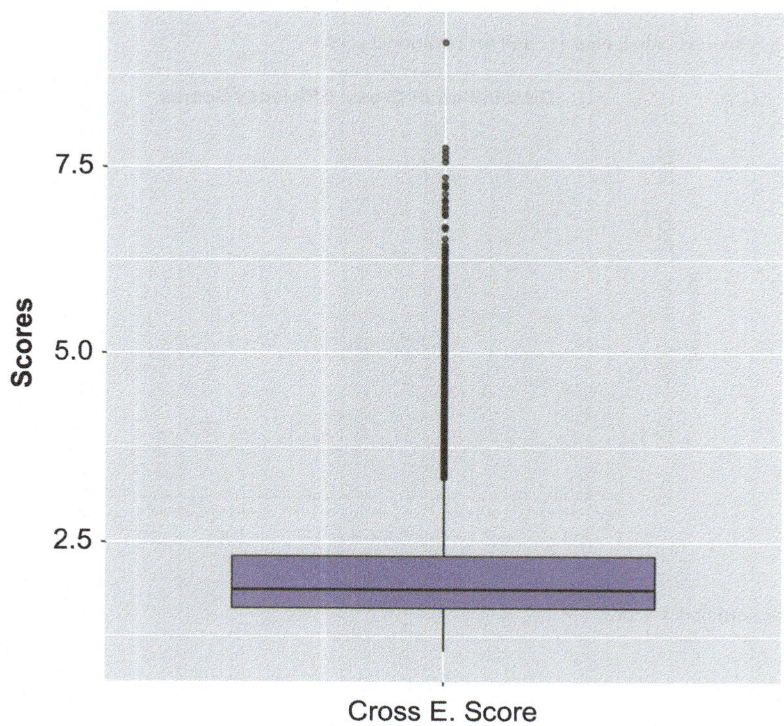

Fig. 4 Distribution of the cross-efficiency scores

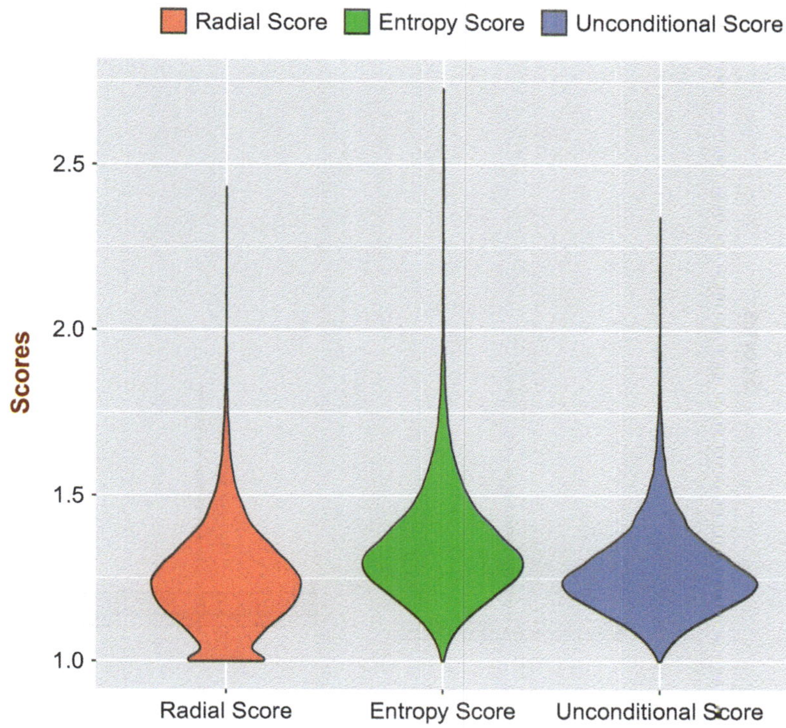

Fig. 5 Distribution of efficiency scores: radial, entropy, and unconditional scores

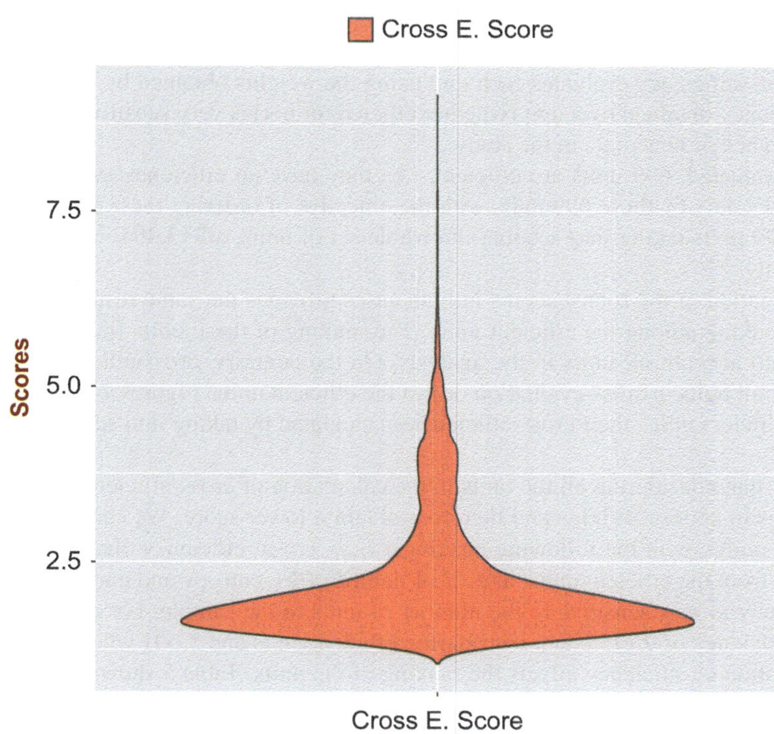

Fig. 6 Distribution of the cross-efficiency scores

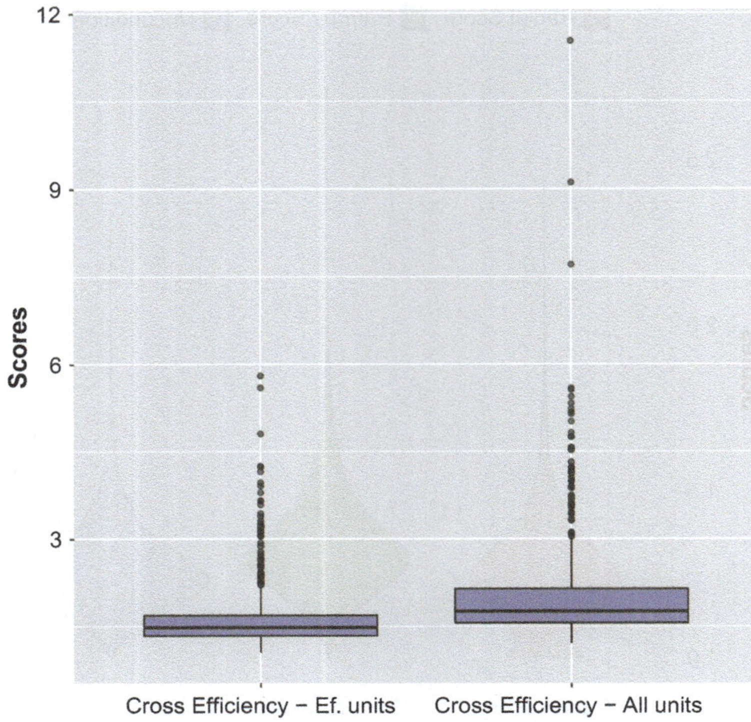

Fig. 7 Distribution of cross-efficiency *scores* for the efficient units

obtained by a unit only depends on its presence in the set of efficient units, i.e., the inclusion of new non-efficient units in the sample does not alter the robust score obtained by an efficient unit.

On the other hand, cross-efficiency evaluates each unit using the weights obtained by the rest of the units in the study. In this sense, the cross-efficiency obtained by a unit (whether efficient or not) is very sensitive to the composition of the sample of units and to the appearance of new units in the study.

Of the 13,494 units evaluated, 699 units are efficient, i.e., they have an efficiency score equal to 1. If we consider the sample of schools formed solely by these 699 units with the objective of ordering these efficient units, we could proceed in two ways. Order these 699 units taking into account the whole set of units, all 13,494, or, order the efficient 699 units and take them into account only.

The result of the calculation of the robust scores in both cases provides the same results, i.e., the same efficiency scores and therefore the same ranking among the efficient units. The ranking of these units (the relative position among them) is not affected by taking into account all units in the analysis. On the contrary, cross-efficiency changes considerably when taking into account either all units in cross-evaluation or just the efficient units. Figures 7 and 8 compare the cross-efficiency distributions of the 699 efficient units, their cross-efficiencies calculated by taking into account either all the units or just the efficient ones.

The first conclusion is that considering all the units in the calculation of cross-efficiency tends to temper the score. Each unit has more possibilities to choose weights and therefore obtain a lower score. We can see this result in Table 4 (20 first units of the 699 efficient units), with the following headings: $\overline{E}_{all}$, cross- efficiency obtained from the 13,494 units; $\overline{E}_{eff}$, cross-efficiency obtained from the efficient units; and $E^{e}(\Phi)$ and $E_{\overline{u}}(\Phi)$, entropy and unconditional scores, respectively. We can see that cross-efficiency is very sensitive to the number of units in the sample. For example, the efficient unit listed in third place has a cross-efficiency of 9.115 when considering efficient units and 5.601 when considering all the units.

To see how the calculation of efficiency affects the ranking of the units, Table 5 shows the order occupied by each of the 20 units reported, depending on the ranking considered. Thus, for example, unit 16 occupies position 101 of the 699 efficient ones when its cross-efficiency is calculated with all units, while it occupies position 464 when compared only to efficient units.

Finally, we can compare the scores and orders of the 699 efficient units. Tables 6 and 7 collect the correlations between the scores and the distances between the orders that induce these scores.

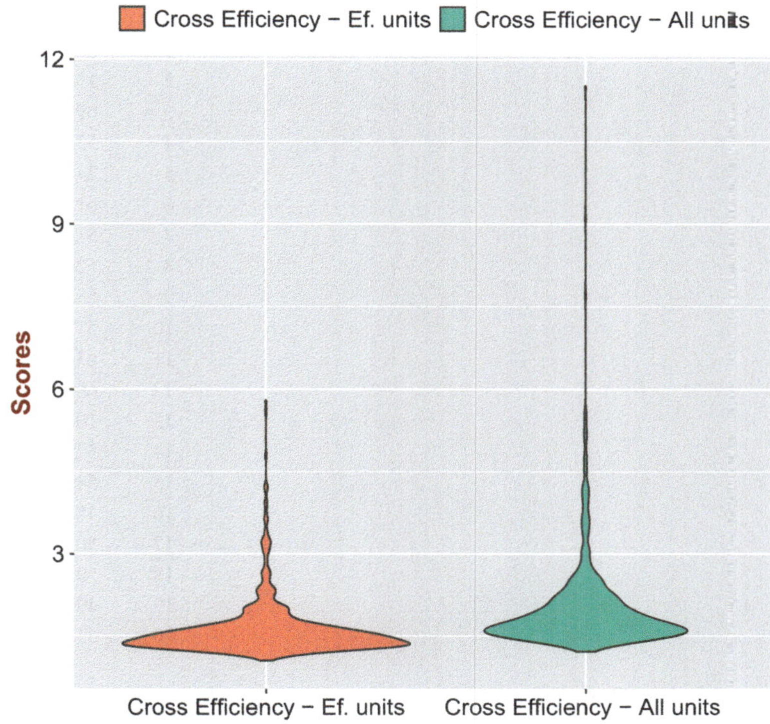

Fig. 8 Distribution of cross-efficiency *scores* for the efficient unitts

Table 4 *Scores* for the first 20 efficient unit orders

	$\overline{E}_{eff}$	$\overline{E}_{all}$	$E^{e}(\Phi)$	$E_{\overline{u}}(\Phi)$
1	2.404	2.374	1.742	1.521
2	1.535	1.486	1.338	1.252
3	9.115	5.601	1.473	1.324
4	2.156	1.999	1.379	1.275
5	1.646	1.472	1.287	1.205
6	2.536	2.272	1.597	1.407
7	2.133	1.826	1.482	1.34
8	2.149	1.693	1.321	1.228
9	2.241	1.403	1.064	1.047
10	2.307	1.502	1.071	1.051
11	2.722	1.713	1.102	1.071
12	4.573	2.267	1.238	1.167
13	1.507	1.186	1.035	1.029
14	2.167	1.384	1.094	1.067
15	2.216	1.377	1.004	1.004
16	1.966	1.299	1.048	1.038
17	2.087	1.52	1.099	1.072
18	2.482	1.423	1.012	1.011
19	2.074	1.57	1.139	1.104
20	2.79	1.671	1.107	1.075

The obvious conclusion is that cross-efficiency provides scores and orders that vary strongly depending on the set of units selected, even if efficient units are maintained, as is the case described.

Table 5 different orders for the first 20 efficient units

	$\overline{E}_{eff}$	$\overline{E}_{all}$	$E^e(\Phi)$	$E_{\overline{u}}(\Phi)$
1	590	655	697	697
2	133	345	616	625
3	698	698	669	666
4	526	612	637	641
5	249	331	569	564
6	611	646	688	688
7	518	577	675	674
8	524	523	598	593
9	552	249	98	96
10	571	365	113	111
11	630	535	181	166
12	685	645	493	464
13	104	17	41	43
14	529	220	167	156
15	541	213	3	4
16	464	101	65	71
17	502	383	176	169
18	597	267	13	13
19	497	434	259	262
20	637	513	189	176

Table 6 Correlation between *scores* for the efficient units

	$\overline{E}_{all}$	$\overline{E}_{eff}$	$E^e(\Phi)$	$E_{\overline{u}}(\Phi)$
$\overline{E}_{all}$: *cross-efficiency scores* (all units)	1	0.910	0.072	0.047
$\overline{E}_{eff}$: *cross-efficiency scores* (eff units)	0.910	1	0.264	0.246
$E^e(\Phi)$: Entropy *scores*	0.072	0.264	1	0.998
$E_{\overline{u}}(\Phi)$: Unconditional scores	0.047	0.246	0.998	1

Table 7 Kendall tau distance between different orders for the efficient units

	$\overline{E}_{all}$	$\overline{E}_{eff}$	$E^e(\Phi)$	$E_{\overline{u}}(\Phi)$
$\overline{E}_{all}$: *cross-efficiency scores* (all units)	0	19.02%	45.30%	46.64%
$\overline{E}_{eff}$: *cross-efficiency scores* (eff units)	19.02%	0	30.60%	31.41%
$E^e(\Phi)$: Entropy *scores*	45.30%	30.60%	0	2.09%
$E_{\overline{u}}(\Phi)$: Unconditional *scores*	46.64%	31.41%	2.09%	0

Table 8 Estimation of the Entropy Score

	Coef	R^2	min diff	max diff	Diff media	$d(\pi_1, \pi_2)$	$d(\pi_1, \pi_2)/n(n-1)/2$
SRS	0.9544	0.9965	0.00001	0.5886	0.0104	13612381	14.95
SS	0.9607	0.9966	0.00014	0.5659	0.0091	13690658	15.03

6.3 Estimation of the Entropy Score

In the previous sections, results have been presented that suggest that robust scores can be a good tool for ordering units. The main disadvantage in the use of robust scores is the large number of problems to be solved and the computational time required. This section presents the results obtained by estimating robust, entropy, and unconditional scores, through statistical sampling.

Table 8 shows the comparison of the entropy score of each unit evaluated with respect to the entropy score obtained by random sampling and stratified sampling. The headings of the table are the following: Coeff, coefficient of the linear regression between the entropy score and its estimation; R^2, coefficient of determination of linear regression; $min\ diff$ and $max\ diff$, least and greatest difference between the entropy score and its estimation for all units; $Avge.\ Diff.$, average of the differences between the scores and the estimations; and $d(\pi_1, \pi_2)$ y $d(\pi_1, \pi_2)/n(n-1)/2$, Kendall tau distance between the ranking induced by the entropy scores and the ranking induced by its estimation.

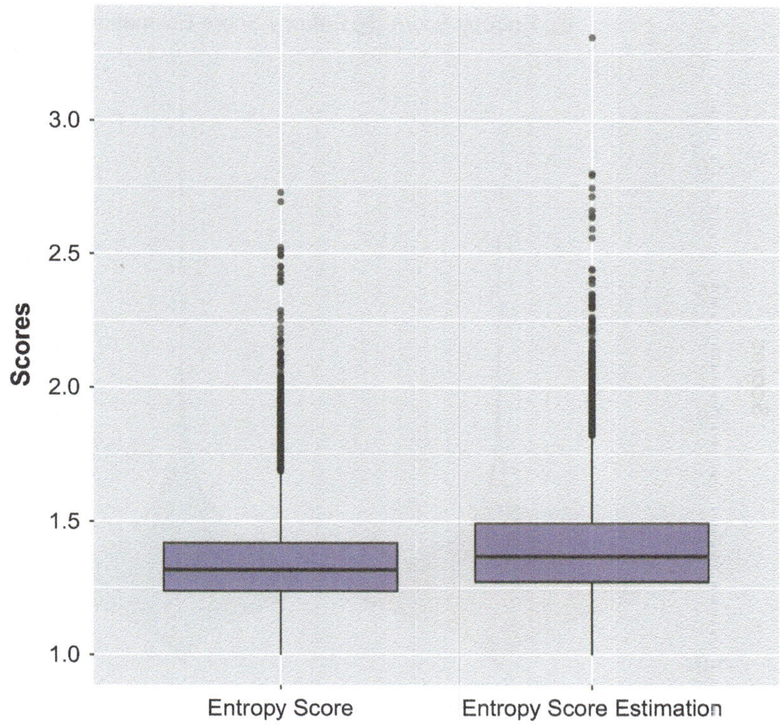

Fig. 9 Distribution for the entropy scores and their estimation

Both types of sampling have provided very close results, being very similar. In view of the results in Table 9, we cannot conclude that stratified sampling supposes a significant advantage over simple random sampling; therefore and due to the simplicity of simple random sampling, we can conclude that this sampling is the most appropriate for the estimation of entropy scores.

Note that the entropy score is the average of the scores for all possible configurations in the selection of variables, so simple random sampling seems the most appropriate method for its estimation.

Figures 9 and 10 show the distributions and densities of the entropy scores and their estimation for the set of units evaluated. We can observe that the distribution of entropy scores and the distribution of their estimates differ slightly. Estimations tend to overestimate the actual entropy score for each unit. The coefficient of linear regression took a value slightly below 1.

6.4 Estimation of the Unconditional Score

For the estimation of unconditional score, a simple random sampling and stratified sampling have also been considered. Table 9 shows the results obtained, where the headers are the same as in Table 8.

The first conclusion we reach is that stratified sampling improves random sampling when the parameter of interest is the unconditional score. We can see how the regression coefficient is closer to the unit, although both samples provide a good fit, with R2 values very close to 1. The other advantage that can be seen in the table is that the differences between the actual values and the estimated values are smaller when stratified sampling is used, the maximum difference being 0.4906, compared to 0.7880 in the SRS.

The difference between the rankings provided by both estimates with respect to the ranking provided by the true unconditional scores hardly shows any differences.

Figures 11 and 12 present the distribution and density of the unconditional scores and their estimations for the set of units evaluated. As in the case of the entropy score, the estimations slightly overestimate the true values, although in this case, it seems that the observed differences are smaller.

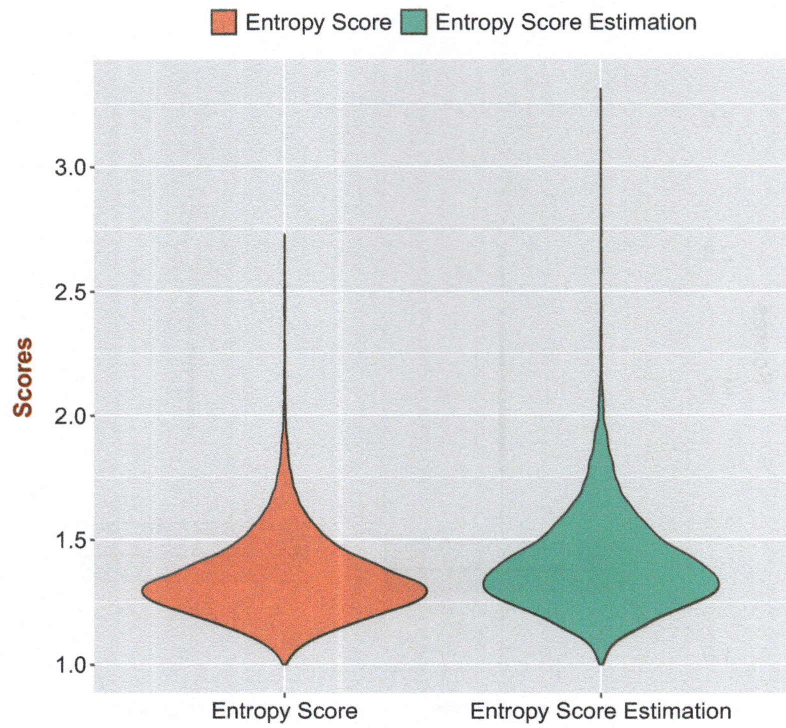

Fig. 10 Distribution for the entropy scores and their estimation

Table 9 Estimation of the unconditional score

	Coef	R^2	min diff	max diff	Diff media	$d(\pi_1, \pi_2)$	$d(\pi_1, \pi_2)/n(n-1)/2$
SRS	0.9232	0.9956	0.00002	0.7880	0.0185	15818481	17.37
SS	0.9617	0.9964	0.00001	0.4906	0.0084	16059723	17.64

6.5 *Comparison of Efficiency Scores*

In this section, the various efficiency scores are calculated, the radial score, the cross-efficiency, the entropy score, and the unconditional score, and the estimations of entropy and unconditional scores will be compared.

Table 10 shows the number of problems and the time needed to obtain each of the different scores.

We can observe that obtaining entropy scores and unconditional scores requires a very high computational time, given the large number of problems that must be solved.

In this application, for each of the 13,496 units evaluated, 213 different problems must be solved, one for each subset of variables, resulting in a total of more than 110 million problems. The estimation of these scores only requires the resolution of approximately 1.3 million problems and 100 subsets of variables (sample size of 100) for each of the 13,496 units. Although the computational time is still high for the calculation of estimates, this time is due to the large number of units to be evaluated.

7 Conclusions

In this work, we have seen how we can use robust scores for the ordering of units and the establishment of a ranking. We have also observed that the ranking provided by the robust scores provides an order closer to the order provided by the radial scores of each unit.

Cross-efficiency is the tool that is usually used in DEA for the comparison of units, since all units are evaluated with the same weights. In the case of a large number of units and variables, such as the application example, cross-efficiency provides

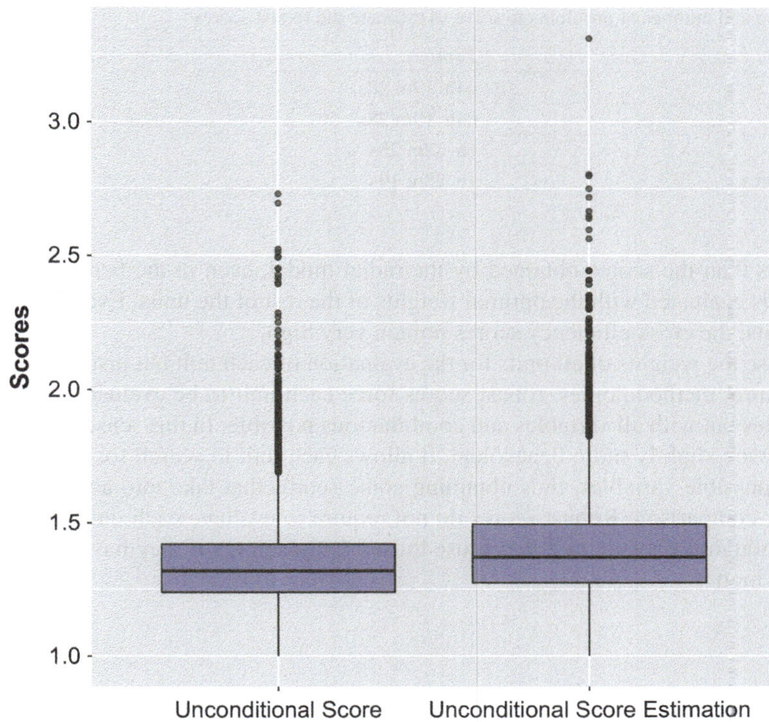

Fig. 11 Distribution for the unconditional scores and their estimation

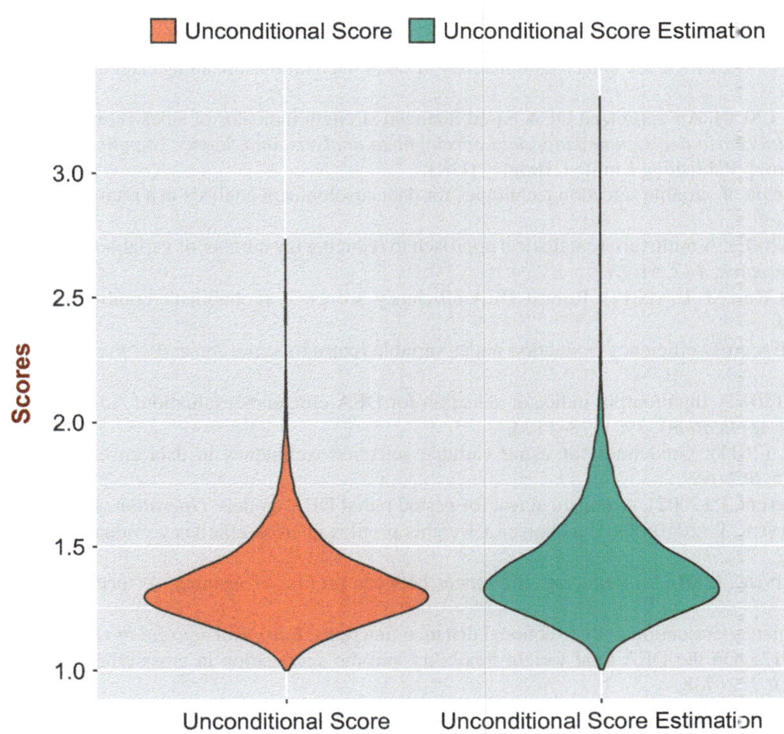

Fig. 12 Distribution for the unconditional scores and their estimation

Table 10 Computational time and number of problems to solve to estimate the robust scores

	$Time$	N_{prob}
Entropy scores	64h 19m 28s	110,542,848
Unconditional scores	64h 19m 28s	110,542,848
Estimated Entropy scores	1h 28m 25s	1,349,400
Estimated Unconditional scores	1h 28m 19s	1,349,400

significantly higher scores than the scores obtained by the radial model, even in the benevolent case of weights selection. This is because each unit is evaluated with the optimal weights of the rest of the units. Even in the application example, with a very large sample of units, the cross-efficiency scores remain very high.

Robust scores do not use the weights of all units for the evaluation of each unit but instead use all the variables. Although they may seem very different methodologies, robust scores force each unit to be evaluated in a DEA model not only with the most favorable variables but with all variables and combinations possible. In this sense, the procedure is similar to cross-efficiency, but since it is even slightly more benevolent, it allows each unit to search for its best weights but restricting the search to each subset of possible variables, thus obtaining some scores that take into account all the variables and allows a common framework for comparison. Robust scores do not require to evaluate each unit in the same way as the unit with which it is compared, although it does require that it use those inputs/outputs if they have been included and considered in the definition of the DEA model.

References

Banker, R. (1993). Maximum likelihood, consistency and data envelopment analysis: A statistical foundation. *Management Science, 39*, 1265–1273.

Banker, R. (1996). Hypotesis test using data envelopment analysis. *Journal of Productivity Analysis, 7*, 139–159.

Charnes, A., Cooper, W. W., & Rhodes, E. (1978). Measuring the efficiency of decision making units. *European Journal of Operational Research, 2*, 429–444.

Doyle, J. R., & Green, R. H. (1994). Efficiency and cross-efficiency in DEA: Derivations, meanings and uses. *Journal of the Operational Research Society, 45*, 567–578.

Edirisinghe, N., & Zhang, X. (2010). An optimized DEA-based financial strength indicator of stock returns for U.S. markets. In K. D. Lawrence (Ed.), *Applications in multicriteria decision making, data envelopment analysis, and finance* (Applications of Management Science, Vol. 14, pp. 175–198). Emerald Group Publishing Limited, Bingley (UK).

Eskelinen, J. (2017). Comparison of variable selection techniques for data envelopment analysis in a retail bank. *European Journal of Operational Research, 259*, 778–788.

Jenkins, L., & Anderson, M. (2003). A multivariate statistical approach to reducing the number of variables in data envelopment analysis. *European Journal of Operational Research, 147*, 51–61.

Landete M., Monge, J. F., & Ruiz, J. L. (2017). Robust DEA efficiency scores: A probabilistic/combinatorial approach. *Expert Systems With Applications, 86*, 145–154.

Lim, S., & Zhu, J. (2015). DEA cross-efficiency evaluation under variable return to scale. *Journal of the Operational Research Society, 66*, 476–487.

Luo, Y., Bi, G., & Liang, L. (2012). Input/output indicator selection for DEA efficiency evaluation: An empirical study of Chinese commercial banks. *Expert System with Applications, 39*, 1118–1123.

Natajara, N., & Johnson, A. (2011). Guidelines for using variable selection techniques in data envelopment analysis. *European Journal of Operational Research, 215*, 662–669.

Pastor, J. T., Ruiz, J. L., & Sirvent, I. (2002). A statistical test for nested radial DEA models. *Operations Research, 50*, 728–735.

Ramón, N., Ruiz, J. L., & Sirvent, I. (2010). On the choice of weights profiles in cross-efficiency evaluations. *European Journal of Operational Research, 207*, 1564–1572.

Ramón, N., Ruiz, J. L., & Sirvent, I. (2011). Reducing differences between profiles of weights: A "peer-restricted" cross-efficiency evaluation. *Omega, 39*, 634–641.

Ruiz, J. L. (2013). Cross-efficiency evaluation with directional distance functions. *European Journal of Operational Research, 228*, 181–189.

Ruiz, J. L., & Sirvent, I. (2012). On the DEA total weight flexibility and the aggregation in cross-efficiency evaluations. *European Journal of Operational Research, 223*, 732–738.

Sexton, T. R., Silkman, R. H., & Hogan, A. J. (1986). Data envelopment analysis: Critique and extensions. In R. H. Silkman (Ed.)., Measuring Efficiency: An assessment of data Envelopment Analysis. San Francisco: Jossey-Bass.

Shannon, C. (1948). The mathematical theory of communication. *The Bell System Technical Journal, 3–4*, 379–423, 623–656.

Sirvent, I., Ruiz, J. L., Borras, F., & Pastor, J. T. (2005). A monte carlo evaluation of several tests for the selection of variables in DEA models. *International Journal of Information Technology and Decision Making, 4*, 325–343.

Wagner, J., & Shimshak, D. (2007). Stepwise selection of variables in data envelopment analysis: Procedures and managerial perspectives. *European Journal of Operational Research, 180*, 57–67.

Part III
Empirical Advances

Corporate Social Responsibility and Firms' Dynamic Productivity Change

Magdalena Kapelko

Abstract This chapter examines the relationship between corporate social responsibility (CSR) and firms' productivity change. The application focuses on panel data of US firms from 2004 to 2015. The chapter uses a dynamic data envelopment analysis (DEA) model to measure productivity change and its technical, technical-inefficiency, and scale-inefficiency change components. A bootstrap regression model relates CSR and its dimensions of social, environmental, and governance CSR with dynamic performance measures. Results support a positive association between CSR and dynamic productivity change. The findings also provide evidence about the relevance of CSR dimensions, as well as the components of dynamic productivity change, adding interesting insights into the relationship between CSR and productivity change.

Keywords Corporate social responsibility · Dynamic productivity change · Dynamic Luenberger indicator · Data envelopment analysis

1 Introduction

Customers, employees, suppliers, community groups, governments, and shareholders have recently inspired companies to invest more in their corporate social responsibility (CSR) activities (McWilliams and Siegel 2001). The concept of CSR is gaining importance, mainly due to increasing awareness regarding sustainable development and the effects of firms' operations on the environment and society. CSR is becoming one of the major issues when crises form a challenge for the financial (such as the crisis of 2008) and environmental (climate change) sustainability domains, as well as because of social needs and preferences. In general, CSR relates to the broad role of business in society and can be defined as voluntary actions, in which the firm goes beyond compliance and engages in "actions that appear to further some social good, beyond the interests of the firm and that which is required by law" (McWilliams and Siegel 2001).

A fundamental question that has arisen in CSR research is: Do firms lose or gain performance as they seek to meet the socially responsible decisions that society has come to expect of them? In this chapter, we try to provide additional insight into this question by focusing on the relationship between CSR and firms' performance while assessing that performance from a dynamic perspective and using the measures of productivity change. In the absence of clear theory linking CSR with productivity growth, it remains an empirical issue.

Numerous studies have attempted to analyze the relationship between CSR and performance. Based on the conjecture that companies engage in CSR activities for anticipated benefits (profits) (McWilliams and Siegel 2001), most academic studies have examined the relationship between CSR and some measure of firms' financial performance. There are two groups of these types of studies. One group uses the methodology of event study to analyze the short-run influence of firms' engagement in socially responsible or irresponsible practices (e.g., Hannon and Milkovich 1996; Wright and Ferris 1997). The second group of studies investigates the relationship between indicators of CSR and firms' long-run performance using measures of profitability (e.g., Waddock and Graves 1997; Orlitzky et al. 2003; Surroca et al. 2010). Both groups show mixed results on the relationship between CSR and firms' performance that is positive, negative, and neutral associations. Margolis et al. (2009) presented a comprehensive review of research on the relationship between CSR and financial performance.

M. Kapelko (✉)
Department of Logistics, Wroclaw University of Economics and Business, Wrocław, Poland
e-mail: magdalena.kapelko@ue.wroc.pl

J. Aparicio et al. (eds.), *Advances in Efficiency and Productivity II*, International Series in Operations Research & Management Science 287, https://doi.org/10.1007/978-3-030-41618-8_9

The literature has only recently recognized the importance of examining the relationship between CSR and measures of firms' efficiency and productivity change that assess the technological and economic relationships between output production and input demand (Morrison Paul and Siegel 2006). Within this line, the research investigated the relationship between technical or cost efficiency and CSR in the semiconductor (Lu et al. 2013), telecommunications (Wang et al. 2014), chemical (Sun and Stuebs 2013), thrift (Vitaliano and Stella 2006), creative (Hou et al. 2017), and manufacturing industries (Jacobs et al. 2016), as well as all economic sectors (Guillamon Saorin et al. 2018). However, none of the studies analyzed the relationship between CSR and productivity change as a measure of firms' performance.[1]

This study fills in the gap in the literature outlined above and investigates the relationship between CSR and productivity change. We further extended the analysis of this association using dynamic models of production, in which current firms' production decisions constrain or enhance future production possibilities. The dynamic measures account for the adjustment costs related to firms' investments in quasi-fixed factors of production (Silva and Stefanou 2003, 2007; Kapelko et al. 2014; Silva et al. 2015). Dynamic productivity change is operationalized in this study by the dynamic Luenberger indicator (Kapelko et al. 2015a; Oude Lansink et al. 2015). We used the data envelopment analysis (DEA) method (Charnes et al. 1978; Banker et al. 1984) to compute the dynamic Luenberger productivity indicator and decompose dynamic productivity change to understand its sources: dynamic technical change, dynamic technical-inefficiency change, and dynamic scale-inefficiency change. The dynamic indicators were then related in the regression analysis with CSR measures, representing overall CSR and its dimensions of social, environmental, and governance CSR. Our empirical focus was on CSR activities of US firms in a variety of economic sectors from 2004 to 2015.

The structure of the chapter is as follows: Section 2 describes the methodology to compute dynamic productivity change and its components. Section 3 presents the dataset and variables used to compute dynamic indicators and applied in the regression analysis. Section 4 describes the empirical results. Section 5 offers concluding comments.

2 The Measurement of Dynamic Productivity Change

The dynamic production framework applied in this chapter has its foundations in the theory of adjustment costs, dating back to Eisner and Strotz (1963), Lucas (1967), Treadway (1970), and Epstein (1981), among others. Based on this theory, the dynamic framework allows for gradual adjustment of quasi-fixed factors of production, due to the presence of adjustment costs. Within this framework, the dynamic Luenberger indicator was developed to measure the change in dynamic productivity (Kapelko et al. 2015a; Oude Lansink et al. 2015), extending the static version of Luenberger indicator by Chambers et al. (1996) and Chambers and Pope (1996). The development of the Luenberger dynamic productivity change indicator and its components presented thereafter largely follows from Kapelko et al. (2015a, b, 2016).

Let us first introduce some mathematical notations. We assumed a data series representing vectors of observed quantities of variable inputs, $\mathbf{x}_t$, quasi-fixed inputs, $\mathbf{k}_t$, outputs, $\mathbf{y}_t$, and gross investments in quasi-fixed inputs, $\mathbf{I}_t$ for $j = 1,..,J$ firms at time t. The Luenberger indicator of dynamic productivity change comprises input-oriented, dynamic directional distance functions: for time t ($\vec{D}^i_t(\mathbf{y}_t, \mathbf{k}_t, \mathbf{x}_t, \mathbf{I}_t; \mathbf{g}_x, \mathbf{g}_I)$); for time $t+1$ ($\vec{D}^i_{t+1}(\mathbf{y}_{t+1}, \mathbf{k}_{t+1}, \mathbf{x}_{t+1}, \mathbf{I}_{t+1}; \mathbf{g}_x, \mathbf{g}_I)$); a mixed-period reflecting the technology at time t, evaluated using the quantities at time $t+1$ ($\vec{D}^i_t(\mathbf{y}_{t+1}, \mathbf{k}_{t+1}, \mathbf{x}_{t+1}, \mathbf{I}_{t+1}; \mathbf{g}_x, \mathbf{g}_I)$); and technology at time $t+1$, evaluated using the quantities at time t ($\vec{D}^i_{t+1}(\mathbf{y}_t, \mathbf{k}_t, \mathbf{x}_t, \mathbf{I}_t; \mathbf{g}_x, \mathbf{g}_I)$). The input-oriented, dynamic directional distance function for time t, with directional vectors for inputs ($\mathbf{g}_x$) and investments ($\mathbf{g}_I$), $\vec{D}^i_t(\mathbf{y}_t, \mathbf{k}_t, \mathbf{x}_t, \mathbf{I}_t; \mathbf{g}_x, \mathbf{g}_I)$, is defined as follows (Silva et al. 2015):

$$\begin{aligned}\vec{D}^i_t(\mathbf{y}_t, \mathbf{k}_t, \mathbf{x}_t, \mathbf{I}_t; \mathbf{g}_x, \mathbf{g}_I) = \max\{\beta \in \Re : (\mathbf{x}_t - \beta\mathbf{g}_x, \mathbf{I}_t + \beta\mathbf{g}_I) \in V_t(\mathbf{y}_t : \mathbf{k}_t)\}, \\ \mathbf{g}_x \in \Re^N_{++}, \ \mathbf{g}_I \in \Re^F_{++}, (\mathbf{g}_x, \mathbf{g}_I) \neq (\mathbf{0}^N, \mathbf{0}^F)\end{aligned} \quad (1)$$

if $(\mathbf{x}_t - \beta\mathbf{g}_x, \mathbf{I} + \beta\mathbf{g}_I) \in V_t(\mathbf{y}_t : \mathbf{k}_t)$ for some β, $\vec{D}^i_t(\mathbf{y}_t, \mathbf{k}_t, \mathbf{x}_t, \mathbf{I}_t; \mathbf{g}_x, \mathbf{g}_I) = -\infty$ when $(\mathbf{x}_t - \beta\mathbf{g}_x, \mathbf{I} + \beta\mathbf{g}_I) \notin V_t(\mathbf{y}_t : \mathbf{k}_t)$.

In the above formulation, $V_t(\mathbf{y}_t : \mathbf{k}_t)$ signifies the input requirement set that is defined as $V_t(\mathbf{y}_t : \mathbf{k}_t) = \{(\mathbf{x}_t, \mathbf{I}_t)$ can produce $\mathbf{y}_t$, given $\mathbf{k}_t\}$ (Silva and Stefanou 2003). The input-oriented, dynamic directional distance function is defined by simultaneously contracting variable inputs and expanding gross investments. It measures dynamic inefficiency of firms,

[1] Sun and Stuebs (2013) and Jacobs et al. (2016) did refer to firms' productivity. However, in fact, they measured technical efficiency. Kapelko et al. (2020) analyzed the productivity change in the CSR context, but using input-specific productivity change measures.

as represented by β. The input-oriented, dynamic directional distance function for time $t + 1$ and mixed-period distance functions are analogously defined to (1).

The dynamic Luenberger indicator is defined in Oude Lansink et al. (2015) as:

$$L = \frac{1}{2}\left\{\begin{array}{l}\left[\vec{D}^{i}_{t+1}(\mathbf{y}_t, \mathbf{k}_t, \mathbf{x}_t, \mathbf{I}_t; \mathbf{g}_x, \mathbf{g}_I) - \vec{D}^{i}_{t+1}(\mathbf{y}_{t+1}, \mathbf{k}_{t+1}, \mathbf{x}_{t+1}, \mathbf{I}_{t+1}; \mathbf{g}_x, \mathbf{g}_I)\right] \\ + \left[\vec{D}^{i}_{t}(\mathbf{y}_t, \mathbf{k}_t, \mathbf{x}_t, \mathbf{I}_t; \mathbf{g}_x, \mathbf{g}_I) - \vec{D}^{i}_{t}(\mathbf{y}_{t+1}, \mathbf{k}_{t+1}, \mathbf{x}_{t+1}, \mathbf{I}_{t+1}; \mathbf{g}_x, \mathbf{g}_I)\right]\end{array}\right\} \quad (2)$$

It is constructed as the arithmetic average of productivity change, measured by the technology at time $t + 1$, and the productivity change measured by the technology at time t.

In the empirical part of the chapter, we used the decomposition of the Luenberger indicator developed by Kapelko et al. (2015a). This decomposition considers three components, dynamic technical change (ΔT), dynamic technical-inefficiency change under variable returns to scale (VRS) (ΔTI), and dynamic scale-inefficiency change (ΔSI), and their contributions to dynamic productivity change:

$$L = \Delta T + \Delta TI + \Delta SI \quad (3)$$

We then define and explain each of these components. Dynamic technical change is calculated as the arithmetic average of the difference between technology at time t and time $t + 1$, evaluated using quantities at time t and time $t + 1$:

$$\Delta T = \frac{1}{2}\left\{\begin{array}{l}\left[\vec{D}^{i}_{t+1}(\mathbf{y}_t, \mathbf{k}_t, \mathbf{x}_t, \mathbf{I}_t; \mathbf{g}_x, \mathbf{g}_I) - \vec{D}^{i}_{t}(\mathbf{y}_t, \mathbf{k}_t, \mathbf{x}_t, \mathbf{I}_t; \mathbf{g}_x, \mathbf{g}_I)\right] \\ + \left[\vec{D}^{i}_{t+1}(\mathbf{y}_{t+1}, \mathbf{k}_{t+1}, \mathbf{x}_{t+1}, \mathbf{I}_{t+1}; \mathbf{g}_x, \mathbf{g}_I) - \vec{D}^{i}_{t}(\mathbf{y}_{t+1}, \mathbf{k}_{t+1}, \mathbf{x}_{t+1}, \mathbf{I}_{t+1}; \mathbf{g}_x, \mathbf{g}_I)\right]\end{array}\right\} \quad (4)$$

This component measures the shift of dynamic production technology due to the firm's exposure to innovation and adaptation of new technologies.

Dynamic technical-inefficiency change is computed as the difference between the value of the dynamic directional distance function in variable returns to scale at time t and time $t + 1$:

$$\begin{aligned}\Delta TI = {} & \vec{D}^{i}_{t}(\mathbf{y}_t, \mathbf{k}_t, \mathbf{x}_t, \mathbf{I}_t; \mathbf{g}_x, \mathbf{g}_I \,|VRS) \\ & - \vec{D}^{i}_{t+1}(\mathbf{y}_{t+1}, \mathbf{k}_{t+1}, \mathbf{x}_{t+1}, \mathbf{I}_{t+1}; \mathbf{g}_x, \mathbf{g}_I \,|VRS)\end{aligned} \quad (5)$$

This component measures the change in the position of the firm, relative to dynamic production technology between time t and time $t + 1$.

Dynamic scale-inefficiency change is calculated as follows:

$$\begin{aligned}\Delta SI = {} & \vec{D}^{i}_{t}(\mathbf{y}_t, \mathbf{k}_t, \mathbf{x}_t, \mathbf{I}_t; \mathbf{g}_x, \mathbf{g}_I \,|CRS) - \vec{D}^{i}_{t}(\mathbf{y}_t, \mathbf{k}_t, \mathbf{x}_t, \mathbf{I}_t; \mathbf{g}_x, \mathbf{g}_I \,|VRS) \\ & - \Big[\vec{D}^{i}_{t+1}(\mathbf{y}_{t+1}, \mathbf{k}_{t+1}, \mathbf{x}_{t+1}, \mathbf{I}_{t+1}; \mathbf{g}_x, \mathbf{g}_I \,|CRS) \\ & - \vec{D}^{i}_{t+1}(\mathbf{y}_{t+1}, \mathbf{k}_{t+1}, \mathbf{x}_{t+1}, \mathbf{I}_{t+1}; \mathbf{g}_x, \mathbf{g}_I \,|VRS)\Big]\end{aligned} \quad (6)$$

This component compares dynamic directional distance functions gauged relative to constant returns to scale (CRS) technology and relative to VRS technology, between time t and time $t + 1$. This captures firms' abilities to move their scale of operations toward CRS.

The positive (negative) value of the dynamic Luenberger indicates growth (decline) in productivity between t and $t + 1$, while positive (negative) values of its components signify positive (negative) contributions of these components to dynamic productivity change.

In this study, we used DEA to measure input-oriented, dynamic directional distance functions that make the dynamic Luenberger indicator and its components. The DEA model used to compute dynamic, directional input distance function for time t in VRS is (Kapelko et al. 2016):

$$
\begin{aligned}
&\overrightarrow{D}_t^i(\mathbf{y}_t, \mathbf{k}_t, \mathbf{x}_t, \mathbf{I}_t; \mathbf{g}_x, \mathbf{g}_I | VRS) = \max_{\beta,\gamma} \beta \\
&s.t. \\
&\mathbf{y}_{tm} \leq \sum_{j=1}^{J} \gamma^j \mathbf{y}_{tm}^j, m = 1, \ldots, M; \\
&\sum_{j=1}^{J} \gamma^j \mathbf{x}_{tn}^j \leq \mathbf{x}_{tn} - \beta \mathbf{g}_{x_n}, n = 1, \ldots, N; \\
&\mathbf{I}_{tf} + \beta \mathbf{g}_{I_f} - \delta_f^j \mathbf{k}_{tf} \leq \sum_{j=1}^{J} \gamma^j \left(\mathbf{I}_{tf}^j - \delta_f^j \mathbf{k}_{tf}^j \right), f = 1, \ldots, F; \\
&\sum_{j=1}^{J} \gamma^j = 1 \\
&\gamma^j \geq 0, j = 1, \ldots, J.
\end{aligned} \tag{7}
$$

in which γ is an intensity vector of firm weights; δ represents depreciation rate of quasi-fixed inputs; and the constraint $\sum_{j=1}^{J} \gamma^j = 1$ reflects the VRS assumption. Computing the dynamic, directional distance functions under CRS is undertaken by dropping the constraint $\sum_{j=1}^{J} \gamma^j = 1$, while distance functions for time $t + 1$ and mixed period distance functions are done analogously to (7) by exchanging the appropriate time subscripts between t and $t + 1$.

Regarding details on the empirical application of dynamic measures, the value of the directional vector used is, for g_x, the actual quantity of variable inputs and, for g_I, 20% of capital stock. Furthermore, it is well known that computing the Luenberger indicator and its components may yield infeasible observations (Briec and Kerstens 2009a, b). In this chapter, we excluded infeasibilities encountered in the empirical analysis from the computation of averages. Finally, dynamic indicators are determined for each firm for a pair of consecutive years and separately for each economic sector (represented by the Standard Industrial Classification [SIC]) to address potential differences in technology between sectors.

3 Dataset and Variables

3.1 Dataset

The CSR data was collected from the Kinder, Lydenberg, and Domini (KLD) database. KLD is a popular source of CSR data in academic research (applied in, e.g., McWilliams and Siegel 2000; Lev et al. 2010; Servaes and Tamayo 2013; Flammer 2015). KLD provides rating data grouped in seven qualitative areas including community, diversity, employee relations, human rights, product, environment, and corporate governance for a large subset of publicly traded firms in the United States. For each dimension, strengths and concerns are measured to assess the positive and negative aspects of CSR by using dummy variables. In particular, KLD assigns a value of 1 when a firm presents a certain strength or concern and a value of 0 otherwise. The examples of strengths include charitable giving, work/life benefits, women and minority contracting, no-layoff policy, indigenous peoples relations, product quality, pollution prevention, and reporting quality. Some examples of concerns are negative economic impact, workforce diversity controversies, workforce reductions, firms' operations in Burma and Sudan, product quality and safety controversies, substantial emissions, and business ethics controversies. The firms included in KLD represent different economic sectors. In this study, we excluded financial firms from the analysis because for such firms efficiency and productivity is measured differently, using specific combinations of input and output variables. As a result, the sectors in our study included construction, manufacturing, mining, retail trade, services, transportation, and wholesale trade (as classified by SIC). Furthermore, KLD has compiled information on CSR since 1991, but we focused our analysis on 2004 to 2015, due to KLD's larger coverage of firms from 2004 onward.

We collected the financial data from COMPUSTAT Global Vantage for 2004 to 2015 to calculate productivity change by DEA, as well as to construct control variables used in the regression. By merging KLD with COMPUSTAT, and excluding observations with missing data, and eliminating outliers (following Simar 2003), we obtained a final sample of 15,753 observations for 3119 firms from 2004 to 2015 (unbalanced panel). Since productivity change is calculated for a pair of consecutive years and the panel is unbalanced, only firms that existed for at least two consecutive years have been included in the analysis.[2]

3.2 Measurement of Variables

As explained in the Results section, dynamic productivity change is the dependent variable in the regression. Consistent with prior research (e.g., Puggioni and Stefanou 2019; Guillamon Saorin et al. 2018), one output (revenues), two variable inputs (costs of goods sold and number of employees), and one investment (gross investments in quasi-fixed input) are distinguished in estimating the Luenberger indicator of dynamic productivity change and its components, using DEA. Quasi-fixed input is measured as the year's beginning value of fixed assets. Hence, gross investments in quasi-fixed inputs are computed as the beginning value of fixed assets in year $t + 1$, minus the beginning value of fixed assets in year t, plus the beginning value of depreciation in year $t + 1$.[3] To facilitate across-period comparisons, all monetary variables were deflated, using the appropriate price indices supplied by the US Bureau of Labor Statistics. In particular, revenues were deflated by the producer price index, adjusted for each specific industry and sub-industry; the costs of goods sold by the indexes, reflecting the prices of supplies to manufacturing and nonmanufacturing industries; and the price indexes for private capital equipment for manufacturing and private capital equipment for nonmanufacturing which were used for investments. Implicit quantity indexes were generated as the ratio of the value to the price index.

Our main independent variable was CSR and our main measure for it was *CSR_Score*, which is the net difference between strengths and concerns along all KLD dimensions of community, diversity, employee relations, human rights, product, environment, and corporate governance. Because the number of categories that comprise the dimensions has evolved over time, we created an adjusted measure of strengths and concerns. We derived this by scaling the strength and concern scores for each firm year, within each CSR dimension, by the maximum number of items of the strength and concern scores of that dimension in each year. This method replicates previous research (e.g., Deng et al. 2013; Servaes and Tamayo 2013). Furthermore, following prior research (e.g., Lys et al. 2015), we looked at the components of *CSR_Score*: social score, *CSR_Soc* (including community, diversity, employee relations, human rights, and product dimensions); environmental score, *CSR_Env*; and governance score, *CSR_Gov*.

We included a set of variables to control for the determinants of productivity change and its components of technical change, technical-inefficiency change, and scale-inefficiency change (Worthington 2000; Dilling-Hansen et al. 2003; Alene 2010; Cummins and Xie 2013; Sun and Stuebs 2013; Curi et al. 2015; Wijesiri and Meoli 2015). In particular, we controlled for *Size*, measured as the natural logarithm of total assets; *Leverage*, defined as the ratio of total debt to total assets; *MTB*, which is the market value of equity divided by the book value of shareholder equity; *ROA*, which is the net income divided by the total assets; *R&D*, defined as R&D expenses scaled by total assets; *Marketing*, measured as marketing expenses divided by total assets; and *Diversification*, assessed as the number of business segments in which a firm operates. In addition, we controlled for time, including year dummies, and sector. Since we used a fixed-effects regression model to analyze the relationship between CSR and productivity change, we could not use sector dummies given that firms do not change sector over time. In this case, the literature tends to introduce the averaged dependent variable (excluding focal firm) for the corresponding sector as an explanatory variable (Surroca et al. 2010). We followed this approach (adopting SIC codes) for our study.

Table 1 provides the descriptive statistics of DEA and regression variables for the study period 2004 to 2015. It is interesting to note that, on average, the dynamic productivity change is positive. Looking at the components of dynamic productivity change, dynamic technical change and dynamic scale-inefficiency change have, on average, positive contributions to productivity change. Conversely, dynamic technical-inefficiency change has a negative contribution. Furthermore, the *CSR_Score* mean is negative, suggesting that, on average, firms in the sample were socially irresponsible. The negative mean of *CSR_Score* can be explained by the negative mean for the social (*CSR_Soc*) and governance (*CSR_Gov*) dimensions of CSR, despite a positive mean for environmental CSR (*CSR_Env*).

---

[2]In general, literature finds that the differences between productivity changes computed with unbalanced and balanced panel can be significantly different depending on the dataset used (Kerstens and Van de Woestyne 2014). However, it is also found that balancing an unbalanced panel results in a substantial loss of information (Kerstens and Van de Woestyne 2014); hence, we decide to use unbalanced panel in this chapter.

[3]Quasi-fixed input (fixed assets) is not applied directly in the DEA model used to estimate dynamic productivity measures. Hence, it is not one of the variables directly used to estimate dynamic measures. Quasi-fixed input is used mainly to compute investments. Also, in the general dynamic DEA model, depreciation is given as a fraction of quasi-fixed input.

Table 1 Descriptive statistics of DEA and regression variables, 2004 to 2015

Variable	Mean	Std. dev.	Coefficient of variation
DEA variables			
Revenues	4334.083	14549.762	3.3571
Costs of goods sold	2606.555	10174.7954	3.9035
Number of employees	0.1831	0.6934	3.7854
Fixed assets	1795.272	6863.1867	3.8229
Investments	356.945	1368.7322	3.8346
Dependent variables			
Dynamic productivity change	0.0010	0.0704	73.4404
Dynamic technical change	0.0030	0.0732	24.4736
Dynamic technical-inefficiency change	−0.0067	0.1038	−15.4542
Dynamic scale-inefficiency change	0.0047	0.0770	16.4321
Variable of interest			
CSR_Score	−0.1586	0.5792	−3.6513
CSR_Soc	−0.1411	0.4774	−3.3839
CSR_Env	0.0178	0.1202	6.7592
CSR_Gov	−0.0353	0.1620	−4.5851
Control variables			
Size	7.3795	1.5896	0.2154
Leverage	0.2002	0.2154	1.0757
MTB	3.4780	32.0795	9.2237
ROA	0.0321	0.1504	4.6926
R&D	0.0423	0.0976	2.3090
Marketing	0.0138	0.0383	2.7826
Diversification	2.8978	1.9629	0.6774

Monetary values (fixed assets, costs of goods sold, revenues, and investments) are in millions of US dollars, constant prices from 2003. Number of employees is in millions

4 Results

We will first summarize the findings regarding the dynamic productivity change indicator and its components of dynamic technical change, dynamic technical-inefficiency change, and dynamic scale-inefficiency change. We will then present results for regression models that analyze the relationship between dynamic productivity change, each of its components, and the measures of CSR.

4.1 Dynamic Productivity Growth per Sector and Quartile

Table 2 presents the quartile-specific and overall means of the dynamic Luenberger productivity indicator and its components of dynamic technical change, dynamic technical-inefficiency change, and dynamic scale-inefficiency change across all industries for the period 2004/2005 to 2014/2015. To compute quartile-specific means, we first computed quartiles for each dynamic measure: the lowest (I), lower-middle (II), upper-middle (III), and the highest (IV). We then calculated the means for each dynamic measure in each quartile.

On average, the overall dynamic productivity change was positive for firms in construction, manufacturing, retail trade, and transportation industries, while companies in mining, services, and wholesale trade sectors had a negative dynamic productivity change. However, looking at the dynamic productivity change quartiles reveals a considerable variation in dynamic productivity change. The largest difference between the lowest and the highest quartile was seen for mining and wholesale trade, so the dynamic productivity change is mostly dispersed for these sectors.

The analysis of the components of dynamic productivity change found that the increase in dynamic productivity change for the manufacturing and retail trade sectors was driven by positive contributions of dynamic technical change and dynamic scale-inefficiency change. In the transportation sector, only dynamic technical change made a positive contribution, and both dynamic technical-inefficiency change and dynamic scale-inefficiency change made positive contributions for construction

Table 2 Dynamic productivity change and its components by industry and quartile group (mean values for 2004/2005–2014/2015)

	Quartile group	Construction	Manufacturing	Mining	Retail trade	Services	Transportation	Wholesale trade
Dynamic productivity change	Lowest (I)	−0.0687	−0.0595	−0.1217	−0.1114	−0.0609	−0.0695	−0.1278
	Lower-middle (II)	−0.0192	−0.0052	−0.0151	−0.0112	−0.0055	−0.0038	−0.0138
	Upper-middle (III)	0.0171	0.0091	0.0149	0.0309	0.0075	0.0172	0.0257
	Highest (IV)	0.0904	0.0630	0.1055	0.0923	0.0539	0.0733	0.0997
	Overall	0.0048	0.0018	−0.0041	0.0002	−0.0012	0.0043	−0.0039
Dynamic technical change	Lowest (I)	−0.0718	−0.0720	−0.0928	−0.1438	−0.1013	−0.0442	−0.1311
	Lower-middle (II)	−0.0301	−0.0074	−0.0211	−0.0025	−0.0108	−0.0009	−0.0329
	Upper-middle (III)	−0.0031	0.0203	0.0143	0.0475	0.0076	0.0269	0.0401
	Highest (IV)	0.0835	0.0715	0.0867	0.1197	0.0686	0.1063	0.1563
	Overall	−0.0056	0.0031	−0.0033	0.0052	−0.0090	0.0220	0.0080
Dynamic technical-inefficiency change	Lowest (I)	−0.0532	−0.1132	−0.1839	−0.0987	−0.0989	−0.1354	−0.0685
	Lower-middle (II)	−0.0047	−0.0224	−0.0187	−0.0183	−0.0128	−0.0302	−0.0056
	Upper-middle (III)	0.0071	0.0104	0.0201	0.0078	0.0097	0.0052	0.0049
	Highest (IV)	0.0684	0.0948	0.1578	0.0778	0.1072	0.0950	0.0579
	Overall	0.0029	−0.0076	−0.0077	−0.0075	0.0013	−0.0164	−0.0004
Dynamic scale-inefficiency change	Lowest (I)	−0.0467	−0.0495	−0.1211	−0.0746	−0.0653	−0.1021	−0.1357
	Lower-middle (II)	0.0011	−0.0037	−0.0104	−0.0125	−0.0064	−0.0093	−0.0133
	Upper-middle (III)	0.0185	0.0081	0.0228	0.0140	0.0090	0.0115	0.0205
	Highest (IV)	0.0567	0.0706	0.1361	0.0831	0.0886	0.0948	0.0959
	Overall	0.0075	0.0064	0.0068	0.0025	0.0065	−0.0013	−0.0079

sector. On the contrary, a decrease in dynamic productivity change in the mining sector came with a regression of dynamic technology and a negative dynamic technical-inefficiency change. The decrease of the dynamic productivity for services was only caused by technical regress. However, in the wholesale trade sector, it was caused by negative changes in both dynamic technical-inefficiency and scale-inefficiency. A closer look at the distribution of the dynamic productivity change components reveals that for almost all sectors dynamic technical change, dynamic technical-inefficiency change, and dynamic scale-inefficiency change showed a positive change for the upper half of the respective distributions and a negative change for the lower half of the respective distributions. The exceptions were dynamic technical change in the construction sector, which showed a regression for the upper 75% of distribution, and the dynamic scale-inefficiency change for this sector which was negative only for the lowest quartile.

4.2 CSR and Dynamic Productivity Change

In the regression analysis that tests the association between the dynamic indicator and CSR, we use the following model, not requiring any causal relationship:

$$\text{Dynamicindicator}_{jt} = \beta_0 + \beta_1 \text{CSR}_{jt} + \beta_2 \text{Controls}_{jt} + \mu_j + \vartheta_{jt}, \quad (8)$$

in which μ is the intercept for each firm (fixed effects), ϑ is an error term, and *Controls* are control variables explained in Sect. 3.2. Fixed effects in the model allow controlling for an unidentified, time-invariant firm characteristic. In total, 16 regression models were estimated, one for each of the dynamic indicators (productivity change, technical change, technical-inefficiency change, and scale-inefficiency change) and each of the CSR measures (*CSR_Score*, *CSR_Soc*, *CSR_Env*, and *CSR_Gov*). To estimate these models, we used panel data linear regression with bootstrap. Such an approach has been adopted in the context of second-stage analysis with productivity change measures estimated using DEA (e.g., Kapelko et al. 2015a, 2016; Skevas and Oude Lansink 2014). A bootstrap approach is applied to address the well-known problem of serial correlation among DEA measures (Simar and Wilson 2007). We used linear regression because DEA dynamic productivity indicators are not truncated, so Simar and Wilson's (2007) truncated regression approach was not suitable in our context.[4] In our analysis, we used 500 bootstrap replications, which allowed for computing bootstrap regression coefficients.

To address the potential problem of endogeneity in estimating the model (8), we applied an endogeneity test of endogenous regressors using the instrumental variables (IV) approach. This test is the regression-based form of the Hausman (1978) test. It compares the models' results using the OLS regression and IV approach, in which the null hypothesis is that the OLS estimator is consistent and fully efficient (Baum et al. 2003). In our application of this test, we analyzed if any CSR measures were endogenously determined. Following previous literature (El Ghoul et al. 2011; Cheng et al. 2014) as instruments for CSR, we used an industry average CSR score (calculated excluding the contribution of the focal firm) and a dummy variable for company loss in the previous year. Following previous research (Cheng et al. 2014), the validity of these instruments were tested using Kleibergen-Paap rk Lm statistic and Kleibergen-Paap rk Wald F statistics (Kleibergen and Paap 2006), which showed that the instruments were appropriate.[5] The results of the endogeneity tests estimated for each regression model (for 16 regression models) indicated that the null hypothesis that CSR (*CSR_Score*, *CSR_Soc*, *CSR_Env*, and *CSR_Gov*) is exogenous could not be rejected. This suggests that the results using linear regression were robust to endogeneity issues.

Table 3 presents the results of the models that examined the relationship between dynamic productivity change and overall CSR score and its dimensions of social, environmental, and governance CSR. The coefficient on *CSR_Score* (Model 1) is positive and significant, which suggests that firms with better CSR performance achieve better productivity change outcomes.

---

[4]We did not apply bootstrap in the first stage when estimating the dynamic productivity change and its components, since no bootstrap approach has been developed in the context of both the static and dynamic Luenberger indicator. Although the bootstrap approach exists for the static directional distance function (see Simar et al. 2012), its adaptation to our context is not straightforward, since it requires previous analysis of the properties (such as consistency, rate of convergence, and asymptotic distributions) of the estimator of dynamic measures. Furthermore, the bootstrap approach exists in the literature for the first stage within the static Malmquist index (see Simar and Wilson 1999), but its adaptation in our context is not straightforward. More importantly, recent papers (Kneip et al. 2018; Simar and Wilson 2019) show that Simar and Wilson's (1999) approach cannot be theoretically justified. Instead, these papers develop new, central limit theorems to allow for inference about Malmquist productivity change and its components. Again, these developments are not directly applicable in our context. Moreover, they allow to analyze if estimated productivity changes are significantly different from 1, which is out of the scope of this chapter.

[5]In total, each statistic was run for each regression model. The under-identification test of the Kleibergen-Paap rk Lm statistic showed that the models were always identified (p-value = 0.0000), while the weak identification test using the Kleibergen-Paap rk Wald F statistic indicated that our instruments were relevant and strong (the F statistics oscillated between 17 and 36, depending on the model).

Table 3 Dynamic productivity change and CSR and its components

Dependent variable	(1) Dynamic productivity change	(2) Dynamic productivity change	(3) Dynamic productivity change	(4) Dynamic productivity change
Variable of interest				
CSR_Score	0.0019*			
	(0.0010)			
CSR_Soc		0.0021*		
		(0.0012)		
CSR_Env			−0.0037	
			(0.0039)	
CSR_Gov				0.0057*
				(0.0031)
Control variables				
Size	0.0022	0.0022	0.0022	0.0022
	(0.0020)	(0.0021)	(0.0021)	(0.0020)
ROA	0.0995***	0.0995***	0.0993***	0.0993***
	(0.0176)	(0.0170)	(0.0173)	(0.0185)
R&D	0.0871**	0.0870**	0.0865**	0.0868**
	(0.0354)	(0.0346)	(0.0360)	(0.0361)
Marketing	0.1120*	0.1122*	0.1113**	0.1112*
	(0.0606)	(0.0605)	(0.0565)	(0.0594)
Leverage	0.0089	0.0090	0.0091	0.0089
	(0.0091)	(0.0094)	(0.0098)	(0.0099)
Diversification	0.0016**	0.0016**	0.0015**	0.0015**
	(0.0007)	(0.0006)	(0.0006)	(0.0006)
Constant	0.4642***	0.4641***	0.4637***	0.4641***
	(0.0608)	(0.0597)	(0.0594)	(0.0579)
Fixed effects	Yes	Yes	Yes	Yes
Industry and year	Yes	Yes	Yes	Yes
Observations	15,753	15,753	15,753	15,753
R^2	0.3619	0.3619	0.3618	0.3619

Bootstrap regression coefficients are reported (from 500 bootstrap replications). Bootstrap standard errors are reported in parentheses
***, **, and * indicate statistical significance at the 1%, 5%, and 10% level, respectively

This result is driven by the social and governance dimensions of CSR (Models 2 and 4), which reflect positive outcomes of social and governance aspects of CSR in increasing firms' productivity. This showed the importance of the effect of CSR activities that mainly benefitted internal stakeholders, such as employee relations or ownership and compensation issues, rather than CSR activities addressed to external stakeholders such as those involving environmental issues. The possible explanation for this finding is that companies engaging in internal CSR achieve better results in their internal dimension of performance, as reflected by the productivity change measure. Additional results in Table 3 related with control variables indicate a significantly positive relationship between productivity change and *ROA* across all models, which is consistent with previous research (Wijesiri and Meoli 2015). Furthermore, the coefficients on *R&D* and *Marketing* across all models are positive and significant, indicating that firms which invest more in R&D and marketing are more likely to achieve better productivity outcomes. This result is also in line with previous research (Worthington 2000; Färe et al. 2008; Pergelova et al. 2010; Aw et al. 2011). The coefficient on *Diversification* is also positive and significant, suggesting that diversification of activities, as proxied by the number of business segments, significantly improves productivity, consistent with previous findings (Cummins and Xie 2013).

Table 4 presents the regression results regarding the relationship between the technical change component of dynamic productivity change and CSR measures (Models 5 to 8). Among overall, social, environmental and governance dimensions of CSR, only the environmental aspect had a significant relationship with dynamic technical change (Model 7). In particular, the coefficient on environmental CSR is negative, indicating that firms which integrate environmental concerns in their operations, such as pollution-prevention policies or recycling programs, experience a negative impact on technical change. The negative sign for environmental CSR can reflect that CSR, having a nature of a large investment, causes technical change to decrease. This finding seems to be consistent with the literature on large investments (spikes) and their relationship with technical change tending to show that investment spikes lead to technical change falling after this investment is made

Table 4 Dynamic technical change and CSR and its components

Dependent variable	(5) Dynamic technical change	(6) Dynamic technical change	(7) Dynamic technical change	(8) Dynamic technical change
Variable of interest				
CSR_Score	0.0003			
	(0.001)			
CSR_Soc		0.0007		
		(0.0014)		
CSR_Env			−0.0144***	
			(0.0052)	
CSR_Gov				0.0034
				(0.0037)
Control variables				
Size	0.0027*	0.0027*	0.0027*	0.0027*
	(0.0016)	(0.0016)	(0.0016)	(0.0015)
ROA	−0.0085	−0.0085	−0.0087	−0.0086
	(0.0072)	(0.0068)	(0.0063)	(0.0069)
R&D	−0.0270	−0.0269	−0.0273	−0.0269
	(0.0229)	(0.0225)	(0.0234)	(0.0246)
Marketing	0.0573	0.0575	0.0581	0.0572
	(0.0588)	(0.0564)	(0.0564)	(0.0566)
Leverage	−0.0041	−0.0041	−0.0038	−0.0042
	(0.0062)	(0.0059)	(0.0059)	(0.0061)
Diversification	0.0007	0.0007	0.0006	0.0006
	(0.0007)	(0.0007)	(0.0007)	(0.0007)
Constant	1.6884***	1.6885***	1.6873***	1.6883***
	(0.2161)	(0.2124)	(0.2218)	(0.2231)
Fixed effects	Yes	Yes	Yes	Yes
Industry and year	Yes	Yes	Yes	Yes
Observations	15,753	15,753	15,753	15,753
R^2	0.4400	0.4400	0.4403	0.4401

Bootstrap regression coefficients are reported (from 500 bootstrap replications). Bootstrap standard errors are reported in parentheses
*** and * indicate statistical significance at the 1% and 10% level, respectively

(Huggett and Ospina 2001; Kapelko et al. 2015b). Whether or not the relation between environmental CSR and technical change modifies in subsequent years (i.e., technical change measured between $t + 1$ and $t + 2$, $t + 2$ and $t + 3$, and so on) is an interesting issue that deserves future investigation. Regarding control variables, *Size* had a positive relationship with dynamic technical change, indicating that larger firms tended to have larger frontier shift effects, which is consistent with prior research (Worthington 2000).

Turning to results for dynamic technical-inefficiency change and its relationship with CSR measures, Table 5 shows that coefficients on all CSR measures (overall, social, environmental, and governance) are positive and statistically significant (Models 9 to 12), supporting a positive relationship between CSR and technical-inefficiency change. This finding suggests that firms with larger CSR obtain better technical-inefficiency change outcomes.[6] Based on this result, positive relationships between dynamic productivity change and overall, social, and governance dimensions of CSR, as reported in Table 3, are driven by the positive relationships of these CSR measures with dynamic technical-inefficiency change. The results for control variables in Table 5 are in line with prior research, *ROA* is positively associated with efficiency (Sun and Stuebs 2013), and the relationship between *R&D* and efficiency is also positive (Dilling-Hansen et al. 2003).

Table 6 summarizes the results for the relationship between the last component of dynamic productivity change—scale-inefficiency change—and CSR measures. Across all CSR indicators, there is a negative association between dynamic scale-

[6]In the regression models on the relation between CSR and dynamic technical and scale-inefficiency changes, the dependent variable is dynamic inefficiency change (in its technical or scale variation), so, on the contrary to dynamic inefficiency itself, the larger the values of dynamic inefficiency change, the more positive change occurs. Therefore, the positive relation between dynamic technical-inefficiency change and CSR could imply that the larger the CSR, the larger the dynamic technical-inefficiency change that is implicitly a positive relation between CSR and dynamic technical-efficiency.

Table 5 Dynamic technical-inefficiency change and CSR and its components

Dependent variable	(9) Dynamic technical-inefficiency change	(10) Dynamic technical-inefficiency change	(11) Dynamic technical-inefficiency change	(12) Dynamic technical-inefficiency change
Variable of interest				
CSR_Score	0.0063***			
	(0.0018)			
CSR_Soc		0.0041**		
		(0.0020)		
CSR_Env			0.0240***	
			(0.0069)	
CSR_Gov				0.0219***
				(0.0053)
Control variables				
Size	−0.0001	−0.0001	−0.0002	−0.0001
	(0.0026)	(0.0027)	(0.0026)	(0.0025)
ROA	0.0982***	0.0980***	0.0979***	0.0976***
	(0.0163)	(0.0162)	(0.0175)	(0.0164)
R&D	0.1416***	0.1408***	0.1406***	0.1408***
	(0.045)	(0.0487)	(0.0451)	(0.0449)
Marketing	−0.0170	−0.0179	−0.0217	−0.0195
	(0.0666)	(0.0676)	(0.0688)	(0.0688)
Leverage	0.0180	0.0184	0.0180	0.0178
	(0.0127)	(0.0128)	(0.0141)	(0.0133)
Diversification	0.0010	0.0010	0.0010	0.0010
	(0.0008)	(0.0008)	(0.0008)	(0.0008)
Constant	−5.6061***	−5.6036***	−5.6039***	−5.6123***
	(0.6053)	(0.5615)	(0.5842)	(0.6114)
Fixed effects	Yes	Yes	Yes	Yes
Industry and year	Yes	Yes	Yes	Yes
Observations	15,753	15,753	15,753	15,753
R^2	0.3883	0.3878	0.3880	0.3885

Bootstrap regression coefficients are reported (from 500 bootstrap replications). Bootstrap standard errors are reported in parentheses
*** and ** indicate statistical significance at the 1% and 5% level, respectively

inefficiency change and CSR (Models 13 to 16). Therefore, companies having larger overall CSR commitment, and in their social, environmental, and governance dimensions, experience more negative scale-inefficiency change. It suggests that good CSR performance is not in line with scale-inefficiency change and the ability of firms to adjust their scale of operations. As a result, firms engaging in more CSR operate farther away from the optimal scale. For example, regulatory constraints related to CSR engagement could negatively influence firms' flexibility in adjusting the size of their operations. Turning to control variables, the coefficient on *Marketing* is positive and significant, indicating that firms with larger marketing expenses are more likely to experience positive scale-inefficiency change contribution to productivity change.

5 Conclusion

The purpose of this study was to examine the relationship between CSR and firms' productivity change. We studied US firms in a variety of sectors, from 2004 to 2015, as covered by the KLD dataset, as an empirical setting of this study. Productivity change was assessed using a dynamic production framework. In particular, a dynamic Luenberger indicator was used to measure dynamic productivity change. It was broken down into the contributions of dynamic technical change, dynamic technical-inefficiency change, and dynamic scale-inefficiency change. We then applied a regression analysis to determine the relationship between dynamic productivity change and its components, and CSR measures, including overall CSR and its dimensions of social, environmental, and governance CSR activities.

Table 6 Dynamic scale-inefficiency change and CSR and its components

Dependent variable	(13) Dynamic scale-inefficiency change	(14) Dynamic scale-inefficiency change	(15) Dynamic scale-inefficiency change	(16) Dynamic scale-inefficiency change
Variable of interest				
CSR_Score	−0.0042***			
	(0.0013)			
CSR_Soc		−0.0030*		
		(0.0016)		
CSR_Env			−0.0124**	
			(0.0059)	
CSR_Gov				−0.0148***
				(0.0044)
Control variables				
Size	0.0003	0.0003	0.0003	0.0002
	(0.0018)	(0.0019)	(0.0019)	(0.0018)
ROA	−0.0030	−0.0028	−0.0027	−0.0026
	(0.0089)	(0.0087)	(0.0093)	(0.0092)
R&D	−0.0413	−0.0409	−0.0405	−0.0408
	(0.0314)	(0.0312)	(0.0353)	(0.0315)
Marketing	0.0765*	0.0770**	0.0794**	0.0782**
	(0.0393)	(0.0383)	(0.0375)	(0.0392)
Leverage	−0.0065	−0.0067	−0.0065	−0.0063
	(0.0071)	(0.0074)	(0.0079)	(0.0072)
Diversification	−0.0001	−0.0001	−0.0001	−0.0001
	(0.0006)	(0.0006)	(0.0006)	(0.0006)
Constant	3.3347***	3.3342***	3.3337***	3.3344***
	(0.3623)	(0.3745)	(0.3730)	(0.3750)
Fixed effects	Yes	Yes	Yes	Yes
Industry and year	Yes	Yes	Yes	Yes
Observations	15,753	15,753	15,753	15,753
R^2	0.4379	0.4376	0.4376	0.4381

Bootstrap regression coefficients are reported (from 500 bootstrap replications). Bootstrap standard errors are reported in parentheses
***, **, and * indicate statistical significance at the 1%, 5%, and 10% level, respectively

Our findings suggest that CSR is likely to be positively associated with dynamic productivity change. Moreover, the evidence emphasizes the relevance of CSR dimensions, as well as the components of dynamic productivity change. In particular, we found that the positive relationship between CSR and dynamic productivity change came from the social and governance dimensions of CSR. In other words, the relationship came from CSR activities of a more internal nature, dedicated in large measure to internal stakeholders. Furthermore, the positive relationships between dynamic productivity change and overall, social, and governance CSR are driven by positive associations between these CSR dimensions and dynamic technical-inefficiency change, despite negative relationships with the dynamic scale-inefficiency component. Interestingly, we found that dynamic technical change was negatively associated with environmental CSR, which could reflect that such a large investment as CSR could initially have a negative effect on dynamic technical change. For example, the investment in environmental CSR can make some production options impossible (such as needing to change production methods to address environmental concerns), which could cause even the situations of technical regress.

The conclusions derived from this study are important from the policy point of view. One policy implication of the findings would be to introduce instruments to encourage firms to invest in CSR as it is associated with better performance outcomes, that is, larger productivity. In other words, the policies aiming at promoting CSR may provide firms' managers with incentives to eventually improve productivity. The examples of such policies could include tax reductions or more favorable lending rates for firms investing in CSR.

Future analyses are needed to assess the robustness of these findings. In particular, assessing if a negative association between technical change and CSR recovers would require conducting the regression analysis with technical change between $t + 1$ and $t + 2$, $t + 2$ and $t + 3$, and so on. Further checks regarding endogeneity can also allow the robustness of our results to be assessed.

Acknowledgments The financial support for this article from the National Science Centre in Poland (grant number 2016/23/B/HS4/03398) is gratefully acknowledged.

References

Alene, A. D. (2010). Productivity growth and the effects of R&D in African agriculture. *Agricultural Economics, 41*, 223–238.

Aw, B. Y., Roberts, M. J., & Xu, D. Y. (2011). R&D investment, exporting, and productivity dynamics. *American Economic Review, 101*(4), 1312–1344.

Banker, R. D., Charnes, A., & Cooper, W. W. (1984). Some models for estimating technical and scale inefficiencies in Data Envelopment Analysis. *Management Science, 30*, 1078–1092.

Baum, C. F., Schaffer, M. E., & Stillman, S. (2003). Instrumental variables and GMM: Estimation and testing. *The Stata Journal, 3*(1), 1–31.

Briec, W., & Kerstens, K. (2009a). The Luenberger productivity indicator: An economic specification leading to infeasibilities. *Economic Modelling, 26*, 597–600.

Briec, W., & Kerstens, K. (2009b). Infeasibility and directional distance functions with application to the determinateness of the Luenberger productivity indicator. *Journal of Optimization Theory and Application, 141*, 55–73.

Chambers, R. G., & Pope, R. D. (1996). Aggregate productivity measures. *American Journal of Agricultural Economics, 78*(5), 1360–1365.

Chambers, R. G., Chung, Y., & Färe, R. (1996). Benefit and distance functions. *Journal of Economic Theory, 70*(2), 407–419.

Charnes, A., Cooper, W. W., & Rhodes, E. (1978). Measuring the efficiency of the decision making units. *European Journal of Operational Research, 2*, 429–444.

Cheng, B., Ioannou, I., & Serafeim, G. (2014). Corporate social responsibility and access to finance. *Strategic Management Journal, 35*, 1–23.

Cummins, J. D., & Xie, X. (2013). Efficiency, productivity, and scale economies in the U.S. property-liability insurance industry. *Journal of Productivity Analysis, 39*(2), 141–164.

Curi, C., Lozano-Vivas, A., & Zelenyuk, V. (2015). Foreign bank diversification and efficiency prior to and during the financial crisis: Does one business model fit all? *Journal of Banking & Finance, 61*, S22–S35.

Deng, X., Kang, J.-K., & Low, B. S. (2013). Corporate social responsibility and stakeholder value maximization: Evidence from mergers. *Journal of Financial Economics, 110*, 87–109.

Dilling-Hansen, M., Strøjer Madsen, E., & Smith, V. (2003). Efficiency, R&D and ownership – Some empirical evidence. *International Journal of Production Economics, 83*(1), 85–94.

Eisner, R., & Strotz, R. H. (1963). *Determinants of business investment*. New York: Prentice-Hall.

El Ghoul, S., Guedhami, O., Kwok, C., & Mishra, D. (2011). Does corporate social responsibility affect the cost of capital? *Journal of Banking & Finance, 35*(9), 2388–2406.

Epstein, L. G. (1981). Duality theory and functional forms for dynamic factor demands. *Review of Economic Studies, 48*, 81–96.

Färe, R., Grosskopf, S., & Margaritis, D. (2008). U.S. productivity in agriculture and R&D. *Journal of Productivity Analysis, 30*, 7–12.

Flammer, C. (2015). Does corporate social responsibility lead to superior financial performance? A regression discontinuity approach. *Management Science, 61*(11), 2549–2568.

Guillamon Saorin, E., Kapelko, M., & Stefanou, S. E. (2018). Corporate social responsibility and operational inefficiency: A dynamic approach. *Sustainability, 10*(7), 2277.

Hannon, J., & Milkovich, G. (1996). The effect of human resource reputation signals on share prices: An event study. *Human Resource Management, 35*, 405–424.

Hausman, J. (1978). Specification tests in econometrics. *Econometrica, 46*(6), 1251–1271.

Hou, C.-E., Lu, W.-M., & Hung, S.-W. (2017). Does CSR matter? Influence of corporate social responsibility on corporate performance in the creative industry. *Annals of Operations Research, 278*, 255–279.

Huggett, M., & Ospina, S. (2001). Does productivity growth fall after the adoption of new technology? *Journal of Monetary Economics, 48*(1), 173–195.

Jacobs, B. W., Kraude, R., & Narayanan, S. (2016). Operational productivity, corporate social performance, financial performance, and risk in manufacturing firms. *Production and Operations Management, 25*(12), 2065–2085.

Kapelko, M., Oude Lansink, A., & Stefanou, S. E. (2014). Assessing dynamic inefficiency of the Spanish construction sector pre- and post-financial crisis. *European Journal of Operational Research, 237*(1), 349–357.

Kapelko, M., Oude Lansink, A., & Stefanou, S. (2015a). Effect of food regulation on the Spanish food processing industry. *PLoS One, 10*(6), e0128217. https://doi.org/10.1371/journal.pone.0128217.

Kapelko, M., Oude Lansink, A., & Stefanou, S. (2015b). Analyzing the impact of investment spikes on dynamic productivity growth. *Omega, 54*, 116–124.

Kapelko, M., Oude Lansink, A., & Stefanou, S. (2016). Investment age and dynamic productivity growth in the Spanish food processing industry. *American Journal of Agricultural Economics, 98*, 946–961.

Kapelko, M., Oude Lansink, A., & Guillamon-Saorin, E. (2020). Corporate social responsibility and dynamic productivity change in the US food and beverage manufacturing industry. *Agribusiness* (forthcoming).

Kerstens, K., & Van de Woestyne, I. (2014). Comparing Malmquist and Hicks–Moorsteen productivity indices: Exploring the impact of unbalanced vs. balanced panel data. *European Journal of Operational Research, 233*(3), 749–758.

Kleibergen, F., & Paap, R. (2006). Generalized reduced rank tests using the singular value decomposition. *Journal of Econometrics, 133*, 97–126.

Kneip, A., Simar, L., & Wilson, P. W. (2018). Inference in dynamic, nonparametric models of production: Central limit theorems for Malmquist indices. In *Discussion paper #2018/10, Institut de Statistique, Biostatistique et Sciences Actuarielles*. Louvain-la-Neuve, Belgium: Université Catholique de Louvain.

Lev, B., Petrovits, C., & Radhakrishnan, S. (2010). Is doing good for you? How corporate charitable contributions enhance revenue growth. *Strategic Management Journal, 31*, 182–200.
Lu, W.-M., Wang, W.-K., & Lee, H.-L. (2013). The relationship between corporate social responsibility and corporate performance: Evidence from the US semiconductor industry. *International Journal of Production Research, 51*(19), 5683–5695.
Lucas, R. E. (1967). Adjustment costs and the theory of supply. *Journal of Political Economy, 75*, 321–334.
Lys, T., Naughton, J. P., & Wang, C. (2015). Signaling through corporate accountability reporting. *Journal of Accounting and Economics, 60*, 56–72.
Margolis, J. D., Elfenbein, H. A., & Walsh, J. P. (2009). *Does it pay to be good... And does it matter? A meta-analysis of the relationship between corporate social and financial performance*. Available at SSRN: https://ssrn.com/abstract=1866371, http://dx.doi.org/10.2139/ssrn.1866371. Accessed 20 Jan 2019.
McWilliams, A., & Siegel, D. (2000). Corporate social responsibility and financial performance: Correlation or misspecification? *Strategic Management Journal, 21*(5), 603–609.
McWilliams, A., & Siegel, D. (2001). Corporate social responsibility: A theory of the firm perspective. *The Academy of Management Review, 26*, 117–127.
Morrison Paul, C. J., & Siegel, D. S. (2006). Corporate social responsibility and economic performance. *Journal of Productivity Analysis, 26*, 207–211.
Orlitzky, M., Schmidt, F. L., & Rynes, S. L. (2003). Corporal social and financial performance: A meta-analysis. *Organization Studies, 24*, 403–441.
Oude Lansink, A., Stefanou, S. E., & Serra, T. (2015). Primal and dual dynamic Luenberger productivity indicators. *European Journal of Operational Research, 241*, 555–563.
Pergelova, A., Prior, D., & Rialp, J. (2010). Assessing advertising efficiency. *Journal of Advertising, 39*(3), 39–54.
Puggioni, D., & Stefanou, S. E. (2019). The value of being socially responsible: A primal-dual approach. *European Journal of Operational Research, 276*(3), 1090–1103.
Servaes, H., & Tamayo, A. (2013). The impact of corporate social responsibility on firm value: The role of customer awareness. *Management Science, 59*(5), 1045–1061.
Silva, E., & Stefanou, S. E. (2003). Nonparametric dynamic production analysis and the theory of cost. *Journal of Productivity Analysis, 19*, 5–32.
Silva, E., Oude Lansink, A., & Stefanou, S. E. (2015). The adjustment-cost model of the firm: Duality and productive efficiency. *International Journal of Production Economics, 168*, 246–256.
Silva, E., & Stefanou, S. E. (2007). Dynamic efficiency measurement: Theory and application. *American Journal of Agricultural Economics, 89*(2), 398–419.
Simar, L. (2003). Detecting outliers in frontier models: A simple approach. *Journal of Productivity Analysis, 20*(3), 391–424.
Simar, L., & Wilson, P. W. (1999). Estimating and bootstrapping Malmquist indices. *European Journal of Operational Research, 115*, 459–471.
Simar, L., & Wilson, P. W. (2007). Estimation and inference in two-stage, semiparametric models of production processes. *Journal of Econometrics, 136*, 31–64.
Simar, L., & Wilson, P. W. (2019). Central limit theorems and inference for sources of productivity change measured by nonparametric Malmquist indices. *European Journal of Operational Research, 277*, 756–769.
Simar, L., Vanhems, A., & Wilson, P. W. (2012). Statistical inference for DEA estimators of directional distances. *European Journal of Operational Research, 220*, 853–864.
Skevas, T., & Oude Lansink, A. (2014). Reducing pesticide use and pesticide impact by productivity growth: The case of Dutch arable farming. *Journal of Agricultural Economics, 65*, 191–211.
Sun, L., & Stuebs, M. (2013). Corporate social responsibility and firm productivity: Evidence from the chemical industry in the United States. *Journal of Business Ethics, 118*(2), 251–263.
Surroca, J., Tribo, J. A., & Waddock, S. (2010). Corporate responsibility and financial performance: The role of intangible resources. *Strategic Management Journal, 31*(5), 463–490.
Treadway, A. (1970). Adjustment costs and variable inputs in the theory of the competitive firm. *Journal of Economic Theory, 2*, 329–347.
Vitaliano, D. F., & Stella, G. P. (2006). The cost of corporate social responsibility: The case of the community reinvestment act. *Journal of Productivity Analysis, 6*(3), 235–244.
Waddock, S., & Graves, S. (1997). The corporate social performance - financial performance link. *Strategic Management Journal, 18*, 303–319.
Wang, W.-K., Lu, W.-M., Kweh, Q. L., & Lai, H.-W. (2014). Does corporate social responsibility influence the corporate performance of the U.S. telecommunications industry? *Telecommunications Policy, 38*(7), 580–591.
Wijesiri, M., & Meoli, M. (2015). Productivity change of micro finance institutions in Kenya: A bootstrap Malmquist approach. *Journal of Retailing and Consumer Services, 25*, 115–121.
Worthington, A. (2000). Technical efficiency and technological change in Australian building societies. *Abacus, 36*(2), 180–197.
Wright, P., & Ferris, S. (1997). Agency conflict and corporate strategy: The effect of divestment on corporate value. *Strategic Management Journal, 18*, 77–83.

A Novel Two-Phase Approach to Computing a Regional Social Progress Index

Vincent Charles, Tatiana Gherman, and Ioannis E. Tsolas

Abstract In recent decades, concerns have emerged regarding the fact that standard macroeconomic statistics (such as gross domestic product) do not provide a sufficiently detailed and accurate picture of societal progress and well-being and of people's true quality of life. This has further translated into concerns regarding the design of related public policies and whether these actually have the intended impact in practice. One of the first steps in bridging the gap between well-being metrics and policy intervention is the development of improved well-being measures. The calculation of a regional Social Progress Index (SPI) has been on the policymakers' agenda for quite some time, as it is used to assist in the proposal of strategies that would create the conditions for all individuals in a society to reach their full potential, enhancing and sustaining the quality of their lives, while reducing regional inequalities. In this manuscript, we show a novel way to calculate a regional SPI under a two-phase approach. In the first phase, we aggregate the item-level information into subfactor-level indices and the subfactor-level indices into a factor-level index using an objective general index (OGI); in the second phase, we use the factor-level indices to obtain the regional SPI through a pure data envelopment analysis (DEA) approach. We further apply the method developed to analyse a single period of social progress in Peru. The manuscript is a contribution to the practical measurement of social progress.

Keywords Data envelopment analysis · Objective general index · Social progress index

1 Introduction

Economic growth is an interesting and puzzling concept. For more than five decades, nations around the world have assessed their general well-being based on this indicator, most commonly captured via the computation of the gross domestic product (GDP); the common view has been that the higher the economic growth, the better the nation's overall performance (Kuznets 1934; Kubiszewski et al. 2013). Governments, businesses and the civil society alike, they have all equated economic growth to progress; it is no wonder then that economic policies around the world have largely been shaped by the end goal of maximising GDP growth. This perception has, nonetheless, been challenged since a long time ago. For example, as early as 1974, Easterlin's paradox (Easterlin 1974) highlighted that at a point in time human happiness varies directly with economic growth both among and within nations, but over time happiness does not trend upward as income continues to grow.

In time, a plethora of economic and statistical research, accompanied by psychological research, have challenged the position of authority of the GDP as an indicator of national progress on a number of fronts, showing the discrepancy between monetary valuation and perceived well-being (Davies 2015). According to Porter et al. (2016, p. 32), 'social progress is the capacity of a society to meet the basic human needs of its citizens, establish the building blocks that allow citizens and communities to enhance and sustain the quality of their lives, and create the conditions for all individuals to reach their

V. Charles (✉)
School of Management, University of Bradford, Bradford, UK

CENTRUM PUCP, Pontificia Universidad Católica del Perú, Lima, Peru
e-mail: c.vincent3@bradford.ac.uk

T. Gherman
Faculty of Business and Law, University of Northampton, Northampton, UK

I. E. Tsolas
School of Applied Mathematics and Physics, National Technical University of Athens, Athens, Greece

J. Aparicio et al. (eds.), *Advances in Efficiency and Productivity II*, International Series in Operations Research & Management Science 287, https://doi.org/10.1007/978-3-030-41618-8_10

full potential'. In line with this definition, there has been a constant increase in the number of calls to address basic human needs, promote equality and opportunity for all people, improve the quality of life of people and protect the environment, among others. What these calls are indicative of is a shortcoming of GDP to capture the essence of inclusive growth, wherein inclusive growth is a combination of both economic and societal progress. There is an increased awareness that GDP has mistakenly been used as a proxy indicator of the citizens' well-being, human progress and overall social and economic health and welfare (Cobb et al. 1995; Stiglitz et al. 2009, 2010). Can a nation register a high rate of economic growth but a slow societal progress at the same time? Evidence points to yes.

Without a doubt, GDP is an important economic instrument for measuring and comparing market activity, but it is only that: a barometer of a nation's raw economic activity. The search for better instruments to measure people's well-being has translated into the creation of various initiatives, most of which materialised in the 2000s. For example, the year 2007 marked a particular point in time when four main bodies, represented by the European Commission, the European Parliament, the Organisation for Economic Co-operation and Development (OECD) and the World Economic Forum (WEF), organised a conference aimed at clarifying 'which indices are most appropriate to measure progress and how these can best be integrated into the decision-making process and taken up by public debate' (European Commission 2007). Further, in 2008, the Commission on the Measurement of Economics Performance and Social Progress (also known as the Stiglitz Commission) was set up, whose main objective was to propose better indicators of social well-being (Stiglitz et al. 2009); interestingly enough, the Commission highlighted the well-being measurement as a necessary accompaniment to GDP. More precisely, the Commission's aim was 'to identify the limits of GDP as an indicator of economic performance and social progress, including the problems with its measurement; to consider what additional information might be required for the production of more relevant indicators of social progress; to assess the feasibility of alternative measurement tools; and to discuss how to present the statistical information in an appropriate way' (Stiglitz et al. 2009). More recently, at a special UN summit in 2015, a document titled 'Transforming Our World: The 2030 Agenda for Sustainable Development' was adopted, which represented a commitment of heads of state and government to eradicate poverty and achieve sustainable development by 2030 worldwide. This document also differentiated between GDP and social progress when it formulated its objective as: 'By 2030, build on existing initiatives to develop measurements of progress on sustainable development that complement gross domestic product, and support statistical capacity-building in developing countries'.

All in all, 'The Beyond GDP' initiative has brought together a large number of countries who found themselves cooperating on developing indicators that are as clear as GDP, but more inclusive of environmental and social aspects of progress. Such efforts further led to the creation of Wikiprogress, the official online platform for the OECD-hosted Global Project on 'Measuring the Progress of Societies' and whose purpose is to share information on the measurement of social, economic and environmental progress. Some of the indices included in The Global Project are Genuine Progress Indicator, Global Peace Index, Happy Planet Index, Human Development Index, Sustainable Society Index, The Climate Competitiveness Index, the Better Life Index, the Legatum Prosperity Index and World Happiness Index, among others. Despite all these efforts, however, there is no single methodology and no general agreement on the existence of a set of standardised or holistic indicators to measure social progress. Here, we join the calls for the development of improved methodologies to measure social progress.

In this manuscript, we show a novel way to calculate a regional social progress index (SPI) under a two-phase approach. In the first phase, we aggregate the item-level information into subfactor-level indices and the subfactor level indices into a factor-level index using an objective general index (OGI); in the second phase, we use the factor-level indices to obtain the regional SPI through a pure DEA approach. The benefits of our proposed method are twofold: on the one hand, we account for the variation in the two stages of the first phase, and on the other hand, we build an index based on relative measures in the second phase. We further apply the method developed to analyse a single period of social progress in Peru. The manuscript is a contribution to the practical measurement of social progress.

2 Social Progress Index

The Social Progress Imperative (Social Progress Imperative 2018), a global non-profit based in Washington, DC, defines social progress as 'the capacity of a society to meet the basic human needs of its citizens, establish the building blocks that allow citizens and communities to enhance and sustain the quality of their lives, and create the conditions for all individuals to reach their full potential'. In line with this definition, the Social Progress Imperative has been calculating a Social Progress Index ever since 2013; this index measures 51 social and environmental indicators, across 3 broad dimensions of social progress: basic human needs, foundations of well-being and opportunity (see Fig. 1). In the words of the organisation itself, 'the index doesn't measure people's happiness or life satisfaction, focusing instead on actual life outcomes in areas from

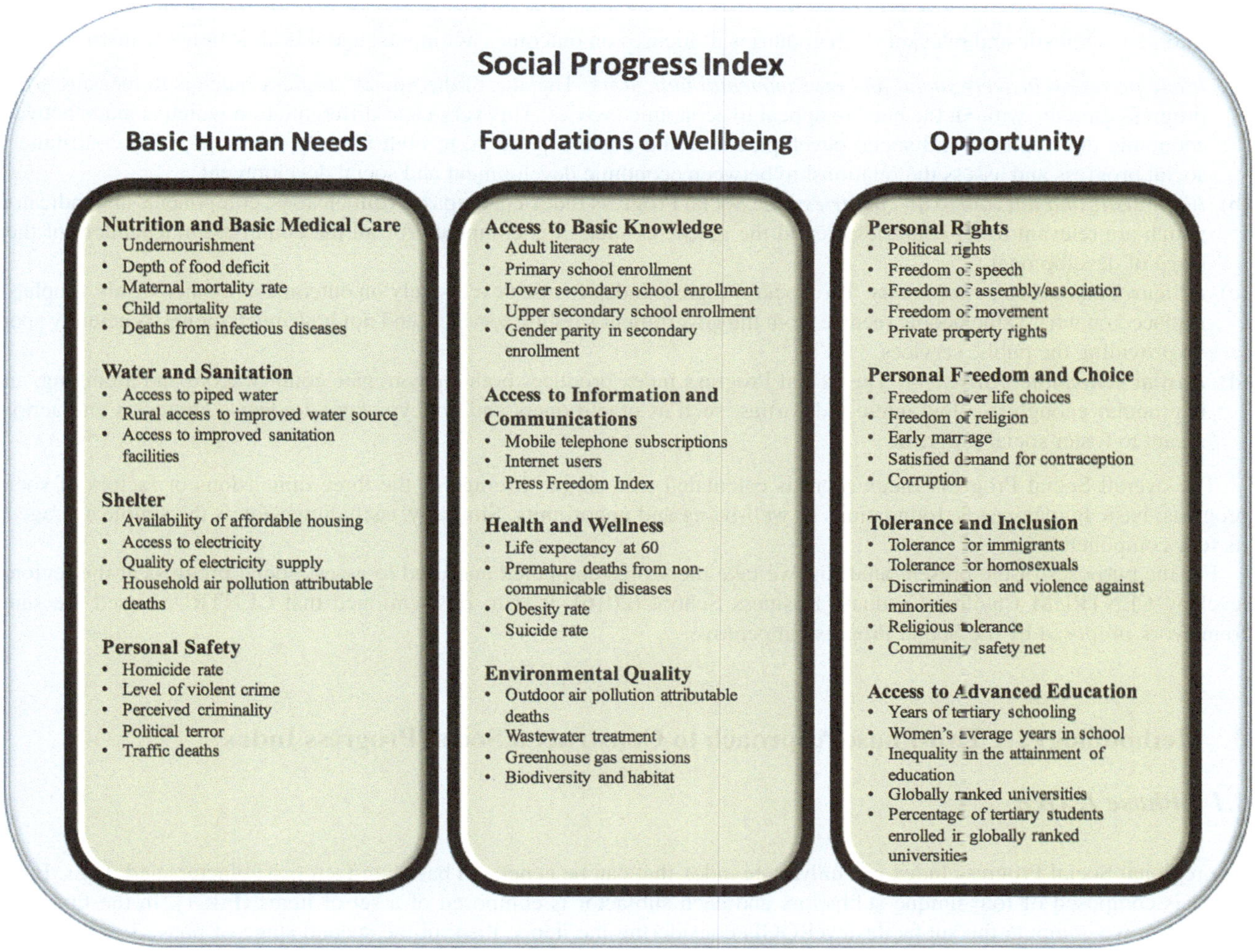

Fig. 1 Social Progress Index framework, as defined by the Social Progress Imperative (2018)

shelter and nutrition to rights and education. This exclusive focus on measurable outcomes makes the index a useful policy tool that tracks changes in society over time.' Below, we proceed to describe the three factors briefly:

1. The *basic human needs* factor 'assesses how well a country provides for its people's essential needs by measuring access to nutrition and basic medical care, if they have access to safe drinking water, if they have access to adequate housing with basic utilities, and if society is safe and secure' (Social Progress Imperative 2018). In other words, it answers the question: Does everyone have the basic needs for survival met?
2. The *foundations of well-being* factor 'measures whether citizens have access to basic education, can access information and knowledge from both inside and outside their country, and if there are the conditions for living healthy lives. Foundations of Wellbeing also measures a country's protection of its natural environment, air, water and land, which are critical for current and future wellbeing' (Social Progress Imperative 2018). It answers the question: Does everyone have access to what is needed to improve their lives?
3. The *opportunity* factor 'measures the degree to which a country's citizens have personal rights and freedoms and are able to make their own personal decisions as well as whether prejudices or hostilities within a society prohibit individuals from reaching their potential. Opportunity also includes the degree to which advanced forms of education are accessible to those in a country who wish to further their knowledge and skills, creating the potential for wide-ranging personal opportunity' (Social Progress Imperative 2018). It answers the question: Does everyone have a chance to pursue their goals, dreams and ambitions?

The design of the Social Progress Index is based on four principles: it comprises exclusively social and environmental indicators, it is holistic and relevant to all countries, it focuses on outcomes not inputs, and it is an actionable instrument:

(a) *It comprises exclusively social and environmental indicators*: The aim of the Social Progress Index is to measure social progress directly, without the need to appeal to economic proxies. This very clear differentiation which is made between economic development and social development would make it possible to both identify the factors that contribute to social progress and assess the relationship between economic development and social development.
(b) *It is holistic and relevant to all countries*: The Social Progress Index encompasses dimensions, components and indicators which are relevant to all countries around the globe; as such, it is computed for all the countries, independent of their stage of development.
(c) *It focuses on outcomes not inputs*: The Social Progress Index focuses exclusively on outcomes; in other words, emphasis is placed on what value people receive from the government's public services, and not how much money is actually spent on providing the public services.
(d) *It is an actionable instrument*: The Social Progress Index produces both an aggregate country score and a ranking, and is granular enough to allow interested parties, such as practitioners and policymakers, to devise strategies and actions meant to foster social progress.

The overall Social Progress Index score is calculated as a simple average of the three dimensions or factors of social progress: basic human needs, foundations of well-being and opportunity. Similarly, each dimension is the simple average of its four components.

For the purposes of the present analysis, we take the scores computed and used to assess social progress at the regional level by CENTRUM Católica Graduate Business School (2016). It is to be mentioned that CENTRUM used the same framework proposed by the Social Progress Imperative.

3 Methodology: A Two-Phase Approach to Construct a Social Progress Index

3.1 Phase I: OGI

The regional Social Progress Index is a univariate index that can be generated based on factors, subfactors and items. Every factor is composed of four unique subfactors and each subfactor is composed of a set of items (Fig. 1). In the first stage of phase I, we compute the subfactor-level OGIs considering the items; then, in the second stage of phase I, we compute the factor-level OGIs considering the subfactor-level OGIs. Upon obtaining the three phase I factor-level OGIs, we further proceed to compute the phase II DEA-based SPI using the phase I factor-level OGIs as inputs. The resulting SPI is referred to as the *Social Progress Index* for the given application. In the subsequent paragraphs, we shall start by highlighting the importance of the OGI and detail the computational procedure and the relevant foundations.

Let us consider a data matrix of n entities (regions) with p variates (could be factors or subfactors or items under subfactors). In order to rank the entities, a general index that combines the p variates into a univariate index should be constructed. If the data are uncorrelated, the general index can be constructed as the sum of standardised scores (Z-scores), and if the data are correlated, the first principal component may be employed as a general index, as it maximises the variance of the index under weight constraints. Nevertheless, one of the undesirable features of such approaches is that these indices can be negatively correlated with some of the variates. To tackle such shortcomings, Sei (2016) proposed an OGI that is always positively correlated with each of the variates. We apply the notion of OGI under a two-stage framework to study the social progress of the regions.

The objective general index (OGI) can be defined in line with Sei (2016) and Charles and Sei (2019) as:

$$G = \sum_{l=1}^{p} w_l X_l, \tag{1}$$

where X_l is the lth random variable and the positive weight vector $\{w_l\}_{l=1}^{p}$ is the solution to equation (2), which is known to have a unique solution as long as the covariance matrix of $X_l's$ denoted by $S_{lm} = E[X_l X_m]$ is not singular (Marshall and Olkin 1968):

$$\sum_{m=1}^{p} w_l S_{lm} w_m = 1, \quad l = 1, \ldots, p. \tag{2}$$

Equation (2) implies that each variable X_l has a positive correlation with the OGI since equation (2) can be rewritten as:

$$E[(w_l X_l)G] = 1. \tag{3}$$

A naive algorithm to obtain the weights is to solve the quadratic equation (2) with respect to $w_l > 0$, given $\{w_m\}_{m \neq l}$ for each l, and repeat this process until convergence. The algorithm is detailed as follows, in line with Sei (2016) and Marshall and Olkin (1968):

Algorithm:
Input: A positive definite matrix $\mathbf{S} \in \mathbf{R}^{\mathbf{pxp}}$, initial value $\mathbf{w}_0 (= \mathbf{1}_p)$ and tolerance $\epsilon > 0$
Output: A vector $0 < \mathbf{w} = (w_1, \ldots, w_p)^T$, such that **DSD** is a bi-unit matrix
(*i.e.* $\mathbf{DSD}_p = \mathbf{1}_p$), where $\mathbf{D} = diag(\mathbf{w})$:

(i) $\mathbf{w} \longleftarrow \mathbf{w}_0$
(ii) For $l = 1, \ldots, p$, in order, solve the quadratic equation (2) with respect to w_l.
(Note: $\mathbf{DSD}_p \equiv \sum_{m=1}^{p} w_l S_{lm} w_m$, where elements of $\mathbf{S}$ are denoted by S_{lm}.)
(iii) If $\|\mathbf{w} - \mathbf{w}_0\| < \epsilon$, output $\mathbf{w}$. Otherwise, $\mathbf{w}_0 \longleftarrow \mathbf{w}$ and go to step (ii).

One can note from Sei (2016) that a weight map $\mathbf{w} = \mathbf{w}(\mathbf{S})$ is said to be consistent if the weight vector $\mathbf{w}$ is positive for any $\mathbf{S}$; and it is said to be covariance consistent if $\mathbf{Sw}$ is positive for any $\mathbf{S}$. The weight map of OGI is both consistent and covariance consistent. By contrast, other index generation methods fail to satisfy the consistency property (such as the $\mathbf{w} = \mathbf{S}^{-1}\mathbf{1_p}$ method), the covariance consistency property (such as the sum of Z-scores) or both (such as the first principal component).

The following lemma characterises the OGI by an orthogonality condition:

Lemma 3.1 (Orthogonality Charles and Sei 2019) *Let* $w_1, \ldots, w_p$ *be positive numbers,* $G = \sum_{l=1}^{p} w_l X_l$*, and* $\Delta_l = w_l X_l - G/p$*. Then, the following two conditions are equivalent:*

(a) *G is the OGI.*
(b) $E[G\Delta_l] = 0$ *and* $E[G^2] = p$.

In the above lemma, we will call Δ_l as *the residual of OGI*.

Let $\{X^i_{jk} \mid i \in I, j \in J_i, k \in K_j\}$ be a set of random variables. In our setting, the index set for social progress factors is $I = \{BHN, FoW, Opp\}$ ={basic human needs, foundations of well-being, opportunity}.

Likewise, the index set for the social progress subfactors for every factor could be considered as follows: J_{BHN} = {nutrition and basic medical care, water and sanitation, shelter, personal safety}, J_{FoW} = {access to basic knowledge, access to information and communications, health and wellness, environmental quality} and J_{Opp} = {personal rights, personal freedom and choice, tolerance and inclusion, access to advanced education}. In the same way, K_j is the set which consists of the jth subfactor's items that are listed in Fig. 1.

Let us define the two-stage OGI as follows:

Definition 3.1 (Two-stage OGI) For the given ith factor for each $j \in J_i$, compute the OGI of $\{X^i_{jk}\}_{k \in K_j}$ by:

$$G^i_j = \sum_{k \in K_j} w^i_{jk} X^i_{jk}, \quad E[(w^i_{jk} X^i_{jk}) G^i_j] = 1, \quad k \in K_j. \tag{4}$$

Then, compute the joint OGI of $\{G^i_j\}_{j \in J_i}$ by:

$$G^i = \sum_{j \in J_i} w^i_j G^i_j, \quad E[(w^i_j G^i_j) G^i] = 1, \quad j \in J_i. \tag{5}$$

The resultant index G^i is the ith *two-stage OGI*.

The two conditions (4) and (5) suggest that each G^i_j is the representative of subfactors X^i_{jk}'s and G^i summarises G^i_j's for every given $i \in I$.

Properties of OGI

Property 3.1 Equation (4) in the definition of the two-stage OGI implies that $E[X^{i}_{jk}G^{i}_{j}]$ is positive.

Property 3.2 Equation (5) in the definition of the two-stage OGI implies that $E[G^{i}_{j}G^{i}]$ is positive.

Lemma 3.2 (Lack of Lag) *In general,* $E[X^{i}_{jk}G^{i}_{j}] > 0$ *and* $E[G^{i}_{j}G^{i}] > 0 \nRightarrow E[X^{i}_{jk}G^{i}] > 0.$

Proof See Charles and Sei (2019) for a counter-example.

The two-stage OGI is considered as a kind of ANOVA (analysis of variance) decomposition.

3.2 Phase II: DEA

Data envelopment analysis (DEA), introduced by Charnes et al. (1978), is a linear programming technique that facilitates the estimation of the efficiency of units within production contexts characterised by multiple outputs and inputs. In time, DEA has gained reputation as an excellent management science tool, supporting decision-making processes in a variety of fields. In the present manuscript, the objective is to rank the regions according to their social progress performance in the various factors, but without imposing an ad hoc valuation (weight) for any of them.

Below, we proceed to introduce two different DEA models, namely, radial and non-radial pure DEA. On the one hand, because the DMUs are evaluated in the best possible light, radial pure DEA focuses on the performance of the factor(s) in which the DMU performs the best; in practice, this means that the built index will end up emphasising few factors or even one single factor and disregard the performance of the others. On the other hand, non-radial pure DEA addresses this issue by focusing on the performance of all the factors (Charles and Diaz 2016). Both models are useful and serve different purposes, and hence, our aim is to provide the readers with a comparison between the two.

3.2.1 Radial Pure DEA

Having obtained the factor-level index for every factor through the two-stage OGI, in line with Lovell and Pastor (1999), the following system would produce the DEA-based index of social progress for region o that has a vector of $|I|$ outputs (the factors) $G_o = (G_o^1, \ldots, G_o^{|I|})$ and belongs to a set of R regions:

$$\begin{aligned} \max_{\phi,\lambda_1,\ldots,\lambda_R} \quad & \phi \\ \text{s.t.} \quad & \phi G_0^i \leq \sum_{r\in R} G_r^i \lambda_r, \quad \forall i \in I \\ & \sum_{r\in R} \lambda_r = 1, \quad \lambda_r \geq 0, \quad \forall r \in R. \end{aligned} \tag{6}$$

The result of this system would produce a vector $(\phi_o, \lambda_{o1}, \ldots, \lambda_{oR})$ for region o. Upon solving System (6) for every region, $r \in R$, we use the results to construct a social progress index $\theta_r^{radial} = 1/\phi_r$ for each of the regions.

3.2.2 Non-radial Pure DEA

Let us consider System (6) in light of the non-radial DEA (Charles and Zegarra 2014), wherein importance has been given to all the factors under study. Similar to the radial approach, we use the factor-level index obtained from the two-stage OGI and plug it into the following System (7). This in turn produces the non-radial pure DEA-based index of social progress for region o, which has a vector of $|I|$ outputs (the factors) $G_o = (G_o^1, \ldots, G_o^{|I|})$ and belongs to a set of R regions:

$$\max_{\Phi^1,\ldots,\Phi^{|I|},\lambda_1,\ldots,\lambda_R} \quad \sum_{i\in I}\Phi^i$$
$$\text{s.t.} \quad \Phi^i G_o^i \le \sum_{r\in R} G_r^i \lambda_r, \quad \forall i \in I$$
$$\sum_{r\in R}\lambda_r = 1, \quad \lambda_r \ge 0, \quad \forall r \in R. \tag{7}$$

The result of this system would produce a vector $(\Phi_o^1, \ldots, \Phi_o^{|I|}, \lambda_{o1}, \ldots, \lambda_{oR})$ for region o. Upon solving System (7) for every region, $r \in R$, we use the results to construct a social progress index $\theta_r^{non-radial} = |I|/\sum_{i\in I}\Phi_r^i$ for each of the regions.

4 Inferences from the Analytics

Table 1 shows the OGI indices for all the three factors of social progress, the social progress indices for the year 2015, as well as the associated ranking, for both the radial and non-radial DEA applied in the second phase of our modelling. It is to be noted that radial DEA refers to the indices obtained by running the pure DEA method with radial expansion (System 6), while the non-radial DEA refers to the indices attained by running the non-radial pure DEA method (System 7).

The interpretation of the results is quite straightforward. First, the table shows the situation of the regions in view of each of the three factors considered, that is, basic human needs, foundations of well-being and opportunity. We can quickly observe that the best performers in the BHN factor are Ica, Callao and Lambayeque, while the worst performer is Madre de Dios, followed by Puno. Similarly, Tacna, Cusco, Huancavelica and Ancash are the best performers in the FoW factor, with Ucayali, Lima Provincias and Loreto as the worst performers. Lastly, in the Opp factor, Moquequa, Ica, Lambayeque, Ancash and La Libertad are the best performers, and Puno, Loreto, Madre de Dios, Pasco, Amazonas, Ucayali and Huanuco are the worst performers.

Second, the table provides the ranking of the regions based on both the radial and non-radial DEA-based SPI. An immediate observation is that, independent of method used and despite some variations, the coastal regions are in general the highest performers in terms of social progress, while the jungle regions tend to be the worst performers. This finding is consistent with previous research (Charles and D'Alessio 2019). A visual representation of the results will yield additional insights, and this is what we proceed to do in the next subsection.

4.1 Visual Analytics

Figure 2 presents the boxplots of factors vs. classifications. With three factors and three classifications, the figure shows a total of nine boxplots, wherein each boxplot represents a specific factor and a specific classification. Furthermore, there are three median lines drawn horizontally in red colour; these represent the respective factor medians and are provided along with their 95% median confidence intervals. Among the three factor medians, the lowest median is recorded in the case of the Opp factor, followed by the BHN factor and then the FoW factor.

Although based on Table 1, one can observe that the standard deviations of the three factors are the same, still, in Fig. 2, we can see that there is a difference in the width of the confidence interval. The variation is high in the case of BHN when compared to the other two factors, FoW and Opp; by contrast, FoW registers a narrower confidence interval. We can observe that in the case of the BHN factor, the median of the coastal region falls outside the interval, while the other two medians of the highlands and jungle regions fall inside the interval. In the case of the FoW factor, the first two medians of the coastal and highlands regions fall inside the interval, while the third median of the jungle region falls outside the interval. Lastly, in the case of the Opp factor, the medians of all the regions fall outside the interval. Overall, the interesting observation to make here is that in two out of three cases (for FoW and Opp), the medians of the third classification (i.e. the jungle) are below the respective factor medians. This means that the jungle regions perform particularly poorly in the FoW and Opp factors. By contrast, in two out of three cases (for BHN and Opp), the medians of the first classification (i.e. the coast) are above the respective factor medians. In other words, the coastal regions are performing particularly well in the BHN and Opp factors.

Table 1 SPI: Ranking of regions based on radial and non-radial pure DEA

DMU	Regions	BHN	FoW	Opp	SPI-R	Rank-R	SPI-NR	Rank-NR
1	Amazonas[c]	18.51	20.77	9.63	0.9168	16	0.8033	19
2	Ancash[a]	18.31	22.02	14.18	0.9956	2	0.9377	7
3	Apurimac[b]	17.59	20.88	12.23	0.9219	15	0.8655	13
4	Arequipa[a]	20.23	21.65	13.57	0.9793	4	0.9526	4
5	Ayacucho[b]	19.93	21.94	12.24	0.9761	7	0.9174	10
6	Cajamarca[b]	17.08	21.64	12.12	0.9453	12	0.8625	15
7	Callao[a]	21.51	19.59	11.34	0.9858	3	0.8818	12
8	Cusco[b]	17.07	22.52	10.08	0.9674	10	0.8139	18
9	Huancavelica[b]	16.71	22.17	12.12	0.9630	11	0.8613	16
10	Huanuco[b]	17.40	21.13	9.76	0.9076	18	0.7953	20
11	Ica[a]	21.82	21.38	14.70	1.0000	1	1.0000	1
12	Junin[b]	17.21	21.32	12.22	0.9364	13	0.8637	14
13	La Libertad[a]	18.05	21.56	14.01	0.9771	6	0.9231	8
14	Lambayeque[a]	21.36	19.88	14.19	0.9789	5	0.9576	3
15	Lima Metropolitana[a]	20.01	21.57	13.25	0.9709	8	0.9401	6
16	Lima Provincias[a]	17.46	16.84	10.54	0.8002	21	0.7665	21
17	Loreto[c]	17.37	16.45	8.51	0.7961	22	0.7004	24
18	Madre de Dios[c]	13.49	17.71	9.51	0.7662	23	0.6864	26
19	Moquegua[a]	20.23	21.76	14.90	1.0000	1	0.9843	2
20	Pasco[b]	16.92	19.33	9.51	0.8470	20	0.7612	22
21	Piura[a]	20.32	21.30	13.40	0.9677	9	0.9450	5
22	Puno[b]	15.49	21.18	7.61	0.9098	17	0.6897	25
23	San Martin[c]	18.80	19.80	11.70	0.8975	19	0.8579	17
24	Tacna[a]	19.39	23.28	12.11	1.0000	1	0.9209	9
25	Tumbes[a]	20.36	18.98	12.28	0.9331	14	0.8836	11
26	Ucayali[c]	16.56	15.16	9.68	0.7589	24	0.7065	23
Statistics	Min	13.49	15.16	7.61	0.7589	1	0.6864	1
	Q1	17.11	19.64	9.84	0.9082	5.25	0.7973	7.25
	Median	18.05	21.18	12.12	0.9453	11	0.8637	13
	Q3	20.18	21.65	13.36	0.9785	17.75	0.9341	19.75
	Max	21.82	23.28	14.9	1.0000	24	1.0000	26
	Mean	18.43	20.45	11.75	0.9269	11.62	0.8569	13.5
	SD	2.00	2.00	2.00	0.0700	7.47	0.0900	7.65

Note: BHN = basic human needs, FoW = foundations of well-being, Opp = opportunity, SPI = Social Progress Index
[a]Coast
[b]Highlands
[c]Jungle

Figure 3 shows the correlations among the three factors, BHN, FoW and Opp. The highest correlation is between BHN and Opp; the correlation coefficient value is 0.683, which is significant at the 0.01 level. The correlation between FoW and Opp is 0.485, which is significant at the 0.05 level. Lastly, the correlation between BHN and FoW is not significant, with p-value = 0.148.

Figure 4 further shows that all the three factors correlate with both the radial and the non-radial DEA-based SPIs. An interesting observation to make, however, is that the FoW factor contributes to a greater extent to the construction of the radial DEA-based SPI (correlation coefficient = 0.872, significant at the 0.01 level), whereas in the case of the non-radial DEA-based SPI, the BHN and Opp factors are the ones contributing more towards its construction (correlation coefficients are 0.814 and 0.947, respectively, at the 0.01 level).

Figure 5 represents the correlations between the radial DEA-based SPI and the non-radial DEA-based SPI. It is to be noted that the legend of the region classifications in the graph is the same as before: 1 is the coast (represented with a circle symbol), 2 is the highlands (represented with a square symbol), and 3 is the jungle (represented with a star symbol). This graph shows a positive correlation between the radial DEA-based SPI and the non-radial DEA-based SPI, with a correlation coefficient of 0.867, which is significant at the 0.01 level. The horizontal and vertical lines represent the averages of the

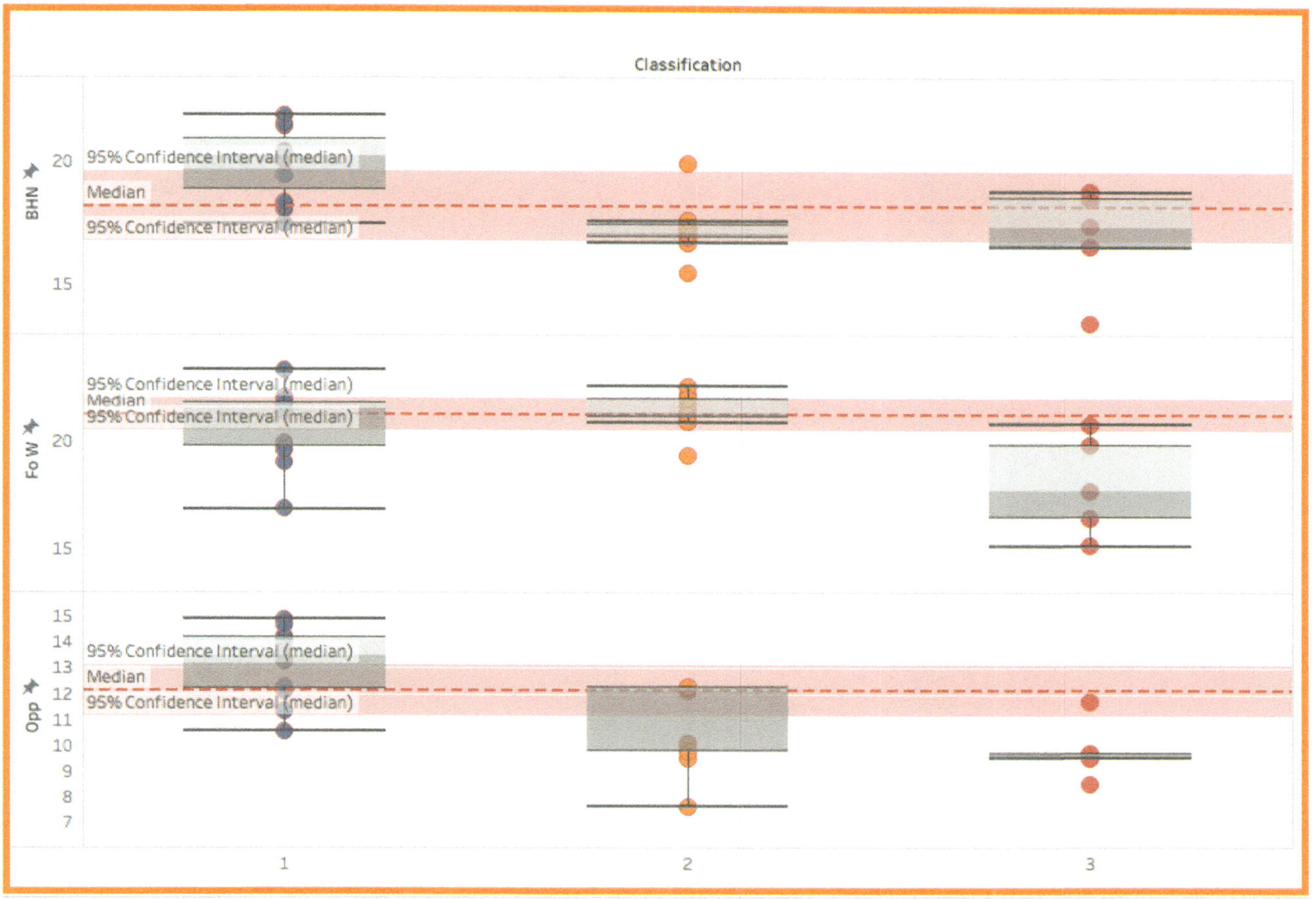

Fig. 2 Boxplots of factors vs. classifications (Note: 1 = Coastal regions; 2 = Highlands regions; 3 = Jungle regions)

non-radial DEA-based SPI and the radial DEA-based SPI, respectively; with the following confidence intervals: 0.8189–0.8948 for the non-radial DEA-based SPI and 0.8970–0.9568 for the radial DEA-based SPI. We also provide the trend line, represented by the dotted line, along with its 95% confidence band. We can observe that the average of the radial DEA-based SPI is higher than the average of the non-radial DEA-based SPI (0.9269 versus 0.8569). Also, the radial DEA-based SPI counts with a higher variation, which can be appreciated from the width of the confidence interval.

Based on Fig. 5, we can draw some noteworthy observations. First, in the case of the non-radial DEA-based SPI, we can notice that except for one region (Lima Provincias), all the coastal regions are above the average. Similarly, in the case of the radial DEA-based SPI, we can notice that except for two regions (Lima Provincias and Tumbes), all the coastal regions are above the average yet again. This indicates that overall coastal regions tend to be better performers in terms of social progress than the highlands and jungle regions. Further, we can notice that while in the case of the radial DEA-based SPI, there is only one highlands region (Ayacucho) situated above the average; in the case of the radial DEA-based SPI, we have four highlands regions that are above the average; this is because these four regions are performing well in a particular dimension, which 'pushes' them into the high-performer category. This happens because, as Charles and Diaz (2016) indicated, the non-radial DEA-based SPI values the performance in every factor, whereas the radial DEA-based index tends to focus almost exclusively on the factors in which the DMU performs better.

Another observation to make is that the regions of Ica, Moquegua, Lambayeque, Ancash, Arequipa, La Libertad, Ayacucho and Tacna are above the averages of both the radial and non-radial DEA-based SPIs; in other words, independent of the type of DEA model used, these regions are the ones that can be said to be high performers in terms of social progress. This observation is noteworthy considering that according to Table 1, some of these regions are ranked in the middle, which would make them to be perceived as average performers instead. For example, see Ayacucho, a region that ranks seventh according to the radial DEA and tenth according to the non-radial DEA or see La Libertad, which ranks sixth according to the radial DEA and eighth according to the non-radial DEA. Despite this, a visual representation clearly indicates that

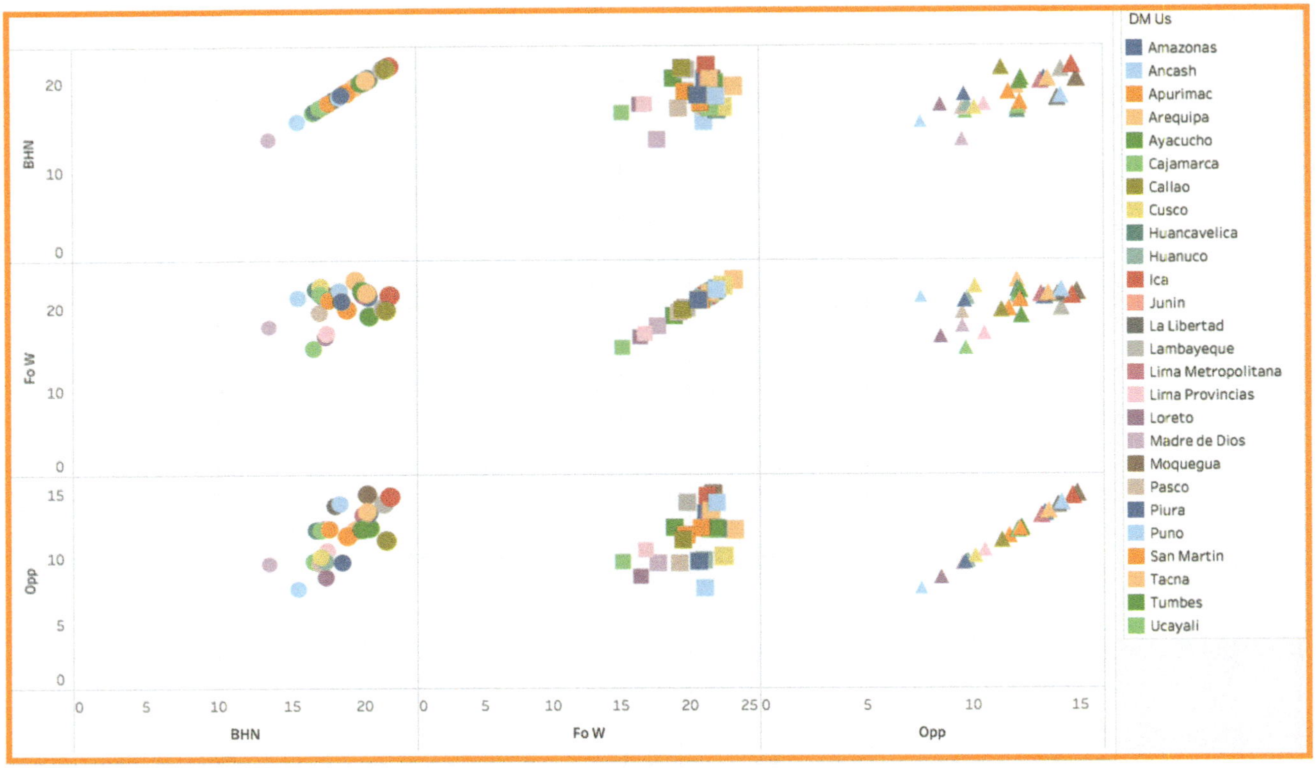

Fig. 3 Factor correlations

Fig. 4 Correlations between factors and radial vs. non-radial DEA-based SPI

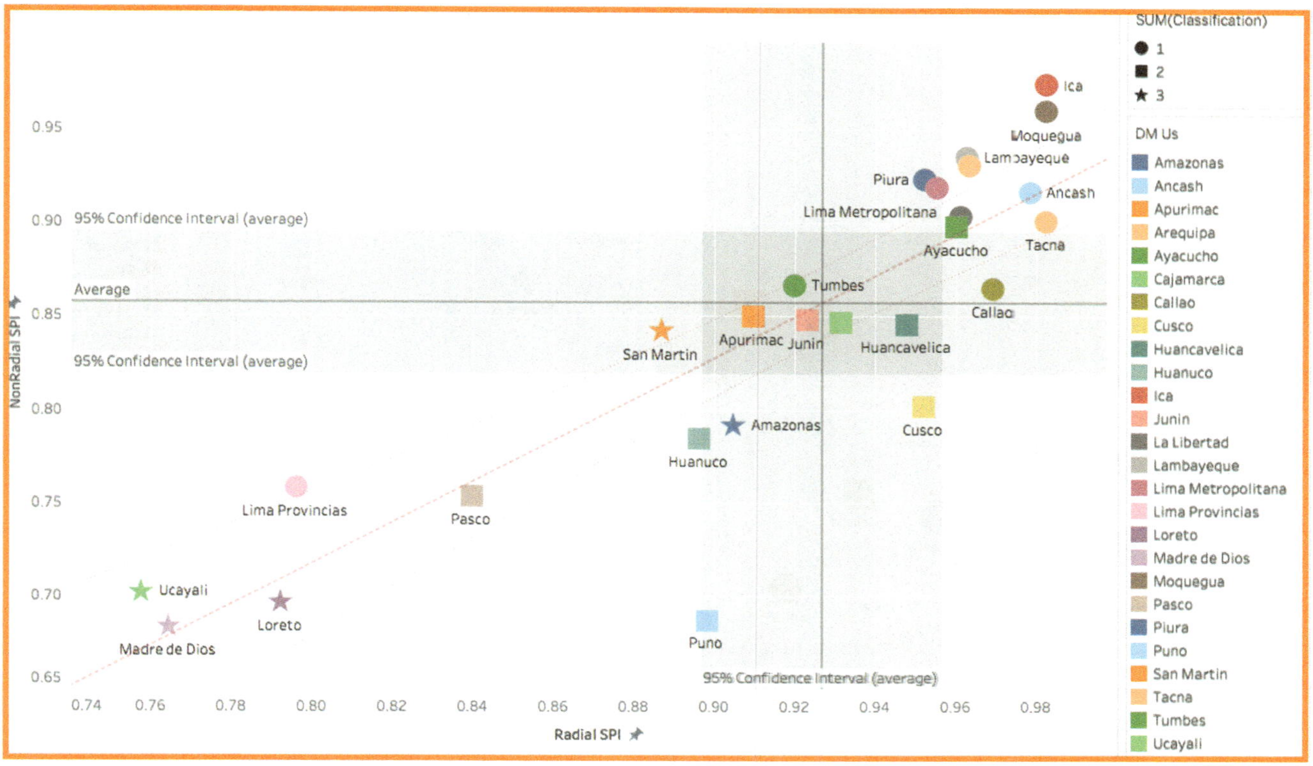

Fig. 5 Correlation between the radial and non-radial DEA-based SPIs

both Ayacucho and La Libertad are high performers, which points towards the cautiousness that should be attached to the interpretation of ranks, in general. Furthermore, Ayacucho is an interesting and isolated case; this is the only highland region that is situated above the averages of both the radial and non-radial DEA-based SPIs, joining the high-performer group of coastal regions.

By contrast, the worst performers are Pasco, Lima Provincias, Loreto, Ucayali and Madre de Dios. These regions are well below the averages of both the radial and non-radial DEA-based SPIs; the reason behind their low performance lies in the fact that they each obtain rather poor scores in at least one factor of social progress. As such, Lima Provincias performs poorly in the FoW factor, Pasco in the Opp factor, Loreto and Ucayali in both FoW and Opp and Madre de Dios in BHN and Opp. In light of this observation, concerned policymakers and regional authorities should give particular attention to these five cases, recommending local strategies, so as to improve the social investment in the mentioned factors and thus increase the regions' social progress level (Charles and D'Alessio 2019). San Martin, Huanuco, Puno, Amazonas, Apurimac and Junin are also located below the mentioned averages. Nevertheless, they are within the confidence interval of the average for either the radial or the non-radial DEA-based SPI; therefore, it can be said that they are average performers in terms of social progress.

Finally, Fig. 6 represents the rank correlations between the radial DEA-based SPI and the non-radial DEA-based SPI. The legend of the region classifications in the graph is the same as in Fig. 5. This graph shows a positive correlation between the SPI radial rank and the SPI non-radial rank, with a correlation coefficient of 0.885, which is significant at the 0.01 level. The horizontal and vertical lines represent the medians of the SPI radial rank (median = 11.5) and the SPI non-radial rank (median = 13.5), respectively, with their median confidence intervals.

At a closer inspection, we can observe that, similar to Fig. 5, the same group of coastal regions dominate the rank (Ica, Moquegua, Lambayeque, Ancash, La Libertad and Arequipa), with the exception of two regions, Ayacucho and Tacna, who find themselves positioned rather as average performers in view of the ranks occupied; also, we can notice that the worst performers are the jungle regions. Overall, Figs. 5 and 6 yield consistent insights. Perhaps the most interesting observations to make here are in relation to Lima Metropolitana and Huancavelica. On the one hand, Lima Metropolitana is generally ranked first in terms of competitiveness (CENTRUM Católica Graduate Business School 2012; Charles and Zegarra 2014), counting with the highest GDP share (53,6%, INEI 2009) and the second highest GDP per capita in the country (S/.12,860, according to INEI 2009), and one of the lowest poverty rates in the country (15.4%, according to INEI 2014). Despite this,

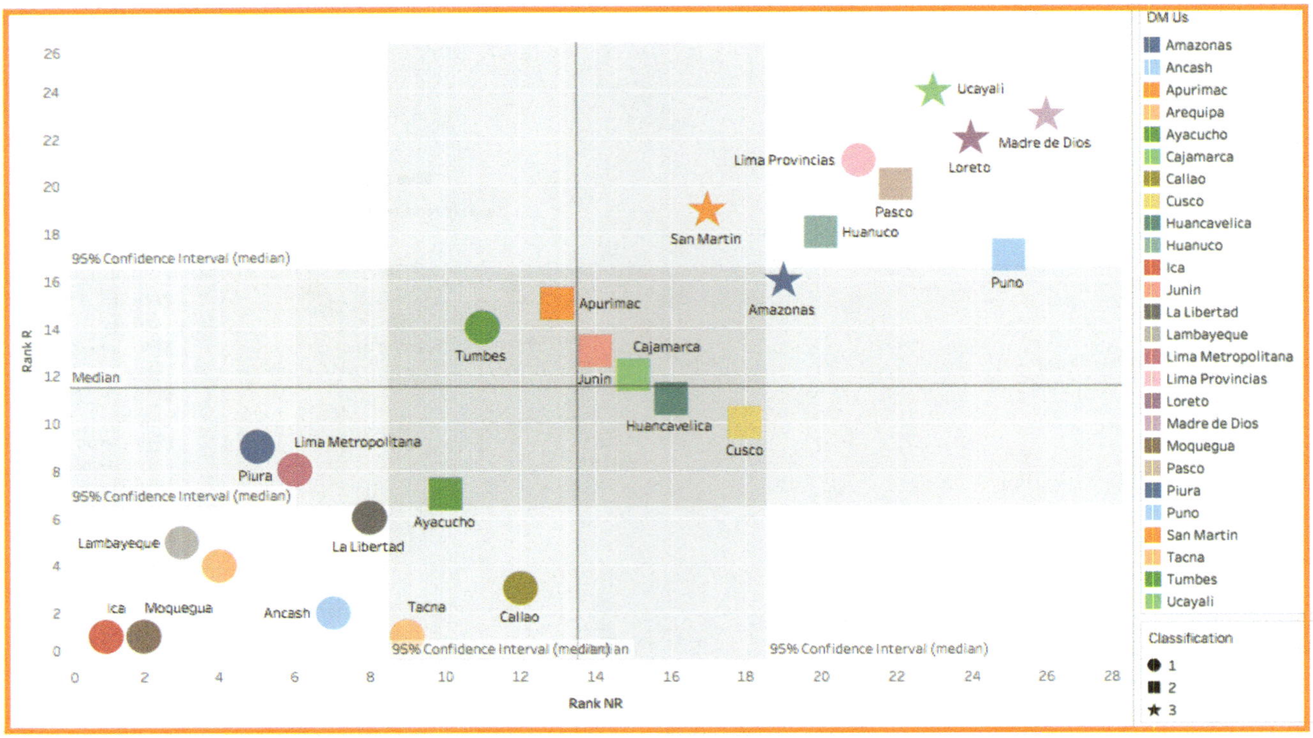

Fig. 6 Rank correlation between the radial and non-radial DEA-based SPIs

however, Lima Metropolitana does not top the rank, being more of an average performer in terms of social progress. On the other hand, Huancavelica is generally considered to be the least competitive region in the country (Charles 2015a,b), counting with the highest poverty rate in the country (77.2%, according to INEI 2009) and one of the lowest GDP per capita (S/.3,453, according to INEI 2014); but then again, despite this, Huancavelica ranks as an average performer in social progress.

Another interesting case is posed by the region of Madre de Dios. This region has a relatively high GDP per capita (S/.7,555, according to INEI 2014) and the lowest poverty rate in the country (12.7%, according to INEI 2009); in terms of social progress, however, it is ranked 23rd in the radial DEA and 26th in the non-radial DEA, making it the worst performer among all the regions. These are fascinating cases, whose results are counter-intuitive, drawing attention to the fact that ranks and scores should always be taken with a pinch of salt. Furthermore, this further supports the necessity to develop better and more refined methodologies for the creation of regional indices for social progress, the kind of indices that can reflect to the reality with higher accuracy.

5 Conclusions

It has been the endeavour of the present manuscript to introduce an improved methodology to measure social progress at the regional level, with an application to the Peruvian regions. Our approach joins together the methodology of the objective general index in the first phase (Sei 2016) with data envelopment analysis in the second phase. This approach to measuring social progress is novel and represents the main contribution of the manuscript. The benefits are twofold: on the one hand, we account for the variation in the two stages of the first phase, and on the other hand, we build an index based on relative measures in the second phase. The approach, however, is not without limitations. From a methodological point of view, while we do account for variation at the subfactor level, we do not account for the same at the factor level; this is an avenue for future research. Furthermore, from a conceptual stand, the framework and variables adopted here are by no means perfect, our analysis being confined to the framework developed by Social Progress Imperative (2018). Despite this, the proposed approach is a step forward towards an improved measurement of well-being and social progress.

The data generated using this approach allowed us both to rank the Peruvian regions more accurately and to determine the sources of competitive strength or weakness of each region. As previously mentioned, some of the results obtained are according to expectations, especially when seen at a more 'macro' level. As such, findings suggest that the most efficient regions in terms of social progress are located on the coast, with the regions of Ancash, Arequipa, Ica, La Libertad, Lambayeque and Moquegua forming the group of high performers in view of both radial and non-radial DEA. In a similar fashion, the worst performers are located in the jungle regions, and the group is composed of Loreto, Madre de Dios and Ucayali. The highland regions are generally average performers. But some other results are counter-intuitive; see the cases of Lima Metropolitana and Huancavelica, for example. Despite being perceived as generally the best and worst regions, respectively, in terms of a variety of aspects such as competitiveness and poverty rate, these regions are both classified as rather average performers in terms of social progress.

Today, there is a plethora of metrics that have been developed to measure social progress. Seen in isolation, each indicator tells a different, yet incomplete story. Overall, there is no single methodology and no general agreement on the existence of a set of standardised or holistic indicators to measure social progress. This highlights that in order to get a more realistic picture of the well-being of a region, it is important to develop more accurate measures of social progress, which do not only consider the expansion of the set of variables considered in the assessment of social progress but also integrate various methods and approaches together, refining, thus, the methodology used to measure social progress. As mentioned, the latter has been the endeavour of the present manuscript.

Economic growth is, for obvious reasons, important. But if economic growth does little to improve social well-being, should it be a primary goal of government policy, as it keeps on being today? This continues to be a fascinating question, given its far-reaching policy implications. The only sure conclusion, as Easterlin (1974) also acknowledged, is that we need much more research on the nature and causes of human welfare. (Bradburn 1969, p. 233) made a similar point when he stated that: 'Insofar as we have greater understanding of how people arrive at their judgments of their own happiness and how social forces are related to those judgments, we shall be in a better position to formulate and execute effective social policies.' Without much doubt, designing measurements that combine objective well-being data with subjective well-being data (Diener 2002; Diener and Oishi 2000) can lead to a much richer notion of a nation's well-being status. We position this as an avenue for future research on the topic. It is the belief of the authors that the proposed social progress index, together with the GDP and other measures of societal progress, can account for the virtuous dynamics of inclusive growth, which is essential to strengthen not only in Peru, but worldwide.

Overall, the present study has important implications for practice. Social progress and well-being throughout the world has arrived at a critical turning point (Estes 2019), so providing a better snapshot of the ranking of the regions in a country in terms of social progress may help policymakers concerned with creating the conditions for nations to satisfy at least the basic social and material needs of their increasing populations (Estes and Morgan 1976) to identify the weaknesses and strengths of each region, the main gaps and the potential for improvement; this, in turn, could further assist them in guiding policies of social investment. Moreover, meaningful comparisons can be made among regions.

Acknowledgements The authors would like to thank the editors and the anonymous reviewers for their valuable feedback on the previous version of this manuscript. The first author would further like to acknowledge and thank the financial support received from the Santander Chair of Efficiency and Productivity in the Center of Operations Research (CIO), at the University of Miguel Hernandez of Elche (Spain), for participating in and presenting the current research at the 2018 International Workshop on Efficiency and Productivity.

References

Bradburn, N. M. (1969). *The structure of psychological well-being*. Chicago, IL: Aldine.

CENTRUM Católica Graduate Business School. (2012). *Índice de competitividad regional del Perú 2011*. Lima, Peru: CENTRUM Católica Graduate Business School, PUCP.

CENTRUM Católica Graduate Business School. (2016). *Índice de Progreso Social Regional Perú 2016*. Lima, Peru: CENTRUM Católica Graduate Business School, PUCP & Social Progress Imperative.

Charles, V. (2015a). Mining cluster development in Peru: Learning from the International Best Practice. *Journal of Applied Environmental and Biological Sciences, 5*(1), 1–13.

Charles, V. (2015b). Mining cluster development in Peru: From triple helix to the four clover. *Strategia, 38*, 33–46.

Charles, V., & D'Alessio, F. A. (2019). An envelopment-based approach to measuring regional social progress. *Socio-Economic Planning Sciences*. In press.

Charles, V., & Diaz, G. (2016). A non-radial DEA index for Peruvian regional competitiveness. *Social Indicators Research, 134*(2), 747–770.

Charles, V., & Sei, T. (2019). A two-stage OGI approach to compute the regional competitiveness index. *Competitiveness Review: An International Business Journal, 29*(2), 78–95.

Charles, V., & Zegarra, L. F. (2014). Measuring regional competitiveness through data envelopment analysis: A peruvian case. *Expert Systems with Applications, 41*, 5371–5381.

Charnes, A., Cooper, W. W., & Rhodes, E. (1978). Measuring the efficiency of decision making units. *European Journal of Operational Research, 2*(6), 429–444.
Cobb, C. W., Halstead, T., & Rowe, J. (1995). If GDP is up why is America down? *Atlantic Monthly, 276*(4), 59–78.
Davies, W. (2015). Spirits of neoliberalism: "Competitiveness" and "Wellbeing" indicators as rivals of worth. In R. Rottenburg, S. E. Merry, S.-J. Park., & J. Mugler (Eds.), *The world of indicators: The making of governmental knowledge through quantification* (pp. 283–306). Cambridge, UK: Cambridge University Press.
Diener, E. (2002). Will money increase subjective well-being? *Social Indicators Research, 57*, 119–169.
Diener, E., & Oishi, S. (2000). Money and happiness: Income and subjective well-being across nations. In E. Diener & E. Suh (Eds.), *Subjective well-being across cultures* (pp. 185–218). Cambridge, MA: MIT Press.
Easterlin, R. A. (1974). Does economic growth improve the human lot? Some empirical evidence. In P. A. David & M. W. Reder (Eds.), *Nations and households in economic growth. Essays in honor of Moses Abramovitz* (pp. 89–125). New York, NY: Academic Press, Inc.
Estes, R. J. (2019). The social progress of nations revisited. *Social Indicators Research, 144*, 539–574.
Estes, R. J., & Morgan, J. S. (1976). World social welfare analysis: A theoretical model. *International Social Work, 19*(2), 29–41.
European Commission. (2007). Beyond GDP. Measuring progress, true wealth, and the well-being of nations. Retrieved from http://www.beyond-gdp.eu/index.html
INEI. (2009). *Censos Nacionales de Población y Vivienda*. Lima, Peru: National Institute of Statistics and Information of Peru.
INEI. (2014). *Censos Nacionales de Población y Vivienda*. Lima, Peru: National Institute of Statistics and Information of Peru.
Kubiszewski, I., et al. (2013). Beyond GDP: Measuring and achieving global genuine progress. *Ecological Economics, 93*, 57–68.
Kuznets, S. (1934). *National Income, 1929–1932*. Cambridge, MA: National Bureau of Economic Research.
Lovell, C. A. K., & Pastor, J. T. (1999). Radial DEA models without inputs or without outputs. *European Journal of Operational Research, 118*(1), 46–51.
Marshall, & A. W., Olkin, I. (1968). Scaling of matrices to achieve specified row and column sums. *Numerische Mathematik, 12*, 83–90.
Porter, M. E., Stern, S., & Green, M. (2016). *Social progress index 2016*. Washington, DC: Social Progress Imperative.
Sei, T. (2016). An objective general index for multivariate ordered data. *Journal of Multivariate Analysis, 147*, 247–264.
Social Progress Imperative. (2018). *Social progress index 2018*. Retrieved from http://www.socialprogressimperative.org/
Stiglitz, J. E., Sen, A., & Fitoussi, J. P. (2009). Report by the commission on the measurement of economic performance and social progress. Retrieved from: https://ec.europa.eu/eurostat/documents/118025/118123/Fitoussi+Commission+report
Stiglitz, J. E., Sen, A., & Fitoussi, J. P. (2010). *Mismeasuring our lives: Why GDP doesn't add up*. New York, NY: The New Press.

A Two-Level Top-Down Decomposition of Aggregate Productivity Growth: The Role of Infrastructure

Luis Orea, Inmaculada Álvarez-Ayuso, and Luis Servén

Abstract In this chapter, we provide evidence as to the effects of infrastructure provision on aggregate productivity using industry-level data for a set of developed and developing countries over the 1995–2010 period. A distinctive feature of our empirical strategy is that it allows the measurement of intra- and interindustry resource reallocations which are directly attributable to the infrastructure provision. To achieve this objective, we propose a two-level top-down decomposition of labor aggregate productivity that extends the decomposition introduced by Diewert (Journal of Productivity Analysis 43:367–387) using a time-continuous setting.

Keywords Productivity growth · Resource allocation · Stochastic frontier analysis · Structural changes

1 Introduction

Understanding the drivers of productivity growth has long been of interest to academics and policy makers given that differences in aggregate productivity are a key source of large cross-country income differentials. Much of the literature on productivity growth decomposition (see Färe et al. 2008) focuses on two productivity sources: the adoption of more productive technologies (technical change) and the existence of diffusion and learning limitations that prevent firms to adopt such technologies (catching-up effect or efficiency change). Another strand of the literature (see Balk 2016a, b) examines the relationship between productivity (growth) measures for low-level production units (industries or firms) and some aggregate productivity measure of such units. This literature concludes that productivity growth at aggregate level at least depends on the change in the individual productivities (plants, firms, industries, etc.) and the shift in the relative size of production units. Restuccia and Rogerson (2008, 2013) find that another key source of productivity (income) differences across countries is the misallocation of resources across plants and firms and that public institutions distort the allocation of resources across firms. Notice in this sense that public investment in highways, electricity distribution, and telecommunication infrastructure has long been considered as one of the public policy decisions exerting the greatest impact on both economic development and aggregate productivity (see, e.g., Crescenzi and Rodríguez-Pose 2012; Qiang and Rossotto 2009; Yang 2000). Given the unequal effect that these sorts of investments might have on the structure of an economy, it is of great interest for both academics and policy makers to examine whether these infrastructure investments have promoted gains in economy-wide productivity through a better allocation of resources across firms and industries.

In this chapter, we provide evidence as to the effects of infrastructure provision on aggregate productivity using industry-level data for a set of developed and developing countries. A distinctive feature of the empirical strategy used in this chapter

This research was partially funded by the Government of the Principality of Asturias and the European Regional Development Fund (ERDF). The authors also thank the Oviedo Efficiency Group, and participants at NAPW 2018 in Miami for their valuable comments to an earlier version of this paper.

L. Orea (✉)
Department of Economics, University of Oviedo, Oviedo, Spain
e-mail: lorea@uniovi.es

I. Álvarez-Ayuso
Universidad Autónoma de Madrid, Madrid, Spain

L. Servén
World Bank, Washington, DC, USA

J. Aparicio et al. (eds.), *Advances in Efficiency and Productivity II*, International Series in Operations Research & Management Science 287, https://doi.org/10.1007/978-3-030-41618-8_11

is that it allows the measurement of the resource reallocation which is directly attributable to the infrastructure provision. In order to achieve this objective, we propose a two-level top-down decomposition of aggregate productivity that somewhat extends and combines several strands of the literature. The first level is a standard top-down decomposition that relies on a productivity measure that first aggregates all individual outputs and inputs and then computes the productivity of the aggregate. This chapter first simplifies Diewert's (2015) decomposition and show that his *output price* effect is an output reallocation effect. This yields a decomposition with the traditional *within* and *reallocation* terms. The second level of our productivity decomposition aims to trace the channels through which private inputs (capital and labor) and other indicators promote economy-wide productivity improvements. In this sense, this chapter extends the literature on aggregate productivity and examines whether specific variables (e.g., infrastructure) have significant impacts on *both* within and reallocation productivity effects.

As it is customary in the literature on regional productivity and infrastructure, we estimate several production models to decompose industry productivity growth. The production models are estimated using stochastic frontier techniques for two reasons. First, as advocated by Straub (2012), this empirical strategy allows infrastructure provision to have a *direct* effect on sectoral production as a standard input and an *indirect* effect as a productivity externality. Second, although we use data at sectoral level, the inefficiency term of our production model frontier allows us to capture the production losses caused by a suboptimal allocation of resources between firms operating in the same industry (Asturias et al. 2017). Thus, while the theoretical model allows measuring inter*industry* reallocation effects, our frontier specification permits measuring inter*firm* reallocation effects. The decomposition of the *within* and *output price* effects into their fundamental sources is carried out using the *same* production model, and hence both decompositions are mutually consistent. The decomposition of our labor-based *reallocation* term is much more challenging because employment is an intrinsically complex phenomenon (see, e.g., Vivarelli 2012) and the computed reallocation effects might change a lot depending on whether, e.g., firms maximize profits or minimize cost. Given that the selection of a proper framework is uncertain, we propose estimating a set of auxiliary regressions to examine the effect of infrastructure provision on both industry labor demands and shares.

The next section outlines the top-down approach used by Diewert (2015) to decompose an aggregate productivity growth using a continuous-time setting. In Sect. 3, we develop a theoretical model that yields mutually consistent decompositions of both within and reallocation effects, once a set of production functions and auxiliary regressions are estimated. We discuss in Sect. 4 the data used in the empirical analysis and its sources. Section 5 presents both the parameter estimates and computed effects. Finally, Sect. 6 presents the conclusions.

2 First-Level Decomposition

Following Diewert (2015), the economy-wide labor productivity (X) can be defined as economy-wide real output (Y) divided by economy-wide labor input (L):

$$X = \frac{\sum_{n=1}^{N} P_n Y_n / P}{\sum_{n=1}^{N} L_n} = \frac{Y}{L} \tag{1}$$

where subscript n stands for industry or sector, Y_n is industry n real output (value-added), L_n is industry n labor input, and P_n is the corresponding industry value-added output price, and P the aggregate output price index. Diewert (2015) shows that it is possible to relate aggregate productivity level (X) to the industry productivity levels ($X_n = Y_n/L_n$) as follows:

$$X = \sum\nolimits_{n=1}^{N} p_n \left(\frac{L_n}{L}\right) X_n = \sum\nolimits_{n=1}^{N} p_n S_{Ln} X_n \tag{2}$$

where industry n real output price, $p_n = P_n/P$, and $S_{Ln} = L_n/L$ is the share of labor used by industry n. Thus, aggregate labor productivity for the economy is a weighted sum of the industry-specific labor productivities where the weight for each industry is its real output price times its share of labor. Next Diewert (2015) develops an expression for the rate of growth of economy-wide labor productivity. Using definition (1) and Eq. (2), aggregate labor productivity growth is equal to[1]:

[1] Using a Bennet-type symmetric method, the discrete-time counterpart of our continuous-time decomposition in Eq. (3) can be written as:

$$\ln\left(\frac{X_t}{X_{t-1}}\right) = \sum_{n=1}^{N} \frac{s_{Ynt-1}+s_{Ynt}}{2} \ln\left(\frac{X_{nt}}{X_{nt-1}}\right) + \sum_{n=1}^{N} \frac{s_{Ynt-1}+s_{Ynt}}{2} \ln\left(\frac{S_{Lnt}}{S_{Lnt-1}}\right) + \sum_{n=1}^{N} \frac{s_{Ynt-1}+s_{Ynt}}{2} \ln\left(\frac{p_{nt}}{p_{nt-1}}\right)$$

$$\dot{X} = WE + LRE + OPE = \sum_{n=1}^{N} s_{Yn}\dot{X}_n + \sum_{n=1}^{N} s_{Yn}\dot{S}_{Ln} + \sum_{n=1}^{N} s_{Yn}\dot{p}_n \tag{3}$$

where a dot over a variable indicates a rate of growth, and s_{Yn} is the *nominal* value-added or output share of industry n in total value-added:

$$s_{Yn} = \frac{P_n Y_n}{\sum_{s=1}^{N} P_s Y_s} = \frac{P_n Y_n}{PY} \tag{4}$$

The first term in (3) can be interpreted as economy-wide labor productivity growth provided that all real output prices and industry relative sizes do not change over time. Notice that this term is just the straightforward aggregation of industry-specific productivity growth rates, and thus it could be labeled as *within effect* (*WE*). The second term measures changes in industry relative sizes; thus, it has to do with transformations of the economy. It just indicates that, even if all industry labor productivity levels remain constant and all industry real output prices remain constant, economy-wide labor productivity growth can change due to changes in industry labor input shares. Therefore, this effect could be labeled the *labor reallocation effect* (*LRE*). Accordingly, if all industry real output prices remain constant, the industries can contribute positively to aggregate productivity change in two ways: if their own productivity level increases or if the industries with above (below) average labor share increase (decrease) in relative size. The last term in (3) indicates that even if industry labor productivity levels and labor input shares remain constant, economy-wide labor productivity growth can change due to changes in industry real output prices. We could label this term as *output price effect* (*OPE*).

Up to this point, our analysis follows that of Diewert (2015), but now our analysis extends his decomposition further more. He links the *OPE* term to changes in the price weights for the industry output growth rates in (2), which in turn affects aggregate labor productivity growth. Notice that the industry n real output price p_n is the industry output price P_n divided by the aggregate output price index P, which can be defined as:

$$P = \sum_{n=1}^{N} P_n \frac{Y_n}{Y} = \sum_{n=1}^{N} P_n S_{Yn} \tag{5}$$

where $S_{Yn} = Y_n/Y$ is the *real* output share of industry n in total output. As the *nominal* output share s_{Yn} defined in (4) can then be rewritten as $s_{Yn} = \frac{P_n}{P} S_{Yn}$, the change of aggregate output price is equal to:

$$\dot{P} = \sum_{n=1}^{N} s_{Yn}\dot{P}_n + \sum_{n=1}^{N} s_{Yn}\dot{S}_{Yn} \tag{6}$$

Rearranging (6), we get:

$$OPE = -\sum_{n=1}^{N} s_{Yn}\dot{S}_{Yn} \tag{7}$$

Therefore, we find that Diewert's output price effect is (the negative) of an *output reallocation effect* that measures changes in the structure of the economy using industry real output shares, instead of using industry labor shares as *LRE*. Both price and quantity definitions of the *OPE* term yield exactly the same number, but the quantity interpretation of *OPE* prevents making assumptions about the forces underlying the output prices if we are willing to decompose it into its basic sources. This will be discussed later on. Moreover, as both *LRE* and *OPE* are measuring reallocation effects, they can be combined into a unique (net) reallocation effect, *NRE* = *LRE* + *OPE*. This yields a decomposition with the traditional within and reallocation terms:

$$\dot{X} = WE + NRE = \sum_{n=1}^{N} s_{Yn}\dot{X}_n + \sum_{n=1}^{N} s_{Yn}\left(\dot{S}_{Ln} - \dot{S}_{Yn}\right) \tag{8}$$

The new reallocation effect treats symmetrically the two variables used to compute aggregate labor productivity, labor, and output. Unlike the traditional labor or output-based reallocation effects often used in the literature (see Balk 2016a), the

We also use a Bennet-type symmetric method to get the discrete-time counterparts of all continuous-time decomposition included in this chapter. Notice that the above productivity decomposition looks like a Törnqvist productivity index. It is worth mentioning that we do not need to introduce in the above decomposition the conventional covariance (or second order) term that appears, for instance, in Baily et al. (1992) and Diewert (2015). The covariance-type terms disappear from the productivity decomposition because the Bennet method is symmetric (Balk 2016a). Diewert (2015) proposed a simplified decomposition with only three terms as in (3) by assigning second- and third-order terms to corresponding first-order terms in a symmetric, even handed manner. He points out in footnote #14 that this assignment scheme is similar to that applied by Bennet (1920).

so-called *NRE* effect takes into account changes in the structure of the economy using two alternative structural variables, i.e., labor and output shares.

We next show that, although the changes in the structure of the economy might be remarkable, their effect on aggregate productivity is expected to be small (i.e., *OPE* and *LRE* tend to be negligible in practice). Regarding *OPE*, it should be first mentioned that the change in real industry output share is $\dot{S}_{Yn} = \dot{Y}_n - \sum_{s=1}^{N} S_{Ys}\dot{Y}_s$. This equation indicates that the change in relative size of industry n depends on how different the change in $\dot{Y}_n$ is with respect to the average change in the economy. Notice that the second term is common to all industries. Thus, if we plug $\dot{S}_{Yn} = \dot{Y}_n - \sum_{s=1}^{N} S_{Ys}\dot{Y}_s$ into (7), we get:

$$OPE = \sum_{n=1}^{N} (S_{Yn} - s_{Yn})\,\dot{Y}_n \tag{9}$$

Therefore, Eq. (9) finally indicates that the *OPE* term mainly depends on the difference between nominal and real output shares. This term vanishes if both output shares coincide. Notice that this happens if all industry output prices P_n are equal to the economy-wide output price P. Interesting enough, although this term capture *changes* in the quantity structure of the economy, it depends on the relative *level* of the industry output prices. As both prices are likely similar in applications using industry-level data because they are indices, we should not expect large *OPE* values in practice. This likely explains why the overall labor productivity contribution term due to changes in industry real output prices found in Diewert (2015) is practically zero.

It is interesting to know whether the above conclusions can be also applied to the *LRE* term, defined as $\sum_{n=1}^{N} s_{Yn}\dot{S}_{Ln}$. The change in the share of labor used by industry n is $\dot{S}_{Ln} = \dot{L}_n - \sum_{s=1}^{N} S_{Ls}\dot{L}_s$. As the second term is common to all industries, we get:

$$LRE = \sum_{n=1}^{N} (s_{Yn} - S_{Ln})\,\dot{L}_n \tag{10}$$

Therefore, Eq. (10) indicates that the *LRE* term mainly depends on the difference of two industry shares. In this sense, the computed *LRE* term tends to be modest in practice. However, Eq. (10) also indicates that *LRE* now depends on industry shares of different nature. As the relative size of an industry in output and labor terms might differ notably in practice, we expect larger values for *LRE* than for *OPE*. This again likely explains why the overall labor productivity contribution term due to changes in industry labor shares found in Diewert (2015) is not zero.

In summary, using the above decompositions, aggregate labor growth can alternatively be decomposed as follows:

$$\dot{X} = \sum_{n=1}^{N} s_{Yn}\dot{X}_n + \sum_{n=1}^{N} (S_{Yn} - s_{Yn})\,\dot{Y}_n + \sum_{n=1}^{N} (s_{Yn} - S_{Ln})\,\dot{L}_n \tag{11}$$

3 Second-Level Decomposition

We next try to decompose the three productivity effects in (11) into its basic drivers using the parametric estimates of a standard production model and the duality theory.

3.1 *Decomposing the Within Effect*

As customary in regional economics, we hereafter assume that industry n output depends on the use of private capital and labor, by industry n, and on a set of country-level variables measuring the provision of different infrastructures such as transport, electricity, information, communication, etc. Moreover, in order to distinguish between pure (e.g., technological) productivity improvements and industry productivity gains caused by a better reallocation of resources between firms operating in the same industry, we propose estimating a stochastic production frontier model for each industry, which may be written as follows:

$$lnY_n = \beta_{0n} + \beta_{Kn}lnK_n + \beta_{Ln}lnL_n + \delta_n t + \gamma_n lnZ + v_n - u_n(Z) \tag{12}$$

where for notational ease we have dropped the standard subscript t indicating time, and a country-specific subscript from the intercept as a fixed-effect-type estimator is used later on to control for unobserved heterogeneity. K_n denotes the capital stock of industry n, and Z is either an indicator measuring traditional infrastructures (e.g., transport, electricity distribution, etc.) or a technological indicator capturing the use of new information and telecommunication networks.[2] Also worth noting is that we have included a traditional time trend in (12) in order to capture improvements in the technology over time (technical change). Finally, it should be mentioned that our Z variables also include a variable measuring human capital.

Equation (12) also includes two error terms, v_n and u_n. While the former term is a symmetric error term measuring pure random shocks, the latter term is a nonnegative error term measuring industry inefficiency, which we link to misallocation of resources between firms. It should be emphasized that not all Z variables in our application will be included as a standard factor of production and as an industry inefficiency determinant due to collinearity issues and the fact that the indirect effect has also to do with misallocation of resources within the industry, an issue with a completely different nature than the technological nature of the industry production frontier. More details about this issue are provided in our data section.

Using the production model in (12), the changes in industry labor productivities can be decomposed as:

$$\dot{X}_n = (\beta_n - 1)\,\dot{K}_n + (1 - \beta_{Ln})\left(\dot{K}_n - \dot{L}_n\right) + \theta_n \dot{Z} + \delta_n \tag{13}$$

where $\beta_n = \beta_{Kn} + \beta_{Ln}$, $(\beta_n - 1)$ is a measure of the returns to scale at industry level, and

$$\theta_n = \frac{\partial lnY_n}{\partial lnZ} = \gamma_n - \frac{\partial u_n}{\partial \ln Z} \tag{14}$$

Equation (13) suggest that the estimated coefficients in (12) can be used to decompose industry labor productivity changes into a *size effect* associated with an increase in the usage of inputs, a *substitution effect* when the input mix varies over time, technical change, and the overall effect of the Z variables. Equation (14) just indicates that the effect of infrastructure provision on industry output is a combination of a *direct* effect through the frontier and an *indirect* effect through the efficiency term. Using (13), we can now decompose the within effect as follows[3]:

$$WE = \sum\nolimits_{n=1}^{N} (\beta_n - 1)\, s_{Yn}\dot{K}_n + \sum\nolimits_{n=1}^{N} (1 - \beta_{Ln})\, s_{Yn}\left(\dot{K}_n - \dot{L}_n\right) + \sum\nolimits_{n=1}^{N} s_{Yn}\delta_n + \sum\nolimits_{n=1}^{N} s_{Yn}\theta_n \dot{Z} \tag{15}$$

3.2 Decomposing the Output Price Effect

We have shown before that Diewert's output price effect can be interpreted as an output reallocation effect that measures changes in the structure of the economy using industry real output shares. We do not need a new theoretical framework to decompose *OPE* because the production model used in Sect. 3.1 to decompose *WE* also provides information on the industry output shares.

Recall that we have found that *OPE* can be defined as $-\sum_{n=1}^{N} s_{Yn}\dot{S}_{Yn}$. Using the production model in (12), the changes in industry output can be decomposed as $\dot{Y}_n = \beta_{Kn}\dot{K}_n + \beta_{Ln}\dot{L}_n + \theta_n\dot{Z} + \delta_n$. Using this decomposition, and considering that $S_{Yn} = Y_n/\sum_{s=1}^{N} Y_s$, the effect of infrastructure provision on the industry n output share is:

$$\frac{\partial lnS_{Yn}}{\partial lnZ} = \theta_n - \sum\nolimits_{s=1}^{N} S_{Ys}\theta_s = \theta_n - \theta \tag{16}$$

This equation indicates that the effect of infrastructure provision on the relative size of industry n depends on how different the within productivity effect is with respect to the average. If the productivity effect of infrastructure provision is the same for all industries, the productivity effect of infrastructure provision through structural changes in the economy disappears.[4]

[2]In our empirical application, we cannot compute K_n for each industry because we do not have the industry volumes for the capital input, just the economy-wide capital level. To address this issue, we will assume that the temporal evolution of K_n is the same in all industries or that $\dot{K}_n = \dot{K}, \forall n = 1, .., N$.

[3]As θ_n is a combination of a *direct* effect through the frontier and an *indirect* effect through the efficiency term, a portion of the within-industry productivity gains captured by *WE* is caused by a better reallocation of resources between firms, and hence the *WE* term cannot be completely interpreted as a term capturing pure (e.g., technological) productivity improvements. The pure productivity within effect can be computed and decomposed using (13) but ignoring the inefficiency term (i.e., using γ_n instead of θ_n).

[4]The output share of each industry also depends on capital and labor and the time trend. Therefore, they also generate interindustry reallocation effects.

Taking into account that *OPE* can alternatively be defined as $\sum_{n=1}^{N}(S_{Yn}-s_{Yn})\dot{Y}_n$, the output price effect attributed to infrastructure provision can be written as:

$$OPE = \sum_{n=1}^{N} (S_{Yn} - s_{Yn}) \left[\beta_{Kn}\dot{K}_n + \beta_{Ln}\dot{L}_n + \theta_n\dot{Z} + \delta_n\right] \tag{17}$$

It should be emphasized that our decomposition of *OPE* is theoretically consistent with the decomposition of *WE* (i.e., they are mutually consistent). In this sense, it is worth mentioning that one simple empirical strategy that has been often used to decompose the *OPE* term is to regress *OPE* on a number of plausible independent variables á la McMillan et al. (2014). In this case, the structural distorts attributable, for instance, to infrastructure provision are represented simply by the parameter estimated for this variable in the auxiliary regression. As McMillan et al. (2014) correctly pointed out, we should view these auxiliary regressions as a first pass through the data, rather than a complete causal analysis based on an explicit theoretical model. Given the somewhat ad hoc nature of such auxiliary regressions, the computations of the structural distorts attributed to infrastructure provision will not be theoretically consistent with the previously computed intra-industry productivity effect.

3.3 Decomposing the Labor Reallocation Effect

Decomposing the industry labor demands that appear in *LRE* is more challenging than decomposing the industry output shares. Indeed, the decomposition of *LRE* requires "endogenizing" the industry-specific labor levels using a theoretical framework. Given that our main interest is measuring the effect of infrastructure provision on *LRE*, in this subsection we adopt a holistic approach and propose using a three-stage procedure.

In the *first stage*, we use standard duality theory to compute the lower and upper bounds for the mentioned effects. We first use a cost framework to "endogenize" the industry labor demands that appear in (10). The *cost-based* effect of infrastructure provision on labor demands is $\Theta_n = -\theta_n/\beta_n$. Notice however that Θ_n is negative in those industries where we have found a positive effect of infrastructure investment on industry production. This somewhat counterintuitive result is caused by the fact that Θ_n is *conditional* on industry output levels. Thus, the estimated adjustments in labor do not take into account the output side of the adjustments that are arising in the economy. We next use a profit framework to "endogenize" the industry labor demands. The profit-based effect of infrastructure provision on labor demand is $\Omega_n = \theta_n/(1-\beta_n)$. Unlike Θ_n, the effect of infrastructure provision on labor demand is *positive* as the output supply increases with infrastructure provision in a profit maximization setting.

The above discussion suggests that the profit-based reallocation effect can be interpreted as an upper bound for the "true" reallocation effect of infrastructure provision because Ω_n tends to be positive, while the cost-based reallocation effect can be interpreted as a lower bound since Θ_n tends to be negative. As we do not know a priori which framework (cost vs. profit-based) is more appropriate, in the *second stage* we carry out the following auxiliary regression to estimate for each industry the weights of the computed bounds that better fit the data:

$$\left(lnL_n - \hat{\Omega}_n Z\right) = \left(a_{0n} + a_{1n}t + a_{2n}t^2\right) - b_n\left(\frac{\hat{\Omega}_n}{\hat{\beta}_n}\right) Z + \varepsilon_n \tag{18}$$

where a_{0n}, a_{1n}, a_{2n}, and b_n are the new parameters to be estimated. As the other determinants of labor demand change with the theoretical framework, we use a time polynomial of degree two with industry- and country-specific parameters (á la Cornwell et al. 1990) to control for the net effect of an unknown set of labor demand drivers that vary over time and across industries and countries.[5] As this empirical strategy is a time-varying extension of the well-known FE estimator, we are likely controlling for any endogeneity issues caused by the underlying variables.

If our intuition is correct, the estimated b_n coefficients must be between zero and one. If $b_n = 0$, the effect is that provided by the profit approach. If $b_n = 1$, the effect of Z is that suggested by the cost approach. The estimated b_n coefficient allows us to compute the following *in-between* effect of infrastructure provision on labor demand: $\Phi_n = \hat{b}_n\hat{\Theta}_n + \left(1-\hat{b}_n\right)\hat{\Omega}_n$.

[5]Notice that we have ignored in (18) the subscript for country to simply the notation.

In the *third* stage of our procedure, we use (10) and the estimated parameters in (18) to decompose the labor reallocation effect as follows:

$$LRE = \sum_{n=1}^{N} (s_{Yn} - S_{Ln}) \left[\Phi_n \dot{Z} + \frac{\partial ln L_n}{\partial t} \right] \tag{19}$$

4 Sample and Data

To illustrate the proposed decompositions, we use a balanced data panel for 39 countries and 5 industries over the period 1995–2010. The industries examined in this chapter are fairly aggregated: agriculture, energy, manufacturing, construction, and services. To simplify the empirical exercise, we have aggregated mining together with electricity, gas, and water supply into one sector. In addition, the services sector includes a large range of services such as wholesale and retail trade, hotels, transport, storage, and communications, finance, and insurance. The dataset includes annual observations on sectoral value-added and prices, physical capital and labor, and our set of Z variables that includes a couple of indicators that have to do with more mature infrastructures, namely, transportation and electricity infrastructures, a technological indicator measuring information and telecommunication assets provision, and a variable measuring the quality of labor. Except industry value-added, output prices, and labor, the remainder variables are measured at country level.

We were forced to drop many countries from the sample given that many years suffered from missing values in value-added or labor at sectoral level or/and in the provision of infrastructures at country level. We found that the (lack of) information in infrastructures and in economic variables did not coincide in most cases. Moreover, in order to work with a reasonable number of observations, we were forced to use the amount of physical capital for the whole country in all the sectoral regressions. Otherwise, the sample size would have been reduced to only 11 countries. Despite these data issues, we were able to work with a sample of countries that belong to different regions in the world (see Appendix A). As these regions exhibit different temporal patterns in their productivity indicators, the relative importance of the intra- and interindustry effects on the observed productivity growth rates will probably vary substantially across regions.

Unlike most of the economic growth literature that adopts a country-wide perspective, we required data collection at sectoral level in order to examine the intra- and interindustry productivity effects of infrastructure provision. In this regard, the *Groningen Growth and Development Centre (GGDC) 10-Sector Database* provides a long-run global set of variables for gross value-added (Y) and labor (L) for each industry. While the output variable Y is measured at constant local currency, the input L is measured in thousands of jobs. Equally, the Penn World Tables (Feenstra et al. 2015) provides capital stock (K) at constant local currency[6] as well as the human capital index (human capital), based on years of schooling. It should be noted that we have not expressed our monetary variables in a unique currency for two reasons. First, because many exchange rates with respect to the US dollar are quite volatile in the sample period (see, e.g., the Argentinian peso). If we used a unique currency, the estimated coefficient for capital will simply be capturing the co-movement of the exchange rates used to deflate both value-added and capital. The second reason has to do with the estimators used in our empirical application. We use fixed-effect-type estimators that ignore the cross-sectional information contained in the data to estimate the parameters of the model. As only the temporal variation of the data is employed, it is not necessary to express our monetary variables in a unique currency.

We have collected from the World Development Indicators (World Bank) a couple of indicators that have to do with more mature infrastructures, namely, transportation and electricity. The first variable (*road network*) is fairly standard and measures the length of the total road network in millions of kilometers. The second variable (*access to electricity*) is the percentage of population that has access to electricity, which can be viewed as a proxy of the available electricity distribution network in the country. These two indicators are included as frontier drivers because, on the one hand, we assume that these two infrastructures are strictly necessary for the production, i.e., they are as important as more conventional inputs such as labor and capital. On the other hand, if we assume as Asturias et al. (2017) that the inefficiency term u_n captures the production losses attributable to an uneven distribution of marginal products of labor across firms due to differences in market power, our variable measuring the provision of transportation infrastructure (*road network*) will likely have also an impact on the allocation of resources within the industry. Indeed, these authors stated that by increasing competition between firms, the distribution of markups in the economy becomes less dispersed, and hence the level of resource misallocation decreases.

---

[6]Notice that this capital variable has been computed using both private and public investments at country level. Therefore, K is likely correlated with our Z variables.

The data on the technological indicator (IT) that have to do with the expansion of information and telecommunication networks are also taken from the World Bank. Our IT indicator simply averages the percentage of cellular subscriptions (which is defined as the weight of mobile cellular subscriptions over the total fixed line and mobile cellular subscriptions) and the percentage of Internet users over the total population. Although this technological indicator has to do with improvements in technology, it is not included as a frontier driver since it is highly correlated with the time trend. Instead it is included as a determinant of u_n because the within-industry misallocation of resources can be also caused by information asymmetries in the labor market (Foster and Rosenzweig 1992) that likely decreases with IT. Information and telecommunication networks might also reduce the differences in labor productivities between firms if they increase a head-to-head competition as well. Moscoso-Boedo and D'Erasmo (2012) show that countries with low stocks of skilled workers are characterized by low firm-level allocative efficiency and lower measured productivity. Thus, our inefficiency term u_n capturing firm-level distortions likely depends on our *human capital* variable. Furthermore, in a cross-country study of Latin American countries, Funkhouser (1996) shows that the mean education level in the formal sector is substantially higher than in the informal sector. Thus, our human capital index also might capture the effect of the existence of informal firms on industry productivity.[7]

Finally, to control for the potential bias caused by replacing an industry-specific variable with its value for the whole economy, we include the share of labor used by industry n as an additional production driver. Notice that the industry-specific but unobserved capital level can be written as $K_n = S_{Kn}K$. Taking logs, this implies that we should only add lnS_{Kn} as an additional production driver in our model. This variable is however not observed. If both labor and capital are substitute inputs, S_{Kn} is likely correlated with S_{Ln}. In particular, we assume in our empirical application that $lnS_{Kn} = \alpha S_{Ln}$, where α is a new parameter to be estimated that captures such a correlation.

Table 1 summarizes the descriptive statistics of the variables used in the empirical application.

Table 1 Descriptive statistics

Variable	Obs	Mean	Std. Dev.	Min	Max
Technological indicators, infrastructures, and human capital					
Capital stock (thousand mil *US$*)	585	2616	7181	0.085	48200
Human capital (years)	585	2.46	0.60	1.130	3.69
Cellular subscriptions (%)	585	0.52	0.28	0	0.99
Electricity access (%)	585	0.78	0.31	0.038	1.00
Internet users (%)	585	0.18	0.24	0	0.91
Roads (Mil. Kms)	585	0.52	1.18	0.002	6.52
Gross Value Added (thousand million US$)					
Agriculture	585	85.5	440.5	0.048	6688.3
Energy	585	67.2	213.0	0.054	2632.1
Manufacturing	585	162.8	339.0	0.216	2641.4
Services	585	420.0	1213.2	0.749	7502.2
Construction	585	64.7	155.2	0.114	1345.6
Labor (million jobs)					
Agriculture	585	20.4	65.6	0.005	366.4
Energy	585	0.6	2.1	0.005	15.7
Manufacturing	585	7.0	19.7	0.027	144.6
Services	585	11.5	20.6	0.081	114.1
Construction	585	3.0	7.9	0.021	52.4
Real output prices (ratio)					
Agriculture	585	1.10	0.21	0.48	2.04
Energy	585	0.95	0.23	0.36	2.13
Manufacturing	585	1.03	0.11	0.73	1.84
Services	585	1.02	0.09	0.81	1.70
Construction	585	0.99	0.22	0.37	2.47

Note: the monetary variables have been expressed in US dollars for the unique purpose of issuing this table

[7] In general, we were not able to find a significant effect for human capital as standard input in previous version of this paper. For this reason, we only include this variable as an inefficiency determinant.

5 Results

5.1 Parameter Estimates

The proposed productivity decompositions rely on the estimation of a heteroscedastic production frontier model for five industries. We have followed Hadri (1999) and estimated a doubly heteroscedastic stochastic frontier production function. In particular, we have assumed that the inefficiency term u_n is distributed as a heteroscedastic half-normal random variable that depends on a subset of Z vector. The noise term is also heteroscedastic, and in order to allow its variance to change with industry and country size, we assume it depends on country capital and industry labor. Moreover, as mentioned above, all the models have been estimated using a set of country-specific dummy variables in order to control for country unobserved heterogeneity. In this sense, our model can be viewed as a heteroscedastic version of the true fixed-effect (TFE) stochastic frontier model introduced by Greene (2005).

The industry-specific parameter estimates are shown in Table 2. Our estimates are consistent with the literature, since both capital stock and labor exhibit positive elasticities in all industries. The simple arithmetic means of the industry-specific elasticities of capital and labor are 0.43 and 0.53, respectively. Therefore, the effect of both inputs follows conventional growth accounting, where labor elasticity is higher (around two-thirds) than the capital elasticity (around one third). We also find significant coefficients for our infrastructure variables. Moreover, quite often the estimated coefficients differ substantially across industries. As shown in Sect. 3.2., the interindustry reallocation effects rely greatly on an uneven distribution of the estimated coefficients associated with the infrastructure variables. This result appears to anticipate the existence of non-negligible interindustry reallocation effects attributable to these variables, at least in some regions.

Access to electricity has a positive and significant effect in *agriculture*, a reasonable result due to the fact that the production of this industry often takes place in rural areas located far away from the main electricity networks. As expected as well, access to electricity has a significant positive effect in the *energy* sector. The infrastructure in roads is a production input with a significant positive effect in all industries. The largest effects are found in *manufacturing* and *services*. It is well-known in the literature that the production activity in the manufacturing sector relies particularly on transportation. The effect on *services* can be likely explained because it includes transportation services. Regarding the time trend, it has a positive effect in *agriculture*, *manufacturing,* and *services*. However, we find that the temporal effects tend to penalize production in the *energy* and *construction* sectors. Finally, notice that the coefficient of industry labor share is negative and highly significant in all sectors. This seems to indicate that our empirical strategy to control for the potential bias caused by replacing the industry-specific capital variable with its value for the whole economy is functioning properly.

Table 2 shows that many of the inefficiency drivers have a negative sign. For instance, the penetration of cellular phones and the Internet in the population tends to reduce inefficiency in all sectors. This seems to indicate that IT networks tend to reduce the degree of interfirm misallocation. In addition to shifting the production frontier, the investment in road network infrastructures has had a catching-up effect. Except in the *agriculture* and *service* sectors, the investment in road infrastructures tends to reduce industry inefficiency. This result clearly supports the hypothesis defended by Straub (2012) and other authors that consider public infrastructures as an efficiency-enhancing externality. This also seems to support the hypothesis defended by Asturias et al. (2017) in the sense that transportation infrastructure increases competition between firms, and thus the level of resource misallocation decreases due to a less dispersed distribution of markups in the industry. Finally, we find a significant positive effect for human capital as industry inefficiency determinant in *manufacturing* and *services* sectors. The effect is negative in the *agriculture* sector. Thus, our results corroborate the theoretical findings of Moscoso-Boedo and D'Erasmo (2012) in the sense that within-industry allocative inefficiency depends on the relative weight of skilled workers. However, except in the *agriculture* sector, our results do not support that low levels of allocative efficiency are correlated with higher levels of skilled workers. This somewhat counterintuitive result might be caused by the fact that our human capital variable has also to do with the existence of informal firms in the industry.

In Table 3, we show the estimated coefficients of the auxiliary regressions defined in Eq. (18). Recall that the coefficients must be between zero and one. Notice that the time-varying fixed effects allow us to almost achieve 100% goodness of fit, indicating that we are controlling quite well for other factors determining industry labor demand. Most coefficients lie between zero and one in all sectors, expect in the *construction* sector that seems to be a maverick industry where the two anchoring (cost and profit-based) models do not provide the proper lower and upper bounds. In *energy*, *manufacturing,* and *services* sectors, the estimated coefficients are equal or close to the unity value, indicating that the cost approach is more appropriate than the profit approach to measure the effect of the Z variables on industry labor demand. Most of the estimated coefficients in the agriculture sector are close to one-half, indicating that the underlying labor generating process is in-between the cost and profit-based coefficients.

Table 2 Maximum likelihood estimates of frontier production functions

	Agriculture			Energy			Manufacturing			Services			Construction		
	Coef.		s.e.	Coef.		s.e.	Coef.		s.e.	Coef.		s.e.	Coef.		s.e.
Frontier															
ln(capital)	0.154	***	0.046	0.682	***	0.097	0.272	***	0.063	0.305	***	0.065	0.759	***	0.069
ln(labor)	0.364	***	0.044	0.319	***	0.059	0.600	***	0.046	0.498	***	0.045	0.899	***	0.052
Road network	0.040	***	0.018	0.098	***	0.031	0.177	***	0.031	0.185	***	0.028	0.139	***	0.023
Access to electricity	0.179	**	0.099	0.592	**	0.204	0.100		0.146	0.020		0.128	−0.124		0.178
t	0.010	***	0.00	−0.015	***	0.00	0.005	*	0.00	0.025	***	0.00	−0.030	***	0.00
Labor share	−0.796	***	0.189	−3.511	*	2.128	−0.983	*	0.537	−1.376	***	0.284	−2.639	***	0.854
Intercept	11.438	***	0.634	5.509	***	1.125	9.031	***	0.709	9.819	***	0.839	2.149	***	0.839
Inefficiency															
Road network	1.224	***	0.205	−0.267		0.197	−0.382	***	0.121	−0.865		0.637	−1.627	*	0.884
IT	−6.709	***	1.639	−6.655	***	1.208	−3.779	***	0.743	−15.253	**	6.323	−2.882	**	0.894
Human capital	−3.333	***	0.567	−0.563		0.367	2.359	***	0.362	12.417	***	4.619	−0.400		0.332
Intercept	1.928	**	0.841	−1.073		0.762	−8.936	***	0.957	−42.713	***	14.879	−2.011	***	0.710
Noise															
ln(capital)	−0.135	***	0.05	−0.068		0.07	−0.605	***	0.19	0.047		0.09	−0.275	***	0.10
ln(labor)	−0.484	***	0.04	−0.161		0.10	0.630	***	0.18	−0.017		0.10	−0.130		0.11
Intercept	−0.065		0.644	−2.744	***	0.714	−2.110		1.411	−5.381	***	0.645	0.031		0.852
LogL	653.12			368.00			605.50			588.78			418.69		

Note: * (**) (***) stands for statistically significance at 10% (5%) (1%)

Table 3 Auxiliary regressions

	Agriculture		Energy		Manufacturing		Services		Construction	
Variable	Coef.	Std. Err.	Coef.	Std. Err.	Coef.	Std. Err.	Coef.	Std. Err.	Coef.	Std. Err.
Access to electricity	0.945	0.246	1.003	0.001	1.086	0.206	0.654	1.033	−1.184	2.905
IT	0.568	0.067	1.000	0.001	0.819	0.049	0.800	0.040	5.224	2.042
Road network	0.488	0.038	1.001	0.001	0.834	0.019	0.786	0.020	1.817	0.544
Human capital	0.509	0.029	1.001	0.001	0.862	0.011	0.803	0.003	5.412	3.561
R-squared	0.9997		0.9999		0.9997		0.9999		0.9985	
#par	120		120		120		120		120	
Time-varying FE	Yes		Yes		Yes		Yes		Yes	

Table 4 Sectoral and aggregate productivity growth (%)

	Obs	Mean	Std. dev.	Min	Max
Sectoral productivity growth rates					
Agriculture	546	2.68	8.53	−54.91	43.69
Energy	546	2.16	13.09	−78.43	60.10
Manufacturing	546	1.78	5.52	−20.52	24.27
Services	546	1.09	4.59	−22.11	16.52
Construction	546	0.14	8.50	−49.14	41.31
Productivity growth decomposition					
Aggregate productivity growth (APG)	546	1.99	3.75	−17.49	13.76
Within effect (WE)	546	1.54	3.70	−12.41	17.01
Labor reallocation effect (LRE)	546	0.46	1.95	−8.43	10.79
Output price effect (OPE)	546	−0.01	0.52	−6.25	2.29

5.2 *First-Level Decomposition*

In this subsection, we first compute the rates of growth of labor productivity for each industry. We next compute aggregate productivity growth and decompose the economy-wide productivity growth rate into Diewert's (2015) main productivity drivers, i.e., WE, LRE, and OPE. Table 4 summarizes the descriptive statistics of the computed rates of growth of labor productivity. The largest (smallest) increase in labor productivity growth is found in the agriculture (construction) sector. This result is mostly caused by labor mobility, from the agriculture sector to the construction sector. The services sector has also employed more labor, but its productivity performance, on the one hand, was better than in the construction sector due to a better performance of its production. On the other hand, the moderate performances of labor productivity in the energy and manufacturing sectors are mainly caused by output increases, given the moderate increase in labor. Aggregating all industry outputs and labor quantities, we obtain economy-wide labor productivity rate of growth of about 2%.

Using Eq. (6), we have decomposed the economy-wide increase in labor productivity into the within effect (WE), the labor reallocation effect (LRE), and the output reallocation effect (captured by minus OPE). As expected, aggregate productivity growth is mainly explained by the within effect, i.e., by improvements in industry-specific productivities. This better performance would yield an increase in labor productivity of 1.5%. The productivity growth attributable to labor reallocation issues is smaller on average (around 0.5%) but positive, indicating that the industries that increase their relative labor demand are larger than the industries that reduce it.

Figure 1 depicts the annual rates of growth computed for the WE, LRE, and OPE terms. Two features of this figure are remarkable. First, the labor reallocation effects tend to strengthen the industry-specific gains in productivity. Second, the LRE effect however varies over time, and both WE and LRE are positively correlated over time, at least on average. In 1998, 2003, and 2008, the reallocation effects are of similar magnitude than the within effects. Overall, this figure suggests that there is room in our empirical application for non-negligible reallocation effects between industries attributable to infrastructure provision. We later on show that both within and reallocation effects also vary across regions.

We finally find that the output price effect is much less important on average. As in Diewert (2015), the aggregate labor productivity contribution term due to changes in industry real output prices is practically zero (around −0.01%). As discussed before, this is an expected result due to the nominal and real output shares are similar in our application (their coefficient of correlation ranges between 90% and 99%). This similarity is caused by the way the output prices have been computed in practice. The industry real output prices P_n are *indices* of the underlying micro-outputs produced in the industry. As all

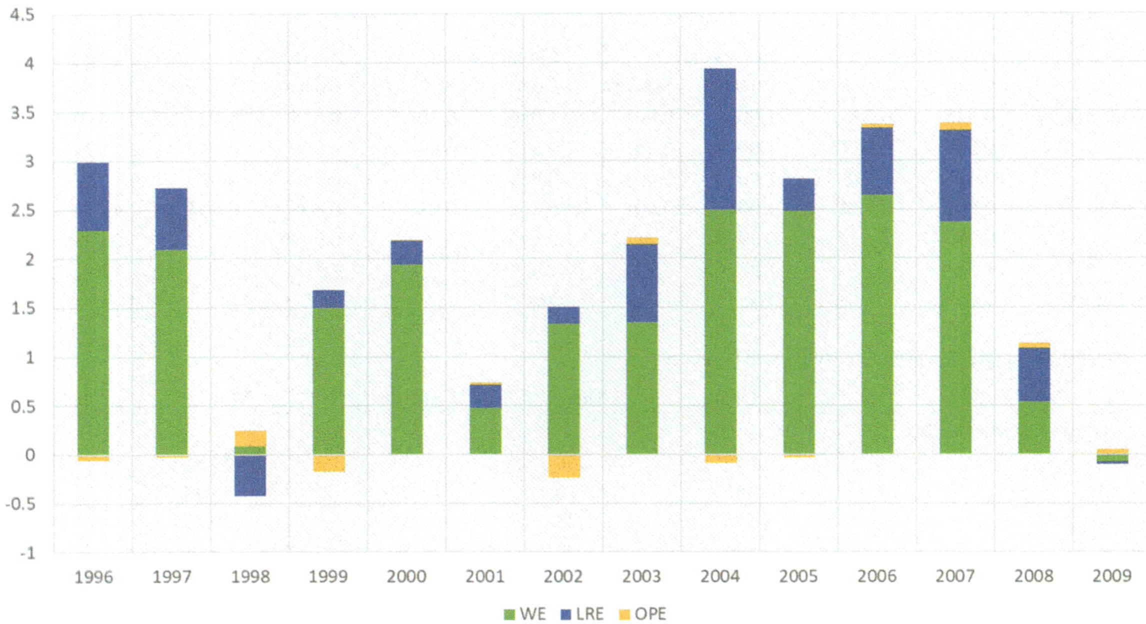

Fig. 1 Diewert (2015) productivity growth decomposition (%)

indices are equal in the base year by construction (in our case, the base year is 2005), their differences before and after the base year are of little magnitude, and hence the computed output reallocation effects associated with the OPE term are much less than the input reallocation effects associated with the LRE term.

5.3 *Second-Level Decomposition*

5.3.1 Decomposing WE

In this subsection, we first decompose the within effects (WE) into industry-level frontier improvements in productivity (PWE) and productivity gains caused by firm-level reallocation effects (FRE). Later on, we examine the impact of infrastructure provision on the overall WE . The results are shown in Fig. 2. This figure shows that the productivity growth attributable to reallocation effects within the industry is of similar magnitude than the productivity growth caused by pure technological improvements in the industry. Moreover, the poor productivity performance found in 1998 and 2009 can be mainly explained by a worse allocation of inputs within the industry.

We next use the parameter estimates of the production frontier models to measure to what extent the WE and OPE effects have to do with changes in the infrastructure provision. To estimate the final effect of our indicators on both industry labor shares and LRE effect, we use the parameter estimates of our auxiliary regressions. To examine the precision of the empirical strategy proposed in this chapter, Fig. 3 compares the computed and estimated WE, OPE, and LRE accumulated indices. All computed and estimated indices follow the same patterns over the sample period, indicating a reasonable "goodness-of-fit" of the empirical strategy proposed in this chapter. Indeed, while the OPE indices are pretty flat as expected, the WE indices are increasing over time due to the within-industry productivity gains are by far the main productivity drivers. The indices capturing labor reallocation effects indicate that the productivity growth attributable to a reallocation of the labor input between industries is smaller, but remarkable. Notice, however, that the estimated LRE values are far from the computed ones. This simply suggests that our set of infrastructure and technological indicators only explains a portion (about one third) of all the productivity growth attributable to interindustry labor reallocation. This is again an expected result given that employment is an intrinsically complex phenomenon and depends on many other factors, which in our auxiliary regressions are captured by the set of time-varying fixed effects.

We next examine the role that our Z variables have played in within productivity growth. The results are shown in Fig. 4. We find that the infrastructure that has promoted industry productivity gains the most in our sample is the investment in IT networks with an average annual rate of growth of 0.30%. Recall that this better productivity performance is caused by a

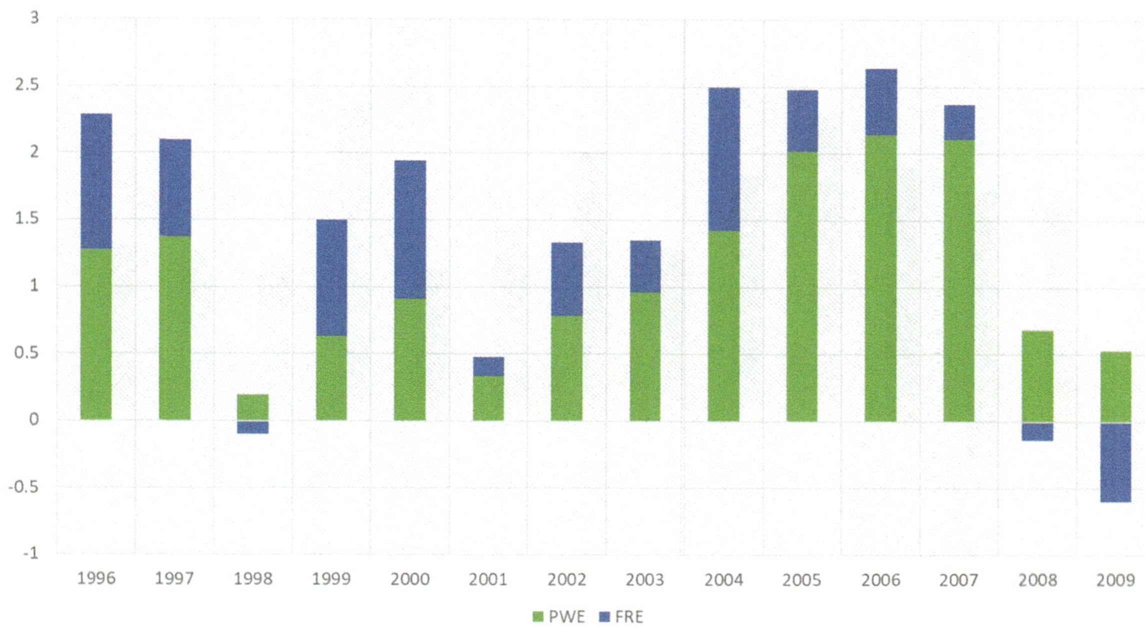

Fig. 2 Pure within effect and interfirm reallocation effect (%)

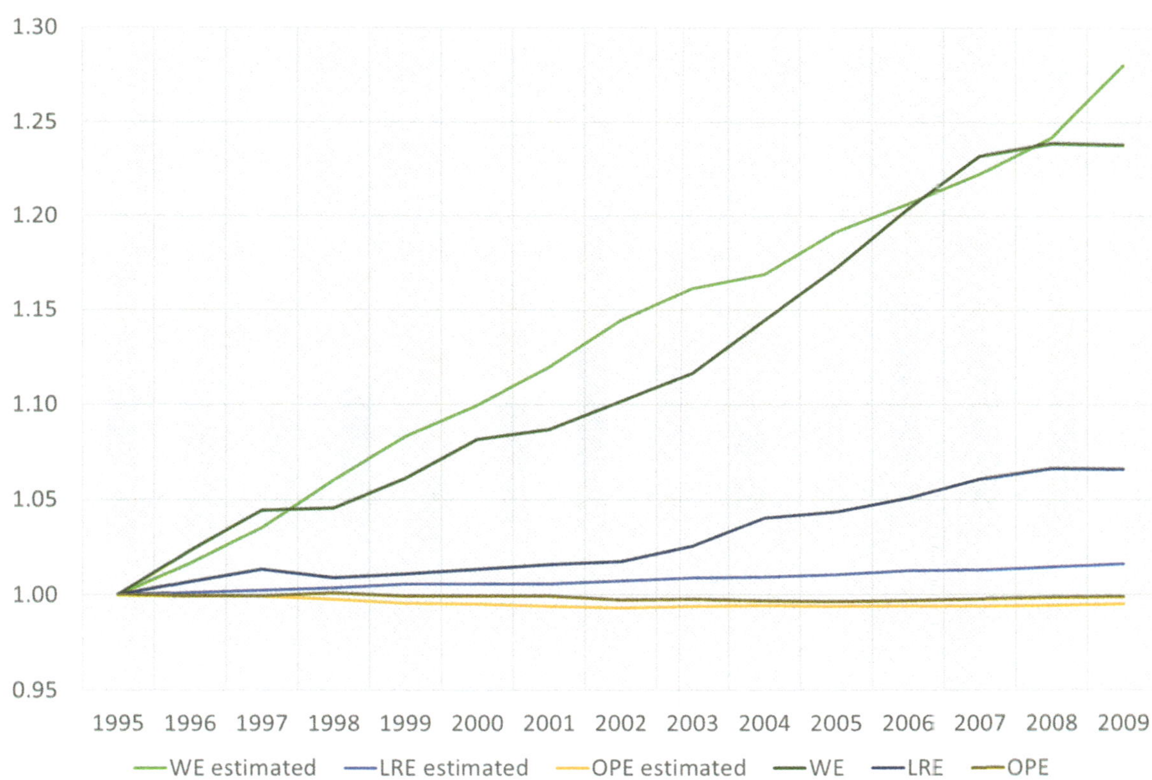

Fig. 3 Computed and estimated productivity effects

better reallocation of resources within the industries. The investment in transport infrastructure and electricity networks has had a more moderate effect on productivity with an average rate of growth of 0.12% and 0.08% per year, respectively. This moderate effect is likely caused by the fact that many countries included in our sample almost completely developed their transportation and electricity networks a long time ago. Finally, the moderate increase in human capital has had small but negative (non-frontier) productivity effects within the industries.

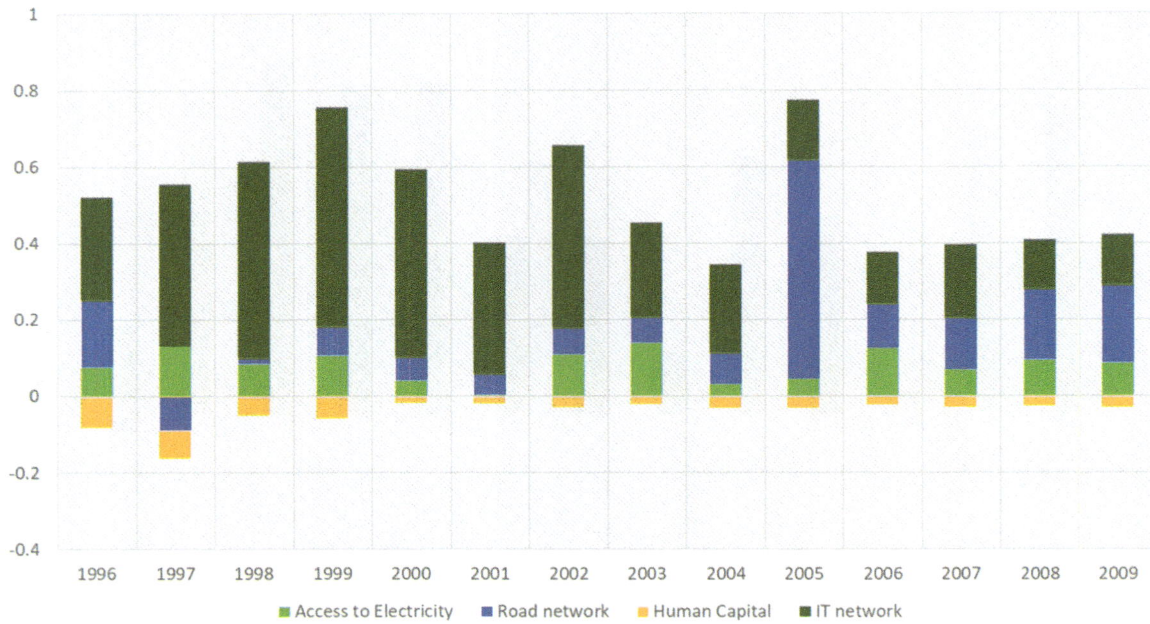

Fig. 4 WE attributable to the Z variables

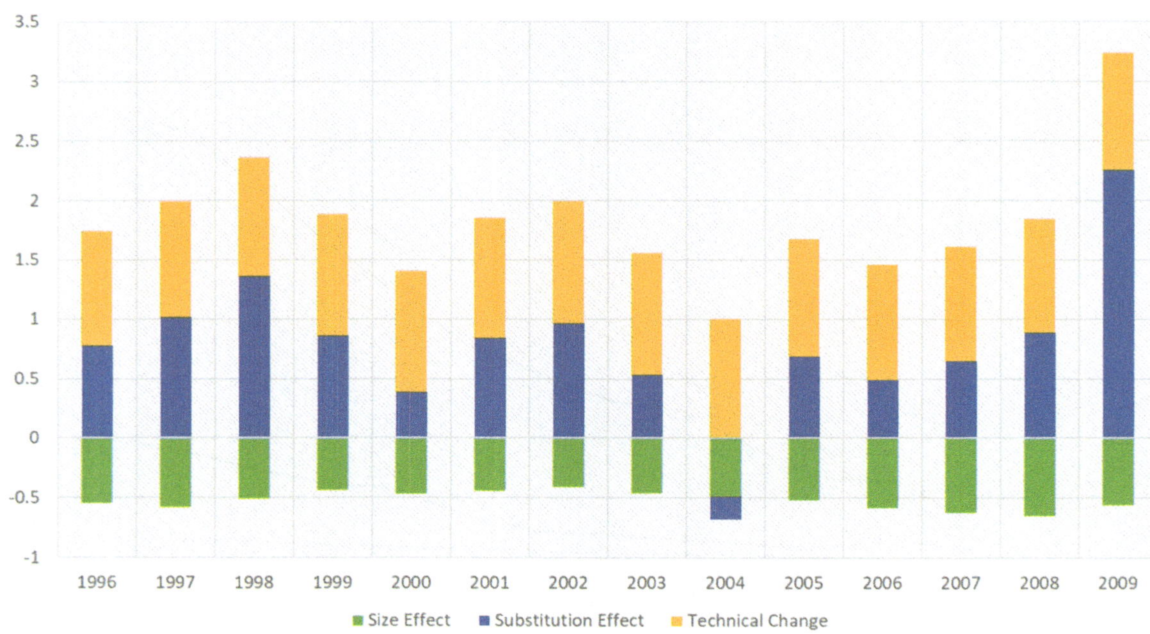

Fig. 5 WE attributable to capital, labor, and technical change

Also using Eq. (16), we have computed the WE term attributable to other factors, such as the increase in the usage of inputs (size effect), changes in the input mix over time (substitution effect), and improvements in industry technology (technical change). Figure 5 shows the size and substitution effects associated with these two inputs. The size effect attributable to a hypothetical increase in all production factors is negative due to the existence of decreasing returns to scale in most industries. The substitution effect however is positive in most years (except in 2004) due to the capital intensification occurred in most countries. Technical change is also one of the most important drivers of industry productivity with an average rate of growth of 1%.

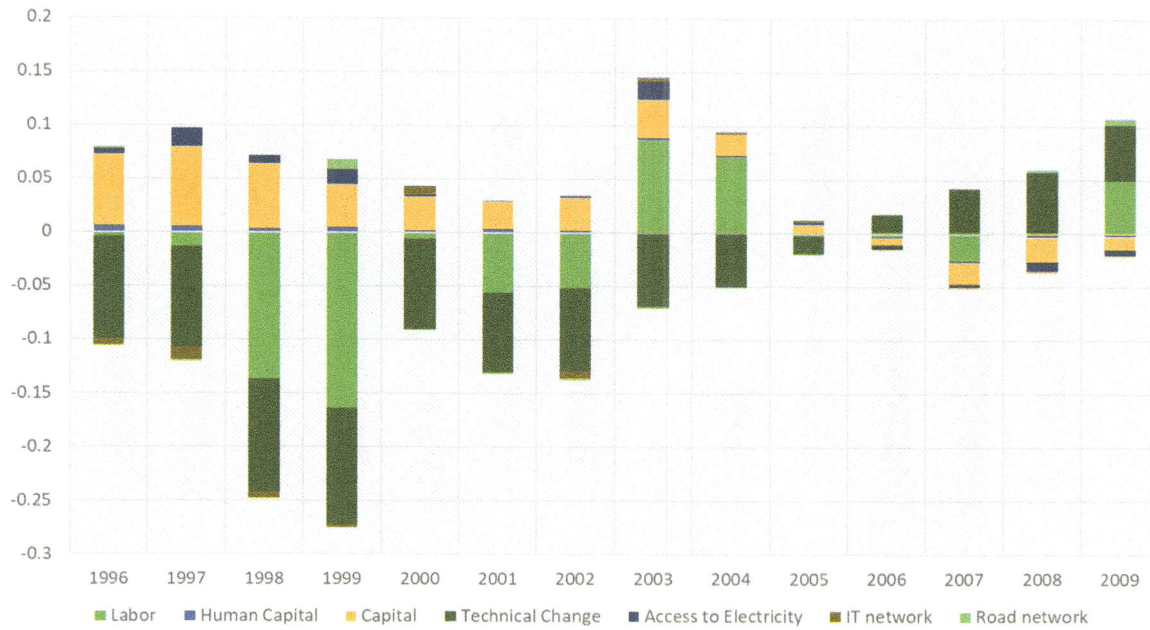

Fig. 6 OPE decomposition

5.3.2 Decomposing OPE and LRE

We next examine the role of capital, labor, technical change, and our set of Z variables have played in interindustry reallocation productivity growth. In particular, we will study to what extent they have generated better (worse) allocations of output and input across the different sectors of the economy.

Figure 6 shows a summary of output reallocation effects associated with the OPE term. The interindustry reallocation effects found are quite small as their final value depends heavily on the differences in nominal and real output shares. In this sense, it is worth mentioning the practically zero value in 2005 and 2006 where all output price indices converge to the unity value. Although the reallocation of value-added across industries is not remarkable on average, the most relevant OPE drivers are labor and capital. This is also an expected outcome since capital and labor are the main production factors and their effect on industry output varies a lot across industries. Technical change and other temporal effects have also generated noteworthy output reallocation effects, first worsening the allocation of valued-added across industries but later on improving the output allocation in the economy. Regarding our infrastructure variables, most of them do not have significant output reallocation effects. Therefore, infrastructure provision seems to improve aggregate productivity through a better allocation of resources between firms operating in the same industry, but not between firms operating in different industries.

The role of infrastructure in determining productivity improvement through better allocations of the labor input across the different sectors of the economy is shown in Fig. 7. Although these numbers just account for one-third of the total labor reallocation effects, the estimated effects of some Z variables are not negligible, and thus they do have not generated similar productivity increases in all sectors. In particular, we find that access to electricity has generated the largest reallocation effect with an annual effect of 0.11%. It is also remarkable the negative but moderate reallocation effects attributable to IT networks. Notice finally that the above numbers are mean values, and this statistic tends to hide relatively large rates of growth that some countries have experienced in specific years.

5.3.3 Regional Productivity Growth Decompositions

Table 5 summarizes the productivity growth decompositions by region. This table shows that the within and reallocation effects vary greatly across regions. The Asian countries show a better performance with an overall increase of 2.8% and a positive and relatively large (0.42%) interindustry labor reallocation effect. Therefore, the traditional within productivity measures tend to underestimate the overall productivity growth in these countries. The set of European countries included in our sample and the USA exhibit a more moderate performance (1.58%). This result is partially attributable to a negative labor reallocation effect (−0.22%) that has partially offset the positive within effect (1.83%). Consequently, the traditional

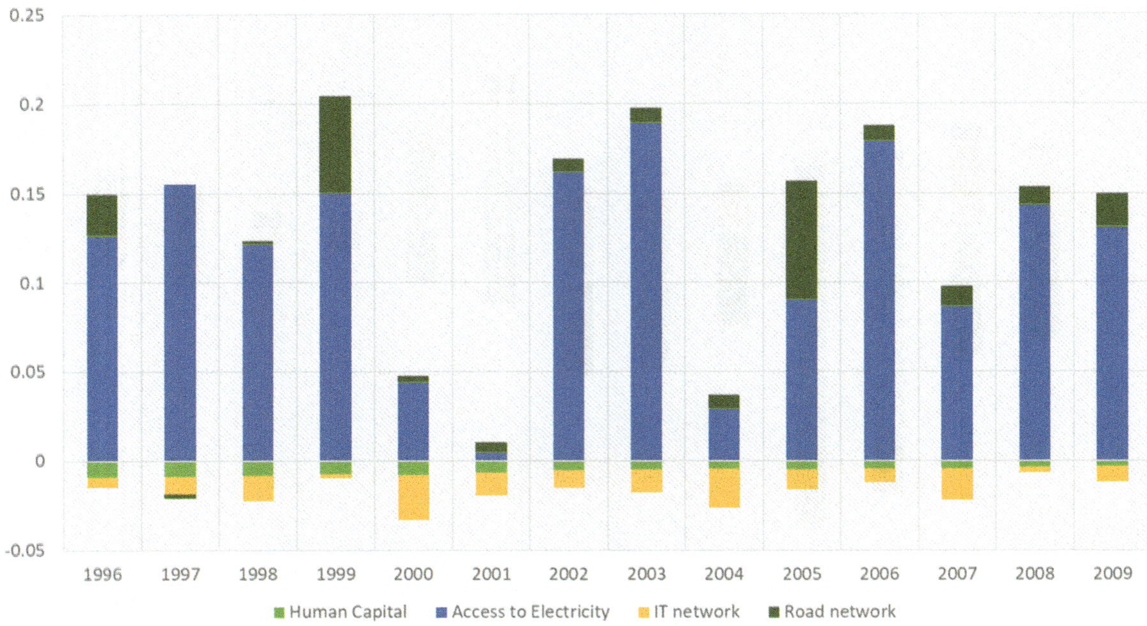

Fig. 7 LRE decomposition

Table 5 Productivity growth decompositions by region

Decomposition level	Asia	EUR and USA	Latin America	Africa	All
First-level					
PAG	2.80	1.58	0.87	2.44	1.99
WE	2.41	1.83	0.55	1.36	1.54
LRE	0.42	−0.22	0.24	1.11	0.46
OPE	−0.02	−0.03	0.07	−0.03	−0.01
Second-level: WE					
Size effect[a]	−0.69	−0.22	−0.43	−0.64	−0.52
Substitution effect[a]	1.70	0.85	0.50	0.32	0.83
Technical change[a]	1.08	1.09	0.91	0.93	1.00
Access to electricity[a]	0.08	0.00	0.07	0.15	0.08
Road network[a, b]	0.36	0.09	0.01	0.02	0.12
IT[b]	0.34	0.79	0.18	0.05	0.31
Human capital[b]	−0.04	−0.17	−0.04	0.06	−0.04
Second-level: LRE					
Access to electricity	0.10	0.00	0.09	0.23	0.12
Road network	0.06	0.00	0.00	0.00	0.02
IT	−0.01	0.01	−0.03	−0.01	−0.01
Human capital	−0.01	−0.00	−0.01	−0.01	−0.01
Other factors	0.19	−0.28	0.20	0.84	0.01
Second-level: OPE					
Capital	0.02	0.02	0.03	0.02	0.02
Labor	−0.00	−0.01	−0.06	−0.01	−0.02
Technical change	−0.02	−0.05	−0.09	−0.02	−0.04
Access to electricity	0.01	0.00	0.00	0.00	0.00
Road network	0.01	0.00	0.00	−0.00	0.00
IT	0.00	−0.02	0.01	0.00	0.00
Human capital	0.00	0.01	0.00	−0.00	0.00

Notes:
[a]Pure within effect through the production frontier
[b]Interfirm reallocation effect measured as a change in industry inefficiency

within productivity measures tend to overestimate overall productivity growth of the most developed countries in the world. The poor performance of Latin American countries is mainly explained by a modest increase in sector productivities. Finally, it is worth emphasizing the remarkable within and labor reallocation effects in the African countries included in our sample. As the labor reallocation effects are as large as the within effects in this region, the traditional within productivity measures tend to seriously underestimate African aggregate productivity growth. We next examine whether the negative reallocation effects found in this region are to any extent caused by investments in infrastructure, among other interesting results.

We start with *Asia*, the region with the largest increase in labor productivity. Regarding the within effect, capital intensification (substitution effect) and improvements in technology are the main drivers of industry productivity with an average rate of growth of 1.70% and 1.08% per year, respectively. However, the size effect is on average equal to −0.69%. Given the existence of diseconomies of scale, the larger use of inputs has had a negative effect on aggregate productivity. We also find that the infrastructure that has promoted aggregate productivity the most in this region is the investment in roads with an average rate of growth of 0.36% per year. This is mainly caused by an annual rate of growth of 3.4% in road networks in these countries. The technological indicator measuring the investment in IT networks is also a relevant productivity driver in Asia (0.34%). Notice that the labor reallocation effect of the investment in both electricity and IT networks is positive with a combined average rate of growth of 0.16%. This implies that both infrastructures have permitted a better allocation of labor across the industries of the economy. Therefore, this reallocation effect should not be ignored in a study measuring the productivity effects of these two infrastructure investments. In other words, the traditional intra-industry measures tend to underestimate the overall productivity effects of road and electricity networks. As expected, the output reallocation effects of all variables are rather small. The moderate increase in human capital did not reveal any relevant intra- or interindustry productivity effect even with the average 2.6% increase in the years of schooling in these countries.

The third column in Table 5 shows the productivity growth rates for the *European* countries and the *USA*. These countries exhibit a more moderate productivity performance than the Asian countries in part due to a negative labor reallocation effect. As these countries developed almost completely their transportation and electricity networks a long time ago, they did not experience productivity effects on their economies during the sample period. For the same reason, both substitution and size effects are less important than in Asia with an average rate of growth of 0.85% and −0.22% per year, respectively. While the productivity gains attributable to technical change (1.09%) are similar to that in Asia (1.08%), the investments in IT networks have promoted much larger increases in aggregated productivity in the European countries with an average rate of growth of 0.79%. Unlike technical change, the estimated effect associated with IT networks only includes the effect through a better allocation of resources between firms operating in the same industry. As the IT indicator was not included in the frontier due to collinearity issues, part of the technical change effect has also to do with the generalization of the Internet in European and American societies. Regarding the (labor) reallocation effects, they are negative but less important than in Asia. Moreover, most of them have to do with other factors (−0.28%) not controlled explicitly in our models.

The fourth column in Table 5 shows the productivity growth rates for the *Latin American* countries. These countries exhibit a poor productivity performance mainly due to a modest increase in sector productivities. As in the European countries and the USA, both substitution and size effects are relatively small with an average rate of growth of 0.50% and −0.43% per year, respectively. While the productivity gains attributable to technical change (0.91%) are only slightly smaller than in Asia, Europe, and the USA, the role of IT networks boosting aggregate productivity is much more moderate in the Latin American countries, with an average rate of growth of 0.18% per year. Fortunately, the labor reallocation effects are positive, but most of them have to do with other factors (0.20%) not controlled in our models with our set of Z variables. Thus, we do not find evidence in these countries supporting the hypothesis that infrastructure provision has permitted a better allocation of labor across the industries of the economy, as we have found in the case of the Asian countries. Interestingly enough, technical change seems to have relatively large output reallocation effects (−0.09%). This suggests that not all sectors in the Latin American countries have benefited equally from these technological improvements. As a result of this, the allocation of industry output across industries has had a negative effect on aggregate productivity.

The last column in Table 5 shows the productivity growth rates for the *African* countries included in our sample. Recall that the labor reallocation effects are as large as the within effects in this region. Regarding the within effect, the improvements in technology are the main drivers of industry productivity with an average rate of growth of 0.93% per year. Notice that while the size effect (−0.64%) is as large as the size effect in the Asian countries, the substitution effect associated with the degree of capital intensification is much less in the African countries (0.32%) than in other world regions. Unlike the previous regions, the use of IT networks in Africa has hardly changed over time during the sample period. This explains the small effect of this technological indicator on aggregate productivity. In line with the other regions, road network investments have been very modest in the African countries included in our sample. However, the improvements in access to electricity in Africa are slightly higher than in other regions. This explains why the investment in electricity networks, which allows larger percentages of population to have access to electricity, has had a relatively large effect on productivity with an average rate of growth of 0.15% per year. It should also be noted that the investment in electricity networks has not only improved individual productivities in all sectors but has also promoted a better allocation of resources across the industries of the economy with an average growth rate of 0.23%. We have found pretty large positive labor reallocation effects in this region. However, we were not able to link these effects to any of our Z variables. Most of them have to do with other factors (0.84%) not controlled explicitly in our models.

6 Conclusion

In this chapter, we have tried to examine the role that infrastructure provision has played in stimulating aggregate productivity through both a better allocation of resources in the economy and as a proper productivity driver. To achieve this objective, we propose a two-step top-down approach that relies on estimating standard production frontier models. To illustrate the proposed decompositions, we have used the sector-level data of 39 countries over the 1995–2010 period.

The average growth rate of labor productivity in our sample is about 2%. As expected, aggregate productivity growth is mainly explained by improvements in industry-specific productivities. The productivity growth attributable to changes in the structure of the economy is small on average but displaying large rates of growth in some countries. We found that the within and reallocation effects also vary across regions. The Asian countries show a better performance, followed by the set of European countries and the USA. The reallocation effects are nontrivial in some countries and have partially offset the improvements in intra-industry productivity.

The above (first-level) productivity components are next attributed to several sources using sectoral production frontier functions. The estimated coefficients vary considerably across industries, a necessary result for non-negligible within (intra-industry) or reallocation (interindustry) productivity effects attributable to infrastructures. We find that the infrastructures that have promoted within-industry productivity the most are the investment in road and telecommunication networks. The latter network has also promoted a better allocation of resources among firms operating in the same industries. Although the interindustry labor reallocation effects are mainly attributed to other factors, the effect of access to electricity is remarkable in most regions. We finally find that the output price effect is practically zero. We show theoretically that we should always expect this result using sectoral-level data.

Some interesting policy implications can be inferred from our results. For instance, Asian policy makers should take into account the non-negligible reallocation effects attributed to infrastructure provision; otherwise, they will underestimate its overall productivity effect. Policy makers in Latin America should improve the quality of their institutions and markets before building costly infrastructures. Aggregate productivity in Africa will likely improve if African policy makers are able to incentive the adoption of capital by the African firms by improving, for instance, the performance of their financial and capital markets. Policy makers in these countries should also be vigilant in the next future to make it easier for African companies to take advantage of the increasingly development of IT networks.

We let for future research to extend our model or our dataset to deal with several empirical issues. For instance, endogeneity problems can arise if economic behaviors are believed to affect both capital and labor inputs (Kumbhakar et al. 2013). Some authors (e.g., Feng and Wu 2018) also argue that public capital is likely to be an endogenous variable due to the likely reverse causality between output and infrastructure. To address this issue, we will follow Amsler et al. (2017) and estimate a set of reduced form equations for the endogenous variables. The frontier parameters will be again obtained once the reduced form residuals are included in our frontier model. We will also try to attenuate some of the weaknesses of our capital variable, which does not distinguish between private and public capital. We will try to avoid this problem using the private capital stock provided by the International Monetary Fund. Finally, we are currently working in a new paper that decomposes a total factor productivity growth measure. While a multifactor measure is a better productivity indicator because it takes into account the growth of all inputs, its computation (and decomposition) is more challenging as it requires using input prices that are not available in our application.

References

Amsler, C., Prokhorov, A., & Schmidt, P. (2017). Endogenous environmental variables in stochastic frontier models. *Journal of Econometrics, 199*, 131–140.

Asturias, J., García-Santana, M., & Ramos, R. (2017). Competition and the welfare gains from transportation infrastructure: Evidence from the Golden Quadrilateral of India. PEDL Research.

Baily, M. N., Hulten, C., & Campbell, D. (1992). Productivity dynamics in manufacturing plants. *Brookings Papers on Economic Activity: Microeconomics, 2*, 187–249.

Balk, B. M. (2016a). The dynamics of productivity change: A review of the bottom-up approach. In W. H. Greene, L. Khalaf, R. C. Sickles, M. Veall, & M.-C. Voia (Eds.),. Proceedings in business and economics *Productivity and efficiency analysis*. Cham: Springer International Publishing.

Balk, B. M. (2016b). *Aggregate productivity and productivity of the aggregate: Connecting the bottom-up and top-down approaches*. Paper prepared for the 34th IARIW General Conference Dresden, Germany, August 21–27, 2016.

Bennet, T. L. (1920). The theory of measurement of changes in cost of living. *Journal of the Royal Statistical Society, 83*(3), 455–462.

Cornwell, C., Schmidt, P., & Sickles, R. C. (1990). Production frontiers with cross-sectional and time-series variation in efficiency levels. *Journal of Econometrics, 46*(1–2), 185–200.

Crescenzi, R., & Rodríguez-Pose, A. (2012). Infrastructure and regional growth in the European Union. *Papers in Regional Science, 91*(3), 487–513.

Diewert, W. E. (2015). Decompositions of productivity growth into sectoral effects. *Journal of Productivity Analysis, 43*(3), 367–387.

Färe, R., Grosskopft, S., & Margaritis, D. (2008). Efficiency and productivity: Malmquist and more, Chapter 5. In H. Fried, K. Lovell, & S. Schmidt (Eds.), *The measurement of productive efficiency and productivity growth*. New York: Oxford University Press.

Feenstra, R. C., Inklaar, R., & Timmer, M. P. (2015). The next generation of the Penn World Table. *American Economic Review, 105*(10), 3150–3182, Available for download at www.ggdc.net/pwt.

Feng, Q., & Wu, G. L. (2018). On the reverse causality between output and infrastructure: The case of China. *Economic Modelling, 74*, 97–104.

Foster, A. D., & Rosenzweig, M. R. (1992). Information flows and discrimination in labor markets in rural areas in developing countries. *World Bank Economic Review, 6*(1), 173–203.

Funkhouser, E. (1996). The urban informal sector in Central America: Household survey evidence. *World Development, 24*(11), 1737–1751.

Greene, W. (2005). Fixed and random effects in stochastic frontier models. *Journal of Productivity Analysis, 23*(1), 7–32.

Hadri, K. (1999). Estimation of a doubly heteroscedastic stochastic frontier cost function. *Journal of Business and Economic Statistics, 17*(3), 359–363.

Kumbhakar, S. C., Asche, F., & Tveteras, R. (2013). Estimation and decomposition of inefficiency when producers maximize return to the outlay: An application to Norwegian fishing trawlers. *Journal of Productivity Analysis, 40*, 307–321.

McMillan, M., Rodrik, D., & Verduzco-Gallo, ´i. (2014). Globalization, structural change, and productivity growth, with an update on Africa. *World Development, 63*, 11–32.

Moscoso-Boedo, H. J., & D'Erasmo, P. N. (2012). Misallocation, informality, and human capital. Virginia economics online papers 401, University of Virginia, Department of Economics.

Qiang, C. Z.-W., & Rossotto, C. M. (2009). *Economic impacts of broadband, information and communications for development 2009: Extending reach and increasing impact* (pp. 35–50). Washington, DC: World Bank.

Restuccia, D., & Rogerson, R. (2008). Policy distortions and aggregate productivity with heterogeneous establishments. *Review of Economic Dynamics, 11*(4), 707–720.

Restuccia, D., & Rogerson, R. (2013). Misallocation and productivity. *Review of Economic Dynamics, 16*(1), 1–10.

Straub, S. (2012). Infrastructure and development: A critical appraisal of the macro-level literature. *Journal of Development Studies, 47*(05), 683–708.

Vivarelli, M. (2012). Innovation, employment and skills in advanced and developing countries: A survey of the literature. Discussion paper series, Forschungsinstitut zur Zukunft der Arbeit, No. 6291, Institute for the Study of Labor (IZA), Bonn.

Yang, H. (2000). A note on the causal relationship between energy and GDP in Taiwan. *Energy Economics, 22*(3), 309–317.

European Energy Efficiency Evaluation Based on the Use of Super-Efficiency Under Undesirable Outputs in SBM Models

Roberto Gómez-Calvet, David Conesa, Ana Rosa Gómez-Calvet, and Emili Tortosa-Ausina

Abstract Although Data Envelopment Analysis models have been intensively used for measuring efficiency, the inclusion of undesirable outputs has extended their use to analyse relevant fields such as environmental efficiency. In this context, slacks-based measure (SBM) models offer a remarkable alternative, largely due to their ability to deal with undesirable outputs. Additionally, super-efficiency evaluation in DEA is a useful complementary analysis for ranking the performance of efficient DMUs and even mandatory for dynamic efficiency evaluation. An extension to this approach in the presence of undesirable outputs is here introduced and then applied in the context of the environmental efficiency in electricity and derived heat generation in the European Union, providing the necessary tool to detect influential countries.

Keywords Efficiency · Energy · Slacks-based measure · Super-efficiency · Undesirable outputs

1 Introduction

Electricity and derived heat concentrate the major part of greenhouse gas (GHG) emissions in the European Union (EU). During the last two decades, the energy sector has clearly shifted to less pollutant primary energy consumption. However, all fossil fuels together (solid, gaseous and liquid) still account for 72.2% of current total primary energy consumption (Eurostat 2015). This large figure shows that most of the primary energy consumed comes from sources with high impact in the environment. Renewable sources have played an important role, but nowadays its share in EU28 primary energy consumption is only 12.6%. The great opportunity to abate GHG emissions comes from the reduction of primary energy consumption, and this can only be accomplished by boosting renewable sources and mainly on behalf of the improvement of the efficiency of the transformation process.

Nonparametric frontier models have been recognised as a powerful tool for efficiency measurement requiring no a priori functional form assumption. One of the most popular nonparametric methods for measuring efficiency is the Data Envelopment Analysis (DEA) estimator. DEA methods combine the estimation of the technology that defines a performance standard (usually called the technology) and the evaluation of the results of a certain decision-making unit (DMU) against the established standard. In the field of energy efficiency and environmental performance, the modeling of undesirable outputs is essential. In this sense, although various techniques for including undesirable outputs have been adopted in Data Envelopment Analysis (DEA) settings, no single one has emerged as the best alternative. According to Yang and Pollitt (2010), there are two main trends in modeling undesirable outputs. The first assumes that undesirable outputs are strongly disposable, so either treat them as inputs or apply a suitable transformation to deal with them. This trend is based on the economic argument that both input and undesirable outputs incur a cost for a decision-making unit (DMU), and hence decision makers usually want to reduce both variables. In the second alternative, the choice is to model undesirable outputs as outputs imposing

R. Gómez-Calvet
Universitat Europea de Valencia, Valencia, Spain

D. Conesa · A. R. Gómez-Calvet
Universitat de València, València, Spain

E. Tortosa-Ausina (✉)
Department of Economics, Universitat Jaume I, Castellón de la Plana, Spain
e-mail: tortosa@uji.es

J. Aparicio et al. (eds.), *Advances in Efficiency and Productivity II*, International Series in Operations Research & Management Science 287, https://doi.org/10.1007/978-3-030-41618-8_12

weak disposability and introduce an environmental performance indicator by decomposing overall productivity into an environmental index and a productive efficiency index (Färe et al. 1989).[1]

A comprehensive analysis on pollution-generating technologies in performance benchmarking can be found in a recent article from Murty and Russell (2018), where authors compile the axiomatic context of by-production technologies previously developed (Murty and Russell 2002; Murty et al. 2012). In line with this but in a nonparametric framework, Dakpo et al. (2016) also present a review on the literature on pollutant-generating technologies. An empirical application from these authors can be found in Dakpo et al. (2017), where an evaluation of the greenhouse gas emissions and efficiency in French sheep meat farming is presented.

When the interest is to perform a joint analysis of inefficiencies from more than one set of variables (i.e., input, outputs and undesirable outputs), a suitable choice is to use *non-oriented* DEA models. Complementarily, *non-radial* DEA models provide more discriminating efficiency measures as they can estimate the optimum target for each variable. Among the non-radial and non-oriented DEA models, we will focus here on the non-oriented slacks-based measure model, a field in which some contributions excel. For instance, based on the DEA Russell measure, Pastor et al. (1999) developed an efficiency measure called the Enhanced Russell Measure (ERM). Simultaneously, and with the same underlying structure, Tone (2001) presented the slacks-based measure (SBM) model, which has been extensively developed by Tone and Tsutsui (Tone 2002; Tone and Tsutsui 2010; Cooper et al. 2007).

The SBM model incorporates slacks for all optimised variables in the objective function, allowing inefficiencies to be taken into account in the full ⟨input, output⟩ space, by providing a *comprehensive* efficiency index. But more interestingly, assuming strong disposability of undesirable outputs, it has the advantage that it can handle these outputs as a third set of variables that appears in the linear problem without the need to transform them. This latter reason is important in situations where undesirable outputs of production processes must be considered and properly included in the evaluation, for instance, when global environmental conservation is a concern. In this particular field, the DEA literature is still evolving, and few contributions can be found (Hu and Wang 2006; Zhou et al. 2006, 2007; Fukuyama and Weber 2010).

Super-efficiency DEA models are a modified version of DEA based upon the comparison of efficient DMUs relative to a reference technology spanned by all other units. These models were introduced among other procedures to rank efficient units (see, for instance, Doyle and Green 1994; Seiford and Zhu 1999; Adler et al. 2002; Banker and Chang 2006). In the context of SBM models, Tone (2002) developed the super-efficiency measure under the basic SBM model. An extension of this model under the oriented version of SBM model can be found in Cooper et al. (2007). Nevertheless, super-efficiency scenarios do not only appear when we are interested in ranking efficient units. Indeed, *super-efficiency* analysis has also proved useful in the context of regulation and incentive schemes (Bogetoft and Otto 2011), influential DMU detection, and dynamic analysis. In line with this, Tone and Tsutsui (2010) have complemented the dynamic DEA originally developed by Färe and Grosskopf (1997) under the SBM framework while also considering carry-over activities between two consecutive periods.

In particular, one of the contexts in which *super-efficiency* analysis turns out to be useful is when the interest is to facilitate an explanation of efficiency over time. The most extended approach for the dynamic analysis is the Malmquist index (see Caves et al. 1982). This index allows measurement not only of the efficiency change over time but also of how much of this change can be attributed to special initiatives of a certain DMU.[2]

But, when analysing situations in which global environmental conservation is a concern, undesirable outputs of production and social activities are issues to be factored into the analysis. In fact, and although it is widely acknowledged in the efficiency analysis literature that analysts should consider the effects of undesirable outputs, it turns out that very few published studies involving productivity change analysis have taken these effects into account.

[1]Examples of the first approach can be found in Seiford and Zhu (2002), where original data was transformed and traditional DEA models were then applied; in Ramanathan (2005), where undesirable outputs are treated as inputs and desirable inputs as outputs; and in Färe et al. (2004), where the DEA model is transformed into a non-linear problem in which normal outputs are maximised and undesirable outputs minimised. With respect to the second approach, the most representative example is Färe et al. (2004). In this study, using the original data, the authors make the assumption of weak disposable reference technology originally suggested by Färe et al. (1996) (this technique has been denoted as environmental DEA technology in Färe et al. (2004)). Nevertheless, it is worth noting Førsund's Førsund (2009) suggestion that the assumption of weak disposability for undesirable outputs has serious formal weaknesses, and, additionally, it does not account for abatement, and he recommends modelling the generation of undesirables as a function of the same set of inputs as in the production of good inputs. In a recent publication (Førsund 2018), he has developed the multi-equation modelling of desirable and undesirable outputs satisfying the physical principle of conservation of material balance.

[2]The use of a Malmquist approach can also be applied to determine the effects of changes other than time. For example, we may use it to evaluate two different ways to organise production, or two technologies, or two different managerial alternatives (see for instance Cooper et al. 2007, p.231).

Taking into account these considerations, our main interest in this study is to analyse the measurement of the productivity change in the electricity and derived heat generation process in the European Union by means of a Super-SBM index that can incorporate the presence of undesirable outputs in the above-mentioned Malmquist index. Our proposal complements some recently proposed approaches in the literature (Du et al. 2012; Wang et al. 2016; Li et al. 2012; Song et al. 2016), while meeting the desirable properties for this type of index: monotonicity, unit independence, and good definition (in the sense that it clearly differentiates efficiency and super-efficiency). This model has been barely used in the context of electricity generation, and, in the specific case of the European Union, on which our application is based, the number of contributions is almost yet to come (see, for instance, Gómez-Calvet et al. 2014). In this sense, as highlighted by (Cagno and Trianni 2013), reducing energy consumption by 20% in 2020 will be a difficult objective if focusing exclusively on the adoption of current EU policies. Therefore, encouraging energy efficiency practices is crucial, and, therefore, research initiatives evaluating different dimensions of energy efficiency in the EU such as the ones considered in this paper are essential.

The paper proceeds as follows. After this introduction, Sect. 2 briefly reviews efficiency theory and presents the SBM efficiency model and super-efficient SBM (SE-SBM) with desirable outputs only. In Sect. 3, we review the SBM including undesirable outputs and present our proposal for a super-efficient SBM with undesirable outputs. In Sect. 4, we illustrate the usefulness of our approach with an application to measure dynamic efficiency for European Union countries (current EU28) during the 2008–2012 period (Sect. 4). Finally, Sect. 5 provides conclusions.

2 Efficiency Concept and Measure Under the SBM Model

In what follows, we firstly review the SBM models introduced by Tone (2001), which extend traditional DEA models by incorporating input excesses and output shortfalls into models that account for both inefficiencies simultaneously. Secondly, we review the model for super-efficiency scenarios proposed by the same author (see Tone 2002). These models deal directly with variable slacks and have the ability to handle both non-oriented and partially oriented models (Cooper et al. 2007).

2.1 *Efficiency and SBM*

The background of the DEA literature is production theory, and the main idea behind it is that compared units have a common underlying technology. In particular, once the inputs and outputs are defined, the technology set or the production possibilities set (hereafter $\mathcal{PPS}$) which models the transformation of inputs $\mathbf{x} \in \mathbb{R}^m_+$ into outputs $\mathbf{y} \in \mathbb{R}^s_-$ is:

$$\mathcal{PPS} = \{(\mathbf{x}, \mathbf{y}) : \mathbf{x} \text{ can produce } \mathbf{y}\}. \tag{1}$$

However, although we seldom know the technology $\mathcal{PPS}$, we can overcome this problem by estimating the technology $\widehat{\mathcal{PPS}}$ from observed data. Throughout this paper, we deal with L Decision Making Units (DMUs, $j = 1, \ldots, L$) having m inputs ($i = 1, \ldots, m$) and s outputs ($r = 1, \ldots, s$). The input and output vectors for the DMU j are denoted by $\mathbf{x}_j$ and $\mathbf{y}_j$ respectively, where $\mathbf{x}_j = (x_{1j}, \ldots, x_{mj})' \in \mathbb{R}^m_+$, $\mathbf{y}_j = (y_{1j}, \ldots, y_{sj})' \in \mathbb{R}^s_+$, while the input and output matrices are denoted by $\mathbf{X} = \{x_{ij}\} \in \mathbb{R}^{m\times L}_+$ and $\mathbf{Y} = \{y_{rj}\} \in \mathbb{R}^{s\times L}_+$. For simplicity, we assume, $\mathbf{X} > 0$ and $\mathbf{Y} > 0$, although this assumption can be relaxed (Cooper et al. 2007).

The estimated production possibility set is defined using the nonnegative linear combination of the L DMUs as:

$$\widehat{\mathcal{PPS}} = \left\{ (\mathbf{x}, \mathbf{y}) | \mathbf{x} \geq \sum_{j=1}^{L} \lambda_j \mathbf{x}_j, 0 \leq \mathbf{y} \leq \sum_{j=1}^{L} \lambda_j \mathbf{y}_j, \;\; l \leq e\boldsymbol{\lambda} \leq u, \;\; \lambda_j \geq 0 \right\}, \tag{2}$$

where $\boldsymbol{\lambda} = (\lambda_1, \lambda_2, \ldots, \lambda_L)'$ is the intensity vector, whereas the parameters u and l refer to the assumption on the returns to scale.[3] This set defines a frontier, delimited by the observed best performers, and represents the reference benchmark for inefficient units. That is, for each inefficient DMU, the distance to the frontier quantifies a measure of inefficiency.

[3]The cases ($l = 0, u = \infty$), ($l = 1, u = 1$), ($l = 0, u = 1$) and ($l = 1, u = \infty$) correspond to the constant (CRS), variable (VRS), non-increasing (decreasing) (NIRS) and increasing (IRS) returns to scale, respectively (see, for instance, Bogetoft and Otto 2011).

A DMU with $(\mathbf{x}_0, \mathbf{y}_0)$ is SBM efficient if there is no vector $(\mathbf{x}, \mathbf{y}) \in \mathcal{PPS}$ such that $\mathbf{x}_0 \geq \mathbf{x}$, $\mathbf{y}_0 \leq \mathbf{y}$ with at least one strict inequality. In order to obtain the estimate of the efficiency for each DMU, Tone's (2001) proposed fractional programming model is:

$$
\begin{aligned}
\rho^* = \min_{(\boldsymbol{\lambda}, \mathbf{s}^-, \mathbf{s}^+)} & \left\{ \frac{1 - \frac{1}{m}\sum_{i=1}^{m} \frac{s_i^-}{x_{i0}}}{1 + \frac{1}{s}\sum_{r=1}^{s} \frac{s_r^+}{y_{r0}}} \right\} \\
\text{s.t. } \mathbf{x}_0 &= \mathbf{X}\boldsymbol{\lambda} + \mathbf{s}^- \\
\mathbf{y}_0 &= \mathbf{Y}\boldsymbol{\lambda} - \mathbf{s}^+ \\
\mathbf{s}^- \geq 0,\ \mathbf{s}^+ \geq 0,\ & l \leq e\boldsymbol{\lambda} \leq u,\ \ \lambda_i \geq 0\,.
\end{aligned}
\tag{3}
$$

The vectors $\mathbf{s}^- \in \mathbb{R}_+^m$, $\mathbf{s}^+ \in \mathbb{R}_+^s$ (usually labeled slacks) correspond to excesses in inputs and shortages in outputs, respectively. The objective value in (3) satisfies the constraint $0 < \rho^* \leq 1$. Among the desirable axioms to be accomplished by efficiency indexes proposed by Färe and Lovell (1978), the SBM shows *indication* of efficiency in input or output bundles (the index is equal to one, if and only if the input and output vector is efficient in the sense of Koopmans 1951), together with weak monotonicity and unit independence.

This fractional program can be solved by transforming it into an equivalent linear program in t using the Charnes-Cooper transformation (Charnes and Cooper 1962) in a similar way as the traditional DEA models:

$$
\begin{aligned}
\tau^* = \min_{(t, \boldsymbol{\Lambda}, \mathbf{S}^-, \mathbf{S}^+)} & \left\{ t - \frac{1}{m}\sum_{i=1}^{m} \frac{S_i^-}{x_{i0}} \right\} \\
\text{s.t. } 1 &= t + \frac{1}{s}\sum_{r=1}^{s} \frac{S_r^+}{y_{r0}} \\
\mathbf{x}_0 t &= \mathbf{X}\boldsymbol{\Lambda} + \mathbf{S}^- \\
\mathbf{y}_0 t &= \mathbf{Y}\boldsymbol{\Lambda} - \mathbf{S}^+ \\
\mathbf{S}^- \geq 0,\ \ \mathbf{S}^+ \geq 0,\ \ & lt \leq e\boldsymbol{\Lambda} \leq ut,\ \ \Lambda_i \geq 0,\ \ t > 0\,.
\end{aligned}
\tag{4}
$$

In particular, if $(t^*, \mathbf{S}^{-*}, \mathbf{S}^{+*}, \boldsymbol{\Lambda}^*)$ is the solution of (4), then we can obtain an optimal solution for (3) using:

$$
\rho^* = \tau^*,\ \ \boldsymbol{\lambda}^* = \boldsymbol{\Lambda}^*/t^*,\ \ \mathbf{s}^{-*} = \mathbf{S}^{-*}/t^*,\ \ \mathbf{s}^{+*} = \mathbf{S}^{+*}/t^*\,. \tag{5}
$$

A DMU with $(\mathbf{x}_0, \mathbf{y}_0)$ is SBM efficient if $\rho^* = 1$. This constraint is equivalent to $\mathbf{s}^{-*} = 0$ and $\mathbf{s}^{+*} = 0$, i.e. no input excess and no output shortfall in an optimal solution.

For an SBM-inefficient DMU $(\mathbf{x}_0, \mathbf{y}_0)$, the improvement of efficiency can be achieved by reducing the input excesses and increasing the output shortfalls. An SBM-inefficient DMU has a projection reference point in the frontier that can be obtained as:

$$
\begin{aligned}
\widehat{\mathbf{x}}_0 &= \mathbf{x}_0 - \mathbf{s}^{-*} \\
\widehat{\mathbf{y}}_0 &= \mathbf{y}_0 + \mathbf{s}^{+*}
\end{aligned}
\tag{6}
$$

The set of indexes corresponding to positive λ_j^* is called the reference set, or peers, for $(\mathbf{x}_0, \mathbf{y}_0)$, and it is denoted by $R = \left\{ j | \lambda_j^* > 0,\ j \in J \right\}$. Graphically the set of peers correspond to those DMUs that build the efficient frontier.

2.2 Superefficiency in the Context of SBM Models

Although under normal circumstances all evaluated DMUs lie inside (inefficient ones) or on the frontier (efficient ones) of the $\widehat{\mathcal{PPS}}$, under certain analysis this might not be true. In situations where, for some reason, an evaluated DMU does not, or should not, belong to the set of DMUs that make up the $\mathcal{PPS}$, the usual procedure needs to be modified to account for what is known as a super-efficiency scenario. This could happen, for instance, in the case of an efficiency evaluation of a newly included DMU within an existing frontier.

In order to account for super-efficiency, the evaluated DMU must first be excluded from the $\mathcal{PPS}$ (if it still contains it), resulting in a smaller $\mathcal{PPS}$ than the original set:

$$\mathcal{PPS}\backslash(\mathbf{x}_0, \mathbf{y}_0) = \left\{ (\bar{\mathbf{x}}, \bar{\mathbf{y}}) \mid \bar{\mathbf{x}} \geq \sum_{\substack{j=1 \\ j\neq 0}}^{L} \lambda_j \mathbf{x}_j,\ 0 \leq \bar{\mathbf{y}} \leq \sum_{\substack{j=1 \\ j\neq 0}}^{L} \lambda_j \mathbf{y}_j,\ l \leq e\boldsymbol{\lambda} \leq u,\ \boldsymbol{\lambda} \geq 0 \right\}, \tag{7}$$

where $\mathcal{PPS}\backslash(\mathbf{x}_0, \mathbf{y}_0)$ means that point $(\mathbf{x}_0, \mathbf{y}_0)$ is excluded from $\mathcal{PPS}$; $\boldsymbol{\lambda} \in \mathbb{R}_+^L$ is the intensity vector; and the l and u parameters determine the return to scale assumption.

Secondly, we define a subset $\overline{\mathcal{PPS}}\backslash(\mathbf{x}_0, \mathbf{y}_0)$ of $\mathcal{PPS}\backslash(\mathbf{x}_0, \mathbf{y}_0)$ as:

$$\overline{\mathcal{PPS}}\backslash(\mathbf{x}_0, \mathbf{y}_0) = \mathcal{PPS}\backslash(\mathbf{x}_0, \mathbf{y}_0) \bigcap \{\bar{\mathbf{x}} \geq \mathbf{x}_0,\ \bar{\mathbf{y}} \leq \mathbf{y}_0\}. \tag{8}$$

Intuitively, $\mathcal{PPS}\backslash(\mathbf{x}_0, \mathbf{y}_0)$ is the original $\mathcal{PPS}$ excluding the evaluated DMU, and $\overline{\mathcal{PPS}}\backslash(\mathbf{x}_0, \mathbf{y}_0)$ is a reduced subset of $\mathcal{PPS}\backslash(\mathbf{x}_0, \mathbf{y}_0)$ as a result of the intersection with the second set of constraints.

The Super-SBM model proposed by Tone (2002) defines an optimal mathematical program with a new objective function and modified constraints based on the new $\mathcal{PPS}$ defined in (8). In particular, the super-efficiency score of a DMU with $(\mathbf{x}_0, \mathbf{y}_0)$ is the optimal objective function value δ^* from the following program:

$$\begin{aligned} \delta^* = \min\nolimits_{(\boldsymbol{\lambda}, \bar{\mathbf{x}}, \bar{\mathbf{y}})} & \left\{ \frac{\frac{1}{m}\sum_{i=1}^{m} \frac{\bar{x}_i}{x_{i0}}}{\frac{1}{s}\sum_{r=1}^{s} \frac{\bar{y}_r}{y_{r0}}} \right\} \\ \text{s.t. } & \bar{\mathbf{x}} \geq \sum\nolimits_{j=1,\neq 0}^{L} \lambda_j \mathbf{x}_j \\ & \bar{\mathbf{y}} \leq \sum\nolimits_{j=1,\neq 0}^{L} \lambda_j \mathbf{y}_j \\ & \bar{\mathbf{x}} \geq \mathbf{x}_0 \text{ and } \bar{\mathbf{y}} \leq \mathbf{y}_0 \\ & \bar{\mathbf{y}} \geq 0,\ l \leq e\boldsymbol{\lambda} \leq u,\ \boldsymbol{\lambda} \geq 0\ . \end{aligned} \tag{9}$$

In the optimum of the above problem, the value of variables $(\bar{\mathbf{x}}, \bar{\mathbf{y}})$ corresponds to the reference point on the frontier, and the optimum of the function (δ^*) is an index that can be interpreted as follows: the numerator is a weighted l_1 distance (also known as Manhattan) from $\mathbf{x}_0$ to $\bar{\mathbf{x}}\,(\geq \mathbf{x}_0)$, and hence it expresses an average expansion rate of $\mathbf{x}_0$ to $\bar{\mathbf{x}}(\geq \mathbf{x}_0)$. In the same way, the denominator shows weighted l_1 distance from $\mathbf{y}_0$ to $\bar{\mathbf{y}}(\leq \mathbf{y}_0)$, and hence it is an average reduction rate of $\mathbf{y}_0$ to $\bar{\mathbf{y}}(\leq \mathbf{y}_0)$. The resulting index is always greater than one, unit invariant, and monotone in both variables (increasing the difference between the observed input, $\mathbf{x}_0$, and the optimum reference input, $\bar{\mathbf{x}}$, raises the index value; a similar trend can be found with the output term).

3 SBM, Super-SBM and Undesirable Outputs

DEA methodology usually assumes that producing more outputs relative to fewer input resources is a criterion of efficiency. Nevertheless, in the presence of undesirable outputs, technologies with more good (desirable) outputs and fewer bad (undesirable) outputs relative to fewer input resources should be recognised as more efficient. When analysing situations in which global environmental conservation is a concern, undesirable outputs of production and social activities are issues to be factored into the analysis.

In our case, we will take advantage of the fact that the SBM can be adapted to take undesirable outputs into account by considering them as a third set of variables that appears in the linear problem without the need to transform them. In particular, the purpose of this section will be to review the SBM with undesirable presence (first subsection) and to introduce a proposal to perform a super-efficiency evaluation in the presence of undesirable outputs (second subsection).

3.1 SBM Efficiency with Undesirable Outputs

Following the same terminology as in the previous section, there are L DMUs each having three sets of factors: inputs, good or desirable outputs, and bad or undesirable outputs, represented by $\mathbf{X} = [\mathbf{x}_1, \ldots, \mathbf{x}_L] \in \mathbb{R}_+^{m\times L}$, $\mathbf{Y}^g = [\mathbf{y}_1^g, \ldots, \mathbf{y}_L^g] \in \mathbb{R}_+^{s_1\times L}$, and $\mathbf{Y}^b = [\mathbf{y}_1^b, \ldots, \mathbf{y}_L^b] \in \mathbb{R}_+^{s_2\times L}$, respectively.

The production possibility set ($\mathcal{PPS}$) is now defined as:

$$\mathcal{PPS} = \left\{ (\mathbf{x}, \mathbf{y}^g, \mathbf{y}^b) | \mathbf{x} \geq \sum_{j=1}^{L} \lambda_j \mathbf{x}_j, 0 \leq \mathbf{y}^g \leq \sum_{j=1}^{L} \lambda_j \mathbf{y}_j^g,\ \mathbf{y}^b \geq \sum_{j=1}^{L} \lambda_j \mathbf{y}_j^b, l \leq e\boldsymbol{\lambda} \leq u \right\}, \tag{10}$$

where $\boldsymbol{\lambda} \in \mathbb{R}_+^L$ is the intensity vector and the l and u parameters determine the return to scale assumption.

A DMU with $(\mathbf{x}_0, \mathbf{y}_0^g, \mathbf{y}_0^b)$ is SBM efficient in the presence of undesirable outputs if there is no vector $(\mathbf{x}, \mathbf{y}^g, \mathbf{y}^b) \in \mathcal{PPS}$ such that $\mathbf{x}_0 \geq \mathbf{x}, \mathbf{y}_0^g \leq \mathbf{y}^g, \mathbf{y}_0^b \geq \mathbf{y}^b$ with at least one strict inequality.

Tone's proposed mathematical program model for SBM including undesirable outputs is (see Cooper et al. 2007):

$$\begin{aligned} \rho^* = \min\nolimits_{(\boldsymbol{\lambda}, \mathbf{s}^-, \mathbf{s}^g, \mathbf{s}^b)} & \left\{ \frac{1 - \frac{1}{m}\sum_{i=1}^{m} \frac{s_i^-}{x_{i0}}}{1 + \frac{1}{s_1 + s_2}\left(\sum_{r=1}^{s_1} \frac{s_r^g}{y_{r0}^g} + \sum_{k=1}^{s_2} \frac{s_k^b}{y_{k0}^b} \right)} \right\} \\ \text{s.t. } \mathbf{x}_0 &= \mathbf{X}\boldsymbol{\lambda} + \mathbf{s}^- \\ \mathbf{y}_0^g &= \mathbf{Y}^\mathbf{g}\boldsymbol{\lambda} - \mathbf{s}^g \\ \mathbf{y}_0^b &= \mathbf{Y}^\mathbf{b}\boldsymbol{\lambda} + \mathbf{s}^b \\ \mathbf{s}^- \geq 0, \mathbf{s}^g &\geq 0, \mathbf{s}^b \geq 0,\ l \leq e\boldsymbol{\lambda} \leq u,\ \boldsymbol{\lambda} \geq 0 \end{aligned} \tag{11}$$

The vectors $\mathbf{s}^- \in \mathbb{R}_+^m$, $\mathbf{s}^b \in \mathbb{R}_+^{s_2}$ correspond to excesses in inputs and bad outputs, respectively, and $\mathbf{s}^g \in \mathbb{R}_+^{s_1}$ expresses shortages in good outputs. The objective function is strictly monotone decreasing with respect to s_i^- $(\forall i)$, s_r^g $(\forall r)$, and s_k^b $(\forall k)$, and the objective value satisfies $0 \leq \rho^* \leq 1$.

This fractional program can be solved in a similar manner as (4) by transforming it into an equivalent linear program again using the Charnes-Cooper transformation (Charnes and Cooper 1962).

An outstanding application of the SBM with undesirable outputs model is the research developed by Choi et al. (2012) which analizes the efficiency of energy-related CO_2 emissions in China. In their study, making use of the dual version of the model, shadow prices of the undesirable output emission are computed. Although it shares some underpinnings with our paper, it has several differences. For instance, although they consider shadow prices, we extend the model to super-efficiency, as we will see in the following section. In addition, whereas they propose and application to China, in our case we focus on the European Union.

As already shown in the super-efficient SBM model, in many circumstances, DEA models require the analysis of DMUs that are not inside the $\mathcal{PPS}$, and the aim of the next subsection is to introduce a proposal for dealing with super-efficiency with undesirable presence.

3.2 SBM Super-Efficiency with Undesirable Outputs

Following the same structure proposed by Tone (2002), we define the $\mathcal{PPS}\backslash\ (\mathbf{x}_0, \mathbf{y}_0^g, \mathbf{y}_0^b)$ spanned by $(\mathbf{X}, \mathbf{Y}^g, \mathbf{Y}^b)$ excluding $(\mathbf{x}_0, \mathbf{y}_0^g, \mathbf{y}_0^b)$ as:

$$\mathcal{PPS}\backslash(\mathbf{x}_0, \mathbf{y}_0^g, \mathbf{y}_0^b) = \left\{ (\bar{\mathbf{x}}, \bar{\mathbf{y}}^g, \bar{\mathbf{y}}^b) | \bar{\mathbf{x}} \geq \sum_{\substack{j=1 \\ j\neq 0}}^{L} \lambda_j x_j,\ \bar{\mathbf{y}}^g \leq \sum_{\substack{j=1 \\ j\neq 0}}^{L} \lambda_j y_j^g,\ \bar{\mathbf{y}}^b \geq \sum_{\substack{j=1 \\ j\neq 0}}^{L} \lambda_j y_j^b,\ l \leq e\boldsymbol{\lambda} \leq u, \boldsymbol{\lambda} \geq 0 \right\}. \tag{12}$$

In the second step, we define a subset $\overline{\mathcal{PPS}} \setminus (\mathbf{x}_0, \mathbf{y}_0^g, \mathbf{y}_0^b)$ of $\mathcal{PPS} \setminus (\mathbf{x}_0, \mathbf{y}_0^g, \mathbf{y}_0^b)$ as:

$$\overline{\mathcal{PPS}} \setminus (\mathbf{x}_0, \mathbf{y}_0^g, \mathbf{y}_0^b) = \mathcal{PPS} \setminus (\mathbf{x}_0, \mathbf{y}_0^g, \mathbf{y}_0^b) \bigcap \{\bar{\mathbf{x}} \geq \mathbf{x}_0,\ \bar{\mathbf{y}}^g \leq \mathbf{y}_0^g \text{ and } \bar{\mathbf{y}}^b \geq \mathbf{y}_0^b\}\ . \tag{13}$$

Intuitively, $\mathcal{PPS} \setminus (\mathbf{x}_0, \mathbf{y}_0^g, \mathbf{y}_0^b)$ is the original $\mathcal{PPS}$ excluding the evaluated DMU, while now $\overline{\mathcal{PPS}} \setminus (\mathbf{x}_0, \mathbf{y}_0^g, \mathbf{y}_0^b)$ is a reduced subset of $\mathcal{PPS} \setminus (\mathbf{x}_0, \mathbf{y}_0^g, \mathbf{y}_0^b)$ as a result of the intersection with the second set of constraints.

Once the $\mathcal{PPS}$ is determined which will serve to define the constraints in the mathematical program, we propose the following index or objective function:

$$\delta = \left\{ \frac{\frac{1}{m+s_2}\left(\sum_{i=1}^{m} \frac{\bar{x}_i}{x_{i0}} + \sum_{k=1}^{s_2} \frac{\bar{y}_k^b}{y_{k0}^b}\right)}{\frac{1}{s_1}\left(\sum_{r=1}^{s_1} \frac{\bar{y}_r^g}{y_{r0}^g}\right)} \right\}. \tag{14}$$

This index can be understood as a quotient between a weighted l_1 distance of inputs ($\mathbf{x}_0$ to $\bar{\mathbf{x}}$) and bad outputs ($\mathbf{y}_0^b$ to $\bar{\mathbf{y}}^b$), which make up the numerator, and a weighted l_1 distance of good outputs ($\mathbf{y}_0^g$ to $\bar{\mathbf{y}}^g$) in the denominator.

It is worth noting that, although other alternatives have been proposed for Super-SBM with undesirable outputs (Du et al. 2012; Wang et al. 2016; Li et al. 2012; Song et al. 2016), a more detailed analysis our index (14) brings up the following properties: it is always equal or greater than one, it is unit independent (it does not depend on the units in which inputs or outputs are measured), and it is monotone (an increase in the difference between an observed input and its optimum, holding other variables constant, leads to an increase in the value of the index).

In a context in which the evaluated process can be clearly split into subprocesses, network DEA models can provide a more precise approach (Huang et al. 2014). In particular, Huang et al. combine network DEA models jointly with a SBM model, providing an alternative objective function where the term linked to undesirable outputs appears in the denominator of the objective function (14). This is a very interesting contribution which differs from ours in several regards. Apart from using a network approach, they consider a different objective function, and, in addition, their focus is the Chinese banking industry, whereas our application deals with energy efficiency in the European Union. It would be interesting to compare both approaches considering the same dataset.

Having defined the objective function in (14) and taking into account its characteristics, our proposed mathematical program is:

$$\begin{aligned}
\delta^* = \min_{(\boldsymbol{\lambda},\, \bar{\mathbf{x}},\, \bar{\mathbf{y}}^g,\, \bar{\mathbf{y}}^b)} & \left\{ \frac{\frac{1}{m+s_2}\left(\sum_{i=1}^{m} \frac{\bar{x}_i}{x_{i0}} + \sum_{k=1}^{s_2} \frac{\bar{y}_k^b}{y_{k0}^b}\right)}{\frac{1}{s_1}\left(\sum_{r=1}^{s_1} \frac{\bar{y}_r^g}{y_{r0}^g}\right)} \right\} \\
\text{s.t. } \bar{\mathbf{x}} & \geq \textstyle\sum_{j=1,\neq 0}^{L} \lambda_j \mathbf{x}_j \\
\bar{\mathbf{y}}^g & \leq \textstyle\sum_{j=1,\neq 0}^{L} \lambda_j \mathbf{y}_j^g \\
\bar{\mathbf{y}}^b & \geq \textstyle\sum_{j=1,\neq 0}^{L} \lambda_j \mathbf{y}_j^b \\
& \bar{\mathbf{x}} \geq \mathbf{x}_0\,,\ \bar{\mathbf{y}}^g \leq \mathbf{y}_0^g \text{ and } \bar{\mathbf{y}}^b \geq \mathbf{y}_0^b \\
& \bar{\mathbf{y}}^g \geq 0\,,\ \bar{\mathbf{y}}^b \geq 0\,,\ l \leq e\boldsymbol{\lambda} \leq u\,,\ \boldsymbol{\lambda} > 0
\end{aligned} \tag{15}$$

This latter mathematical program in (15) can be converted into an equivalent one by introducing the following variables $\phi \in \mathbb{R}^m$, $\psi \in \mathbb{R}^{s_1}$, and $\gamma \in \mathbb{R}^{s_2}$, where

$$\begin{aligned}
\bar{x}_i &= x_{i0}(1+\phi_i) \quad (i = 1, \ldots, m) \\
\bar{y}_r^g &= y_{r0}^g(1-\psi_r) \quad (r = 1, \ldots, s_1) \\
\bar{y}_k^b &= y_{k0}^b(1+\gamma_k) \quad (k = 1, \ldots, s_2)
\end{aligned} \tag{16}$$

The resulting new program in terms of ϕ, ψ, and γ is:

$$\delta^* = \min_{(\boldsymbol{\lambda},\boldsymbol{\phi},\boldsymbol{\psi},\boldsymbol{\gamma})}\left\{\frac{1+\frac{1}{m+s_2}\left(\sum_{i=1}^{m}\phi_i+\sum_{k=1}^{s_2}\gamma_k\right)}{1-\frac{1}{s_1}\left(\sum_{r=1}^{s_1}\psi_r\right)}\right\}$$
$$\begin{aligned} \text{s.t. } & \textstyle\sum_{j=1,\neq 0}^{L} x_{ij}\lambda_j - x_{i0}\phi_i \le x_{i0} \\ & \textstyle\sum_{j=1,\neq 0}^{L} y_{rj}^{g}\lambda_j + y_{r0}^{g}\psi_r \ge y_{r0}^{g} \\ & \textstyle\sum_{j=1,\neq 0}^{L} y_{kj}^{b}\lambda_j - y_{k0}^{b}\gamma_k \le y_{k0}^{b} \\ & \phi_i \ge 0\,(\forall_i),\ \psi_r \ge 0(\forall_r),\ \gamma_k \ge 0(\forall_k),\ \lambda_j \ge 0 \\ & l \le e\boldsymbol{\lambda} \le u\ ,\boldsymbol{\lambda} \ge 0 \end{aligned} \tag{17}$$

As mentioned above, the optimal solution of program (17) is always greater than or equal to one, is unit invariant, and has monotonicity in the input, bad output increase, and output reduction.

Again using the Charnes-Cooper transformation (Charnes and Cooper 1962), the program becomes linear in the following way:

$$\begin{aligned} \tau^* = \min_{(\boldsymbol{\Lambda},\boldsymbol{\Phi},\boldsymbol{\Psi},\boldsymbol{\Gamma})} & \left\{t+\frac{1}{m+s_2}\left(\sum_{i=1}^{m}\Phi_i+\sum_{k=1}^{s_2}\Gamma_k\right)\right\} \\ \text{s.t. } & 1 = t-\frac{1}{s_1}\left(\sum_{r=1}^{s_1}\Psi_r\right) \\ & \textstyle\sum_{j=1,\neq 0}^{L} x_{ij}\Lambda_j - x_{i0}\Phi_i - x_{i0}t \le 0 \quad (i=1\ldots m) \\ & \textstyle\sum_{j=1,\neq 0}^{L} y_{rj}^{g}\Lambda_j + y_{r0}^{g}\Psi_r - y_{r0}^{g}t \ge 0 \quad (r=1\ldots s_1) \\ & \textstyle\sum_{j=1,\neq 0}^{L} y_{kj}^{b}\Lambda_j - y_{k0}^{b}\Gamma_k - y_{k0}^{b}t \le 0 \quad (k=1\ldots s_2) \\ & \Phi_i \ge 0\,(\forall_i),\ \Psi_r \ge 0(\forall_r),\ \Gamma_k \ge 0(\forall_k),\ \Lambda_j \ge 0, \\ & lt \le e\boldsymbol{\Lambda} \le ut,\ \boldsymbol{\Lambda} \ge 0,\ t > 0 \end{aligned} \tag{18}$$

The optimal solution of this linear program ($\boldsymbol{\tau}^*, \boldsymbol{\Phi}^*, \boldsymbol{\Psi}^*, \Gamma^*, \boldsymbol{\Lambda}^*, t^*$) allows us to calculate the solution of the fractional problem, using:

$$\rho^* = \tau^*,\ \boldsymbol{\lambda}^* = \boldsymbol{\Lambda}^*/t^*,\ \boldsymbol{\phi}^* = \boldsymbol{\Phi}^*/t^*,\ \boldsymbol{\psi}^* = \boldsymbol{\Psi}^*/t^*,\ \boldsymbol{\gamma}^* = \boldsymbol{\Gamma}^*/t^*. \tag{19}$$

And therefore, the solution of the original super-efficiency SBM is given by:

$$\begin{aligned} \bar{x}_{i0}^* &= x_{i0}(1+\phi_i^*) \quad (i=1,\ldots,m) \\ \bar{y}_{r0}^{g*} &= y_{r0}^{g}(1-\psi_r^*) \quad (r=1,\ldots,s_1) \\ \bar{y}_{k0}^{b*} &= y_{k0}^{b}(1+\gamma_k^*) \quad (k=1,\ldots,s_2) \end{aligned} \tag{20}$$

This optimal solution provides not only the super-efficiency score but also the reference point in the empirical frontier and provides a measure for each variable of the distance between the evaluated DMU and the efficient frontier.

In this line of research, recent contributions from Fang et al. (2013) have developed an alternative approach for the super-efficiency estimation in the SBM framework based on a two-stage analysis. Their proposal overcomes the possibility of having reference points in the super-efficient frontier that may not be strongly Pareto efficient. Simultaneously, Chien-Ming (2013) has tackled the same problem using a joint computational model based on the SBM and the Super-SBM combined in a mixed-integer linear problem. Both alternatives may be implemented under the presence of undesirable outputs in the SBM DEA model (17) proposed in this paper.

4 Measuring the Energy and Environmental Dynamic Efficiency of EU-28 Countries

Our interest in this section is to analyse the performance in the context of energy and environment related to the European Union. In particular, we evaluate how electricity and derived heat from non-renewable sources were produced in the 28 EU countries from 2008 until 2012. In this specific context, with more than 80% of electricity generation coming from non-renewable sources with important negative externalities (Eurostat 2015), the impact of pollution and future risk is an important factor to bear in mind, and the efforts devoted to increasing energy efficiency and reliable replacement with renewable energy sources are key objectives for EU climate policies. This implies that it will be relevant not only to include the appropriate sets of inputs and outputs but, more importantly, the undesirable by-products generated during the production process, for which the SBM models we use fit particularly well.

This context gains further importance if we factor in the EU commitment to combat climate change with the specific—and binding—objectives of reducing overall greenhouse gas emissions. Actually, the EU was the the *first* geopolitical region that adopted a binding target (Böhringer et al. 2009).[4]

4.1 Data and Sources

Data for the analysis was obtained from the "Environment and Energy" section of the Eurostat database and the European Environment Agency (EEA). The period analysed covers 5 years, which we split into two periods (2008–2010 and 2010–2012). A brief summary of the data is shown in Table 1. Since the study focuses on the country level, each EU country will be considered as a DMU that chooses from different alternatives the way it produces electricity and derives heat. Each country's energy mix will be based on its resource availability and its environmental policy.

Electricity and derived heat comes from other primary sources of energy and also from renewable energy. Therefore, in this study we consider one desirable output, namely, electricity and derived heat obtained from non-renewable sources[5] in the electricity generation process. On the input side, we consider three variables: (i) the total primary energy *consumed* (fossil fuel combustion and heat produced in nuclear reactors), (ii) the installed capacity (physical capital), and (iii) the number of employees (labour).[6]

The variable used to represent the factor exerting pressure on the environment is the emission of GHG into the environment. It is measured in CO_2 equivalent[7] emissions, which are responsible for global warming. This variable will be included in the model as *undesirable* outputs linked to the production process.

In the energy efficiency literature, many authors have considered pollutants like CO_2 in their analyses (Zhou et al. 2008; Arcelus and Arocena 2005; Zofio and Prieto 2001). Others have also considered additional pollutants such as SO_2 or NO_x (Färe et al. 1986). As the amount of emissions responsible for acid rain (SO_2 and NO_x) have been greatly reduced (Vestreng et al. 2007), our aim in this analysis is to focus on the GHG emissions' issue, making an attempt to find those peers that may help to establish a benchmark or reference for the rest.

[4]Regarding the specific objectives, the sixth Environment Action Program (EAP), adopted in 2002, is a policy program for the environment in the EU for the period 2002–2012. This program has four key priorities, the first one "Tackle climate change" with two objectives: (i) to achieve the EU target of reducing greenhouse gas emissions by 8% by 2008–2012 and (ii) to target more radical global emission cuts in the order of 20% by 2020. These long-term objectives require efforts from EU countries in terms of efficiency improvement and energy saving, and the evaluation of energy and environment efficiency in the EU member countries allows references to be identified for dissemination and provides evidence of the results achieved.

[5]In this study, we account for the electricity and derived heat generated from conventional thermal plants (fossil fuels) and nuclear plants

[6]An approach with several similarities has been considered in (p.375–376 Cooper et al. 2007) in the context of US electric utilities.

[7]A metric measure used to compare the emissions from various greenhouse gases (i.e. methane, carbon dioxide, fluorine gas, HFCs, nitrous oxide, PFCs, and SF_6) based upon their global warming potential (GWP). Carbon dioxide equivalents are commonly expressed as "million metric tons of carbon dioxide equivalents ($MMTCO_2Eq$)". The carbon dioxide equivalent for a gas is derived by multiplying the tons of the gas by the associated GWP. Nevertheless, the most important greenhouse gas linked with the energy sector is CO_2, although most of the literature lacks a precise definition of this term.

Table 1 Data summary

		Inputs			Output	Bad output
		Primary energy (thousand, TOE)	Total electrical capacity (megawatt)	Labor force (thousand, workers)	Output (thousand, TOE)	GHG emissions (Tg: million; tones grams)
Year 2008	Average	24,738.221	30,953.536	54.532	11,004.543	47.169
	Median	11,324.400	15,280.500	25.150	5,001.800	19.626
	Std. Dev.	35,240.262	41,070.702	68.243	14,588.035	70.908
Year 2009	Average	23,232.818	31,862.893	57.932	10,376.450	43.505
	Median	10,433.750	15,331.000	25.850	4,689.000	19.059
	Std. Dev.	32,845.721	42,456.066	76.021	13,538.542	65.472
Year 2010	Average	23,977.000	33,394.679	58.018	10,832.325	44.031
	Median	10,374.650	15,774.000	25.600	4,648.200	18.818
	Std. Dev.	34,363.286	44,958.381	78.515	14,295.294	67.431
Year 2011	Average	23,529.861	35,761.607	57.704	10,497.779	43.396
	Median	10,360.100	16,450.500	24.400	4,911.400	16.553
	Std. Dev.	33,375.605	49,683.942	78.527	13,738.913	66.808
Year 2012	Average	23,259.775	36,666.786	58.121	10,272.489	43.763
	Median	10,220.800	17,104.000	24.650	4,674.450	15.091
	Std. Dev.	33,331.351	50,481.797	80.548	13,598.318	69.846

4.2 Results

Previously to analysing productivity change, we performed an influential DMU detection analysis following the methods proposed by Banker and Chang (2006). For this, we adopted preselected screen value of 1.3. That is, if an efficient DMU has a super-efficiency score equal to or greater than this value, it will be considered a potential candidate as an outlier.

Results from the efficiency analysis are depicted in Fig. 1 and summarized for the whole set of countries in a boxplot in Fig. 2. For each country, the score obtained represents its efficiency. In the case of *peer* countries (the efficient ones), we have obtained their super-efficiency scores following the model presented in Sect. 3.2. Only two *peer* countries have shown a super-efficiency score above the proposed screen value of 1.3. These are Finland and Sweden. Among the efficient countries, we also find Denmark, France, Latvia, and Lithuania. Closer analysis of the energy sector in Finland shows a country with an ambitious program for renewable energy (with the objective of 38% for 2020) and also happens to be one of the few countries in Europe planning to expand its nuclear capacity. The other selected super-efficient country is Sweden. In this country we also find strong commitments towards decarbonisation of the energy sector. It also shows a large share of electricity from nuclear power plants.

In the second stage of the analysis, we have computed a new set of efficiency scores, excluding these two influential countries (Finland and Sweden). Results of this study are shown in the second plot of Fig. 1. Based on the same screen value (super-efficiency score equal or greater to 1.3), we have found that nearly half of the countries become efficient, and one of them (France) yields a score above 1.3. Actually, France's energy sector presents large differences from the rest of countries; its nuclear power plants currently provide 75% of electricity, but with a plan to reduce this share to 50% by 2025.

On the third stage, France has been excluded and new efficiency scores computed for the rest of countries. Results are plotted in the third picture of Fig. 1. In this scenario, efficiency and super-efficiency scores are similar to the second picture (excluding Finland and Sweden), and all super-efficiency scores are below 1.3.

In summary, the previous analysis show three countries (Finland, Sweden, and France) which are highly influential, and in this particular case, these three countries account for the largest share of electricity from nuclear power plants. In other words, the super-efficiency analysis may be revealing technological differences among the evaluated DMUs. In Fig. 2 we report boxplots for efficiencies in the three scenarios mentioned above. We observe that, without excluding the influential units, the obtained scores have lower discrimination power, that is, there is a set of efficient units and other set of non-efficient units with very low efficiency scores. Once these three units have been excluded, the range of efficiencies is wider providing a better assessment.

Complementarily to the super-efficiency analysis, we have also evaluated productivity change. This analysis is based on Malmquist index and requires the use of a model that can deal with super-efficiency. In this case, the evaluation has covered three periods, namely, 2008–2010, 2010–2012, and the entire period of 2008–2012. The results are reported in Table 2, which

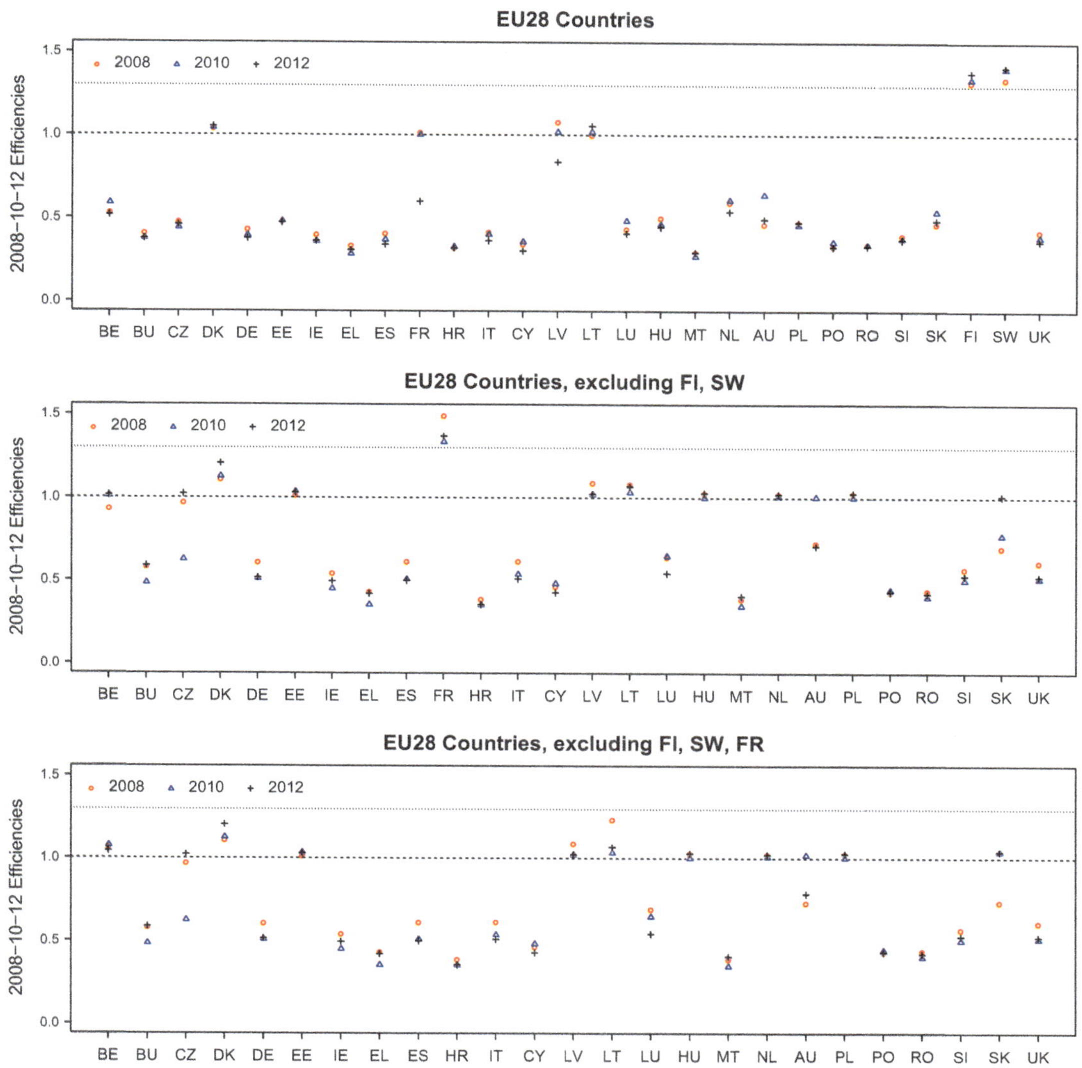

Fig. 1 Year efficiencies for the three scenarios

reports productivity change indices and its components, namely, technical change (TC) and efficiency change (EC), for all countries and periods under analysis.

Additionally, the last rows in Table 2 present different measures of central tendency for the whole set of countries and for each period and variables. Among the four central tendency measures reported, we will focus on the weighted mean. One of the reasons we prefer to use this moment is that the weighted mean is a constructed using the country's electricity production as weight, giving more influence to large countries when calculating the average. Also, we can observe that some small economies show relatively large and/or low values that might be considered outliers. This would be the case of, for instance, Cyprus, Malta, and Luxembourg. When considering the weighted mean, the (likely) influence of small countries is limited.

As indicated in the last rows in Table 2, the values for all summary statistics point to a stagnate productivity change (which we will refer to as MPI, i.e. Malmquist Productivity Index) during the first period (2008–2010) and a decrease on the second period (2010–2012). The results for the whole period show a slight decrease. In the first period, the driver for the productivity has been the technical change (TC), meanwhile the efficiency change has been negative. Regarding the second period, we found that efficiency change (EC) has been greater than TC. The analysis of the whole period (2008–2012) shows a decrease in productivity where TC and EC have decreased.

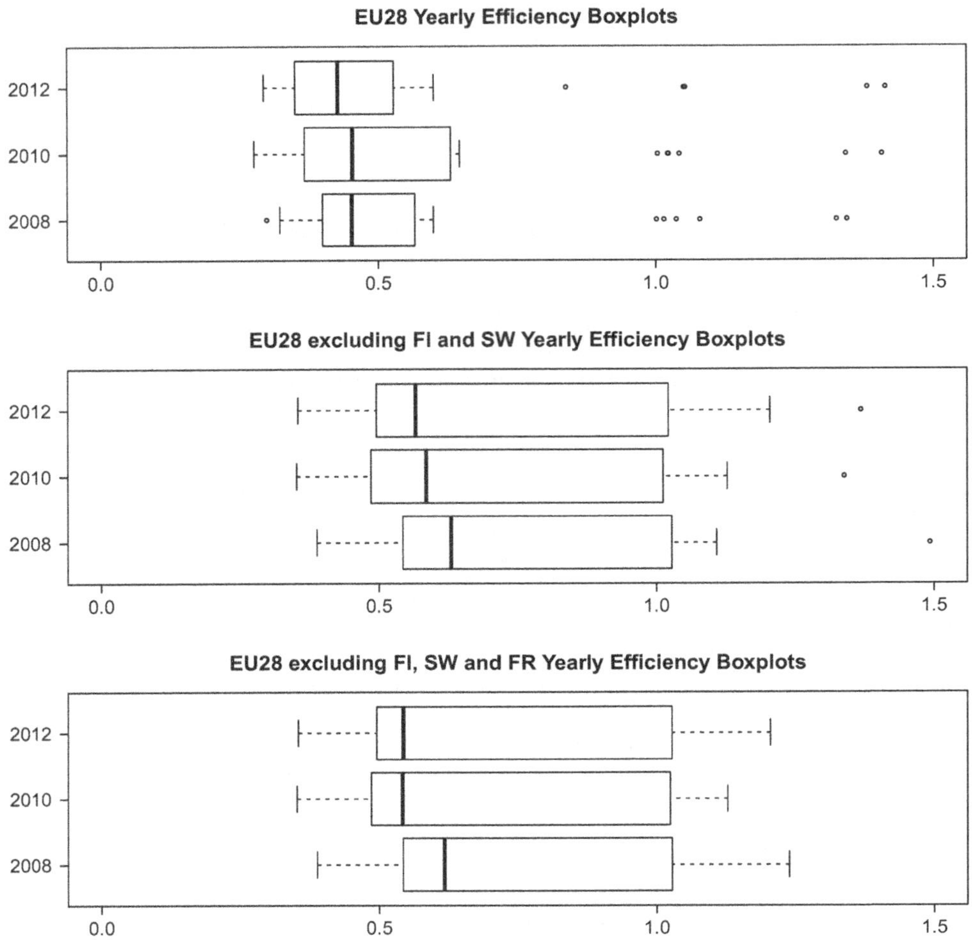

Fig. 2 Yearly efficiency boxplots for the three scenarios

A graphical illustration of the results for the Malmquist index and its decomposition is also available in Figs. 3, 4, and 5, which reports maps for each of these variables for Europe. It shows that the lowest efficiency change (Fig. 3 tends to concentrate in Eastern Europe (i.e., countries whose economic systems have transited from planned economies to capitalism), a tendency which is less exacerbated for the technical change (Fig. 4) and, consequently, productivity change (Fig. 5).

5 Conclusions and Discussion

Today, in economies with a strong fossil fuel demand from developing countries, and considering the threats of nuclear power, the movement towards renewable energies, energy savings, and energy efficiency improvements is likely to emerge as particularly relevant. In this upcoming scenario, the availability of rigorous tools that enable the accurate modelling of complex realities might prove to be essential.

In this context, frontier techniques have been recognised as an appropriate tool for efficiency measurement. Among the different options, nonparametric methods such as DEA represent one of the most widespread alternatives. Traditionally, radial and oriented approaches have been used in a large proportion of these analyses. These approaches generally consider improvements in the inputs or outputs employed in similar proportions. However, when the problem involves variables of a different nature, this assumption might not provide a real solution for performance enhancement, and, under these circumstances, the use of slacks-based measure (SBM) models represents an interesting alternative. Additionally, non-oriented models such as the original SBM also provide an added advantage, since they can simultaneously detect inefficiencies for all sets of variables.

Table 2 Productivity change and its decomposition (2008/2010, 2010/2012 and 2008/2012)

Country		2008–2010			2010–2012			2008–2012		
		Technical change	Efficiency change	Productivity change	Technical change	Efficiency change	Productivity change	Technical change	Efficiency change	Productivity change
Austria	AU	1.021	1.361	1.390	1.290	0.785	1.012	1.271	1.068	1.358
Belgium	BE	1.093	1.000	1.093	0.967	1.000	0.967	1.003	1.000	1.003
Bulgaria	BU	1.123	0.836	0.938	0.723	1.212	0.876	0.785	1.013	0.795
Croatia	HR	1.093	0.916	1.001	0.975	0.995	0.970	1.048	0.911	0.955
Czech Rep.	CZ	1.039	0.648	0.674	0.608	1.592	0.968	0.802	1.032	0.828
Cyprus	CY	1.091	1.046	1.142	0.647	0.878	0.568	0.923	0.919	0.848
Denmark	DK	1.104	1.000	1.104	0.956	1.000	0.956	1.001	1.000	1.001
Estonia	EE	1.140	1.000	1.140	0.821	1.000	0.821	0.900	1.000	0.900
Germany	DE	1.105	0.842	0.930	0.884	1.008	0.891	0.882	0.848	0.748
Greece	EL	1.083	0.824	0.893	0.861	1.178	1.014	0.931	0.971	0.904
Hungary	HU	0.912	1.000	0.912	0.756	1.000	0.756	0.800	1.000	0.800
Ireland	IE	1.098	0.835	0.917	0.887	1.094	0.970	0.968	0.913	0.884
Italy	IT	1.145	0.878	1.005	0.922	0.940	0.867	1.034	0.825	0.854
Latvia	LV	1.019	1.000	1.019	0.991	1.000	0.991	1.005	1.000	1.005
Lithuania	LT	0.948	1.000	0.948	1.023	1.000	1.023	0.966	1.000	0.966
Luxembourg	LU	1.392	0.940	1.308	0.770	0.832	0.640	1.173	0.781	0.916
Malta	MT	1.087	0.897	0.974	0.852	1.155	0.984	0.926	1.036	0.959
Netherlands, The	NL	1.088	1.000	1.088	0.791	1.000	0.791	0.852	1.000	0.852
Poland	PL	1.088	1.000	1.088	0.859	1.000	0.859	0.930	1.000	0.930
Portugal	PO	1.107	1.031	1.141	0.927	0.961	0.891	1.013	0.990	1.003
Romania	RO	1.102	0.917	1.010	0.926	1.036	0.959	1.008	0.950	0.957
Spain	ES	1.174	0.836	0.981	0.924	0.971	0.897	1.003	0.812	0.815
Slovenia	SI	1.11.1	0.885	0.983	0.858	1.047	0.898	0.853	0.926	0.790
Slovakia	SK	0.864	1.358	1.174	1.001	1.000	1.001	0.778	1.358	1.056
United Kingdom	UK	1.110	0.842	0.935	0.882	1.019	0.899	0.952	0.858	0.817
Weighted mean		1.101	0.896	0.983	0.881	1.027	0.895	0.936	0.911	0.850
Arithm. mean		1.085	0.956	1.031	0.884	1.028	0.899	0.952	0.968	0.918
Geom. mean		1.081	0.945	1.022	0.874	1.019	0.891	0.946	0.963	0.911
Median		1.093	0.940	1.005	0.884	1.000	0.899	0.952	1.000	0.904

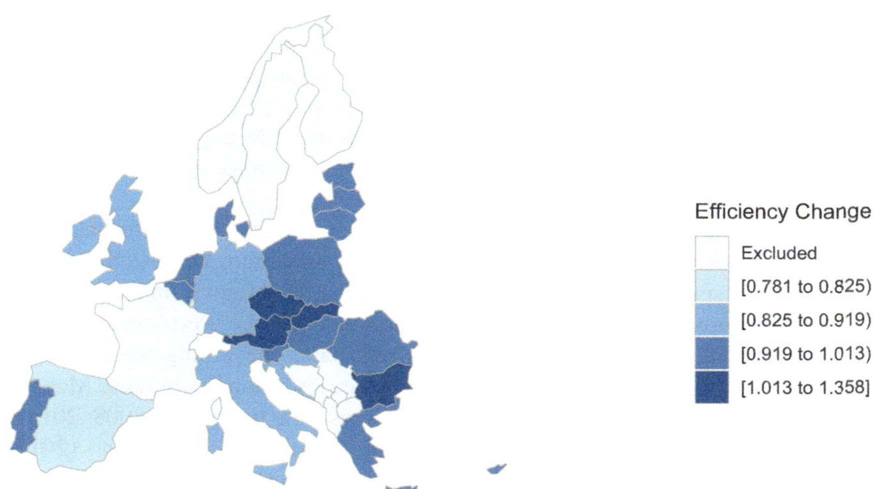

Fig. 3 Efficiency change (2008–2013)

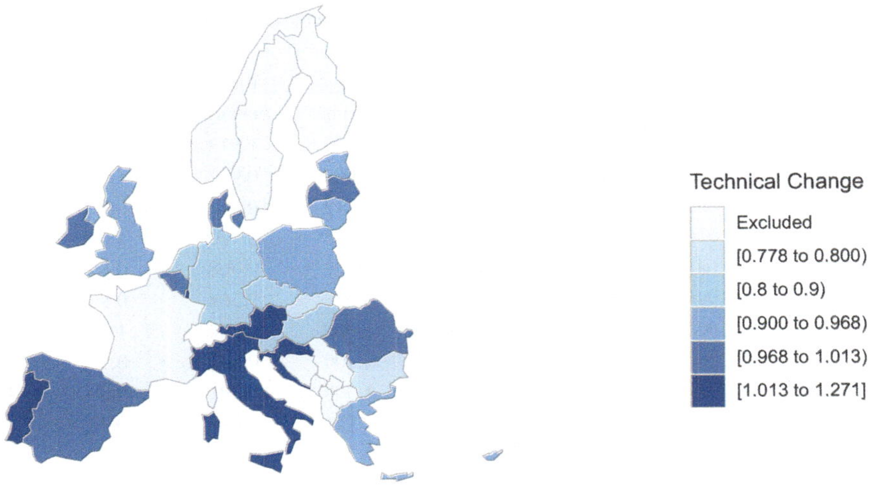

Fig. 4 Technical change (2008–2013)

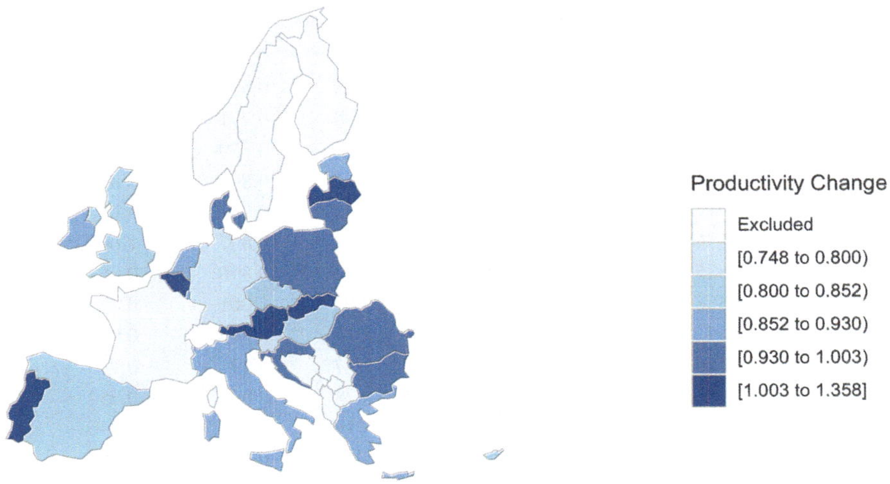

Fig. 5 Productivity change (2008–2013)

When evaluating performance and its evolution across several periods, the analysis gains interest and complexity. These dynamics have been modelled using the Malmquist Productivity Index. In this context, controlling for super-efficiency has attracted less attention than it should. This particular contribution adds an SBM approach to this relatively unexplored field and also takes into account the presence of undesirable outputs. As far as we know, to date, this combination has barely been contemplated by the literature.

In empirical analyses of dynamic efficiency, the detection of influential DMUs is a relevant a priori step, particularly in data-driven problems, and their results may help to focus attention on certain DMUs, contributing to isolate abnormal influences in the analysis. In our specific analysis based on the evaluation of environmental efficiency in electricity and derived heat generation in the European Union, Finland, Sweden, and France were classified as influential, and all of them have a great share of electricity generation from nuclear power plants. Regarding productivity change in the analysed period, the gains are moderate, although there are remarkable disparities among countries. More specifically, during the analysed period (which was characterised by the beginning of the crisis), the first years (2008–2010) were characterised by modest productivity change (on average) and mainly based on *technical change*. The final years (2010–2012) showed poorer performance, as there was actually productivity decline, mainly driven by technical regress.

Acknowledgements David Conesa would like to thank the Ministerio de Educación y Ciencia (Spain) for financial support (jointly financed by the European Regional Development Fund) via Research Grant MTM2016-77501-P, and Emili Tortosa-Ausina acknowledges the financial support of Ministerio de Economía y Competitividad (ECO2017-85746-P), Universitat Jaume I (UJI-B2017-33) and Generalitat Valenciana (PROMETEO/2018/102). The usual disclaimer applies.

References

Adler, N., Friedman, L., & Sinuany-Stern, Z. (2002). Review of ranking methods in the data envelopment analysis context. *European Journal of Operational Research, 140*, 249–265.

Arcelus, F., & Arocena, P. (2005). Productivity differences across OECD countries in the presence of environmental constraints. *Journal of the Operational Research Society, 56*, 1352–1362.

Banker, R., & Chang, H. (2006). The super-efficiency procedure for outlier identification, not for ranking efficient units. *European Journal of Operational Research, 175*, 1311–1320.

Bogetoft, P., & Otto, L. (2011). *Benchmarking with DEA, SFA, and R* (International series in Operations Research and Management Science). Dordrecht: Springer.

Böhringer, C., & Löschel, A., Moslener, U., & Rutherford, T. F. (2009). EU climate policy up to 2020: An economic impact assessment. *Energy Economics, 31*, S295–S305.

Cagno, E., & Trianni, A. (2013). Exploring drivers for energy efficiency within small-and medium-sized enterprises: First evidences from Italian manufacturing enterprises. *Applied Energy, 104*, 276–285.

Caves, D., Christensen, L., & Diewert, W. (1982). The economic theory of index numbers and the measurement of input, output, and productivity. *Econometrica: Journal of the Econometric Society, 50*, 1393–1414.

Charnes, A., & Cooper, W. (1962). Programming with linear fractional functionals. *Naval Research Logistics Quarterly, 9*, 181–186.

Chien-Ming, C. (2013). Super efficiencies or super inefficiencies? Insights from a joint computation model for slacks-based measures in DEA. *European Journal of Operational Research, 226*, 258–267.

Choi, Y., Zhang, N., & Zhou, P. (2012). Efficiency and abatement costs of energy-related CO_2 emissions in China: A slacks-based efficiency measure. *Applied Energy, 98*, 198–208.

Cooper, W., Park, K., & Pastor, J. (1999). Ram: A range adjusted measure of inefficiency for use with additive models, and relations to other models and measures in DEA. *Journal of Productivity Analysis, 11*, 5–42.

Cooper, W. W., Seiford, L. M., & Tone, K. (2007). *Data envelopment analysis: A comprehensive text with models, applications, references and DEA-solver software*. New York: Springer Science & Business Media.

Dakpo, K. H., Jeanneaux, P., & Latruffe, L. (2016). Modelling pollution-generating technologies in performance benchmarking: Recent developments, limits and future prospects in the nonparametric framework. *European Journal of Operational Research, 250*, 347–359.

Dakpo, K. H., Jeanneaux, P., & Latruffe, L. (2017). Greenhouse gas emissions and efficiency in French sheep meat farming: A non-parametric framework of pollution-adjusted technologies. *European Review of Agricultural Economics, 44*, 33–65.

Doyle, J., & Green, R. (1994). Efficiency and cross-efficiency in DEA: Derivations, meanings and uses. *Journal of the Operational Research Society, 45*, 567–578.

Du, J., Chen, C. M., Chen, Y., Cook, W. D., & Zhu, J. (2012). Additive super-efficiency in integer-valued data envelopment analysis. *European Journal of Operational Research, 218*, 186–192.

Eurostat. (2015). *Energy, transport and environment indicators* (2015 Edition). Publications Office of the European Union. https://doi.org/10.2785/547816.

Färe, R., Grosskopf, S., & Tyteca, D. (1996). An activity analysis model of the environmental performance of firms–application to fossil-fuel-fired electric utilities. *Ecological Economics, 18*, 161–175.

Fang, H. H., Lee, H. S., Hwang, S. N., & Chung, C. C. (2013). A slacks-based measure of super-efficiency in data envelopment analysis: An alternative approach. *Omega, 41*, 731–734.

Fukuyama, H., & Weber, W. L. (2010). A slacks-based inefficiency measure for a two-stage system with bad outputs. *Omega, 38*, 398–409.

Färe, R., & Grosskopf, S. (1997). Intertemporal production frontiers: With dynamic DEA. *Journal of the Operational Research Society, 48*, 656–656.

Färe, R., & Lovell, C. A. K. (1978). Measuring the technical efficiency of production. *Journal of Economic Theory, 19*, 150–162.

Färe, R., Grosskopf, S., & Pasurka, C. (1986). Effects on relative efficiency in electric power generation due to environmental controls. *Resources and Energy, 8*, 167–184.

Färe, R., Grosskopf, S., Lovell, C. A. K., & Pasurka, C. (1989). Multilateral productivity comparisons when some outputs are undesirable: A nonparametric approach. *Review of Economics and Statistics, 71*, 90–98.

Färe, R., Grosskopf, S., & Hernández-Sancho, F. (2004). Environmental performance: An index number approach. *Resource and Energy Economics, 26*, 343–352.

Førsund, F. R. (2009). Good modelling of bad outputs: Pollution and multiple-output production. *International Review of Environmental and Resource Economics, 3*, 1–38.

Førsund, F. R. (2018). Multi-equation modelling of desirable and undesirable outputs satisfying the materials balance. *Empirical Economics, 54*, 67–99.

Gómez-Calvet, R., Conesa, D., Gómez-Calvet, A. R., & Tortosa-Ausina, E. (2014). Energy efficiency in the European Union: What can be learned from the joint application of directional distance functions and slacks-based measures? *Applied Energy, 132*, 137–154.

Hu, J. L., & Wang, S. C. (2006). Total-factor energy efficiency of regions in China. *Energy Policy, 34*, 3206–3217.

Huang, J., Chen, J., & Yin, Z. (2014). A network DEA model with super efficiency and undesirable outputs: An application to bank efficiency in China. *Mathematical Problems in Engineering, 2014*, 1–4.

Koopmans, T. (1951). Analysis of production as an efficient combination of activities. In Koopmans, T. (Ed.), *Activity analysis of production and allocation* (pp. 33–97). New York: Wiley.

Li, H., Fang, K., Yang, W., Wang, D., & Hong, X. (2012). Regional environmental efficiency evaluation in China: Analysis based on the super-SBM model with undesirable outputs. *Mathematical and Computer Modelling*.

Murty, S., & Russell, R. (2002). *On modeling pollution-generating technologies*. Department of Economics, University of California, Riverside. Discussion papers series.

Murty, S., & Russell, R. R. (2018). Modeling emission-generating technologies: Reconciliation of axiomatic and by-production approaches. *Empirical Economics, 54*, 7–30.
Murty, S., Russell, R. R., & Levkoff, S. B. (2012). On modeling pollution-generating technologies. *Journal of Environmental Economics and Management, 64*, 117–135.
Pastor, J., Ruiz, J., & Sirvent, I. (1999). An enhanced DEA Russell graph efficiency measure. *European Journal of Operational Research, 115*, 596–607.
Ramanathan, R. (2005). An analysis of energy consumption and carbon dioxide emissions in countries of the Middle East and North Africa. *Energy, 30*, 2831–2842.
Seiford, L., & Zhu, J. (1999). Infeasibility of super-efficiency data envelopment analysis models. *Infor, 37*, 174–188.
Seiford, L., & Zhu, J. (2002). Modeling undesirable factors in efficiency evaluation. *European Journal of Operational Research, 142*, 16–20.
Song, M., Zheng, W., & Wang, Z. (2016). Environmental efficiency and energy consumption of highway transportation systems in China. *International Journal of Production Economics, 181*, 441–449.
Tone, K. (2001). A slacks-based measure of efficiency in data envelopment analysis. *European Journal of Operational Research, 130*, 498–509.
Tone, K. (2002). A slacks-based measure of super-efficiency in data envelopment analysis. *European Journal of Operational Research, 143*, 32–41.
Tone, K., & Tsutsui, M. (2010). Dynamic DEA: A slacks-based measure approach. *Omega, 38*, 145–156.
Vestreng, V., Myhre, G., Fagerli, H., Reis, S., Tarrasón, L., et al. (2007). Twenty-five years of continuous sulphur dioxide emission reduction in Europe. *Atmospheric chemistry and physics, 7*, 3663–3681.
Wang, J., Zhao, T., & Zhang, X. (2016). Environmental assessment and investment strategies of provincial industrial sector in China—Analysis based on DEA model. *Environmental Impact Assessment Review, 60*, 156–168.
Yang, H., & Pollitt, M. G. (2010). The necessity of distinguishing weak and strong disposability among undesirable outputs in DEA: Environmental performance of Chinese coal-fired power plants. *Energy Policy, 38*, 4440–4444.
Zhou, P., Ang, B., & Poh, K. (2006). Slacks-based efficiency measures for modeling environmental performance. *Ecological Economics, 60*, 111–118.
Zhou, P., Poh, K., & Ang, B. (2007). A non-radial DEA approach to measuring environmental performance. *European Journal of Operational Research, 178*, 1–9.
Zhou, P., Ang, B., & Poh, K. (2008). Measuring environmental performance under different environmental DEA technologies. *Energy Economics, 30*, 1–14.
Zofio, J. L., & Prieto, A. M. (2001). Environmental efficiency and regulatory standards: The case of CO_2 emissions from OECD industries. *Resource and Energy Economics, 23*, 63–83.

Probability of Default and Banking Efficiency: How Does the Market Respond?

Claudia Curi and Ana Lozano-Vivas

Abstract The paper attempts to analyze whether shareholders value as intangible assets the management decisions of bank production plan, in terms of cost efficiency, and risk associated to bank portfolio composition, in terms of probability of default (PoD). To test the market response to both management decisions, we employ a regression equation for bank valuation, using the panel regression model estimation procedure with country and year fixed effects, for the listed banks of 15 European countries, during the period 1997–2016. The results show that shareholders value both the efficiency of the production plan and the default risk. In particular, shareholders positively value banks' cost efficiency and negatively value those banks with high PoD. These findings have important policy implications and show that the market value performance allows for the provision of more insights than book value into potential drivers of banks' system stability and potential mechanisms for regulators and supervisors to maintain and control bank stability.

1 Introduction

The entire banking sector is facing significant challenges to survive technical, regulatory, and economic changes, globalization, and new competitors that have been emerging over time. Banks respond to these changes by reassessing and adjusting their assets and liabilities, in order to accommodate their business model to the new environment they face. Such amendments have triggered an increase in bank complexity, whereby banks have shifted from being traditional intermediaries to more market-oriented players (Abuzayed et al. 2009), providing a wider range of products and services. Such movement has led banks to raise intangible or hidden assets in their operations. These are assets not reflected on the bank book value, and to some extent, they explain the gap between banks' book values and market values. Kane and Unal (1990) prove that whenever the economic market values of bank assets and liabilities differ from their accounting and book value, it is explained by the fact that the firm has substantial hidden assets. In this sense, Ang and Clark (1997) assert, even before the crisis, that the conventional wisdom that market value reflects perfectly the bank book value has become increasingly invalid, given the important reorientation of banks as result of their new asset and revenue mix. The aftermath of the financial crisis reinforces this view. In this vein, Calomiris and Nissim (2014) emphasize that, since the US financial crisis (2006–2009), financial markets have changed their perception of the valuation of bank intangibles. For instance, mortgage servicing fees were valuable before the crisis but have declined their value since the crisis, due to persistent, adverse, expected changes in the extent of mortgage refinancing and origination activity, mortgage default rates, and expected interest income earned on the mortgage servicing-related float. This change in market expectation has contributed to widening the gap between bank book value and market value and lowering the value of intangible assets.

Although book and market values are proven to be different from each other, because book value neglects information about expected future cash flows associated with intangible assets and liabilities, regulators and supervisors focus on book values for scrutinizing financial fragility. The omission of such pieces of information does not enable book values to reflect accurately the bank rent and its vulnerability, from a long-term perspective. In this vein, Calomiris and Nissim (2014) argue the fact that, after the crisis, banks displayed market-to-book ratios below 1 indicate that banks' investments are projected to generate negative economic profits in the future. Thus, the projection of a bank's investment was neglected in the evaluation

C. Curi
Free University of Bozen-Bolzano, Bolzano, Italy

A. Lozano-Vivas (✉)
University of Málaga, Málaga, Spain
e-mail: avivas@uma.es

J. Aparicio et al. (eds.), *Advances in Efficiency and Productivity II*, International Series in Operations Research & Management Science 287, https://doi.org/10.1007/978-3-030-41618-8_13

of financial fragility during the crisis by regulators and supervisors because they neglected the market value of banks while focusing, instead, on the book value of a bank's activities, employing accounting measures from balance sheets and income statements. Consequently, it seems that a market value-based metric allows for the provision of more insight into the potential drivers of system stability of banks and the mechanisms available to supervisors and regulators to maintain stability.

To the extent that investors value banks through pricing bank intangible assets, this paper aims to investigate how intangible assets, which are under the control of managers, are valued by market investors. More specifically, we consider two intangible assets: the first is the overall bank risk, as an outcome of the manager's decision in selecting a bank business model; the second is a bank performance metric, as an outcome of the manager's decision in developing the bank production plan. Accordingly, our main purpose is to analyze how financial markets value banks, depending on the PoD and cost efficiency as proxies of overall bank risk and performance, respectively. With this analysis, the purpose of the paper is to contribute to the debate started in the literature by Kane and Unal (1990), Ang and Clark (1997), and Calomiris and Nissim (2014), among others, about the superior information that market value has compared to book value due to the fact that the former takes into account intangible assets. The particular contribution of the paper is to prove whether shareholders evaluate two particular manager decisions, cost efficiency and default risk, decisions that represent banks' hidden assets.

Given that the banks that are best able to survive are those that can achieve a strategic position that best enhances their franchise value (Ang and Clark 1997), in this paper we use the franchise value as the measure of how banks create value. Franchise value is a long-term concept of firm rent and gives information about divergences between the book and the market values. In particular, we define it as the Tobin's Q, which is a forward-looking and market-based measure to appraise shareholder value for banks.

In terms of a bank performance metric, we use bank cost efficiency. Although firm performances are usually ratios fashioned from financial statements, these measures do not bring out the effects of differences in exogenous firm-specific conditions that may affect firm value but are beyond management's control. Therefore, financial ratios cannot reflect accurately the problem of agency costs (Berger and Di Patti 2006). By using the cost efficiency measure instead of financial performance indicators, we can gain an accurate measure of agency cost generated by the decision of managers on implementing the bank production plan.[1] Our methodological approach is underpinned by Leibenstein (1966), who showed how different principal-agent objectives, inadequate motivation, and incomplete contracts become sources of inefficiency.

Regarding overall bank risk, we use the PoD. The management decision of choosing a given business model, i.e., in terms of the composition of their portfolio assets, funding, and revenue, is one of the most relevant determinants of risk-taking for the banks, where a wrong selection of debt portfolio for running the business plan leads to a bank defaulting. In the literature of corporate finance, there is a stream that analyzes, theoretically and empirically, the relationship between default risk and stock return. Chava and Purnanandam (2010) expose that if default risk is regarded as systemic, then the investor claims a risk-premium for bearing this risk. These authors, by using analysts' forecasts as a measure of the market's ex ante expectations in place to realize stock return, found a strong positive relation between default risk and stock return. However, other empirical studies (i.e., Dichev (1998) and Campbell et al. (2008)) suggest that, in the post-1980 period, the cost of equity capital decreases with default risk, i.e., there exists a negative relationship between default risk and realized stock returns. In general, the default risk is related to stock return, though the direction of the relation is unclear.

Our research is oriented to evaluate the response of financial markets, i.e., how shareholders value banks' hidden assets, for 15 countries of the EU, during the period 1997–2016. This long time span allows us to track changes in the franchise value, in the hidden assets entailed by banks, and in their shareholder valuation during the banking industry deregulation, the financial crisis, and after the crisis periods. Additionally, this period allows us to analyze, systematically, the decision of managers in terms of determining the amount of riskiness of their operations and the efficiency of their production plans. To perform our empirical analysis, we use a panel regression model with country and year fixed effects, with standard errors clustered at the bank and year levels (Petersen 2009). The regression equation links Tobin's Q with cost efficiency and PoD for each bank from 1997 to 2016. The main results show that shareholders value the cost efficiency and the PoD; that is, they value the two intangible assets that are decisions under the control of bank managers. While the bank Tobin's Q increases with bank cost efficiency, it decreases with higher PoD. Thus, it seems that the cost efficiency and the PoD are drivers of the bank Tobin's Q for the banking industry of the EU.

Our study contributes to the literature on the determinants of bank value creation or bank market value in several ways. First, we attempt to analyze whether two important decisions under the control of the managers, i.e., cost efficiency and default risk, are valued by shareholders. Although there exists in the literature some studies that consider bank efficiency

[1]The agency cost appears in banking when the goal of the manager is not aligned with one of the shareholders, since, while the goal of shareholders is to maximize the firm's market value, the managers pursue maximizing their own utility. This nonaligned goal leads to outcome inefficiency in the production process.

and shareholder value,[2] there is a scarcity of studies in the banking literature relating to risk and shareholder's value.[3] To our knowledge, this is the first study that takes a market-based perspective to study the joint impact of two decisions under the control of managers, cost efficiency, and PoD, on long-term performance. Second, while most of the studies on the determinants of bank value creation have been oriented to one single country's banking industry or limited to only a few countries, the present study analyzes the 15 countries of the EU. Third, this is one of the few papers in the literature that uses the Tobin's Q as total bank value. Only De Jonghe and Vander Vennet (2008) and Fu et al. (2014) also use this measure. Lastly, the long time period (20 years) used in our analysis provides us with the opportunity for giving some insights on whether banks change intangible assets and, concurrently, whether the shareholders change their perceptions over time and the reaction of banks and shareholders before, during, and after the financial crisis.

The paper is structured as follows: Section 2 explains the methodology used for our empirical exercise. Section 3 shows the data and variables used jointly, with a descriptive analysis of the key variables of the empirical exercise. Section 4 presents the empirical results, while Sect. 5 provides the conclusion.

2 Methodology

In order to investigate the relationship between bank market valuation, cost efficiency, and the probability of default, we use as the dependent variable the Tobin's Q, which is defined as the ratio of the market value of a firm to the replacement cost of its assets. In this paper, for each bank *i* and year *t*, Tobin's Q ($TQ_{i,\,t}$) is defined as:

$$TQ_{i,t} = \frac{Market\ value\ of\ Common\ Equity_{i,t} + Book\ Value\ of\ Total\ Liabilities_{i,t}}{Book\ Value\ of\ Total\ Assets_{i,t}} \tag{1}$$

Cost efficiency for each bank *i* and year *t* (CE_{it}) has been obtained using the nonparametric approach (data envelopment analysis, DEA). The main argument for using DEA instead of other approaches lies in two key advantages. First, DEA provides an ordinal ranking or relative cost efficiency compared to the Pareto-efficient frontier (the bank best practice benchmark). Instead, parametric methods, such as the stochastic frontier approach, estimate the efficiency relative to the average performance. Second, DEA does not impose an explicit weighting structure to inputs and outputs in the estimation of the efficiency scores. This implies that banks using a less than optimal mix to reach the same level of output will be valued with an efficiency score of less than 1.

As a specification model used to estimate the frontier, we follow the intermediation approach, which was originally developed by Sealey and Lindley (1977) and posits that total loans and other earning assets are outputs, whereas deposits along labor and physical capital are inputs.[4] Specifically, the output variables capture the traditional lending activity of banks (total loans) and investment banking activities of banks (other earning assets), respectively. The input variables used in this study are the cost of labor (personnel expenses/total assets), costs of deposits (interest expenses/total deposits), and physical capital (total noninterest expenses—personnel expenses/total fixed assets).

The PoD for each bank *i* and year *t* (PoD_{it}) are taken from the database, Risk Management Institute database (National University of Singapore). The PoD is calculated in this database based on the call option theory of the Merton (1974) model. And it is available at the daily frequency. We therefore compute the average per year in order to assign to each bank *i* the PoD corresponding to the corresponding year *t*.

Since we deal with a panel database, we use panel regression models with the country and year fixed effects, with clustering at bank and year level (Petersen 2009). In this approach, the standard errors clustered by a bank capture the unspecified correlation between observations on the same bank in different years, and standard errors clustered by year capture the unspecified correlation between observations in different banks in the same year.

The regression equation for the bank valuation is given by:

[2] There is some studies analyzing the relationship between market value and bank efficiency, for instance, Fu et al. (2014), Abuzayed et al. (2009), Pasiouras et al. (2008), Beccalli et al. (2006), Eisenbeis et al. (1999), Adenso-Diaz and Gascon (1997), and Chung and Pruitt (1996).

[3] The pioneer work on this area is the Demsetz et al. (1996) study. The authors relate the franchise value of the banks not with probability of default but with other bank risks as the solvency risk and the portfolio risk.

[4] In the banking literature, there are three alternative approaches to measuring bank outputs and inputs based on the classical microeconomic theory (production, intermediation, and user-cost approaches). Based on the intermediate role that banks play in the economy, we use the intermediation approach—approach widely used in the banking empirical analysis.

$$TQ_{it} = \beta_0 + \beta_1 CE_{i,t-1} + \beta_2 PoD_{i,t-1} + \sum \beta Controls_{it-1} + country\ FE + year\ FE + \varepsilon_{i,t} \quad (2)$$

where TQ_{it} represents Tobin's Q of bank *i* at time *t*, $CE_{i,\,t-1}$ is the efficiency score for bank *i* at year *t-1*, and $PoD_{i,\,t-1}$ represents the probability of default of bank *i* at year *t-1*. This variable aims at approximating the fragility of banks. Finally, as control variables, we use three variables which characterized the banks' business models. First, we include size proxied by the log of total assets. Size is often thought to affect valuation, through economies of scale. For instance, Hughes and Mester (2013) and Wheelock and Wilson (2012) find evidence of economies of scale for US banks. To account for the mixture of activities conducted by each bank and, therefore, to identify the relation between valuation and diversification, we include also the ratios of deposits over total liabilities and loans over total assets (e.g., Laeven and Levine (2007). Bank valuation might be impacted by the deposits/liabilities ratio, as a higher deposits/liabilities ratio implies that the bank has access to low-cost, subsidized funding (with deposits generally being an inexpensive source of funding and deposits often enjoying government-subsidized insurance) and, in turn, a higher deposits/liabilities ratio might signal higher valuations. Moreover, banks that engage in more traditional activities, such as activities that generate interest income, are generally valued less than banks that are more specialized in making activities that require investments in assets other than loans. This effect is captured by loans/total assets ratio.

3 Data and Variable Statistics

This research carries out an empirical analysis of how bank valuation responds to PoD and cost efficiency for European-listed banks from the 15 countries of the European Union (EU15) during the period 1997–2016. The sample represents more than 75% of bank total assets in EU15. To answer our research question, we rely on three data sources: Bankscope, to obtain balance sheet and other accounting items, Datastream (Thomson Reuters), to collect stock market data, and Risk Management Institute database (National University of Singapore), to obtain data on PoD. We fill in missing data by hand-collecting details of individual bank financial statements from corporate sources and websites. Given the different sources of information used for the empirical exercise, the registers of the three databases were manually matched, bank by bank.

We present, in this section, a descriptive analysis of the variables used in our empirical exercise. The aim is to deeply understand, from the raw data, not only the evolution of the variables but also whether there exist some insight into the type of relationship among the main variables of our analysis, i.e., Tobin's Q, cost efficiency, and PoD. Table 1 provides descriptive statistics for the sample dataset, by year (Panel A) and by country (Panel B). The average market capitalization is \$13.604 bn (median \$1.653 bn), while the average equity book value is \$10.093 bn (median \$1.887 bn). Thus, consistent with Ang and Clark (1997), market value does not perfectly reflect bank book value. Along the period, it is possible to observe how the market capitalization has fallen, tremendously, since 2008.[5]Before this year, the average market capitalization was higher than the equity book value; however, the trend reversed from 2008, with market capitalization much lower than equity book value. Thus, as Calomiris and Nissim (2014) emphasize, the global financial crisis leads to a market-to-book ratio below 1, indicating that the average projection of a bank's investments is of negative economic profits creation in the future. In terms of Tobin's Q, banks, on average, were overvalued in terms of both average and median values. Over the sample period, the average Tobin's Q was greater than 1 each year—except in 2016—meaning that, on average, banks were overvalued. A different picture emerges if we consider the median Tobin's Q: up to 2008, values are greater than 1, while from 2009 and thereafter the median Tobin's Q turns to lower than 1, meaning that 50% of the banks were undervalued; although at the mean value for the sample as a whole, the banks show up overvalued.

The average size bank measured in terms of total assets is \$232.055 bn (median \$22.750 bn). The average (and median) bank in the sample is a bank with total assets increasing over time, reaching its peak in 2008, followed by a decline until 2016. Thus, it seems that total assets decline with a year lag with respect to market capitalization and, while total equity has an increasing trend during the time span, total assets increased until 2008 but after 2008, the trend reverses. Thus, after 2008, the total equity to total assets ratio, an indicator of the solvency of banks, is higher, due to new capital regulation following the financial crisis.

Panel B shows that the largest banks, by market capitalization, are located in the UK, Spain, and Sweden, while in terms of totals assets, the UK, Spain, Belgium, Sweden, and Germany report higher average total assets. In terms of Tobin's Q, both average and median values are less than 1 in Belgium, Finland, France, and Germany, while 8 out of 14 countries

[5]During the sampling period, the average market capitalization increased until 2007, followed by a significant decline in 2008 and thereafter. A similar pattern is found in the median value, although, from 2013, the median market capitalization slowly rebounded.

Table 1 This table shows descriptive statistics of the EU15 bank sample 1997–2016

Panel A									
		Total assets ($bn)		Total equity ($bn)		Market capitalization ($bn)		Tobin's Q	
Year	Number of banks	Mean	Median	Mean	Median	Mean	Median	Mean	Median
1997	43	81.741	23.605	3.465	1.477	6.166	2.612	1.101	1.022
1998	48	85.494	23.897	3.526	1.376	7.629	3.053	1.125	1.048
1999	54	98.502	23.675	4.021	1.801	9.919	2.762	1.117	1.05
2000	54	107.149	24.167	4.976	1.597	12.481	2.7	1.103	1.05
2001	58	112.559	19.946	5.43	1.387	12.384	2.139	1.071	1.043
2002	72	103.733	9.222	4.941	0.774	9.593	0.836	1.135	1.036
2003	72	117.011	11.558	5.745	0.921	10.899	1.498	1.208	1.026
2004	75	156.892	14.237	7.388	1.11	13.865	1.556	1.264	1.03
2005	75	166.329	15.429	7.811	1.286	15.075	1.542	1.337	1.039
2006	77	230.341	18.882	10.113	1.641	21.032	2.582	1.414	1.05
2007	78	290.995	23.111	12.152	2.019	23.697	2.701	1.356	1.038
2008	78	345.235	28.435	13.109	2.343	15.825	1.919	1.176	1.013
2009	80	339.971	32.681	13.975	2.318	13.798	1.589	1.07	0.989
2010	80	323.352	31.547	15.362	2.322	13.51	1.15	1.068	0.984
2011	82	321.244	31.524	15.097	2.359	11.683	1.07	1.075	0.984
2012	84	321.271	26.505	14.54	2.164	10.682	0.797	1.049	0.978
2013	82	322.437	33.324	15.369	2.467	14.911	1.289	1.065	0.985
2014	81	309.814	28.262	15.713	2.823	17.21	1.354	1.113	0.991
2015	80	284.947	26.321	15.542	2.954	13.924	1.407	1.095	0.981
2016	78	235.486	24.586	13.583	2.611	10.541	1.268	0.954	0.96
Whole sample		**217.725**	**23.546**	**10.093**	**1.887**	**13.241**	**1.791**	**1.145**	**1.015**
Panel B									
Austria	99	19.103	7.931	1.354	0.387	1.272	0.445	1.019	0.987
Belgium	33	244.288	237.476	10.006	7.786	7.481	1.746	0.998	0.964
Denmark	311	32.120	1.101	1.333	0.120	10.324	0.711	1.700	1.527
Finland	48	16.348	9.806	0.974	0.430	1.041	0.331	0.997	0.997
France	291	319.548	19.912	12.792	2.295	9.369	0.195	0.932	0.909
Germany	76	608.242	215.735	18.610	8.444	14.369	3.742	0.998	0.993
Greece	93	45.728	27.236	3.059	1.326	4.139	1.982	1.057	1.037
Ireland	20	157.636	159.992	7.450	8.618	9.745	9.322	1.030	1.040
Italy	196	180.178	36.684	12.319	2.791	9.496	2.096	1.007	0.993
Netherland	13	3.159	3.905	0.476	0.598	1.090	0.970	1.454	1.106
Portugal	37	78.039	87.116	5.069	5.051	5.649	5.047	1.021	1.027
Spain	75	485.114	322.616	31.061	18.528	37.915	30.342	1.041	1.014
Sweden	60	219.555	235.583	9.690	9.336	14.731	13.008	1.025	1.028
UK	79	973.569	681.777	43.204	38.079	71.733	51.396	1.071	1.055
Whole sample		232.047	97.843	10.780	5.354	13.634	6.134	1.156	1.102

Panel A shows summary data (mean and median) across sample years (1997–2016): number of banks, total assets ($bn), total equity ($bn), market capitalization ($bn), and Tobin's Q. Panel B shows summary data (mean and median) by country for the whole period (1997–2016): number of observations, market capitalization ($bn), total equity ($bn), total assets ($bn), and Tobin's Q

show a median Tobin's Q greater than 1. Thus, while in former countries the average bank is undervalued, in the remaining European countries, banks are perceived well and, therefore, overvalued.

Figure 1 depicts the evolution of PoD over the sample. We observe an increase in the PoD during the financial crisis (2008–2009) and the sovereign financial crisis (2010–2012). In Fig. 2, across the different 15 European countries, Greece shows the higher mean (and median) values, followed by Belgium and France.

Table 2 shows the descriptive statistics of output and input variables used to estimate the cost efficiency measure for the sample dataset during the period 1996–2016. In terms of total loans, UK and Spain exhibit the highest volume of loans, while in terms of other earning assets, the UK and Germany are the highest. The price of physical capital seems to be higher in Finland, Germany, Netherland, and Sweden, while the labor price is higher in the Netherlands, Greece, and Denmark.

Fig. 1 The figure presents statistics (mean and median expressed in percentage terms) of the probability of default (PoD) across sample years (1997–2016)

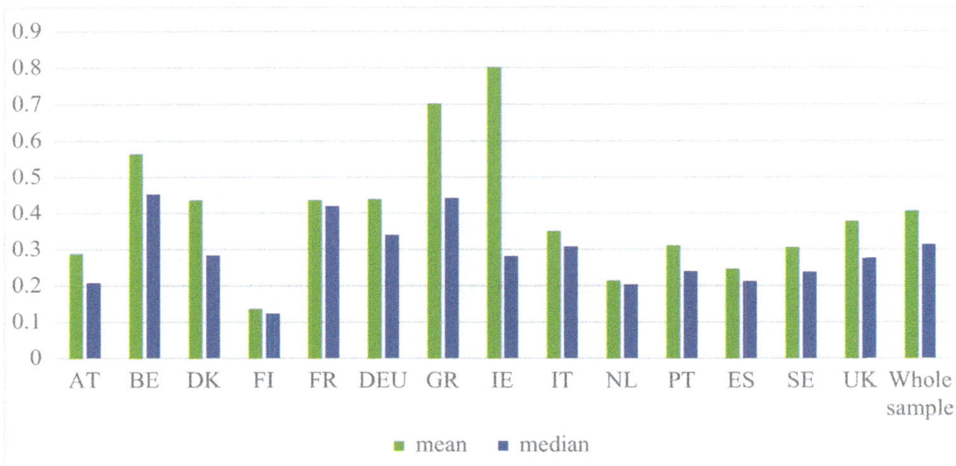

Fig. 2 The figure presents statistics (mean and median) of the probability of default (PoD) by country across sample years (1997–2016)

Finally, higher deposit interests are found to be in France, Portugal, and Sweden. The price of physical capital and labor presents a positive trend until 2006; however, the opposite is true for deposit interest rate. Finally, while total loans steadily increase until 2010, the other operating assets have a positive trend until 2009, with both having decreased since 2010 and 2009, respectively.

The evolution of the EU15 bank cost efficiency over the period 1997–2016 is reported in Table 3. It is interesting to note that the overall sample mean and median cost efficiency are 0.756 and 0.754, respectively. Starting from 2006, the median value of cost efficiency decreases over time, although not continuously, and never rebounds to the 2005 cost efficiency level. The efficiency reduced in 2008 and 2009. Countries that exhibit the more cost-efficient banks are Netherlands and the UK, followed by Austria and Germany (see Fig. 3).

From the descriptive statistical analysis, we observe that, as Calomiris and Nissim (2014) emphasize, after the crisis, financial markets changed their valuation of bank intangibles, contributing to the increase in gap between bank book and market value, which is reflected in the deterioration of the franchise value, i.e., Tobin's Q. Interestingly, while the franchise value declines, PoD increases and cost efficiency declines. Thus, it seems from the simple data descriptive statistic that there may be a negative (positive) relationship between franchise value and probability to default (cost efficiency). Whether or not shareholders value the two proxies of manager decision as intangible assets and reflect them as drivers of franchise value is not able to be inferred from the raw data. We need to resort to the econometric method designed in our methodology to prove whether this relationship likely exists and is statistically significant.

The next section presents the results obtained from the estimation of our regression equation for bank valuation.

Table 2 This table reports descriptive statistics of output (total loans ($mil), other earning assets ($mil)) and input (physical capital, labor cost, and interests on deposits) variables of the EU15 bank sample 1997–2016 used to estimate the cost efficiency measure

Panel A											
		Outputs				Inputs					
	Number of	Total loans ($mil)		Other earning assets ($mil)		Physical capital		Labor		Deposit interests	
Year	banks	Mean	Median	Mean	Median	Mean	Median	Mean	Median	Mean	Median
1997	43	40.029	10.560	33.727	10.334	0.748	0.625	0.013	0.013	0.055	0.053
1998	48	39.883	12.139	37.157	8.545	0.870	0.658	0.014	0.013	0.053	0.047
1999	54	44.885	13.170	43.212	6.330	0.958	0.807	0.013	0.013	0.044	0.042
2000	54	47.812	12.697	46.516	7.294	0.927	0.789	0.013	0.013	0.052	0.047
2001	58	47.505	12.469	51.497	5.309	0.933	0.851	0.013	0.012	0.048	0.043
2002	72	43.882	6.024	47.340	2.378	0.984	0.820	0.014	0.013	0.038	0.033
2003	72	49.139	8.196	53.877	2.733	1.237	0.853	0.014	0.012	0.030	0.028
2004	75	66.840	10.305	74.730	2.538	1.460	0.907	0.014	0.012	0.026	0.025
2005	75	69.902	9.835	84.228	2.675	1.518	0.980	0.013	0.011	0.028	0.026
2006	77	90.722	11.502	124.788	4.896	1.575	1.033	0.013	0.011	0.034	0.030
2007	78	115.176	15.055	157.143	5.275	1.359	0.950	0.011	0.010	0.044	0.040
2008	78	131.603	17.839	191.491	4.528	1.321	0.959	0.011	0.010	0.048	0.043
2009	80	135.004	18.681	180.397	6.219	1.433	1.055	0.011	0.009	0.194	0.029
2010	80	135.195	17.232	162.162	5.815	1.324	1.079	0.011	0.010	0.187	0.023
2011	82	132.332	17.102	161.341	5.901	1.235	1.070	0.011	0.009	0.182	0.025
2012	84	129.244	19.279	160.713	6.589	1.385	0.951	0.011	0.009	0.026	0.025
2013	82	129.362	20.931	160.048	8.305	1.192	0.885	0.010	0.009	0.022	0.021
2014	81	122.823	19.425	155.462	8.246	1.723	0.883	0.011	0.009	0.019	0.018
2015	80	113.572	18.043	141.969	6.069	2.001	1.086	0.011	0.010	0.027	0.014
2016	78	99.476	16.523	110.795	5.153	1.956	1.085	0.016	0.010	0.036	0.010
Whole sample		**89.219**	**14.350**	**108.930**	**5.757**	**1.350**	**0.920**	**0.012**	**0.011**	**0.060**	**0.031**
Panel B											
Austria	99	11.282	5.095	6.377	2.000	0.764	0.417	0.010	0.011	0.037	0.026
Belgium	33	109.798	90.135	119.081	91.683	0.937	0.821	0.007	0.007	0.035	0.031
Denmark	311	17.676	0.677	13.001	0.283	1.244	1.043	0.017	0.017	0.022	0.018
Finland	48	6.918	4.899	7.615	3.402	2.467	1.252	0.010	0.008	0.853	0.032
France	291	95.970	15.314	192.465	3.427	1.246	1.090	0.011	0.009	0.043	0.032
Germany	76	155.426	110.663	400.605	110.422	3.480	1.484	0.008	0.007	0.037	0.028
Greece	93	27.970	13.071	12.271	10.617	0.667	0.543	0.015	0.013	0.037	0.031
Ireland	20	104.846	102.036	42.839	44.115	1.241	0.915	0.008	0.007	0.033	0.033
Italy	196	104.656	26.676	59.313	10.615	1.172	0.614	0.014	0.013	0.032	0.028
Netherland	13	0.440	0.508	2.151	2.735	3.736	2.524	0.024	0.015	0.009	0.007
Portugal	37	52.098	54.885	18.445	17.111	0.885	0.873	0.009	0.009	0.045	0.043
Spain	75	279.805	157.612	150.698	109.510	0.618	0.606	0.010	0.009	0.034	0.029
Sweden	60	135.402	147.217	65.559	59.560	2.479	2.094	0.006	0.005	0.045	0.042
UK	79	364.959	293.908	532.180	281.729	1.245	1.130	0.009	0.009	0.025	0.024
Whole sample		**94.615**	**49.770**	**116.726**	**36.007**	**1.350**	**0.920**	**0.012**	**0.011**	**0.061**	**0.028**

Panel A shows summary data (mean and median) across sample years (1997–2016). Panel B shows summary data (mean and median) by country for the whole period (1997–2016)

4 Results

As we presented in Sect. 3 we used as the dependent variables the Tobin's Q (regressed against the lagged cost efficiency and the probability of default), cost efficiency$_{t-1}$, and PoD$_{t-1}$, respectively, for each bank *i* at year *t*, as our main variables. As control variables, we included the bank size, defined as the logarithm of total assets, Ln (total assets); the ratio of loan to total assets, loans/total assets; and the ratio of deposits to total liabilities, deposits/total liabilities. All the independent variables are included as lagged variables, to control for potential endogeneity, since the intangibles, as defined in previous sections, are deliberate decisions of the bank management and, therefore, not random. We estimated the panel data with

Table 3 This table reports descriptive statistics (mean and median) of the cost efficiency measure for the entire sample over the period (1997–2016)

Year	Whole sample	
	Mean	Median
1997	0.806	0.816
1998	0.758	0.722
1999	0.729	0.737
2000	0.759	0.755
2001	0.775	0.756
2002	0.739	0.730
2003	0.780	0.784
2004	0.721	0.727
2005	0.824	0.838
2006	0.797	0.782
2007	0.751	0.729
2008	0.706	0.677
2009	0.682	0.630
2010	0.766	0.743
2011	0.799	0.787
2012	0.763	0.722
2013	0.777	0.743
2014	0.750	0.726
2015	0.730	0.738
2016	0.722	0.716
Whole period	**0.756**	**0.744**

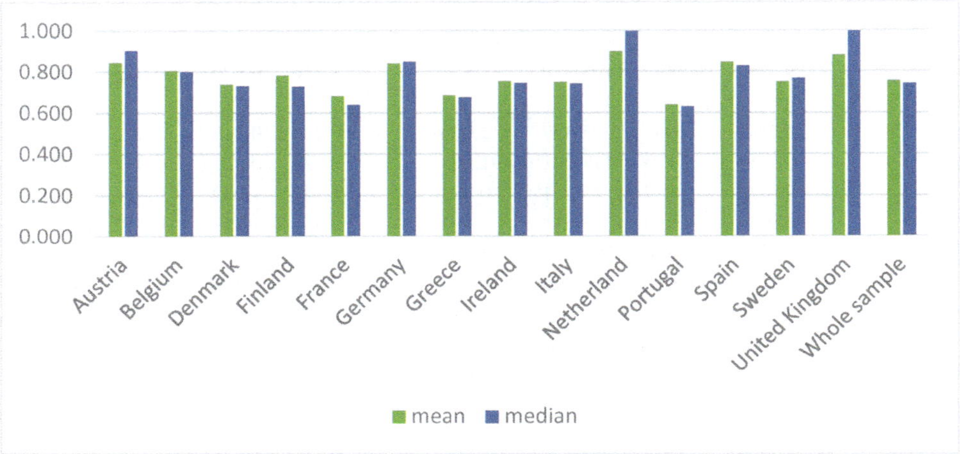

Fig. 3 The figure presents statistics (mean and median) of the cost efficiency by country across sample years (1997–2016)

the year and country fixed effects by using clustering at country and year level (Petersen 2009). The estimation of the regression equation (2) is displayed in Table 4. Overall, the results show that the PoD and cost efficiency affect significantly the Tobin's Q. In particular, while the PoD maintains a negative relationship with the Tobin's Q, the cost efficiency holds a positive relationship. Thus, our results obtained in the econometric model validate our conjectures stemmed by the descriptive analysis. The results of the positive effect of cost efficiency and shareholder value are consistent with the findings of Fiordelisi and Molyneux (2010) on European banks and Fu et al. (2014) on Asia Pacific banks.

The results for the whole time span, 1997–2016, indicate that bank valuation is affected by both bank risk of default and the efficiency of the production plan. While bank value is positively affected when managers attempt to minimize the production cost, given their technology, those banks which have investment portfolios that contribute to increasing the bankruptcy probability are valued negatively. If, as we enunciated in the introduction, we assume that PoD and cost efficiency are proxies of two intangible assets under management control, then the regression results suggest that both assets are under the scrutiny of financial investors and valued accordingly. Since none of them is incorporated in financial statements of the bank, then the market value is given more insight about the driver of bank stability through the projection of a bank's investment, in terms of future economic profits.

Table 4 Equation of bank value estimation for the whole period (1997–2016), pre-crisis period (1997–2007), crisis period (2008–2012), and post-crisis period (2013–2016)

	1997–2016	1997–2007	2008–2012	2013–2016
$PoD_{i,t-1}$	−0.083***	−0.038*	−0.081***	−0.107***
	(0.014)	(0.021)	(0.017)	(0.037)
$CE_{i,t-1}$	0.336***	0.363***	0.174***	0.211***
	(0.043)	(0.065)	(0.054)	(0.062)
Ln (total assets) $_{i,t-1}$	−0.024***	−0.047***	0.001	−0.001
	(0.005)	(0.009)	(0.006)	(0.005)
Loans/total assets $_{i,t-1}$	−0.118***	−0.228***	−0.171***	0.044
	(0.045)	(0.082)	(0.038)	(0.080)
Deposits/total liabilities $_{i,t-1}$	0.081	0.194*	0.301***	−0.091
	(0.067)	(0.111)	(0.079)	(0.092)
Constant	0.698***	1.428***	0.249	0.196
	(0.172)	(0.343)	(0.244)	(0.282)
Country fixed effects	Yes	Yes	Yes	Yes
Year fixed effects	Yes	Yes	Yes	Yes
Observations	1237	586	370	281
R-squared	0.684	0.755	0.701	0.701

Robust standard errors are shown in parentheses
Significant at 10%
*Significant at 5%
**Significant at 1%

Regarding bank valuation during the pre-crisis period (1997–2007), the crisis period (2008–2012), and the post-crisis period (2013–2016), we observe, in Table 4 (columns 2–4), that the PoD holds its negative relationship along the three sub-periods, which is statistically significant. Interestingly, the intensity of the effect is larger during the post-crisis period compared to the periods during the crisis and before the crisis, when the impact had a lower magnitude. Thus, it seems that the default risk is a more important driver for bank market value after, rather than before, the crisis. These results can be explained by the social cost generated by the global financial crisis and the "new" perceptions that banks are worth less if they incur in higher default risk. Therefore, the market only recently seems to discount more the probability of default that banks might take, compared to the period before the financial crisis. In terms of cost efficiency, the positive relationship between cost efficiency and Tobin's Q holds along the three sub-periods, with the peculiarity that, during the crisis, the estimated parameter of cost efficiency is not statistically significant. Apparently, during the crisis, given the restructuring of the banking system and the failure and rescue of many of them, the market neither discounted nor provided a premium to cost efficiency, which, instead, would have been a suitable indicator to monitor for bank valuation. However, before and after the crisis, the cost efficiency contains enough information and credible information to be valued by the market.

Regarding the control variables, during the whole period, Ln (total assets) presents a negative and statistically significant relationship with the Tobin's Q. This result could be imputed to diseconomies of scale and scope, as large banks might engage in managing several subsidiaries and branches and/or multiple activities, which intensify agency problems and lead to destroying value. Thus, it seems that larger banks are less worth than smaller banks. However, this effect arose before the crisis, since during and after the crisis, the bank size became not statistically significant. This new finding may be related to the too-big-to-fail (TBTF) paradigm. Since the larger banks are more protected by the regulators, in order to impede failure, given their important impact on the economy as a whole, it seems that the markets do not value it.

The negative and statistically significant sign of loan/total assets suggests that the market has discounted some activities more than others; in particular, commercial activities (or more lending-oriented business models) were valued less than banks, which are more specialized in activities turning their investments into assets other than loans (Laeven and Levine 2007). In terms of the impact of the ratio deposits to total liabilities, our additional control variable, it is positive but not statistically significant. Since this is maintained for the whole period and the three sub-periods, it seems that the market does not value a higher reliance on deposit funding.

Tables 5 and 6 present the results of the estimation of bank value equation for large and small banks,[6] for the whole period and the pre-crisis, crisis, and post-crisis periods. We performed these regressions to deeply analyze the effect of size on bank

[6]We consider as large banks those banks with total assets larger than $20 bn.

Table 5 Equation of bank value estimation for larger banks for the whole period (1997–2016), pre-crisis period (1997–2007), crisis period (2008–2012), and post-crisis period (2013–2016)

Large banks				
	1997–2016	1997–2007	2008–2012	2013–2016
$PoD_{i,t-1}$	−0.032***	−0.047***	−0.037***	−0.020***
	(0.007)	(0.015)	(0.013)	(0.006)
$CE_{i,t-1}$	0.057***	0.092***	0.018	−0.006
	(0.020)	(0.032)	(0.031)	(0.018)
Ln(total assets)$_{i,t-1}$	−0.016***	−0.039***	0.000	−0.002
	(0.006)	(0.009)	(0.009)	(0.005)
Loans/total assets$_{i,t-1}$	−0.157***	−0.243***	−0.157***	−0.311***
	(0.030)	(0.057)	(0.040)	(0.072)
Deposits/total liabilities$_{i,t-1}$	0.005	0.135	0.058	0.148***
	(0.032)	(0.098)	(0.046)	(0.054)
Constant	1.312***	1.910***	0.854***	0.968***
	(0.217)	(0.386)	(0.318)	(0.122)
Country fixed effects	Yes	Yes	Yes	Yes
Year fixed effects	Yes	Yes	Yes	Yes
Observations	662	294	204	164
R-squared	0.663	0.732	0.646	0.890

Robust standard errors are shown in parentheses
*Significant at 10%
*Significant at 5%
**Significant at 1%

Table 6 Equation of bank value estimation for small banks for the whole period (1997–2016), pre-crisis period (1997–2007), crisis period (2008–2012), and post-crisis period (2013–2016)

Small banks				
	1997–2016	1997–2007	2008–2012	2013–2016
$PoD_{i,t-1}$	−0.127***	−0.049*	−0.101***	−0.205***
	(0.023)	(0.028)	(0.031)	(0.059)
$CE_{i,t-1}$	0.558***	0.557***	0.162	0.462***
	(0.081)	(0.126)	(0.098)	(0.140)
Ln(total assets)$_{i,t-1}$	−0.068***	−0.113***	0.005	−0.019
	(0.010)	(0.014)	(0.021)	(0.020)
Loans/total assets$_{i,t-1}$	0.269**	0.426***	0.049	0.338
	(0.107)	(0.157)	(0.139)	(0.207)
Deposits/total liabilities$_{i,t-1}$	0.042	0.188	0.900***	−0.107
	(0.093)	(0.159)	(0.255)	(0.113)
Constant	0.923***	2.198***	−0.574	−0.388
	(0.320)	(0.466)	(0.637)	(0.518)
Country fixed effects	Yes	Yes	Yes	Yes
Year fixed effects	Yes	Yes	Yes	Yes
Observations	575	292	166	117
R-squared	0.732	0.793	0.745	0.750

Robust standard errors are shown in parentheses
*Significant at 10%
*Significant at 5%
**Significant at 1%

value. Regarding Table 5, we observe that our two variables of interest, PoD and cost efficiency, retain the same effect as that for the whole sample, a negative (positive) relationship between PoD (cost efficiency) and Tobin's Q. For large banks, this relationship holds for all the sub-periods for PoD; however, compared to regressions which include the entire sample, the cost efficiency became statistically insignificant in the post-crisis period. Thus, since the financial crisis, the markets are not valuing cost efficiency of larger banks. On the contrary, Table 6 shows that, while the PoD effect for small banks follows the same patterns of large banks, after the financial crisis, information was conveyed to the market which in turn impacted bank valuation. Additionally, comparing the estimated parameter of the two key variables for larger and small banks, it is observed that the magnitude effect of both variables is higher for smaller than for larger banks.

Finally, focusing now on the effect of the control variables for the case of large and small banks, the most relevant result to emerge is the opposite relationship between loan to total asset ratio and Tobin's Q for the case of larger and small banks. While, for the former, the relationship is negative and statistically significant, the opposite is true for the case of small banks. Thus, it seems that the orientation of business models of banks is differently valued by markets, depending on the bank size. Large banks are more highly valued if they engage less in loans activities; instead, small banks are better valued if they are more focused on loans activities. Interestingly, the deposit to total liabilities appears statistically significant just for small banks, and only for the case of the crisis period.

5 Conclusion

This study investigates the market valuation of banks by considering two intangible assets, namely, bank cost efficiency and the probability of default, for listed banks of 15 European countries during the period 1997–2016. We complement previous studies by calibrating the impact, not only of the effect of cost efficiency but also of the effect of PoD, of how the market values banks under the assumption that cost efficiency and PoD are two good proxies of two manager decisions, that is, the manager's decision of developing the production plan and the outcome of the decision of the manager on selecting the business model, respectively. Considering such decisions as intangible assets that arise due to the decision of the bank manager, the paper attempts to bring into line the effect of them on the market valuation of banks.

The aim of the paper is to contribute to the current debate in the literature about the superior information that market value has concerning book value given that the former take into account intangible assets. Thus market value contains superior information than book value which may be useful for detecting potential drivers of bank system stability. The particular contribution of the paper is to consider cost efficiency and bank default risk jointly as bank's hidden assets as proxies of manager decisions and to prove whether shareholders evaluate such intangible assets.

Exploiting a wide database from three different sources and matching them manually, the paper estimates a regression equation for bank valuation using the panel regression model estimation procedure with country and year fixed effects. Using as proxy of market value the Tobin's Q, estimating the cost efficiency by means of the data envelopment analysis (DEA) approach, and using information of PoD based on the call option theory of Merton model (1974), the results show that the market values both the default risk and the efficiency of the production plan. That is, bank market value is explained by bank cost efficiency and PoD, and each intangible asset plays an important role before, during, and after the global financial crisis.

In particular, considering the whole sample period, the results show that more cost-efficient (default risk) banks have a higher (lower) Tobin's Q. On the other hand, when the exercise is performed by corresponding sub-periods before, during, and after the financial crisis, the results show that the positive impact of the more cost-efficient banks on Tobin's Q disappears during the crisis but exists before and after the crisis period. On the other hand, the PoD increases its impact, extensively, after the crisis and on average. Finally, performing the analysis for large and small banks, the results show that more cost-efficient banks have a higher impact on Tobin's Q for small banks than for larger banks. Additionally, we find a higher impact of the PoD on small than on large banks. These results explain, to some extent, the hypothesis of the too-big-to-fail (TBTF) hypothesis.

In conclusion, the results suggest that cost efficiency and PoD drive and contribute to a bank's value. It seems that cost efficiency and PoD impact more on value creation for small than large banks. More efficient banks are more likely to survive, over time, since the results show that the market regards them as more likely to realize rents associated with their charter value over a long horizon (Furlong and Kwan 2006). Overall, the results suggest that keeping market participants well-informed of cost efficiency and PoD will reward a risk-conscious management strategy by credit institutions in their asset allocation decisions.

The results have important policy implications and expand the existing knowledge on the important and superior information that the market value has with respect to the book value. The findings show that the market value performance allows the provision of more insights than book value does into potential drivers of bank system stability and the mechanism for regulators and supervisors to maintain and control bank stability. Insight into the causes of the evolution of the Tobin's Q may also be interesting for the third pillar of the Basel III framework, which advocates for the adoption of market discipline mechanisms into prudential supervision. Thus, it seems that regulators should pay attention to market value with respect to book value, in order to scrutinize bank stability.

Acknowledgment The authors are very grateful to the participants of the Second Santander Chair International Workshop of Efficiency and Productivity 2018, the 8th International Conference of The Financial Engineering and Banking Society, and the X North American Productivity Workshop for the comments received. We also thank an anonymous reviewer for their valuable and insightful suggestions. Claudia Curi acknowledges the financial support from the Free University of Bozen-Bolzano. The authors acknowledge the financial support from the Spanish research national program (grant reference RTI2018-097620-B-I00).

References

Abuzayed, B., Molyneux, P., & Al-Fayoumi, N. (2009). Market value, book value and earnings: is bank efficiency a missing link? *Managerial Finance, 35*(2), 156–179.

Adenso-Diaz, B., & Gascon, F. (1997). Linking and weighting efficiency estimates with stock performance in banking firms. *The Wharton Financial Institutions Center* WP 97/21.

Ang, J. S., & Clark, J. A. (1997). The market valuation of bank shares: with implications for the value additivity principle. *Financial Markets, Institutions & Instruments, 6*(5), 1–22.

Beccalli, E., Casu, B., & Girardone, C. (2006). Efficiency and stock performance in European banking. *Journal of Business Finance & Accounting, 33*(1–2), 245–262.

Berger, A. N., & Di Patti, E. B. (2006). Capital structure and firm performance: A new approach to testing agency theory and an application to the banking industry. *Journal of Banking & Finance, 30*(4), 1065–1102.

Calomiris, C. W., & Nissim, D. (2014). Crisis-related shifts in the market valuation of banking activities. *Journal of Financial Intermediation, 23*(3), 400–435.

Campbell, J. Y., Hilscher, J., & Szilagyi, J. (2008). In search of distress risk. *The Journal of Finance, 63*(6), 2899–2939.

Chava, S., & Purnanandam, A. (2010). Is default risk negatively related to stock returns? *The Review of Financial Studies, 23*(6), 2523–2559.

Chung, K. H., & Pruitt, S. W. (1996). Executive ownership, corporate value, and executive compensation: A unifying framework. *Journal of Banking & Finance, 20*(7), 1135–1159.

De Jonghe, O., & Vander Vennet, R. (2008). Competition versus efficiency: What drives franchise values in European banking? *Journal of Banking & Finance, 32*(9), 1820–1835.

Demsetz, R. S., Saidenberg, M. R., & Strahan, P. E. (1996). Banks with something to lose: The disciplinary role of franchise value.. *Federal Reserve Bank of New York. Economic Policy Review, 2*(October), 1–14.

Dichev, I. D. (1998). Is the risk of bankruptcy a systematic risk? *The Journal of Finance, 53*(3), 1131–1147.

Eisenbeis, R., Ferrier, G, & Kwan, S. (1999). The informativeness of stochastic frontier and programming frontier efficiency scores: Cost efficiency and other measures of bank holding company performance. *Working Paper Series (Federal Reserve Bank of Atlanta)* 99-23, pp 1–38.

Fiordelisi, F., & Molyneux, P. (2010). The determinants of shareholder value in European banking. *Journal of Banking & Finance, 34*(6), 1189–1200.

Fu, X. M., Lin, Y. R., & Molyneux, P. (2014). Bank efficiency and shareholder value in Asia Pacific. *Journal of International Financial Markets, Institutions and Money, 33*, 200–222.

Furlong, F. T., & Kwan, S. (2006). *Sources of bank charter value*. Manuscript, FRB San Francisco.

Hughes, J. P., & Mester, L. J. (2013). Who said large banks don't experience scale economies? Evidence from a risk-return-driven cost function. *Journal of Financial Intermediation, 22*(4), 559–585.

Kane, E. J., & Unal, H. (1990). Modeling structural and temporal variation in the market's valuation of banking firms. *The Journal of Finance, 45*(1), 113–136.

Laeven, L., & Levine, R. (2007). Is there a diversification discount in financial conglomerates? *Journal of Financial Economics, 85*(2), 331–367.

Leibenstein, H. (1966). Allocative efficiency vs. "X-efficiency". *The American Economic Review, 56*(3), 392–415.

Merton, R. C. (1974). On the pricing of corporate debt: The risk structure of interest rates. *The Journal of Finance, 29*(2), 449–470.

Pasiouras, F., Liadaki, A., & Zopounidis, C. (2008). Bank efficiency and share performance: Evidence from Greece. *Applied Financial Economics, 18*(14), 1121–1130.

Petersen, M. A. (2009). Estimating standard errors in finance panel data sets: Comparing approaches. *The Review of Financial Studies, 22*(1), 435–480.

Sealey, C. W., & Lindley, J. T. (1977). Inputs, outputs, and a theory of production and cost at depository financial institutions. *The Journal of Finance, 32*(4), 1251–1266.

Wheelock, D. C., & Wilson, P. W. (2012). Do large banks have lower costs? New estimates of returns to scale for US banks. *Journal of Money, Credit and Banking, 44*(1), 171–199.

Measuring Global Municipal Performance in Heterogeneous Contexts: A Semi-nonparametric Frontier Approach

José Manuel Cordero, Carlos Díaz-Caro, and Cristina Polo

1 Introduction

Improving the efficiency and effectiveness of public services and at the same time reducing public deficit have become an important concern in the public sector. Undoubtedly, local governments could benefit from adhering to these objectives. They play an important role in providing public goods and services to citizens in many countries, since they are the closest political level to the population and their needs. Moreover, local authorities and public managers are increasingly under pressure to conform to the standards demanded by the general public in terms of both quantity and quality. Nevertheless, the resources to fulfill the demand for more and better local public services are scarce, especially after the cutbacks and debt constraints imposed by the economic and financial crisis. In this framework, the assessment of municipal efficiency has become a very important factor in providing additional guidance for policy makers worldwide.

This study refers to the particular case of municipalities in the Spanish region of Catalonia. For this purpose, we selected a sample of 154 medium-sized municipalities (with a population from 5000 to 50,000 inhabitants) that provide similar public services.[1] Our aim is to measure and quantify their overall efficiency for an 8-year period (2005–2012) stretching from the years leading up to the economic crisis to the early years of recovery. Likewise, in our estimation we account for the potential effects of the context in which those local governments operated, represented by a set of socioeconomic and geographical indicators. The consideration of these contextual variables in the estimation of the efficiency scores is crucial in order to make sure that municipalities rated as inefficient really are poor performers or fail to achieve the targets that others manage to attain due to factors that are beyond the control of local authorities.

For that purpose, we employ a novel approach, the so-called stochastic semi-nonparametric envelopment of data (StoNED) developed by Kuosmanen and Kortelainen (2012), which allows for combining the advantages presented by parametric techniques together with the flexibility of nonparametric techniques. Hence, we consider both inefficiency and noise in the deviations from the estimated function in a flexible framework using convex nonparametric least squares (CNLS, Hildreth 1954). Moreover, the proposed method can also be extended in order to account for the influence of contextual factors (StoNEZD, Johnson and Kuosmanen 2011). As far as we know, this methodological approach has not yet been applied to assess the global efficiency of municipalities neither in Spain nor in any other country, which makes this study clearly innovative.

[1]According to the National Law that regulates the competencies attributed to the municipalities, this group of municipalities includes two levels of competencies powers divided as follows: local governments with a population from 5000 to 20,000 inhabitants and local governments with a population from 20,000 to 50,000 inhabitants, but the divergences are minimal.

J. M. Cordero (✉)
Universidad de Extremadura, Badajoz, Spain
e-mail: jmcordero@unex.es

C. Díaz-Caro
Universidad de Extremadura, Cáceres, Spain

C. Polo
Universidad de Extremadura, Plasencia, Spain

J. Aparicio et al. (eds.), *Advances in Efficiency and Productivity II*, International Series in Operations Research & Management Science 287, https://doi.org/10.1007/978-3-030-41618-8_14

The organization of the chapter is as follows: Sect. 2 reviews the related literature. Section 3 presents the methodology applied, including the extensions regarding its application to both panel data and exogenous variables. Section 4 describes the main characteristics of the database used and the variables selected to conduct the proposed empirical analysis. Section 5 reports and discusses the empirical results, and Sect. 6 concludes.

2 Literature Review

The literature about local government efficiency is relatively recent, since the pioneering works did not emerge until the early 1990s (Van Den Eeckaut et al. 1993; De Borger et al. 1994; De Borger and Kerstens 1996a, b). Since then, a wide range of studies have analyzed the efficiency of municipalities from multiple perspectives, although we can mainly distinguish between two strands of empirical research. On the one hand, some works focused on the evaluation of a particular local public service, such as refuse collection and street cleaning (Bosch et al. 2000; Worthington and Dollery 2000a; Simões and Marques 2012; Benito et al. 2014; Pérez-López et al. 2018), water provision (Picazo-Tadeo et al. 2009; Byrnes et al. 2010), police services (García-Sánchez 2009), street lighting (Prado-Lorenzo and García-Sánchez 2007), or public libraries (De Witte and Geys 2011, 2013). On the other hand, many articles adopt a global perspective, since local authorities provide a wide variety of services and facilities from the same municipal budget. A major drawback of the first type of studies is that it is difficult to sort out which parts of the municipal inputs are assigned to each specific service. In this chapter, therefore, we focus on the literature addressing global local government efficiency. This approach has been applied to assess the performance of municipalities in multiple countries, as showed in Table 1.[2]

Most studies estimate the global efficiency of units using nonparametric techniques like data envelopment analysis (DEA, Charnes et al. 1978) or its nonconvex version free disposal hull (FDH, Deprins et al. 1984). They formulate the technological features from certain assumptions about the structure of the production technology (e.g., free disposability, convexity, etc.); thus, they are more flexible and generalizable and can be easily adapted to the characteristics of public service provision. Moreover, they can easily handle multi-input and multi-output analysis in a simple way (Ruggiero 2007). Nevertheless, these methods also present several drawbacks, such as their deterministic nature (all deviations from the frontier are considered as inefficient and no noise is allowed) or suffering the well-known curse of dimensionality, that is, the lack of discrimination power between efficient and inefficient units when the number of variables included in the model (inputs and outputs) is high in relation to the number of observations available.

Table 1 Summary of papers assessing efficiency of local governments (by countries)

Countries	Studies	Countries	Studies
Australia	Worthington (2000)	Japan	Nijkamp and Suzuki (2009)
	Worthington and Dollery (2000b)		Nakazawa (2014)
	Fogarty and Mugera (2013)		Otsuka et al. (2014)
Belgium	Geys and Moesen (2009)	Korea	Sung (2007)
	Ashworth et al. (2014)	Italy	Boetti et al. (2012)
Brazil	Sousa and Ramos (1999)		Settimi et al. (2014)
	Sousa and Stošić (2005)		Agasisti et al. (2016)
Chile	Pacheco et al. (2014)	Turkey	Kutlar et al. (2012)
Greece	Athanassopoulos and Triantis (1998)	Spain	Prieto and Zofío (2001)
Portugal	Afonso and Fernandes (2006)		Balaguer-Coll et al. (2007)
	Afonso and Fernandes (2008)		Giménez and Prior (2007)
	Cruz and Marques (2014)		Balaguer-Coll et al. (2010)
	Cordero et al. (2017a)		Zafra-Gómez and Muñiz (2010)
Norway	Borge et al. (2008)		Bosch et al. (2012)
	Bruns and Himmler (2011)		Balaguer-Coll et al. (2013)
	Sørensen (2014)		Cuadrado-Ballesteros et al. (2013)
Finland	Loikkanen and Susiluoto (2005)		Pérez-López et al. (2015)
Germany	Geys et al. (2010)		Cordero et al. (2017b)
	Kalb et al. (2012)		

Source: Own elaboration

[2] Narbón-Perpiñá and De Witte (2018a, b) provide a recent and detailed review of those empirical contributions.

On the other hand, we can also find various studies using parametric approaches, that is, they assume a specific functional form of the boundary of the production set with constant parameters to be estimated (i.e., Cobb-Douglas or translog). Their main strength is that their deviations from the efficiency frontier can be decomposed into inefficiency and a noise term by applying stochastic frontier methods (SFA, Aigner et al. 1977; Meeusen and Vandenbroeck 1977). Moreover, they perform well with panel data, because they take into account unobserved heterogeneity, thanks to the use of econometric techniques. Some examples are the empirical works conducted by Geys and Moesen (2009), Kalb et al. (2012), Otsuka et al. (2014), Pacheco et al. (2014), or Niaounakis and Blank (2017).

Although those approaches are frequently identified as competitors, actually they are complements, since, in the trade-off between them, something must be sacrificed for something to be gained (Kuosmanen et al. 2015). As a result, many authors have tried to remove differences between the two competitors DEA and SFA by relaxing some assumptions or proposing semi-parametric or semi-nonparametric methods. In the present study, we apply the StoNED method, which accommodates the main advantages of both DEA and SFA in a unified framework.

The selection of variables included in the model to calculate efficiency measures of local governments' performance usually depends on the specific services provided in each country as well as the availability of data. The variables most widely used as inputs are indicators representing budget expenditures (total or distinguishing between current and capital expenses) and personnel. On the other hand, the indicators representing outputs are usually represented by infrastructures and communal services as well as the total population, which is considered as a common standard in the literature to represent the basic administrative tasks performed by municipal governments through the service general administration.[3]

Likewise, researchers are primarily concerned with exploring how external factors potentially influence the local governments' performance. Municipalities face different contextual conditions in terms of social, demographic, economic, political, financial, geographical, and institutional, among others (see Cruz and Marques 2014, for a detailed review of these factors). These factors can have a huge impact on the efficiency measures despite that they are beyond the control of local authorities; therefore, performance analysis should control for this heterogeneity.[4]

To do this, the common practice of studies using nonparametric methods is to apply a second-stage analysis where the efficiency scores estimated in a first stage are regressed on a set of covariates representing the main characteristics of the external environment in which the local governments are operating. This model has been traditionally estimated using conventional inference methods such as Tobit or OLS (e.g., Loikkanen and Susiluoto 2005, Giménez and Prior 2007, Afonso and Fernandes 2008, or Balaguer-Coll and Prior 2009). However, the results yielded by the above approaches are usually biased and inconsistent due to the existence of serial correlation among the estimated efficiencies obtained with nonparametric methods (see Simar and Wilson 2007, 2011 for details). Therefore, in more recent literature, it is common to find studies using the algorithms based on truncated (and not censored) regression models and bootstrap methods proposed by Simar and Wilson (2007) to avoid this problem (e.g., Bönisch et al. 2011; Bosch et al. 2012; Doumpos and Cohen 2014; Cruz and Marques 2014; Pérez-López et al. 2015). Moreover, we can also find some studies using the conditional measures of efficiency developed by Daraio and Simar (2005, 2007), which allows for incorporating the effect of external or contextual factors directly into the estimation of efficiency measures using a probabilistic formulation (e.g., Asatryan and De Witte 2015; Cordero et al. 2017a, b).

The empirical studies using parametric approaches to estimate efficiency measures of local governments' performance usually accommodate exogenous variables as part of the error term. Those models can be estimated using a single stage, that is, considering the effect of those variables when obtaining efficiency scores (e.g., Geys and Moesen 2009; Geys et al. 2010, 2013; Kalb et al. 2012; Nakazawa 2013, 2014; Cuadrado-Ballesteros and Bisogno 2018), or using two-stage models in which, as explained above for nonparametric methods, the efficiency scores obtained in a first step via parametric methodologies are regressed in a second step using OLS or a Tobit censored regression (De Borger and Kerstens 1996a; Worthington 2000).

In this work we adopt a novel approach suggested by Johnson and Kuosmanen (2011) that relies on regression interpretation of DEA, which allows us to combine a nonparametric DEA-style frontier accounting for the contextual variables with a parametric treatment of the inefficiency and noise, under less restrictive assumptions than those required by traditional two-stage approaches. To the best of our knowledge, this method has not been previously employed to measure the global efficiency of local governments, which makes this study clearly innovative. In the following section, we provide a detailed explanation of this methodology and its main advantages with respect to traditional methods applied in previous literature.

---

[3]Although this variable is not a direct output, most empirical studies include it in their models (e.g., Afonso and Fernandes 2006; Balaguer et al. 2007; Balaguer and Prior 2009; De Borger and Kerstens 1996a; Geys et al. 2010; Giménez and Prior 2007).

[4]Aiello and Bonanno (2018) perform a meta-regression analysis using data from a substantial number of studies and quantify the impact of potential sources of heterogeneity on local government efficiency.

3 Methodology

In this chapter, we apply a recently developed technique, the so-called StoNED method, which combines the main advantages of parametric and nonparametric approaches. This model can be described as the regression interpretation of data envelopment analysis (DEA) proposed by Kuosmanen and Johnson (2010) to combine the key advantages of two approaches into a unified approach: the piecewise linear DEA-type nonparametric frontier with the probabilistic treatment of inefficiency and noise in stochastic models. As a result, StoNED is more robust to outliers, data errors, and other stochastic noise in the data than DEA, since all observations influence the benchmark. Moreover, as we are interested in exploring the potential influence of a set of social and economic variables on efficiency levels, we apply an extension of this method known as StoNEZD (stochastic semi-nonparametric envelopment of Z variables data, Johnson and Kuosmanen 2011) that incorporates an average effect of the operational context common to all the evaluated units. One of the main advantages is that the StoNEZD methodology estimates jointly the production frontier and the influence of the contextual variables. In the following lines, we introduce the key concepts of this technique.

In the production function framework, technology is represented by a frontier production function $Ø(x)$, which indicates the maximum output that can be produced with inputs $\boldsymbol{x}$. The observed output (y) may deviate from the frontier due to random noise (v), inefficiency ($u > 0$), and the effect of contextual factors (z). As suggested by Johnson and Kuosmanen (2011), this can be formally defined as a multiplicative model:

$$y_i = Ø(x_i) \cdot e^{\varepsilon_i}$$

$$\varepsilon_i = \delta z_i + v_i - u_i \tag{1}$$

No distributional assumptions for u and v are necessary in this stage, but u, v, and z are assumed to be uncorrelated. According to this definition of the composite disturbance term, $\boldsymbol{\delta z}_i - u_i$ can be interpreted as the overall inefficiency of a unit, being $\boldsymbol{\delta z}_i$ the part of technical inefficiency explained by the contextual variables, which is identical for all firms, and u_i the inefficiency that remains unexplained. Therefore, it is implicitly assumed that the exogenous variables have influence on the output level, so the estimated efficiency scores will incorporate the impact of the heterogeneous context in which the units are operating.

This model can be adapted to a dynamic context when longitudinal data are available, that is, when different observations are available for the same unit in different time periods ($t = 1, \ldots, T$). Therefore, we can define a time invariant production frontier model as

$$y_{it} = Ø(x_{it}) \cdot e^{\varepsilon_{it}}$$

$$\varepsilon_{it} = \delta z_{it} + v_{it} - u_i \tag{2}$$

where y_{it} is the observed output of firm i in time period t, $\boldsymbol{x}_{it}$ is a vector of inputs consumed by firm i in time period t, z_{it} is a vector of contextual variables, and $Ø$ is a production function that is time invariant and common to all units. This model can be estimated using the fixed effects approach suggested by Schmidt and Sickles (1984), in which we assume that inefficiency term (u_i) that does not change over time but the disturbance term can (v_{it}). Likewise, we assume that u_i and v_{it} are independent of inputs $\boldsymbol{x}_{it}$ and of each other.

The StoNEZD method estimates efficiency in two stages. In the first stage, the shape of the frontier can be obtained by minimizing the squared residuals in a quadratic programming problem, which does not need to presuppose a priori any assumption about the functional form, but it is built upon constraints like monotonicity and convexity [5]:

[5]Kuosmanen and Johnson (2010) show that this problem is equivalent to the standard (output-oriented, variable returns to scale) DEA model when a sign constraint on residuals is incorporated to the formulation ($\varepsilon_i \leq 0 \;\forall\; i$) and considering the problem subject to shape constraints (monotonicity and convexity).

$$\begin{aligned}
&\min \sum_{t=1}^{T} \sum_{I=1}^{n} \varepsilon_{it}^2 \\
&\textit{subject to} \\
&y_{it} = \alpha_{it} + \beta'_{it} x_{it} + \delta' z_{it} + \varepsilon_{it} \quad \forall i = 1, \ldots, n \quad \forall t = 1, \ldots, T \\
&\alpha_{it} + \beta'_{it} x_{it} \le \alpha_{ht} + \beta'_{it} x_{hs} \quad \forall h, i = 1, \ldots, n \quad \forall s, t = 1, \ldots, T \\
&\beta_{it} \ge 0 \quad \forall i = 1, \ldots, n \quad \forall t = 1, \ldots, T
\end{aligned} \tag{3}$$

where ε_{it} represents the residuals of the regression in time period t. The parameters α_{it} and $\boldsymbol{\beta}_{it}$ characterize the tangent hyperplanes of the estimated production function, which are specific to each unit in each time period. Thus, the frontier is estimated with as many as nT hyperplanes. Likewise, $\boldsymbol{\delta}$ represents the average effect of contextual variables z_{it} on performance, and the term $\boldsymbol{\delta}' z_{it}$ represents the portion of inefficiency that is explained by the contextual variables.

The parametric part of the regression equation containing the contextual variables is analogous to standard OLS. However, this approach avoids the potential bias and inconsistencies that may arise in the well-known two-stage approaches, where DEA efficiency estimates are subsequently regressed on the contextual variables (see Wang and Schmidt 2002; Simar and Wilson 2007 for details), when the inputs are correlated with the contextual variables. The StoNEZD method does not require that those $z$variables are uncorrelated with the explanatory variables (here outputs y), because the syntax of the model directly incorporates the environment in the formulation; thus, the correlations between y and z are explicitly taken into account in the estimation of the frontier (Johnson and Kuosmanen 2011). In our empirical analysis, the contextual factors are represented by socioeconomic and demographic factors that should be affecting the output, so the ability of the StoNEZD approach to deal with such correlations represents a main advantage with respect to the conventional DEA two-stage model (Eskelinen and Kuosmanen 2013).

Given the CNLS residuals ε_{it}, it is possible to estimate the individual efficiency scores in a second stage by using parametric tools that have been widely used in previous literature. Firstly, in order to disentangle inefficiency from noise, we use the well-known method of moments (Aigner et al. 1977). The use of this technique requires additional parametric assumptions regarding the distributions of inefficiency and noise. We assume a half-normal distribution for the inefficiency term and a normal distribution for the noise term. As is typical in most regression models, the CNLS residuals sum to zero; thus, the second and the third central moments of the residual distribution are

$$\begin{aligned}
\widehat{M}_2 &= \textstyle\sum_{i=1}^{n} \left(\hat{\varepsilon}_{it}\right)^2 / (n-1) \\
\widehat{M}_3 &= \textstyle\sum_{i=1}^{n} \left(\hat{\varepsilon}_{it}\right)^3 / (n-1)
\end{aligned} \tag{5}$$

The second moment is simply the variance of the distribution, and the third is a component of the skewness:

$$\begin{aligned}
M_2 &= \left[\tfrac{\pi-2}{\pi}\right] \sigma_u^2 + \sigma_v^2 \\
M_3 &= \left(\sqrt{\tfrac{2}{\pi}}\right) \left[1 - \tfrac{4}{\pi}\right] \sigma_u^3
\end{aligned} \tag{6}$$

Note that the third moment only depends on the parameter σ_u. Thus, given the estimated $\hat{M}_3$,we can estimate σ_u and σ_v as

$$\begin{aligned}
\hat{\sigma}_u &= \sqrt[3]{\frac{\hat{M}_3}{\left(\sqrt{\frac{2}{\pi}}\right)\left[1-\frac{4}{\pi}\right]}} \\
\hat{\sigma}_v &= \sqrt{\hat{M}_2 - \left[\tfrac{\pi-2}{\pi}\right] \sigma_u^2}
\end{aligned} \tag{7}$$

Subsequently, parametric techniques can be used to estimate inefficiency measures of performance. Originally, Johnson and Kuosmanen (2011) proposed the well-known firm-specific inefficiency estimator developed by Jondrow et al. (1982). However, Andor and Hesse (2014) emphasized that it is not a consistent estimator of μ_{it}, so they proposed to use the Battese and Coelli (1988) estimator:

$$\hat{E}\left(\exp\left(-u_{it}\right) | \hat{\varepsilon}_{it}\right) = \frac{\Phi\left(\hat{\mu}_{*it}/\hat{\sigma}_{*u} - \hat{\sigma}_{*v}\right)}{\Phi\left(\hat{\mu}_{*it}/\hat{\sigma}_{*u}\right)} \cdot exp\left(\frac{1}{2}\hat{\sigma}_*^2 - \hat{\mu}_{*it}\right) \tag{8}$$

where Φ is the cumulative distribution function of the standard normal distribution, with $\mu_* = -\varepsilon_{it}\sigma_u^2/\sigma^2$, $\sigma_*^2 = \sigma_u^2\sigma_v^2/\sigma^2(\sigma^2 = \sigma_u^2 + \sigma_v^2)$ and being $\varepsilon_{it} = \hat{\varepsilon}_{it} - \hat{\sigma}_u\sqrt{2/\pi}$ the estimator of the composite error term. As we have different estimations of efficiency for each unit ($\hat{u}_{i,t}$), the average efficiency of each unit i during the whole time period considered is calculated as the mean of estimates for different periods: $\hat{u}_i = \frac{1}{T}\sum_{t=1}^{T}\hat{u}_{i,t}$.

Finally, it is worth mentioning that the StoNEZD estimator for $\boldsymbol{\delta}$ has some desirable properties, since it is shown to be statistically unbiased, consistent, asymptotically normally distributed, and converge at the standard parametric rate ($n^{1/2}$) (see Kuosmanen et al. 2015 and Yagi et al. 2018 for details). Therefore, standard techniques from regression analysis like t-tests or confidence intervals can be easily applied to test the statistical significance of $\boldsymbol{\delta}$ effect.

4 Data and Variables

We use a sample of 154 Spanish municipalities from the region of Catalonia with a population between 5000 and 50,000 inhabitants. Although there are many more municipalities in this region (735 with less 5000 inhabitants and 55 with more than 50,000 inhabitants), the database has been confined to these municipalities in order to assure some level of homogeneity with respect to both local government organization and structure and their respective competencies. Moreover, sampling was conditioned by the availability in the different consulted information sources of information on the variables accounted for in the empirical application for the entirety of the period under review, as discussed below. Table 2 reports a classification of the municipalities into three categories according to their population size.

The database has a panel structure, covering the eight-year period from 2005 to 2012; thus, we have a total number of 1232 observations. The selected period can be divided into two subperiods: one of economic prosperity and a term where the availability of local government resources shrank with the advent of the global financial crisis. Note, in this respect, that the start of the crisis is usually dated in the year 2008. However, it did not actually affect local authority budgets until 2010 because the amount of resources provided to municipalities through the intergovernmental transfer system depends on the trend in the state tax revenue growth rate, and the definitive value of this indicator is calculated with a lag of 2 years.

Regarding the selection of variables included in our model, the inputs used are personnel expenditures, other current expenditures (these are expenditures in goods and services, financial expenditures, and current transfers), and capital expenditures (real investments and capital transfers). All inputs used are measured in euros and should approximate the cost of the municipal services offered. Additionally, the inclusion of capital expenditure accounts for the level of local investment in regular services, as well as the maintenance and new equipment available throughout the period. These inputs are in line with most previous empirical studies conducted in the Spanish context (e.g., Balaguer et al. 2007; Balaguer and Prior 2009; Zafra-Gómez and Muñiz 2010, or Bosch et al. 2012). The data were gathered from the budget settlements of the municipalities compiled by the Ministry of Finance and Public Administration. Original values were denominated in millions of nominal euros, but they have been converted to real values using a deflator (2010 = 100) according to the evolution of the consumer price index.

A more complex task is to select variables to represent the output, as local public services are troublesome to measure due to their intangibility and indivisibility, plus the nonexistence of market prices serving as a reference (De Borger and Kerstens 1996a). Most studies use proxy variables related to services offered by local governments as a possible solution. In our case, we have selected four variables representing the local services provided, including the number of light points, tons of collected waste, length of the water pipeline section, and kilometers of surfaced main roads and streets. The information regarding all these variables was collected from the Infrastructure and Local Equipment Survey conducted by the Ministry of Finance and Public Administration.[6] In addition, we also gathered information about the seasonal population of the

Table 2 Number of municipalities and population size

Size	Number of municipalities
5000–10,000 inhabitants	73
10,000–20,000 inhabitants	47
20,000–50,00 inhabitants	34

Source: Own elaboration

[6]The Infrastructure and Local Equipment Survey provides information for municipalities with a population of less than 50,000 inhabitants. Unfortunately, information on the Catalan municipalities for the years 2006, 2007, and 2012 is missing from this database. On this ground, we were obliged to impute the values for the above years based on the information from adjacent years. In fact, for 2006 and 2007, we calculated

Table 3 Correlation coefficients among output variables

Correlations	Population	Streetlights	Waste	Water	Roads
Population	1.0000				
Streetlights	0.6761	1.0000			
Waste	0.7410	0.6041	1.0000		
Water	0.3245	0.3861	0.4020	1.0000	
Roads	0.4190	0.5042	0.4483	0.3671	1.0000

Source: Own elaboration

Table 4 Results of the principal component analysis for the output factor

	Initial eigenvalues			Squared sums of saturations		
Component	Total	Variance %	Aggregate %	Total	Variance %	Aggregate %
1	2.874	68.526	68.526	2.874	68.526	68.526
2	0.586	16.459	84.985			
3	0.409	9.758	94.743			
4	0.179	3.706	98.449			
5	0.028	1.551	100.000			

Source: Own elaboration

municipality from the Catalan Statistics Institute. This variable is commonly used in the literature to approximate the wide range of general services for which there is no special-purpose measure (Narbón-Perpiñá and De Witte 2018a).

All these indicators were highly correlated among themselves (see Table 3); thus, we have aggregated all the variables into one composite indicator following the same criterion adopted in many previous studies (e.g., Nijkamp and Suzuki 2009; Bosch et al. 2012; Nakazawa 2014; Yusfany 2015; Cordero et al. 2017b). To do this, we applied principal component analysis, according to which we identified one factor that explains 67.312% of the variance of the analyzed outputs (see Table 4). In our model, this component accounts for the output representing all the different services offered by local governments.[7]

We also gathered information on several variable indicators representing the context or environment in which the municipalities operate that may have an influence on their efficiency levels, as inferred from the evidence reported in previous literature (Narbón-Perpiñá and De Witte 2018b). First, we account for the income level of the population living in the municipality (z_1), since we presume that the demand for local public services may vary with income (De Borger et al. 1994; Hayes et al. 1998). However, we cannot anticipate whether this influence will be positive or negative, since some authors argue that higher-income citizens who pay greater taxes will be more demanding to require a more efficient provision of local services, while others consider that those citizens may be less motivated to monitor expenditures, which would lead to lower levels of efficiency.

Second, we also include the population density (z_2), that is, the number of inhabitants of each municipality divided by its extension expressed in square kilometers. Again, the influence of this variable is not, a priori, clear since we consider different alternatives on the effect it can have on efficiency. On the one hand, we can expect that municipalities with higher values of this variable should be more efficient, since they can take advantage of the reduced costs associated to economies of scale when population is more concentrated. On the other hand, if the population concentration is larger, problems of agglomeration might arise; thus, the provision of municipal services would be less efficient. Likewise, we consider the levels of net debt (z_3) compiled by the Ministry of Finance and Public Administration.[8] In this case, we expect that municipalities with higher levels of debt will be more inefficient, since they have to employ more resources to attend debt interests and amortization payments; thus, they cannot devote them to the provision of local services.

However, it is also possible that this variable can have a positive influence on efficiency, since debt can be the result of past investments on equipment that enhance current efficiency. Finally, we also incorporate a dummy variable representing the location of the municipality and, more specifically, whether it is located along the coast (z_4). Our intuition is that coastal municipalities are economically more attractive and should have more prospects of increasing their tax receipts; thus, they should be able to achieve higher levels of efficiency. Thus, being placed in a coastal location should have a positive relation

moving averages using information with respect to 2005, 2008, and 2009, whereas, for 2012, we projected the value according to the average annual growth rate for 2010 and 2011.

[7]The component values were rescaled by adding the maximum negative value to all the values to assure that the variable values accounted for in the model are all positive.

[8]The variable used is outstanding local authority debt as of 31/12 of the current year according to the Public Finance and Debt System.

Table 5 Descriptive statistics of the variables (2005–2012)

			2005	2006	2007	2008	2009	2010	2011	2012
Outputs	Seasonal population	Mean	13,809	14,244	14,860	14,908	15,132	15,247	15,200	15,480
	(inhabitants)	S.D.	10,046	10,367	10,994	10,736	10,813	10,864	10,961	11,034
	Streetlights	Mean	2636	3854	3854	2906	2907	2914	2974	2864
		S.D.	2337	8259	8259	3652	2665	2669	3129	2404
	Waste	Mean	9992	9944	9947	10,263	9199	8179	7591	7838
	(tons)	S.D.	10,246	9633	9632	12,819	9341	8619	7677	7951
	Water	Mean	14,663	15,114	15,114	15,565	17,076	15,644	16,246	15,901
	(length in meters)	S.D.	17,382	17,841	17,841	19,995	25,029	18,971	19,507	19,037
	Main roads	Mean	53,308	54,020	54,020	54,731	57,202	57,138	56,549	56,944
	streets (squared kms)	S.D.	36,465	36,025	36,025	38,806	42,079	42,075	42,395	42,169
	Composite	Mean	1.25	1.28	1.30	1.31	1.34	1.32	1.28	1.31
	indicator	S.D.	0.93	0.98	0.98	1.03	1.05	1.04	0.99	1.02
Inputs	Personnel expenditure	Mean	4,069,524	4,525,104	4,861,945	5,413,495	5,746,083	5,786,543	5,678,651	5,132,663
	(euros)	S.D.	2,929,805	3,238,969	3,413,241	3,759,177	4,016,684	3,996,612	3,896,236	3,539,385
	Current expenditure	Mean	5,400,360	6,175,236	7,007,991	7,623,797	7,672,987	7,422,577	7,338,642	7,371,398
	(euros)	S.D.	4,227,028	4,862,012	5,463,351	6,013,976	6,132,659	5,909,017	5,716,280	5,767,001
	Capital expenditure	Mean	2,730,953	3,945,966	4,924,731	4,534,084	6,136,431	4,962,174	3,165,297	1,486,436
	(euros)	S.D.	2,266,032	3,338,553	3,821,738	3,674,354	5,346,296	4,340,435	2,912,134	1,652,129
Contextual factors	Income pc	Mean	15,416	16,411	17,143	17,875	17,941	16,619	16,661	16,674
	(euros)	S.D.	2732	3223	3181	3274	3608	2346	2236	3441
	Population density	Mean	856	958	973	935	951	979	890	968
	(inhabitants)	S.D.	1387	1434	1432	1418	1408	1475	984	1480
	Coastal area	Mean	0.29	0.29	0.29	0.29	0.29	0.29	0.29	0.29
		S.D.	0.46	0.46	0.46	0.46	0.46	0.46	0.46	0.46
	Debt pc	Mean	3.14	3.05	2.96	2.85	3.21	3.35	3.31	3.39
	(euros)	S.D.	4.77	4.65	4.52	4.37	4.94	5.00	4.84	5.36

Source: Own elaboration

to efficiency. However, the sea municipalities can be subject to seasonality, which would imply having a negative correlation with efficiency.

Table 5 presents the descriptive statistics of all the variables used in our empirical analysis for each evaluated year. The structure of most of the output indicators is similar, that is, there is widespread growth up to the maximum values about halfway through the studied period, followed by a slight drop. The inputs evolve similarly; thus, it can be observed that, during the period of the peak of financial crisis (2009–2012), the inputs have been decreased on average terms alongside with municipalities' income levels. On the other hand, the socioeconomic indicators are much more constant, although the income experienced a small decrease after the crisis, while the levels of debt have slightly increased.

5 Empirical Results

In this section we present the efficiency scores estimated, taking into account the contextual variables using the StoNEZD method described in Sect. 3. Table 6 summarizes the main descriptive statistics (median, maximum, minimum, and standard deviation, along with first- and third-quartile values) of all the units evaluated in a dynamic context, that is, 154 municipalities over an eight-year period. We can observe that the mean efficiency is 0.70, which implies that there is still room for improvement in many municipalities. We can also observe that the standard deviation is relatively low (5%), which implies that most units have efficiency values close to the mean. This can be seen much better in Fig. 1, which displays the distribution of efficiency estimates obtained using nonparametric kernel density methods. This allows us to identify a higher concentration of units positioned left to the mean value represented by the vertical line.

Table A1 included in the Appendix reports the ranking of municipalities according to their average estimated efficiency score and their population size. Here we can observe that most of those placed in the top positions are municipalities with a relatively high number of inhabitants, while those placed in the bottom have a smaller size. This evidence can be summarized

Table 6 Descriptive statistics of efficiency estimates

Mean	SD	Min	1Q	Median	3Q	Max
0.7058	0.0529	0.5743	0.6694	0.7022	0.7364	0.8534

Source: Own elaboration

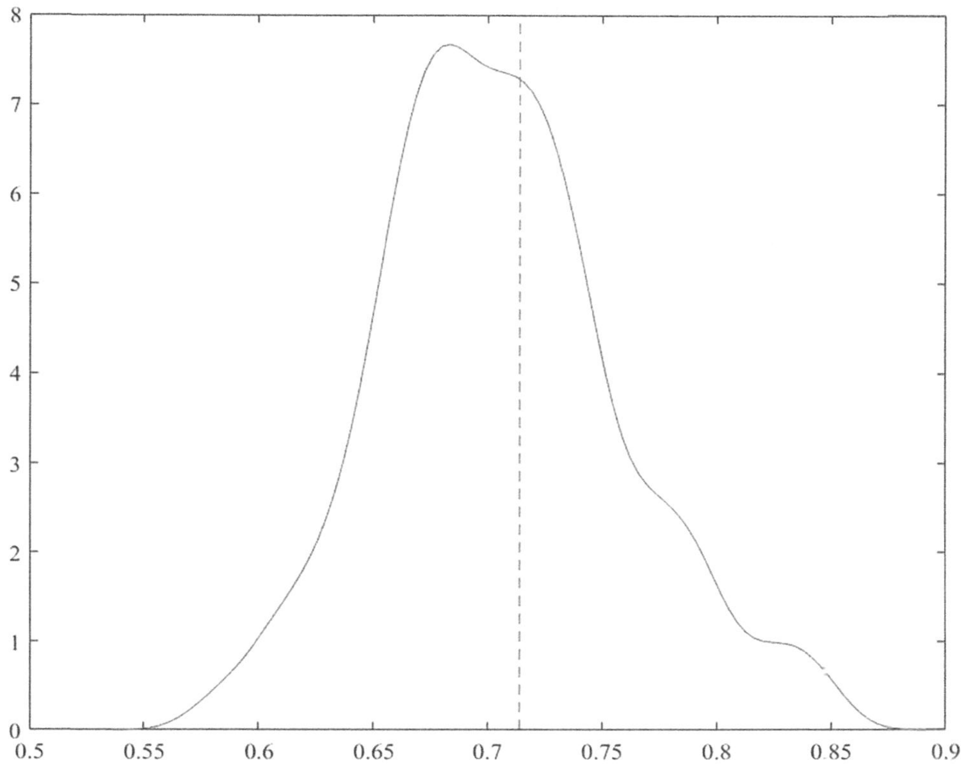

Source: Own elaboration

Fig. 1 Distribution of efficiencies. (Source: Own elaboration)

Table 7 Average efficiency levels for different sizes

Size of municipalities	Mean efficiency
5000–10,000 inhabitants	0.6831
10,000–20,000 inhabitants	0.7085
20,000–50,000 inhabitants	0.7615

Source: Own elaboration

by the average efficiency scores displayed in Table 7, in which we distinguish among three categories in order to compare their efficiency levels. We notice that large municipalities clearly outperform small and medium municipalities (the gap between small/medium municipalities is less than 2%, but the difference widens to almost 6% when compared to larger ones). The primary explanation for these results is that larger municipalities are better able to exploit economies of scale, as shown by several previous studies (e.g., Revelli 2010 or Pérez-López et al. 2015). Moreover, they are better able to increase their resources through tax revenues, whereas both small and medium municipalities are more dependent on government funding.

As we consider the dynamic structure provided by using panel data, we are also able to examine how they have evolved over the analyzed period. Figure 2 reveals that efficiency estimates declined during the initial years and then remained almost stagnant with the onset of the crisis. However, we can observe a small improvement in the last year, although it was not enough to regain the values reached at the beginning of the period. Again, if we explore the evolution of efficiency considering different types of municipalities depending on their size (Fig. 3), we can also notice that larger ones have maintained higher efficiency levels than the rest throughout the period. Actually, larger local governments have hardly experienced any changes in their efficiency levels, while small- and medium-sized municipalities suffered a slight decrease in the first years, then maintained stable when the economic crisis arrive, and, finally, experienced a small improvement in the last year (2012).

Source: Own elaboration

Fig. 2 Evolution of average efficiency levels for all municipalities. (Source: Own elaboration)

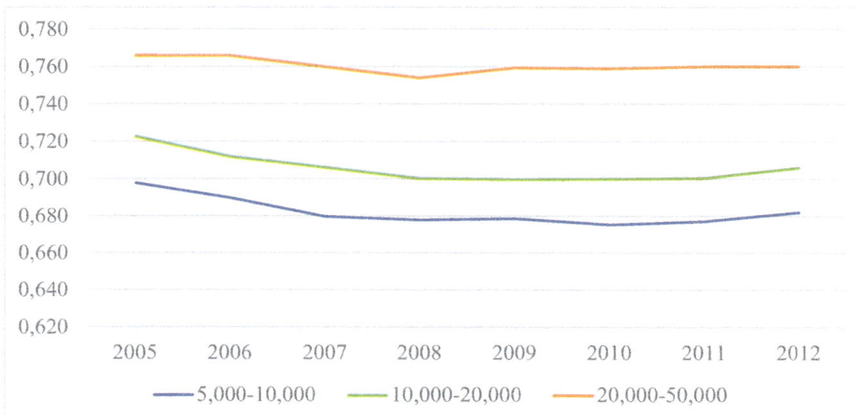

Source: Own elaboration

Fig. 3 Evolution of average efficiency levels by population size. (Source: Own elaboration)

Finally, in order to examine the average effect of economic and demographic variables included as contextual variables in the model, Table 8 reports the values of the δ parameter estimated for each variable and the related statistics. We find that all contextual variables (income, population density, debt, and location in a coastal area) have a highly significant effect on efficiency levels. The estimated parameters of the first three variables have a positive value, which implies a negative effect on efficiency. Specifically, with respect to incomes, this result corroborates previous evidence already reported in several empirical studies, demonstrating that relatively richer municipalities exercise less control over municipal activities (Bosch et al. 2012; Ashworth et al. 2014; Cruz and Marques 2014). Regarding the population density, although the influence on municipal efficiency is also negative, the value of the coefficient is so small that we can consider that this effect is practically nonexistent. This is a finding that matches other earlier studies referred to Spanish municipalities (Giménez and Prior 2007) and also for other countries (e.g., Ashworth et al. 2014 or Cordero et al. 2017a). For the debt, the result obtained also confirm our intuition about the negative influence of devoting larger amounts of resources for interest payment and debt repayment, as demonstrated in some previous works (e.g., Geys and Moesen 2009; Bönisch et al. 2011 or Cruz and Marques 2014). Finally, we identify a clearly positive effect (negative coefficient) for the location of the municipality in a coastal area, which leads us to consider that the positive effects of their higher levels of development appear to be greater than the potential negative effects that seasonality might generate as previously demonstrated in other empirical studies (e.g., Cordero et al. 2017a).

Table 8 Effect of contextual variables (δ)

Contextual variable	$\hat{\delta}$	t-statistic
Income per capita	0.012174***	93.2467
Population density	0.000124***	23.7644
Debt per capita	0.028717***	22.9907
Coastal area	−0.224653***	22.5435

Source: Own elaboration

6 Concluding Remarks

In this chapter, we have evaluated the global efficiency of a sample of medium-sized municipalities (with a population ranging from 5000 to 50,000 inhabitants) from the Spanish region of Catalonia over a period of 8 years (2005–2012) in which there have been important changes in their economic situation due to the financial crisis. To conduct this empirical analysis, we used an innovative approach known as StoNEZD, which allows us to account for the potential existence of noise in data and also distinguish the effect of contextual variables affecting local performance in a dynamic framework. This option is a remarkable improvement upon most of the empirical studies reported in previous literature, which frequently fail to incorporate information about contextual variables in the estimation of the efficiency measures of performance. Therefore, they usually overlook the existing heterogeneity across local authorities. Additionally, it is also worth mentioning that most previous studies which focused on analyzing the global efficiency of local governments are based on cross-sectional data; thus, they are not able to examine the trend over a period of time.

Our results show that municipalities experienced a slight decrease in their efficiency levels during the economic boom phase until 2008, then remained almost stagnant during several years, and, finally, show a small improvement in the last year evaluated (2012). Therefore, it seems that local governments were able to react to the changes produced by the financial crisis, managing to maintain similar levels of local service provision despite having fewer resources. However, this evidence can only be considered as a preliminary approximation of the potential influence of the financial crisis on the performance of Spanish municipalities; thus, it would be necessary to extend the analysis to municipalities from other regions (apart from Catalonia) and also explore the evolution in the more recent years of economic recovery. Unfortunately, this was not possible in our study because data about local public services provided by local authorities as well as several economic indicators were not available. Likewise, we would be better able to fine-tune our findings if we had access to qualitative data that allows us to make a better assessment of municipal services provision and round out the results of this study based solely on quantitative indicators.

Other relevant finding is that larger municipalities, that is, those with population higher than 20,000 inhabitants, are clearly more efficient than those of smaller population size throughout the period under review. This leads to the conclusion that clustering into larger-sized municipalities may help to provide more efficient services, since that would imply benefit from lower administrative costs, increased purchasing power, and improved utilization of equipment (Andrews and Boyne 2009). This is a topic that has attracted the attention of many researchers in recent years, especially after the processes of merging municipalities that have taken place in several countries such as Australia (Marques et al. 2015; McQuestin et al. 2018), Denmark (Blom-Hansen et al. 2016), Portugal (Cordero et al. 2017a; Afonso and Venâncio 2019), or Switzerland (Steiner and Kaiser 2017).

Regarding the contextual variables, we find that all the economic and geographical variables representing the operational environment in which municipalities operate have a significant effect on their efficiency. In particular, the factor with the most relevant effect on municipal performance is the location in a coastal area, although the level of income and debt also exert a significant influence. These results lead us to conclude that the estimation of measures indicative of local government performance that do not take into account contextual factors beyond the control of local authorities will be of very limited value.

Finally, it is worth to recognize some potential limitations of our study and some ideas for further research. First, we cannot interpret our results in a causal way, since it would entail neglecting the potential presence of endogeneity in data arising from selection bias or unobserved heterogeneity across municipalities. Thus, more research based on quasi-experimental methodologies is still needed as suggested by Narbón-Perpiña and De Witte (Narbón-Perpiñá and De Witte 2018a). Second, the StoNEZD method used for estimating efficiency measures presents the same peculiarities to be developed in a multi-output context with that of parametric methods since it is partially based on the SFA methodology. However, this issue has been tackled by Kuosmanen and Johnson (2017), who propose that the multi-output technology can be modeled within directional distance functions; thus, it seems that this limitation might be overcome in future empirical works. Likewise, the StoNEZD approach do not allow us to identify fully efficient units, since it imposes inefficient behavior on all the evaluated units in the sample; thus, we could also explore the possibility of using some alternative methods that can accommodate the presence of both efficient and inefficient firms in the sample such as the zero inefficiency stochastic model proposed by Kumbhakar et al. (2013) or the Bayesian approach suggested by Rho and Schmidt (2015).

Acknowledgments The authors would like to express their gratitude to the Regional Government of Extremadura (*Junta de Extremadura*) for supporting this research through grants IB16171 and GR18106. Carlos Díaz-Caro would also like to acknowledge the funding received from the Institute of Economics of Barcelona (IEB) and the Provincial Government of Barcelona through the Catalan Local Government Research Aid.

Appendix

Table A.1 Rank of municipalities according to their efficiencies estimated with StoNEZD

Municipality	Efficiency score	Population
Olot	0.8464	33,813
Vic	0.8368	41,191
Vilafranca del Penedès	0.8223	39,035
Lloret de Mar	0.8165	40,837
Gavà	0.8150	46,488
Sant Feliu de Llobregat	0.8083	43,671
Sant Pere de Ribes	0.8043	29,149
Sitges	0.7962	29,039
Sant Vicenç dels Horts	0.7961	28,084
Sant Quirze del Vallès	0.7947	18,994
Palau-solità i Plegamans	0.7901	14,484
Tortosa	0.7890	34,734
Figueres	0.7843	45,262
Calafell	0.7837	24,672
Roses	0.7809	19,896
Blanes	0.7795	39,785
Igualada	0.7761	39,198
Salou	0.7729	26,601
Matadepera	0.7704	8669
Malgrat de Mar	0.7670	18,504
Cervelló	0.7623	8666
Martorell	0.7540	2807
Corbera de Llobregat	0.7530	14,231
Mont-roig del Camp	0.7506	12,702
Llinars del Vallès	0.7504	9477
Vila-seca	0.7483	22,052
Palafrugell	0.7477	2288
Santa Perpètua de Mogoda	0.7471	25,606

(continued)

Table A.1 (continued)

Municipality	Efficiency score	Population
Banyoles	0.7465	19,341
Premià de Dalt	0.7458	10,289
Tordera	0.7455	16,318
Caldes de Montbui	0.7430	17,271
Móra d'Ebre	0.7423	5704
Valls	0.7384	25,084
Vallirana	0.7374	14,549
Maçanet de la Selva	0.7341	7175
Tàrrega	0.7340	16,731
Calonge	0.7337	10,851
Castell-Platja d'Aro	0.7336	10,527
Pineda de Mar	0.7320	26,066
Castellar del Vallès	0.7304	23,363
Manlleu	0.7297	20,416
Montcada i Reixac	0.7293	34,689
Cervera	0.7277	9444
Esparreguera	0.7275	21,856
Parets del Vallès	0.7270	18,492
Sant Vicenç de Castellet	0.7267	9314
Sant Joan Despí	0.7262	32,792
Castelló d'Empúries	0.7259	11,794
Torelló	0.7254	13,883
Cabrils	0.7238	7140
Almacelles	0.7228	6728
Abrera	0.7197	11,870
Taradell	0.7196	6212
Bigues i Riells	0.7191	8781
Cambrils	0.7173	33,535
Torredembarra	0.7173	1531
Sant Feliu de Guíxols	0.7167	21,961
Santa Coloma de Farners	0.7158	12,448
Berga	0.7139	16,845
Balaguer	0.7137	16,952
Vacarisses	0.7129	6231
Alcarràs	0.7128	8755
Amposta	0.7117	21,434
Barberà del Vallès	0.7116	32,436
Olesa de Montserrat	0.7109	2398
Vidreres	0.7108	7732
Lliçà d'Amunt	0.7107	14,584
Santa Maria de Palautordera	0.7099	9196
Ripoll	0.7096	10,904
Argentona	0.7083	11,914
Santa Margarida de Montbui	0.7082	9689
Sant Antoni de Vilamajor	0.7066	5699
Cunit	0.7056	12,626
Sant Carles de la Ràpita	0.7045	15,232
Sils	0.7041	5702
Guissona	0.7028	6763
Sant Andreu de la Barca	0.7021	27,306
Sentmenat	0.7021	8521

(continued)

Table A.1 (continued)

Municipality	Efficiency score	Population
Sant Sadurní d'Anoia	0.7015	12,482
Sant Fost de Campsentelles	0.7012	8441
Cassà de la Selva	0.7009	9925
Sant Fruitós de Bages	0.6990	8227
Deltebre	0.6990	12,316
Santa Margarida i els Monjos	0.6960	7121
Navarcles	0.6958	5973
Moià	0.6946	5793
Puigcerdà	0.6936	8957
Begues	0.6936	6520
Alcanar	0.6935	10,658
Canet de Mar	0.6923	14,183
Roquetes	0.6923	8333
Agramunt	0.6922	5633
Cardedeu	0.6912	17,427
Masquefa	0.6875	8373
Artés	0.6861	5566
Viladecavalls	0.6849	7411
Alella	0.6848	9610
Santa Coloma de Cervelló	0.6837	7964
Ulldecona	0.6822	7372
Cubelles	0.6819	14,375
Alpicat	0.6814	6203
Calella	0.6802	18,529
Caldes de Malavella	0.6797	7071
Centelles	0.6797	7282
Tona	0.6796	8108
Canovelles	0.6788	1609
Sant Just Desvern	0.6769	15,874
Vilafant	0.6739	5523
Arenys de Mar	0.6735	1503
Vielha e Mijaran	0.6731	5454
Pallejà	0.6719	11,255
Palamós	0.6714	17,813
Vilassar de Dalt	0.6714	8865
Riudoms	0.6706	6530
Súria	0.6705	6218
Arenys de Munt	0.6703	8530
Montornès del Vallès	0.6702	16,192
Sallent	0.6687	6875
Llagostera	0.6687	8157
Vilanova del Camí	0.6686	12,585
Torrelles de Llobregat	0.6684	5740
Solsona	0.6679	9201
Arbúcies	0.6676	6741
Piera	0.6674	15,009
Polinyà	0.6671	8106
Mollerussa	0.6666	14,729
Cardona	0.6664	5064
Torroella de Montgrí	0.6655	11,494
Teià	0.6652	6154

(continued)

Table A.1 (continued)

Municipality	Efficiency score	Population
Montblanc	0.6647	7356
Sant Vicenç de Montalt	0.6639	5878
Sant Hilari Sacalm	0.6632	5753
Lliçà de Vall	0.6605	6394
Alcover	0.6598	5143
Sant Joan de Vilatorrada	0.6573	1078
Premià de Mar	0.6489	28,145
Anglès	0.6467	5719
Llançà	0.6442	5105
Montgat	0.6423	10,859
Sant Andreu de Llavaneres	0.6407	10,541
Capellades	0.6402	5439
Castellbisbal	0.6378	12,407
Roda de Ter	0.6377	6172
Montmeló	0.6354	8830
Tossa de Mar	0.6307	5952
Vilassar de Mar	0.6273	19,918
Palafolls	0.6262	9027
Sant Pol de Mar	0.6156	5073
Sant Esteve Sesrovires	0.6141	7510
Constantí	0.6108	6774
Tremp	0.6040	6515
Tiana	0.5961	8151
Vandellòs i l'Hospitalet de l'Infant	0.5838	5985

References

Afonso, A., & Fernandes, S. (2006). Measuring local government spending efficiency: Evidence for the Lisbon region. *Regional Studies, 40*(1), 39–53.

Afonso, A., & Fernandes, S. (2008). Assessing and explaining the relative efficiency of local government. *The Journal of Socio-Economic, 37*, 1946–1979.

Afonso, A., & Venâncio, A. (2019). *Local territorial reform and regional spending efficiency*. Local Government Studies, 1–23.

Agasisti, T., Dal Bianco, A., & Griffini, M. (2016). The public sector efficiency in Italy: The case of Lombardy municipalities in the provision of the essential public services. *Economia Pubblica, 26*, 59–84.

Aiello, F., & Bonanno, G. (2018). Explaining differences in efficiency: A meta-study on local government literature. *Journal of Economic Surveys, 33*, 999.

Aigner, D., Lovell, C. K., & Schmidt, P. (1977). Formulation and estimation of stochastic frontier production function models. *Journal of Econometrics, 6*(1), 21–37.

Andor, M., & Hesse, F. (2014). The StoNED age: The departure into a new era of efficiency analysis? A Monte Carlo comparison of StoNED and the "oldies" (SFA and DEA). *Journal of Productivity Analysis, 41*(1), 85–109.

Andrews, R., & Boyne, G. A. (2009). Size, structure and administrative overheads: An empirical analysis of English local authorities. *Urban Studies, 46*, 739–759.

Asatryan, Z., & De Witte, K. (2015). Direct democracy and local government efficiency. *European Journal of Political Economy, 39*, 58–66.

Ashworth, J., Geys, B., Heyndels, B., & Wille, F. (2014). Competition in the political arena and local government performance. *Applied Economics, 46*(19), 2264–2276.

Athanassopoulos, A., & Triantis, K. (1998). Assessing aggregate cost efficiency and the related policy implications for Greek local municipalities. *Information Systems and Operational Research, 36*(3), 66–83.

Balaguer-Coll, M. T., & Prior, D. (2009). Short-and long-term evaluation of efficiency and quality. An application to Spanish municipalities. *Applied Economics, 41*, 2991–3002.

Balaguer-Coll, M. T., Prior, D., & Tortosa-Ausina, E. (2007). On the determinants of local government performance: A two stage nonparametric approach. *European Economic Review, 51*, 425–451.

Balaguer-Coll, M. T., Prior, D., & Tortosa-Ausina, E. (2010). Decentralization and efficiency of local government. *The Annals of Regional Science, 45*(3), 571–601.

Balaguer-Coll, M. T., Prior, D., & Tortosa-Ausina, E. (2013). Output complexity, environmental conditions, and the efficiency of municipalities. *Journal of Productivity Analysis, 39*, 303–324.

Battese, G. E., & Coelli, T. J. (1988). Prediction of firm-level technical efficiencies with a generalized frontier production function and panel data. *Journal of Econometrics, 38*(3), 387–399.

Benito, B., Solana, J., & Moreno, M. (2014). Explaining efficiency in municipal services providers. *Journal of Productivity Analysis, 42*, 225–239.
Blom-Hansen, J., Houlberg, K., Serritzlew, S., & Treisman, D. (2016). Jurisdiction size and local government policy expenditure: Assessing the effect of municipal amalgamation. *American Political Science Review, 110*(4), 812–831.
Boetti, L., Piacenza, M., & Turati, G. (2012). Decentralization and local governments' performance: How does fiscal autonomy affect spending efficiency? *FinanzArchiv: Public Finance Analysis, 68*(3), 269–302.
Bönisch, P., Haug, P., Illy, A. & Schreier, L. (2011). Municipality size and efficiency of local public services: Does size matter?. *IWH Discussion papers*, 18/2011, Halle (Germany)
Borge, L. E., Falch, T., & Tovmo, P. (2008). Public sector efficiency: The roles of political and budgetary institutions, fiscal capacity, and democratic participation. *Public Choice, 136*(3–4), 475–495.
Bosch, N., Espasa, M., & Mora, T. (2012). Citizen control and the efficiency of local public services. *Environment and Planning C: Government and Policy, 30*(2), 1–248.
Bosch, N., Pedraja, F., & Suárez-Pandiello, J. (2000). Measuring the efficiency of Spanish municipal refuse collection services. *Local Government Studies, 26*(3), 71–90.
Bruns, C., & Himmler, O. (2011). Newspaper circulation and local government efficiency. *Scandinavian Journal of Economics, 113*(2), 470–492.
Byrnes, J., Crase, L., Dollery, B., & Villano, R. (2010). The relative economic efficiency of urban water utilities in regional New South Wales and Victoria. *Resource and Energy Economics, 32*(3), 439–455.
Charnes, A., Cooper, W. W., & Rhodes, E. (1978). Measuring the efficiency of decision making units. *European Journal of Operational Research, 2*(6), 429–444.
Cordero, J. M., Pedraja-Chaparro, F., Pisaflores, E. C., & Polo, C. (2017a). Efficiency assessment of Portuguese municipalities using a conditional nonparametric approach. *Journal of Productivity Analysis, 48*(1), 1–24.
Cordero, J. M., Díaz-Caro, C., & Polo, C. (2017b). Measuring efficiency in Catalan municipalities using a dynamic conditional model. *Revista de Economía Aplicada, 25*(75), 29–51.
Cruz, N. F., & Marques, R. C. (2014). Revisiting the determinants of local government performance. *Omega, 44*, 91–103.
Cuadrado-Ballesteros, B., García-Sanchez, I. M., & Prado-Lorenzo, J. M. (2013). Effect of modes of public services delivery on the efficiency of local governments: A two-stage approach. *Utilities Policy, 26*(2), 23–35.
Cuadrado-Ballesteros, B., & Bisogno, M. (2018). Efficiency as a determinant of financial condition: An assessment of Italian and Spanish local governments. *International Public Management Journal*. https://doi.org/10.1080/10967494.2018.1476426.
Daraio, C., & Simar, L. (2005). Introducing environmental variables in nonparametric frontier models: A probabilistic approach. *Journal of Productivity Analysis, 24*(1), 93–121.
Daraio, C., & Simar, L. (2007). Conditional nonparametric frontier models for convex and nonconvex technologies: A unifying approach. *Journal of Productivity Analysis, 28*(1–2), 13–32.
De Borger, B., & Kerstens, K. (1996a). Cost efficiency of Belgian local governments: A comparative analysis of FDH, DEA and econometric approaches. *Regional Science and Urban Economics, 26*, 145–170.
De Borger, B., & Kerstens, K. (1996b). Radial and non-radial measures of technical efficiency: An empirical illustration for Belgian local Governments using an FDH reference technology. *Journal of Productivity Analysis, 7*, 41–62.
De Borger, B., Kerstens, K., Moesen, W., & Vanneste, J. (1994). Explaining differences in productive efficiency: An application to Belgian municipalities. *Public Choice, 80*(3–4), 339–358.
Deprins, D., Simar, L., & Tulkens, H. (1984). Measuring labor inefficiency in post offices. In P. Marchand, P. Pestieau, & H. Tulkens (Eds.), *The performance of public enterprises: Concepts and Measurements* (pp. 243–267). Amsterdam: North Holland.
De Witte, K., & Geys, B. (2011). Evaluating efficient public good provision: Theory and evidence from a generalised conditional efficiency model for public libraries. *Journal of Urban Economics, 69*(3), 319–327.
De Witte, K., & Geys, B. (2013). Citizen coproduction and efficient public good provision: Theory and evidence from local public libraries. *European Journal of Operational Research, 224*(3), 592–602.
Doumpos, M., & Cohen, S. (2014). Applying data envelopment analysis on accounting data to asses and optimize the efficiency of Greek local governments. *Omega, 46*, 74–85.
Eskelinen, J., & Kuosmanen, T. (2013). Intertemporal efficiency analysis of sales teams of a bank: Stochastic semi-nonparametric approach. *Journal of Banking & Finance, 37*(12), 5163–5175.
Fogarty, J., & Mugera, A. (2013). Local government efficiency: Evidence from Western Australia. *Australian Economic Review, 46*(3), 300–311.
García-Sánchez, I. M. (2009). Measuring the efficiency of local police force. *European Journal of Law and Economics, 27*(1), 59–77.
Geys, B., Heinemann, F., & Kalb, A. (2010). Voter involvement, fiscal autonomy and public sector efficiency: Evidence from German municipalities. *European Journal of Political Economy, 26*(2), 265–278.
Geys, B., Heinemann, F., & Kalb, A. (2013). Local government efficiency in German municipalities. *Raumforschung und Raumordnung, 71*(4), 283–293.
Geys, B., & Moesen, W. (2009). Exploring sources of local government technical inefficiency: Evidence from Flemish municipalities. *Public Finance and Management, 9*, 1–29.
Giménez, V. M., & Prior, D. (2007). Long-and short-term cost efficiency frontier evaluation: Evidence from Spanish local governments. *Fiscal Studies, 28*(1), 121–139.
Hayes, K. J., Razzolini, L., & Ross, L. B. (1998). Bureaucratic choice and nonoptimal provision of public goods: Theory and evidence. *Public Choice, 94*(1–2), 1–20.
Hildreth, C. (1954). Point estimates of ordinates of concave functions. *Journal of the American Statistical Association, 49*(267), 598–619.
Jondrow, J., Lovell, C. K., Materov, I. S., & Schmidt, P. (1982). On the estimation of technical inefficiency in the stochastic frontier production function model. *Journal of Econometrics, 19*(2–3), 233–238.
Johnson, A. L., & Kuosmanen, T. (2011). One-stage estimation of the effects of operational conditions and practices on productive performance: Asymptotically normal and efficient, root-n consistent StoNEZD method. *Journal of Productivity Analysis, 36*(2), 219–230.
Kalb, A., Geys, B., & Heinemann, F. (2012). Value for money? German local government efficiency in a comparative perspective. *Applied Economics, 44*(2), 201–218.

Kumbhakar, S. C., Parmeter, C. F., & Tsionas, E. G. (2013). A zero inefficiency stochastic frontier model. *Journal of Econometrics, 172*(1), 66–76.
Kuosmanen, T., & Johnson, A. L. (2010). Data envelopment analysis as nonparametric least-squares regression. *Operations Research, 58*, 149–160.
Kuosmanen, T., & Johnson, A. L. (2017). Modeling joint production of multiple outputs in StoNED: Directional distance function approach. *European Journal of Operational Research, 262*(2), 792–801.
Kuosmanen, T., & Kortelainen, M. (2012). Stochastic non-smooth envelopment of data: Semi-parametric frontier estimation subject to shape constraints. *Journal of Productivity Analysis, 38*(1), 11–28.
Kuosmanen, T., Johnson, A. L., & Saastamoinen, A. (2015). Stochastic nonparametric approach to efficiency analysis: A unified framework. In J. Zhu (Ed.), *Data envelopment analysis. A handbook of models and methods* (pp. 191–244). New York: Springer.
Kutlar, A., Bakirci, F., & Yüksel, F. (2012). An analysis on the economic effectiveness of municipalities in Turkey. *African Journal of Marketing Management, 4*(3), 80–98.
Loikkanen, H. A., & Susiluoto, I. (2005). Cost efficiency of Finnish municipalities in basic service provision 1994-2002. *Urban Public Economics Review, 4*, 39–64.
Marques, R. C., Kortt, M. A., & Dollery, B. (2015). Determining the optimal size of local government: The case of Tasmanian councils. *Australian Journal of Public Administration, 74*(2), 212–226.
McQuestin, D., Drew, J., & Dollery, B. (2018). Do municipal mergers improve technical efficiency? An empirical analysis of the 2008 Queensland municipal merger program. *Australian Journal of Public Administration, 77*(3), 442–455.
Meeusen, W., & Vandenbroeck, J. (1977). Efficiency estimation from Cobb-Douglas production functions with composed error. *International Economic Review, 18*(2), 435–445.
Nakazawa, K. (2013). Cost inefficiency of municipalities after amalgamation. *Procedia Economics and Finance, 5*, 581–588.
Nakazawa, K. (2014). Does the method of amalgamation affect cost inefficiency of the new municipalities? *Open Journal of Applied Sciences, 4*, 143–154.
Narbón-Perpiñá, I., & De Witte, K. (2018a). Local governments' efficiency: A systematic literature review–Part I. *International Transactions in Operational Research, 25*(2), 431–468.
Narbón-Perpiñá, I., & De Witte, K. (2018b). Local governments' efficiency: A systematic literature review–Part II. *International Transactions in Operational Research, 25*(4), 1107–1136.
Niaounakis, T., & Blank, J. (2017). Inter-municipal cooperation, economies of scale and cost efficiency: An application of stochastic frontier analysis to Dutch municipal tax departments. *Local Government Studies, 43*(4), 533–554.
Nijkamp, P., & Suzuki, S. (2009). A generalized goals-achievement model in data envelopment analysis: An application to efficiency improvement in local government finance in Japan. *Spatial Economic Analysis, 4*(3), 249–274.
Otsuka, A., Goto, M., & Sueyoshi, T. (2014). Cost-efficiency of Japanese local governments: Effects of decentralization and regional integration. *Regional Studies, Regional Science, 1*(1), 207–220.
Pacheco, F., Sanchez, R., & Villena, M. (2014). A longitudinal parametric approach to estimate local government efficiency. *MPRA paper*, 54918. http://mpra.ub.uni-muenchen.de/54918/
Pérez-López, G., Prior, D., & Zafra-Gómez, J. L. (2015). Rethinking new public management delivery forms and efficiency: Long-term effects in Spanish local government. *Journal of Public Administration Research and Theory, 25*(4), 1157–1183.
Pérez-López, G., Prior, D., & Zafra-Gómez, J. L. (2018). Temporal scale efficiency in DEA panel data estimations. An application to the solid waste disposal service in Spain. *Omega, 76*, 18–27.
Picazo-Tadeo, A. J., González-Gómez, F., & Sáez-Fernández, F. J. (2009). Accounting for operating environments in measuring water utilities' managerial efficiency. *The Service Industries Journal, 29*(6), 761–773.
Prado-Lorenzo, J. M., & García-Sánchez, I. M. (2007). Efficiency evaluation in municipal services: An application to the street lighting service in Spain. *Journal of Productivity Analysis, 27*(3), 149–162.
Prieto, A. M., & Zofio, J. L. (2001). Evaluating effectiveness in public provision of infrastructure and equipment: The case of Spanish municipalities. *Journal of Productivity Analysis, 15*, 41–58.
Revelli, F. (2010). Spend more, get more? An inquiry into English local government performance. *Oxford Economic Papers, 62*(1), 185–207.
Rho, S., & Schmidt, P. (2015). Are all firms inefficient? *Journal of Productivity Analysis, 43*(3), 327–349.
Ruggiero, J. (2007). A comparison of DEA and the stochastic frontier model using panel data. *International Transactions in Operational Research, 14*(3), 259–266.
Schmidt, P., & Sickles, R. C. (1984). Production frontiers and panel data. *Journal of Business and Economics Statistics, 2*(4), 367–374.
Settimi, C., Vidoli, F., Fusco, E., & Ballanti, D. (2014). Estimating technical efficiency in the Italian Municipalities. *Procedia Economics and Finance, 17*, 131–137.
Simar, L., & Wilson, P. W. (2007). Estimation and inference in two-stage, semi-parametric models of production processes. *Journal of Econometrics, 136*(1), 31–64.
Simar, L., & Wilson, P. W. (2011). Two-stage DEA: Caveat emptor. *Journal of Productivity Analysis, 36*(2), 205.
Simões, P., & Marques, R. C. (2012). On the economic performance of the waste sector. A literature review. *Journal of Environmental Management, 106*, 40–47.
Sørensen, R. J. (2014). Political competition, party polarization, and government performance. *Public Choice, 161*(3–4), 427–450.
Sousa, M. C., & Ramos, F. S. (1999). Measuring public spending efficiency in Brazilian municipalities: A nonparametric approach. In G. Westermann (Ed.), *Data envelopment analysis in the service sector* (pp. 237–267). Wiesbaden: Deutscher Universitäts-Verlag.
Sousa, M. C., & Stošić, B. (2005). Technical efficiency of the Brazilian municipalities: Correcting nonparametric frontier measurements for outliers. *Journal of Productivity Analysis, 24*(2), 157–181.
Steiner, R., & Kaiser, C. (2017). Effects of amalgamations: Evidence from Swiss municipalities. *Public Management Review, 19*(2), 232–252.
Sung, N. (2007). Information technology, efficiency and productivity: Evidence from Korean local governments. *Applied Economics, 39*(13), 1691–1703.
Van Den Eeckaut, P., Tulkens, H., & Jamar, M. A. (1993). Cost efficiency in Belgian municipalities. Cost efficiency in Belgium municipalities. In H. Fried, C. Lovell, & S. Schmidt (Eds.), *The measurement of productive efficiency: Techniques and applications* (pp. 300–334). New York: Oxford University Press.

Wang, H. J., & Schmidt, P. (2002). One-step and two-step estimation of the effects of exogenous variables on technical efficiency levels. *Journal of Productivity Analysis, 18*, 129–144.
Worthington, A. C. (2000). Cost efficiency in Australian local government: A comparative analysis of mathematical programming and econometric approaches. *Financial Accountability and Management, 16*(3), 201–224.
Worthington, A. C., & Dollery, B. E. (2000a). Measuring efficiency in local governments' planning and regulatory function. *Public Productivity & Management Review, 29*(2), 469–485.
Worthington, A. C., & Dollery, B. E. (2000b). An empirical survey of frontier efficiency measurement techniques in local government. *Local Government Studies, 26*(2), 23–52.
Yagi, D., Chen, Y., Johnson, A. L., & Kuosmanen, T. (2018). Shape-constrained kernel-weighted least squares: Estimating production functions for Chilean manufacturing industries. *Journal of Business & Economic Statistics*. in press. https://doi.org/10.1080/07350015.2018.1431128.
Yusfany, A. (2015). The efficiency of local governments and its influence factors. *International Journal of Technology Enhancements and Emerging Engineering Research, 4*(10), 219–241.
Zafra-Gómez, J. L., & Muñiz, M. (2010). Overcoming cost-inefficiencies within small municipalities: Improve financial condition or reduce the quality of public services? *Environment and Planning C: Government and Policy, 28*, 609–629.

The Impact of Land Consolidation on Livestock Production in Asturias' Parishes: A Spatial Production Analysis

Inmaculada Álvarez, Luis Orea, and José A. Pérez-Méndez

Abstract This chapter evaluates the impact of the land consolidation (LC) processes that have taken place in Asturias during the period 2001–2017. These processes have received European funds as they help to improve the economic activity in rural areas. In particular, the LC processes involve very localized public investments in infrastructures that favour accessibility and development not only in the local but also in adjacent areas. To evaluate the effect of LC processes on milk and beef production, we treat the parishes in Asturias as production units and estimate a set of multi-output distance functions. Our results indicate that LC contributes to increase parishes' livestock production, although those processes not always are accompanied by an increase in the number of farms. We also find that the (indirect) effect from LC processes implemented in neighbouring parishes is positive and even more relevant than the (direct) effect on the local LC processes.

Keywords Land consolidation · Multi-output distance function · Spatial effects

JEL Codes C21, C23, D24, Q15

1 Introduction

Land consolidation (LC) has been acknowledged as an effective instrument to add new farmland, improve land productivity and promote sustainable land use (see Zhou et al. 2019 and the references therein). It consists of two main components: land reallocation aiming to reduce land fragmentation (LF) and rural planning encompassing the provision of relevant infrastructure, e.g. roads and irrigation networks (Demetriou 2018). Although LC policies usually had agricultural goals initially, they have increasingly become instruments of rural sustainable development in Europe and in many countries around the world (Crecente et al. 2002).

The studies on LC and its effects are of great interest to those responsible for designing agrarian and rural development policies as well as for farmers and rural inhabitants. See the Appendix for a summary of the most recent literature on this topic. The literature on LC presents multiple approaches, and it is also related to research on the effects of LF and on the efficiency and productivity of agricultural holdings.

The effect of LF on agriculture has worried policymakers for a long time because it is expected to be a negative effect. LC policies are frequently implemented to soften the degree of LF. LF is expected to affect farm production negatively for several reasons. LF causes an increase in travelling time between fields, which induces both lower labour productivity and

The authors would like to thank the financial support obtained from the Regional Government of the Principality of Asturias in conjunction with FEDER (Grant FC-15-GRUPIN14-048). This chapter was also supported by the Spanish Ministry of Economics, Industry and Competitiveness (Grant MINECO-18-ECO2017-85788-R).

I. Álvarez (✉)
Department of Economics, Universidad Autónoma de Madrid, Madrid, Spain
e-mail: inmaculada.alvarez@uam.es

L. Orea
Department of Economics, University of Oviedo, Oviedo, Spain

J. A. Pérez-Méndez
Department of Accounting, University of Oviedo, Oviedo, Spain

J. Aparicio et al. (eds.), *Advances in Efficiency and Productivity II*, International Series in Operations Research & Management Science 287, https://doi.org/10.1007/978-3-030-41618-8_15

higher transport costs for inputs and outputs; LF reduces the efficiency of machines use; and land is lost when forming plot boundaries and access routes. Most empirical studies conclude that fragmentation negatively affects agricultural production (Wan and Cheng 2001; Rahman and Rahman 2008). In the case of the dairy sector, Del Corral et al. (2011) evaluate the effect of LF on milk production in a sample of Spanish farms located in Asturias and found a negative influence of LF on milk production. Additionally, based on a previous paper, Orea et al. (2015) found not only a significantly larger impact of LF on the productivity of extensive farms compared to intensive ones but also that LF significantly reduces the probability of using extensive milk production processes.

Regarding the LC literature, it generally finds that LC has exerted broad impacts on promoting agricultural production scale and increasing the competitiveness of agricultural products in Europe and other countries. For instance, Hiironen and Riekkinen (2016) evaluate a dozen of LC projects in Finland using standard statistical methods and production cost analyses. They found that LC improved the property structure and costs decreased 15%. Crecente et al. (2002) evaluate the economic, social and environmental effects by comparing consolidated and non-consolidated areas in Galicia, an autonomous region located in north-west Spain that is adjacent to the region examined in our paper (i.e. Asturias). A dominant traditional agricultural economy and a historical tradition of property inheritance by subdivision within families have produced a high degree of LF in these two regions. They show that LC contributes to retaining farmland in agricultural use and improves the population evolution in rural areas, although they observe changes in use from cropland to pasture land. Also using very disaggregated geospatial data at parish level, Miranda et al. (2006) conclude that LC has improved agricultural land structure by reducing the number of plots per holding, has reduced the generalized decline in the number of active holdings and has reduced the decline in the population of rural areas.

In recent years, there has been great interest in the study of the effects of LC processes in China. For instance, Wu et al. (2005) used a production function approach and farm-household data to evaluate the effectiveness of LC projects in China. They found that the LC processes have improved land quality and the productivity of household crop production. Using detailed geospatial information for a large set of Chinese LC projects, Jin et al. (2017) found however that the overall effectiveness of these LC processes in improving agricultural productivity is low, existing clear regional differences.

As pointed out by Crecente et al. (2002), there is no specific methodology that is generally accepted for the evaluation of LC. Our review shows that the methodologies used in this literature vary from country to country, due to lack of data availability (see, e.g. Hiironen and Riekkinen 2016), differences in both data disaggregation (e.g. farm/household-level vs. geospatial data) and data collection (gathered via questionnaires or by the public administration involved in the LC processes), the existence of different objectives of land-use policy (land productivity, rural development, nature protection, etc.) or different categories of LC effects (e.g. agricultural production effects, transportation effects, effects on drainage and similar measures, the impact on ecological environment or the social and regional economic effects). Furthermore, there are inconsistent conclusions on the impact of LC on several of the above categories. For instance, Zhou et al. (2019) point out that while some studies showed that LC has a negative impact on the ecosystem services value and landscape diversity (see, e.g. Zhang et al. 2014), other papers found a positive ecological effect (see, e.g. Yu et al. 2010; Hartvigsen 2014).

In summary, there are studies that analyse the effects of LF and LC at a micro-level or farm level (Wu et al. 2005; Manjunatha et al. 2013; Orea et al. 2015; Nilsson 2018), while others carry out the analysis at a spatial level, taking the municipalities or regions as units of study assessing the effect on spatial distribution of economic activities (Crecente et al. 2002; Du et al. 2018; Dudzińska et al. 2018), even focusing on the socio-economic improvement of rural areas and the reduction of poverty in these territories (Zhou et al. 2019).

This chapter evaluates the impact of the LC processes that have taken place in Asturias in recent decades. As regional policymakers strongly believe that the high degree of LF in Asturias prevents local farms to be competitive, they have promoted the implementation of 279 public LC processes in this region since the 1960s to soften the degree of LF. According to the information provided by the Principality of Asturias, the LC processes carried out in Asturias over this period have involved more than 28,000 owners and about 60,000 hectares of land, and the average investment amounts to 2300 euros per hectare. Moreover, these processes have been able to reduce the number of plots from 224 to 58,000 plots. These processes have been receiving European funds because of their potential to improve the economic activity in rural areas, increase farmer income and stabilize their population.

Figure 1 shows the number of LC processes carried out in Asturias over the period 1963–2017. Notice that the number of LC processes has intensified since 2000. This large enforcement is likely caused by the new public LC mechanisms allowed by recent regulation in Asturias. On the one hand, in particular, the Legal Decree 80/1997 established the conditions under which farmers can request the regional government to initiate a LC process. This regulation avoids negotiation and legal costs and allows the public administration to change access routes to the new plots. On the other hand, and following the

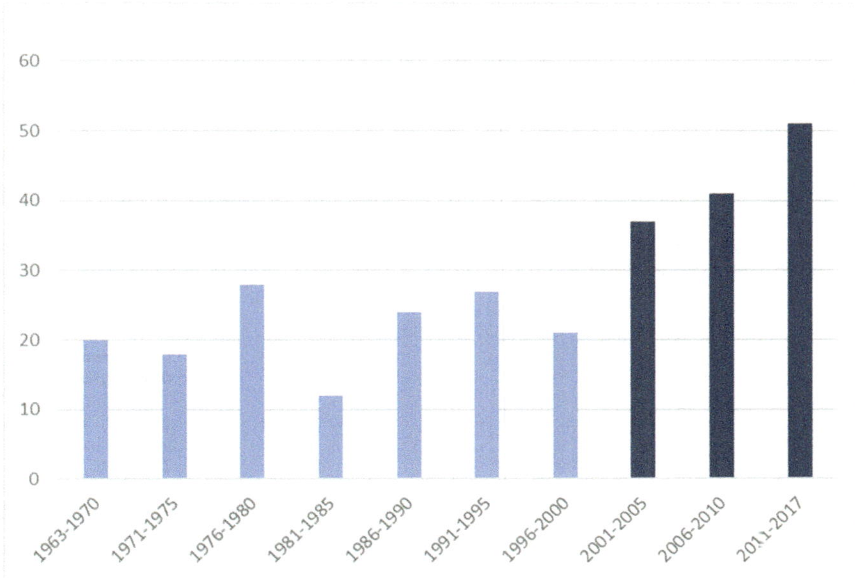

Fig. 1 Number of LC processes in Asturias (1963–2017)

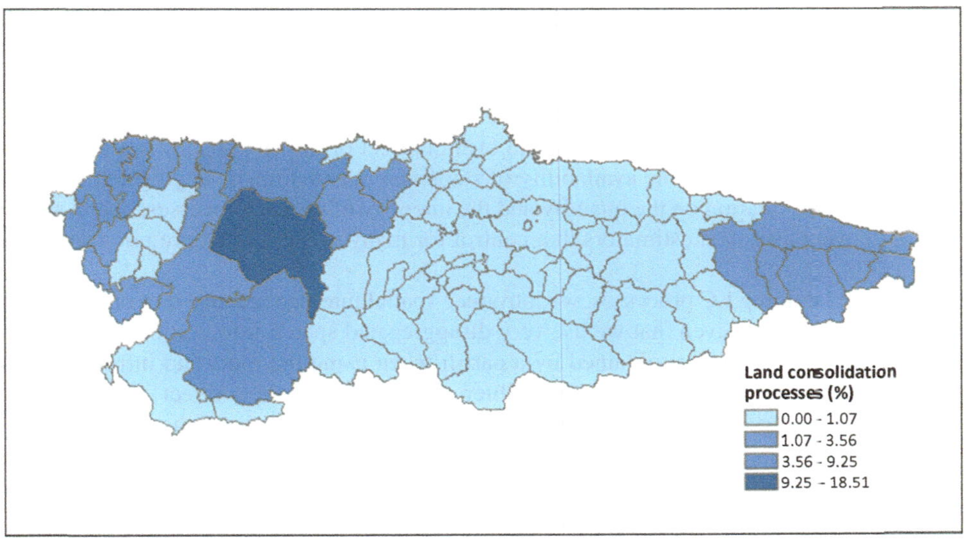

Fig. 2 Land consolidation processes in Asturias (1963–2000)

principles established in the Agrarian Regulation and Rural Development Law of 1989, the public administration itself can also promote a local LC process.[1]

This chapter evaluates the impact of a set of Asturian LC projects during the period 2001–2017 due to the large enforcement of the LC policy since 2000 and because there is not reliable data on parishes' farms activity in previous decades. The study is focused on western Asturias because, as shown in Figs. 2 and 3, the LC processes were implemented with great intensity in the western municipalities and parishes of Asturias, especially since 2000. We also do not have information about public investment in many of the LC processes carried out in East Asturias.

Like Wu et al. (2005), we use a production function approach to evaluate the effectiveness of the LC processes. However, while these authors use farm-household data, we use detailed geospatial data of Asturian parishes with and without LC

[1]The above two regulations can be found in the Asturias' Official Bulletin (https://sede.asturias.es/portal/site/Asturias/menuitem.048b5a85ccf2cf40a9be6aff100000f7/?vgnextoid=c0c756a575acd010VgnVCM100000bb030a0aRCRD&i18n.http.lang=es&calendarioPqBopa=true)

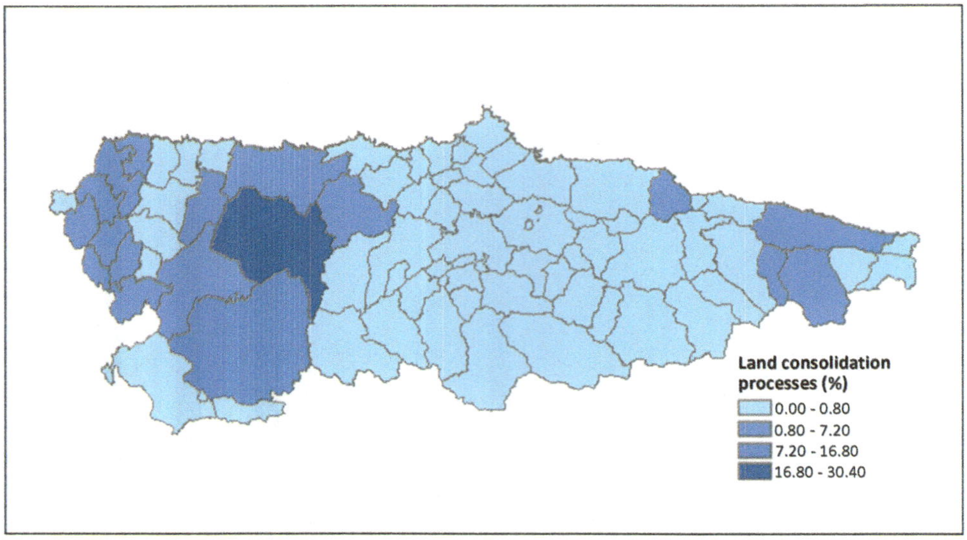

Fig. 3 Land consolidation processes in Asturias (2001–2017)

processes, as in Crecente et al. (2002) and Miranda et al. (2006). We treat the parishes in Asturias as production units to evaluate the effect of LC processes on milk and beef production. Given the multi-output nature of the parishes' production technology, we take advantage of the production theory and estimate a set of distance functions that can be viewed as multi-output productions functions. Due to lack of data, we use parishes' dairy and beef herd as proxies for both livestock production in each parish. In addition, we analyse the effect of LC on parishes' farm numbers using a set of auxiliary regressions. This allows us to compute, and decompose, an overall effect of LC on parishes' livestock production.

This work has been possible, thanks to the availability of statistical information disaggregated by parishes on farms and livestock, as well as specific information on the quantity and the intensity of the LC processes, over a sufficiently long period of time. This allows us to use panel data estimators that control for many variables that are not available at parish level but likely time-invariant.

Unlike previous papers examining LC processes, we introduce spatial interdependence into our analysis by adding the LC indicators of neighbouring parishes. Given that we use very disaggregated spatial information, we expect substantial spatial spillover effects, understood as the benefits obtained by a parish when using the plots and infrastructures existing in other parishes. One stylized result from the regional economics literature is that the direct effect of own variables on production reduces when the territorial disaggregation of locations increases (i.e. administrative units are smaller) (see, e.g. Álvarez-Ayuso et al. 2016). This happens in our application as our observations are parishes, i.e. Christian territorial entities that are much smaller than the standard municipalities (provinces) used in urban (regional) economics. For this reason, it is critical to take into account spatial spillover effects when analysing the impacts of our LC indicators. There is a literature at micro-level (farms) that introduce spillover effects based on the idea that large farms can benefit neighbouring smallholders via different channels (Deininger and Xia 2016; Ali et al. 2019). However, to the knowledge of authors, there are no studies that analyse these effects in the case of LC processes.

2 Empirical Method

Our first empirical models aim to measure the economic impact of LC processes on parishes' livestock production using a primal representation of *parishes' production* technology. The effects estimated here can be interpreted as an effect on farms' average size because they are *conditional* on the number of farms of each parish. In order to get an overall effect, we next estimate a set of *auxiliary regressions* to examine the effect of our LC variables on the number of farms.

2.1 *Parishes' Production Model*

Our production models are inspired in three different but complementary approaches: (i) the panel data estimators that control for unobserved heterogeneity, (ii) the spatial econometric models that aim to capture indirect effects generated by LC processes in neighbouring parishes and (iii) the production theory that allows us to examine changes in parishes' dairy and beef production using a singly equation.

Regarding the first two approaches, Demetriou (2018) points out that the standard regression analysis in LC evaluations ignores two important issues: spatial heterogeneity and spatial dependence. Indeed, there are many characteristics that affect parishes' production but which are unobserved at parish level or omitted variables (e.g. geographic conditions, population structure, distribution of economic activities, network characteristics). If these omitted variables are correlated with our regressors, we have an endogeneity problem. If this issue is ignored, we will get both biased parameters and biased effects attributed to LC processes. However, notice that many of the above unobservable variables are likely to be time-invariant or rarely changing variables. In this case, the endogeneity issue can be addressed by adding a set of parish-specific intercepts α_i that are treated as parameters to be estimated using the fixed-effect (FE) estimator.

It should be mentioned that the FE estimator only uses the temporal variation of the data to get the parameter estimates. In this sense, our empirical strategy to measure the effects of LC can be viewed as a difference-in-differences (DiD) method. DiD is a panel data statistical technique that calculates the effect of a treatment (explanatory variable) on an outcome (response variable) by comparing the average change over time in the outcome variable for a "treatment group", compared to the average change over time for a "control group". DiD requires data measured at two or more different time periods, viz. before and after "treatment". In our application, the LC variables included in the model allow us not only to identify the before and after periods but also how intense was the LC process (i.e. the treatment). As in Du et al. (2018), our method can also be viewed as a before-and-after method. However, in our case, the difference between the before and after periods is not the difference of two simple means but a function of several covariates.

The second issue is spatial dependence. Spatial dependence is known to be particularly severe for small spatial units, such as parishes and municipalities (da Silva et al. 2017). The small size of parishes implies that local factors affecting parishes' production tend to affect production dynamics of neighbouring parishes. Therefore, another weakness of the standard regression analysis in LC evaluation is neglected spatial dependence. To address this issue, we simply enlarge the set of explanatory variables of the model with observed LC variables of neighbouring parishes or locations in the same fashion as a standard spatial lag model (SLX) does.

As it is customary in regional economics, we treat each parish as a production unit. Thus, our observations are not individual farms as in most papers examining the effect of LF on farms' productivity and efficiency (see, e.g. Orea et al. 2015), rather aggregate production units comprising many farms. In this sense, we will hereafter assume that our production units "employ" farms (and other *unobserved* inputs captured by the parish-specific effects) to produce dairy and beef products. While an adequate indicator to assess dairy (beef) production is the production of milk (beef) in litres (kilograms) or the farmers' sales in monetary units, there is no data source from which these volumes can be measured directly at parish level. We use parishes' dairy and beef herd sizes as proxies, respectively, for parishes' dairy and beef production.[2] In this sense, it should be pointed out that most of the literature in agricultural economics shows that the most important input in dairy (beef) production is the dairy (beef) livestock number, and thus both variables are highly correlated.

Although it is possible to split the overall number of farms in a parish into dairy-, beef- and mix-oriented farms, we cannot allocate the observed dairy and beef livestock to each farm type. This issue forces us to treat each parish as a multi-output production unit. In this sense, we find it very useful the well-known concept of "distance function" in production economics as this primal representation of parishes' production technology allows us to study the effect of the LC processes on both dairy and beef production using a single equation. The basic model with no LC effects can be represented by the equation:

$$lny_{1it} = \alpha_i + \alpha_t + F\left(x_{it}, y_{2it}/y_{1it}, z_{it}\right) + \varepsilon_{it} \tag{1}$$

where i stands for parish; t stands for periods; y_{1it} and y_{2it} are, respectively, the number of dairy and beef livestock at the parish level; x_{it} is the number of farms located in a parish; z_{it} is a maturity indicator of cattle that has to do with the existence of traditional (e.g. extensive) farms in a particular parish; α_i is a parish-specific fixed effect aiming to capture time-invariant unobserved heterogeneity at the parish level; α_t is a time effect that is included in the model in order to capture the general reduction in farms' activity observed in the last decades; and ε_{it} is an error term measuring random shocks. Finally, in our empirical application, we use a Translog (TL) form for the deterministic function $F(\cdot)$. The Translog distance function is a quadratic function in lnx_{it}, $ln(y_{2it}/y_{1it})$ and z_{it} that provides a more general (*flexible*) representation of parishes'

[2]This is not the first time where input and output variables are used for the same purposes. For instance, the relative size of a particular industry is often given by either its value-added share or its labour share (see, e.g. Balk 2016).

production technology (see Diewert 1971). The estimated elasticities in the TL specification are parish-specific as they are linear functions of lnx_{it}, $ln(y_{2it}/y_{1it})$ and z_{it}.[3]

The basic model in (1) is next extended using a set of variables that try to capture not only the number but also the strength of the LC processes implemented in the parishes included in our sample. The extended specification can be represented by the equation:

$$lny_{1it} = \alpha_i + \alpha_t + F\left(x_{it}, y_{2it}/y_{1it}, z_{it}, LC_{it}\right) + \varepsilon_{it} \quad (2)$$

where again $F(\cdot)$ is a TL representation of parishes' production technology and LC_{it} is a vector of three variables, e.g. $LC_{it} = N_{it}, A_{it}, lnIH_{it}$. N_{it} is a count variable that measures the cumulative number of LC processes in parish i at period t, and A_{it} is the time elapsed since the last LC process. As N_{it}, this variable takes zero values before the first LC process. The third LC-based variable $lnIH_{it}$ is the cumulative public investment (per hectare) involved in LC plans. As the two previous LC indicators, this variable takes zero values before the first LC process because the logged variable is defined as $lnIH_{it} = ln\,(IH_{it} + 1)$. While N_{it} aims to capture the effect of one or more "representative" LC processes, $lnIH_{it}$ tries to distinguish between weak and intensive LC processes.

It is worth mentioning that the effects of the LC variables are parish-specific as we use a TL representation of parishes' production technology. Although the main focus of this chapter is whether LC matters as a whole, the individual coefficients allow us to capture differences among LC processes. The interactions with parishes' characteristics allow us to identify which parishes have benefited the most from the LC processes.

To illustrate how we calculate the effect of LC on parishes' dairy and beef production once (4) has been estimated, let us show the TL formulation of our distance functions with and without LC-based variables. While the TL specification of (1) is

$$\begin{aligned} lny_{1it} = \Big[&\alpha_i + \alpha_t + \beta_x lnx_{it} + \beta_y \ln\left(y_{2it}/y_{1it}\right) + \beta_z lnz_{it} + \tfrac{1}{2}\beta_{xx}(lnx_{it})^2 + \\ &\tfrac{1}{2}\beta_{yy}(\ln\left(y_{2it}/y_{1it}\right))^2 + \tfrac{1}{2}\beta_{zz}(lnz_{it})^2 + \beta_{xy} lnx_{it}\ln\left(y_{2it}/y_{1it}\right) + \\ &\beta_{xz} lnx_{it} lnz_{it} + \beta_{yz}\ln\left(y_{2it}/y_{1it}\right) lnz_{it}\Big] + \varepsilon_{it} \end{aligned} \quad (3)$$

the TL specification of (2) can be written as:

$$\begin{aligned} lny_{1it} = &TL\left(x_{it}, y_{2it}/y_{1it}, z_{it}, \alpha_i, \alpha_t\right) + \gamma_1 LC_{it} + \tfrac{1}{2}\gamma_2 LC_{it}^2 + \gamma_x LC_{it} lnx_{it} + \\ &\gamma_y LC_{it}\ln\left(y_{2it}/y_{1it}\right) + \gamma_z LC_{it} lnz_{it} + \varepsilon_{it} \end{aligned} \quad (4)$$

where $TL(x_{it}, y_{2it}/y_{1it}, z_{it}, \alpha_i, \alpha_t)$ is the term in brackets in (3).[4] The direct effect of LC on parishes' farm production (hereafter DLCE)[5] is then computed using the following difference of two *conditional* expected productions:

$$\begin{aligned} &DLCE_{it} = \\ &E\left[lny_{1it}|x_{it}, y_{2it}/y_{1it}, z_{it}, LC_{it}, \alpha_i, \alpha_t\right]_{N_{it}\ge 1} - \\ &E\left[lny_{1it}|x_{it}, y_{2it}/y_{1it}, z_{it}, LC_{it}, \alpha_i, \alpha_t\right]_{N_{it}=0} \end{aligned} \quad (5)$$

This equation measures the effect of LC as the difference between the expected production of a parish that has been involved in a LC process (i.e. when $N_{it} \ge 1$) and the expected production of a *similar* but *hypothetical* parish that has the same explanatory variables (and coefficients) than the above parish but it has not been involved in any LC process (in this case N_{it} should take a zero value). Notice that (5) is conditional on both parish effects, α_i. Therefore, we are controlling for time-invariant differences between the two mentioned parishes. In this sense, our empirical strategy can be viewed as a DiD method. We are also controlling in (5) for differences in the value of α_t before and after the first LC process took place. This prevents us to wrongly attribute to the LC processes the change in parish' production that has to do with exogenous factors that are common to all farms and parishes.

Notice that while the first conditional expectation in (5) is equal to (4) once we drop the noise term, all LC-based variables take the zero value when $N_{it} = 0$, and then the second conditional expectation in (5) is equal to (3) once we drop again the noise term. As both (3) and (4) include $TL(x_{it}, y_{2it}/y_{1it}, z_{it}, \alpha_i, \alpha_t)$, $DLCE_{it}$ in (5) can be alternatively rewritten as follows:

[3]We do not take logs in z_{it} as this indicator already takes values between zero and one, and changes in z_{it} can be interpreted as rates of growth.

[4]If more than one LC-based variable is used, the equation (4) should be extended with the proper linear and quadratic terms (including interactions) associated with the new LC-based variables.

[5]Why we have added the "direct" label to this effect is explained below in this section.

$$DLCE_{it} = \gamma_1 LC_{it} + \frac{1}{2}\gamma_2 LC_{it}^2 + \gamma_x LC_{it} lnx_{it} + \gamma_y LC_{it} \ln(y_{2it}/y_{1it}) + \gamma_z LC_{it} lnz_{it} \tag{6}$$

A common feature of the above two specifications is that they ignore the spatial structure of the data. In other words, (5) and (6) are only capturing a *direct* effect on parishes' production as they ignore that the local LC processes might have also an *indirect* impact on neighbouring parishes' production. To address this issue, we follow the standard SLX model in regional economics and enlarge the set of explanatory variables that appears in (2) with the LC variables of neighbouring parishes:

$$lny_{1it} = \alpha_i + \alpha_t + F(x_{it}, y_{2it}/y_{1it}, z_{it}, LC_{it}) + \lambda W_i LC_t + \varepsilon_{it} \tag{7}$$

where LC_t is a vector of $Px1$ LC-based variables, P is the number of cross-section parishes in our sample and W_i is a known $1xP$ spatial weight vector with elements that are equal to zero if a particular parish j is not a neighbour of parish i and equal to one if the two parishes are neighbours or adjacent. Equation (7) is a model that now includes a set of spatially lagged variables, i.e. $W_i LC_t$.[6] Therefore, (7) resembles a conventional spatial SLX model, where the term λ is a coefficient that measures the effect of neighbours' LC processes on the production of a parish.[7] Once λ has been estimated, we can measure the *indirect* or *spatial* effect of neighbours' LC processes as follows:

$$ILCE_{it} = \lambda W_i LC_t \tag{8}$$

Finally, the *total* effect of LC on parishes' farm production is then simply computed by adding both direct and indirect effects:

$$LCE_{it} = DLCE_{it} + ILCE_{it} \tag{9}$$

2.2 Auxiliary Regressions

Our previous empirical models aim to measure the economic impact of LC processes at the parish scale, conditional on the number of farms. To get an overall view of the subject, we need to estimate the effect of our LC-based variables on the number of farms. In order to take into account the different composition of the farms located in each parish, we split the sample into dairy-, beef- and mix-oriented parishes and propose estimating the following auxiliary regression for each type of parish:

$$lnx_{it} = \alpha_{ji} + \alpha_{jt} + \delta_j LC_{it} + \tau_j W_i LC_t + v_{jit} \tag{10}$$

where j stands for parish type (j = dairy-, beef- and mix-oriented), x_{it} is the number of farms, α_{ji} and α_{jt} are two fixed effects aiming to capture the effect of parish-specific (but time-invariant) and time-specific (but common to all parishes) unobserved variables on x_{it} and v_{jit} is an error term measuring random shocks. In the same fashion as LCE_{it}, the effect of LC on parishes' farm numbers is computed as follows once (10) has been estimated:

$$XLCE_{it} = \delta_j LC_{it} + \tau_j W_i LC_t \tag{11}$$

2.3 Overall Effects

In order to get an overall effect of LC on parishes' production, we need to combine somehow the conditional LCE_{it} effect (i.e. the effect of LC on lny_{1it} and lny_{2it} given x_{it}) and $XLCE_{it}$ (i.e. the effect of LC on x_{it}). A very simple method to achieve

[6]Notice again that $W_i LC_t$ is a vector of three LC-based variables, e.g. $W_i LC_t = (W_i N_t, W_i A_t, W_i lnIH_t)$.

[7]Halleck-Vega and Elhorst (2015) provide a comprehensive overview of the strengths and weaknesses of different spatial econometric model specifications in terms of spillover effects. Based on their overview, they advocate taking the SLX model as point of departure in case a well-founded theory indicating which model is most appropriate is lacking.

this objective is estimating a distance function without x_{it}, and use the parameter estimates of this unconditional model to compute (6) and (9). This model is misspecified because a significant explanatory variable has been dropped. Indeed, if we omit x_{it} (and its square and interactions) from Eq. (4), the estimated coefficients associated with the LC-based variables will be (on purpose) biased because they will be capturing both the conditional effect on parishes' production and the effect via a reduction (increase) in the number of farms, an omitted variable in this specification.[8] As Orea (2010), we take advantage of this misspecification to combine both effects.

3 Sample and Data

The data used in our study comes from two complementary sources and has allowed us to have a panel of parishes from 2001 to 2017. On the one hand, SADEI has provided us with annual information at the parish level that contains the following variables: population, parish's total land area, number of bovine farms, total bovine herd (both beef and dairy) and livestock units (see SADEI, 2011).[9] On the other hand, the Principality of Asturias has provided us with information on the processes of LC carried out from 1963 to the present, with data about the parishes and municipalities affected, the treated hectares, the starting and ending plots number, the date of taking possession of the new plots, the volume of public investment in the development and implementation of the LC processes, etc.

The variables used to estimate our distance functions are defined as follows. The two outputs of the distance functions (3) and (4) are y_{1it} and y_{2it}, i.e. the total number of dairy and beef bovine animals, respectively. The main input of the parishes' distance function is the total number of bovine farms, x_{it}. This variable includes dairy-, beef- and mix-oriented farms. As mentioned in Sect. 2, it is not possible to allocate the observed dairy and beef livestock to each farm type because all of them uses dairy and beef cows, but in different proportions. In particular, the farms are classified as dairy farms when the dairy livestock units (LU) only exceed 2/3 of the total livestock units.[10] Therefore, beef livestock units in some of these farms might represent up to 33% of the total LU. Similar comments deserve the other two categories.[11]

To distinguish between traditional (extensive) and non-traditional (intensive) farms in each parish, we have included in our distance function the ratio livestock units to total bovine herd, z_{it}. Total bovine herd is the sum of dairy livestock and beef livestock. The z-ratio is a maturity indicator of farms' cattle. z_{it} is less than unity since the total of the bovine herd includes all bovine animals whether they are adult cows, heifers and young calves. Adult cows count as one livestock unit, while younger animals count less than one livestock unit. A ratio equal to 1 would imply that all the bovine animals would be adult cows. The higher the value of the ratio, the less weight the younger animals have in the herd of cattle (calves and heifers). It is worth mentioning that z_{it} can also be viewed as an indicator of the traditional (extensive) character of livestock in each parish. In the case of dairy farms, the lower the z-ratio, the more weight the heifers have. This reflects that the farms require a high rate of annual replacement of cows because dairy cows of high production usually have a shorter productive life. Therefore, on the one hand, in the case of milk orientation at lower value of z-ratio, there is greater intensification of productive activity (cows with higher production, with more feed consumption per cow, etc.). On the other hand, in the case of beef farms, the lower the z-ratio, the more weight the calves have (breeding and baiting). The higher the value of the z-ratio, the lower the weight of the calves in the cattle. This could indicate that the meat holdings have few calves in the process of bait, and this would be the case of farms that decide to sell the calves after a few months of life to be fattened in other more professional farms (feedlots) outside the parish.

The effect of LC on parishes' production is measured using three variables capturing the quantity and the intensity of the LC processes. The first LC variable is the cumulative number of LC processes, N_{it}. This variable does not necessary begin with a zero value in 2001 because it also considers the LC processes that were implemented in the 1990s. N_{it} (and its square) is *originally* included in the model in order to examine if the LC processes have had a positive but decreasing effect on parishes' dairy and beef production. As this effect is conditional on the number of farms, it can alternatively be interpreted

[8]A more comprehensive method to combine both effects relies on the following differential equation that requires computing the elasticity of lny_{1it} with respect to lnx_{it}: $\frac{dlny_{1it}}{dLC_{it}} = \frac{\partial lny_{1it}}{\partial LC_{it}} + \frac{\partial lny_{1it}}{\partial lnx_{it}} \cdot \frac{\partial lnx_{it}}{\partial LC_{it}}$

[9]See http://www.sadei.es/datos/sad/vacas/vacas.aspx

[10]The livestock unit sometimes abbreviated as LU (or LSU) "is a reference unit which facilitates the aggregation of livestock from various groups of age as per convention, via the use of specific coefficients established initially on the basis of the nutritional or feed requirement of each type of animal". This definition was obtained from Eurostat website (see https://ec.europa.eu/eurostat/statistics-explained/index.php/Glossary:Livestock_unit_(LSU)).

[11]While the farms are classified as beef farms when the beef livestock units exceed 2/3 of the total LU, the mix-oriented farms are those farms with beef and dairy livestock units less than 2/3 of the total LU.

Table 1 Descriptive statistics

Variable	Description	Obs	Mean	Std. Dev.	Min	Max
y_1	Dairy livestock	4964	283.6	454.3	0	2779
y_2	Beef livestock	4964	333.9	338.0	0	3317
x	Dairy-, beef- and mix-oriented farms	4964	23.3	18.4	0	153
z	Livestock units/(total bovine herd+1)	4912	0.71	0.10	0	0.89
D_{beef}	Dummy variable for beef-oriented parishes	4964	0.48	0.50	0	1
D_{milk}	Dummy variable for dairy-oriented parishes	4964	0.14	0.35	0	1
D_{mix}	Dummy variable for mix-oriented parishes	4964	0.38	0.49	0	1
N	Number of LC processes	1056	1.46	0.78	1	5
A	Time elapsed since the last LC process	1056	7.76	5.77	1	27
IH	Public investment per hectare	1056	1595	1200	0	6170
WN	Neighbours' average number of LC processes	1056	0.73	0.65	0	3.8
WA	Neighbours' average time elapsed since the last LC process	1056	3.11	2.51	0	14
WIH	Neighbours' average public investment per hectare	1056	725.7	778.4	0	4293

as an effect on farms' average size.[12] The effect of N_{it} is a bit uncertain in practice because it might be also controlling for the discontinuity of the other two LC variables. The second LC-based variable is the time elapsed since the last LC process, A_{it}. This variable is included in the model due to a new LC process might not have an immediate effect on parishes' production (and average farms' size) but a delayed impact.[13] Notice as well that the time trend measuring the time elapsed since the last LC process is reset and starts up again taking the unity value each time a new LC process takes place. Thus, A_{it} exhibits a discontinuity each time N_{it} increases. The third LC-based variable is the natural logarithm of the cumulative public investment (per hectare) involved in LC plans, $lnIH_{it}$. While N_{it} simply measures the quantity of LC processes, $lnIH_{it}$ measures their intensity. This variable begins to take (high) positive values when we move from zero processes to unity. Thus, $lnIH_{it}$ exhibits a discontinuity when $N_{it} = 1$ the first time.

Table 1 shows the descriptive statistics of 292 parishes over the period 2001–2017. The total sample size is 4964 observations; 1056 observations have been involved in one or more LC processes. As all LC variables in a parish take a zero value before the first LC process is implemented, the descriptive statistics of these three variables are computed using 1056 observations. For comparison grounds, we also provide the descriptive statistics of spatial lags of these LC variables for 1056 observations.

Our output distance functions are conditional on the number of farms and hence the estimated parameters of the time dummy variables measure here the "natural" tendency of parishes' average farm size over time. Similar comments deserve the parameters of the time dummy variables of our auxiliary regressions. As the parameters of the time dummy variables are not shown in next section, we provide in Fig. 4 the annual parish average farm size (measured as average cows per farm) and farm figure. This figure shows a persistent decline in the number of farms over the last 17 years. This evolution just captures the increasingly cessation of livestock activity in the Asturian rural areas.[14] This figure also shows that the above restructuration of livestock production has favoured concentration and intensification of production on larger farms.

4 Results

4.1 Conditional LC Effects

The parameter estimates of four different specifications of the output distance functions in (4) are shown in Table 2. First, we provide in column (1) the Translog function with a linear function of LC variables capturing direct effects on parishes' production. In column (2), we extend the model including interactions between LC indicators. Here we only consider the number of farms as an input to "produce" milk, the beef-to-dairy livestock ratio to control for substitution effects between

[12] It also might capture an effect on farms' structure if it is interacted with y_{2it}/y_{1it}.

[13] Crecente et al. (2002) conclude that data from two consecutive years are insufficient to evaluate properly the effects of LC. In this sense, for a project completed in period t, Du et al. (2018) consider the period $(t-6, t-1)$ as before consolidation and $(t+1, t+6)$ as after consolidation.

[14] Due to this cessation, the number of farms and the livestock numbers are zero at the end of the sample period in a few parishes.

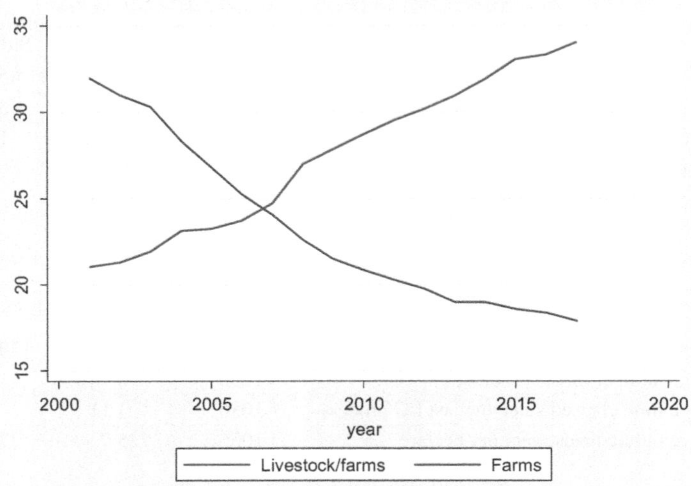

Fig. 4 Temporal evolution of farms size and farm numbers

dairy and beef products and z_{it} (or z-ratio) as control variable. In addition, we introduce the three variables capturing the quantity and the intensity of the LC processes. The third model allows examining non-neutral effects of the LC variables as they are interacted with the production determinants of the distance functions. These interactions let us to know whether, e.g. the effect of the LC processes is more intensive in large parishes (i.e. with many farms), in parishes more oriented to dairy production or in parishes with more traditional farms. The last model adds spatial lags of the LC variables in order to capture indirect effects from neighbouring parishes. The explanatory variables have been divided by the geometric mean of the parishes involved in one or more LC processes. This transformation has no effect on the estimation but allows the first-order coefficients to be interpreted as elasticities for a "representative" parish involved in LC processes. The F statistic of joint significance in Table 2 indicates that all production parameters (including time dummies) are significant. The above-mentioned specifications have been estimated using the fixed-effects estimator in order to control for parish-specific but time-invariant unobserved variables for the researcher. The performed F-tests also reject that all $\alpha_i = 0$, indicating that there are significant differences in unobserved environmental conditions among parishes. The estimated fixed effects (not shown) capture not only other relevant inputs for farms' production but also other geographical and socio-economic variables that condition farms' size.

The similarities in the coefficients between the different specifications confirm the robustness of our specifications. On the one hand, as expected, we find a negative and significant relationship between parishes' beef and dairy production, conditional on the number of farms. The estimated elasticity is on average less than unity in absolute terms, indicating that parishes "adjust" dairy cattle less than beef cattle. On the other hand, we find a positive effect of the number of farms on dairy and beef livestock. This is also an expected result. Again the estimated elasticity is on average less than unity, indicating the existence of decreasing returns to scale at parish level. In other words, parishes with more farms tend to have smaller farms in terms of beef and dairy cattle. Furthermore, the negative coefficient associated with z_{it} implies that more extensive (and traditional) farms tend to be smaller as they on average use less beef and dairy cows than more intensive farms. The quadratic and interaction terms are also very similar in all specifications of the distance function (4). Except for z_{it}, the quadratic terms are negative. The negative coefficient for the beef herd indicates that the underlying production possibility curve is concave to the origin as it is customary in the economic production theory. The effect of the number of farms on dairy (and beef) herd adopts a form of inverted U due to the first-order effect is positive and the quadratic term is negative. The opposite result is observed for z_{it}. Finally, it is worth mentioning that the parameters of the interaction terms are significant but with different signs. Therefore, the above-mentioned effects are sometimes attenuated (if the sign is negative) or intensified (positive sign) by other production determinants.

We have also included three different LC indicators in our models to measure the effect of LC processes on parishes' dairy and beef production. In particular, we consider the number of processes, an indicator that collects the time elapsed between processes, and the investment per hectare measuring the intensity of the LC processes. Although we are more interested in the overall effects than in individual effects because each LC process is a complex phenomenon, we find that the first-order coefficient of N_{it} is not significant in most specifications. Moreover, it has a negative coefficient when the model does not include second-order coefficients. As anticipated before, the discontinuity of the other two LC variables might explain counterintuitive or non-significant results associated with this variable when estimating both our distance

Table 2 Parameter estimates of the distance functions

	Model 1			Model 2			Model 3			Model 4		
Variable	Coef.		s.e.	Coef.		s.e.	Coef.		s.e.	Coef.		s.e.
lny$_2$	−0.721	***	0.009	−0.721	***	0.009	−0.749	***	0.011	−0.748	***	0.011
lnx	0.826	***	0.022	0.830	***	0.022	0.872	***	0.031	0.876	***	0.031
z	−0.933	***	0.228	−0.953	***	0.228	−0.651	*	0.385	−0.531		0.388
1/2(lny$_2$)^2	−0.062	***	0.003	−0.062	***	0.003	−0.061	***	0.003	−0.061	***	0.003
1/2(lnx)^2	−0.166	***	0.018	−0.161	***	0.018	−0.159	***	0.018	−0.156	***	0.018
1/2z^2	4.003	***	0.987	4.089	***	0.988	4.543	***	0.984	4.482	***	0.984
lny$_2$·lnx	−0.066	***	0.005	−0.068	***	0.005	−0.074	***	0.005	−0.075	***	0.005
lny$_2$·z	0.489	***	0.049	0.490	***	0.049	0.426	***	0.049	0.425	***	0.049
lnx·z	−1.236	***	0.161	−1.253	***	0.161	−1.258	***	0.163	−1.236	***	0.163
N	−0.032	***	0.013	−0.016		0.021	0.020		0.023	0.003		0.024
A	0.007	***	0.002	0.006	***	0.002	0.009	***	0.002	0.007	***	0.002
lnIH	−0.003		0.003	−0.024		0.018	−0.053	***	0.019	−0.054	***	0.019
1/2N^2				0.011		0.015	0.023		0.016	0.020		0.016
1/2A^2				−0.014	***	0.006	−0.018	***	0.006	−0.018	***	0.006
1/2(lnIH)^2				0.001	***	0.000	0.001	*	0.000	0.001	*	0.000
N·A				0.009		0.009	0.005		0.009	0.007		0.009
N·lnIH				0.005	**	0.002	0.005		0.003	0.004		0.003
A·lnIH				0.000		0.002	−0.001		0.002	−0.002		0.002
lnx·N							0.076	***	0.025	0.084	***	0.025
lnx·lnIH							−0.003		0.006	−0.005		0.006
lnx·A							−0.004	*	0.002	−0.003		0.003
lny$_2$·N							−0.013		0.008	−0.011		0.008
lny$_2$·lnIH							0.004	*	0.002	0.003		0.002
lny$_2$·A							−0.005	***	0.001	−0.005	***	0.001
z·N							0.169		0.364	0.255		0.371
z·lnIH							0.200	**	0.090	0.194	**	0.091
z·A							−0.183	***	0.046	−0.185	***	0.046
WN										0.067	***	0.022
WA										0.007	***	0.003
WlnIH										−0.011	**	0.005
Intercept	−0.060	***	0.022	−0.055	**	0.026	−0.025		0.027	−0.013		0.027
Time dummies	Yes			Yes			Yes			Yes		
Fixed effects	Yes			Yes			Yes			Yes		
Significance F-test[a]	1294.1	***		1069.8	***		868.4	***		813.8	***	
F-test that all $\alpha_i = 0$	96.2	***		95.7	***		97.1	***		95.7	***	
Degrees of freedom	4644			4638			4629			4626		
Obs.	4964			4964			4964			4964		
# parameters	320			326			335			338		
# function parameters	13			19			28			31		
# fixed effects[b]	291			291			291			291		
# time dummies[b]	16			16			16			16		

[a]This F-test includes the distance function coefficients (except the intercept) and the set of time dummy parameters
[b]One effect is excluded due to an intercept being estimated
Note: *, **, *** indicate significante at the 10, 5, 1% level, respectively

functions and auxiliary regressions. The first-order coefficient of A_{it} is positive and significant. This result seems to indicate that, on average, the LC processes do not have an immediate effect on Asturias parishes' production (and on average farm size) but a delayed impact. However, the quadratic coefficient of A_{it} is negative. Therefore, there is an inverted U-shaped effect associated with the time elapsed since the last LC process, indicating that the effect tends to vanish after several years. In contrast, we find a proper U-shaped effect associated with $lnIH_{it}$. The investment tends to have a negative effect on parishes' livestock production for small investments levels, but positive when the investment involved in the LC process is sufficiently large. However, our LCE figures shown later in this section seem to indicate that this quadratic effect is not enough to compensate the first one. It is also worth noting that the interactions between the LC indicators are not statistically significant in our more comprehensive models.

Models 3 and 4 include interactions between our LC indicators and the production determinants of the distance function. The coefficient of $lnx_{it}N_{it}$ is always positive and statistically significant, indicating that adding new LC processes is more effective in parishes with many farms. This result indicates the existence of some synergies between LC processes when the number of farms located in such a parish is large. Therefore, this finding seems to suggest policymakers to accumulate LC processes in large parishes rather than in small parishes with few farms. Another statistically significant and negative interaction is $ln(y_{2it}/y_{1it})A_{it}$. This coefficient indicates that the effect of the LC processes is less intensive in beef-oriented parishes than in parishes more oriented to milk production. As most of the dairy livestock is in coastal municipalities, the effects of LC on livestock production will be larger in littoral areas. Another remarkable result is the positive and statistically significant coefficient of $z_{it}lnIH_{it}$. This coefficient indicates that the public investments in infrastructures tend to have a larger (positive) effect in parishes where the local farms use more traditional systems of livestock production. The negative coefficient of $z_{it}A_{it}$ suggests, however, that this effect is less intense over time.

A common feature of the first three models in Table 2 is that they ignore the spatial structure of the data. In other words, they only capture *direct* effects on parishes' production. In order to capture *indirect* effects associated with LC processes implemented in neighbouring parishes, Model 4 enlarges the set of explanatory variables with spatial lags of LC variables. We observe that the spatial spillover (or between parishes) LC effects are as relevant as the internal (or within parishes) LC effects, thereby confirming the importance of considering the notion of spatial interactions in studies that rely on very disaggregated spatial information. The positive and significant coefficients of the average number of neighbouring LC processes and their age confirm the existence of positive spillovers coming from the neighbouring parishes. Therefore, the quantity of LC processes in neighbouring parishes affects positively local livestock production. On the contrary, we observe negative spillover effects in terms of investment per hectare, which may arise through competition in financial support between parishes. They are indicative of backwash Myrdal's effects (Gude et al. 2018). However, our LCE figures shown later in this section seem to indicate that such an effect is not enough to compensate the positive effects associated with the number of neighbouring LC processes and their age. In spite of the results obtained in relation to the investment in LC processes, the public investment effort might have positive effects on other variables not considered in our model, such as the satisfaction of the inhabitants of rural areas with the improvements made on roads and access to plots and villages.

In summary, as in Deininger and Xia (2016), we find significant spillover effects in Asturias as the effect of a localized LC project expands beyond the area in which such measure has been implemented. This finding first indicates that the LC effects are likely underestimated if we only examine the local economic impacts of such processes. Another important implication of the above result is that Asturian policymakers should likely initiate *wide* LC processes involving simultaneously several parishes if they aim to promote livestock (or economic) activity in a particular rural area, rather than initiating *dispersed* or poorly coordinated LC processes.

We next proceed to calculate the effect of LC on parishes' dairy and beef production using the parameter estimates of Model 4 in Table 2, our more comprehensive model. While the *direct* effect of each parish is computed using (6), the *indirect* (spatial) impact is computed using (8). The *total* effect of LC on parishes' livestock production is then simply computed by adding both parish-specific direct and indirect effects, i.e. using (9). Figure 5 presents the distribution of the total effect as well as its disaggregation into direct and indirect effects, understood as the effects from LC processes performed inside the parishes and those from the surrounding ones. They all have been computed using the complete sample of parishes. We can conclude from these distributions that the LC effects are generally positive. The average total effect from the LC processes is around 10.8 percent. Its decomposition into direct and indirect effect is on average positive as well: 7.1% and 3.8%, respectively. As is shown in Table 1, the average age of the processes is around 8 years. This implies an annual total effect of 1.4%, which is divided into a direct annual effect of 0.9% and an indirect effect of 0.5% per year. The positive (and relative larger) magnitude of the direct effect corroborates the previous literature that finds a positive contribution of LC processes on rural economic activity (see, e.g. Crecente et al. 2002, for Galician parishes).[15] The indirect effect hence accounts for around 40% of the total impact, corroborating, in line with Deininger and Xia (2016), the importance for accounting for both types of effects and particularly the spatial LC spillover effects generated in neighbouring parishes.

The previous results can be interpreted as "average effects" as they all have been computed using the whole set of parishes in our sample. We differentiate between parishes in Fig. 6 according to several criteria. Our criteria have to do with the number of LC processes (one vs two or more), the time elapsed from the previous process (recent or distant),[16] the localization of parishes (inland vs coast), the intensity of the LC processes (small vs large investment),[17] the specialization of the farms

[15]It is worth highlighting that the distribution of the direct effect is quite disperse, indicating that our DLCE estimates are rather inconclusive due to the presence of large negative and positive point estimates.

[16]The *distant* group includes parishes where the last LC process finished one decade ago or more. Otherwise, it is included in the *recent* group.

[17]The *small* (*large*) investment group includes parishes with less (more) investment per hectare than the sample average.

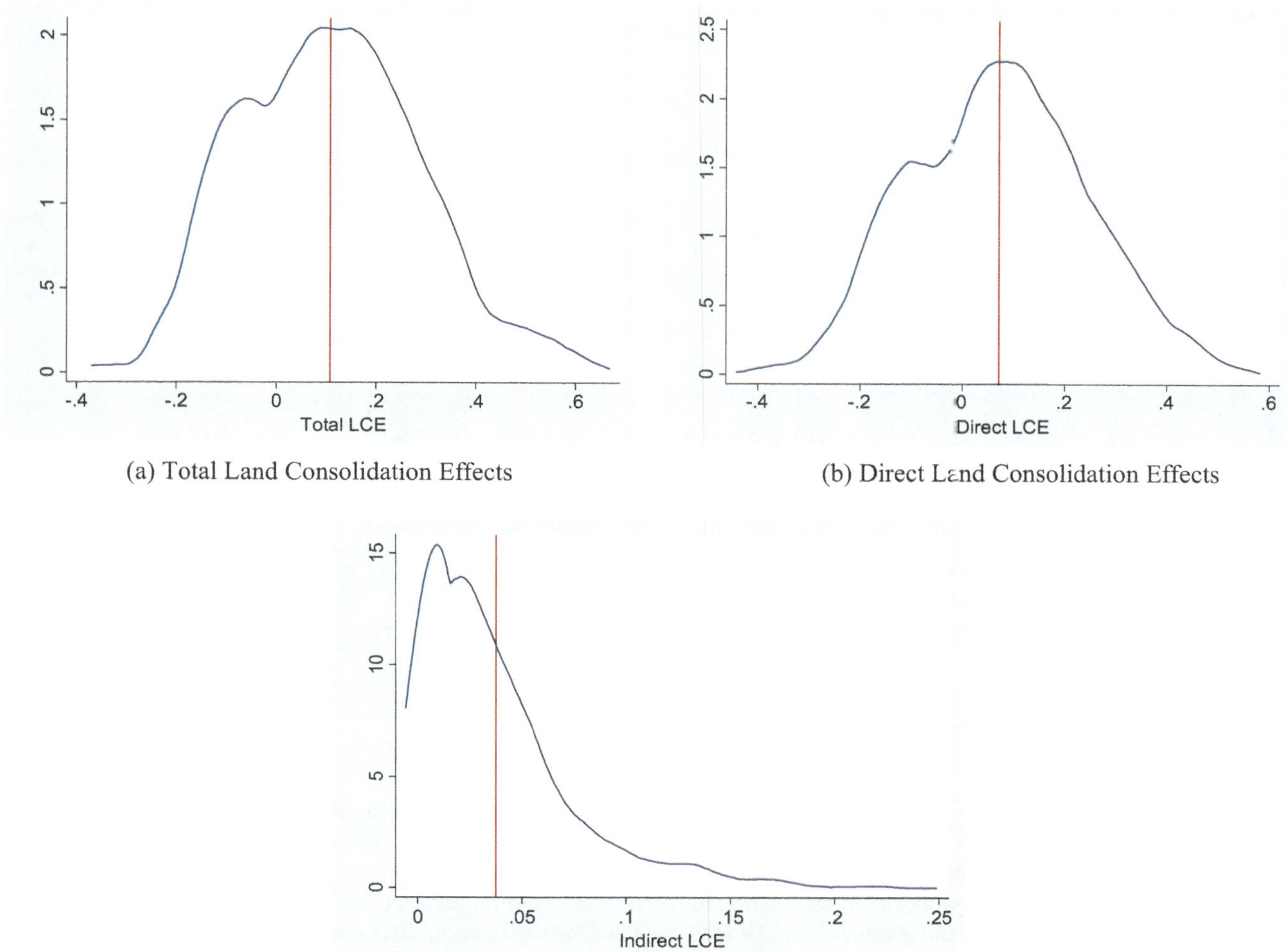

(a) Total Land Consolidation Effects

(b) Direct Land Consolidation Effects

(c) Indirect Land Consolidation Effects

Fig. 5 Distribution of LC effects

located in parishes (beef-, dairy- and mix-oriented) and the use of traditional system of livestock production (traditional vs non-traditional).[18] This allows us to get a more accurate assessment of the magnitude of the LC impact across different types of parishes.

We obtain interesting findings once we split the sample into several groups. For instance, we find that the positive effect of LC is as expected more intensive in parishes that either have experimented two or more LC processes or the last process finished one decade ago or more. The later result thus confirms the Crecente et al. (2002, p. 142) findings in the sense that a two-year period is not enough to capture the final LC effects. The third distribution considers whether the parishes are in inland or coastal municipalities. We find that the coastal parishes are the most benefited by the LC processes. As most of the dairy livestock is located in coastal municipalities, this result is confirmed by the next distribution that shows the different effects between parishes with a greater percentage of farms specialized in beef, milk or both types of livestock production. This distribution suggests the existence of a positive effect in parishes mainly specialized in dairy farms, while those specialized in beef herd present a negative effect. Interestingly, LC processes are mainly observed in those parishes where the dairy-oriented farms predominate. Therefore, it seems that the Asturian policymakers have already considered that the effect is larger in these parishes than in beef-oriented parishes. The fifth distribution has to do with the intensity of the LC processes. We find here that a greater investment does not necessarily imply more livestock production at parish level. Finally, the sixth distribution distinguishes the effect of LC processes between parishes with extensive farms using traditional

[18]The *traditional* (*non-traditional*) group includes parishes with more (less) z-ratio than the sample average.

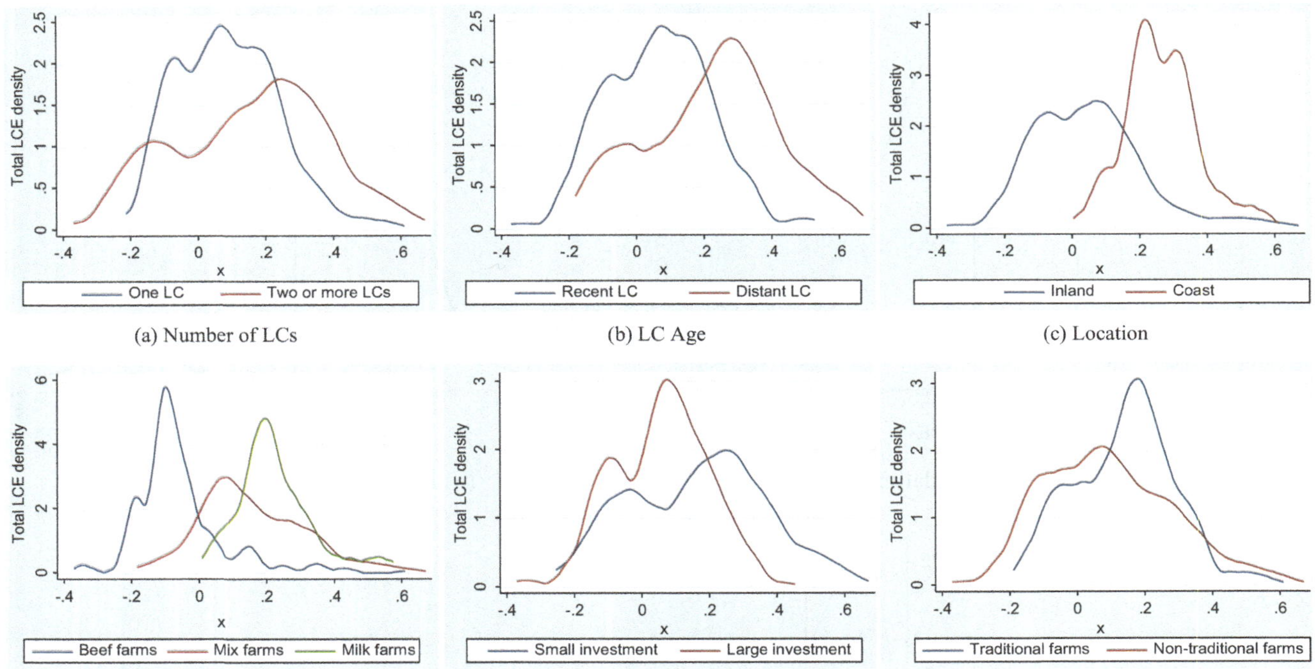

(a) Number of LCs (b) LC Age (c) Location

(d) Farms´ Orientation (e) Investment Effort (f) Livestock Production System

Fig. 6 Total LC effects by groups

systems of livestock production and parishes with more intensive farms. As in previous studies, we find that the effect is more relevant for extensive farms. For instance, Orea et al. (2015) also concluded that the LC processes would particularly improve extensive farms' profits rather than the returns of the intensive farms.

In general, these findings corroborate previous researches focused on rural areas at spatial level (see, e.g. Crecente et al. 2002 for Spain, Du et al. 2018 and Zhou et al. 2019 for China or Dudzińska et al. 2018 for Poland) as we also find that the LC processes are key policies to promote the socio-economic conditions in rural areas.

4.2 Unconditional LC Effects

As previously discussed, LC processes might affect Asturian parishes' livestock production via the number of farms. To explore this possibility, we have estimated a set of *auxiliary regressions* that include both internal LC indicators and their spatial lags as explanatory variables of the number of farms. The parameter estimates of these regressions are presented in Table 3. In order to take into account the different composition of the farms located in each parish, we have split the sample into dairy-, beef- and mix-oriented parishes. Once again, the regressions are performed including time dummies and parish-specific effects. The F-test corroborates the joint significance of both the explanatory variables and the fixed effects.

If we use the complete sample of observation, we do not get significant direct effects of the LC processes on the number of farms (only a very slightly negative effect from the number of projects). Nevertheless, these results confirm the positive spillovers coming from the LC processes in adjacent parishes. Therefore, the most remarkably indirect effect is the positive one emerging from the number of processes in surrounding areas. So, we can conclude in this sense that the increase in the number of farms has been mainly incentivized for the LC processes carried out in other but nearby parishes.

In order to obtain a more precise measure of this impact, the next columns in Table 3 present the same specification for beef-, dairy- and mix-oriented parishes, respectively. It is worth noting that beef-oriented parishes represent 48% of the total sample of parishes, while mix- and dairy-oriented parishes represent 38% and 14%, respectively. Although we are again more interested in the overall effects than in individual effects, the group-specific estimates show that a positive farm effect of both the number and age of the LC processes emerges in mix production-oriented parishes. Distant LC processes also have a significant and positive effect on the farms of beef-oriented parishes. In contrast, the number of LC processes affect negatively farm figures in both beef- and dairy-oriented parishes. It should also be highlighted that the indirect or spatial spillover effects are quite significant. Moreover, we next show that the indirect effect is even more relevant than the direct effect.

Table 3 Parameter estimates of the auxiliary regressions (dep. var.: number of farms)

	All parishes			Beef-oriented			Dairy-oriented			Mix-oriented		
Variable	Coef.		s.e.	Coef.		s.e.	Coef.		s.e.	Coef.		s.e.
N	−0.030	*	0.016	−0.115	**	0.032	−0.137	***	0.038	0.037	*	0.012
A	0.002		0.002	0.016	***	0.004	0.005		0.002	0.000	**	0.001
lnIH	−0.001		0.003	−0.002		0.007	0.025		0.006	−0.007		0.002
WN	0.066	***	0.024	0.177	***	0.046	−0.003		0.046	0.036	**	0.020
WA	−0.006	*	0.003	0.035	***	0.008	−0.005	***	0.004	0.000	***	0.002
WlnIH	0.007		0.006	−0.057		0.013	0.041	*	0.009	0.029	***	0.005
Intercept	3.185	***	0.012	2.746	***	0.022	3.631	***	0.019	3.525	***	0.011
Time dummies	Yes			Yes			Yes			Yes		
Fixed effects	Yes			Yes			Yes			Yes		
Significance F-test[a]	165.7	***		31.69	***		134.4	***		295.6	***	
F-test that all $\alpha_i = 0$	238.1	***		165.1	***		327.1	***		497.5	***	
Degrees of freedom	4650			2202			650			1754		
Obs.	4964			2363			714			1887		
# parameters	314			161			64			133		
# fixed effects	291			138			41			110		
# time dummies	16			16			16			16		

[a]This F-test includes the coefficients of all LC variables and the set of time dummy parameters
Note: *; **; *** indicate signficance at the 10, 5, 1% level, respectively

Table 4 Overall LCE effects

		All parishes		
LCE	Obs	Unconditional	Conditional	Farms
Total	1056	16.36	10.82	1.77
Direct	1056	4.90	7.08	−3.43
Indirect	1056	11.46	3.75	5.21
		Beef-oriented parishes		
LCE		Unconditional	Conditional	Farms
Total	308	−5.55	−5.92	0.82
Direct	308	−14.51	−8.98	−4.85
Indirect	308	8.96	3.06	5.67
		Dairy-oriented parishes		
LCE		Unconditional	Conditional	Farms
Total	223	30.24	22.50	16.79
Direct	223	21.06	19.59	6.42
Indirect	223	9.18	2.91	10.36
		Mix-oriented parishes		
LCE		Unconditional	Conditional	Farms
Total	525	23.32	15.68	14.37
Direct	525	9.42	11.19	0.81
Indirect	525	13.90	4.50	13.56

The last column in Table 4 provides the direct and indirect effects of LC on parishes' farm numbers that have been computed using (11) and the parameter estimates in Table 3. This column shows that the indirect effect of LC on farm numbers is on average positive (5.2%) for the whole set of parishes that were involved in LC processes. This favourable effect is partially offset by the negative direct effect (−3.4%). The total effect is thus slightly positive (1.7%). This decomposition changes when we have a look at the three groups of parishes in terms of specialization. Indeed, while the direct effect on farm numbers is negative (negligible) for beef-oriented (mix-oriented) parishes, the LC processes have clearly stimulated the creation of new dairy farms. Notice that a positive effect here does not imply that the number of farms increases over time due to the increasingly negative coefficients of the time dummies included in our auxiliary regression. They rather indicate that the decline in the number of farms is attenuated by the LC processes.

Table 4 also provides the overall and conditional effects of LC on parishes' livestock production. We have used the parameter estimates of an unconditional distance function model to get the overall effects on parishes' livestock production.

This model (not shown) captures both the conditional LC effect examined in the previous subsection and the LC effect via a reduction (increase) in the number of farms. Conditional on the number of farms, as shown in Sect. 4.1, this table provides positive direct and indirect LC effects on parishes' livestock production for the whole set of parishes involved in LC processes (7.1% and 3.7%, respectively). Again, this decomposition changes when we examine the three groups of parishes in terms of specialization. Indeed, while all conditional effects are positive for dairy- and mix-oriented parishes (i.e. the total effects are 22.5% and 15.7%, respectively), both the total and direct conditional effects for the beef-oriented parishes are negative (−5.9% and − 8.9% respectively). Notice that the negative effects do not imply that beef-oriented farm size decreases over time due to the increasingly positive coefficients of the time dummies included in our distance function. They rather indicate that the increase in size of these farms is less than in dairy- and mix-oriented farms.

Regarding the overall (unconditional) effect of LC, we find that parishes' livestock production increases about 16.3%, mainly thanks to the positive indirect effects associated with both farms' size and numbers. This result represents annual increases of 2.1% in parishes' livestock production. To test the stability of this result, we split the sample of parishes involved in LC processes into beef-, dairy- and mix-oriented parishes. As previously discussed, beef-oriented parishes are less benefited from LC. If we divide the cumulative total effect for this group (−5.5%) by the average age of the processes average, we get an annual deterioration in parishes' beef production of 0.7% due to the negative direct effects associated with both farms' size and numbers. In this case, the indirect effects offset partially but not totally the adverse direct effect on parishes' beef production. The unconditional results for dairy- and mix-oriented parishes change considerably as they all are positive, with cumulative increases of 30% and 23%, respectively, which in turn represent annual increases of 3.1% and 3.3% in parishes' livestock production.

The above-mentioned effects can be considered as a lower bound of the overall effect attributed to LC processes because we still have not examined the indirect effects on parishes that have never implemented any LC process. In this sense, we have found a slightly less but positive indirect effects for these parishes. For instance, the computed unconditional indirect effects attributed to neighbouring LC process are on average 8.2%. The effect via number of farms and the conditional effect on farms size are also remarkable, about 3.5% and 2.5%, respectively.

5 Conclusion

The objective of this research is to evaluate the impact of the land consolidation (LC) processes that have taken place in Asturias during the period 2001–2017. During the last decades, and particularly during the period under study, Asturias has received European funds to promote concentration processes for three reasons. First, the land has traditionally been fragmented in Asturias. Second, previous research often has found that the LC processes are important tools to improve the economic activity in rural areas, increase farmer income and stabilize their population. Finally, recent regulation in Asturias has contributed to encourage those processes.

We first base our estimation in a production approach using parishes' dairy and beef herd as proxies for livestock production and several LC-based variables that aim to capture the quantity and intensity of the LC processes implemented in each parish. In addition, we analyse the effect of LC-based variables on the number of farms using auxiliary regressions. The overall effect is then computed combining both effects. Our main contributions to this literature have to do with the panel data techniques used to estimate all models and the spatial interdependence that has been incorporated into our analysis by adding the LC indicators of neighbouring parishes. This last feature allows us to decompose the total effects attributed to LC into direct and indirect effects.

In summary, we find an annual effect of about 2.1% on parishes' livestock production attributed to LC processes in Asturias, which has mainly benefited parishes with dairy- and mix-oriented farms. These improvements can be attributed to different sources. While the positive effect in dairy-oriented parishes is mainly due to the direct effect generated by internal LC processes, the livestock production gains in the mix-oriented parishes are caused by indirect or spatial effects generated in neighbouring parishes. It should also be highlighted that the 2.1% increase above is only a lower bound as it ignores the non-negligible indirect effects on parishes that have never implemented any LC process. Although the contribution of LC processes to parishes' livestock production is positive, we find that their impact is not homogenous. For instance, the positive effect of LC is more intensive in parishes that either have experimented two or more LC processes or the last process finished one decade ago or more. The effect is also larger in coastal parishes and in parishes with dairy farms. In addition, we find that the LC effect is more relevant in parishes with more extensive and traditional farms.

Overall these results advocate using spatial econometrics techniques in the empirical examinations of economic effects attributed to LC processes. They also advocate using coordinated LC measures by the regional governments in order to take full advantage of this important policy. Policymakers should also be aware that the impact of their LC processes might depend on parishes' characteristics and that the expected effects might be underestimated if the spatial spillover effects of such measures are ignored.

Appendix: Literature Review on Land Consolidation (LC)

Paper	Objective	Sample	Methodology	Results
Burger (2001)	Analyse the agricultural transformation, land redistribution and land tenure and the role of agriculture in the Hungarian economy	309 farms in 11 counties of Hungary in 1998	Questionnaire	LC has taken place mainly by renting. Rented land increases with the increasing farm size
Coelho et al. (2001)	Proposition of a model that incorporates methods for the evaluation of the performance of the agricultural system before and after the LC project	The model was applied to the Valenca LC in 1989, before project execution, and in 1995 after implementation	The model evaluates each effect of the project (land, irrigation and drainage and road reconstruction) on a technical and social basis and estimates its economic impacts	The results suggest that a multidisciplinary approach, supported by robust models, can be used as a reliable basis for the evaluation and decision- making process of LC projects
Crecente et al. (2002)	Review the process of LC in Galicia analysing economic, social and environmental effects	Parishes with and without LC processes. Cases of two municipalities	Comparative analysis of consolidated and non-consolidated areas in Galicia	LC contributes to retaining farmland in agricultural use and improves the population evolution in rural areas, although there are changes in use from cropland to pasture land
Vitikainen (2004)	Discuss the similarities and differences in the LC procedure in various European countries	Objectives and contents of LC in Finland, Germany, the Netherlands and Sweden	Comparison of the organization, objectives, legal procedure, costs and financing and the development of LC between countries	The demand for LC arises from the need for promoting the appropriate use of the land. There are differences in the objectives and procedures of LC between countries related to factors like historical trends, culture, tradition and legislation
Wu et al. (2005)	Examine and measure the impact and cost-effectiveness of the comprehensive agricultural development program on Chinese agriculture	Data collected from a survey to 227 Chinese farm households	This paper uses a production function approach	The program has improved land quality and the productivity of household crop production, and overall has been cost-effective
Lerman and Cimpoieş (2006)	Examine LC within of process of agrarian reform	Several surveys in Moldova, made in different years and previously published	Analysis of several surveys	LC leads to better economic performance. Land leasing is used as a market mechanism for consolidation
Miranda et al. (2006)	Examine the geographic, agricultural, socio-economic and environmental effects of LC in Galicia since the 1950s	Databases related to 315 Galician municipalities and 3793 parishes. Data from 1129 LC processes related to the period 1950–2001	Methodology drawn up by the European Union for evaluation of its socio-economic programs	LC has in general made a positive contribution to slowing rural depopulation
Yu et al. (2010)	Identify and classify the ecological risks in LC. Develop a framework of the theory and method to assess the change of ecological risk degree before and after LC	A case study of a LC project in Chongyang County, Hubei Province, China	Analytical hierarchical processing (AHP) method to the data resources from the LC project in Southern China to allocate weightings to the indices of ecological risk (ER) and to set up an integrated index system for the ecological risk identification. This integrated index system encompasses the ecological risks with three factors (water, soil and biology) and 14 indices	The ER is reduced from 58.02 to 28.8 after LC and the degree of ecological risk is down from degree III to degree IV. The water ER is reduced from 21.53 to 6.16; its contribution to reduce the ecological risk is 53%. The reduced ERs of soil and biology are, respectively, 12.79 and 1.06; their contribution of ecological risk reduce is lower than water

(continued)

Paper	Objective	Sample	Methodology	Results
Hartvigsen (2014)	Study of land reform in 25 countries in Central and Eastern of Europe from 1989 and onwards and provide an overview of applied land reform approaches	Land reform approaches applied in 25 countries in Central and Eastern Europe from the Baltic and Central European countries in the West to Russia and the small Trans-Caucasus countries in the east, and to the Balkan countries in the south	With a basis in theory on land fragmentation, the linkage between land reform approaches and land fragmentation is explored	Land fragmentation is often hampering agricultural and rural development when both landownership and land use is highly fragmented
Lisec et al. (2014)	Investigate the opinion of LC participants about LC	Responses to a questionnaire of 254 landowners from 3 areas of Slovenia in 2011	Survey conducted on a sample of private landowners involved in selected LC projects	The active participation of landowners contributes to their comprehension of the aims and to their satisfaction with the results of the LC
Zhang et al. (2014)	Identify the changes resulting from the LC implementation and to develop a parametric approach to assess the resource-environment effects	Case study of Tianmen LC project in Hubei Province of China	Use of indexes to assess the different effects of LC	LC causes positive and negative effects. Positive effects were demonstrated in agricultural production capacity and in its costs. The negative effects were expressed by the ecosystem services value, landscape diversity and human disturbance intensity
Guo et al. (2015)	Identify and measure the effect of LC on the multifunctionality of cropland ecosystems	Analysis of county scale LC projects in the 31 provinces of China (period 2006–2012)	Set pair analysis methodology. Variable fuzzy sets analysis	LC have significantly improved the production function of cropland, driven investment in agriculture, promoted development of the rural agricultural economy, maintained food security and stability in the rural area. However, it also impaired rural ecological benefits in some provinces
Wang et al. (2015)	Understand how LC affects landscape patterns and ecosystems investigating the ecosystem service value and the ecological connectivity in a consolidated area of Da'an City from 2008 to 2014 using a revised ecological connectivity index	Consolidated area of Da'an City from 2008 to 2014 (China)	Use an ecosystem service evaluation and a revised ecological connectivity index	LC has certain negative influences on the ecosystem services. LC could change the ecological connectivity as well as the land-use structure
Hiironen and Riekkinen (2016)	Evaluate agricultural impacts and profitability of LC	12 LC projects implemented in Finland	Standard statistical methods, production cost calculations and feasibility analyses	LC is an effective and feasible land management tool for the improvement of property structure. Due to the improvement of property structure the average production costs decrease 15%

(continued)

Paper	Objective	Sample	Methodology	Results
Jiang et al. (2017)	Propose an assessment model to estimate the improvement of land productivity potential via LC	Region of Shenyang City (China)	Use of a system for assessing the cultivated land productivity potential before and after LC	The effect of the concentration is based on an increase of more than 20% in the potential productivity of the land
Jin et al. (2017)	Evaluation of the effectiveness of LC policy	Detailed geospatial information for 5328 LC projects implemented between 2006 and 2010 in China	Generalized linear mixed model (GLMM) to predict project effectiveness incorporating selected biophysical, social-economic variables as fixed effects and province variables to model random effects	The overall effectiveness of LC in improving agricultural productivity is low. There are also clear regional differences
Luo and Timothy (2017)	Evaluation of the performance of LC in terms of rural households' levels of satisfaction in rural China	Data gathered via questionnaires in the regions of Hangzhou, Changsha and Guiyang (China)	Probit model	The overall satisfaction rate was 76.5%. Residents' satisfaction with LC depends, among others, on farmers' level of education, family size, level of agricultural mechanization and their participation in rural production cooperatives
Demetriou (2018)	Present and discuss the development, implementation and evaluation of two different automated valuation models (AVMs) for a case study LC	Case study area in Cyprus	Estimation of two hedonic price models combined with a geographical information system (GIS)	The AVM is highly efficient compared to conventional land valuation methods and provides transparency
Du et al. (2018)	Propose a straightforward method to assess agricultural productivity changes using remote sensing data	Moderate Resolution Imaging Spectroradiometer NDVI time series from 2001 to 2013 and data on LC projects completed in China in 2006 and 2007	Two indexes were used to evaluate the effects of LC: the rate of change in the mean annual NDVI and the coefficient of variation of this variable before and after consolidation	78.67% of projects in 2006 and 78.32% of those in 2007 proved effective at either improving or stabilizing productivity
Dudzińska et al. (2018)	Assessment of the socio-economic effects of consolidations at the meso-level in rural areas	Polish communes in which both traditional and infrastructural consolidations had been implemented over an area of at least 15% of the commune's area	The level of socio-economic development was assessed based on an indicator of the rate of changes, calculated as the difference between the levels of commune development indicator for the years 2004 and 2016	Implementation of traditional consolidations of agricultural land is one of the factors contributing to an increase in the level of socio-economic development of rural areas
Li et al. (2018)	Investigate the challenges in implementing LC in rural China and to pose policy implications for rural sustainability	LC project in a village community of Shandong Province (China)	Analysis and reflection on the process of LC	LC is needed to coordinate and improve the changing human-land relationship in rural China. It is needed an expanded rural land market. LC should be implemented by respecting local stakeholders' willingness and request
Nilsson (2018)	Examine the role of land use consolidation on agricultural productivity among smallholder farmers in Rwanda	Random sample of 1538 households across Rwanda of which 25 per cent participated in land use consolidation between 2010 and 2014	Household-level data are used to estimate a fixed-effects model with matched control groups to mitigate selection bias	Positive association between land use consolidation and crop yields (among farms with landholdings greater than one hectare)

(continued)

Paper	Objective	Sample	Methodology	Results
Shi et al. (2018)	Research on LC projects by integrating landscape pattern analysis with production, living, and ecological benefit assessments	Two municipal LC projects in China were selected for analysis	By an evaluation index system, the authors quantitatively estimate the dynamic changes in the production, life and ecological benefits of the two project areas	LC has directly or indirectly improved landscape ecological patterns. LC has improved the balanced distribution of cultivated land and the concentrated distribution of construction land in the project area
Zeng et al. (2018)	Evaluate the impacts of LC on agricultural technical efficiency of producers	Data from a field survey executed during July 2010 and July 2016. A total of 900 producers were chosen randomly from 30 LC projects in the Jiangsu Province (China)	Stochastic frontier analysis production function	Land tenure transfer, land fragmentation, non-agricultural income and crop diversity have undergone significant changes after LC. The overall agricultural technical efficiency of producers had also increased considerably after LC
Zhang and Zhang (2018)	Analyse the interference by human activities caused by LC engineering in terrestrial ecosystems	Analysis of a project area located in Mugong Village in Guanling County (China)	GIS technology, ecological values, landscape pattern indexes and an ecological risk evaluation were used to construct an ecological sensitivity evaluation index	The project area was divided into sensitivity zones according to the results that provide suggestions for future land management decisions
Colombo and Perujo-Villanueva (2019)	Propose a methodology for assessing ex-ante the most suitable areas in which LC initiatives could be carried out	The case study focuses on olive groves in the Andalusia region (Spain). Interviews to 72 landowners	Interviews to 72 landowners and use of a methodology for assessing ex-ante LC projects	LC procedure in the areas identified would bring about a noticeable improvement in the property structure and production cost savings of between 5.8% and 15.3%
Janus and Markuszewska (2019)	Verify the hypothesis of persistence of favourable basic parameters of LF and other factors affecting the efficiency of agricultural production after LC	Jabłonka commune located in the southern Poland	Comparison of indicators for all villages from the commune selected	There is a multigenerational and positive impact of LC on the development and functioning of rural areas. This is evident regarding the average plot size, the road accessibility, the land fragmentation indicators and the lowest level of land abandonment
Zhou et al. (2019)	Analyse the mechanism and path behind LC boosting poverty alleviation	Data on LC in Fuping County (China)	Revision of the evolution of China's land policies related to poverty alleviation since 1978. Case study method	LC has contributed to increasing cultivated land area, promoting agricultural production scale, improving rural production conditions and living environment, alleviating ecological risk and supporting for rural development and poverty alleviation

References

Ali, D., Deininger, K., & Harris, A. (2019). Does large farm establishment create benefits for neighbouring smallholders? Evidence from Ethiopia. *Land Economics, 95*, 71–90.

Álvarez-Ayuso, I., Condeço-Melhorado, A. M., Gutiérrez, J., & Zofío, J. L. (2016). Integrating network analysis with the production function approach to study the spillover effects of transport infrastructure. *Regional Studies, 50*(6), 996–1015. https://doi.org/10.1080/00343404.2014.953472.

Balk, B. (2016). Chapter 2: The dynamics of productivity change: A review of the bottom-up approach. In W. Greene, L. Khalaf, R. Sickles, M. Veall, & M.-C. Voia (Eds.), *Productivity and efficiency analysis* (pp. 15–49). Cham: Springer.

Burger, A. (2001). Agricultural development and land concentration in a central European country: A case study of Hungary. *Land Use Policy, 18*, 259–268.

Coelho, J., Pinto, P. A., & Silva, L. M. (2001). A systems approach for the estimation of the effects of land consolidation projects (LCPs): A model and its application. *Agricultural Systems, 68*, 179–195.

Colombo, S., & Perujo-Villanueva, M. (2019). A practical method for the ex-ante evaluation of land consolidation initiatives: Fully connected parcels with the same value. *Land Use Policy, 81*, 463–471.

Crecente, R., Alvarez, C., & Fra, U. (2002). Economic, social and environmental impact of land consolidation in Galicia. *Land Use Policy, 19*, 135–147.

da Silva, D. F. C., Elhorst, J. P., & da Mota Silveira Neto, R. (2017). Urban and rural population growth in a spatial panel of municipalities. *Regional Studies, 51*(6), 894–908.

Deininger, K., & Xia, F. (2016). Quantifying spillover effects from large land-based investment: The case of Mozambique. *World Development, 87*, 227–241.

del Corral, J., Perez, J. A., & Roibas, D. (2011). The impact of land fragmentation on milk production. *Journal of Dairy Science, 94*, 517–525.

Demetriou, D. (2018). Automating the land valuation process carried out in land consolidation schemes. *Land Use Policy, 75*, 21–32.

Diewert, W. E. (1971). An application of the Shephard duality theorem: A generalized Leontief production function. *Journal of Political Economy, 79*, 461–507.

Du, X., Zhanga, X., & Jinb, X. (2018). Assessing the effectiveness of land consolidation for improving agricultural productivity in China. *Land Use Policy, 70*, 360–367.

Dudzińska, M., Bacior, S., & Prusc, B. (2018). Considering the level of socio-economic development of rural areas in the context of infrastructural and traditional consolidations in Poland. *Land Use Policy, 79*, 759–773.

Gude, A., Alvarez, I., & Orea, L. (2018). Heterogeneous spillovers among Spanish provinces: A generalized spatial stochastic frontier model. *Journal of Productivity Analysis, 50*, 155–173.

Guo, B., Jin, X., Yang, X., Guan, X., Lin, Y., & Zhou, Y. (2015). Determining the effects of land consolidation on the multifunctionality of the cropland production system in China using a SPA-fuzzy assessment model. *European Journal of Agronomy, 63*, 12–26.

Halleck-Vega, S., & Elhorst, J. P. (2015). The SLX model. *Journal of Regional Science, 55*(3), 339–363.

Hartvigsen, M. (2014). Land reform and land fragmentation in Central and Eastern Europe. *Land Use Policy, 36*, 330–341.

Hiironen, J., & Riekkinen, K. (2016). Agricultural impacts and profitability of land consolidations. *Land Use Policy, 55*, 309–317.

Janus, J., & Markuszewska, I. (2019). Forty years later: Assessment of the long-lasting effectiveness of land consolidation projects. *Land Use Policy, 83*, 22–31.

Jiang, G., Zhang, R., Ma, W., Zhou, D., Wang, X., & He, X. (2017). Cultivated land productivity potential improvement in land consolidation schemes in Shenyang, China: Assessment and policy implications. *Land Use Policy, 68*, 80–88.

Jin, X., Shao, Y., Zhang, Z., Resler, L. M., Campbell, J. B., Chen, G., & Zhou, Y. (2017). The evaluation of land consolidation policy in improving agricultural productivity in China. *Sci Rep, 7*, 2792, www.nature.com.

Lerman, Z., & Cimpoieş, D. (2006). Land consolidation as a factor for rural development in Moldova. *Europe-Asia Studies, 58*(3), 439–455.

Li, Y., Wu, W., & Liu, Y. (2018). Land consolidation for rural sustainability in China: Practical reflections and policy implications. *Land Use Policy, 74*, 137–141.

Lisec, A., Primozic, T., Ferlan, M., Sumrada, R., & Drobne, S. (2014). Land owners' perception of land consolidation and their satisfaction with the results – Slovenian experiences. *Land Use Policy, 38*, 550–563.

Luo, W., & Timothy, D. J. (2017). An assessment of farmers' satisfaction with land consolidation performance in China. *Land Use Policy, 61*, 501–510.

Manjunatha, A. V., Anik, A. R., Speelmand, S., & Nuppenaua, E. A. (2013). Impact of land fragmentation, farm size, land ownership and crop diversity on profit and efficiency of irrigated farms in India. *Land Use Policy, 31*, 397–405.

Miranda, D., Crecente, R., & Alvarez, M. F. (2006). Land consolidation in inland rural Galicia, NW Spain, since 1950: An example of the formulation and use of questions, criteria and indicators for evaluation of rural development policies. *Land Use Policy, 23*, 511–520.

Nilsson, P. (2018). The role of land use consolidation in improving crop yields among farm households in Rwanda. *The Journal of Development Studies*. https://doi.org/10.1080/00220388.2018.1520217.

Orea, L. (2010). The effect of legal barriers to entry in the Spanish retail market: A local market approach. *Hacienda Pública Española, 193*(2), 49–74.

Orea, L., Pérez-Méndez, J. A., & Roibás, D. (2015). Evaluating the double effect of land fragmentation on technology choice and dairy farm productivity: A latent class model approach. *Land Use Policy, 45*, 189–198.

Rahman, S., & Rahman, M. (2008). Impact of land fragmentation and resource ownership on productivity and efficiency: The case of rice producers in Bangladesh. *Land Use Policy, 26*, 95–103.

Shi, Y., Cao, X., Fu, D., & Wang, Y. (2018). Comprehensive value discovery of land consolidation projects: An empirical analysis of Shanghai, China. *Sustainability, 10*(6), 2039.

Vitikainen, A. (2004). An overview of land consolidation in Europe. *Nordic Journal of Surveying and Real Estate Research, 1*, 25–44.

Wan, G. H., & Cheng, E. (2001). Effects of land fragmentation and returns to scale in the Chinese farming sector. *Applied Economics, 33*, 183–194.

Wang, J., Yan, S., Guo, Y., Li, J., & Sun, G. (2015). The effects of land consolidation on the ecological connectivity based on ecosystem service value: A case study of Da'an land consolidation project in Jilin province. *Journal of Geographical Sciences, 25*(5), 603–616.

Wu, Z., Liu, M., & Davis, J. (2005). Land consolidation and productivity in Chinese household crop production. *China Economic Review, 16*, 28–49.

Yu, G., Feng, J., Che, Y., Lin, X., Hu, L., & Yang, S. (2010). The identification and assessment of ecological risks for land consolidation based on the anticipation of ecosystem stabilization: A case study in Hubei Province, China. *Land Use Policy, 27*, 293–303.

Zeng, S., Zhu, F., Chen, F., Yu, M., Zhang, S., & Yang, Y. (2018). Assessing the impacts of land consolidation on agricultural technical efficiency of producers: A Survey from Jiangsu Province, China. *Sustainability, 10*(7), 2490.

Zhang, Q., & Zhang, T. (2018). Land consolidation design based on an evaluation of ecological sensitivity. *Sustainability, 10*(10), 3736.

Zhang, Z., Zhao, W., & Gu, X. (2014). Changes resulting from a land consolidation project (LCP) and its resource–environment effects: A case study in Tianmen City of Hubei Province, China. *Land Use Policy, 40*, 74–82.

Zhou, Y., Guoc, L., & Liu, Y. (2019). Land consolidation boosting poverty alleviation in China: Theory and practice. *Land Use Policy, 82*, 339–348.

Index

J. Aparicio et al. (eds.), *Advances in Efficiency and Productivity II*, International Series in Operations Research & Management Science 287, https://doi.org/10.1007/978-3-030-41618-8

T

U

V

The manufacturer's authorised representative in the EU is Springer Nature Customer Service Centre GmbH, Europaplatz 3, 69115 Heidelberg, Germany. If you have any concerns regarding our products, please contact ProductSafety@springernature.com

Printed and bound by CPI Group (UK) Ltd, Croydon, CR0 4YY
30/09/2026
02225271-0002

The book series *International Series in Operations Research and Management Science* encompasses the various areas of operations research and management science. Both theoretical and applied books are included. It describes current advances anywhere in the world that are at the cutting edge of the field. The series is aimed especially at researchers, doctoral students, and sophisticated practitioners. The series features three types of books:

- *Advanced expository books* that extend and unify our understanding of particular areas.
- *Research monographs* that make substantial contributions to knowledge.
- *Handbooks* that define the new state of the art in particular areas. They will be entitled

Recent Advances in (name of the area). Each handbook will be edited by a leading authority in the area who will organize a team of experts on various aspects of the topic to write individual chapters. A handbook may emphasize expository surveys or completely new advances (either research or applications) or a combination of both.

The series emphasizes the following four areas: *Mathematical Programming:* Including linear programming, integer programming, nonlinear programming, interior point methods, game theory, network optimization models, combinatorics, equilibrium programming, complementarity theory, multiobjective optimization, dynamic programming, stochastic programming, complexity theory, etc. *Applied Probability:* Including queuing theory, simulation, renewal theory, Brownian motion and diffusion processes, decision analysis, Markov decision processes, reliability theory, forecasting, other stochastic processes motivated by applications, etc. *Production and Operations Management:* Including inventory theory, production scheduling, capacity planning, facility location, supply chain management, distribution systems, materials requirements planning, just-in-time systems, flexible manufacturing systems, design of production lines, logistical planning, strategic issues, etc. *Applications of Operations Research and Management Science:* Including telecommunications, health care, capital budgeting and finance, marketing, public policy, military operations research, service operations, transportation systems, etc.

More information about this series at http://www.springer.com/series/6161

International Series in Operations Research & Management Science

Volume 287